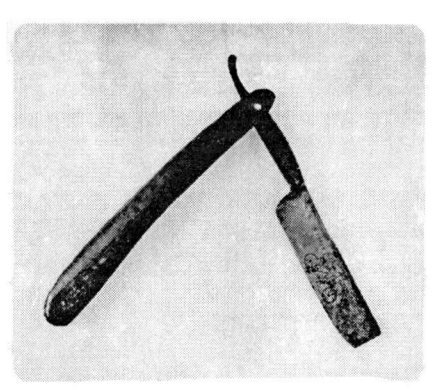

Nobody owns life, but anyone who can pick up
a frying pan owns death.
William S. Burroughs

It is my belief, Watson, founded upon my experience, that the lowest and vilest alleys in London do not present a more dreadful record of sin than does the smiling and beautiful countryside.
Arthur Conan Doyle

A farm is a manipulative creature. There is no such thing as finished. Work comes in a stream and has no end. There are only the things that must be done now and things that can be done later. The threat the farm has got on you, the one that keeps you running from can until can't, is this: do it now, or some living thing will wilt or suffer or die. Its blackmail, really.
Kristin Kimball

But these backwaters of existence sometimes breed, in their sluggish depths, strange acuities of emotion...
Edith Wharton

All great and precious things are lonely.
John Steinbeck

It is from the Bible that man has learned cruelty, rapine, and murder; for the belief of a cruel God makes a cruel man.
Thomas Paine

The monstrous act by definition demands a monster.
Rick Yancey

One situation - maybe one alone - could drive me to murder: family life, togetherness.
Patricia Highsmith

I have no desire whatever to reform myself. My only desire is to reform people who try to reform me. And I believe that the only way to reform people is to kill 'em.
Carl Panzram

Finally, this being America, there is the constant possibility of murder.
Bill Byrson

DEAD MEN DO TELL TALES SERIES

FEAR THE REAPER

America's Rural Mysteries, Hauntings & Horrors
BY TROY TAYLOR & RENE KRUSE

© Copyright 2014 by Troy Taylor, Rene Kruse
& Apartment 42 Productions
All Rights Reserved, including the right to copy or reproduce this book, or portions thereof, in any form, without express permission from the author and publisher

Original Cover Artwork Designed by
© Copyright 2014 by April Slaughter & Troy Taylor

This Book is Published By:
Whitechapel Press
A Division of Apartment 42 Productions
Decatur, Illinois   1-888-GHOSTLY
Visit us on the internet at http: www.whitechapelpress.com

First Edition - May 2014
ISBN: 1-892523-90-6

Printed in the United States of America

INTRODUCTION
BY TROY TAYLOR

Eighty years later, it was still the most famous murder and suicide in the small town where I grew up. I lived on an Illinois farm during my adolescent and teenage years, and the closest town to us was a place called Moweaqua a Native American word that was said to mean "muddy water." It was a rural community, built up around farming and a coal mine that closed down after a disaster in 1932 that killed fifty-four miners. But the Portwood Murder was still whispered about after eight decades and was still distantly recalled as one of the dark spots in the town's history.

It happened on September 10, 1905. Henry Portwood was a wealthy retired farmer who had owned a large farm about two miles east of town until 1903. He was respected and generally well-liked in the community. He had served in the Union Army during the Civil War, enlisting in 1862 at age seventeen, and was a quiet and industrious man. After he retired from farming, he purchased a home from H.C. O'Dell, which was located on the northeast edge of Moweaqua. On Sunday morning, September 10, he cut the throat of his fourth wife – nearly severing her head, the newspaper said - before slashing his own throat with a straight razor. Mrs. Portwood died quickly but her husband lived for several hours, first claiming that "God" had killed his wife and then confessing when he was told that his son would be blamed for the crime. The boy, Everett, age nine, had discovered his father and step-mother lying in pools of blood on their bedroom floor and was the first to raise the alarm about the tragic event. Ironically, it was Everett who was the source of the problems between the husband and wife, which led to the murder-suicide.

The newspapers stated, "Moweaqua is greatly excited because of the awful deed of the enraged husband."

Portwood had been a widower three times over. All of his previous wives had died, including Everett's mother, who passed away in 1902. This never generated much sympathy from his fourth wife, Mollie. Just twelve years younger than her husband, Mary Helen Doyle, who went by the name of Mollie, was born in Bunker Hill, Illinois, and had moved to Moweaqua with her family when she was a child. As far as I can learn, she had never been married before becoming engaged to Portwood, who began courting her the same year that his third wife passed away. It was a troubled marriage, and Mollie never got along with Everett. She constantly complained about the boy, perhaps because he served as a reminder of Portwood's previous marriage or because of the boy's behavior, since those who knew the family stated that she was often angry because Portwood would never allow her to discipline the boy.

The constant disagreements about Everett led to the couple separating for a brief time in July 1905. They stayed apart for about two weeks and then reconciled. According to friends and witnesses, they seemed to be getting along well, even as little as an hour before the murder took place. The Portwoods had been visiting with neighbors that Sunday morning and they seemed in good spirits, the neighbors later told police.

But around 10:30 a.m., something occurred in the Portwood home that would never be revealed. Henry Portwood took the true reason for his wife's murder to the grave. A half-hour later, young Everett walked into his parent's bedroom and found them lying there, surrounded by blood. Screaming for help, the horrified child ran out of the back door and gave the alarm to the closest neighbors. Several men ran into the Portwood house and discovered the awful scene.

The newspapers stated, "The room looked like a slaughterhouse." Mollie was lying on the floor near the window. Her head had nearly been severed from her body by the brutal force of the cut. Blood was still flowing from the gaping wound and she twitched and gurgled, still showing signs of life. The damage that had been done to her throat prevented her from her speaking. With a wound to his neck almost as deep as his wife's, Portwood was lying a short distance away, almost in the doorway to the parlor. He was still alive, his feet kicking and his legs twisting as he thrashed about in his own blood. He was obviously in terrible condition, but he was in better shape than his wife.

Looking about, the men could see that a struggle had taken place in the room. Furniture was knocked over and the bed covers were twisted onto the floor. Everything in the room, from the bed to the walls, with spattered with blood. It was, the newspaper said, "a scene more terrible than can be described."

Mollie had evidently been sitting at the north window of the bedroom, dressing her hair, when she was attacked by her husband. Bloodstains showed that she rose from her chair after she was cut. After his wife had been dealt with, Portwood had then turned the razor on himself, cutting fast and deep across his own throat.

Seeing that Portwood was still alive, one of the man pressed a cloth to his throat to try and stop the bleeding. The straight razor was on the floor, just inches from Portwood's hand. It was obvious to everyone what had happened. Cyrus Mitchell, one of the first to arrive on the scene, asked him why he had killed Mollie. But Portwood's replies were nonsensical, claiming that he had not killed his wife and that he had not been hurt. Mitchell told him that his throat had been cut, as had his wife's, and that he must have done it. He replied, "Nobody cut my throat, did they? I did not do anything to my wife or myself."

Pressed to explain, Portwood insisted, "I did not do it, God must have done it."

But Mitchell didn't let up. He insisted that Portwood confess to what he had done, even stating that the police might believe that it was Everett who committed the murders if Portwood died before admitting to what had happened. Apparently, this worked because the dying man made one more statement: "Yes, I did it. But it don't make any difference why. It is all right."

And those were the last words that Portwood would speak about the murder. Dr. Pratt was summoned to try and save the man's life. He sewed up the wound in his neck, but his jugular had been severed and there was little he could do for him. Henry Portwood died later that afternoon - a killer and a suicide. He never explained what had caused him to snap and murder Mollie. To this day, the motivations for the crime remain a mystery.

The bodies of the Portwoods were later examined by the Shelby County coroner and then an inquest was held on Monday. The verdict was as expected: murder and suicide. Henry was buried in Hayes Cemetery, outside of Moweaqua, and Mollie was buried separately in West Cemetery. They were divided, even in death.

As for Everett, he was taken in by his sister, Mrs. Frank Clark, Portwood's daughter with his second wife, Almira, who had died in 1883. She promised to take care of him, assuring the newspapers that he would be "well raised." From there, Everett seems to vanish from history. I could find no trace of what became of the boy whose life was shattered by a single bloody event.

The idea for this book came to René and me while we were driving from her home in southwest Pennsylvania to Gettysburg one spring during one of our annual outings. When we travel anywhere together, it always turns into a "multi-hour gabfest," as René calls it. She told me about the White Rocks Murder, which is included in this book. I told her that she needed to write that story up for inclusion in some future book, but I had no idea what book it would be. At that time, we had recently written our first book on American disasters and hauntings *And Hell Followed With it* and were in the midst of planning the sequel. The idea for *Fear the Reaper* was still coming, and when I put it together, I asked René to not only contribute the story of the White Rocks Murder, but to co-author the book with me.

It was an easy fit. We have been friends for going on two decades now and had written two other books together, but that wasn't all there was to it. Both of us had grown up on farms although, as I often say, MANY years apart in Illinois for myself and Kansas for René. We were both very familiar with the loneliness and the isolation of rural life and we are both well aware of the dark things that can happen in what seems like an idyllic setting. We had both grown up hearing many blood-curdling stories of murder and depravity that people mistakenly believe only happen in the "big city."

Trust me when I assure you that the farms, fields and woods of America's rural countryside have been drenched with blood.

But it wasn't just isolation that led to murder. Many of the tragedies that occurred on farms in years past were carried out at the hands of the hired help. Farmhands were among the scariest-looking folks around in the nineteenth and early twentieth centuries - and the most dangerous.

Many of them developed sinister reputations in local communities and on neighboring farms; usually with good reason. Farmhands were essentially field laborers, uneducated and scarred by rough outdoor conditions. They often slept in barns, outhouses or packed into a farmhouse's cramped spare bedroom. They drank heavily and had little in the way of worldly possessions. They would do just about anything for money, ranging from back-breaking labor to murder.

One had only to glance at nineteenth-century execution records to realize the danger inherent in transient workers. The death penalty was in heavy use during those years. Men went to the gallows on a weekly basis. Farmhands were frequently hanged for murder in all parts of the country.

In 1874, a farmworker named Marshall Martin, who worked in Martinez, California, in the San Francisco Bay area, murdered his work supervisor with an axe. He had been put up to it by the supervisor's wife. Martin was convicted and sentenced to death, while his boss' wife went to an insane asylum. His hanging, the last in Martinez, was particularly gruesome, during a time when such things were public spectacles. The noose was so tight that it popped his head off his neck like a grape being plucked from a vine. A newspaper article stated, "Although there was a drop of only six feet, the body dropped headless to the ground. His head rebounded a distance of six feet."

Another farmhand who was hanged was Joseph Waltz. He was a troubled young man who worked as a grounds-keeper for his parents near Catskill, New York. He was frequently in trouble for robbing school houses and setting fires. A local newspaper reported that he had built a stone tower on his parents' property, from which he intended to make speeches to gatherings of interested onlookers.

One night, a travelling scissor-grinder was given lodging at the Waltz house. Joseph Waltz entered the man's bedroom, smashed his head several times with a hatchet, cleaned up the crime scene and buried the body on the farm. Waltz later confessed to the murder by saying, "an evil spirit came over me." He led the police to where the body was buried and was later hanged. Before his sentence could be carried out, though, Waltz killed again. Confined to a jail cell, he managed to pull an eighteen-inch iron bar from the flooring and used it to beat one of his guards to death. "Joe won't hurt me," the guard had confidently and erroneously said when asked why he allowed the prisoner to be loose in his cell without leg irons.

He should have known better. Across the country, bitter and angry farmhands were committing murder for seemingly pointless reasons. Some of them killed because they had been fired or because they were hired by someone else and had a grudge against their previous employer. Some killed out of greed or imagined slights. Some killed over jealousy and others because someone looked at them funny.

But despite their misdeeds, farmworkers were essential in rural life. Unless a farmer had a large brood of children, he needed help to plant seeds, harvest the crops or tend the farm animals. Farmhands were physically strong. They were necessary and they knew the land because it was the nature of their work. In most farm communities, they were a common thread. They knew almost everyone because they worked for almost everyone, but when they disappeared, they left no trace behind.

But not all of those who committed murders in the countryside were strangers and drifting farmhands - far from it. Many of the killers were members of the victim's family and the most common weapon seemed to be an axe. It was a tool that was indispensable for rural life. It was used to clear the land, cut down trees and chop the wood that provided heat and warmth for homes. It was also handy for lopping the heads off chickens and other domestic fowl. In the nineteenth and early twentieth centuries, the vast majority of rural murders were committed with an axe.

On November 20, 1894, a brutal mass murder occurred outside the small village of Wellsville, Missouri. It was carried out by Thomas Portercheck, who allegedly went insane and slaughtered his mother, two sisters and a brother before killing himself. The family, who lived in humble circumstances, occupied a small house about a half-mile east of downtown Wellsville. On the afternoon of November 19, Portercheck began acting strangely and gave, the newspaper stated, "indications that his mind was deranged." He labored under the idea that his neck was broken and insisted that someone call a doctor. His family tried to convince him that he was mistaken and to persuade him to go to bed. But he refused to lie down, insisting on sitting up all night. Late that Sunday night, the family finally went to bed, exhausted, leaving Portercheck sitting in a chair, slowly rocking back and forth, staring at the wall.

At around 3:00 a.m., one of the sisters, Mary, was awakened by an agonizing scream from her mother. When she emerged from her bedroom, she found her mother lying on the floor and Portercheck standing over her with an axe in his hands. The floor was covered with blood. In an adjoining room, she could hear her other brother moaning in what turned out to be his death throes. Mary ran through the house in a panic. After finding all of the doors locked, opened a window and jumped to the ground. Her murderous brother never noticed that she left. Through the glass, she watched in horror as he seized a can of coal oil, poured it all over the floor and then set it on fire. From the kitchen, he took a butcher knife and, standing in the midst of the flames, cut his own throat. He collapsed to the floor next to the body of his mother. The fire spread so quickly that in less than ten minutes, the entire house was engulfed in flames.

Mary's screams awakened the neighbors and they rushed to the scene, but the fire had already finished the work that the maniac had started. When the remains of the house were cool enough for the ruins to be searched, four bodies were found, blackened and charred among the timbers. They were those of Mrs. Portercheck, her youngest daughter, son James and the killer, Thomas.

The investigation showed that the mother, daughter and son had been horribly mutilated by an axe and it was surmised that it had probably been Thomas' intention to kill Mary too, but her life was saved by the screams of her mother.

"No theory is advanced for the sudden fit of insanity which overcame the young man," the newspaper said. It was simply another gruesome tragedy in rural America.

In other cases, those who lived in the isolated conditions of the heartland fell prey to passing strangers, who chose their victims because the families lived far away from help from neighbors or the law. In far too many cases, such crimes went unsolved. Murderous strangers passed through, never seen by the distant neighbors, and vanished without a trace. But when they were caught, the vengeance extracted could be brutal.

In 1870, one of the most horrific murders in Missouri's history occurred on a farm near the small town of Potosi. On November 21, David and Louisa Lapine, along with their two children and Mrs. Lapine's sister, Mary Christopher, and her child, were found shot and hacked to death with an axe. The family had been murdered by two brothers, Leon and Charles Jolly, and a third man, John Armstrong. The drunken trio had called at the Lapine cabin and at some point, a disagreement erupted between Armstrong, Charles Jolly and Mrs. Christopher. David Lapine got between them, attempting to stop the argument, and Jolly pulled out a revolver and shot him four times. He then struck Louisa, knocking her to the floor. Armstrong, in the meantime, had snatched up an axe, killed Mary with it, and then attacked the children. The heads were severed from all of their bodies. After the murders, the men set fire to the cabin to try and hide the evidence, but the bodies were found in the ruins the following morning and clear evidence pointed an accusatory finger at the Jollys and John Armstrong.

The men were quickly arrested and jailed. Leon Jolly, who did not participate in the murders, agreed to testify against his brother and Armstrong in the upcoming trial. But some of the local residents didn't want to wait for the legal system to act. Five days after the murders, a mob gathered outside the jail and demanded that the pair be given over to them to be hanged. When the sheriff refused, the angry townspeople attacked the building. When it was over, six residents had been wounded and one killed by the sheriff and his deputies as they defended the jail and their prisoners.

The case went to trial and made headlines in the state and beyond, with reporters gleefully referring to the case as "The Missouri Horror." On December 21, 1870, Charles Jolly and John Armstrong were found guilty and sentenced to death by hanging. The punishment was carried out on January 21, 1871. Surrounding newspapers proclaimed the event the "Day of the Double Hanging," and families came from all over the region to see justice carried out. The men were led to the gallows and nooses were placed around their necks. The trapdoor was sprung and the two plunged to their deaths. Jolly died instantly as his head was nearly ripped completely from his body. Armstrong was not so lucky. The heavy man dangled with his toes scraping the ground. His neck had not broken and because the rope was stretched from his weight, he slowly strangled to death.

The deaths of the Lapine family had finally been avenged.

You'll find many such stories - and many much worse - in the pages ahead. For those who believe that the most horrendous crimes in American history were confined to major cities like New York, Los Angeles and Chicago, you'll be both frightened and shocked by events that occurred in the bucolic countryside, along peaceful back roads, in the dark woods and in the small farming communities of America.

But you will not be surprised by the number of ghosts that are lingering behind.

Keep the lights on while you're reading this one!
I can promise that René and I did while we were writing it!

Troy Taylor
Spring 2014

1782: THE FAMILY ANNIHILATOR

In 1995, author Daniel Cohen wrote "Something strange and horrible happened in a number of American households of the early republic. In a series of curiously clustered incidents, a handful of men, loving husbands and affectionate fathers, took axes from under their beds, or off their mantelpiece, and slaughtered their wife and children."

The public was transfixed by these bloody tragedies, even though they were fairly rare until the early decades of the nineteenth century, when "the rate of wife murder increased fivefold" throughout the north, according to Karen Halttunen, a professor of history at the University of Southern California. At the same time, printed accounts of family murders began to appear with increasing frequency. Such stories offered detailed descriptions of butchery that bordered on the obscene. Those who believe that today's popular culture is unusually graphic in its depictions of violence might consider this passage from an 1857 true crime book called *The Triple Murderer*. It recounted the crimes of a Midwestern killer named Reuben Ward. After he killed his wife, Olive, on their family farm he then disposed of the corpse in the most grisly - although efficient -- way imaginable:

I tore the clothes open from the throat down. I then took a small pocket knife and opened the body, took the bowels out first, and then put them in the stove upon wood; they being filled with air would make a noise in exploding, so I took my knife and pricked holes through them to prevent the noise; then took out the liver and heart... I then took out the blood remaining in the cavity of the body by placing a copper kettle close to the same and cupping it out with my hands... I broke off the ribs and took out the breast bone, and threw it into a large boiler; unjointed the arms at the shoulders, doubled them up and placed them in the boiler; then severed the remaining portions of the body by placing a stick of wood under her back and breaking the back bone over the same, cutting away the flesh and ligaments with a knife.

According to crime historians, men who committed family homicide during this period were generally driven by an intolerable sense of mortification that they had somehow failed in the eyes of society - and their families. By the middle 1800s, increasingly high expectations had been placed on married men. It was no longer enough just to have a house; one had to have a *nice* house. Having a job was no longer enough; a man had to have an upwardly rising career that would support a wife and children in comfort. Husbands were expected to be more than just good providers; they had to be sober, upstanding and respectable. When men could not meet the expectations placed on them by society, they often turned on those closest to them -- their wives and families - who were the most persistent reminders of their failures.

The rise of the so-called "family annihilators" began in the late 1700s, when formerly loving fathers and husbands hideously slaughtered their families in a sudden fit of homicidal frenzy. Perhaps the most infamous of these nightmarish figures was a man named William Beadle, the perpetrator of what one contemporary report called "a crime more atrocious and horrible" than any ever committed in New England "and scarcely exceeded in the history of man."

William Beadle was born in England in 1730 and immigrated to America at the age of thirty-two. He settled in the village of Wethersfield, Connecticut, where he operated a country store that was regarded as having a "handsome assortment of goods." Beadle enjoyed early success, which must have enhanced his initial view of himself. Even though he was a quiet man with unprepossessing looks, he thought of himself as far superior to the ordinary run of humanity. In one journal entry, he wrote, "My person is small and mean to look on and my circumstances were always narrow, which were great disadvantages in the world. But I have great reason to think my soul is above the common mould." In his mind, he believed himself to be "a diamond among millions of pebbles."

His business thrived for several years. Very proud of his success, he maintained a handsome farm outside of town and entertained his guests in great style. His neighbors held him in high esteem. They saw him as an honorable tradesman, a generous host, a loving husband and a proud father.

In the years that immediately followed the Revolutionary War, however, Beadle suffered a number of reverses that left him in dire financial straits. Unable to bear the idea of being thought of as being poor and dependent, he struggled to keep up the outward appearance of his former situation. Eventually, it became too much for him and he succumbed to his despair. The thought of being perceived as a failure by his neighbors was more than he could tolerate. He wrote, "If a man who once lived well, meant well, and done well, falls by unavoidable accident into poverty and submits to be laughed at, despised, and trampled on by a set of mean wretches as far below him as the moon is below the sun; I say, if such a man submits, he must become meaner than meanness itself."

Deciding that suicide was less shameful than poverty, he decided to kill himself - and his family. Like so many others before and after him who committed acts of horror, he justified this intended atrocity as prompted by kindness, even love. He wrote in his journal, "I mean to close the eyes of six persons through perfect humanity and the most endearing fondness and friendship; for mortal father never felt more of these tender ties than myself." At first, he thought he might spare his wife. After much deliberation, though, he concluded that it would be "cruel to leave her behind to languish out a life of misery and wretchedness." If she was faced with having to mourn the loss of her entire family, death would undoubtedly be merciful.

As he began to formulate his plan, he kept hoping that "providence would turn up something to prevent it, if the intent were wrong." Instead, he saw that every circumstance served to convince him that destroying his family was the only logical course. For a while, he prayed each night that his twelve-year-old son and three young daughters might be killed accidentally, thus sparing him the necessity of taking their lives. To facilitate that end, he removed the protective wooden cover from the well in the back yard and encouraged them to swim in the deepest and most treacherous parts of the river. When the children survived these dangers, stubbornly clinging to life, Beadle resolved to take more direct action.

Uncertain at first how and when to carry out this "great affair" as he described the planned massacre , he had no doubt that he would not falter when the time came. He wrote, "How I shall really perform the task I have undertaken I know not till the moment arrives. But I believe I shall perform it deliberately and as steadily as I would go to supper, or to bed."

He eventually decided on November 18 as the day he would kill his family. He first "procured a noble supper of oysters, that my family and I may eat and drink together, thank God, and then die." He was forced to abandon this plan, however, when the maid - who had been sent away on an errand - returned unexpectedly.

A few weeks later, he made another aborted attempt, which he described in his journal:

On the morning of the sixth of December, I rose before the sun, felt calm, and left my wife between sleep and wake, went into the room where my infants lay, found them all sound asleep; the means of death were with me, but I had not before determined whether to strike or not, but yet thought it was a good opportunity. I stood over them, and asked my God whether it was right or not now to strike; but no answer came; not I believe ever does to a man while on earth. I then examined myself, there was neither fear, trembling, nor horror about me. I then went into a chamber next to that to look at myself in the glass; but I could discover no alteration in my countenances of feelings; this is true as God reigns, but for further trial I yet postponed it.

Five days later, in the early morning hours of December 11, 1782, Beadle finally carried out his bloody act. Slipping into the second-floor bedchamber shared by his four children and the housemaid, he shook the latter awake, and then "ordered her to rise gently without disturbing the children" and come downstairs with him. When she appeared a few minutes later, he handed her a note to give to the family's physician, Dr. Farnsworth, who lived a short distance away. Beadle told her that his wife had been ill all night. The maid was to go straight to Farnsworth's home at once, give him the note, and remain there until the doctor returned to the Beadle house with her.

As soon as the maid left on this imaginary errand, Beadle hurried into his bedroom, where he had already stashed a freshly sharpened axe and carving knife. He slipped to the edge of the bed and swung the axe with a swift hand, smashing his sleeping wife's skull. He then slit her throat with the knife, taking care to drain the blood into a pitcher so that he did not stain the bed sheets. After covering her face with a cloth, he went to the children's room and killed all of them in the same way. He left his little boy lying in bed, while the slaughtered girls were placed side by side on the floor - "like little lambs" - covered with a blanket.

Leaving a trail of blood behind him on the stairs, Beadle went down to the kitchen, where he placed the axe and knife - "reeking with the blood of his family" - on the table. He then seated himself in a chair next to the fireplace. Several weeks earlier, in preparation for this moment, he had taken his two flintlock pistols to the village gunsmith for repair. He now took a pistol in each hand and, bracing his elbows on the arms of the chair, he pressed the muzzles against his ears and pulled both triggers at the same time, "splattering his brains against the walls and wainscoting."

By then, Dr. Farnsworth had been roused from his sleep and the Beadles' maid had handed him the note, which "announced the diabolical purpose of the writer." Even though Farnsworth found it impossible to believe that any man would "adopt so horrible a design," he immediately alerted his neighbor, the Hon. Stephen Mix Mitchell, who later became chief justice of the state and wrote an account of the atrocity in 1805. The two men rushed to the Beadle house, where they were greeted by the tragic scene.

Soon, the news of the massacre had spread to the village. Men, women and children flocked to the Beadle house for a look at the carnage. The scene was described by Judge Mitchell in an account that become one of the best-selling true crime pamphlets of its day:

The very inmost souls of the beholders were wounded at the sight and torn by contending passions. Silent grief, with marks of astonishment, were succeeded by furious indignation against the author of the affecting spectacle, which vented itself in incoherent exclamations. Some old soldiers, accidentally passing through the town that morning on their way from camp to visit their friends, led by curiosity, turned into view the sad remains. On sight of the woman and her tender offspring, notwithstanding all their firmness, the tender sympathetic tear stealing gently down their furrowed cheeks betrayed the anguish of their hearts. On being showed the body of the sacrifice, they paused for a moment, then muttered forth an oath or two of execration, with their eyes fixed on the ground in silent sorrow, they slowly went their way. So awful and terrible a disaster wrought wonderfully on the minds of the neighborhood. Nature itself seemed ruffled and refused the kindly aid of balmy sleep for a time.

The people of Wethersfield shared the old soldiers' anger with Beadle, refusing to allow him a Christian burial in the local churchyard. Tying the bloody carving knife to his chest, they dragged him on a small sled to the riverbank, dug a grave in unconsecrated ground, and tossed his ragged body into the hole "like the carcass of a beast." A few days later, after deciding that the site was too close to the ferry landing, a few locals dug up the corpse and moved it "with utmost secrecy" to an "obscure spot." Despite their precautions, some children discovered the place and the body was exhumed again and moved to yet another spot "where it is hoped mankind will have no further vexation with it."

In contrast to the way that the wicked murderer's corpse was treated, the funeral for his victims was a ceremonious affair. One observer wrote, "The remains of the children were borne by a suitable number of equal age, attended with a sad procession of youths of the town, all bathed in tears. Side by side, the hapless woman's corpse was carried in solemn procession to the parish churchyard, followed by a great concourse who, with affectionate concern and every token of respect, were anxious to express their heartfelt sorrow in performing the last mournful duties."

MURDER BALLADS

Even though William Beadle was denied a decent burial or any marker for his forgotten grave, he was granted a kind of immortality in the form of a widely circulated broadside ballad, illustrated with a woodcut of a knife-wielding Beadle stalking his innocent children.

Murder ballads have an unusual place in American history. Long before the advent of tabloid journalism, accounts of sensational homicides were often told through such ballads - crudely written poems that were dashed off in the aftermath of some grisly killing or cruel slaughter, printed on page-long sheets known as broadsides and sold for a few pennies. Since most of the people who composed there verses were talentless hacks - interested more in making money from the public's morbid fascination with violent crime than making art - they rarely signed their work. One exception was the author of a ballad called "The Thirtieth Street Tragedy," who proudly identified himself as "The Saugerties Bard."

Thanks to grueling research by author John Thorn, we know that this prolific ballad writer was Henry Sherman Backus. Born in upstate New York in 1798, Backus came from a military background - his father was a major who died during the War of 1812 - and he developed an early love of martial music, become adept at the fife, drum and bugle. After teaching school for a number of years, he moved to Saugerties, a town in Ulster County, New York, where he married a local woman and had five children with her. After a series of personal tragedies, which included the death of his wife and an infant daughter, he had a breakdown and was confined to a lunatic asylum. His children were sent away to various foster homes. When he was released, he abandoned his old life and became a wandering musician. Roaming from small town to small town, he performed his self-composed ballads in taverns and roadhouses and peddled cheaply printed copies of them to his audiences. Eventually, he made his way to New York, where he continued to produce, print and distribute his ballads of popular crimes. How many ballads Backus wrote is unknown, but scholars have discovered at least three dozen.

And Backus was not alone. Would-be poets and musicians in towns and on farms across the country composed their own ballads about local crimes. Some of them were clever, others were terrible, rarely rising above the level of doggerel.

The murder ballad of William Beadle fits easily into the category of a poorly constructed verse that was composed to take advantage of the public's thirst for horror. A handful of the better and by that we mean "more interesting" ballads will appear within in the pages of this book. Since Beadle's story provided our introduction to murder ballads, the verse written in his honor is as follows:

> A bloody scene I'll now relate,
> Which lately happen'd in a neighboring state
> A murder of the deepest dye, I say.
> O be amaz'd for surely well you may.
> A man unworthy of name who slew
> Himself, his consort, and his offspring too;
> An amiable wife with four children dear,
> Into one grave was put - Oh drop a tear!
>
> Soon in the morning of the fatal day,
> Beadle, the murd'rer sent his maid away,
> To tell the awful deed he had in view;
> To their assistance the kind neighbors flew.
>
> It truly gives me pain for to pen down,
> A deed so black, and yet his mind was sound.
> Says he, "I mean to close six persons' eyes.
> Through perfect fondness and the tend'rest ties."
>
> Detest the errors to this deed him drew,
> And mourn the hapless victims whom he slew;
> And pray to God that Satan be bound,
> Since to deceive so many he is found.
>
> Fly swiftly round, ye circling years,
> Hail the auspicious day,
> When love shall dwell in every heart -
> Nor men their offspring slay!

At least one murder ballad was allegedly written not only by the woman who committed the crime, but she calmly composed it while on the gallows as a crowd of locals gaped at her from below the scaffold. Her name was Frankie Silver and she was the first woman ever hanged in North Carolina. She lived with her husband and baby daughter in a cabin at Deyton Bend, Toe River Valley, in the particularly cold winter of 1831-32. On December 22, Frankie asked her husband, Charlie, to chop plenty of wood before he went hunting, as he might be gone for several days. That night, worn out from his hard work with the axe, Charlie lay down on the floor in front of the fireplace and went to sleep with his daughter in his arms.

The next morning, Frankie walked over the ridge to see her husband's mother and sisters. She found them washing clothes and said to them, "Well, you're up and at it early. I've been working myself, since before daylight, and have my cabin all redded up meaning that she had cleaned it ." This was apparently a surprise to the Silvers since Frankie was not known for her industrious housekeeping. She also asked her in-laws to help her look for her husband, who, she said, had gone across the river the day before to get his Christmas liquor and had not returned. The family was unconcerned, knowing that Charlie was apt to spend some time away, chatting with his old cronies on the other side of the river.

But Charlie did not return. A few days later, a group of men got together to look for him. Many feared the worst. It was unlike him to not return and a big man like Charlie Silver didn't just disappear. Jake Cullis, one of Charlie's old friends, decided to take a look around the family's cabin. He took Charlie's little sister with him and they carefully examined the place. Poking about in the fireplace, they were startled to find bones and teeth among the ashes. When a rock was pried loose, they found bloodstains under the freshly scrubbed hearth.

The discovery was reported to Sheriff John Boone and Frankie was arrested, tried, convicted and sentenced to be hanged for the murder of her husband. With the help of a cousin, she managed to escape from the jail one night, but was captured and brought back. She claimed she was innocent to the authorities, but friends told a different story. After Frankie was hanged, one of her friends reported that Frankie told her how she had taken the baby from her husband's arms and then had struck him a terrible blow with the heavy axe, nearly severing his head from his body. Charlie leapt up and began thrashing about the room, but Frankie dodged him until he collapsed. Once he did, she hacked his body into pieces and burned them in the fireplace, using the wood that her husband had cut for her. There is no record of what became of her daughter.

Frankie Silver was executed on July 12, 1833. Legend says that she mounted the scaffold with a piece of cake in one hand. After she recited her ballad, the hangman asked if she was ready. She replied that she would be as soon as she finished the cake, which she then proceeded to eat. Surprisingly, Frankie's impromptu ballad survived in the Toe River Valley as late as the 1930s, when author Muriel Early Sheppard discovered it being sung to a mournful tune. A portion of the ballad relates the particulars of the crime:

> The jealous thought that first gave strife
> To make me take my husband's life.
> For days and months I spent my time
> Thinking how to commit this crime.

And on a dark and doleful night
I put his body out of sight;
With flames I tried him to consume
But time would not admit it done.

Judge Donnell has my sentence passed;
These prison walls I leave at last;
Nothing to cheer my drooping head
Until I'm numbered with the dead.

Farm communities seem to offer more than their share of murder ballad stories, like one that comes from Pennsylvania in August 1838. Joshua Jones was a farmer who lived between Andrews Settlement and Ellisberg, in north central Pennsylvania. He shot his wife to death one morning while she was still asleep in bed. Then he went out and brought in his cows from the pasture, milked them and returned to the house. Pretending to be shocked at finding his wife's body, he called for help. He then tried to make his neighbors believe that his wife had committed suicide. Needless to say, no one was fooled. Jones was arrested and put on trial for the crime. He was convicted and sentenced to hang on May 29, 1839. Facing death, Jones sold his body to Dr. Amos French for $10, using the money to purchase better food for the remainder of his prison stay. When the day of execution arrived, he still had $1 left, so he placed it between two pieces of bread and ate it.

Dr. French had promised Jones that, as soon as his body was taken from the scaffold, he would do what he could to restore his life. By law, no man could be hanged twice, so if he could be resuscitated, Jones would be a free man. If that failed, Dr. French promised to care for Jones' son. When the revival failed, French took the boy into his home and educated him. Unfortunately, the boy died a few years after his father's execution. French and two other doctors carried Jones' body to Whitesville, where they boiled off the flesh to make a skeleton for the doctor's use. The ballad that was written was in protest to this procedure carried out in the interest of medicine, rather than a lament over the crime of murder. It was circulated locally for many years and was told from the point of view of Jones' ghost. Here are a few stanzas:

Come list ye doctors all to me
For Jones' ghost I truly be -
Come look at me now if you can,
I am that slaughtered, mangled man.
When on earth my name was Jones,
Composed like you of flesh and bones,
But for the murder of my wife
The people they did take my life.

Then we can skip ahead to the stanza that really lies at the root of the story:

> You did not do as you agreed
> Before my death, when you did plead.
> You let me hang an hour almost
> Until that I gave up the ghost.
> You took me down with wicked hands
> Conveyed my corpse to distant lands,
> There to dissect this frame of mine -
> When you did mangle like the swine.

Perhaps the most plentiful of the various murder ballads that made the rounds - especially in rural areas during the nineteenth and early twentieth centuries -- were what many folklorists and "songcatchers" have classified as "Murdered-Girl Ballads." It's a subgenre, of sorts, that almost always seems to involve a trusting young woman who is done in by a cold-hearted seducer. There are four elements that usually made up a murdered-girl ballad: an innocent woman is seduced by an unscrupulous lover; when she becomes pregnant, he arranges a tryst on the pretext of discussing plans for their marriage; over her protests, he lures her to a secluded area; and even though she begs for mercy, he kills her in a terrible manner and then disposes of the body.

There were a couple of very well-known American murdered-girl ballads, including a tear-jerking ditty about Pearl Bryan whose murder is recounted later in this book and another called "Poor Naomi Wise" or "Poor Omie." During the peak of folk music's popularity in the late 1950s - when the pop charts were filled with vocal groups singing "This Land is Your Land" and just about everyone could hum along to "Kumbaya" - the song was a standard in coffeehouses. Scores of artists, including Bob Dylan, have recorded it.

The song was, of course, based on a real-life murder. Naomi Wise was a real person who loved and lost her life in the early 1800s. An orphan, she lived with a farmer named William Adams and his wife near Asheboro, North Carolina. She was nineteen years old and said to be a great beauty, which attracted many of the young men in the region. Naomi's most persistent suitor was a young man named Jonathan Lewis and Naomi fully expected to become his bride. However, Jonathan was rather unexpectedly given hope that he might make a more propitious marriage with Hattie Elliott, the sister of his employer. He had to get rid of Poor Omie, who was demanding that he marry her instead.

One night in the summer of 1808, Naomi tied her few pitiful belongings into a small bundle and hid them outside the farmhouse. Then, carrying a bucket with her as through she was going to get water from the nearby spring, she went out. She quickly snatched up her bundle and went to the spring, where, it is believed, Jonathan had promised to meet her and take her off to be married.

Later, investigators found a stump near where a horse had stood, found Naomi's footprints going to the spot, and decided that she had met someone there, mounted the horse, and ridden away of her own free will, as she probably had. In the night, the family living near the mill pond on the Deep River heard screams, but they soon faded away and nothing more was thought of the incident until the body of Naomi Wise was found in the stream the next day. The water was fairly shallow at this point in the river, but the girl's skirts had been pulled up over her head and tied so that she had been literally thrown into the river in a sack from which she could not escape.

Jonathan Lewis was immediately suspected. He was taken from his home and brought to view the body. He put out a hand and gently smoothed back Naomi's wet, tangled hair from her pale white face - a gesture that infuriated those who had gathered at the scene, who wanted to hang the man immediately. He was jailed, but escaped and it was not until 1815 that he was captured and brought to trial. By that time, even though the story of the murder had been kept vivid by the ballads sung in the region, there was no real evidence against him and a jury found Lewis not guilty. Legend says that he confessed to Naomi's murder many years later on his deathbed, but we'll never known for sure.

What we do know if that Naomi has been kept alive for the last two centuries by the ballads that were sung about her. There were several variations, but here's a portion of the most popular one, which for some reason renames the villain "George Luther." Other versions call him John Lewis or young Lewis. This version goes:

> She met him as promised, they went for a ride;
> Then that villain choked her till Poor Omie died.
> He threw her in the river, below the mill dam;
> And he rode back to his home like an innocent man.
>
> When Omie was missing and could not be found,
> The whole county gathered and searched all around.
> They found her poor body tossed up on the rocks.
> They thought that George Luther had killed Omie Wise.
>
> They found him and they took him to see Omie Wise.
> He lifted the hair out of Poor Omie's eyes.
> They took him to court but no one could say
> That he killed Poor Omie on that fatal day.
>
> Yet when he was dying, so I have heard tell,
> He confessed to the murder to save him from Hell.

Then, as now, stories of horrific crimes had a peculiar fascination for most people, so they were often recounted in ballad form by local artists, poets and musicians - probably far more often than surviving ballads indicate. Unless the crime was a particularly noted one, so that the story was told over and over again, or unless the poet had verses printed to sell, most ballads were lost to future generations. They may seem simple to us today, but they were very moving when they were written.

Murder ballads, despite their often creaky and antiquated style, are an authentic look at the crimes of yesterday and paint a vivid - and often bloody picture - of what life in America was like for the generations that came before us. They were generations that were just as fascinated by crime and murder as we are today.

1810: A DEATH AT WHITE ROCKS
The Murder of Polly Williams

Polly Williams 1792-1810
Behold with Pity you that pass by
Here for the Bones of Polly Williams Lie
Who was cut off in Tender Youth
By a vile wretch, her pretended groom

A fitting epitaph for a beautiful young woman who met her end at the foot of White Rocks, tossed aside by a faithless fiancé.

Mary Williams was a local beauty, described as fair-haired and blue-eyed. She was a hard worker with a kind and loving heart. Sadly, her heart was also a trusting one, and she longed to make a home as the wife of the man she loved.

When Mary, known to everyone as "Polly," was fifteen, she moved with her family to the tiny hamlet of New Salem in the hills of southwest Pennsylvania. Her parents were poor European immigrants who sought employment in the coal and coke region of the state. They chose New Salem because a wealthy relation had settled in the area and Polly's father believed that this connection would help them gain a better life. Their chosen village of New Salem was less than a decade old, but residents in the area quickly added a nickname. New Salem was made up almost entirely of poor immigrants working the nearby coal mines and coke ovens. So many "lost" sheep found their way into New Salem, and subsequently onto the hungry worker's tables, that their hometown became known as "Muttontown."

Shortly after her family settled into their new home, Polly moved in with her aunt and uncle, Major and Mrs. Jacob Moss. She was to help with the cooking, cleaning, and caring for their children. She was a lovely, hard-working girl and was soon thought of as part of their family, so much so that she stayed behind with the Mosses when her parents decided to move farther west in 1808 to find work away from the coal mines. Both she and the Mosses were happy with their new situation. In fact, Mrs. Moss and Polly became very close and held each other's confidences.

Time passed and Polly was introduced to a young bachelor who lived with his parents nearby. Phillip Rogers was immediately taken with the lovely young Polly. Her charm and gentle manners were impossible for him to resist, despite her station in life being decidedly below his. He must have seemed like a godsend to the penniless Polly, who had little to look forward to in her future beyond serving wealthy people as a maid or housekeeper. Phillip represented a reprieve from her otherwise inescapable lower class life. They made for a strange couple: she, a slender beauty with a head of long golden curls and he, homely, squat and stout. But the differences between them didn't stop there. Not only was Phillip from a higher social class than Polly, but he was five years older. Her solid work ethic and sweet temperament was in stark contrast to his domineering and manipulative personality. Nevertheless, they fell in love, or at least, Polly fell in love with Phillip. It's hard to say if he ever loved her, or if he had simply found someone whom he could manipulate.

As soon as was acceptable, the two young lovers became engaged, though Phillip insisted that they keep their engagement a secret. Undoubtedly, he wished to keep word of their betrothal from his class-conscious mother. Polly, on the other hand, confided in her aunt, Mrs. Moss, who was immediately suspicious of Phillips motives. But Polly would hear no words against her beloved. She was willing to keep their relationship from the rest of the community until he was ready to publish the news because she now had a happy future ahead of her with a man she loved.

Because of the secrecy, Phillip insisted that they not attend any gatherings as a couple. Instead, they should only meet in out-of-the-way, secluded spots. A favorite meeting place was a large natural formation known as White Rocks, three miles distant from their respective homes. White Rocks was positioned on a north-facing slope in the Appalachian foothills. It was massive, with some of the rocks towering nearly seventy feet above the steep, almost sheer face that ran to the base of the structure. The highest peak was known by the locals, even in 1810, as "lovers' leap." It was high atop lovers' leap where the two young people met most often, and it was there where the first cracks in their relationship began to form.

Polly happily went along with Phillip's demands, but after the first year had come and gone, Polly was becoming impatient. She had waited long enough and was eager to set a date for their wedding. She was ready to start their life together but Phillip was deaf to her entireties and postponed the date time and again. They began to argue often but he continued to put her off. Word had leaked out that Phillip's parents had heard of the relationship and were violently opposed to a marriage between their son and this impoverished, low-class girl. As the second year of their secret engagement was drawing to a close, Polly began to suspect that Phillip had never intended to marry her at all. She confided her fears and concerns to her aunt. Mrs. Moss was concerned for her niece, fearing that she was being badly used, and begged her to break off the engagement. Polly was nearly inconsolable as she refused her advice. As she sobbed into her aunt's shoulder, she explained that no matter what Phillip did, she simply couldn't live without him. She would always give him one more chance...

Finally Phillip, then twenty-four, seemed to be coming around to see things as Polly did. On August 13, 1810, he sent a message to eighteen-year-old Polly at the Moss home. He was ready for them to marry. He had arranged for a squire, living on the distant Chestnut Ridge in Woodbridgetown, to perform the ceremony. If she would meet him at White Rocks that morning, they would walk the fourteen miles together to meet the squire. Polly was thrilled! The day she had waited so long for had finally arrived. She donned her best frock and packed a few items in a small bag. Mrs. Moss still distrusted Phillip and did her best to discourage Polly from meeting him, but Polly was determined. With a smile on her lips and a skip in her step, she set off for White Rocks to meet her beloved. Mrs. Moss hung her head in disappointment. She saw only sorrow in her dear niece's future, but she had no idea how terribly short that future would be.

The Lovers' Leap cliff at White Rocks

Polly had no intention of keeping her fiancé waiting, so she hurried along her way. She arrived at their appointed rendezvous spot before Phillip. As she waited for him to arrive, she paced nervously back and forth at the precipice of the lovers' leap, probably imagining a blissful life with the man she had waited for so patiently. A few couples approached her on the path, nodded their hellos, and passed on by. When at long last, her Phillip arrived, all was apparently not well. A strolling couple who had seen Polly waiting alongside the path as Phillip arrived, later reported that they had heard the two speaking in excited voices and the young woman sobbing. Not wishing to intrude on a lovers' spat, they walked on, leaving the two alone.

Polly did not return home that night or the following morning, but Mrs. Moss was not concerned. She believed that her niece would be married by then. She would be staying with her new husband in her new home. So Mrs. Moss set about her day, sadly adjusting to Polly's absence.

That August day was a lovely one, though a bit hot. Seeking the cool shade of the woods, four young girls set out to pick berries. As they searched for blackberry bushes, they came upon a shocking sight. In the shadow of White Rocks, crumpled and bloody, lay the body of a young woman. In her hand, she still held fast to a slim branch, torn from a laurel bush as she plummeted from the top of the precipice. The girls ran screaming to tell their fathers.

The woman's body was taken to the Nixon Tavern in Fairchance, the nearest village. The Fayette County sheriff and coroner were sent for from nearby Uniontown, the county seat. The men who had carried the woman from White Rocks could only speculate that she had lost her footing and fallen to her death. When the coroner arrived however, he had a different opinion. What he saw were injuries far more devastating than could be explained by a fall. The body was indeed mangled and twisted, but she had also been struck repeatedly in the forehead with what must have been a rock. The upper part of her face was crushed from the blows. The men had found a bloody rock lying near the woman's feet. They now believed that she and her killer had been standing at the top of White Rocks. He must have struck her down, beat her about the head with a rock, then thrown her over the ledge, tossing the bloody rock after her. The sprig of laurel clutched in her hand was evidence of her feeble attempt to save herself as the brute forced her over the edge.

No one local knew the young woman, so she remained unidentified. After two more days, she was buried in a local cemetery. The people of Fairchance had embraced the unknown woman and had tried to give her a decent burial. As word of the nameless, murdered woman spread across the countryside, the story fell upon the ears of Major and Mrs. Moss. They had not seen nor heard a word from Polly after she had left their home. They were concerned that the murdered woman might be the missing Polly. Major Moss traveled to Uniontown and contacted Sheriff Jacob Harbaugh. The woman's description matched that of Polly Williams, right down to the dress she was wearing when she was last seen. Moss insisted that the sheriff open the grave, and he found that it was indeed Polly Williams, lying on the pine boards of the coffin.

Major Moss told the sheriff how Polly had set out to meet her fiancé the morning of the thirteenth and she had not been seen since. Sheriff Harbaugh immediately set out for the Rogers' home to speak to Phillip. As the sheriff questioned him about Polly, Phillip's mother grew angry and openly admonished him for "taking up with such trash." Phillip denied harming Polly. He told the sheriff that they had quarreled and he had left her where they had met. He implied, without saying so directly, that she must have gotten lost, and in trying to find her way home, she must have fallen off the cliff. The sheriff didn't believe such a flimsy story. Because of the coroner's opinion that she had been bashed about the head before her fall, he arrested Phillip Rogers for the murder of Polly Williams.

On November 22, 1810, Phillip Rogers went on trial for murder. Phillip's parents were determined that their son would not be sent to jail, or worse. Having the means to do so, they spared no expense in providing a defense. They hired Senator James Ross from Pittsburgh as their son's lawyer. There was no real evidence of Phillip's guilt, after all, only speculation and supposition. He admitted to meeting Polly that day atop the cliff, but denied causing her any harm. Phillip was vilified by every prosecution witness but no one had witnessed the murder. No one could verify the bloody rock that struck her had been in his hands. The judge admonished the jury that the evidence was "very strong" but the jury could find no solid evidence with which to convict. Phillip Rogers was acquitted of the murder of Polly Williams. The trial had taken less than one full day.

The jury had acquitted Phillip, but he had been found guilty in the court of public opinion. Following the trail, he tried to go back to the life he had lived before his arrest. His former friends and neighbors would not let this happen. He may have gotten away with murder, but he would not be allowed to live among decent folk. With persistent accusations, insults and violent threats against his life, they drove him from their midst. Phillip packed up and left his parents' comfortable home and made his new home in Greensboro, Green County. He adopted a trade and earned a living as a stone mason, a far fall from the life of wealth and privilege he had grown up with. After a few years in his new home, he married a young woman and raised a family. Phillip Rogers died at the age of seventy-four.

It is unlikely that Phillip rested in peace in death, as he had not had a moment of peace in life. After leaving Fayette County, he had become distrustful and paranoid. He left home each morning for work, but when the sun went down, his home became a fort. He double-bolted the doors and shuttered the windows on the inside. It was not uncommon for him to sit up in a rocking chair, just inside the front door, with a loaded shotgun across his lap. These vigils would last through the night and he would not relax again until the sun was shining through the cracks in the shutters. His wife recalled that he never slept more than a few hours at a time and would often wake screaming, as if the very hounds of hell were after him. He was certain that someone or something was out to get him. Phillip Rogers went to his grave having never admitted his guilt.

After Polly's body had been identified by Major Moss, she was reinterred in the plot that had been provided for her by the people of Fairchance. They had chosen a peaceful spot under a large shade tree in what is now known as Little White Rock Cemetery in the yard of the Little White Rock Church. It seemed that Polly could not escape White Rocks. Her grave remained unmarked until sometime before 1860, when an anonymous gentleman purchased a gravestone for a woman he had never known. Upon the stone, an epitaph was carved that befit her untimely death.

The murder and trial was big news in the area. One newspaper proclaimed it "The Trial of the Century," even though the century was only ten years old and the trial lasted but a day. The story of Polly Williams was carried across the years through a folk music murder ballad and through poems telling of sweet Polly's violent death and the heartless devil in human form who cut her life short. American folk music and fanciful poems were a powerful means of relating stories such as Polly's, but facts were often ignored or contorted to fit the tale to the format.

With the persistent notoriety accorded the murder at White Rocks, Polly was not forgotten. Strangers traveled for many miles to visit White Rocks and to read Polly's epitaph. Soon after her gravestone was erected, visitors began chipping away pieces as a morbid memento. Within thirty years, so many visitors had carried away chips that nothing remained of the stone. A wooden plank replaced the original stone to mark her grave, but even that was carved away by time. Then in 1927, the Polly Williams Sunday School Class at the Little White Rock Church collected enough money to replace the remaining stub from the wooden marker with a new stone. This stone carried the same epitaph as the first, but it didn't take long before chips started appearing in the second stone as well. It took another forty-five years, but in 1972, another group of children attending the Polly Williams Sunday School Class erected a third stone. Once again, Polly's grave marker bore the same epitaph as the first two.

Polly Williams' third and final grave stone.

Polly's third gravestone remains unscathed, and her eternal resting place has finally been left at peace. Sadly though, Polly herself doesn't seem to be at peace. White Rocks remains a popular spot where hikers, boy and girl scouts, picnickers, and even a few die-hard historians visit White Rocks to gaze across the tree-carpeted foothills and down past the ledge to the rocks below. It has been over two centuries since Polly's poor broken body was found at the base of White Rocks. Her corpse was removed but it seems her spirit has remained. Unsuspecting visitors, interested only in the glorious view from the top of White Rocks have reported seeing a young woman, her long skirt brushing the ground, pacing back and forth at the top of lovers' leap, looking up and down the path as if impatiently waiting for someone. After a moment, she fades away to nothing and the witnesses release their long-held breath. Could it be that Polly does not know she has died? Has she been waiting for Phillip for over two hundred years? Or could she be waiting for someone to come along and save her from a terrible fate on the rocks below.

The blood-stained rock that was used to crush Polly's head had been held by the sheriff as evidence of the murder. After the trial concluded, he didn't know what to do with it, so he gave it to the Moss family. They agreed to take the rock, for reasons known only to them. A few nights after the trial, the family was startled awake by the piercing sound of a woman's scream. Unable to find the source of the disturbance, the family went back to bed. Several nights later, there was a repeat of the scream in the night. Again, no explanation was found. By the time they were roused from their sleep for a third time, they began to suspect that the scream was coming from the stone. Not wanting to keep the haunted stone in their home, they offered it to a neighbor. The neighbor accepted the grisly artifact, perhaps thinking it would make an interesting conversation piece. After several nights of being jolted awake by a woman's scream, the neighbor passed the stone on to someone else. After passing through several homes, no one was willing to take custody of the haunted stone. It was finally decided to return it to the base of White Rocks, whereupon, according to legend, the screams ceased.

POLLY WILLIAMS
by - Unknown

Come all ye good people, wherever you be,
Come listen awhile to my sad tragedy.
It is of a young lady that was worthy of praise --
At the age of nineteen she ended her days.

Long time she'd been courted, as I have heard say,
And her lover to delude her took many a way.
For soon as he found that her love he had gained,
Her company he slighted and her love he disdained.

And then to destroy her he contrived a plan:
To this mountain conveyed her, as I understand.
Oh, this innocent creature his mind did not know,
And in hopes to be married with this traitor did go.

And when to this mountain he did her convey,
Oh, he left her fair body for the varmints a prey.
She was cruelly treated and shamefully used
By this cruel tyrant - how could him excuse!

Which caused old and young to weep and to cry,
And to find out this traitor they each on did try.
He was apprehended, his cause to bewail --
Straightway he conducted to Uniontown jail.

There by judge and by jury he was proven out clear,
And he now takes Polly Clayton, and he calls her his dear.
But, like a deceiver, he'll live in despair
Till the day of strict judgment when all must appear.

Oh the judge and the jury they all will be there,
And with one accord the truth will declare.
Oh, the impartial judge he will pass the decree,
And this cruel tyrant condemned will be.

Come all ye good people who saw this object,
Don't add nor diminish, deceive nor correct.
This honored young lady was found in a gore,
And her flesh by this traitor all mangled and tore.

Oh, it's every temptation is the future of some snare,
And of all such false lovers I would have you beware.
Oh, beware of false lovers who court in deceit,
Lest, like Polly Williams, it will prove your sad fate.

To be brought by a lover to shame and disgrace.
And lose your sweet life in some wilderness place.
They will hug you and kiss you, and call you their own,
And when your back is turned they will leave you to mourn.

1840: "THE INHUMAN BUTCHER"

In 1817, when he married his first wife, Rosanna, William Brown had just turned thirty-seven. He was a veteran of the War of 1812 and was known for his gruff manner and quick temper. Eleven years later, the couple settled in Huntingdon County, Pennsylvania, after purchasing a farm of one hundred and twenty-six acres on the east slope of Jack's Mountain. By that time, they were the parents of two girls and four boys. The family shared a rough, one-story cabin that Brown had built with his own hands.

By the spring of 1840, only four of the children still lived at home: Betsy, age seventeen, and the three youngest boys, David, Jacob and George, who ages ranged from ten to sixteen. Their older brother, John - after years of increasingly violent quarrels with their father - had moved four miles away to Shirleysburg, where he worked for a farmer named Samuel Carothers. The oldest of the Brown children, twenty-two-year-old Peggy, lived in a small cabin on her father's land with her husband, Robert McConaghy, and their three small children.

Apart from his age - which was thirty-one when he committed what contemporary accounts called "the most awful atrocity in the annals of crime" - little information survives about Robert McConaghy, none of it good. It is known that he could barely read, occasionally drank too much, and often used coarse language. He also had a seething resentment toward his father-in-law. Even though he certainly could not be considered wealthy, William Brown was a man of substance in the small community. His farm, which included his house, barn and outbuildings, was valued at roughly $4,000 - more than $100,000 in today's dollars. McConaghy not only coveted his father-in-law's property, he felt entitled to it. He later confessed, "I thought I had as good a right to it as any of them." He knew, however, that it would never be his, unless his wife inherited it.

And for that to happen, the rest of her family would have to die.

By the middle of May 1840, McConaghy had devised a plan to wipe out his wife's entire family in a single bloody stroke. The first step was to lure young John Brown back home.

McConaghy knew about a handsome one-year-old colt that was among the Browns' livestock. John had been eager to own the horse since the time it was foaled, but due to the antagonism between them, his father refused to sell the animal to him, let alone make a gift of it to him.

Late on the Friday afternoon of May 29, while John was out plowing his employer's corn, his brother-in-law showed up unannounced at the Crothers farm. To John's surprise, McConaghy told him that he had a message from John's father. The old man had decided to let John have the colt for $15. The price was a little higher than John had expected, but he wanted the horse badly so he agreed to the terms and said that he would come and fetch it in a few days, after the plowing was finished. McConaghy shook his head, nearly betraying his own impatience. He should try and get there sooner, he told the young man, before Brown had a change of heart. John finally promised that he would come the following day.

During this era, there were more than one hundred iron furnaces operating throughout Pennsylvania. One of these was the Matilda Furnace, located in Mt. Union, about ten miles from the Brown farm. To supplement his income, Brown worked regularly at the furnace, often staying in Mt. Union for a number of days at a time. Early in the afternoon of May 30, having been away from his farm for nearly a week, William Brown packed up his things and started home on foot.

He was in no hurry. He stopped along the way to eat and to visit with a few acquaintances, making it just past 5:00 p.m. when he approached his farm. As he crossed over from his neighbor's land to his own, he heard his "dog bark and howl." The dog kept up the commotion, which was unlike the animal's usual behavior. Brown later admitted to being very surprised to hear it.

He was surprised again when he stepped up to the door and reached to open it only to find that the handle was missing. Puzzled, he turned to look around. As he glanced toward the barn, he saw a flash of light from the hayloft, followed by the crack of a rifle, and felt a bullet whistle past his head. A few second later, another shot rang out. This time, the bullet grazed his jaw and took off a part of his ear.

Brown whirled about and jumped down from the cabin's stoop. Bravely, he ran directly toward the barn. As he did, a bareheaded man in dark clothing jumped down from the hayloft and bolted for the woods. Brown screamed after him, "You damned infernal rascal! What are you doing here?" By then, the man had vanished into the trees.

Inside the barn, Brown found the missing door handle. It was lying next to two of his own flintlock rifles, which were normally kept in the house. Grabbing the weapons, he ran back to the house for his shot pouch, intending to reload the guns and pursue his would-be assassin. When he burst into the front room, though, he saw a body lying face-down on the floor. Brown said later, "It was my son John. I put my hand on him and turned him round on his back. He was all stiff. His face was black, and blood was running out of each side of his mouth." He had been shot in the chest.

Leaving the rifles, Brown ran up the road, where he found two of his neighbors, William Atherton and John Taylor, cutting wood in an orchard. "My God, what's happened to you?" Atherton cried, seeing Brown's frantic, disheveled look, and noting the blood on his clothing and his mangled ear. Brown told them that he'd been shot and his son John had been killed. While Atherton hurried off to raise the alarm, Taylor and Brown returned to the latter's farmhouse. It was Taylor who first spotted the bulky form under a quilt in the bedroom. He grimly told Brown that he had better look in the bed. Brown silently approached, steeling himself as he pulled aside the quilt and found his wife lying in a pool of blood. Her skull had been crushed and her throat had been slit with an axe blade.

The four youngest children weren't found until the following day, when neighbors scouring the property found their corpses, partly covered by sticks and leaves, hidden in different places around the farm. Fourteen-year-old Jacob had been shot in the back of the head. Sixteen-year-old George had been savagely beaten by some blunt instrument, and then strangled. Betsy, eighteen, was found with her skull crushed by stones. Eleven-year-old David had been strangled and shot. The bullet had been fired between his legs and according to the testimony of the physician who conducted the postmortem "circumcised him, as it were."

Surrounded by his neighbors, the gruff and surly William Brown wept openly. He pitifully choked through his tears, "I don't know what injury I ever done to a man that he should kill off my family so." As for the man's identity, Brown had no doubts at all. He had gotten a clear look at the killer before he leapt down from the hayloft and fled. It was his son-in-law, Robert McConaghy.

The dried blood of his victims was still caked under his fingernails when McConaghy was arrested the next day. He was locked up in the county jail, protesting his innocence the entire time. When asked, though, he could give no accounting of his whereabouts at the time of the murders. He was convicted after a brief trial in mid-November 1840 and was sentenced to death. The judge spoke harshly as he handed down the death sentence, "Your case is without parallel in criminal jurisprudence. For barbarity, treachery, and depravity, your cruelty and wickedness have not been surpassed by the pirates of the West Indies or the savages of the wilderness."

McConaghy continued to claim that he was innocent right up until the day of his execution, having somehow gotten it into his head that "he would not be hung unless he confessed to the murder." His spiritual advisors, the Rev. George L. Brown and the Rev. John Peebles, assured him that God would have no mercy on his soul unless he confessed his sins, but to no avail. Reverend Brown wrote later, "He denied it again and again."

On the morning of Friday, November 16, 1840, after a sleepless night spent in agonized prayer, McConaghy, dressed in his funeral clothes, was led to the scaffold. His legs were shaking so badly that he had to be supported on each side by Sheriff Joseph Shannon and a deputy. Taking him by the hand, Reverend Brown made one last attempt to elicit a confession from him. But McConaghy only cried out, jerking his head violently, "Oh, do not bother me, I can tell no more!" A few moments later, the hangman released the trap and McConaghy plunged downward.

But then something happened that, in the view of astonished observers, seemed like an act of God, or what Brown called, "a Providential occurrence."

As the condemned man's bound and hooded body plummeted downward, the rope around his neck snapped. McConaghy hit the ground on his feet and then toppled over onto his back.

Stunned but very much alive, McConaghy was filled with sudden hope. "They ought to let me go clear," he exclaimed to the startled clergymen. It was not until he was informed that the execution would be tried again did he finally seem to accept the inevitable. While another noose was made ready, he asked the two ministers to lean down and listen to his confession. Speaking in a trembling voice, he offered them a brief, chilling account of the methodical slaughter of his mother-in-law and her five children.

He had killed George first. He beat him and then, finding him still alive, he choked him to death. He then took David into the woods, knocked him down with a stick and choked him to death. After that, he went to the house and told Jacob that the boys were shooting in the woods. He shot him in the back as he walked toward the woods. After dragging the bodies into the brush and covering them with leaves and sticks, he went to the house to fetch Elizabeth. He led her out to gather strawberries and then beat her with stones and choked her to death. "I then went back to the barn and sat there a spell, waiting for the old woman to come out," he told the ministers. "She came near the door and I shot her and hit her in the arm, and she ran about the house holding her arm. I then ran to the house and asked her if she knew who had done it. She said she did not know. I told her to go into the room and go to bed. I said this for fear that she would faint."

McConaghy told his mother-in-law that he would fetch her a glass of water, but he brought the axe with him instead. Rosanna was sitting on the edge of the bed when he walked in and he swung hard, striking her with the blunt side of the axe just over her right eye. When she fell over, he cut her throat with the axe blade, "to put her out of her misery," and covered her with the quilt.

Opening a trunk in the front room, McConaghy pocketed some of the contents: seven or eight dollars, tobacco, percussion caps and some lead. He went to the barn and hid the items after washing the blood off the axe. He then shut the door to the house and removed the handle, taking it with him to the barn. Casually, apparently unshaken by the murders he had just committed, he walked to his own home, got some water to drink, and washed out his clothes with soap and water. He hung them up to dry in the sun and changed his clothing. McConaghy then sat down to wait until John came home, looking for the horse that his father had promised to sell him, or so he believed.

When John went to the door, he found the handle missing and could not get it open. He turned toward the barn and McConaghy shot him in the chest. He cautiously approached the house, prepared to shoot him again - but the young man was dead. He dragged the body into the house and then went through his pockets, stealing his cash, before returning to the barn to wait for William Brown's arrival. When the old man came home, he shot at him and missed, and then shot again. When Brown ran towards him, McConaghy fled.

He ended his statement, like so many other killers, trying to justify what he had done. "I did not like Brown and murdered them for their little bit of property. I thought I had as good a right to it as any of them. If I had killed Brown, I intended to put him in the house and burn them all up. I was near making a confession three or four times before but didn't like to do it because it would be a disgrace to my family."

Having finally unburdened himself, McConaghy desperately looked at the two ministers. "Can I be saved?" he cried. They directed him to pray as McConaghy climbed up the scaffold again. Before the hood was drawn over his head for the second time, he called to William Brown and begged him for his forgiveness. Brown shook his head and turned away.

A moment later, the trapdoor opened again and he fell once more. This time, the rope held firm.

1866: "THE MONSTER IN THE SHAPE OF A MAN"

During the nineteenth century, dime museums could be found in almost every major city in America. These garish showplaces - sort of a brick and mortar carnival sideshow - were places where visitors could see curios, relics and oddities, human and otherwise. Such places offered venues for magicians, freaks and people with unusual talents to perform. Display cases held Egyptian mummies, African animals, dinosaur fossils, mechanical marvels, waxworks and even replicas of medieval torture devices. They were designed to entertain, enthrall and in some cases, titillate. A few of the more tawdry dime museums specialized in biological displays: preserved fetuses called "pickled punks" in sideshow lingo ; wax models of diseased genitalia; deformed taxidermy specimens like multi-legged animals and cows with three eyes; skulls and skeletons and allegedly authentic anatomical relics of historical figures.

One of the most famous of the "medical museums" of the era was the New York Museum of Anatomy, located on Broadway. Advertising flyers claimed that it contained twenty thousand "novel and astounding" objects, including the preserved head of a Hungarian man with "a perfect deer head growing out of his forehead, a "child with one body, two arms, two heads and four legs," George Washington's deathbed, a genuine hermaphrodite and - printed in large bold letters - "the head and right arm of Anton Probst, Murderer of the Deering Family, Amputated after Execution!"

Such advertisements - and public displays – once again makes stories of the so-called "good old days" blatant fiction. For those who believe that our modern-day culture has hit rock bottom, we can assure you that the past was even worse, especially when displaying the severed body parts of an executed criminal was seen as a socially acceptable form of entertainment. The advertisement highlighted another fact of the era - that Anton Probst, while almost forgotten today, was one of the most notorious murderers of his time. He was regarded as a fiend that perpetrated a deed so heinous that he became known as "the Monster in the Shape of a Man."

Anton Probst

Anton Probst, described as a "sullen, brutish youth" who was "never brought up in any trade," was born in Baden, Germany, in 1842. He arrived in the United States in May 1863, disembarking from the boat in New York and making the nearest saloon his first stop. While drinking beer, he was approached by a Union Army recruiter and was persuaded to enlist after being promised an immediate cash bounty. Six weeks later, Probst deserted. A short time later, looking to collect another bounty, he enlisted in a different regiment. He repeated this swindle a few more times until he was discharged in the spring of 1865 after accidentally shooting off his right thumb while on guard duty in Richmond, Virginia.

Heading for Philadelphia, he soon blew through all of his money in taverns and brothels, then stayed around the area for a few months, working at manual labor jobs until he became ill and ended up in the poorhouse. He had recovered by fall and while wandering the area south of Philadelphia, looking for work. That's when he happened on the farm of Christopher Deering.

Deering was also an immigrant. The thirty-eight-year-old man had come to America in 1849 to escape the potato famine in Ireland. In 1855, he married Julia Duffy, a fellow Irish immigrant and together, they had five children in quick succession. Settled in the rural, sparsely populated area south of Philadelphia that was locally known as "The Neck," he raised and sold cattle in partnership with a man named Theodore Mitchell, who supplied the funds for the cattle enterprise and split the profits with Deering.

Needing an extra hand on the farm, Deering hired Probst for a salary of $15 a month, plus room and board. It was a good salary for that time and that type of work, but to earn it soon proved to be more work than Probst wanted to do. Even though he was well-built for farm chores, the brawny Probst had never enjoyed manual labor. He quit working for Deering after just three weeks because, as he later explained, his employer asked him to work in the fields "on a rainy, very rough day." Deering's wife, Julia, was happy to see him go. According to subsequent accounts, Probst's "conduct and manner" had made her very uneasy.

As he had always done in the past, Probst quickly blew through the money he had earned on liquor and prostitutes. Penniless again, he spent a few days doing menial chores in a saloon and then spent another stretch in the poorhouse before showing up at the Deering farm again on February 2, 1866.

After Probst explained that he had no money and no prospect of work in his heavily accented English, Deering agreed to re-hire him. It was a perfect example of the farmer's kindly nature but there was no way that he could have known that Probst - who, during his previous time at the farm had seen his employer counting cash on several occasions - had really returned "to get hold of his money."

Early on Saturday morning, April 7, Christopher Deering drove his buggy into the city, leaving behind his wife, four of his children, and his two employees - Probst and a seventeen-year-old farmhand named Cornelius Carey. Deering was going to pick up his cousin, Elizabeth Dolan, a forty-nine-year-old spinster from Burlington, New Jersey. Miss Dolan was a frequent visitor to the Deering farm and she had taken the 7:00 a.m. steamboat for Philadelphia. She was wearing "furs and a black coat," sporting a gold chain and carrying a black carpetbag that, in addition to her personal effects, contained a pocketbook with $100 in cash.

While on his way to fetch his guest, Deering stopped to take care of several errands. At around 8:30 a.m., he made his weekly visit to the stand of a street peddler named Jane Greenwell to purchase six pounds of meat for his family. He then went to the home of his partner, Thomas Mitchell, to take

The Deering farm, where the murders took place

care of some business. Short of cash, he borrowed $10 from Mitchell. Then, after checking his pocket watch and noting that he was running late, he hurried off to the steamboat landing.

By the time he had arrived, the boat had already docked and its passengers had been left off onto the docks. Driving along Second Street, he spotted his cousin and pulled up to the curb beside her. A passerby, a Mrs. Wilson, saw Miss Dolan climb into the buggy next to Deering, who then drove off toward Front Street in the direction of his farm.

With this brief sighting, Mrs. Wilson became a key part of the story: she was the last person to see Christopher Deering and his cousin alive.

The Deerings' farm was an isolated place. One of their nearest neighbors was Abraham Everett, whose farm was about one-quarter mile away. Everett, who liked to keep up with the news, subscribed to several Philadelphia newspapers. Every Saturday afternoon, Deering's eight-year-old son, John, walked over to Everett's home and borrowed the previous week's papers for his father.

On Saturday, April 7, though, John never showed up. And he did not appear on the days that followed. By Wednesday, Everett was concerned enough to stop at the Deering farm on his way into town. There was no one in sight when he rode up to the house. Getting down from his horse, he went to the door and knocked loudly. There was no response. The entire farm had an eerie silence about it. It was enough to make Everett feel very unnerved.

Leaving the house, he walked out to the barn and was shocked to find Deering's horses "in a state of starvation and nearly dead from thirst." He immediately grabbed a bucket, hurried out to a water-filled ditch and began tending to the animals. He later stated, "I gave one five buckets of water, another four buckets. I then put water in the trough and another drank the whole lot of it. Another I turned out into the yard and he drank, I suppose, for a full fifteen minutes out of the ditch." Everett then turned the adult horses out into the meadow to feed and brought an armful of hay to a starving colt that was tied up in the stable.

After taking care of the animals, he returned to the house, climbed onto the porch and peered into the window. He was startled to see that, as he put it, "things looked as if they had been knocked around considerably inside. The house looked as if someone had ransacked it." Everett managed to force open the window and climbed inside. He looked around and then started upstairs. He found the rooms on the upper floor in the same state of disorder. The beds had been turned over, clothing was scattered about and bureau drawers had been ransacked.

Everett's feelings of unease had now turned into a state of great concern. He dashed downstairs and headed for the home of the next-closest neighbor, Robert Wyles. When he saw Wyles' farmhand, John Gould, working in a meadow, Everett called to the young man and hurried with him back to the Deering farm. Inside the barn, Gould spotted something that Everett, in his attention to the horses, had missed. Sticking out from under a pile of hay was an object that Gould first thought was a stocking. When he bent to pick it up, however, he discovered "to his amazement and horror" that there was a foot inside it.

Gould broke into a run, speeding back to his employer's farm. When he told Wyles what he had found, Wyles immediately made for the nearest police station. Within a short time, several officers had arrived on the scene, led by the city's chief of detectives, Benjamin Franklin, a longtime veteran of the department with a rather familiar name. When Franklin and some of his colleagues cleared the hay away from the protruding limb, they made a horrifying discovery.

The newspapers reported, "There lay a man who was recognized as Mr. Deering He was extended on the floor cross-wise with the length of the barn. He was dressed in a suit of dark gray clothes, the same in which he had been seen and known on the last day of his life. His head was crushed into pieces, almost to powdered bone, and his throat was cut, nay chopped, from ear to ear. Beside him was a young woman, unknown to these neighbors, whose appearance showed that she had met her fate in the same way. Her head and throat revealed the same wounds as were seen on the man by whose side she was lying."

Another, even more terrible discovery awaited them. Not far from the spot where the two brutalized corpses were found was a small corn crib, about five feet wide and eight feet long, half-filled with hay. Pulling the hay aside, Franklin and his men found a scene so appalling that they were unable to speak. Lying in the corn crib was the decomposed body of Julia Deering, her skull bashed in and her throat cut open to the spine. Surrounding her and upon her "were her four little

A contemporary illustration of Probst slaughtering the entire Deering family

ones, slaughtered in the identical manner. The little babe in death, lay upon its mother's breast as if had done in life so often - a sight to make strong men weep."

The entire Deering family had been slaughtered - with the exception of their oldest child, ten-year-old Willie. He was only spared because he happened to be visiting his grandparents in Schuylkill. No one present could recall a crime of such magnitude. It was, in the view of one observer, an atrocity that was without "parallel in the catalog or mere private murders in the annals of the world."

News of the Deering massacre, which made headlines in newspapers across the country, began a predictable frenzy at the farm. The place was soon overrun by thousands of morbid curiosity-seekers. One journalist was amazed "to see vast numbers of persons on foot or running as if it were a race of life and death. There were old men who would not have to travel far to find their graves, and young men who were making a holiday excursion of the fearful pilgrimage. A minister of the gospel passed on horseback, trotting rapidly along. A cripple on crutches swung his distorted legs over the dusty road, making slow progress. But the women outnumbered the men of all ages, and in all attires from the fashionably dressed lady in her barouche to the poor seamstress on foot." A contingent of police officers made sure that no one in the mob entered the house, but a crowd of ghoulish souvenir hunters managed to get into the barn and make off with handfuls of bloody straw.

It was one of these souvenir hunters who spotted something strange on the property: a man's shirt and a pair of drawers lying next to a large haystack about three hundred yards from the barn. He informed a police officer named Dawson Mitchell, who went to investigate. After walking all the way around the haystack, Mitchell noticed a spot that had been hollowed out of the straw. He thrust his hand inside and immediately came into contact with a human body. Mitchell rummaged around in the straw, grabbed hold of an arm and tugged it free. A corpse tumbled out of the haystack – the decomposed body of the Deerings' seventeen-year-old farmhand, Cornelius Carey. Like the family, his skull had been crushed and his throat had been hacked open from ear to ear.

By this time, the police had found the implements that had obviously been used as murder weapons: a bloody hammer that had been tossed into the hay just inside the entrance to the barn; a small hatchet, encrusted with blood, lying in a ditch near the house; and a full-sized axe with blood splashed on the blade, which had been left in the woodshed.

They had also identified the Deerings' other employee as their prime suspect in the slaughter. None of the neighbors knew much about him, but they offered a fair description: "about thirty, bull-necked, missing his right thumb. His English was poor and his first name was believed to be 'Anthony.'"

One might think that a man who had methodically murdered eight people, including three small children and a fourteen-month-old infant, would lose no time in putting as much distance between himself and the crime scene as possible. For all his low cunning, though, Anton Probst was incapable of rational thought in such matters. Indeed, from all available evidence, he thought nothing beyond the gratification of his immediate physical needs.

On the evening of Saturday, April 7, just hours after he had slaughtered the Deering family and their hired hand, he showed up at a brothel on Front Street, carrying a black carpetbag that contained, along with other items, two watches, a gold chain, a snuffbox, a pistol and a powder flask. After a night of "dissipation and debauchery" with a prostitute named Lavinia Whitman, he left Sunday morning, paying her $3 in greenbacks. He next took a room at a tavern on Newmarket Street, a place he often frequented, which was run by a man named William Leckfeldt. For the next five days, he was in and out of the tavern, drinking beer and shooting dice when he wasn't making brief excursions around the city to pawn his stolen goods for pocket money.

At around 7:00 p.m. on Thursday, April 12, five days after the massacre, he was seated in the barroom of Leckfeldt's when two police officers walked in to ask the proprietor if he had seen a "suspicious-looking man." Pulling his slouch hat down over his eyes and sinking into his seat, Probst made himself as inconspicuous as possible until the policemen departed. The moment they were gone, he leapt from his seat and, without bothering to collect his possessions, he hurried out into the evening.

A short time later, an officer named James Dorsey spotted a burly man with his hat pulled low on his head walking quickly toward the Market Street Bridge. There was something furtive about the man's bearing that made Dorsey suspicious. Looking closely, he saw that the man was missing his right thumb. He was convinced that it was Probst and quickly overtook him. Dorsey snatched the man's hat off for a better look at his face. "Good evening," he said to the man.

"How de do," Probst replied.

Hearing his accent, Dorsey asked him, "You're a Dutchman?"

Probst's reply would become famous in local legend. He said, "No, me a Frenchman."

"You are, are you?" Dorsey said and grabbed Probst by the arm. "Take a walk with me."

At the Sixth District station, Probst's pockets were turned out and the police found Christopher Deering's pistol and snuffbox. The police also quickly determined that Probst was wearing Deering's clothes, having exchanged them for his own blood-soaked pants and shirt before he fled the crime scene. The black carpetbag, retrieved from Leckfeldt's tavern, was identified as the one that Deering's cousin Elizabeth Dolan had been carrying on her visit. Every item found inside of it, including two straight razors, several spools of thread, and a few "five-penny children's trinkets," had been taken from the Deering home.

Probst, while being interrogated by Mayor Morton McMichael, first made a number of predictable protestations of innocence. Then he admitted that he had killed Cornelius Carey, but insisted that the other seven victims were slain by an accomplice, a Swiss cutthroat named Gautner, who had served with him in the Union Army. Needless to say, no one believed him.

Once word of his arrest reached the public, an enraged mob began to gather outside of the station, demanding that Probst be turned over to them. Eventually, he was transferred for his safety to Moyamensing Prison to await trial.

The trial began on Wednesday, April 25, just two weeks after the murders were discovered. Faced with an impossible task, Probst's court-appointed attorneys, John P. O'Neill and John A. Wolbert, admitted that their client was guilty of larceny but argued that any evidence of murder was very circumstantial and not strong enough to establish his guilt. It seemed that even they knew their efforts were worthless - it took the jury less than twenty minutes to convict Probst.

When delivering his sentence, Judge Joseph Allison put into words the feelings of anger that were shared by the entire community: "You have been found guilty of the commission of one of the most appalling crimes of which the records of civilized jurisprudence make any mention. Almost without motive eight innocent victims you slew; not suddenly, not in a tempest of resistless passion, but in the coolness of a premeditated design - one by one, at intervals, with solemn pause, with calm deliberation, and with a quenchless thirst for blood, you ceased not until all that you set out to do was fully accomplished, and when you found yourself alone with the dead, your felt your triumph was complete. And with what horrid mockery of life you grouped these dead together - mother and children gathered close to each other: cheek pressed to cheek as if in calm repose; and like one who lays him down as a sentinel to keep his silent watch, husband and father, in company with his friend and relative, you placed, as if to guard his wife and little ones from harm. How all these ghastly countenances and rigid forms and glaring, sightless eyes condemned you, as on them you looked and claimed the work as all your own! Justice now claims you as its own. And that which it requires to be done shall not be long delayed!"

With that said, Judge Allison ordered Probst to be "taken to the place of execution" and "there hung by the neck until dead." The sentence was scheduled to be carried out in five weeks, on June 8, 1866.

While awaiting execution, Probst continued to insist that he was innocent of all but one of the eight murders. He had killed Carey, he said, but not the Deering family. However, after many meetings with his spiritual advisor, the Rev. Gunther of St. Alphonsus' Church, he agreed to make a full confession. On the morning of May 7, he dictated two separate statements, one to Chief of Detectives Benjamin Franklin, and the other to his attorneys, Wolbert and O'Neill. Although they differed slightly in language, the documents agreed in every detail and were equally chilling in the matter-of-fact way that Probst described his annihilation of the Deering family. Reclining on the cot in his cell, fingering a rosary, he was, in the words of one man present, "quiet, undemonstrative, cool and unembarrassed," sharing his "bloody reminiscences without the least trace of shame or remorse."

According to Probst's confession, his original intention had only been to rob Christopher Deering by sneaking into the house and taking all of the money that he could find. He never had a chance, however, because someone always seemed to be around. Finally, on the Saturday morning of the murder, he decided to kill the entire family because he could not, he explained, "get the money any other way."

That morning, he and Cornelius Carey were out in the field near the haystack, loading wood on a cart to take to the barn. There was a large axe in the cart, used for cutting tree roots. It was raining a little that morning and Carey was sitting down under a tree, talking about work. Probst came up behind him and hit him in the side of the head with the axe. Carey never cried out. He simply fell to the ground, where Probst hit him one or two more times and then cut his throat. He then hid his body inside of the haystack, where it would be later found.

With this deed accomplished, Probst began the rest of the slaughter. He walked to the stable, taking the large axe, the hatchet and the hammer and placing them all at the corner of the door, where they could be handy. He went to the house and found there children were all inside. Julia Deering had gone to fetch some water.

Probst explained what happened next: "I took the oldest boy, John, and told him to go over to the stable and help me with something. I went inside the door, got the little axe in my hand, and then he comes in. I knocked him down and he fell inside. I gave him one or two more of the same and cut and chopped his throat. I carried him to the crib and hauled him inside and put a little hay over him. Then I put the axe at the same place by the door."

Julia Deering was next. Probst told her that something was wrong with a colt in the barn and she came in a few minutes to see the problem for herself. Probst struck her in the side of the head. When she fell, he crushed her skull and then cut her throat. Lifting her onto his shoulder, he also placed her in the corn crib. Leaving the axe by the door, he went to the house and fetched Thomas, telling him that his mother wanted him in the barn. When he walked inside, Probst struck him too. Another body was added to the corn crib.

He continued with his horrific tale: "Then I went over to the house and took Annie. I told her mother wanted to see her in the stable. She did not say a word. Then I took the baby on my arm. The little girl walked alongside of me. I left the baby in the corner as you go into the stable, playing in the hay. Then I picked up the little axe and went over to Annie as she looked about for her mother. I knocked her down with one blow and cut her throat the same as the others. Then I went back and got the little baby and gave it one on the forehead. Then I took the sharp side of the axe and chopped its throat. Then I hauled then into the crib and covered them up with hay. I guess it took me a half an hour to kill the family. Then I went in the house and stayed there, watching for Mr. Deering to come home."

Christopher Deering and Elizabeth Dolan arrived at the farm around 1:30 p.m. As the carriage came into the yard, Probst walked out from behind the house and told Deering that he needed him in the barn. A steer was sick, he claimed, and he needed him to look at it. He followed Probst to the barn while Miss Dolan went into the house. Once inside of the barn, Probst came up behind him with the hatchet and buried it in the back of Deering's skull. He made no sound as he fell forward onto his face. Probst turned him over and hit him twice more in the head and then cut his throat, as he had done the others. He spread some hay over him and left him on the floor, as Deering was too heavy to carry and dump into the corn crib.

When he stepped out of the barn, Elizabeth Dolan called him over to the house, asking him where Julia and the children were. Probst told her that they were all in the barn and, in fact, Mr. Deering wanted to see her there too. When she stepped into the stable, Probst hit her in the back of the head with the hammer, sending her to her knees. When she fell flat on the floor, he smashed her skull and cut her throat.

After hiding her body under the straw on the floor, Probst returned to Deering's body and removed his watch and wallet, placing both in his own pockets. He also removed Deering's boots and took those as well. His butchery then complete, Probst returned to the house, ransacked the place, then washed, shaved and changed his bloody garments for some of Deering's clothes. Hungry from his exertions, he fixed himself some bread and butter and relaxed until the sun went down, then he sneaked away from the property and headed into the city.

Probst smiled when he finished his story. "I feel much better now that I have told the truth about this thing. I feel relieved."

When asked by Chief Franklin why he had done such a terrible thing, Probst gave a half-hearted shrug. "I only wanted the money. I killed the Cornelius boy first so that he could not tell on me. I killed the two oldest children so that would not afterwards identify me. I killed the youngsters as I did not wish to leave them in the house alone without someone to care for them." He truly appeared to believe that he was not responsible for his actions. Probst had no conscience whatsoever and had no guilt about what he had done. He added, "I had no ill feeling to anyone in the family. They always treated me well."

Being locked in prison apparently agreed with Probst. He slept soundly each night and ate so heartily that in the five-week span between his sentencing and execution date, he gained twelve pounds. Visitors to his cell noted that he had "changed greatly in spirit since giving his full confession. He seemed to realize the enormity of the crime he had committed and often expressed himself as not only willing but anxious to undergo any punishment which the law required." More likely, prison was the perfect place for someone like Probst; he had a bed to sleep in, food to eat and he could lie around and do nothing all day. He needed no mental stimulation; he was not built that way. His basic needs were met and he didn't have to do anything to earn them. It was the perfect situation for a man who was barely a step away from being a beast.

If Probst was truly looking for his punishment, the moment for it arrived on June 8, 1866. After a solid night's sleep - his rest was never troubled by the conscience that he lacked - he awoke at 5:00 a.m. and had two soft-boiled eggs, three slices of bread and a large cup of coffee for breakfast. Father Gunther then administered the rite of Holy Communion and led him in prayer for more than an hour.

Shortly before 10:30 a.m., Sheriff Howell and Warden Perkins appeared at the door to his cell. Probst was dressed in simple prison garb: coarse gray pants and muslin shirt, brogans and blue socks. He clutched a crucifix to his chest as he was taken from his cell and escorted to the gallows, which had been built on the western side of the prison yard, out of the view of the convicts' cell windows. Probst slowly climbed the wooden stairs and then knelt in prayer with Father Gunther, who administered the rite of absolution. Then, without showing any sign of fear, he rose to his feet and bent his head so that the noose could be properly adjusted around his neck. A white cowl was then slipped over his head. Father Gunther recited a few final words of prayer, then signaled to the sheriff who immediately released the drop.

Probst plunged to his doom. His body twisted and thrashed for several minutes, and then went still. He was allowed to dangle at the end of the rope for twenty-five minutes before he was finally cut down and carried to the prison's paint room.

Probst was so universally hated that the newspapers abandoned any pretense of journalistic objectivity when reporting about his death. "Anton Probst - the greatest criminal of the nineteenth century - shuffled off his mortal and disreputable coil this morning at 10:46 o'clock," wrote the correspondent for the *New York Times*. "For such a thing it was difficult to feel sympathy or pity. His death was easy, and his ugly carcass swung in the breeze."

In keeping with the custom of the time - when, as a form of sort-of postmortem punishment, the bodies of executed murderers were handed over to anatomists for dissection - Probst's corpse was soon given to Drs. Pancoast, Rand and McCrea of the Jefferson Medical College. Seated upright in a chair in the prison paint room, Probst's naked body was first subjected to a series of bizarre medical experiments, designed to test the "force of galvanism to include post-mortem muscular action." In other words, it was like zapping dead frogs with electricity to see them jump. One pole of a powerful battery was inserted into the dead man's mouth and the other into an incision in his face, causing it to assume "various expressions." The battery was then applied to various muscles of the arms and legs, making them "move wildly about."

After that, the corpse was transported to the medical college, where, at 4:00 p.m. on Saturday, it "was dissected before a crowded audience, composed of men of all professions and vocations." Probst's brain turned out to be of "remarkably small size" - a mere two pounds, four ounces, far below the average weight of three pounds, two ounces - accidentally confirming a quip by a reporter from the *New York Times* who wrote that the killer was "as destitute of brain as he was of heart."

1870: THE MURDEROUS MEDIUM
Katie Bender & Her "Bloody" Family of Killers

Men sometimes vanished on the Kansas prairie. Some of them rode off in search of their fortunes, in search of women, or perhaps to lose themselves on purpose. Some vanished one step ahead of the law, leaving wives, children, dead men, and bad debts behind them. A man could lose himself in the West of the 1870s. It was a chance to start over again, free of the laws and society of the Eastern states. It was not uncommon for men to ride off into the wilds of the prairie and never be seen again.

Little thought was given to such disappearances in the southeastern part of the state, until it was realized just how many men vanished near the same place: a roadside tavern on the Osage Mission Road, between Independence and Fort Scott. This was no mere restaurant or drinking establishment. In addition to offering food and rest for the weary traveler, the proprietors also offered "spiritualistic communion" with the ghosts of the dead. The medium in charge of such things was said to be an attraction herself. Professor Miss Katie Bender, as she was called, was a beautiful young woman who was said to be gifted with the ability to heal all manner of diseases, including blindness and deafness, as well as being able to contact the dead. She traveled about the area, entertaining crowds in small Kansas towns with her spiritualistic show. She was very popular with the male members of the audience, and some of these men traveled to the tavern near the small town of Cherryvale to see her again.

But they, like so many luckless travelers, vanished without a trace.

In late April 1873, a mob of men from southeastern Kansas descended on the roadside tavern with all of the tools necessary to plant a crop for the spring. George Mortimer, harnessed to his horse and plow, cut furrows in the soft dirt as other men worked with shovels and spades. This was no spring planting, though. It was harvest time at the Bender homestead - and not the sort of harvest that the farmers of Kansas reaped every autumn. This was a grim and horrible task, and while many of the men feared the worst, they were totally unprepared for what they were about to discover.

One of the men, the leader of the group, Ed York, surveyed the area around the ramshackle Bender tavern. As he looked around the recently planted apple orchard, his eyes settled on several rectangular depressions scattered among the immature fruit trees. "I see graves," he called out, and several of the men followed in the direction that he pointed.

The men converged on the ground between the apple trees, digging feverishly with their shovels. The metal of their tools clanged together as they worked side by side, crowding one another. Before long, their spades made contact with something hard and the dirt was cleared away. Carefully, they pushed aside the dark earth until the first body lay exposed to the sunlight. The men could see clearly that someone had bashed in the dead man's skull. One of the men pushed through his fellow workers and bent down to move the corpse's head to the side. There was a deep gash across the throat. Someone in the group moaned aloud. The killer had knocked the man senseless and then had cut his throat.

A *Harper's Weekly* illustration of the unearthing of bodies on the Bender property

A sinking feeling fell over Ed York, although neither he nor anyone else could identify the body right away. Too much dirt and dried blood covered the dead man's face and the corpse was too decomposed to be moved. One of the men severed the head so that the face could be washed clean. As the dirt was carefully wiped away and the dead man's hair was parted, York's worst fear was realized. He was looking into the lifeless face of Dr. William York, his brother.

Dr. William H. York's disappearance two weeks earlier had brought his brother and friends to the Bender property on that crisp spring morning. Dr. York had left Fort Scott on horseback, headed for his home in Independence, on March 9. Somewhere along the way, he vanished. More than two weeks later, a local newspaper gave a brief account of his disappearance and the story was quickly picked up by other newspapers in the state. There was considerable speculation that York might have been murdered. He was a respectable man and an upstanding member of the community who would not just disappear on his own. He was also thought to have been carrying a large amount of money at the time he mysteriously vanished.

A search party was soon formed to try and locate him. The searchers were led by the missing man's brothers, Ed York and Kansas Senator Alexander York. Using Fort Scott as a starting point, Ed and Alexander traced their brother's movements along the Osage Mission Road. Rivers were dragged, possible spots of ambush were searched, but there were no signs anywhere as to how he might have met his death, or even that he was dead at all. A number of people living along the road told the pair that they recalled seeing their brother. One man even mentioned the doctor's intention to go to the Bender's tavern, nearly 80 miles southwest of Fort Scott. This was as far as they could trace him - to the small town of Cherryvale, about 50 miles from the southern state line of Kansas. There, his trail seemed to end.

Ironically, Dr. York had been on the road due to an earlier disappearance in the state. In the winter of 1872, a man named George Loncher and his daughter had vanished without a trace. It seems that the doctor had sold the Lonchers a wagon and a team that soon turned up abandoned, with no sign or word from the father or daughter. Dr. York left his home on Fawn Creek and traveled north to Fort Scott to identify the team. When his task was completed, he had mounted his horse and headed toward home. When he didn't show up, his brothers started searching for him - only to find his body in a shallow grave in the Benders' apple orchard.

The horrible discovery of Dr. York's body turned out to be only the beginning. The Benders, with brutal and cold-blooded efficiency, claimed scores of victims near Cherryvale during the early 1870s. The diggers soon harvested many other bodies of unwary travelers who had fallen victim to their attacks. The family would soon become universally known as the "Bloody Benders," and for good reason. Even the most psychotic killers who roamed the West after the Civil War could not compare to the depravity of Katie Bender and her family of fellow serial killers.

In the early 1870s, Cherryvale was a small, sparsely settled community that had only been in existence for a short time when the Benders arrived from somewhere back East. Shortly after the end of the Civil War, federal authorities relocated the Osage Indians to Indian Territory present-day Oklahoma and homesteaders flocked to Kansas' Labette County. In 1870, the Benders were among the families that took advantage of the vacated area, building a modest wooden home and tavern on a 160-acre claim along the Osage Mission Road.

The tavern, where travelers could buy a meal or a drink, stood about 100 yards from the road. Over the door was a sign marked "Groceries." The house was made up of one large room that was divided by a canvas curtain. This separated the grocery store and dining area from the family's living quarters in the back. The living area was sparsely furnished with two beds and a few articles of furniture.

The origin of the Bender family is shrouded in mystery and a great deal of the material that has been written about them is based more on legend than upon established fact. One story is that they came from a German settlement in Pennsylvania, having been driven out by their neighbors because Mrs. Bender and her daughter, Kate, were suspected of *hexeri*, or witchcraft. The Benders were allegedly German, although Germans who spoke with them in Kansas said that they spoke the dialect of the Pennsylvania Dutch, who originally came to America from southwestern Germany, Switzerland, France and the Netherlands. Some have suspected that they had been part of the large Amish community there, but had been forced out for some reason. Based on the advertisements that Kate later placed about her magical healing properties and skill at speaking with the dead, perhaps it was believed that she was a witch after all. The early settlers in Kansas were superstitious about some things, but as a class they were not inclined to believe in witchcraft. The fact that such stories were circulated at all shows that there was something peculiar about the Bender family.

When the Benders came to Labette County in 1870, there were four persons in the family. John Bender, the apparent head of the family, was somewhere around 60 years of age. He was a short, stocky man and described as having a ruddy complexion. He wore his sandy hair rather long and had a full mustache and beard, as was common at the time. He was, by all accounts, sullen and ill-tempered. He talked little, at least when strangers were around, and only spoke in German. It was believed that he understood English, but there is no report that he ever spoke a word of it.

John Bender's wife, known in every account as "Ma" Bender or Mrs. John Bender, was a short, rather stout woman who looked every bit of her 50-plus years and was just as unfriendly as her husband. She spoke broken English as well as German, but was never talkative. None of her neighbors ever knew what her first name was and there is no mention of it in any of the records pertaining to the family.

The younger John Bender, thought to be the old man's son, was somewhat more neighborly than his parents. He had brown hair and blue eyes and spoke English fluently, but with a German accent. He seemed to be a likable sort, but there was something about him - perhaps his odd grin and often inappropriate laughter - that suggested he was simpleminded, or at least not quite right in the head, as neighbors later recalled. He had his own land claim to the north of his father's, but he never lived on it or built any structures on it.

The Bender family, from left to right: Kate, John Jr., Mrs. Bender and the John Sr. The illustrations were created many years after the murders and there is no indication as to their accuracy.

According to accounts, Kate was the "leading spirit of her murderous family." Outgoing and aggressive, the young woman, who was probably no more than 20 years of age, spoke excellent English and was affable and glib when talking to any stranger who took her fancy. She seemed cut from a different cloth than the rest of the family. She didn't act much like a farm girl. For one thing, she became well known in the region as a psychic medium, one that could contact the spirits of the dead and even cure sickness in return for a generous donation. After the misdeeds of the

Bender family were later discovered, Kate was described in numerous reports: "Her hair was a dark, rich auburn. She had deep, grayish-blue or dark-gray eyes. She was over medium height, some five feet six or seven inches tall, slender, well-formed in a voluptuous mould, fair skin, white as milk, rose complexion. She was a good-looking, remarkably handsome woman, rather bold and striking in appearance, with tigerish grace and animal attraction, which but few men could resist. She was a fluent talker, with fine conversationalist powers, but she did not display any educational advantages of a high order. She used good English with very little, if any, German accent."

The true nature of the relationships between the Benders has always been uncertain. For example, it remains unknown whether Pa and Ma Bender were actually husband and wife. Some accounts state and the younger John Bender and Kate were the children of Mrs. Bender from a previous marriage to a man named Gebhardt, but they both used the name Bender in Kansas. Some newspaper writers of the time asserted that John and Kate were not brother and sister at all but that John was Kate's lover who had followed the Benders to Kansas from Pennsylvania. Others have said that John and Kate were brother and sister, but that they had an incestuous relationship.

There was no question that Kate fascinated men. In fact, one of her affairs led to the end of a partnership that the elder John Bender had with another grocer and fellow German in the area named Rudolph Brockman. He fell in love with Kate and was sure that he was going to marry her. She encouraged this belief, but postponed their wedding until Easter Sunday 1873 when, she claimed, the planets would be in the right conjunction for them to marry. The marriage had already been postponed several times because Kate had shown Brockman some complicated astrological charts, and explained that it would never do for them to marry until the various planets were in what she called the "proper nuptial conjunction." Meanwhile, she milked Brockman for money and jewelry until the "engagement" ended and the Benders fled the region. Brockman had no idea that they were gone until several days after the fact, but as soon as he heard about it, he began asking questions of everyone in the area.

Brockman fell under suspicion by those seeking the Benders because of his relationship with Kate, but many wondered if the relationship was still ongoing by spring of 1873. Rumor had it that the affair had ended months before when the grocer discovered the incestuous relationship between Kate and her brother, John. Several people later claimed to witness a fight between the two men when Brockman accused John Bender of being his "rival" for Kate's affections. Even if there had been a falling-out, the relationship between Brockman and Kate was still fresh enough in the minds of the locals that he was accused of being an accomplice in the Benders' crimes.

He answered the accusations against him frankly enough. He said that he had been in love with Kate, and certainly intended to marry her, but had no idea that the Benders were a gang of murderers. He said that Kate intimated to him that her father, in his younger days, had killed a man back in Pennsylvania. This led the family to flee to Michigan and then to the Kansas prairie, but it was many years ago. Brockman said that he had overheard some of their conversations in German, which the Benders used in the presence of guests, but there had been no mention of robbery or murder.

Brockman's house was searched and a gold ring inscribed "To Kate" was discovered, along with a tintype picture of her in a little black frame with gold edges. They also found some love letters from Kate, but there were written mostly in German. Brockman refused to translate the letters, but a German named Biedewolf looked them over despite Brockman's protests, and laughed at what he called their "foolishness." But, he testified, there was nothing about murder or robbery in the letters.

The mob was not satisfied. They needed someone on which to take out their frustrations and Brockman was as good a target as any. He was taken from his home and the crowd tried to force a confession from him. A rope was thrown over a beam and tied around his neck. As he was pulled off his feet, he was ordered to confess his guilt. Witnesses later stated that his face turned nearly black and he was almost dead when he was cut down. Brockman swore that he was innocent and he was pulled into the air again. Once more, he was taken down and revived. This time, he was so confused that he seemed to not understand what the crowd demanded from him. A witness statement noted, "It was an eerie sight. The yelling crowd, the mutilated and butchered dead, the flickering and swirling torches, spluttering in the night wind, the stern set faces of his executioners..." Brockman was hoisted aloft again and this time, only released when we was unconscious. The mob finally rode away, leaving the man dangling at the end of a rope.

Friends cut him down and he survived, although it's possible the mob was not as wrong as his friends assumed. Nothing was ever proven about Brockman in connection with the Benders, but it would later turn out that he was brutal enough to have been involved in their crimes. Years after, his daughter died from treatment that she received at his hand and he was indicted for her murder.

Perhaps the Benders' murderous ways had rubbed off on him after all.

When the Benders first came to Kansas, they lived on an isolated farm somewhere near Parsons. Dr. George W. Gabriel, who also lived in Parsons, remembered them well. He later wrote:

The first time that I recall meeting any of the Benders was in the fall of 1871 at the home of sick family named Boyd. The old woman and Kate were there. The Benders were German and talked the language considerably. When outsiders were present they often carried on a conversation among themselves in their native tongue. Kate talked glibly in English also and was active in what she termed Spiritualism.

Dr. Gabriel did not say so, but he knew what Kate and the old woman were doing at the Boyd home. They were accustomed to visiting the sick all over the neighborhood and claimed to cure illnesses by supernatural means.

It was in late 1871 when the Benders left the farm and moved to a place about seven miles northeast of Cherryvale. This was on the main road used by travelers between Fort Scott and Independence, Kansas, and onwards to the southeast into the Indian Territory. The Bender cabin had only one room, but as they saw many prosperous-looking travelers pass by on the Osage Mission

Road, they decided to go into the tavern business. The Benders might not have been the friendliest folks around, but they welcomed visitors with money in their pockets.

The cabin was divided into two rooms by a canvas curtain, and in the front room they placed a small stock of groceries, canned goods, preserved fruits, tobacco and assorted dry goods. The rear room was a combined kitchen and dining room, as well as living quarters for the Benders. Mrs. Bender cooked meals for the guests, but since there were no extra beds, travelers were allowed to camp in the yard when the weather was fine. In case of a sudden storm, they could bring their blankets into the house and bed down on pallets on the floor.

The food and lodging offered at the Benders' tavern was certainly nothing elaborate, but it was better than sleeping out on the open prairie and cooking over a campfire. There was a rough barn not far from the house, where young John fed and attended to traveler's horses. There were many such places on the Kansas prairies in those days, when everyone went around on horseback or in wagons.

A photograph taken of the Bender tavern after the murders were discovered

Kate was definitely an attraction when the Benders opened their tavern. Not only did her stunning looks appeal to the men who came to the place, but many came strictly because of her alleged mediumistic powers. Those who came for a séance at the tavern, or who came for dinner, were seated with their backs to the canvas curtain that stretched across the room. In the darkened room, Kate made all sorts of strange manifestations appear, likely with her family's assistance, and managed to keep the sitters transfixed for an extended period of time. However, some of the sitters became unnerved while seated with their backs against the canvas wall. Two men later told of dining at the tavern, and after hearing strange sounds behind them, took their meals to the counter to eat. Until then, Kate had been charming and affable, but now she began to abuse them and call them names. This made them even more suspicious and they hastily left the tavern. Later on, they were certainly happy that they did.

Unfortunately, many travelers were not so discerning.

Kate's reputation as a Spiritualist medium spread across the area. Old Mrs. Bender still visited the sick and worked charms and healing witchcraft occasionally, but Kate turned it into a regular business. Several of her professional cards and printed handbills were scattered about southeastern Kansas.

There were many residents of the area who truly believed that Kate Bender had supernatural powers of one kind or another. They said that she not only cured illnesses, but located lost articles, understood astrology and numerology, read palms, told fortunes, worked spells against evil women, sold infallible good-luck charms and love potions, and spoke with the dead.

A number of even wilder stories circulated. Some said that the Benders had no milk cows, but always served milk and homemade cheeses at the tavern. Since they did not leave the tavern for weeks at a time, people could not understand where these dairy products came from. Legend had it that a local man peeked in the window of the tavern one day, hoping to see the shapely Kate in the act of undressing. Instead, he saw Kate and the old woman hang some old rags on a wire in front of the kitchen stove, and squeeze several gallons of milk out of them! A farmer who lived several miles away claimed that his cows were being milked without his knowledge or consent and that, on one occasion, he had actually seen the udders of two cows diminish in size as if they were being milked, although no one was within reach of them. Those who heard the story believed that the Benders had done it by supernatural means.

Another fantastic story told about Kate Bender is that she was accustomed to visiting a certain farmer who lived about two miles away, in the form of a cat. Once inside his cabin, she would resume her normal form and spend the night with him. When she wanted to leave, she turned back into a cat again, returned to the Bender tavern, and was transformed into a woman before any member of the family even realized that she had been absent.

A family named Weissbrod, who came to Kansas from central Missouri, spread the story that a witch could always be detected by fixing a sharp nail to the seat of her chair and then getting her to sit down on it. If the woman was truly a witch she would not feel the point of the nail, but if she jumped up and cried out, she was innocent. The story goes that one of the Weissbrod boys tried this on Kate Bender and succeeded in getting her to sit down on a piece of pointed wire. She sprang up immediately, knocked the young man down and kicked him several times before he could get away.

In spite of this, the family continued to maintain that Kate was indeed a witch and offered their neighbors methods on protecting themselves against her magical powers. One highly recommended procedure was to drive three nails in a door in the form of a triangle to represent the Father, Son and Holy Ghost. Another was to paint the outside of a door blue, which would also keep goblins out of a household. Some Kansans nailed a horseshoe up above their doors, which not only kept away witches but also warded off bad luck. Other pioneers nailed up two sticks in the shape of a cross, believing this was more effective than the horseshoe. There is no doubt that all of these primitive acts of folk magic were done in southeastern Kansas in the early 1870s, but it is by no means certain no matter what the Weissbrods claimed that they were directed at Kate Bender. A few people evidently regarded Kate as a witch, and it may be that they suspected the Benders of murdering their guests, but they said little about it at the time. After they were exposed in the spring of 1873, many people appeared to claim that they had tried to warn people about the "Bloody" Benders, but that no one listened to their warnings.

But not everyone saw Kate as evil - at least when it came to her supernatural powers.

An elderly couple named Gould, who lived in Girard, Kansas, in the 1890s, often told extraordinary stories about the Benders. Although they had never met the family, they received their information from their friends, a group of people who were interested in Spiritualism, table-tipping, automatic writing, astrology, psychic healing, witchcraft and other occult matters. When the Goulds joined this group of amateur psychical investigators, they found that several of their friends had visited Kate Bender in 1872 and thought highly of her abilities as a medium. One woman who lived on a farm between Girard and Fort Scott had lost two valuable rings under mysterious circumstances. She was alone in the house when the rings disappeared and it seemed impossible that anyone could have stolen them. The rings were truly missing, though, and a search of the house failed to reveal their whereabouts.

When the woman went to the Bender tavern, Kate talked with her for a while and then went into some sort of trance. While in her trance, she said that both rings would be found in the wooden gutter attached to the roof of the house. When the woman got back home, she was rather ashamed of having made the trip and regarded the $5 fee that she had given Kate to be a waste of money. But she got a ladder and climbed up on the roof - where she found one of the rings just where Kate told her it would be. She told her husband about the incident and he mounted the ladder, and searched carefully, but did not locate the second ring. Late that night, it occurred to him to check the rain barrel, into which the gutter drained. The man and woman got out of bed, lighted a lantern and went out into the yard. The woman reached down into the barrel and groped around until she found her second ring in the silt at the bottom. It had evidently been in the gutter, but had been washed out by a recent rain.

Since Kate was so successful in finding lost jewelry and locating strayed and stolen livestock, it was only natural that people should call on her for information about their missing friends and relatives. There were - which was no surprise to the murderous medium - a number of men who had gone missing in southeastern Kansas. These mysterious vanishings were noted in the newspaper, but Kate was unable to solve any of them. There was no evidence of foul play in any of these cases. The fact that Kate was consulted about them indicates that no one, at that time anyway, suspected the Bender family of any connection with the missing persons, beyond the fact that a few of them were known to have stopped at the Bender tavern for a meal or a night's rest.

Kate told most of the people who consulted her that the missing men were alive and well, on their way to Texas, the Indian Territory, or some other region. She even wept as she told one distraught woman that her vanished husband had run away with an Indian girl to what is now

Oklahoma and that she would never see him again. Despite Kate's brilliant success in other fields, there is no record that she ever located a single one of the travelers who disappeared in Labette County between 1871 and 1873. It was not lack of knowledge that caused her failure, however. The truth was that Kate and her family had murdered a score of these travelers and had buried them in the Bender orchard, only a few yards from the building in which Kate pretended to console their distressed relatives.

The Benders went about their business of murder with a typically Germanic thoroughness. The Bender tavern was just a short distance from a well-traveled road, set out on the open prairie without so much as a large tree to shelter it from prying eyes. Obviously, it was not practicable to carry dead bodies out of the house in the daytime, so the Benders created a hiding place for corpses under the building. They dug a pit in the kitchen and hinged a trapdoor into the rough floor. The Benders did not do much farming, but they planted an orchard of apple trees behind the tavern - a place where the ground always seemed to be freshly plowed. A little stream called Drum Creek twisted over the prairie not far from the orchard and Big Hill Creek was a few miles away.

The Benders' method of murder and body disposal was simple enough, although it was learned over time. Initially, they didn't do much to cover up their crimes, which could have been a fatal mistake. In 1872, the body of a man was found in Big Hill Creek, about four miles from the tavern, but no one was able to identify him. A doctor who examined the corpse said that the man had been murdered - knocked on the head with something like a hammer and then stabbed in the throat with a large knife. Crimes of violence were not uncommon on the Kansas frontier, so the body was buried on the prairie and little else was said about it.

Then, a month or so later, another body was found floating in the Verdigris River, not far from Cherryvale. This time, the local people were upset and tried to identify the corpse as that of a man who had recently gone missing. An inquest was held in Cherryvale, but little came of it and the body was soon buried.

No one thought of connecting either of these crimes to Kate or the other Benders. They were regarded as peculiar people, and not very neighborly, but no one suspected that they were cold-blooded killers. Even so, the discovery of the bodies brought the murders almost to the Benders' doorstep and Kate realized that they needed a new method of disposing of their victims. They required a place that was both well-hidden and where they could watch over and guard against accidental discovery. Soon, their new plan of murder and body disposal was born.

Keep in mind, though, that the Benders did not murder the majority of their guests. In most cases, men who traveled in company, or who arrived at the tavern when other guests were present, were perfectly safe at the Benders' place. Kate was the mastermind behind the operation and she did not believe in taking chances. She realized that no lone man was a match for four people who caught him unawares, but if the Benders should attack a party of two or three men at a time, there was always a danger that one of them might escape. And one escape, of course, would ruin the family's murderous enterprise.

When a solitary rider was seen approaching, the family quickly made all of the necessary preparations. Kate quickly put on one of her best dresses and fixed her hair, while Mrs. Bender stirred up the fire in the cook stove and contrived to warm up something that would give off an appetizing scent.

Once the traveler had stopped at the tavern the family then had to discover whether or not the guest had any money, whether in his pockets or hidden in his wagon or saddlebags. John always took care of the horses and while he was feeding the animals, he looked for hidden pockets, which were commonly used on the frontier by those carrying large sums of money. It was common for travelers to carry large sums of money in those days, when banks were few and far between. Some men carried money in their pockets, but most experienced travelers preferred a money belt, which was worn around the waist under their clothing. Kate was a very attractive woman and could behave quite provocatively when she wanted to. A little playful touching would quickly reveal whether a man wore a money belt, or whether his wallet was fat or thin. A man with little money was allowed to leave the tavern unharmed, but a one with a belt or wallet that was thick with cash was not so lucky. That man's fate was sealed.

If possible, the Benders waited until nightfall before carrying out their nefarious deeds, when the traveler could be lured out into the darkness on some pretext or another. If he was old, or more interested in food than sex, the Bender males attended to this part of the business. If the fellow was amorously inclined, Kate arranged to meet him in the shadows behind the house. In either case, one of the Bender men hit the fellow over the head with a heavy hammer. This was more than enough to kill an ordinary man, but the Benders took no chances. Immediately after the man was hit, Kate would cut the man's throat from ear to ear with a sharp knife from the kitchen. In some instances, she stabbed the man in the breast as well, or, as it was learned from examination of one body, she disemboweled him and sliced away the man's sex organs.

Once the man was dead, the Benders lost no time in removing his valuables. Then John and the old man carried the body out into the orchard. Usually, a shallow grave had been prepared in advance. The body was then pitched into the grave and covered with dirt, as best as they could in the darkness. The two men then returned to the orchard at dawn, leveled off the grave and carefully removed any blood that might have been spilled unseen in the night. Neighbors remarked on how often the Benders plowed their little orchard, dismissing their winter work as "a fool Dutch notion," never realizing that it was being done to hide secret burials.

If the Benders murdered a man during the daytime, they killed him in the house. The methods varied, but all resulted with Kate distracting the man while John and the old man killed him. She would sometimes throw her arms around him, or would hold a séance to keep his attention. With the victim's back to the canvas curtain, it was simple for John or Pa Bender to sneak up behind him and smash his skull with the hammer. If anything went wrong, Kate was always close enough to stab the man before he could do any damage to the Benders. The body was then dragged back beneath the canvas and stripped. A trap door that led to the earthen cellar was opened and the body was unceremoniously dumped in. Legend had it that Kate would then leap into the pit and cut the victims' throats, ensuring that they were dead. It only took a few minutes for Kate and the old woman to wipe away any blood that had been spilled. Another traveler who entered the place just three minutes after the fatal blow was struck would see nothing out of the ordinary, and certainly no evidence of a bloody murder.

The body in the pit was left there until after dark, when the Benders searched it for valuables and then buried it in the orchard with the others. Although no record was ever found, the Benders likely had some sort of connection with horse thieves or outlaws in the Indian Territory, who took away the horses, wagons, saddles and harnesses left behind by the murdered travelers. Some of the horses and wagons belonging to men murdered at the Bender tavern were of distinct appearance, and would have been easily recognized by many people along the roads of southeast Kansas. However, not one of these horses, or a single piece of equipment, was ever seen after the owner's disappearance. The animals and the rest of the equipment would have fetched a considerable sum for the Benders, so it's unlikely they would have killed the horses or destroyed the wagons and carriages, but whatever became of them remains a mystery.

After the Benders' crimes were exposed in 1873, many people came forward with strange tales of their own narrow escape from death at the hands of the murderous family. One of these was a Catholic priest, Father Paul Ponziglione, whose story was printed in a local newspaper. The story related:

On a windy day toward dusk, Father Paul arrived at the Bender place and decided to put up there for the night. His suspicions were aroused when he happened to see old man Bender place a heavy curtain, just back of the supper table. Later he observed the old man and Kate holding a low, whispered conversation. The hard and forbidding features of the Benders, the lonely surroundings, and the moaning of the wind had a far from soothing effect on the priest's mind. He remembered reading about the strange disappearances of persons in that part of the state, of whom no trace had ever been found. The more he studied over the matter, the more uneasy he became. Some warning voice within seemed to urge his immediate departure. Finally, under the pretext of looking after his horses, he left the house, hurriedly hitching his team to the spring wagon and drove rapidly away. Long afterward, Father Paul often told the story of his escape from the terrible Benders, and he always added that he owed his safe deliverance to a Higher Power.

While the priest's story has the ring of truth to it, many others told wilder and more fantastic tales, like that of a schoolteacher from Paola, Kansas. The man said that he rode up to the Bender tavern at dusk and was ready to dismount when he suddenly saw a gigantic skull and crossbones appear in the sky. It was "exactly like the sign on poison bottles in the drugstore!" he exclaimed. This frightful apparition so alarmed him that he spurred his horse back to the main road and fled toward Independence at a full gallop, never stopping until the horse was completely exhausted.

Another story was told of a young couple who came in a wagon with their mentally handicapped child, a boy of about 10 who had never learned to speak. The husband pulled his team up to turn into the Bender place when suddenly the boy jumped up from the bed of the wagon, where he had been resting on a pile of hay under an old quilt. The boy shrieked "Blood! Blood!" and tried to climb out of the wagon. The astounded parents soothed the child and drove on, having decided to camp by the roadside instead of staying at the Bender tavern.

One traveler testified that he had approached the tavern one stormy night and knocked on the door without getting any response, although he could hear music and voices inside. Finally, he pushed open the door and entered the building to see a group of people who stood about playing guitars and "funny flutes." In a little space in the center of the room, Kate Bender and another girl were dancing. They were completely naked except for some jewelry "which seemed to have feathers fastened to it." The spectators who were jammed into the tavern were dark, black-eyed people, wearing outlandish, gaudy clothes and speaking in a foreign language. The traveler could not understand a word that anyone was saying, but could tell that it was neither English nor German. He said that it "might be some kind of Injun talk," although the people were not like any Indians he had ever seen. Local law officers later came to believe that the people the man had seen were Gypsies, since some of them had been reported at Fort Scott a month before this encounter. They linked this traveler's tale with a theory that Kate and Mrs. Bender were not Pennsylvania Dutch at all, but Gypsies who had come from some German-speaking part of Central Europe. The theory conveniently linked the Benders with a band of criminals who helped them dispose of the valuables and horses taken from their victims - and of course, with the stories that Kate had supernatural powers.

Over the course of nearly two years, the Benders were likely very successful in their efforts to obtain ill-gotten wealth. Two of the men who disappeared in the region, Ben Brown and W.F. McCarthy, were known to have carried more than $5,000 in cash between them, besides jewelry and other valuables. A man named McCugsey, who disappeared about the same time, was believed to have had at least $2,000 with him. There were several others, including a woman who vanished with several valuable antique rings. The spoils from their numerous robberies, the fairly good income made from the steady sale of food and accommodations, and the money made by "Prof. Miss Kate Bender" from her supernatural healing and other occult practices would suggest that the Benders must have done very well financially.

If Kate had been smart enough to spare the life of Dr. William H. York, the Benders could probably have continued to ply their bloody trade for many years to come without much danger of discovery. However, Kate had not been smart enough and their profitable business soon came to an end.

In March 1873, Ed and Alexander York, along with a party of men, were diligently searching the Kansas countryside for any trace of the missing doctor. They stopped at every house within two or three miles of the Osage Mission Road and asked the farmers whether they had seen a man answering Dr. York's description, or a horse that resembled his. They described the doctor's saddle, his watch, his revolver, his wallet, and anything else they could think of that might jog someone's memory. They found many people along the road to Fort Scott who had seen the man pass, but no one south or west of the Bender place knew anything about him.

Late in the month of March, accompanied by twelve men from around the area, Ed York rode up to the Bender tavern and asked the same questions that he had been asking along the road. Kate was extremely cooperative and even offered to contact the spirit world on the missing doctor's behalf to see if some clue could be obtained as to his present whereabouts. York had little interest in her offer, but said that should all of his searches come up empty, he'd be happy to pay her for her help. When he questioned John and Old Man Bender, he gained more information, although all of it was useless. The old man, who was reading a German Bible on the porch, spoke to John, who translated for the search party. Both men said that they vaguely recalled seeing the doctor and that he had arrived around noon, had eaten dinner and then left about an hour later. He had talked little, said nothing of where he was going, but the Benders assumed that he was on his way to Independence, since he rode off in that direction.

But John Bender wasn't able to stop his storytelling there. He told York that somebody had seen some strangers near Drum Creek, not far from the Bender home, and suggested that perhaps they had something to do with the doctor's disappearance. He concocted a far-fetched tale about how he had been waylaid recently and suspected the strangers had something to do with it. He even went as far as to take York to the supposed site of the attack and to the place where the strangers had allegedly camped. There was a deep hole in the creek just at this point, so several of the men dragged the creek on the chance that the missing doctor's body might be concealed beneath the muddy water. John Bender helpfully pitched in and assisted them, but nothing was found.

Meanwhile, Ed York, finding little credence in John's theories, continued his search.

Soon after this encounter with Ed York, the residents of nearby Harmony Grove assembled in the weathered clapboard schoolhouse for the annual school board election, held each year on the second Tuesday in April. On that day, April 8, 1873, the election was hurried along. There was a more pressing business that needed to be talked about: namely missing people. The discussion became heated, one voice rising over another, but all of them calling for some sort of action. The men who were gathered there clenched their fists and promised some sort of punishment for those responsible for the missing local residents. Pa Bender and young John were present at the meeting that day, and when one man demanded that every foot of the nearby farms be searched, a cold sweat must have gripped the guilty pair.

A short time after the meeting at the schoolhouse, a neighbor of the Benders named Billy Tole was driving his cattle past the tavern and saw no sign of the family. The place appeared to be deserted. He stopped to investigate and found their livestock were unattended, having been left with no feed or water. A number of animals had been tied up and had no way to fend for themselves. One poor calf, tied to a post in the stable, had been unable to free itself and had died of thirst. Its mother was nearby, her udders burst. Tole checked the house and found it empty and in great disorder, as if the Benders had left in a hurry. Dirty dishes and pieces of cooked food were scattered all over the place. Pictures had been pulled down off the walls and the canvas curtain that had separated the cabin into two rooms was lying in a heap in one corner. The stove was filled with ashes and it looked as though a number of papers had been hurriedly burned. Tole called out, but there was no reply. The Benders had cleared out and they didn't appear to be coming back. Where had they gone?

News traveled slowly on the Kansas border in those days and the Benders had been gone nearly two weeks before Ed York heard about it. At this point, no one suspected them of murder, but people were up in arms about the mistreatment of their animals. Ed York, though, sensed something more sinister about the Benders' disappearance. He came down from Fort Scott with several friends and they broke into the tavern. It was York himself, legends say, who discovered the crude trapdoor with the leather strap hinges in the kitchen. He went down into the cellar and was met with the stench of death. There were no bodies in the pit, but the ground had been soaked with blood. The men searched the house and found three hammers, a knife that was hidden inside a clock, and pieces of jewelry, cufflinks and trinkets that belonged to some of the missing people, although no one knew it at the time. Scattered across the kitchen floor, they found some of Kate Benders' advertising broadsides.

York also found strange designs scratched into the floor of the front room, which he studied for a long time. There were twelve distinct characters arranged in a circle, about three feet in diameter, with several columns of figures beside them. Eventually, it was decided that these figures were meant to represent the signs of the Zodiac and had likely been used by Kate in some of her astrological prognostications. Half-burned in the stove were two little wooden figures with nails driven into them. They were probably "spite dolls," which practitioners of folk magic often used to bring death or pain upon the persons the dolls are supposed to represent.

Drawn by the putrid smell and congealed blood in the cellar, York and about fifty men from the township began their grim search for bodies there, but they found no bodies under the floor. By afternoon, the crowd of diggers and the morbidly curious had swelled to several hundred. Inside the house, York found a pair of spectacles and recognized a solder repair to the silver frame. They were his missing brother's glasses. Crestfallen, he went outside for some fresh air and sat down on the seat of a wagon in the yard. This slight elevation gave him a good view of the premises. As he gazed moodily into the orchard that the Benders had so carefully tended, he saw something that chilled his blood.

"Boys," he shakily called out. "I see graves."

The men soon set to the work of their dark harvest. Heavy metal rods were driven into the ground, especially into the irregularly shaped mounds located among the trees. As the rods were withdrawn, it was discovered that some of them were matted with hair and putrefying flesh. Shovels were used to carefully move away the soil and within a few minutes, the first body - that of the missing Dr. York - was uncovered. As the corpse was pulled from the ground, its head was removed and Ed York numbly identified the gray and rotting face of his brother. The dead man's skull had been smashed and his throat had been cut all of the way to the spine.

The men continued the grim harvest of bodies the next morning and it soon became apparent that the Benders were not among those buried in the apple orchard. The men likely doubted by this time that the missing Benders were innocent murder victims. Quite the contrary; the true extent of the family's depravity was just being uncovered.

Men excavating for bodies at the Bender tavern

By nightfall, the diggers had turned up the remains of at least nine other people in the orchard, including the pair for whom Dr. York himself had been searching: George Loncher and his daughter. Loncher's skull had been crushed and his throat cut, but it was the state in which they found the girl, said to be around eight years old, which left the hardened settlers horrified. She had a broken arm, but her skull was intact and she was not otherwise injured. The men believed that she had been thrown alive into the grave and her father's body was dropped on top of her. Loncher's wife had died a short time before he and his daughter had disappeared and they were in the process of moving to Iowa when they vanished. Sadly, their journey never extended beyond the Bender tavern.

Some of the corpses found were in the last stages of decomposition, but others still held enough flesh to be recognized. Among those subsequently identified were two men from Cedarville, who, on different dates, had apparently stopped off at the Benders' for a meal. One had been contesting a land case in Independence and the other was a horse trader who was only recognized by a silver ring that he wore. A third man had been missing since December 5, 1872. He had been traveling to Independence to take up residence there. His sister was only able to identify him from his clothing. A number of the bodies were never identified, although one of them, Henry McKenzie, was cousin to a neighbor's wife. He had been on his way to Independence to see his sister and was last seen on

November 6, 1872. Like most of the other corpses found in the orchard, his skull had been smashed in at the back and then his throat had been cut to ensure that he was dead.

But the horrifying discoveries were not yet over. The remains of a second child were found the following day. This time, it was the body of a girl who had been so badly mutilated that her age could only be estimated to be around eight years old. Her breast bone had been driven in, her right knee wrenched from its socket and the leg doubled up under the body. After she had been exhumed, someone cut off her golden hair and fashioned it into a wreath, a ghoulish but not unusual mourning custom at the time. The wreath is still on display in a Cherryvale museum.

The remains of a man named Johnny Boyle were discovered sitting upright in an old shallow well, and the bodies of at least four unidentified men were found off the Bender property. Exactly how many people the Benders killed between 1871 and 1873 remains unknown, but estimates range to well over twenty victims. It is also uncertain how much money the family made by robbing their prey. Some of their victims carried thousands of dollars, while others had no more than pocket change.

It seems apparent that the Benders' bloodlust was fueled by more than just greed.

The news soon spread about the deadly deeds of the "Bloody Benders," as they became known, and curiosity-seekers flocked to the house. The grisly finds in the apple orchard shook those who lived in and around Cherryvale and Harmony Grove, but the killings also created a thirst for vengeance. Rewards were offered and vengeful groups of riders were formed and began searching throughout Kansas for any trace of the family. They questioned anyone they believed had a connection to the Benders, like the grocer Rudolph Brockman, who was lucky to survive the ordeal. A preacher from Parsons named A.M. King, who knew and befriended the Benders when they had lived there, was taken into custody for a while, but was eventually released. Accusations flew and many were accused of aiding the Benders in some way, but none of the suspected individuals were able to offer any clue as to the murdering family's whereabouts.

The hunt for the Benders soon took on a life of its own. Ed York offered a $1,000 reward for information that would lead to their arrest. Kansas Governor Thomas A. Osborn followed in May 1873 with a $2,000 reward for the apprehension of the foursome. Search parties - some sanctioned, but most not - had little luck. Bounty hunters, lawmen and amateur detectives descended on the region, all hoping to track down the Benders and take home the reward for their capture.

Others came to Kansas on the trail of a sensational news story. Reporters and photographers from as far away as New York and Chicago converged on the scene, all looking for grisly details to thrill their readers. Others came to pillage macabre souvenirs from the Bender homestead. The relic hunters soon dismantled the entire tavern and barn. One week after the discovery of the bodies, the Thayer newspaper reported, "Thousands of people daily visit the grounds. Last Sunday it was estimated that there were 3,000 people on the grounds at one time." Fortunately, Osage Township Trustee LeRoy Dick had preserved some of the evidence, including a knife and three hammers that were thought to be murder weapons. On June 25, 1873, the *Thayer Head Light* ran a follow-up to its earlier story, noting, "The whole of the house, excepting the heavy framing timbers on the Bender farm and even the few trees, have been carried away by relic hunters." The newspaper also addressed the disappearance of the Bender family, suggesting, "The murderers themselves are probably in the middle of China by this time and will never be heard from."

The Benders' wagon was about the only thing that ever turned up. It could be traced to them because the sign that had once hung over the tavern's front door - on which John had scrawled "Grocry" on one side and Kate had correctly printed "Groceries" on the other - had been used to make a repair of the wagon's bed. The wagon had been found abandoned near Thayer, Kansas, in a deeply wooded valley. The horses had been unhitched, but were tied to the wagon. An old shotgun was found next to the seat, but there was no sign of any blood or that anyone had been hurt. The occupants of the wagon had simply vanished.

After the discovery of the wagon, Marshal Jim Snoddy from Fort Scott and posse members Colonel C.J. Peckham and Henry Beers went to Thayer and inquired in town about train departures. Four people who matched the Benders' description had boarded a train there for Humboldt, Kansas. The Humboldt station manager said that from there, John and Kate had taken a train south, while Ma and Pa Bender carrying a trunk that was speculated to have been filled with money , had taken another train to St. Louis. Snoddy, Peckham and Beers chased the train to St. Louis and learned that an elderly couple assumed to be the Benders had taken a carriage from the train station to a house in the city, but were long gone. The three lawmen returned to Kansas and, while checking the Southeastern rail lines, came across a baggage master on the Frisco line that had checked a trunk like the one the Benders had reportedly carried through to Vinita in the Indian Territory. Following that lead, the three men boarded a train for Vinita.

Meanwhile, Albert Owens, who owned a rooming house in Denison, Texas, reported that a tall young German railroad worker and his wife had recently pitched a tent near his establishment, where an older couple visited them from time to time. They were planning to head for another town on the Texas-New Mexico border. LeRoy Dick intercepted Peckham and Beers Marshall Snoddy had since returned to his duties at Fort Scott in Vinita and shared the new report with them. Changing direction, the two men traveled to Texas and picked up the trail of the alleged Benders, first 200 miles west of Denison and then again in El Paso and into the Chihuahua desert of Mexico, before giving up the chase. Some believe the Benders permanently vanished over the border, but there is no real proof of that.

Wherever they went, the Benders had completely disappeared. Some would go on chasing them for the next fifty years but officially, the family was gone forever.

But, of course, there were the tall tales, the erroneous reports and the legends that may or may not be tinged with truth.

One widely reported story was that the Benders had boarded a train for Kansas City after leaving Thayer, knowing that it would connect them to the east. James Ransom, a conductor on the train, reported in 1908 that, "While the posses were racing around the country, the Benders were on their way to Europe."

As the years passed, various newspapers reported sightings of Bender family members. A dispatch from Florence, Arizona, which was picked up by the *New York Times* on February 13, 1875, firmly stated that a man who was one of the Benders was arrested after being tracked through West Texas. This went hand in hand with a story in the *San Antonio Express* for July 7, 1873 that said the two Bender women had been arrested in Winterset, Iowa. Nothing ever came of these or other supposed sightings.

Osage Township Trustee LeRoy Dick had his own ideas about what happened to the Benders. According to his story, Kate and John realized that they had been lucky when eluding the lawmen that followed them into Texas and stayed on in Mexico. In the fall of 1874, Old Man Bender and his wife went to Michigan, where they lived quietly for five years. Then, in 1879, Dick flatly stated that Old Man Bender had killed himself. While no record of any suicide exists, it appears that many people believed that between 1879 and 1889, Kate and Mrs. Bender were living together in Michigan.

According to a story in the October 31, 1889 edition of the *Chicago Daily Tribune*, two women were arrested for larceny near Niles, Michigan, and were identified as Ma and Kate Bender. The women gave their names as Mrs. Frances E. McCann and Mrs. L. Davis, but someone was sure they were the Benders. In fact, the evidence of this was so compelling that LeRoy Dick traveled to Niles, arrest warrants in hand, and transported the prisoners to Oswego, Kansas. Several old-timers from the Cherryvale area traveled to the jail at Oswego and identified the women as Mrs. Bender and her daughter, Kate. The women indignantly denied everything, but were afraid that they might be lynched before they could establish their identities. Authorities held the women for a few months, but after a hearing with sixteen witnesses seven who said the women were the Benders, seven who said they weren't, and two that weren't sure , a judge decided that the county had incurred enough expense in the matter, and since the evidence against them was insufficient to prosecute them anyway, he released them. Although the authorities never proved that the women were Ma and Kate, LeRoy Dick went to his grave believing that they had located them - and that they had escaped from justice.

But not everyone believed this. In fact, most people believed that the Benders did indeed get what they had coming to them and that their punishment was outside of the law. It was a general belief among most Kansans that a posse managed to catch up to the Benders and had killed them. The killers were all sworn to silence, which is the reason that the story has never been confirmed, and yet a few who talked managed to keep the legend of their death alive.

One story stated that the Benders had all been killed, with one of the men in the posse firing four shots into Kate's body and watching her die on the ground. Members of his family prized this pistol for many years because, as far as they were concerned, it was the gun that killed the Kansas murderess. According to the story, the posse overtook the Benders near what is now the Kansas-Oklahoma line. The Benders jumped out of the wagon they were riding in and fled across a corn field, firing back at their pursuers as they ran. The posse tried to take the Benders alive, but John and the old man were killed early in the fight. Mrs. Bender was captured, but as the men approached, she fired a pocket pistol at them and was immediately shot to death. Kate Bender came near to escaping, but one of her pursuers pushed ahead of the others and found her hiding between the rows of corn. As he approached, she fired at him with a Colt revolver and he was wounded in the leg. He returned fire with his own gun and Kate fell to the ground. She was still alive, however, but in a fury, he limped forward and fired three more shots into her body. The beautiful, sinister Kate Bender was dead - or so the story went.

There were several versions told about the death of the Benders at the hands of the numerous bands of riders that pursued them across the Great Plains. In some stories, they were shot, in others they were lynched. One such story came from a rather unlikely source. Famed *Little House on the Prairie* author Laura Ingalls Wilder spoke of the Benders during a speech that she gave in Detroit in 1937. In it, she told of her own family's possible connection to the fate of the Bloody Benders. It was a disturbing tale that sheds a new light on the author's adored father. During her lecture, Wilder said:

Every story in this novel Little House on the Prairie , all the circumstances, each incident are true. All I have told is true but it is not the whole truth. There were some stories I wanted to tell but would not be responsible for putting in a book for children, even though I knew them as a child.

There was the story of the Bender farm that belonged in the third volume, The Little House on the Prairie. The Benders lived halfway between it ffithe Ingalls' homesteadffl and Independence, Kansas. We stopped there, on our way in to the Little House, while Pa watered the horses and brought us all a drink from the well near the door of the house. I saw Kate Bender standing in the doorway. We did not go in because we could not afford to stop at a tavern. On his trip to Independence to sell his furs, Pa stopped again for water, but did not go in for the same reason as before.

There were Kate Bender and two men, her brothers, in the family and their tavern was the only place for travelers to stop on the road south from Independence. People disappeared on that road. Leaving Independence and going south they were never heard of again. It was thought they were killed by Indians but no bodies were ever found.

Then it was noticed that the Benders' garden was always freshly plowed but never planted. People wondered. And then a man came from the east looking for his brother who was missing. He made up a party in Independence and they followed the road south, but when they came to the Bender place there was no one there. There were signs of hurried departure and they searched the place.

The front room was divided by a calico curtain against which the dining table stood. On the curtain back of the table were stains about as high as the head of a man when seated. Behind the curtain was a trap door on the floor and beside it lay a heavy hammer. In the cellar underneath was the body of a man whose head had been crushed by the hammer. It appeared that he had been seated at the table back to the curtain and had been struck from behind it.

A grave was partly dug in the garden with a shovel close by. The posse searched the garden and dug up human bones and bodies. One body was that of a little girl who had been buried alive with her murdered parents. The garden was truly a grave-yard kept plowed so it would show no signs.

The night of the day the bodies were found a neighbor rode up to our house and talked earnestly with Pa. Pa took his rifle down from its place over the door and said to Ma, "The vigilantes are called out." Then he saddled a horse and rode away with the neighbor. It was late the next day when he came back and he never told us where he had been.

For several years there was more or less of a hunt for the Benders and reports that they had been seen here or there. At such times Pa always said in a strange tone of finality, "They will never be found." They never were found and later I formed my own conclusions why.

Many stories were told of the Benders being hunted down and killed, but there just as many that were spread about their miraculous escape. Most of these appeared in the pages of cheaply printed true-crime thrillers that were published in Philadelphia and New York - far away from the Kansas frontier. There were several books that appeared in the years that followed, purporting to have inside information about the Bender murders. It has been said that garbled accounts of the Benders' crimes were published as far away as Britain and France and translated into several foreign languages.

There were even those who claimed that Kate Bender survived into the 1930s. Mrs. Bender was supposed to have died in Texas in 1882 or 1883. Another story claimed that Kate married a U.S. Deputy Marshal, one of the men who pursued her family when they fled from Texas. In the early 1900s, people were always claiming to have met Kate on the street somewhere - in New Orleans, Key West, Mexico City, Havana, New York and even once, in Paris. She was always described as a distinguished-looking old woman, slender and well-dressed. In 1910, it was claimed that she was living in Kansas City and several people even wrote to the newspapers about her. In 1938, a weekly magazine stated, as if it were a historical fact, that John Bender died in Amarillo, Texas.

The Benders were a mystery - an unsolved enigma that intrigued anyone with an interest in historical crime. What really happened to them? How many people did they actually kill? No one knew then or now and for this reason, people across the country refused to believe that they had been killed.

Those were the tales told in far-off cities and in distance places, but in every story told by the pioneers of the 1870s especially those related by residents of Labette County, Harmony Grove and Cherryvale the Benders always received their just desserts at the hands of the vigilantes who hunted them down. Many old-timers from the area, as late as the 1920s, claimed to have positive proof that the Benders had been killed. They told of seeing old guns, watches and money belts in the possession of pioneer families, who told them in confidence that the objects were relics of the "Bloody Benders." At least a dozen men swore that they were there on the day that Kate Bender was shot to death, her body riddled with scores of bullets.

But could they have truly told the tale any other way?

Those who lived near the Bender farm were unnerved by the fact that savage murders had been carried out literally right under their noses and that no one had ever suspected the family in the mysterious disappearances that had taken place all around the region. Once the Benders had disappeared, the locals needed to believe that the family was dead. In order for them to sleep at night, the Benders *had* to be dead - no one wanted to think about them ever coming back. For the people of Cherryvale and Harmony Grove, the Benders would always be the "boogeymen," the monsters under the bed, lurking in the dark and waiting for their unsuspecting prey.

For most of us, the phrase "going on a bender," just makes us think of a drinking spree, but in southeastern Kansas, it would always have a different meaning.

Finally, the legends of the Benders would not end with their deaths. The story of Kate Bender remained alive in Kansas for more than a century after the family had vanished. She was a monster in life, most believed, so why would she not linger after death?

By 1886, the house in which the Benders had lived was reduced to nothing more than an empty hole that had once been the cellar. Relic-seekers had carried away every last remnant of the building, even taking the stones that lined the cellar walls. Only memories of the dark deeds of the Bender family remained to provide evidence that they had ever existed: memories - and ghosts.

The stories claimed that the ghosts of the Benders' victims haunted the ruins of the house and later, the earthen hole that was all that remained. Those who wandered out to site hoping to bring back some gruesome souvenir were often frightened off by strange, glowing apparitions and the moaning and keening sounds that came out of the darkness. Some of these spirits still reportedly wander the area today.

If they do, they may not walk alone. Some legends say that Kate Bender returned to haunt the lonely land where she took so many lives. She is, perhaps, doomed to roam the earth as some sort of black penance for her horrific crimes.

Many claim that these stories were nothing more than grim folklore, but few of even the most skeptical dare to walk the roadways near the location of the old tavern at night in order to find out.

1872: THE NORTHWOOD MURDERER

It is a common misconception that serial murder or "repeat killing" as it was once known is a relatively recent phenomenon that began roughly around the time of the sensational Jack the Ripper slayings in London's impoverished Whitechapel district in 1888, or with the murders of H.H. Holmes in the 1890s in America. But this couldn't be further from the truth. Historical evidence makes it depressingly clear that humans have been butchering one another since the days when our ancient ancestors dined on each other's brains and collected human body parts as hunting trophies. That our species has always indulged in barbaric behavior is made clear in everything from the Greeks myths like the story of Atreus who slaughtered his brother's sons and cooked them in a pie to fairy tales like "Little Red Riding Hood," which to many historians reflects the atrocities of real-life lycanthropes like Peter Stubbe, a lust killer who attacked and killed more than a dozen children, ripping them to pieces like a wolf.

Many years before Jack the Ripper embarked on his bloody spree in London, a sexual murderer that was every bit as monstrous as the terrible British fiend was at large in America. Precisely why he has been largely forgotten over the years, while less terrifying killers have achieved mythic status remains a mystery. According to his confession, he killed just as many as the Ripper and his savagery was no less extreme. In fact, the nature of his crimes was even more shocking because he preyed primarily on children.

His name was Franklin Evans, and in the eyes of his contemporaries, he was "the most monstrous and inhuman criminal of modern times - or indeed of any time."

On Monday, June 12, 1865, fifteen-year-old Isabella Joyce and her twelve-year-old brother, John - children of a recently widowed seamstress who lived in Lynn, Massachusetts - went to visit their grandmother in Roxbury, a neighborhood of Boston. At around 11:00 a.m., they asked for permission to go and explore a nearby wooded area called May's Woods, which was popular locally as a picnic spot and recreation ground. After some initial reluctance, their grandmother agreed to let them go. She packed them a lunch, gave them ten cents each for trolley fare, and told them to return no later than 2:00 p.m. She never saw them alive again.

When the children did not return, their grandmother became frantic. For the next five days, search parties scoured the forest outside town. It wasn't until Sunday, June 18, however, that two men, John Sawtelle and J.F. Jameson - while hiking In nearby Bussey's Woods, not May's Woods where the children said they planned to go - stumbled across the remains of the two missing children.

From the scene, it seemed clear that Isabella and her brother had been playing contentedly in the woods, creating little hillocks of moss and fashioning wreaths out of oak leaves and twigs, when they were unexpectedly attacked. The assailant - which the newspapers called a "fiend in human shape" - attacked the girl first, cutting her savagely with a knife, tearing off her undergarments and raping her. The coroner found twenty-seven stab wounds in her torso and another sixteen in her neck. The ground around her body was saturated with blood. She had apparently put up a desperate fight, grabbing the long blade of the knife and trying to wrest it from the attacker's hands. The index finger of her right hand was completely severed and the rest of her fingers were mangled, bloody and hanging loosely by bits of skin. Her clothing was soaked in her blood and clumps of grass and dirt had been roughly shoved in her mouth to try and stifle her cries.

Apparently, poor John had stood paralyzed for a few moments in terror, watching the attack on his sister. When he finally turned to run, it was too late. He was found lying face down in the dirt, possibly having tripped over a tree root when he was attempting to escape. The killer had pounced on the boy's back and stabbed him a half dozen times. The wounds were so deep that, in several instances, the blade had gone all the way through the young boy's body and pierced the earth beneath him.

There were two houses within a few hundred yards of the murder scene, but the occupants were so used to hearing shouts, laughter and yells from the nearby picnic area that, as the newspapers noted, "They would not have paid any attention even if they heard screams on this occasion."

The horrific savagery of the Joyce murders provoked a tremendous response throughout the state. From church pulpits, ministers pointed to the murders as a sign that the country was descending into a deplorable state of vice, immorality and crime. Rewards totaling more than $4,500 more than $60,000 in today's money were offered by local residents, while an enormous manhunt was started for the "inhuman wretch" that was responsible for the outrage. Newspapers issued confident predictions that the perpetrator would be "speedily arrested" and "subjected to summary vengeance." But, even though a number of likely suspects were interrogated in the wake of the murders, no arrests were made.

A break in the case seemed to finally be imminent in March 1866 when an inmate at Charlestown State Prison, a small-time crook who went by the colorful nickname of "Scratch Gravel," told a cellmate that he had "done that job in Roxbury." In the end, though, Scratch Gravel turned out to be nothing but a "blustering braggart" who had not even been in Massachusetts at the time of the murders. As months - then years - passed with no arrests in the case, it seemed that the murder of the Joyce children - which newspapers called "one of the most horrible and revolting crimes which has ever occurred in New England" - would remain forever unsolved.

Time moved on and for the most part, the murders were mostly forgotten. But in the early summer of 1872, seven years after Isabella and John Joyce had been brutally slain, a new string of events was set into motion when Franklin Evans came to board with his elderly sister, Mrs. Deborah Day, at her farmhouse in Northwood, New Hampshire.

Evans, a gaunt and grizzled sixty-four-year-old ne'er do well, had led a shiftless existence for most of his adult life. A contemporary writer later said of him, "He belonged to that numerous class of deadbeats that are always broke." Wandering the New England countryside, he survived by sponging off his adult children, "borrowing" small amounts of money from relatives and acquaintances and blatantly seeking handouts from strangers.

What little honest money he made came from supplying a Manchester physician, Dr. F.W. Hanson, with healing roots and herbs that he scrounged up in the forest. His vagabond life had given the old man a deep knowledge of the land and "his reputation for obtaining medicinal products of the woods and fields was unsurpassed." Even in this line of work, though, Evans could not keep from betraying his lazy and dishonest nature. Claiming that he himself was a "botanical physician," he peddled worthless cures to rural families.

He also passed himself off as an itinerant preacher. Taking advantage of the religious fervor of the era, he joined the Second Advent Society, declared that he was a minister of the Gospel and managed to raise a little money from his brethren to support himself while on his sacred mission. The religious society naturally took offense, however, when he was arrested for consorting with prostitutes. And this incident wasn't his only brush with the law. At various times, he was charged with petty theft, attempting to pass crudely forged $10 bills and - most seriously - scheming to defraud the Traveler's Insurance Company of Boston of $1,500.

If these crimes were the worst of his transgressions, Evans would have been nothing more than a small-time scoundrel, a snake oil salesman and a con artist. But as the country would eventually learn -much to its horror --- he was something far worse: a creature so depraved that, to the people of his time, his crimes seemed the work of a supernatural evil - "too horrible," as one newspaper stated, "for anything in human form to have perpetrated."

There were four people living at his sister's farm when Evans showed up there that summer: Mrs. Day and her husband, Sylvester; their widowed daughter, Susan Lovering, and Susan's daughter, Georgiana. This poor young woman - Evans' grand-niece - immediately became the object of the depraved old man's lust. Within days of his arrival, he began trying to seduce the girl. When she repulsed his advances, he concocted a diabolical scheme. It was, as one account stated, "A deeply laid plan designed for no other purpose than to lure his victim into his lecherous grasp."

Near the Day farmhouse was a deep forest, the largest tract of woodland in the county, covering an area of more than two thousand acres. Late on Monday, October 21, 1872, after being away from the farm for most of the day, Evans returned to his sister's home, explaining that he had been off in the forest setting snares for partridges. The following morning, he invited his niece to accompany him into the woods to see if he had caught anything. For reasons unknown, she agreed. The traps turned out to be empty, but he showed Georgiana how they worked - little hoops concealed inside the hedges, designed to snag birds by the throat as they scrambled through the foliage. Georgiana was intrigued by the snares, never suspecting that their purpose was actually to trap her.

Early Friday morning, October 25, Evans asked the young woman for a favor. He had agreed to take care of some chores for a neighbor, a farmer named Daniel Hill, and would be gone all day. He asked Georgiana if she would mind going into the woods and check the partridge traps for him. Surely he must have caught something by now. She was reluctant at first, but allowed herself to be persuaded. Evans left soon afterward, presumably for Hill's farm several miles away. A short time later, Georgiana stuck a comb into her thick brown hair to hold it in place, threw on a shawl and disappeared into the forest.

When Georgiana failed to return by lunchtime, her grandfather went to look for her. Unable to find any sign of her, he came back home and told her mother, who immediately became alarmed. The two of them hurried back into the woods. As they frantically made their way along the forest paths, shouting girl's name, they spotted her shawl on a tree branch. A short distance away, they discovered her comb, broken in half, with strands of her hair still tangled in its teeth. The earth all around had been trampled with footprints - one made by a man's boots, the other by a girl's shoes - evidence, Sylvester Day would later testify, of a "squabble." Terrified now, Day and his daughter pushed deeper into the trees, but found no other signs of the missing girl.

The two of them ran home, alerting the neighbors as they went. Throughout the weekend, all day on Saturday and Sunday, hundreds of people scoured the woods, but found nothing. By then, however, suspicion had fallen on Franklin Evans. The authorities checked with Daniel Hill and found that Evans' story didn't hold up. He had not asked him to help with chores that day. In fact, he hadn't seen him for more than a week. Another witness, a young man named James Pender, testified that he had seen Evans cross into the forest at around 8:30 a.m. on Friday morning, just a half hour before Georgiana had disappeared into those same woods.

County Sheriff Henry Drew grilled Evans but the old man could offer no convincing account of his whereabouts on the day that his grand-niece went missing. He was promptly taken into custody. Inside Evans' pockets, Drew later stated, he found "a wallet, money, obscene books, a bottle of liquor, and a common bone-handled knife with two blades, blood-stained and keen as a razor."

Even after he was arrested, Evans denied knowing anything about what had happened to Georgiana. But when Drew assured him that "no harm would come to him if he confessed," Evans changed his story. Georgiana, he insisted, was alive and well. He had arranged to have her "carried away by a man from Kingston," a farmer named Webster who wanted her for his bride and was willing to pay for her.

Although Sheriff Drew was skeptical, he immediately started for Kingston, where he quickly confirmed the story was a "base falsehood." Back at the jailhouse, he continued to badger Evans, plying him with liquor and even telling him that he would help him escape to Canada if he told him the truth. Finally, on October 31, the old man gave in. When Drew asked him "whether the girls was cold in death or not," Evans replied: "She is, and I've done wrong."

At midnight that Halloween night, six days after her disappearance, Evans told the sheriff he would accompany him to the place where the body had been left. Through the dark forest they silently made their way along, over rocks and logs and along narrow trails. Then, in a clearing at one of the deepest points of the woods, Evans took the sheriff and an assembled group of deputies to a spot underneath the roots of an upturned tree. He pointed a shaking finger at a pile of dried leaves and quietly murmured, "There she is." The sheriff gently brushed away the leaves and by the dim light of his lantern, he saw the pale face and mangled remains of Georgiana Lovering.

Two townsmen who were at the scene, Eben J. Parsley and Alonzo Tuttle, had brought the local physician, Dr. Caleb Hanson, with them. Gaping in shock at the body of the naked, savaged girl, Parsley couldn't help by speak. He demanded of Evans, "How did you come to do such a bloody deed?"

The old man shrugged as he replied, "I suppose the evil one got the upper hand of me."

Dr. Hanson bent down to examine the dead girl. A glance at her face, with its bulging eyes, swollen and protruding tongue, and dark bruises at her throat, told him that she had been strangled. Her body had been hideously mutilated. Evans later confessed that he had raped her corpse and then had torn open her belly with his bone-handled knife to get to her uterus. He had also excised her vulva, which he carried away with him and hid under a rock. When a stunned Sheriff Drew asked him why he had committed such butchery, the old man calmly replied that he did it "to gain some knowledge of the human system that might be of use to me as a doctor."

As he was dragging the man back to jail, Drew had one more question for him: "What did you set those snares for, Frank?"

Evans answered with a self-satisfied smirk: "I set them to catch the girl - and I catched her."

Franklin Evans' trial opened on February 3, 1873, but it was a perfunctory affair. The outcome was a foregone conclusion to everyone involved, including the defendant. Only one dramatic moment occurred during its three-day duration. Early on the morning of Tuesday, February 5, while his guard was off fetching him a glass of water, Evans took one of his suspenders, tied it around his neck, attached the other end to a clothes hook on the wall of his cell and tried to hang himself. Just then, the newspapers reported, the guard returned, "seized Evans and disengaged him from the hook."

Most observers believed that the man's half-hearted suicide attempt was nothing more than a ploy to set up an insanity defense. If that was the case, the effort failed. He was convicted of murder in the first degree and sentenced to hang on February 17, 1874. For "his unnamable and incredible crimes, he will be swung like a dog," celebrated one local newspaper, which went on to recommend that those wishing to attend the hanging should make "early application in order to secure 'reserved seats,' which will be scarce."

Accompanied by the high sheriff of Rockingham County, J.W. Odlin, Evans was transported by train to the state prison at Concord. A crowd of more than eight hundred people gathered at the station to get a glimpse of him. One newspaper stated that they were "excited to a remarkable pitch of feeling." This frenzied fascination was not entirely based on Evans' notoriety as the killer of Georgiana Lovering. By then, he had confessed to other crimes as well - atrocities that marked him as one of the most appalling killers of the era.

Evans began his murderous career nearly fifteen years earlier, when he was visiting Derry, New Hampshire. Passing by the home of a family named Mills, he peeped in a window and spotted a little girl, approximately five years of age, playing on the floor. There were no adults nearby. Possessed by the urge to "procure a body for surgical purposes," he snuck into the house, snatched the child, then took her off into the woods and strangled her. When he stripped off her clothing, though, he discovered that "one hip and part of her spine were deformed." Filled with revulsion, he abandoned his plans to "examine her" - the name he gave to postmortem rape and sexual mutilation - and buried the corpse under a rotten tree stump.

Three years later, while in Augusta, Maine, he snatched a fourteen-year-old girl named Anna Sibley on her way to school. Carrying her deep into the woods, he raped her, cut her throat, and then hid her corpse under a pile of leaves. In May 1872, just weeks before arriving at his sister's home in Northwood, Evans raped and murdered a woman whose body was found in the woods near Fitchburg, Massachusetts.

His most sensational confession, though, was that he had killed little John and Isabella Joyce in Lynn, Massachusetts. While some of the law officers involved in the case were skeptical of his claim, and through Evans himself retracted it shortly before his death, the similarities between the Lovering murder and the murders in Bussey's woods convinced most lawmen that the crimes had indeed been perpetrated by the same person. Headlines around the country spread the news that the eight-year-old Joyce murder mystery had finally been solved.

Franklin Evans spent the last night of his life quietly, falling asleep around midnight with the Rev. Church of Providence, Rhode Island at his side. Around 5:30 a.m., he ate a hearty breakfast and drank a cup of tea. When Church asked him if he had any last-minute statements to make, he replied, "I have confessed everything. If the people don't believe it, I can't help it."

A large, excited crowd gathered outside the prison walls as the hour of execution drew near. At 10:50 a.m., they were admitted into the building, where the gallows had been set up in the corridor between the guardroom and the cells. Within minutes, every available space was packed with spectators, some of them standing on the stairways leading up to the cells, others crowding around the scaffold.

At 11:00 a.m., Evans, dressed in a black suit, was led through the crowd by the prison warden. He climbed the scaffold on his own and muttered something under his breath as his arms and legs were tied. He appeared "quite calm and possessed," although the people who were standing closest to the gallows later reported that his knees were trembling. The noose was adjusted around his neck and a black hood was pulled over his head. After reading the death warrant, Sheriff Odlin placed his foot on the spring that controlled the drop and - at exactly 11:06 a.m. on Tuesday, February 17, 1874 - the elderly serial killer was "launched into eternity."

He dangled in the air, slowly strangling, for nearly twenty minutes before his heart stopped beating and the attending physician declared him dead. Ironically, since he claimed that his murders were committed so that he could gain anatomical knowledge to "aid him as a doctor," his corpse was donated to the Dartmouth Medical College so that it could be dissected by the students there.

The murder of Georgiana Lovering became the subject of one of the previously mentioned "murdered-girl ballads," which hold a unique place in American history. Franklin Evans was still awaiting trial when a local man named Byron DeWolfe composed and printed a broadside ballad about the sex slaying of the unfortunate young woman. Unlike the typical ballads of this sort, which tend to play fast and loose with the facts, DeWolfe's piece, despite its rampant sentimentality, offers an almost journalistic account of the crime. Consisting of more than two-dozen eight-line stanzas, it is too long to reprint in full here, though a few pieces from it appear below:

> Dark were the eyes of a beautiful maiden,
> Like music her voice, and her cheeks were in bloom;
> Her mind seemed to be with the purest thoughts laden,
> Her breath was as sweet as the rose's perfume;
> Her mother worked hard for her child's education,
> And brought with her many a well-written tome;
> Her father had died for the flag of his Nation,

And she was the sunlight and comfort of home!

She had an uncle too deep steeped in error
To learn in her presence the way to improve;
His sinister look would fill the children with terror;
Few hearts could towards him affectionate move;
He looked sanctimonious for certain occasions,
And words big with honor came to him at ease,
Yet he was her uncle, and she must have patience,
And do all she could to relieve him and please.

In the wild wood had her grandfather sought her,

The mother, too, searched for her beautiful daughter,
Until she was ready with anguish to die;
How wildly - how deeply her mother lamented,
And said, "Tell me, Georgie, where you roam!"
No wonder the woman was almost demented,
When she found the apron, and with it her comb!

And when Sheriff Drew at last forced the confession
From Evans, the uncle a fiend among men,
That he had done great wrong, and great was his transgression,
That search was abandoned, but not until then!
Abandoned! But 'twas for the sake of another,
To be in the night - in the darkness intense;
For one that would bring a dead child to its mother,
But for a lost idol make small recompense.

There the fiend stopped, ay, he was almost kneeling,
He scraped away leaves and there was something white!
The sheriff the form of the dead girl was feeling!
Feeling it there on that terrible night!
Feeling it there with her murderer near him,
And standing as calm as a man at his gate,
Feeling it there! Was he wild? Was he dreaming?
He thought even this was a terrible fate.

Assistance was near, for that had been provided;

> Men came to the spot just as quick as they could;
> The prisoner, surely, by that time decided
> That nothing about was foreboding him good;
> There lay the form of the girl he had strangled,
> And probably dragged to that horrible spot;
> There last the body, all lifeless and mangled,
> A, never a tiger such bad work had wrought.

This was not quite the end of the story, at least in regards to the murders of the Joyce children. A few years after Franklin Evans went to the gallows for the murder of Georgina Lovering, a ghost story came to be connected to the murders of the children in Bussey's Woods. The murders had a tremendous effect on the local community. As one local resident wrote in 1878, "Of the many dark deeds of blood which have disgraced this age few have been fraught with more harrowing details than the one enacted right here."

Isabella and John Joyce vanished on June 12, 1865 but were not found until the following Sunday, when their bodies were accidentally discovered by hikers in Bussey's Woods. The woods were part of an old four-hundred-acre farm, located on both sides of Bussey Street, that was given by Benjamin Bussey to Harvard College for the horticultural institute. In time, one hundred and twenty acres of the farm and woods would become the Arnold Arboretum with the Bussey Institute on one side. The Joyce children had sought the high ground of the woods for their picnic.

Isabella had been raped and stabbed repeatedly and her brother was found a quarter-mile away by Bussey Brook in a condition that sickened the was-hardened Civil War veterans who saw the body. It was surmised that just before noon, he had left his sister, fallen, and finally been attacked by his sister's murderer.

The children were brought back to Lynn for burial. The funerals became the scene of public sorrow, especially since they occurred just two months after the assassination of President Lincoln. Rewards were offered by the authorities and seven suspects were interrogated and released. Visitors to the girl's murder site raised a memorial cairn. In the process, any further clues were obliterated, although what could have been discovered during those days of primitive forensics remains unknown. For the protection of the public, a police beat was established in the Bussey Woods.

In March 1866, the *Boston Weekly Voice* reported a possible break in the case. A man of violent disposition had been arrested in August 1865 for burglary. While being held for trial in Fitchburg, he plotted to murder his guard and to escape with other prisoners. Known as "Scratch Gravel," he stated that any man who had done "the Roxbury job" would not hesitate to kill again. His bravado about the children's murder revolted another prisoner, who foiled the escape by telling authorities about Gravel's entire conversation.

When Gravel was moved to the state prison for his burglary conviction, officials there tried to get him to speak more about the Joyce murders, but he refused. He was transferred to a light work detail in hopes that he might talk with a trusted prisoner, but he still refused. Finally, an undercover detective was placed in Gravel's cell in February 1866. Gravel liked his cellmate, and soon they were hatching a plan for escape. Gravel referred to "the Roxbury children" but never confessed to their murders.

Gravel - whose real name was Charles Aaron Dodge - was loosely tied to the murders by the prison warden. A man resembling him was seen at Taft's hotel in Roslindale, less than a mile from Bussey's Woods. The knife taken from him at Fitchburg could have wounded the Joyce children. The Boston police were not convinced, though. All his information could have come entirely from newspaper reports, they said. In time, they realized that Gravel was nothing more than a braggart who embellished the basic information in the newspapers for his own twisted reasons.

It was there that the matter of the area's most heinous and unsolved murder rested until it took another bizarre turn some thirteen years later.

"The details of our area's terrible atrocity and barbarity fueled a feeling of unprecedented horror," wrote an author of a book about the murders, published in Boston in 1878. The book asked how a crime so terrible could ever have happened, "In a section as civilized, a community so guarded, a population so abundant, in the marginal outline of a great city."

The book's author was Henry Johnson Brent, founder and editor of the New York City magazine, *Knickerbocker*, which was widely enjoyed from 1833 through the Civil War. In June 1865, he happened to be staying with friends who lived within a few hundred yards of the murders. He wrote his book, "*Was It A Ghost?*" to focus attention again on the twin murders that had gone unsolved for more than a decade.

Brent himself had immediately become a suspect in the case when a boy told police that he had often seen a man of Brent's description in the Bussey's Woods with a knife and gun. Fortunately for Brent, he was an artist, whose palette knife and target-shooting practice was known in the neighborhood. He was also acquainted with members of the police force. The police quickly dismissed him as a suspect.

By the end of June 1865, the search for the killer had grown cold. A week or so later, in a bizarre personal twist, Brent saw the ghost of a man on the far side of his host's property between Bussey and Motley Woods. Brent truly felt that the event was something beyond his ability to reconcile by the usual rules of explanation and that it deserved publication.

He had gone down to meet his host returning from Boston via Forest Hills, only to learn later that he had returned home via Centre Street at 10:00 p.m. Brent revisited the site where he spotted the apparition at 9:00 p.m., within half an hour of the event, but nothing more was seen nor found. Initially, Brent connected the apparition with his host, whom he feared might have met with some kind of misfortune, but during this second visit, which included a walk to the rock where Isabella Joyce had been murdered, Brent suddenly connected it with the murders.

He took his story to a perplexed police chief, who urged him to publish it. The chief asked whether Brent recognized the ghost. Could it have been the children's recently deceased father? Was the spirit perhaps a witness to the murders?

H.J. Brent detailed his encounter with the spirit in chapter ten of his book. An abridged version of it appears below:

Upon a still and clear night I went out of the cottage, and, taking two dogs with me, strolled down through the stable yard and past the garden, until I came to the brow of the hill that formed the apex of my friend's grasslands. The brow of the hill was flat all about me and at the base ran off into a meadow, the opposite side of which was overlooked by the Bussey Woods.

From where I stood, several pines rose out of the even surface of the forest, marking as with an uplifted hand spread out the place where the girl's murder had been done. On my left was Motley's Woods, drawing up with its intense shadows close to the dividing wall. From the wall to where I stood all was clear and distinct, save where the shadows fell over the ground.

The wall and the wood on my left ran down to that corner at Bussey Creek, which was only a short distance about 50 feet from the spot where the boy had fallen. Some 250 yards away and close to the corner just mentioned was a clump of trees, and then straight before me without an intervening object, the dark wood gloomed over the rock of the girl's death. My purpose was simply to take the cooling air from the winnowing trees.

It was the habit of my host, who did business in Boston, of leaving the train at Forest Hills Station at 9 o'clock as a general thing and keeping to South Street until he got to the bottom of the hill near to where the brook crosses the road. He would then enter the lowlands at the outskirts of Bussey Woods and thence follow the path and up the hillside covered by Motley's Woods, keeping close to the wall until he reached the point of the wall near which I was standing, pass over it and be home.

Knowing that my host was irregular as to his hours of return home at night, I was not surprised when I saw a figure lean over the wall for an instant within about 20 feet of me, pause a moment, and then cross over to the side on which I was. Seeing that he stopped, I spoke aloud these words, "Hello, Dan, is that you?"

Though I could discover the figure and recognize its movements, there was too great a shade thrown over the wall to enable me to distinguish a face so familiar to me. To my appeal there was no reply, and then in an instant the impression came upon me that if it really was my friend, he was testing my nerves. Up to this moment I never had a thought apart from him.

While I stood perfectly motionless, waiting for some recognition of my appeal, the figure advanced slowly in a direct line from the wall, leaving the shadow, and stopped before me and not 20 feet away from me. I saw at once that it was somebody I had never seen before. When in the light without even a weed to obstruct my vision, as soon as he stopped, I called, "Speak or I will fire!"

It was at this period that I observed especially the behavior of the dogs. Up to this time they had been quiet, lying on the grass, but now they both got up, and I felt on each side of me the pressure of their bodies. They were evidently frightened, and I saw that they were looking with every symptom of terror at the figure that stood so near us without a motion.

The figure never once turned its head directly toward me but seemed to fix its look eastward over where the pine-trees broke the clear horizon on the murder-hill. This inert pose was preserved but for a moment, for as quick as the flash of gunpowder it wheeled as upon a pivot and, making one movement as of a man commencing to step out toward the wall, was gone!

To my vision it never crossed the space between where it had stood and the outline of the shade thrown by the trees upon the ground. One step after turning was all I saw, and then it vanished. What I saw I relate exactly as it happened. Can I describe this figure you will ask?

It looked like painted air. There was no elaborate appearance, indeed I could not make out the fashion of the garment. I was more occupied in the effort to recognize a human being in the figure that was before me. He looked dark grey from head to foot. Body he had, legs, arms, and a head, but the face I could not distinctly see, as he turned it from me.

Brent published his book long after interest had died in the case and it is believed that many local residents never accepted Franklin Evans claims that he had killed the Joyce children, despite the similarities to his other crimes. Brent hoped that his book would stir up a renewed investigation and would goad the murderer, if still alive, into remorse and confession. The ghost story is the centerpiece of his book, and rightly so, given the title.

Many local residents must have had theories about the murders. Brent, believing the murderer was still alive, did not state his complete details. The change of the picnic from May's Woods - where the children told their grandmother they were going -- to the more secluded Bussey's Woods prompted a suspicion that the children were accompanied by someone they knew. The coins their grandmother had given the children to ride the streetcar were found lying near the girl's body. Someone else had apparently paid their fare.

Brent's book alternates between a detailed description of the double murder and an argument for the existence of ghosts. He even noted the results of séances that had recently occurred in which letters were read that were alleged to be written by the murdered girl and her father. A communication purportedly from the boy also was circulated. Though unacquainted with Spiritualism, Brent felt that he had to include these reports with his ghostly account. Brent maintained a terrible feeling of guilt over the fact that he had been in Bussey's Woods painting and target shooting on the day that the murders took place and yet had seen nothing.

Unfortunately, his unorthodox look at the murders - weaving together the crime and the ghost stories - drew scorn from many contemporary reviewers. One of them wrote, "We are disposed to consider this a very unsubstantial pretext for making a book. What good it accomplishes, what end it serves, it is impossible to discover. It does not help the identification of the murderer. It throws no light on the supernatural speculations so prevalent these days. The curious public will probably hang with fresh interest on the horrible details of the crime. But no one, as far as we can see, will be benefited by its perusal."

1874: "THE DEMON FROM THE BOTTOMLESS PIT"

Less than two years after Franklin Evans was hanged for the horrific sex murder of Georgina Lovering, another shockingly similar crime occurred in New Hampshire. This time, the killer was a French Canadian woodcutter named Joseph Lapage. Like Evans, he was a sexual psychopath who attacked his victim with the ferocity of a wild animal and unspeakably mutilated the corpse. For those who believe that such killers are of a more recent vintage, we'll stress once again that the "good old days" weren't always so good.

Lapage fit the modern definition of a classic lust killer, but his contemporaries described him in less clinical terms as a "fiend incarnate" and a "demon of the bottomless pit." For the people of rural New Hampshire, it was nearly impossible to believe that a human being could be capable of the things that Lapage did. Such acts, they insisted, could only be carried out by a true monster from hell.

And perhaps they were right.

The killer who would come to be regarded as the "fiend incarnate" was born Joseph Paget in 1837 on a farm about fifty miles northwest of Montreal. At the age of twenty, he married a local woman three years his senior from a family named Rousse. They had five children over the course of almost as many years. Around 1862, he and his family moved to Saint Beatrice, a small provincial town in the hills of Quebec. By then, as the *New York Times* would later report, "he had gained a very bad reputation. He abused his wife shamefully and associated with the vilest company." It was during his years in Saint Beatrice that he committed his first known sex crime: the rape of his wife's thirteen-year-old sister, Julienne, a girl he had known since her earliest childhood.

The rape occurred in June 1871. At around 7:00 a.m. that day, Julienne - who did housework for a family name Lajeunesse --- went to milk the cows, her usual morning chore. She was walking through an isolated corner of the pasture when she was stopped in her tracks by a sinister sight. About fifty feet away from her stood a man dressed in a red flannel shirt and baggy linen trousers, held up by a black leather belt. Beneath his hat, his face was concealed by a mask that had been fashioned from buffalo skin. In his hand, he carried a wooden cudgel about two and a half feet long and as thick as Julienne's arm. Suddenly, the man came running toward her, moving so fast that his hat flew off his head.

Julienne screamed as she turned and ran, but she was not fast enough. When the man caught her and spun her around, the young girl reached up and tore away his grotesque mask. It was Joseph, her brother-in-law, she later testified, his face contorted in a grimace of savage lust.

Lapage, as he later became known, gripped Julienne around the throat and threw her to the ground. He straddled her and as she tried to cry out, he reached for a handful of sandy soil and shoved it into her mouth to try and silence her. He ground more of it into her eyes. He lifted her skirt, tore away her underclothes and brutally entered her. She lost consciousness while he was raping her.

When she awoke, she found herself alone in the pasture. She staggered back to her employer's house and told Joseph Lajeunesse what had happened to her. Alarmed and angry, he immediately contacted the police. An arrest warrant was issued for Lapage, but he managed to escape the authorities. Julienne, unable to first to keep down any food or drink, took a "long month" to recover from her physical injuries. By then, her attacker had fled Canada with his wife and children.

Joseph Lapage had vanished - at least for a time.

Three years later, on the afternoon of Friday, July 27, 1874, a young schoolteacher, Miss Marietta Ball of St. Albans, Vermont, closed up her one-room schoolhouse for the day and started off down a lonely stretch of road to visit a friend on the south side of the small community. She never arrived.

The following day, search parties scoured the woods for any sign of her and some of them came upon a horrible sight. Several of the men found Marietta's naked corpse - "hideously violated and mangled in a most fiendish manner - lying in a little gully beneath a pile of leaves. At the inquest, the coroner, Dr. H.H. Farnsworth, determined that her skull had been crushed with a rock. She had been raped, but whether it was before or after her death it was impossible to say.

Determined to discover who had killed this well-liked young woman, her neighbors put together all the money they could and hired a detective from Boston to look into the matter. The detective began interviewing everyone who knew Marietta, including her students, and soon learned about a suspicious character who had been asking the schoolchildren about Miss Ball's route home in the weeks prior to her disappearance. This same man allegedly had bruises and scratches on his face immediately after her murder. Known for his generally crude demeanor, especially toward women, the suspect had been living in St. Albans' "French settlement" since his arrival from Quebec three years earlier. The man's name was Joseph Lapage.

Lapage was promptly arrested, but he managed to produce witnesses who were willing to testify that he was working in a hayfield at the time of the murder and supported his claims that his face had been scratched by thorns while he was berry picking. With no hard evidence against him, he was released. The following March, he and his family suddenly packed up and left town. A short time later, they showed up in Pembroke, New Hampshire, where Lapage found work as a woodcutter for a man named Joe Daniels, who supplied wood to power the steam engines in the Pembroke mills.

In late September 1875 - just six months after the Lapage family moved to Pembroke - a number of people reported a strange figure lurking along the country road that led to the local school. Seventeen-year-old Clarence Cochran was one of them. He was headed to class on the last Friday of the month when, he later testified, he "saw a man jump into the bushes on the left side of the road" about fifty feet ahead of him. Believing that it was his friend John Colby, a practical joker who liked to hide in the bushes and spring out at his unsuspecting friends, Cochran shouted at him: "Get out of there, you long-legged son of a gun, you can't scare me!" But when Clarence reached the spot where the figure had vanished into the underbrush, no one was there.

The following day, Mrs. Albersia Watson, and her youngest daughter, Annie, a student at Pembroke Academy, were walking along the same lonely stretch of road. Suddenly sensing that

Academy Road as it looked in 1875

someone was behind them, they turned and saw "a man standing by the side of the road about one hundred feet away, holding a stick in his right hand." Mrs. Watson couldn't make out his features, but she could see that he was of stocky build with "black hair and whiskers, tan-colored overalls and a black slouch hat." As the mother and daughter hurried on their way, the man quickly followed them. Throwing a protective arm around her daughter - who was now whimpering in fear - Mrs. Watson hurried the girl along. By now, the man was "partly running." He was almost upon them when, rounding a bend, Mrs. Watson spotted a neighbor, George Mack, picking berries in a nearby field. As Mrs. Watson steered her daughter toward Mack, she threw a quick glance over her shoulder and saw the man who was pursuing them duck into the woods and disappear.

That same weekend, Hiram Towle, and his wife, Harriet, were driving their buggy along Academy Road when they saw "a man coming, carrying a stick behind him in a peculiar way." As they drew up beside him, he glanced at Mrs. Towle with a look that made her shake with fear. She later testified, "I thought me might be crazy. I felt afraid of the man." Even though she had never seen Franklin Evans, she had read the description of the infamous "Northwood Monster" in the newspapers. Now, as they drove past the dirty, club-wielding man who was making his way towards the school, Mrs. Towle turned to her husband and said: "I should think that was old Evans himself if he was still alive."

By the time that Mr. and Mrs. Towle had passed him on the road, Lapage had already set his sights on another victim. It was not a teacher this time, but one of the students attending Pembroke Academy. Exactly which student is planned to kill is unclear. It appears that his original plan had been to kill Litia Fowler, the sixteen-year-old daughter of a farmer named Trueworthy Fowler, or her schoolmate, Sarah Prentiss.

On September 22, while working as a field hand for Fowler, Lapage saw Litia as she crossed the front yard and entered the house. He immediately began asking her twenty-year-old brother, Andrew, about the girl - who was she, where did she go to school, what road did she take to get there? Oblivious to how inappropriate and sinister these queries were, Andrew obligingly answered him and even pointed out the school when he and Lapage drove a wagon past it a few days later.

Sarah Prentiss also caught Lapage's eye while he was working for Fowler. When he saw her walking past the farm, he pulled aside a thirteen-year-old boy named Edwin Mahuir and questioned him about the girl, asking her name, where she lived and "who was going with her." When he made a crude remark about "certain parts of the girl's anatomy, young Edwin was so startled that he turned and fled."

Evidence suggests that Lapage intended to attack either Litia Fowler or Sarah Prentiss on the morning of October 4, 1875, as they made their way to school. For some reason, his plan was never carried out. Both Sarah and Litia made it safely to school, but their classmate Josie Langmaid was not so lucky.

Just two months shy of her eighteenth birthday, Josie was a "pretty and popular girl" who usually made the two-and-a-half-mile walk to school with her sixteen-year-old brother, Waldo. On that morning, though, Josie had promised to wait for a friend. Waldo, growing impatient, waited with his sister for as long as he could, but then headed off to school by himself. When the first bell tolled at the academy, summoning students to class, Josie gave up on her wait and started off to school on her own. At around 9:00 a.m., five minutes after the final bell had sounded, a farmer named Bernard Gile passed her as she was hurrying in the direction of the school. He was the last person - except for the killer - to see her alive.

When Waldo returned home from school that afternoon and told his parents that his sister had never shown up, an anxious Mr. Langmaid hurried around to neighboring homes to see if Josie might be with one of her friends. Except for Bernard Giles, however, no one had seen her all day. Within an hour, news of her disappearance had spread throughout the community. Dozens of men began searching the countryside and as darkness fell, the search continued by lantern light.

At around 8:00 p.m., a farmer named Daniel Merrill became the unlucky man who stumbled on Josie's savaged corpse in a marshy patch of woods about eighty feet from the road. The body was "lying on its back with the right arm doubled under and the left crossed over the breast," Merrill later testified. "The right foot was drawn up. The clothing appeared to have been removed and thrown back, all saturated with blood. The breast was bare." Josie's vulva had been cut away and carried off by the killer. It was never found. Her head had been cleanly severed and was not found at the scene.

The following morning, another searcher, Horace Ayer, discovered Josie's head, rolled in her blue cloak and dumped in the woods about a quarter mile from where the body had been found. During the postmortem examination, it was revealed that before he cut her head off with an ax, the

Left Pembroke Academy   Right The unfortunate Josie Langmaid

killer had crushed her skull with a club, and then stomped on her face for good measure, leaving a clear print of his boot heel on one cheek. The young woman had been so badly beaten that every bone in her left hand had been shattered as she tried to shield her head from the blows.

The first suspect in the murder was a twenty-four-year-old stonemason named William Drew, who - though married with children - was reported to have made "improper advances" toward a number of schoolgirls, including Josie Langmaid. It turned out, though, that witnesses supported Drew's claim that he had been mending a wall on a neighbor's farm at the time of the murder.

A few days later, officials in Pembroke received a letter from the coroner in St. Albans, Vermont, who had read about the Langmaid case in the newspaper. He noted the striking similarity to the rape and murder of Marietta Ball that had occurred a year and a half earlier. The police immediately paid a visit to the home of Ball's accused killer and a search of Lapage's bedroom turned up a blood-soaked overcoat, a bloody hat, and a pair of trousers "bespattered with blood from the belt line all the way down to the cuffs." A comparison of his boots to the tracing of the heel print that had been left on Josie's face revealed a perfect match.

Lapage insisted that he had been "lost in the woods" at the time of the murder, but a high school girl named Hattie Gault swore that she had seen him walking on Academy Road with an axe in his hand at 8:30 that morning. Another witness, Thomas Gardiner, told the police that on the afternoon of October 4 - after Josie was reported missing, but her body had not yet been found - he and his wife received a visit from Lapage. When Mrs. Gardiner remarked on Josie's disappearance, Lapage allegedly blurted, "It's too bad that girl has been killed." Then - seemingly aware that he had revealed information he wasn't supposed to know - he turned and "hurried away as quick as he could."

Depraved killer Joseph Lapage

Lapage was taken into custody and was indicted for murder, rape and the mutilation of Josie Langmaid. During his incarceration, a newspaper reporter sought out Lapage's wife and questioned her about the murder of Marietta Ball. She claimed that she had "no evidence that would link him" to the crime, "but since she had foiled an attempt by him to ravish their own fifteen-year-old daughter, she had to admit that he was capable of committing it."

Meanwhile, Lapage was trying hard to dig his way to freedom with a makeshift tool that he had fashioned from a piece of his metal bed frame. He managed to pry seventeen bricks from the wall of his cell before his jailers became aware of his efforts.

A huge crowd showed up at the Concord City Hall for the start of Lapage's trial on Tuesday, January 4, 1876. Before the actual proceedings began, the jurors, along with the defendant, were taken to the scene of the murder. As Lapage looked on with little interest, the dozen men were taken into the woods and shown exactly where the headless body of the young woman had been found. A large stake, marking the spot, had been driven into the earth and the surrounding trees and bushes had been draped with pieces of black cloth - tokens of mourning from Josie's friends and neighbors. The makeshift memorial was eventually turned into a permanent monument, a fifteen-foot stone obelisk that was erected by local townsfolk. The stone still stands near the spot where Josie's headless corpse was found. Inscribed on the stone are the words:

Erected by the citizens of Pembroke and vicinity, to commemorate the place of the tragic death and memory of Josie A. Langmaid, a student of Pembroke Academy who was murdered on her way to school, on the 4th day of October, 1875, aged 17 years, 10 months and 27 days.

Also included are helpful directions to the precise spot in the woods where her decapitated head was found.

From the somber place where Josie's body was found, the jurors were taken to the place where the head was discovered. On a nearby tree, someone had whittled away a section of bark and, on the exposed wood, had inscribed the following with a lead pencil: "J. Langmaid's head found here, October 5, 1875. Poor Josie, may her soul rest in peace."

The trial lasted for six days and was highlighted by the appearance of Julienne Rouse, Lapage's French-speaking sister-in-law, who testified through a translator and told of the terrifying morning five years earlier when Lapage had attacked and raped her. In the end, the jury took only ninety minutes to convict him. Unfortunately for the prosecution, the appeals court ruled that Judge Foster had erred in admitting Julienne's testimony since it had no direct bearing on the Langmaid murder. The reversal, though, was only a temporary setback for the state. A second trial in March 1877 ended with another swift conviction.

A year passed before Lapage's execution on March 15, 1878. According to the *New York Times*, Lapage was a "perfectly docile" prisoner while confined at the state prison in Concord, New Hampshire. He gave no trouble to the warden, never complained about his treatment or asked for anything. On the Monday before his scheduled hanging, he had a final meeting with his family, but - apart from a few tears shed by one of his daughters - "little emotion was manifested by any of them. At parting, he kissed his wife and daughters but only shook hands with his two boys."

On the evening before the execution, Lapage received a visit from two priests, J.E. Barry and J.B. Millette. They prayed together in his cell until nearly midnight. Almost as soon as they left, Lapage - who had maintained that he was innocent through his trial and incarceration - summoned the warden to his cell. Falling to his knees and speaking in broken English, he tearfully confessed to the murders of the two young women. He stated that he felt "greatly relieved" after his confession.

When the priests returned early the next morning, they found Lapage eating a hearty breakfast. After receiving the sacrament, he was led to the gallows, which had been erected in the corridor of the prison's north wing. A large crowd had assembled, including Josie Langmaid's father, James, who was not only still devastated by the murder of his daughter, but also by the death of his thirteen-year-old son, Waldo, who had died from tuberculosis only two months after Josie had been killed.

At just after 11:00 a.m., Lapage was led to the scaffold by Sheriff Dodge, who read aloud the death warrant and adjusted the noose around the prisoner's neck. He drew the back hood over

Lapage's head, tied his arms and legs and then sprang the trapdoor. Lapage plunged downward, bouncing once with the snap of his neck. The *New York Times* reported, "A slight twitching of the legs was the only motion observable after he fell." Officiating physicians, Drs. A.H. Crosby, C.P. Gage and J.W. Barney, monitored his fading heartbeats and pronounced him dead after nearly twenty minutes. His corpse was taken to a local undertaker and he was buried without ceremony at Blossom Hill Cemetery.

But he did not rest there in peace.

Two weeks later, a "party of young scamps" stole into the graveyard at midnight, exhumed the corpse and left it hanging from a water pipe in the yard of the statehouse. It greeted the citizens of Concord the next morning - April Fools' Day.

1881: "THE GIRL HAD SET HIM CRAZY"
The Story of Johnny Coyle

The Accomac Inn sits on a slight rise overlooking the majestic Susquehanna River, just east of what is now York, Pennsylvania. The Inn itself isn't terribly old, but the land upon which it sits is historically significant. In 1722, the land was part of a 200-acre tract of land in a thick hardwood forest that was surveyed and granted to two gentlemen named Philip Syng and Thomas Brown, who called the tract "The Partner's Adventure." For decades, the area continued to be largely populated by Native Americans, with several small villages springing up along the banks of the river in both directions. This area was enveloped by hundreds of thousands of acres of virgin forests, and thus far, virtually untouched by European settlements.

Controversy surrounded the opening of these lands for settlers and as to who the rightful holders were. Both the Pennsylvania and Maryland colonies claimed to be the proprietors and each offered land grants with differing restrictions. On a few occasions, each colony granted the same land to different people. Pennsylvania would not grant land patents until after the land had been secured by treaties from the appropriate Native American tribes. Maryland held to no such requirements and granted land patents as it wished. As a result, it took nearly a decade for Syng and Brown to receive patents from both colonies granting them ownership of The Partner's Adventure.

Syng and Brown had a very good reason for why they worked so hard and waited so long to move forward with their land development. The spot they chose on the west bank of the Susquehanna River was an ideal location for a ferry landing. By 1736, the last of the Native American claims to the land west of the Susquehanna were eliminated by treaties. New European settlements were immediately planned for these western lands. The Partner's Adventure was in a prime location to prosper from the impending migration.

The land was later sold to James Anderson and in 1742, Anderson received an official charter for his ferry landing. At this time, the landing became officially named Anderson's Ferry. Anderson improved the river landing and operated his prosperous ferry and landing, later building the

Anderson's Ferry Inn. He also owned much of the land surrounding what had been "The Partner's Adventure" and was involved with some farming and logging. His only real claim to anything historically notable, even as just a footnote, was that he fathered a child with a Delaware Indian woman. This child went on to achieve acclaim as the great Chief Anderson of Anderson, Indiana, the chief of the Delaware "Turkey" group.

The endeavor became even more prosperous when a new road, the Accomac Road, was surveyed and built. For decades, Anderson's Ferry and the Accomac Road carried nearly all of the settlers traveling south and west from the New England states and the area became known as simply "Accomac."

During 1777 and 1778, the ferry became a strategic crossing point for military dignitaries and members of the Continental Congress during the American Revolutionary War. Likewise, the inn that was next to the landing played host to many of these notables, including the Marquis de Lafayette, who wrote favorably of his accommodations while spending several days there.

Most often, ferries consisted of poled or rowed flat-bottom boats. However, in 1825, an historical first brought national attention to Accomac. John Elgar built America's first iron steamboat which he christened *The Codorus*, after a creek near Accomac. Hundreds arrived at the Accomac to look at or ride on *The Codorus*, making it an even more popular resting place for travelers.

The ferry and the inn passed through several owners, including a period where the name changed to Keesey's Ford. There was never a time when the Accomac was not both popular and prosperous. Eventually, in 1864, the property was purchased by John Coyle, Sr. Coyle, his wife Mary, and their young son, John "Johnny" Coyle, Jr., changed the name of the ferry to Coyle's Ferry and the inn to the Accomac Inn, then moved in and took up operations.

Over the next eighteen years, the Accomac Inn became more than just a stopover for the ferry landing. It had become a popular resort along the Susquehanna River for sportsmen, hunters, and gamblers. Also during this time, young Johnny Coyle had become an expert ferryman. In fact, locals believed him to be the best on the water. He was said to know "every pothole and shallow for a mile up and down the landings."

But a fine ferryman was not all there was to Johnny Coyle. As he grew older, he grew stranger and stranger. Most of the people from the surrounding area believed him to be, in the parlance of the era, simple-minded. Though usually a gentle man, he could be moody and temperamental. No one ever knew if Johnny's outbursts were caused by bouts with insanity or his love of alcohol. His history of erratic behavior led his friends and customers to be wary whenever they were alone on the water with him.

Mary, Johnny's mother, knew from his toddler years that he was different, that he wasn't like other children. She and John Sr. had not had their child until later in life so they put much of their love and energy into their odd son. As he grew to adulthood, they struggled to make him behave and he drove them crazy with worry. He often seemed to waver between foolishness and insanity. He would disappear into the woods for days at a time and they never knew when, or if, he would return. They took Johnny to see two physicians specializing in diseases of the brain. Each prescribed every treatment imaginable but none seemed to help. One doctor went as far as to tell Johnny's parents that if they weren't able to take care of him, he would lose his mind entirely. At one point, they became so concerned that they hired a man to watch over their son through the winter, paying him with room and board at the inn.

Johnny also displayed an obsessive personality. In his teens, he accidentally shot himself in the leg while duck hunting. Though the injury was relatively minor, he constantly complained and expressed anxiety about being a "cripple" for life. As his leg healed, he suffered from typhoid fever for nearly three months. His father believed that the fever, combined with Johnny's alcoholism, drove him to severe depression, which in turn led him to several half-hearted suicide attempts...or possibly just the appearance of suicide attempts. They were mostly threats to shoot himself, or slash his own throat, but there was never a drop of blood shed.

He was also unlucky in love. This was largely because no woman was courageous enough, or crazy enough, to consider spending her life with Johnny. Miss Emily Robbins had the misfortune of drawing Johnny's attention. Without prelude, he confronted her, demanding that she marry him. Thinking to forestall him, she said she would only marry in a silk dress. Johnny promptly ran to his mother's closet and pulled from it her best silk dress. Running back to Miss Robbins, he thrust it at her exclaiming that they should marry that same afternoon. Completely taken aback, she stammered that she had not been serious and could never marry him, realizing that "he could not be of sound mind." Coyle did not take the rejection well, and fumed to a friend that he was not finished with her yet.

George Spangler had on occasion gone hunting with Johnny, that is until the day that Johnny "turned crazy" on him. They were deep in woods, hunting rabbits, when Spangler spotted a rabbit and aimed his gun. Suddenly, Coyle aimed his own gun at Spangler and threatened to shoot him if he dared shoot the little rabbit. He kept his gun pointed at Spangler until he lowered his gun. Spangler later reported that Johnny's eyes were popping out as he made his threat. They walked out of the woods without speaking a word. It was their last hunting trip together.

In Marietta, the small town across the river from the Accomac Inn, a man named John Campbell operated the local hotel. Johnny occasionally visited Campbell when he was in town collecting the mail. Campbell explained that Johnny would come into his place carrying letters. They were love letters written to Johnny. He would either read the letters to Campbell, or insist that Campbell read the letters to him. He always believed that Johnny had written the letters to himself, creating imaginary love interests.

The stories of Johnny's exploits and outbursts were common among the folks living along the Susquehanna River, usually affording amusement and head-shaking at the odd young man's antics. One of those stories, however, seemed to be an ominous portent of things to come.

By 1881, Mary Coyle was getting older and she struggled with all the work it took to keep the inn running. Mary and her husband decided to hire a young woman to help out. They found Emily Myers, a young orphan girl from Chambersburg, and hired her to come to the inn to work. Johnny was immediately taken with her and her lovely raven hair, but Emily was only interested in her work. She needed the money. As an orphan, she had to make her own way in the world. And besides, she had seen enough of Johnny to know that she needed to keep her distance.

Johnny had decided that Emily Myers was going to be his wife and told her so. Emily declined this strange proposal as politely as she could, not wanting to anger him. She had seen what could happen when he got angry. He left, dejected but still determined. He soon decided that it was time to try again. He cornered her and proposed again. Emily's reply remained the same and she returned to her work. Johnny stormed off, growing angrier as he went. Returning to the ferry, he found John Warfield waiting to cross the river. As they crossed the river toward Marietta, he suddenly exclaimed: "I want to get married, but have not got the means. I have asked the maid twice and she has refused me. I intend to ask here again and if she refuses...by God, before she shall marry any other man, I will shoot her." Warfield, a little shaken by this sudden and violent outburst, did his best to persuade Coyle that this plan could only end badly, with Emily's death and his own execution. Johnny looked downcast and replied that whiskey and bad women had ruined him. He just didn't care anymore.

On May 30, 1881, just three days after his conversation with John Warfield, Johnny was determined to once again ask for Emily's hand in marriage. Waking very early in the morning, just after 5:00 am, he walked to the barn where he knew Emily would be milking the cows. He once again demanded that she agree to marry him. Emily, growing weary of his persistence, told him that she would not marry him and asked him to just leave her be. Whether out of frustration or rage, Johnny took a few steps toward her, pulled a pistol from his pocket and without a second thought, shot her through the heart. She fell dead upon the straw-strewn floor. Johnny then raised the pistol to his head and fired several times. When he fired upon himself, he used just powder and paper wadding, not bullets. It was another insincere suicide attempt. He only succeeded in breaking the skin enough to create thin rivulets of blood, running down his forehead, along his neck and onto his shirt.

Inside the inn, Mary called for Emily to bring the milk. It was time for them to prepare breakfast for their guests. Instead of Emily, however, Johnny walked into the kitchen and faced his mother. Seeing the blood, Mary began to panic, asking him what had happened. What had he done? Her son looked at her, his eyes "large and glaring like fire." He told her that he had shot Emily dead in the barn. He said that he had gone into the barn to confront her, hoping to verify that she still intended to marry him. No one knew if Johnny, in his own mind, believed that Emily had agreed to marry him, or if he was attempting to justify causing her death. Mary later testified that "my son...told me that the girl had ruined him and set him crazy."

Unwilling to face what he had done, or fearing the consequences of his actions, Johnny ran from the inn and into the forest, where he stayed hidden for ten days. He was ultimately found and brought back to face legal charges. He was charged with first-degree murder, an offense punishable by death.

His trial began on October 19 of that same year. His attorney had decided to try a novel defense for his actions. He was to plead not-guilty because he was feeble-minded, and possibly even insane at times. The strategy was a failure, although the defense presented a string of witnesses, including both his parents, who testified as to Johnny's odd behaviors, and his bizarre and unpredictable reactions to different situations. He also stressed Johnny's diminished mental capacity due to the effects of his alcoholism. In the end, Johnny's own statements proved to be his undoing. After the murder, Henry Shad, the publisher of the *Marietta Register* had heard him pronounce: "My God, I wish I had shot and killed myself first, and then shot the girl." Although this statement may, to some, indicate a level of insanity, or at least clearly distorted thinking, the prosecution used it to support their theory that he had willfully and intentionally shot poor Emily Myers. Even in jail, Johnny simply could not keep quiet. He tried to explain what he had done by telling the jailer that he had been crushed when Emily had repeatedly rejected him. He insisted that when he had pulled his gun on her in the barn that early morning, she had taunted him, daring him to shoot her.

The general public had no sympathy for Johnny Coyle and his eccentricities. They'd had to cope with his outlandish behaviors for so many years and they were fed up. He had finally gone too far and taken the life of an innocent young woman. This attitude was apparent to the jury as well. During the trial, the prosecution had placed Emily's sister at the prosecutor's table, attempting to draw sympathy her way, though there was no way to know if the two young women had even associated much with each other. The ploy seemed to be working but the prosecution had a real shock planned for the jury. On the last day of their case, they brought Emily's actual heart into the courtroom, preserved and sealed in a large jar. Her heart was accompanied by the dress she had worn the day she died. It was stained dark brown with blood, and had a large hole where her heart would have been.

The murder case had been a sensation, commanding screaming headlines in every newspaper in the area. Coyle's defense was a long shot. The prosecution's case had been strong. It was of little surprise when, after only three hours of deliberation, the jury returned with a guilty verdict and Johnny was to be executed by hanging.

The defense was not finished yet, however. Johnny's attorney took his appeal all the way to the Pennsylvania Supreme Court. They heard the case in October of 1882, almost exactly one year after his trial. The defense claimed that the judge had not instructed the jury properly on what evidence they should consider in order to acquit him based on a finding of insanity. The court granted Coyle a new trial. Based on the extreme amount of publicity over the first trial, he was also granted a change of venue for his re-trial. Johnny would be tried for murder a second time in Gettysburg.

Johnny was found guilty once again following his second trial on May 5, 1883. Emily had been dead nearly two years when he was sentenced to death in Gettysburg. His second trial had the same result as his first. It had again taken the second jury just three hours to decide his fate. His mother cried out in anguish, "Oh gentlemen, how could you take away my only son from me? May God forgive you for it." Johnny Coyle would face the gallows and this time, there would be no reprieve.

When the judge in Gettysburg prepared to pass sentence, Johnny attempted one last time, to lay blame for his actions at another's door. He bitterly spat out an accusation aimed at his father. Everything was his father's fault because he had not raised him properly and had not treated him right! The judge shook his head in disgust and told Johnny that he had broken many moral laws. He should not worry so much about the past, but should make his peace with God instead.

It has been said that there are no atheists on death row. This certainly held true for Johnny Coyle. True to form, while awaiting his execution, he became a devout Christian. During his final weeks, clergymen and advisors visited him often, praying with him and discussing the hereafter. As Johnny awaited the hangman, his parents had not given up hope. They hired medical experts to visit him in jail to evaluate his sanity. Each doctor judged him insane, and collectively traveled to Harrisburg with his lawyers to plead with the governor for a stay of execution. Some followers of the case began to believe that Johnny might indeed be spared the ultimate penalty. But after considering each entreaty, Governor Robert E. Pattison decided to allow the execution to go forward. When he heard the news, Johnny reportedly dropped to his knees and wept uncontrollably.

Johnny's last day arrived on April 22, 1884. It was nearly three years after he had taken the life of Emily Myers, the young woman who simply wanted to do the work she had been hired to do. The day was to be an exciting one for the Gettysburg's citizens and visitors alike. Thousands of people had arrived at the jail early that morning, hoping to get a glimpse of the condemned man. If they were especially lucky, they would get the opportunity to watch him drop through the trap door in the floor of the gallows. The jail yard was not nearly big enough to hold the throng of people waiting outside the wall. Scalpers were on hand and tickets allowing the holder admission inside the jail walls were sold for as much as five dollars.

When the appointed time arrived, twenty-nine-year-old Johnny Coyle was taken from the jail, hands bound behind his back. His aging mother and father, now gray and haggard looking, stepped forward. Together, they held their son between them for a long moment, tears streaming down their faces and onto his shirt. Nodding their last good-byes, they stepped back and Johnny walked slowly but steadily toward the gallows along the back wall of the jail yard.

After mounting the thirteen steps up onto the gallows, Johnny was asked if he had any final words. He looked out across the crowd and quietly said that he forgave all his enemies and he held no ill will towards anyone. He was led to a spot over the trap door, his head draped with a black hood. The thickly wound noose was slipped over his head and tightened at his neck. With a nod from the sheriff, the trap door was released and the prisoner dropped with a shudder. Johnny Coyle breathed no more.

Loaded onto a wagon and parked behind the jail, a coffin waited. When Johnny's corpse had been taken down, the wagon was pulled forward and he was loaded into the coffin. His parents were taking him home. But there would be one last indignity they would have to face as the wagon slowly rolled toward through the jail yard gate. A man had taken the hangman's rope, cut it into pieces, and was selling the souvenirs of the hanging. Mary Coyle, upon realizing what he was doing, chastised him, saying that someday his own son might meet his fate on the gallows.

The coffin was transported by train from the Gettysburg station to Hallem, the nearest station to Accomac. As the train traveled through the countryside, people lined up at each station, hoping to catch a glimpse of the coffin as it passed. When it was unloaded at Hallem, members of the eager crowd awaiting their arrival asked the Coyles if they would lift the lid so they could see Johnny's body. Angered by the callous request, John responded, "None of you false witnesses shall see Johnny!"

Johnny was home for the first time in nearly three years. His body was laid to rest in a private grave about fifty feet from the inn in a wooded spot. It would be several nights before John Sr. would be able to sleep through the night. As soon as Johnny was in the ground, and the sun set, his father would be positioned where he could stand guard. He knew that grave robbers would soon be there to steal his son's remains, and he was right. When the darkly dressed men crept toward the mound under which Johnny lay, John Sr. fired a shot into the air and the men scattered into the trees. After the first few nights of this morbid ritual, the *York Press*, having become aware of the situation, called for it to stop and let the parents mourn their son in peace.

Soon after his burial, a stone marker was placed over Johnny's grave bearing the epitaph "Weep not Mother, for I am not dead, but merely sleeping." As time went by, this would prove to be more literal that figurative.

Johnny Coyle's grave stone near the Accomac Inn

A few years later, the Coyles retired from the inn and it passed into the hands of new owners, then it was sold yet again. A new era was ushered in with the invention of the automobile. As they became more popular and more affordable, a new purpose for places like the Accomac Inn was realized. It was now possible for a family to load up into their Ford, drive to a scenic location for lunch or dinner, and drive home…all in the same day! As a result, the Accomac Inn became a popular dining destination and less as a place for travelers to spend the night. Despite its changing role, the inn remained a favorite place to visit for people from near and far. Until, that is, the night of May 16, 1935 when the inn burned to the ground.

The next day, the following was reported in the *York Dispatch*:

OCCUPANTS FLEE FROM HOTEL ACCOMAC BLAZE: The Accomac hotel along the Susquehanna River, north of Wrightsville, was destroyed by fire shortly before midnight last night at a loss estimated at about $15,000. Norman T. Pickle, the proprietor, Lester Goodling, Theodore Caracher and Norman Smith, who were asleep in the structure when the blaze was discovered, were aroused by a neighbor and escaped with only the clothes on their backs. The fire, believed to have been caused by a short circuit in an electric light line, started on the porch of the tavern.

Almost before the ashes had cooled, Norman Pickle began making plans to rebuild the inn. Using stone from the original inn, he built a beautiful three-story structure that was advertised to have every modern amenity. Just four months after the fire, on September 21, 1935, the doors of the newly re-built Accomac Inn opened to welcome customers once again.

The Accomac Inn as it appears today

Johnny Coyle's solitary grave was left untouched during this time of excitement and rebuilding. It remains today as a reminder of the past and the tragic murder of an innocent young woman. It is difficult to read the engraving on his grave marker as time and weather have worn away the stone. But the epitaph carved into the surface may lend an explanation to some of the strange things that go on inside the inn. As it happens, Johnny did not rest in peace, and apparently, neither did Emily.

For years, employees and guests have spoken of bizarre, unexplainable events that have been witnessed throughout the inn. It is impossible to know for sure, but they believe that Johnny is ether still angry or he is just demanding their attention. He has been held responsible for breaking dishes, knocking glasses from tables in the dining room, opening and closing doors, and other petty nuisances. One of Johnny's most common pranks is to leave a room in disarray, just after it has been cleaned and arranged. Dining room tables set for dinner may be completely jumbled when a worker's back is turned. Though no one has ever felt threatened by Johnny or whatever else is performing these pranks, many people have related experiencing odd, creepy feelings when they were alone in parts of the building.

Emily has made herself known in softer, more feminine ways. Someone might hear the swish of a long skirt behind them in a hallway or on a stair, and turn to find no one there. People feel a gentle presence at times early in the morning. Late at night, they are greeted by soft music and a woman's voice, coming from everywhere and nowhere.

Just a few years back, an employee at the inn opened the door to an upstairs storage room and saw the slowly fading image of a man and woman, dressed in nineteenth-century garb, embracing. No one knows how Johnny looked at the time of his death, and there are no known photographs of Emily, but that image had caused some to wonder if Emily had finally given into Johnny's dogged attempts to win her over. Whether she has surrendered to him, or continues to keep her distance, both Johnny and Emily seem to be held fast to the beautiful Accomac Inn on the western shore of the Susquehanna River.

1894: "ATROCIOUS MURDER!"

There is an old Missouri Ozark folk song that begins, "I'm one of Mister Meeks' little girls, and if you'll lend and ear, I'll tell you all the saddest tale you ever did hear..."

It's a tale that begins just before dawn on May 11, 1894 when Sallie Carter, who lived four miles southwest of Browning, Missouri, heard someone knocking at the front door of her home. She rose from her bed and found a bedraggled little girl of six or seven years standing on her doorstep. The girl's clothing was torn and caked with mud and blood. She had a large gash on her forehead. Mrs. Carter was aghast at the state of the child, and brought the girl into the house to tend to her needs. She questioned the child about how she came to be there and the story that was told remains one of the most bizarre in the annals of Missouri history.

Nellie Meeks

The little girl said that her name was Nellie Meeks and she had spent the night in a haystack. In garbled, often incoherent sentences, she explained that someone had killed her Papa and Mama and Hattie and the baby and left them in the hay.

Mrs. Carter was shocked by the news but with no husband at home, she awoke her nine-year-old nephew, Jimmy, and she sent him to see if the story was true. The woman tended to the child until Jimmy returned and he told her that he had not found anything. Little Nellie stood up and walked out the front door. I'll show you where they lie, she said. She led them to the haystack - where she herself had been left for dead - and brushed away the straw to uncover the faces of her murdered family.

Gus Meeks, a thirty-three-year-old farmer, his wife, Delora, his daughter, Hattie, age four, and baby Mary, only eighteen months old, had been murdered. Nellie had been beaten with a rock and left for dead with the others. The bodies were found on the farm of a man named George Taylor, in a field that was freshly planted with corn. In the center of the field was an old haystack that had been worn and eaten down by livestock until it was not more than three feet deep. It was under the edge of this straw, which had been turned and rolled back, where the bodies were buried. A few shovels of dirt had been tossed over their faces and a bit of straw had been scattered over them by the wind and the hands of the killers.

The terrible tale of the Meeks murders remains one of the most horrific crimes ever committed in the region, even after more than a century has passed.

Gus and Delora Meeks

Young Jimmy Carter was the first to see the bodies of the Meeks family that day, but he would not be the last. After the truth of Nellie Meeks' story was revealed, Mrs. Cater sent Jimmy to spread the news to the neighbors. Passing through the field, the unsuspecting boy caught sight of George Taylor harrowing around the old haystack in an attempt - it was last discovered - to erase the wagon tracks that he had left at the site the night before. The boy innocently walked over to him and informed him that there were dead people in the stack and that Taylor should be careful not to harrow over them.

Taylor apparently thought very quickly about what to do next. He took Jimmy with him to his house and told him to sit down. He would be inside to fetch him just as soon as he put his team away and then they would go and investigate the haystack together. Jimmy waited for quite some time, but Taylor never came into the house. As soon as Jimmy went inside, he saddled a horse and rode off to Browning to find his brother. The two of them quickly left the area.

As the investigation into the case began, it was soon discovered that the circumstances leading up to the horrible crime was a matter of court record in Linn and Sullivan counties.

George and William Taylor were well-known in the region. They were ambitious young men with a number of ongoing enterprises. William was a graduate of the Missouri University School of Law and had served in the Missouri General Assembly. After that, he worked as a cashier for the People's Exchange Bank in Browning. Both men were popular, and George, the younger brother, was known for being exceedingly handsome.

Throughout the late 1880s, the Taylor brothers prospered and eventually the locals discovered why. In 1891, they were charged with forgery, larceny, arson, cattle rustling and writing false bank drafts. Gus Meeks was indicted along with them, and he later entered a guilty plea and was sent to the state penitentiary. But about one month before Meeks was murdered, the governor pardoned him on the condition that he testify against the Taylors in court.

The Taylor brothers heard about these plans and became anxious to get rid of Meeks - one way or another. They told him that they wanted him to leave the area so that he would not be around to testify when their case went to trial, although some believe that they planned to kill him all along. Whatever the case, the Taylors arranged with Meeks that he would receive $1,000, along with a wagon and team with which to leave Missouri. Meeks agreed. He would leave with the Taylors on the night of May 10, 1894 and his family would join him later, after he was settled.

The Taylors were foolish enough to put their arrangement in writing. Gus Meeks' mother, who lived in Milan, knew about the plan and she told the authorities that Gus had received a letter from the Taylors on Thursday. It was discovered in the Meeks house on Saturday, after the murders. The letter read:

Browning, Mo. May 10, 1894.
Be ready at 10 o'clock, everything is right, xxx

The letter had been written on stationary from the People's Exchange Bank in Browning, where William Taylor had been a cashier. The letter was addressed to Meeks and was received in Milan at 2:00 p.m. on May 10. The handwriting on the letter and the envelope were later traced to William Taylor.

On Thursday night, Meeks did not go to bed. Instead, he lay down with his clothes on. When the Taylor brothers came to pick up her husband around midnight, Delora Meeks refused to let him leave without her. Fearing for her husband's life, she reasoned that the Taylors would not harm him if the family was along. She had already packed their meager belongings and so she gathered the children and prepared them to get into the wagon.

Nellie Meeks, the only living witness to what happened that night was not yet seven years old at the time of the murders. She was bright and intelligent, though, and both lawmen and reporters accepted her version of events, which began with two men coming to move the family away. They got into a large wagon with the two men in the spring seat and the family perched in the rear of the wagon. Nellie later recalled, "When we were going up the hill, the man without whiskers said his feet were cold and got out and walked along the side of the wagon and shot Papa, and Papa jumped out and started to run, then Mamma screamed and started to jump when they shot Mamma and sister, then they hit me in the head and I went to sleep."

The murders were committed on Jenkins Hill, a short distance east of Browning. George Taylor had jumped down from the wagon, pulled a gun and shot Gus Meeks. When Delora started to jump out of the wagon, he shot her too. Hattie was also shot, while the baby and Nellie were beaten with rocks. The baby was beaten to death and Nellie, also bludgeoned, was assumed to be dead too.

Investigators found prints on the side of the road where the bodies had fallen and large pools of blood on the grass and leaves next to the road. They even recovered a pistol with three chambers empty and the bloody rock that had been used to beat the smallest children.

The brothers then loaded the bodies back into the wagon and drove them about two miles to a field just past George Taylor's house. They drove out into a freshly planted corn field to the old straw pile, where a makeshift grave for Gus Meeks had already been prepared. They hadn't counted on so many occupants for the hole, but they were determined to make do. Meeks was placed lengthwise into the shallow grave and Delora was placed in the reverse way next to her husband. The baby was under her and at the side, while Hattie was placed next to her father. There was no way to determine where Nellie was placed since she miraculously survived the slaughter.

After Nellie "went to sleep," as she called it, she knew no more until she was thrown out of the wagon at the haystack, which seemed to cause her to regain consciousness. She could hear everything, she later reported, but could say nothing or cry out. She told investigators, "When the man put me in the straw the one with the whiskers kicked me on the back and said, 'They are all dead now, the damn villain sons of bitches.'" The doctor who examined Nellie found the bruises on her back from where William Taylor had kicked her.

She continued, "They covered me up and I could not breathe good. I heard them say, 'It would not burn,' as it would not catch." Nellie thought they were talking of burning the straw, but a woolen blanket was buried at one side of the grave, about ten feet away. It had been on fire and was still smoldering when the family's grave was discovered the next morning. The blanket had been part of the bedclothes that Delora Meeks had brought along for the children on what she thought was a trip they were making out of the county.

There were some interesting theories that made the rounds as to how Nellie arrived at the Carter house the following morning. The George Taylor home and the Carter home were at equal distances from the haystack. She could have just as easily stumbled to the Taylor home where she "rose from the grave" and ended up losing her life when it was discovered that she had survived. Some simply stated that it was "providence" that guided her to Mrs. Carter, but many believed that it was something else. Many claimed that Nellie heard the ghostly voice of her dead mother guiding her that morning and it was her spirit that told her which way to go. Obviously, we will never know for sure, but if not for her walking in one direction instead of the other, the gruesome fate of the Meeks family might have never been discovered.

The bodies of the Meeks family

The bodies remained in the field all day until about 5:00 p.m. It was dark when the coroner finally arrived and an inquest could be held. After it was over, the bodies were placed in rough wooden coffins and moved to Milan. A writer for the local newspaper stated, "Be it said to the eternal disgrace of Linn County that the woman's and children's bodies were placed in those unlined boxes with all that dirt, blood and old clothes they had lain in all day, and unwashed, and with only 'furniture packing,' and old clothes stuffed around them."

The bodies arrived in Milan at about 11:00 p.m. on that Saturday night and were placed in the courthouse yard. The undertaker, a man named Schoene, opened the coffins in view of a crowd of onlookers and the outrage of the newspaper reporter was shared by those present as to the state of the bodies. The coffins were crude and unfinished and the bodies had not yet been washed. There was no one looking for forensic evidence in those days, and it was considered common courtesy for bodies to be washed and treated with dignity, which many felt was lacking in this situation. To the credit of the undertakers and several female volunteers, the bodies were removed from the crude coffins, the blood was gently washed off, and the Meekses were dressed in shrouds. Schoene took the coffins to his undertaking parlor, where he lined them. They were placed in the corridors of the courthouse, where during the rest of the night and Sunday morning, the remains were viewed by hundreds of people who filed past, coming from the town and the surrounding countryside. Many learned for the first time that Delora Meeks had been pregnant when she was killed. When the jumped from the wagon on Jenkins Hill, she suffered a miscarriage and her unborn child had been thrown in the grave with the rest of the family.

At 9:00 a.m. on Sunday morning, the coffins were placed in wagons and the funeral procession traveled to Bute Cemetery, about five miles southeast of Owasco. The crowd at the funeral was estimated to number in the thousands. It was nearly six hours before the funeral service finally took place, conducted by the Rev. Pollard of Milan. The grave that was dug was ten feet wide and all of the bodies were placed in a single grave.

Needless to say, the people of the area had never experienced anything so horrible before.

Meanwhile, after the coroner's inquest, the Taylor brothers were charged with murdering the Meeks family, although by this time, neither of them could be found. Pursuing parties made up of men from all of the surrounding counties were organized, and by Saturday night there were more than five hundred men in search of the Taylors. Bloodhounds from various places were brought in to help with the search. By Monday morning, there were believed to be at least one thousand well-armed men on the hunt.

In spite of the number of searchers involved, the Taylor brothers were not tracked down for weeks. On June 26, 1894, William and George Taylor were captured by Jerry South in Batesville, Arkansas. South wired Sheriff Barton of Linn County with the news. According to the Taylors, they had immediately fled to Springfield, Missouri, spent a few days there, and then had gone on to Chadwick, spending six weeks staying in hotels in the southern part of the state and in Arkansas, living in relative comfort. Astonishingly, they claimed that they were not on the run - they were merely traveling - and would have come home eventually. The Taylors were returned to Linn County by train, traveling through Macon, Moberly and St. Joseph. Sheriff Barton had been notified that there would be a mob to meet them at Brookfield, which is why he arranged for the roundabout route.

At the approach of the train, a shout went up through Brookfield. Twenty-five men rode down the street with the lower part of their faces covered with handkerchiefs. All of them were heavily armed and most carried Winchester rifles. They rode to the depot and began to dismount. Several dozen people joined their ranks, calling out for the Taylors to be turned over to them. They were determined to take the brothers from the train and hang them. They were thwarted in their thirst for rough frontier justice, however, because Sheriff Barton had managed to slip past them and soon had the Taylors safely locked up in the county jail.

The Linn County Court was asked to set bail but refused.

The Taylor brothers' trial began on March 18, 1895 in Carollton, Missouri. Carloads of people came in on the railroad from all over Linn, Sullivan, Grundy and Livingston counties. They jammed into the courthouse, taking every available seat. Hundreds of others gathered outside. At 9:30 a.m., George and William Taylor were brought into court. They were well-dressed and smiling, apparently not nervous at all. They maintained that they were innocent and seemed confident that they would be cleared. The newspapers wrote, "Both men have the appearance of intelligent business men who have dropped in as spectators to the trial. Inside the bar railing, the space was uncomfortably crowded by the attorneys in the case, visiting attorneys, court stenographers, members of the local press and reporters from the St. Louis and Kansas City dailies."

A jury was chosen and Judge Rucker instructed them not to talk with anybody about the case. They were told they must not read the newspapers and were not to "string out over town."

The prosecuting attorney was T.M. Bresnehen. He began his opening statement at 11:00 a.m. He told the story of the murder of the Meeks family on the night of May 10, 1894, and said the state would prove beyond all doubts that the crime was committed by William and George Taylor, that the state would present witnesses who saw the Taylors driving in a wagon on the night of the murder, that they stopped at Gus Meeks' house, that the Meeks family came out, got into the wagon with the Taylors and drove off.

He continued, telling the jurors about how, on the morning of May 11, little Nellie Meeks went to a farm house near George Taylor's farm and told the story of the murder. A boy was sent to the stack to see if the story were true, and how the boy saw George Taylor harrowing in a nearby field and asked Taylor to go to the haystack with him. George told the boy he did not have time, took the boy to the house with him, then saddled a horse and rode off to Browning, where he held a hasty consultation with his brother. The two Taylor brothers then fled the area, leaving local residents to wonder why the Taylors left so suddenly after news of the murder reached town.

Bresnehen described the position of the dead bodies. After that, he told the jury that he had a witness who hauled wood for George Taylor who said that he had gone to Taylor's house early on the morning of May 11. He had found George rubbing and currying his horses, which had been out in the mud and rain the night before. The witness saw the wagon bed covered with clotted blood, some of which had trickled through the wooden boards of the bed and had stained the axles. The witness would testify, Bresnehen said, that an effort was made to burn the wagon bed, and that the clothing of the Meeks family was also burned. He would also talk about the cattle stealing case in which Gus Meeks and the Taylors were implicated and how Meeks was pardoned by the governor on the condition that he testify against the Taylors, and how William Taylor had said that he must be gotten rid of.

Bresnehen's statement was both startling and compelling and it's likely that the defense attorney, Colonel John Hale, knew there was little he could say to compete with it in the early moments of the trail. He declined to make an opening statement but asked the judge that witnesses be excluded from the courtroom during the trial. The judge granted his request. The afternoon was spent with witnesses being called by the state and cross-examined by Colonel Hale.

The first witness of the day was W.H. McCullom. He recalled how he had seen the dead bodies tumbled into a heap, the two children lying on top of their father and mother, all of them covered with blood. Dr. Van Wye, the coroner of Sullivan County, made similar testimony. Harris Wilson told of his visit to the Jenkins Hill, two miles north of Browning, and seeing the trail of blood on the ground by the roadside. He described the spot where the murder was committed, and told how the bodies were hauled two miles in the wagon and buried in the straw stack. Wilson found a revolver at the scene of the murder that had three shots fired from it. These men were followed by several others who had seen the bodies, been to the murder scene on Jenkins Hill, and had seen the state of the field around the haystack where the bodies were discovered. Mrs. Kitty Edens came to the stand and testified that she had heard five shots just after midnight during the early morning hours of May 11.

Mrs. Martha Weeks, Gus' mother, took the stand around 3:00 p.m. She had lived at the Meeks home with her son and his family, and she told of the frequent visits to the house by the Taylors. She told how George had come to the house the night after Gus had returned from the penitentiary and asked that Gus come outside as William was there to see him. Mrs. Meeks said she always felt apprehensive around the Taylors, fearing they would murder Gus and his family and kill her, too. She testified that she told Gus not to go outside and meet them. Gus refused to go, but George Taylor back to the door three times to ask him to come out. When Gus still refused, William came inside and Mrs. Meeks overheard him offer Gus $1,000 to pull up stakes and leave.

She recalled that on May 10, Gus received a letter written on letterhead from the People's Exchange Bank of Browning, where William Taylor was a cashier. The letter, dated May 10, read, "Be ready at 10 o'clock. Everything is right." There were three stars where the signature would usually be. Gus handed his mother the letter and said he was going to take the $1,000 and leave that night. Mrs. Meeks said she tried to persuade him not to go, fearing he and his family would be killed. That night a wagon drove up, George Taylor came in and helped Gus carry out the household goods. Gus told his mother that William was outside, but she did not see him.

On cross examination, Hale tried to weaken her testimony by attempting to prove that she didn't know the Taylor brothers very well, but Mrs. Meeks pointed to each brother and identified him. The letter spoken of earlier was brought into court and the writing was identified as that of William Taylor.

The damning testimony continued. W.H. Jones of Browning told about seeing George Taylor drive out toward the Milan road at dusk on the evening of May 10. John I. Russell, a neighbor of William Taylor, testified to the same thing. E.M. McCullum not only said he saw George Taylor drive out in a wagon toward the scene of the murder, he also saw William Taylor walking down the railroad tracks in Browning in a direction to intersect the route taken by George.

The following day was Wednesday, and court opened at 8:00 a.m. The same throng crowded the building, filling all of the seats in the gallery, sitting squeezed in, shoulder to shoulder. Many more waited expectantly outside, hoping to hear news of what was taking place in the courtroom.

D.C. Pierce was called as the first witness. He testified to a conversation he had with George Taylor when Meeks was pardoned. He Pierce had spoken to George about Meeks coming home to testify against him and William in the cattle stealing case, George replied, "We will get the --- out of the way."

A.R. Dillinger, who lived six miles north of Browning, related a conversation he had with William Taylor about Gus Meeks testifying against him and George. He said Taylor threatened to kill Meeks. Dillinger's testimony could not be shaken by Colonel Hale.

Mrs. John Carter, whose house Nellie Meeks went to on the morning after the murders, gave the most compelling testimony so far for the state. She said she had been at home on the morning of May 11 when Nellie arrived at her door after crawling out of the shallow grave where she had been buried with her parents. She testified, "I got up at 4 o'clock on the morning of May 11. Between 5 and 6 in the morning a little girl came crying to the door. When asked where she had slept, she said in a straw stack. When asked where the straw stack was she pointed out a straw stack about 75 yards away on the George Taylor farm. The little girl's face was covered with blood and dirt. She had a gash cut in the top of her head and her hair was clotted with blood. She kept crying and telling about her little sister being in the straw stack. I sent my nine-year-old nephew, Jimmy Carter, to find the straw stack and report to me. I asked her name and she said it was Nellie Meeks, Gus Meeks' child and her pa and ma were lying up the road.' I stepped out to see where Jimmy was and saw him walking across a field with a man that looked like George Taylor." Mrs. Carter said she had also seen the dead bodies in the haystack.

Young Jimmy Carter was the next to give testimony. The boy told the court, "I first saw Nellie Meeks coming up the walk crying. She said her sister was in the straw stack and my aunt sent me to see about it. In the field on the way I met George Taylor and told him what the little girl had said. I asked him to go with me but he said to wait, I must go to the barn lot and let someone else go to the stack. He made me hold the team. He asked if the little girl said anything about her father and mother, I told him she said her pa and ma were lying down there in the road. He put a saddle on a horse in the barn lot and rode away. I then went to the straw stack, pushed the straw back and saw the bodies."

James L. Harris, who worked as a hired hand for George Taylor, took the stand next. He stated he went from George Gibson's house to Taylor's at about 5:30 in the morning of May 11. He found George Taylor washing the mud from his horses as if they had been out the night before in the rain. Harris said he had hitched up Taylor's team to haul wood. He noticed the wagon's bed and axles were bloody and that there was a strong odor of coal oil coming from the wagon bed. He saw that an attempt had been made to burn out the bloodstains.

On cross-examination, Harris admitted that he had been arrested in the wake of the murders. He was bound over to the grand jury, but he said that he didn't know the charges that had been filed against him. Apparently, Prosecutor Bresnehen had him arrested in order to bring him before the grand jury to testify. Colonel Hale asked Harris if he had not been arrested on suspicion of having been implicated in the Meeks murder. He said he had been closely questioned by a number of men who wanted to know where the Taylors had gone, and he did not know. Hale was hoping that he could cast suspicion on Harris and away from his clients.

John B. Harris, James' brother, also testified to seeing the bloodstains in Taylor's wagon, as did Linn County Sheriff Edward Barton. The defense counsel had an explanation for the fire in the wagon, though. According to Jim Taylor, the father of the defendants, some children had been playing in some straw in the wagon bed and had set fire to it, thus explaining away the charge that somebody had tried to burn out the bloodstains. Of course, this did not explain how the blood got there in the first place.

Jerry South, a member of the Arkansas legislature, took the stand. An audible whisper went through the crowd: "That's the fellow who captured the Taylor boys!"

South was questioned by A.W. Mullins of the prosecution. He stated his home was in Mountain Home, Arkansas, and he was serving his third term in the Arkansas legislature. He first saw the defendants in Buffalo City, Arkansas, on June 20 or 21, 1894. He saw them again on June 25, also in Buffalo City. The Taylors were staying at a house run by a man the name of Hays, as there were no hotels in Buffalo City. One of the men said his name was Edwards, the other called himself Price. South said he knew everyone in the county and the men were strangers to him. At dinner that evening, William Taylor seemed very nervous and South said that he watched him suspiciously. He said, "I remembered something I had read about the Meeks and Taylors in *The St. Louis Republican*. I checked in a newspaper office and found pictures and descriptions which fitted the Taylors."

A short time later, South ran into the Taylors in a store and he became convinced they were the fugitives that he had read about. He went after them with his shotgun, catching up with them on the road and ordering them to stop. Both men were in their shirtsleeves, he said, and he could clearly see their guns. William reached for his revolver, but South had his shotgun leveled at them. They gave up without incident. When South showed them their photographs in the newspaper they acknowledged they were the Taylor brothers. South took them to Little Rock, and from there to St. Louis, where he was met by Sheriff Barton of Linn County.

In conversation with their captor, William asked South what he had heard about them. South mentioned the letter and William admitted writing it, but claimed to have an alibi for the murder. He insisted he had given the money, wagon and team to Meeks, and someone else had murdered the family and buried them on the Taylor farm to throw suspicion on the Taylors. When asked why, if they were innocent, they had left Browning so hurriedly, William told him that they had fled to escape a possible lynch mob.

When cross-examined, South said the Taylors admitted they went to Milan on the night of May 10 and got the Meeks family, but left them alive in the wagon at 2:00 a.m. They also told him that

George helped Gus Meeks carry out the household goods while William remained in the wagon. South continued, "At that time, I was convinced the Taylors were innocent and I gave them honest advice. I told them not to deny writing the letter to the Meeks family because someone would prove he had. I told them they would better predicate their defense on some other theory. They knew I was a lawyer and listened attentively."

South admitted that he was paid $1,500 by Linn County for the capture of the Taylors, but Governor Stone told South that he would not be paid the $600 offered by the state of Missouri unless the Taylors were convicted. Hale tried to hint that Stone was only testifying for the defense so that he could get the additional $600. After two hours of questioning, South left the stand. His was the final testimony for the state.

With Colonel Hale supervising, the questioning of the defense witnesses was led by Virgil Conkling, a big, bluff, Democratic politician. He was assisted by A.W. Myers, a venerable lawyer from Brookfield, whose chief duty seemed to be hunting down witnesses for the defense and inducing them to sign their names to written statements.

Most of the defense testimony was given by relatives of the Taylors. Beverly Gibson, whose wife was a sister of the Taylors, said that he had visited the haystack, had seen the dead bodies, had examined the wagon bed, and had followed the wagon tracks from the haystack to the George Taylor farm. He said the wagon bed had once been painted red and the paint had worn off leaving only patches of red paint. This was the reason that some people had "mistaken" the stains in the wagon for blood. John H. Gibson, a cousin of George Taylor's wife, gave essentially the same testimony given by Beverly Gibson. He additionally said that he found some bed clothing over the bodies at the haystack and that it had been on fire.

Mrs. James J. Taylor, the mother of the defendants took the stand next. While she was on the stand, William Taylor acted very nervous, courtroom spectators later said, and began chewing on strips of notebook paper. George, however, stayed calm as usual, sitting very still in his chair. Mrs. Taylor swore that she was at home on May 11 when she heard the news of the murders and the accusations that her sons were involved. She said she went out and looked at the wagon bed and saw no bloodstains, just spots of red paint.

William Gibson, an uncle of George Taylor's wife, swore that he had visited the haystack, saw the bodies, and heard the crowd accusing the Taylor brothers. He had found no blood on the wagon. He did admit, however, that there was red clay in George Taylor's barnyard, which had fallen from off the wagon. The Milan road to the Meeks house was over red clay roads. He also admitted, when cross-examined, that the wagon tracks led from the haystack to George's farm.

Charles Taylor, the youngest brother of the defendants, took the stand. On the night of the murder, he was at his father's house and later heard about what had taken place. He went to see the haystack and heard the crowd accuse his brothers. He told Virgil Conkling that he had examined the wagon and saw no bloodstains.

Jim Taylor, the defendant's father, agreed. He hadn't seen any bloodstains either. After hearing the accusations against his sons, he went to the haystack and someone in the crowd gathered there said that the murdered bodies had been hauled in George Taylor's wagon. He said he went home and examined the wagon, but saw no bloodstains. He testified that the wagon bed had been burned when some of his grandchildren were playing around a fire under a kettle and accidentally set the bed of the wagon alight.

Mr. Taylor said he saw no wagon tracks and had not gone over to George's house for three or four days after the murder. He denied he ever told Daniel Nichols, a neighbor, that he thought his wagon had been used to haul the Meeks family, which was something that Nichols had claimed. He also said that when George's hired hand, James Harris, returned the wagon on May 11, he never mentioned anything about bloodstains. However, Taylor was later accused of trying to persuade John Harris, James' brother, into making a statement he had seen no blood on the wagon either.

Mrs. David Gibson, George Taylor's mother-in-law, gave some of the most confusing testimony of the day. She claimed George was at home at times when even he admitted to being away and she gave various times as to when she saw George ride away from home on the morning of May 11. She said she returned to George's house but did not see Jimmy Carter holding George's team and she did not go to the Carter house a short distance away to see little Nellie as everyone else was doing.

The next witnesses were brought to try and discredit the testimony of Martha Meeks. Mrs. Anna Cooper, who lived a few blocks away from Mrs. Meeks, stated that on the morning of May 11, Mrs. Meeks told her that she did not know who rode away with her son and his family the night before, but "supposed it was the Taylor boys."

Mrs. George Taylor took the stand carrying her fussy baby. Perhaps this explained why she became confused - or outright lied - when testifying that her husband was home all night on May 10 and never left her side. By this time, George had already admitted to taking the Meeks family in the wagon, but claimed that he had left the Meekses alive at 2:00 a.m.

William's wife, Maude, also testified. She claimed that William had been at home on the night of the murders. He had gone downtown after supper, she claimed, and was back home by 10:00 p.m. He had gone to bed, gotten up at 5:00 a.m. and was having breakfast at 6:00 a.m. She did say that George had supper with them on May 10 and afterwards, had left in a wagon. During cross-examination, Maude was asked if she had not told the Rev. P.M. Best a few days after the murders that her husband had been away from home that night and did not return home until morning. She then told Best that she had prayed her husband would be cleared of all previous charges against him, but had lost hope. Maude denied having the conversation with Best. She also denied knowing anything about plans to take the Meeks family out of the country.

William Taylor then took the stand in his own defense. After giving some information about himself and his education, he explained what he had done on the night of the murder.

George Taylor, my brother, came in with some wagon wheels in a wagon about 4 o'clock in the afternoon of May 10, 1894. He ate supper at my house and about dark hitched up his team and went home to the country. I remained in the house about an hour and went downtown to the bank. I frequently had work to do in the bank at night, for I attended to nearly all the work there.

I left the bank about 10 o'clock that night and went home and stayed there all night in bed. I arose about 5 o'clock next morning, went downtown and bought some soda. I went downtown that morning again about 8 o'clock to open the bank and a few minutes later George came up and said there were some dead people down on his place and he thought the man was Gus Meeks. He wanted to get an officer to take down there. After talking the matter over I advised him not to get an officer. I told him I believed Meeks had been murdered and placed on his place in order to get us in trouble and we should better wait and see what developed.

Taylor admitted that Meeks was planning to testify against them for the cattle stealing case, but there was nothing to it. He had been pushed into testifying by the brothers' "many enemies." Taylor believed those same enemies had killed the Meeks family and wanted the Taylors to flee when people started accusing them of the murders so that they would look guilty.

When he was cross-examined, Taylor admitted that Gus Meeks had already testified against him in an arson case. Taylor said, "He told me he had promised to swear to anything they wanted him to swear against me in the cattle stealing case. I met Meeks and assisted him in his preparation to leave the country, because I was quite willing that he should go."

Asked about the letter to Meeks stating, "Be ready at 10 o'clock everything is all right." Taylor admitted he wrote it. Asked who had informed George about the murder, Taylor said, "George told me a little boy came up to him in the field where he was harrowing and told him there were dead bodies in the straw stack. George said he harrowed on around the field until he came to the stack, when he looked and saw the body of a man and knew it was Gus Meeks. He then saddled his horse and came to Browning to tell me."

Like his brother, George Taylor was cool and collected on the stand. He told the same story that William did, reiterating that he had indeed eaten supper with his brother's family, but now he claimed that he had gone home afterwards and stayed there the entire night. The next morning, he was harrowing in his freshly planted corn field when Jimmy Carter came to him told him about the dead bodies in the haystack. Taylor said, "I drove the harrow on around the land until I came to the stack, and stopped. I kicked away some straw, and saw the face of the dead man whom I recognized as Gus Meeks. I went to the house, got on a horse and rode to town and had a talk with Bill. We concluded that it was a job set upon us to get us into trouble and we thought it best to get away. We had a great many enemies and we thought there would be trouble. Bill and I rode our horses south of Browning and left them with our father and brother in the timber and then proceeded on foot."

When cross-examined, George denied telling Jimmy Carter to go with him to the house when the boy told him about the murder, and then taking off without telling him where he was going. He also said that he had he found no bed clothes on fire. After he recognized Gus Meeks, he drove the harrow across the field to the barn lot. He said he made only a brief search of the haystack, seeing only the face of Gus Meeks. He then left without looking any further.

The state followed the Taylors' testimony with a string of rebuttal witnesses about the character of the two men. Gus Corbin, circuit clerk and recorder for Adair County, testified he had an indictment against William and George Taylor for passing a forged check for $2,000. Israel Wood of Milan took the stand to impeach the testimony of Mrs. Johnson, a defense witness. He said Mrs. Johnson was promiscuous, as if that had anything to do with her integrity as a witness. J.A. Niblo of Milan, who was serving his second term as sheriff of Sullivan County, went him one better, swearing that not only was Mrs. Johnson's a loose woman, she was also a liar. C.S. Hart, a grocer at Milan, said the same, as did Theodore S. Poole, who swore that Mrs. Johnson was "a bad egg".

After the state concluded with its final witnesses, the case was given to the jury on Tuesday night, April 9, 1895. Arguments in the jury room led to a stalemate and the jurors were eventually dismissed without reaching a verdict. The state announced that it would be trying the case again. On a side note, a special grand jury was called on April 29 to investigate charges of bribery against the jury in the original case. There were also charges of perjury filed against some of the defense witnesses.

At this point, the case against the Taylors was shaping up to be an enormous mess.

On July 25, 1895, the business of selecting a new jury began. Not a great deal of new evidence was introduced in the second trial. Gus Meeks' pistol that was found on Jenkins Hill was brought to court. The most damaging testimony was that of D.C. Pierce, who said George Taylor had told him that he George had no fear of Gus Meeks, as they would get him out of the way.

Many of the other prosecution witnesses returned, including Sallie Carter, whose home Nellie Meeks had gone to after she had crawled out of the makeshift grave. Nellie herself made an appearance in court during the second trial. She went to the prosecution table and actually climbed up into the lap of Prosecuting Attorney Pierce! He and his wife had become the wards of the orphaned little girl. When Nellie entered the courtroom, the newspapers reported that William Taylor looked over at her but George only glanced at her with a cold, hard look.

During the new testimony of the second trial, a detective named Freeman spoke of how he discovered the remains of a fire in the woods pasture on the farm of James Taylor, father of the defendants. He gathered the fragments found in the charred embers, sealed them in an envelope, and kept them in a bank vault until they were introduced at the trial. They were a piece of cloth from a pair of trousers, a scrap of bed ticking, pieces of a pocket book an old-fashioned term for a man's wallet , and pieces of a comb and picture frame. Mrs. Meeks, Gus Meeks' mother, stated that Gus packed a pair of trousers in his trunk when he left to go with the Taylors, and that the piece of cloth from the fire looked like it came from them. The part of the pocket book looked like his, she added, but she wasn't sure. She noted that the ticking of the feather bed that was found looked like the one her son and his family took with them in the wagon. She could not positively identify the pistol found on Jenkins Hill, but she said Gus took his with him the night of the murders.

The defense brought in additional witnesses to say that they had not seen any blood in the bed of the wagon. The two brothers also testified again, repeating the same statements that they had made at the first trial.

Both sides rested and the case was given to the jury on July on August 2, 1895. The newspapers opined that the strain of the trial was starting to show on the Taylors - especially after the jury returned with a guilty verdict, after only deliberating for an hour and a half. After the jury was polled and discharged, the judge sentenced the defendants to hang.

On March 3, 1896, the Missouri Supreme Court upheld the verdict and the execution date was set for April 30. Reporters on the scene wrote that George Taylor as usual, took the appeals verdict in stride, but William looked as though all hope was now lost.

But the Taylors weren't giving up just yet. On the night of April 11, 1896, they attempted to escape the Carrollton jail. George succeeded but William was quickly recaptured. At about 8:30 that evening, a night watchman named Shelton went out into the back yard of the jail. He was talking to a friend when he heard a noise on the other side of the building. He rushed around the corner and saw a man named Lee Cunningham, who was in jail for murder, sliding down a hose to the ground, at which point Shelton quickly captured him at gunpoint. William Taylor, who was about halfway down the hose, shouted to Shelton not to shoot, he would give himself up. He told Shelton that George was still on the roof. Shelton stood guard but George never showed. He had evidently gone down the hose first and his brother's fib gave him enough time to get away.

During the investigation into the escape, it would found that a bolt had been cut in the back of one of the cells and a bar knocked off. This gave the prisoners access to the corridor. They climbed up on top of the cage, into the garret, and onto the roof. They took a fifty-foot hose with them which they fastened to the roof.

A posse was quickly organized and farmers with bloodhounds were rushed to the jail to try and find George's trail, but no substantial lead was found. The dogs were only able to track him to the back gate, where it was believed he was picked up in a buggy. Detectives discovered that Yound Leonard from Norborne, Missouri, a brother-in-law of William Taylor, was in Carrollton that day. Late that evening, he took a rig from the livery stable and drove out of town. A telephone message from Norborne said that a team arrived there at 10:00 p.m. that evening and it had been driven hard, but the identity of the driver was never discovered.

On April 13, William Taylor was transferred to the Kansas City, Missouri, jail for safe-keeping. In an interview with newspaper reporters, Taylor, who was locked up in the jail's "murderer's row" said, rather poetically, "I tasted the air of freedom for a few moments. It was the sweetest breath for many a weary day. A man has to be penned up in jail to appreciate liberty, free air and the lights of heaven. If I had been a moment sooner or a minute later I should be with George now. He is having lots of hardships and I would like to help bear them. We were unfortunate the deputy sheriff discovered us by accident. We had our escape well-planned and had got clear of the jail and had not been missed when one of the two deputies who were on guard walked outside the jail and discovered us. He cornered me but George was still on the roof. It was 25 feet to the ground but George jumped off the opposite side of the jail." It was thought that George may have escaped by climbing down the smokestack of the furnace on the east side of the jail, which was out of sight of Shelton, the deputy who captured William Taylor and Lee Cunningham.

The people of Carrollton were in an angry mood after the escape, as were many in Linn and Sullivan counties. It was widely believed that it had been carelessness on the part of Sheriff Stanley that allowed the escape to occur. With little effort made to recapture George, more angry men converged on Carrollton. Rumors spread that the Taylors were buying their way out of trouble. As threats to lynch William Taylor began to be made, Sheriff Stanley thought it was best to move him quickly out of town.

As it happened, though, a lynching would have only brought about William Taylor's death a few days early. After being returned to Carrollton, he went to the gallows on April 30, right on schedule. When he arrived back in town on the evening before, hundreds of people were there to meet the train. Taylor was handcuffed and guarded by thirteen deputies when he stepped off the train. He was loaded into a wagon, followed by guards armed with shotguns and rifles, and taken to the jail. When he arrived there, he was thoroughly searched and a folded card was found in possession that contained enough strychnine to kill him. It was unknown where he had acquired it. As he was being stripped, guards noticed him trying to get the poison into his mouth. The card was taken away and Taylor was not given the chance to beat the hangman.

Before his death, he was allowed to leave the following written statement:

To the Public:

I have only this additional statement to make. I ought not to suffer as I am compelled to do. Prejudice and perjury convicted me. By this conviction my wife to be left a lonely widow, my babies are made orphans in a cold world, my brothers mourn and friends weep. You hasten my gray-haired father and mother to the grave. The mobs and the element have haunted me to the grave. I had hoped to at least live till the good people realized the injustice done me but it cannot be so. I feel prepared to meet my God, and now wing my way to the great unknown, where I believe everyone is properly judged. I hope my friends will meet me all in heaven. I believe I am going there. Goodbye all.

W.P. Taylor.

A short time before the execution, Taylor and Father Kennedy, his spiritual advisor, knelt together in prayer. Taylor was absolved of his sins and kissed the crucifix. At 6:00 a.m. the following morning, he was given a breakfast of two fried eggs, three buttered biscuits and a tin cup of coffee. At 7:30, a mass was held for him and the last sacrament was administered.

William went to the gallows at 11:00 a.m. He walked onto the scaffold, stood alone while the straps were put on, remaining calm, cool and collected. He moved his head for the rope to be adjusted. A priest prayed while the trap was sprung. He died instantly at the end of the rope.

Taylor, who had only recently been baptized into the Church, was buried after a Catholic funeral in Carrollton. Only his immediate family attended the service. Today, he is largely forgotten, except as a figure in a few old folk songs that still survive about the murders.

The last photograph of William Taylor - on the gallows

As for George Taylor, he was never captured, although his appearance was reported at various times around the country over the years. Several men confessed on their death beds to being George Taylor, but no proof of their claims were ever offered. There were the usual rumors, of course. Some said that he fought honorably in Cuba during the Spanish-American War, others said he left the country, while some said he returned and visited his family in Missouri on many occasions and was seen around the area. We'll never know for sure. We can only know that he was never apprehended and in time, was lost to history.

Nellie Meeks, the sole survivor of the massacre, was raised by her grandmother and reportedly grew to be a pretty and charming young woman. She married Albert Spray of North Salem in 1906, but her happy life only lasted a few more years. In 1910, she died of complications from childbirth after her daughter, Hattie, was born.

It was a sad ending to a life that had barely escaped the grave once before.

1896: THE MURDER OF PEARL BRYAN

Although the details of the case have long since faded into obscurity, one of the grisliest and most highly publicized American murders of the late nineteenth century began in an apple orchard in northeastern Kentucky. Over the years, the story of the murder has spawned more than its share of legends. Most of these horror stories are now connected to a small nightclub in Wilder, Kentucky, which marks the site where a grisly piece of evidence in the murder was allegedly disposed of. If there is any truth to these tales, then the place may be one of the most haunted, and most sinister, locations in the region.

The building that stands today as Bobby Mackey's Music World has a long and bloody history in the northern Kentucky and Cincinnati area. It started out as a slaughterhouse in the 1850s and was one of the largest packing houses in the region for many years. Only a well that was dug in the basement, where blood and refuse from the animals was drained, remains from the original building. The slaughterhouse closed down in the early 1890s but it gained lasting notoriety a few years later when it became a part of two of the most spectacular murder trials ever held in the state of Kentucky. The trials were so large that tickets were sold to the public and more than five thousand people stood outside the courthouse waiting eagerly for information about what was taking place inside. The trials, and the murder that spawned them, have become an integral part of the old building's history.

The victim in the case was Pearl Bryan, the attractive, young daughter of a wealthy farmer from Greencastle, Indiana. She was one of the most popular girls in the area and was considered to be beautiful, well-educated and delicate. Even before she finished school, she was courted by many of the young men in the region, but she spurned most of them. The only man that she was close to was her cousin, William Wood, a medical student at DePauw University. The two of them were more like brother and sister than cousins and Pearl considered him her closest friend. So, when Will introduced her to his friend, Scott Jackson, a dental student, Pearl was immediately taken with him. Her family was impressed with the young man as well. He came from a good family and he was always polite and courteous when he called on Pearl, but all was not what it seemed.

The smooth-talking Jackson quickly seduced the innocent Pearl. Unknown to her friends and the polite members of Greencastle society, Pearl became pregnant. In her desperation, she turned to her trusted cousin, Will Wood, who took the news to Jackson. Jackson was enraged and made immediate plans to remedy the situation. Wood, who was not as trustworthy as Pearl thought he was, went along with his pal's plans. Confused and unsure of what to do, Pearl let Wood convince her to have an abortion. Jackson made arrangements for the operation with a friend named Alonzo Walling. He was also a dental student and attended the Ohio College of Dental Surgery in Cincinnati.

Pearl left her parents' home on January 31, 1896, telling them that she was going to Indianapolis. Instead, she made plans to meet with Jackson and Walling in Cincinnati. It would be the last time her parents would ever see her alive.

Pearl Bryan

Early on Saturday morning, February 1, 1896, sixteen-year-old Jack Hewling, a hired hand for a farmer named James Lock who owned a large amount of property near Fort Thomas, Kentucky, was cutting across his employer's property when he saw a woman sprawled out in the grass beneath some apple trees. The orchard was about two hundred feet from the Alexandria Turnpike and less than two miles from an abandoned slaughterhouse. Hewling was not especially startled by the sight - at least not at first. After a night on the town, carousing soldiers from the fort often brought their girls out into the fields for a tumble, and on more than one occasion, Hewling had come across a female sleeping off the effects of too many drinks the night before.

But this time was different.

As he got closer, he realized to his shock that the woman's head had been removed. It was obvious from the blood that had been spattered on the grass that a furious struggle had taken place. A man's torn and bloody shirtsleeve was lying nearby. Hewling ran to the nearby house of Wilbert Lock and, along with a man named Mike Noonan, returned to the scene. After viewing the bloody scene, they went immediately to the fort and notified the commander, Colonel Cochran, who called the Newport police headquarters. The call brought Sheriff Jule Plummer, Coroner Robert Tingley and several other county and city officials to the scene.

Tingley examined the scene. The coroner later stated that the woman's head had been "cleanly" cut off and, horribly, that she had been alive at the time the beheading occurred, based on the

The murder site where Pearl's body was found.

presence of blood on the underside of some leaves at the murder scene. When he turned the body over, he found that her outer clothing had been ripped open and her corset torn off, exposing her breasts. The palm and fingers of her left hand had been sliced nearly to the bone. A large pool of blood had soaked the ground beneath the body.

While Tingley was inspecting the body, Sheriff Plummer and one of his deputies examined the crime scene. They soon discovered several sets of footprints. From these markings and other physical evidence - the scattered clothing, trampled ground, and widely spattered blood - they deduced that the dead woman had a male companion and that they "had walked side by side for a short distance when, for some reason, the woman had attempted to flee." Overtaking her, the murderer had "choked her into silence and dragged her toward a bushy bank. She struggled desperately and he tore handfuls of clothing from her dress. He threw her to the ground and slid over the bank with her." Drawing a knife, he "slashed her throat." Fighting for her life, she clutched the blade with her left hand and it "laid her palm and fingers open to the bone. Her struggles were useless, and in a moment her life blood was pouring from the gaping wound in her throat." Afterward, the killer had sawn through her neck below the fifth vertebra and carried off her head.

While the body was being loaded onto a wagon and driven to an undertaker's establishment in Newport, police officers set to work trying to identify the dead woman. Two detectives from Cincinnati, Cal Crim and John McDermott, were assigned to the case and soon arrived at the murder scene. By the time they arrived, though, they were stunned to find hundreds of souvenir hunters, curiosity-seekers and soldiers from the nearby fort roaming around and picking up everything that had blood on it. The crowd, along with heavy rains that moved in later that afternoon, wreaked havoc on the crime scene.

The scene outside of W.H. White's undertaking parlor in Newport was equally frenzied. A newspaper reported, "All day long and up to a late hour at night, the place was besieged with people anxious to get a look at the remains of the unfortunate woman." With Coroner Tingley and several other physicians in attendance, Dr. Robert Carothers conducted a postmortem examination, which revealed that the victim was between four and five months pregnant. The fetus, which had been alive when the victim was butchered, was removed and taken to a nearby pharmacy, where it was placed in alcohol for preservation. The stomach was also excised and turned over to Dr. W.H. Crane of the Ohio Medical College, who was able to ascertain that the victim had ingested seventeen grams of cocaine shortly before her death. All of the victim's blood loss had occurred through her open neck: there was not a single drop remaining in her veins, arteries or heart.

Following the autopsy, Dr. Carothers issued a statement that proved to be uncannily accurate: "I judge that it was a premeditated and cold-blooded murder. The girl, in my opinion, was from the country and comparatively innocent. She was brought to Cincinnati to submit to a criminal operation. Once here, she was taken to Fort Thomas and murdered. Her head was taken away, horrible as it may seem, merely to prevent the identification of her body."

News of the gruesome murder made newspaper headlines across the country. "The awful deed struck horror to the hearts of the people, and they were worked up to a pitch that had never been witnessed," one observer wrote. "The entire country was startled from center to circumference and aroused as it never had been before. Telephones and telegraph were called into service, and the finding of the headless body of a young and doubtless beautiful woman in a sequestered spot near Fort Thomas was flashed around the world."

With criminal science still in its early stages - even the forensic use of fingerprints was still more than a decade away in America - detectives resorted to the only means at their disposal. They contacted Arthur Carter of Seymour, Indiana, who owned a set of bloodhounds named Jack, Wheeler and Stonewall that had been used by other investigators across the Midwest. The dogs had helped to capture twenty fugitives who were then spending time in various penitentiaries. The dogs were given the scent of the murdered woman's clothing and then released at the crime scene - where they found nothing useful. The thousands of visitors to the site had ruined any chance of a good trail.

The only hope the detectives had was to find someone who could identify the body. Every woman missing in the entire country was considered and then ruled out. They decided to open the doors of the undertaker's establishment in Newport and allow people to view the corpse, in hopes that someone might recognize her. This, of course, created another circus-like scene as morbid crowds formed for a look at the nude, headless body. Several times, the body was identified, but each time the "identified" person was found to be alive and well.

In the end, it was the victim's shoes that broke the case open. They bore the imprint of Louis and Hays, a shoe company in Greencastle, Indiana. Detectives found that only a dozen pairs of the same shoes had been sold and quickly accounted for all but two of them. This information made the newspapers and caused concern for Mrs. Alexander Bryan, Pearl Bryan's mother. She mentioned it to her son, Fred, and he went to the Western Union office and telegraphed some of Pearl's friends in Indianapolis to ask if she was all right. The manager of the telegraph office, A. W. Early, read the telegraph and the reply stating that Pearl had never arrived in Indianapolis. Early was shocked and became suspicious. He hurried to the hotel where the detectives were staying and told them what he knew. Early had only been living in Greencastle for a few months but had become close friends with Will Wood, Pearl's cousin. The two men often shared their letters with one another and Early recalled a letter that Wood had received from a man named Scott Jackson. In the letter, Jackson admitted that he had gotten Pearl pregnant and asked for Wood's advice on some remedies for her condition. He also told the detectives that Pearl was to travel to Cincinnati for an illegal operation.

By this time, it was midnight but the detectives left their hotel and went to the home of the manager of Louis and Hayes. They traveled to the store to check its records and discovered that Pearl Bryan had indeed purchased a pair of the company's shoes. The next morning, the men arrived at the Bryan house with the clothing taken from the body of the unidentified woman. Mrs. Bryan began to sob when she recognized her daughter's dress. Her description of her daughter, including a scar on her right hand, proved the body's identity.

A telegram was sent at once to Cincinnati, ordering the police to arrest Scott Jackson. The detectives left Greencastle and departed for South Bend, Indiana, where William Wood was supposed to be staying with his uncle. Meanwhile, officers were sent to Jackson's home, which was located on Ninth Street next to Robinson's Opera House. They staked out the apartment and a nearby saloon for almost seven hours before getting word that Jackson had been seen at the Palace Hotel. They followed a man who matched Jackson's description back to Ninth Street but he stood on the street, not going up to his room. Finally, one of the officers approached him and asked if he was Scott Jackson. The man said that he was and the policeman told him that he had been looking for him. Jackson turned pale and began to tremble as he was taken into custody. Chief Dietsch of the Cincinnati Police Department greeted Jackson when he arrived at headquarters. He said, "Well, we have got you."

Jackson replied, "Yes, it looks like it."

Jackson was ushered into a room filled with police detectives, city officials and newspapers reporters to be questioned. He admitted that he knew Pearl Bryan but claimed that he had last seen her during the holidays. He also knew Will Wood and said he had last seen him around January 6. Chief Dietsch then read the arrest warrant aloud and asked him for a response. Jackson claimed that the accusations were all false rumors and that he knew nothing about Pearl being murdered except what he had read in the newspaper. On Friday night, when the murder occurred, he said he had been eating supper and studying in his apartment. On Saturday, he had gone to the theater with a friend. He was shocked and sickened when he read about the murder but he claimed that he did not know that Pearl was even in Cincinnati.

Chief Dietsch listened to Jackson's story and then surprised him with a strange question, "Do you remember leaving a valise in Legner's Saloon on Saturday night?" Jackson stated that he did but thought that it was empty or did not know what was in it. He claimed that he loaned it to another student named Hackleman, but later admitted to lying about that. Witnesses remembered him having the case but it was not found when Jackson's home was searched.

Jackson was booked on suspicion of murder. Detective Bill Bulmer held his arm as he took him into the Newport police station's booking room. A number of water works employees and janitors followed them up the steps and the receiving room was filled with curious onlookers. Jackson was booked and then searched. His pockets revealed two carriage tickets that proved that he had crossed the Central Newport Bridge into Kentucky. After that, he was taken back to his cell, where Bulmer ordered that he be strip searched. This provided more damning evidence. On Jackson's right arm were two scratches. One of them ran from his elbow to the wrist and the other was about three inches long. Jackson claimed that he had scratched some insect bites but the detectives knew that Pearl Bryan had been found with blood and skin under her nails after she had struggled with her killer.

Even with this evidence, there was nothing to prove that Jackson had killed anyone. This all changed on Thursday morning at 3:30 a.m. when Alonzo Walling was arrested. The police did not originally believe that Walling had anything to do with the murder but Jackson revealed otherwise around 2:00 a.m. that morning. After a restless night of trying to sleep, he asked the guard outside of his cell if Walling had been arrested yet.

The guard asked, "Why should he be arrested?"

Jackson immediately went silent, realizing that he had made a mistake. Detectives roused Walling out of bed and peppered him with questions. He admitted that he had been with Jackson at a saloon on Friday night but he claimed to know nothing about the murder. They arrested him anyway and took him down to the station.

That same morning, a telegram arrived in Newport stating that Will Wood had been arrested in South Bend, Indiana. He confessed that he had arranged for Pearl to go to Cincinnati for an abortion. He believed that the operation caused her death and that her head must have been removed to prevent her from being identified. He named Jackson and Walling as the perpetrators of the crime.

When word spread that arrests had been made in the murder of the headless woman, hundreds of people flocked to the police station. Additional officers had to be called in to handle the crowds as Walling was taken to the chief of police's office for interrogation. Walling startled the police by admitting to his role in the crime. He recounted a conversation on Christmas Day between himself and Jackson, when his friend admitted to getting Pearl pregnant. He went on to tell of the botched abortion and the plan to get rid of the girl. Walling said that Jackson had purchased the cocaine and had injected the girl with it. On Friday night, he said, he took Pearl Bryan to Fountain Square and was instructed to wait until Jackson came back. In ten or fifteen minutes, Jackson arrived and then left again. Jackson later brought him a valise and asked him to take it but Walling refused. Walling also confessed that Jackson told him, just hours before he was arrested, that he was going to go to the Palace Hotel and write to Will Wood, sending him a fake letter that was supposed to be from Pearl Bryan. Wood was to mail the letter in Indianapolis on his way home from South Bend. That way, it would look like Pearl was still alive when her family received the letter.

The authorities immediately telegraphed the postmaster in South Bend and instructed him to seize all of Will Wood's letters and send them to Newport. Unfortunately, Wood had already received the letter and destroyed it, a fact that would not become known until later.

Chief Dietsch then decided to try and trick more information out of the dental student. He told Walling that he knew he was lying, that Jackson had already told them that Walling had performed the abortion on Pearl. Walling became enraged that Jackson was supposedly blaming him for everything. He swore that it was Jackson who was guilty.

The following day, the chief brought Jackson into the interrogation room and asked him if he wanted to make a confession. He told him that Walling had shifted all of the blame onto him. Jackson was very upset by this and tried first to blame Wood, then Walling, for the crime. He also claimed that it had been Wood who had gotten Pearl pregnant and that Wood had asked for his help because he was studying medicine. Dietsch then told him that he had been seen near Fort Thomas with Walling on Friday night but Jackson swore this was not true. He then asked Jackson who he believed had committed the murder and the young man now blamed it on Alonzo Walling. Jackson even went as far as to say that Walling had taken Jackson's trousers with him when he butchered the girl.

Crowds continued to descend on the police station. By 9:00 p.m., detectives had arrived with William Wood in custody. Wood was questioned, and after his side of the story was recorded, he was sent to the Grand Hotel with his father. The mob outside was in a volatile state. There were angry suggestions made that Jackson and Walling should hang in the streets and plans were formed to lynch them. Inside the station, the police feared the worst and they closely guarded the prisoners. Eventually, the mob settled down and slowly dispersed.

A short time later, the case took another turn. John Kugel, a saloon keeper, walked into the station, claiming to have Jackson's mysterious leather valise. The police knew about the case but did not know what had become of it. Kugel carried it into the station and turned it over to the detectives. They found it was empty but was stained with blood. Jackson was brought in and questioned about the valise. He pretended not to know that the interior was soaked with gore but looked very nervous and upset when Kugel identified him and said that Jackson told him that he wanted to get rid of the case. Kugel had taken it and then was shocked to find the blood inside.

Jackson was seen with the case on Friday evening by a porter named Allen Johnson. He had seen Jackson with Pearl Bryan and Alonzo Walling on Friday evening, leaving Wallingford's saloon in a carriage. The case had been with them at the time and it was thought to belong to Pearl Bryan. On Saturday, Jackson returned with the valise and Kugel took it when Jackson left it behind.

On Saturday, February 8, more evidence against Jackson was discovered when his blood-stained coat was removed from a sewer at the corner of Richmond and John streets. A detective found tansy flower seeds in the pockets, which were reported to cause miscarriages. Alonzo Walling had placed

Alonzo Walling Left and Scott Jackson

the coat in the sewer at the request of Scott Jackson, he said. Further evidence was found in Jackson's locker at the Ohio Dental College. When detectives opened it, they found muddy trousers with bloodstains on the legs. Jackson and Walling each claimed that the pants were the property of the other.

Later that evening, Jackson provided directions to where Pearl's clothing could be found in a sewer on Richmond Street. Jackson claimed that Walling had been the one who put it there. This caused Walling to tell the police how he believed Jackson had killed Pearl. For several days, he said, Jackson had been reading medical books, looking for the best poison. He chose four grams of cocaine mixed with sixteen drops of water. If he made her drink it, her vocal cords would be impaired and she could not scream. He then said Jackson told him that he was going to cut off her head.

Confronted with this story, Jackson admitted that he had purchased the cocaine but, he swore, he had given it to Walling. At this, the two men were brought together and they continued to blame one another for the murder. The men were asked what had become of Pearl's head but neither of them would say.

With both men shifting the blame back and forth, it was realized that without a confession, or more evidence, no one could be definitively charged with the crime. Keeping that in mind, the authorities devised a rather dramatic plan that they believed would force a confession out of one -- or both -- of the men. Jackson and Walling were brought in to a room that contained the body of Pearl Bryan. They were stationed at each end of the coffin and forced to face Pearl's brother and sister. Jackson was terribly excited and nervous but Walling remained calm and cool, except for the quiet tapping of his foot. Chief Dietsch asked Walling if he recognized the body. He said that it was Pearl Bryan but that he only knew that because Jackson had told him. Walling began to shout and the grotesque scene erupted into cries and accusations. The two men both continued to insist that the other had committed the murder. Finally, when she could stand it now more, Pearl's sister demanded to know what had become of Pearl's head. She wept as both of them refused to answer her. The attempt to force a confession had failed.

Eventually, Walling and Jackson were moved to the Hamilton County Jail for their safety and on Tuesday, February 11, a jury was selected for a formal inquest. Police detectives and officials testified as to how the identity of the dead woman had been determined and doctors gave their opinions on the cause and manner of Pearl's death. Detective Crim told of how he had been assigned to the case and what he had learned from the crime scene. They had come to the conclusion, the detective stated, that the victim had been murdered at the spot and that she had been alive when her throat was cut. Blood had soaked the surrounding trees and bushes and had seeped into the ground to a depth of eight or nine inches. Crim was then asked, to the best of his knowledge, who he believed had committed the crime. There was a deep silence in the courtroom.

Finally, Detective Crim answered: "Scott Jackson and Alonzo Walling."

The detective went on to testify as to how the men had been accounted for on Friday evening up until the time that Pearl Bryan accompanied them in the carriage from Wallingford's Saloon. Neither of them was seen again until 3:00 a.m. on Saturday morning and they could not account for their whereabouts during that time. He also told about the blood-stained valise before he was excused from the witness stand.

Dr. Robert Carothers followed with his postmortem report and the chemist who tested the contents of her stomach, Dr. W.H. Crane, testified to the presence of cocaine. After a few other witnesses told of the state and condition of the corpse, the inquest was completed. The jury debated for less than an hour and unanimously determined that the remains were those of Pearl Bryan. They also found that Pearl had been given cocaine, had been decapitated while she was still alive, and that she was last seen in the company of Scott Jackson and Alonzo Walling. The jury asked that these conclusions be filed with their verdict.

On Wednesday, February 12, a Campbell County grand jury, in session in Newport, returned an indictment against Scott Jackson and Alonzo Walling, charging the two men with Pearl Bryan's murder. The state of Kentucky had to obtain the proper papers to extradite the pair from Cincinnati, where they were being jailed, and authorities in Ohio granted several continuances in the case to allow them the time to do so. The men were basically being kept away from Newport for fear of another lynch mob. When Kentucky came through with the indictment, papers were approved by the Ohio governor to grant the release of the two men to Kentucky. When the papers were served on the authorities in Hamilton County, the attorneys for Jackson and Walling began a bitter fight to keep their clients in Ohio. Kentucky was the only place that the men could be put on trial, since the murder took place in that state, but the lawyers hoped to prove that Kentucky was not safe for their clients. Governor William O'Connell Bradley offered the full command of the state militia to Sheriff Plummer in Newport to protect the men from any lynch mobs, but this was not enough. The attorneys fought the extradition, tying up the courts and causing delay after delay.

The defense had chosen Judge M.L. Buchwalter of the Hamilton County Court of Common Pleas to hear their case because they knew that the judge had recently refused to turn over a prisoner in another murder case. At this point, one of Kentucky's most acclaimed lawyers, Colonel Robert T. Nelson, volunteered his service for the prosecution. The judge's bias against Kentucky was no match for the skills of Colonel Nelson and the public sentiment in the case. It took until March 17, but Jackson and Walling were finally turned over to the authorities in Newport. That afternoon, a patrol wagon backed up to the door of the Hamilton County Jail and the two men were hustled inside. They were each handcuffed to either Detective Crim or Detective McDermott. Crowds of people followed the wagon down Sycamore Street to Eighth and the sheriff had the wagon stop at Cincinnati's Central Police Station for their safety. The men stayed for a few hours and then slipped away in another wagon to cross Central Bridge and end up at the Newport Jail.

On that same day, the body of Pearl Bryan was finally laid to rest in a vault at the Forest Hill Cemetery in Greencastle, Indiana. Her white casket had been followed to the cemetery by a long procession of her classmates, grieving family members and sympathetic townspeople. It was one of the largest funerals in the history of the town.

On March 23, Jackson and Walling were both arraigned on charges of murder and asked for a plea. The attorneys for both men entered pleas of not guilty. Colonel George Washington, Walling's lawyer, asked the court for separate trials and L.J. Crawford, the attorney of record for Jackson, agreed. Jackson's trial was set for April 21 and Walling's for May 5.

Scott Jackson was prosecuted by M.R. Lockhart and he immediately began calling witnesses, starting with Jack Hewling, who told of finding the body. The second witness, Coroner Tingley, provided damaging forensic testimony, detailing how Pearl had been alive when she was beheaded. He also identified the clothing that belonged to the victim.

Lockhart stumbled on the second day when he brought a headless dummy into the courtroom, dressed in Pearl's blood-soaked clothing. The jury, along with the spectators in the courtroom, was offended by this gruesome sight and the defense attorney petitioned to have it removed. The judge ordered it taken out of the courtroom.

Pearl's sister, Mary Stanley, was the next witness called. She identified Pearl's clothing and her valise. Pearl's mother also took the stand, both to identify Pearl's clothing and to evoke sympathy from the jury. Lockhart then called the bartender from Wallingford's Saloon, who recognized Pearl's clothing as that worn by the young woman who accompanied Jackson and Walling on the Friday night of the murder. Next, George Jackson testified to driving the carriage out of Cincinnati while Walling gave him directions. He further testified that he heard what sounded like a woman crying out in pain coming from the back and a struggle that caused a window to break. Jackson said he went to hand the reins over to Walling so that he could see what was going on, but when he turned, Walling was pointing a gun in his face. He threatened the driver, ordering him to stop the carriage, climb down from the seat and turn around. Jackson said he climbed down but instead of stopping, because he feared that he would be shot, he ran away.

The next important witnesses were detectives Crim and McDermott. They gave testimony about the crime scene and the investigation, noting that some of Pearl's clothing had been found in Jackson's possession. John Kugel, the saloon-keeper from Wallingford's, was presented next and he testified about the valise that Jackson had left behind in the tavern.

Will Wood was the next witness called to the stand. All of the charges that had been filed against Wood as an accessory to the crime had been dropped on the condition that he testify against his friends. He said that Jackson and Pearl were intimate and that she had become "sick," meaning that she was pregnant. Jackson suggested remedies that failed to cause her to miscarry, followed by suggesting she have an abortion. Wood was told to arrange to get Pearl to Cincinnati but claimed that he did not make the arrangements. He also testified that he had received a letter from Jackson that warned him to stick by him and Walling, or there would be trouble.

The last prosecution witness was Cincinnati Police Chief Colonel Dietsch, who testified about his interrogations of Walling and Jackson. He also went on to tell of a phone conversation that took place between the two defendants but this conversation, because it was illegally obtained, was ruled inadmissible. No record of what was said during this conversation exists today.

After Colonel Dietsch, the defense took over and Scott Jackson was put on the stand. Jackson calmly answered all of the questions that were put to him without hesitation. He continued to place all of the blame for the murder on Alonzo Walling and on William Wood, for sending Pearl to Cincinnati in the first place. Jackson claimed that he ran into Pearl on the street and offered to help her find a place to live. He said that this was the only reason that he had some of her clothing. Jackson was followed on the stand by his landlord, Rose McNevin, who claimed that Jackson was home at the time of the murder. She was his only defense witness and apparently, the jury didn't believe either one of them. On May 14, the jury deliberated for only a few minutes before finding Jackson guilty of murder in the first degree.

Alonzo Walling's trial, which had originally been scheduled for May 5, finally began on May 29. The events in this case almost exactly mirrored those of Jackson's trial, including the verdict. Walling was also found guilty of first-degree murder. The prisoners were remanded to the Newport Jail during their appeal process, but all of the appeals were turned down. They were sentenced to hang on March 20, 1897. Because of the temper of the public, the prisoners were first transferred to the Covington jail and then were finally housed in Alexandria, which was considered safer. They would be returned to Newport for the hanging.

Legends still persist claiming that Jackson and Walling were both offered life sentences instead of execution if they revealed the location of Pearl's head. Both men refused. They went to the gallows behind the courthouse in Newport on March 20. It was the last public hanging in Campbell County.

Three minutes before the executions were to take place, Jackson announced that Walling was innocent of the crime. An appeal was sent to the governor, who stated that if Jackson were to confess to everything, Walling would be released. Jackson refused to do it. He was still maintaining his own innocence and to admit that he had committed the murder, and not Walling, would be the same as a confession. He told the county officials that he had nothing else to say.

The two men were marched to the gallows just before 11:30 a.m. and Sheriff Plummer asked Jackson if he had any last words. Jackson replied, "I have only this to say: that I am not guilty of the crime for which I will pay the penalty with my life."

When it came to be Walling's turn, he stated, "I have nothing to say, only that you are taking the life of an innocent man, and I call upon my God to witness the truth of what I say."

At 11:40 a.m., the trap was sprung beneath the gallows but the drop was too short. The men's necks did not break. Instead, they slowly strangled to death. The crowd that had gathered to witness the execution began to stir and cries of horror went up from the women in the audience. It took three minutes for Jackson's fingers to stop twitching and four minutes for Walling to stop struggling for air. Finally, both men died.

Stories and rumors ran rampant after the hangings and while many stated that they felt Jackson and Walling got what they deserved, others were not so sure. They had nagging doubts brought on by Jackson's last-minute claims of Walling's innocence. Walling's possible innocence started more stories and one newspaper reporter commented later that Walling, as the noose was being slipped over his head, threatened to come back and haunt the area after his death. The same writer also stated a few days later, in an article in the *Kentucky Post*, that an "evil eye" had fallen on many of the people connected to the Pearl Bryan case. Legend has it that many of the police officials and attorneys involved in the case later met with bad luck and tragic ends.

The greatest mystery that lingered in the region for years was the location of Pearl Bryan's missing head. Nearly everyone speculated about it and stories ranged from the head being dumped into the sewers under Cincinnati, thrown into the river or buried somewhere in the woods.

One of the most persistent rumors stated that Pearl's head had been thrown into the depths of the well at the old slaughterhouse, located a short distance from the murder site. The slaughterhouse was a place largely avoided by local residents. It had been empty for years but legend had it that the place was far from abandoned. Locals said that the packing house was a meeting place for occultists and that the old well was used to hide the remains of small animals that were butchered during their ceremonies. This occult group was allegedly made up of society people from Cincinnati and the surrounding area, and some claimed that Scott Jackson and possibly Alonzo Walling might have been involved with it. Their familiarity with the area was what was said to have drawn them across the river to commit Pearl's murder and, because they knew of the old slaughterhouse, they left the head in the well, assuming that it would never be found. It's further been claimed that the two men were afraid of what might happen to them if they revealed the location of Pearl's head. Some of the occultists were said to be powerful people in the region, including county officials, judges, attorneys and even members of law enforcement. Whether or not these legends had any truth to them, the simple fact remains that Pearl's head was never found - and many people believe that it vanished into the depths of the slaughterhouse.

After the trials and hangings, the building was silent and empty for many years. It was eventually torn down and a roadhouse was constructed on the site. During the 1920s, the place became known as a speakeasy and as a popular gambling joint. Local lore has it that during this period, a number of murders took place in the building. None of them were ever solved because the bodies were normally dumped elsewhere to keep attention away from the illegal gambling and liquor operation.

After Prohibition ended in 1933, the building was purchased by E.A. Brady, better known to his friends and enemies alike as "Buck." Brady turned the building in a thriving tavern and casino called the Primrose. He enjoyed success for a number of years but eventually the operation came to the attention of syndicate mobsters in Cincinnati. They moved in on Brady, looking for a piece of the action. Brady refused offers for new "partners" and ignored demands to buy him out of the Primrose. Soon, the tavern was being vandalized and customers were being threatened and beaten up in the parking lot. The violence escalated until Brady became involved in a shooting in August 1946. He was charged, and then released, in the attempted murder of a small-time hood named Albert "Red" Masterson. This was the last straw for Buck and he gave in and sold out to the gangsters. It was said that when he left, he swore the place would never thrive again as a casino. Brady committed suicide in September 1965.

After Brady sold out, the building re-opened as a nightclub called the Latin Quarter. It was during this period that the legends about the building gained another vengeful ghost. According to the stories, the daughter of the club's owner, a young woman named Johanna, fell in love with one of the singers who was performing there. Her resulting pregnancy made her father furious. Thanks to his criminal connections, he had the singer killed. Johanna became so distraught that she attempted to poison her father and failed. She then took her own life. Her body was later discovered in the basement of the club. According to the autopsy report, she was five months pregnant at the time.

Business did not fare well after this. During the early 1950s, new owners of the bar were arrested several times on gambling charges. In 1955, Campbell County deputies broke into the building with sledgehammers and confiscated slot machines and gambling tables. Apparently, Brady's prediction had come true.

Bad luck continued to plague the owners of the tavern. In the 1970s, it became known as the Hard Rock Café, but authorities closed it down in early 1978 because of some fatal shootings on the premises.

Finally, the building was turned into the bar and dance club that it is today. Bobby and Janet Mackey became the new owners in the spring of 1978 with the intention of turning it into a country western bar. Mackey was a well-known as a singer in northern Kentucky and had recorded several albums. He scrapped his plans to record in Nashville in order to renovate the old tavern. Once the bar was opened up, it immediately began to attract a crowd. Despite a number of years of Mackey's success with the place, the good times have never been able to erase the "taint" caused by the location's history of tragedy and death.

Carl Lawson was the first employee hired by Bobby Mackey. He was a loner who worked as a caretaker and handyman. He lived alone in an apartment upstairs and spent a lot of time in the sprawling building after hours. When he began reporting that he was seeing and hearing bizarre things in the empty building, people around town first assumed that he was simply crazy. Later on, though, when others started to see and hear the same things, Lawson didn't seem quite so strange after all.

He later reported, "I'd double-check at the end of the night and make sure that everything was turned off. Then I'd come back down hours later and the bar lights would be on. The front doors would be unlocked, when I knew that I'd locked them. The jukebox would be playing the 'Anniversary Waltz' even though I'd unplugged it and the power was turned off."

Soon, the odd events went from strange to downright frightening. The first ghost that Lawson spotted in the place was that of a dark, very angry man behind the bar. Even though others were present at the time of the sighting, they saw nothing. A short time later, Lawson began to experience visions of a spirit who called herself "Johanna." She would often speak to Lawson and he was able to answer her and carry on conversations. The rumors quickly started that Lawson was "talking to himself." Lawson claimed that Johanna was a tangible presence, though, often leaving the scent of roses in her wake.

Odd sounds and noises often accompanied the sightings and Lawson soon realized that the spirits seemed to be the strongest in the basement, near an old-sealed up well that had been left from the days when there was a slaughterhouse at the location. The lore of the area, Carl knew, stated that the well had once been used for occult rituals. Some of the local folks referred to it as "Hell's Gate." Although he wasn't a particularly religious man, Lawson decided to sprinkle some holy water on the old well one night, thinking that it might bring some relief from the spirits. Instead, it seemed to provoke them and the activity in the building began to escalate.

Soon, other employees and patrons began to have their own weird experiences. They began to tell of objects that moved around on their own, lights that turned on an off by themselves, disembodied voices and laughter and other strange events. Bobby Mackey was not happy about the ghostly rumors that were starting to spread around town. He said, "Carl starting telling stories and I told him to keep quiet about it. I didn't want it getting around, because I had everything I owned stuck in this place. I had to make a success of it." Mackey was not one to believe in ghosts or the supernatural and he didn't want his customers thinking that his staff was crazy. He was sure there was nothing more to the stories than wild imaginations. However, when his wife, Janet, revealed that she had also encountered the club's resident spirits, Mackey was no longer sure what to think. Janet told him that she had seen the ghosts, had felt their overwhelming presences and had even smelled Johanna's signature rose scent. She also had a very frightening encounter in the basement. While she was there, she was suddenly overcome by the scent of roses and felt something unseen swirl around her. She later recalled, "Something grabbed me by the waist. It picked me up and threw me back down. I got away from it, and when I got to the top of the stairs there was pressure behind me, pushing me down the steps. I looked back up and a voice was screaming 'Get Out! Get Out!'"

Once Janet admitted that she had seen the ghosts in the building, other people began to come forward with their own tales to relate. Roger Heath, who often worked odd jobs in the club, remembered a summer morning when he and Carl Lawson were working alone in the building. Heath was removing some light fixtures from the dance floor and Lawson was carrying them down to the basement. Just before lunch, Lawson came up the stairs and Heath noticed that he had small handprints on the back of his shirt. It looked just like a woman had pressed her hands onto his back. Erin Fey, a hostess at the club, also confessed to encountering the ghost they called "Johanna." She had laughed one day at Lawson when he was talking to the ghost. She stopped laughing when she got a strong whiff of the rose perfume.

Once the stories starting making the rounds, they caught the attention of a writer named Doug Hensley. He decided to investigate and started hanging around the club, striking up conversations with the regular customers. No one was anxious at first to talk about ghosts. Hensley said, "When I first talked to these people, almost every one of them refused to be interviewed." After he talked to Janet Mackey, though, other people came forward. Soon, Hensley had thirty sworn affidavits from people who said they had experienced supernatural events at the club.

He continued to collect stories and reports of sightings, intrigued by the various spirits who had been seen, including a headless ghost who was dressed in turn-of-the-century woman's clothing. Strangely, independent witnesses provided matching descriptions of the phantom, never knowing that others had seen her. That was when Hensley turned to historic records to shed some light on the building's history. He was stunned to discover that events of the past were closely connected to the hauntings of the present. In old newspaper accounts, he found the story of Pearl Bryan and heard the rumors or her head being tossed down the well in the basement. None of the witnesses to the haunting activity were even vaguely aware of the Pearl Bryan case or what connection it might have to the building.

And neither was a psychic whom Hensley later brought in to get her impressions of the club. The psychic later reported that the nightclub was one of the scariest places that she had ever been to. She claimed to have seen a vision of a woman named Pearl, who was holding her head in her hands, as well as a male ghost named Scott who kept repeatedly yelling at her that it was her fault that he was dead. The psychic swore that she knew nothing about the history of the place when she reported these visions to Hensley.

Strange activity continues to occur at Bobby Mackey's Music World, despite several attempted exorcisms. It's as though the dark and bloody history of this place refuses to let go of its hold on the present. And that bloody past will likely continue reaching out from the grave for many, many years to come.

1900: "PROMINENT FARMER KILLED"

Around midnight on a moonlit night in early December 1900, a prosperous Iowa farmer named John Hossack was attacked and mortally wounded in his bed. The assassin struck the victim in the head with an axe. Hossack lived through the night, partly conscious but unable to speak well enough to name his attacker. He died the next morning, about ten hours after the attack.

The Hossack family

Hossack and his wife, Margaret, had nine children, including five, ranging in age from thirteen to twenty-six, who were in the house at the time of the attack. Margaret Hossack told investigators that she had been asleep next to her husband when an unidentified intruder struck the fatal blows. But reports soon surfaced that Hossack had abused and threatened his family. For years, his wife had complained to neighbors about his violent and erratic behavior. Warren County authorities quickly decided that Hossack's abuse of his wife constituted a motive for murder and the investigation began to be targeted toward Margaret Hossack. Four days after the murder, as she was leaving her husband's burial, Margaret was arrested and charged with the crime.

As it was, though, there were many other suspects. Evidence that the family dog had been drugged on the night of the crime suggested that an outsider had been involved. All of the Hossack children had reason to fear and dislike their father. Several neighbors had tried to intervene in family disputes, and at least two of them had spoken about the possibility of sending Hossack to an insane asylum. Another neighbor had a history of quarrels with Hossack. Rumors hinted at the possibility that Hossack might have had improper relations with another woman. Complicating things further, a mysterious rider was seen on horseback leaving the Hossack property shortly after the attack.

At the coroner's inquest, most of the Hossacks and their neighbors were tight-lipped about their knowledge of the turbulent family history. In 1900, communities, especially rural ones, largely ignored or tolerated domestic abuse and no one talked publicly about it. A code of discreet silence prevailed. Conflict between a man and his family was deemed a private matter, something not spoken of with outsiders.

The tragedy and subsequent legal proceedings against Margaret Hossack divided, horrified and mesmerized the community. The family hired William H. Berry, a distinguished lawyer and former state senator, to defend the accused. He was pitted against George Clammer, a young and ambitious county attorney, who asked that Margaret be convicted of first-degree murder and sentenced to death. Overflowing crowds packed the courthouse to watch the legal drama in progress.

And so it was that a murder, a trial and a horror-filled litany of events galvanized a small farming community in the dawning days of the twentieth century. It would, according to later residents of the Hossack house, leave a lingering spirit behind.

John Hossack arrived in Warren County, Iowa, in October 1867. The young farmer had made an agreement with John and Indiana Hollis to purchase one hundred and twenty acres of rolling, fertile land - rich black dirt where he would plant crops, earn a living and raise a family. He built a fine, sturdy house at the highest point of the farm, took a wife and raised a large family, which included sturdy sons to help him with the planting, chores, and the harvest.

There was no way that he could know in those early days of the grim fate that lay ahead of him.

On the last day of his life, John Hossack rose before dawn and woke up his youngest son, Ivan, to help him bring back coal from an exposed vein a few miles east of their family farm. It was a cold morning and they put on heavy coats when they left the house at 8:00 a.m.

Hossack was no longer the robust young man that he was when he built the farm in 1867. He was now fifty-nine years old and had his share of ailments - heart trouble, stomach problems and what some called "nerves" - but he was fit for his age, still capable of handling livestock and working next to his sons in the fields. He raised corn, longhorn cattle and hogs. He kept a close eye on his fences, buildings, and tools, which required constant attention and needed frequent repair.

Hossack loved his farm, which he had tended for more than three decades. He was proud of his reputation in the community as a smart landowner and businessman. Known for being outspoken, he had firm convictions, and as a long-time subscriber to the local newspapers, he was well-informed on the issues of the day. In the summer of 1898, he was convinced to run for the Republican Party nomination for county treasurer. He came within two votes of securing the post, losing to the candidate who went on to win in the general election. Hossack took the loss in stride, admitting to friends that his farm kept him busy enough.

On the morning of Saturday, December 1, Hossack was not feeling well. The weather had turned bitterly cold and the sky was a steely gray, signaling the approach of a storm. He knew that the full force of winter would soon be on them, and the days had already shortened to the point that evening chores were being completed in the dark.

Hossack's son, Ivan, who accompanied him to fetch coal that morning, had just turned thirteen. He was the youngest in a family of nine children and perhaps because of the disturbing things that he had seen during his short life, he was apt to stay quiet around his father. He knew how quickly the man's mood could change, and was cautious not to provoke him. His father was prone to sudden and unpredictable bursts of rage, fits that were easily triggered by some trivial action by Ivan's mother and older siblings, especially his brother Johnnie. When such a mood was coming, his father's eyes would turn wild, with a strange and detached look that served as a warning to anyone nearby.

One of the worst family quarrels had occurred just over a year before, on Thanksgiving Day of 1899. Furious, Hossack had ordered his wife to go upstairs and stay out of his sight. She later secretly left the house on foot, walking to a neighbor's house in the rain, and coming home the next evening with Ivan's oldest sister, Annie, and her husband, Ev Henry. Hossack was enraged that Margaret had spent the night with the Henrys and he screamed at his son-in-law, shouting at him to get off his property and never return. Henry drove away, leaving the women at the house. A few minutes later, two of Hossack's friends, Mr. Johnston and Mr. Keller, came to the house and gathered everyone in the sitting room. The two men knew what had happened and they urged the family to try and live together more peaceably. Then the men took Ivan and his siblings into the kitchen and spoke to them separately, asking them to be more respectful of their father and honor his wishes. Before leaving, both Johnston and Keller told the children and their mother that they must stop talking to their neighbors about their troubles. Things like that were private and should be settled without help from outsiders. This was how domestic disputes were handled in those days and the admonishment to keep their troubles private seemed perfectly sensible to the family, no matter how upset and frightened they might be.

The visit from Johnson and Keller brought a welcome calm to the household, which made the subsequent year a largely peaceful one. Hossack had repaired his relationship with Ev Henry and in the spring, two of Ivan's siblings moved out of the house. Johnnie - at twenty-two, the oldest of the boys at home - went to live a few miles away at Alger Truitt's farm, where he began working as a hired hand. For Johnnie, who did not get along well with his father, it was a relief to be out of the household, although he still visited his family on most weekends. In late March, Ivan's sister, Louie, married Alger Truitt's stepson, Joe Kemp, and made a new home with him.

With Johnnie gone, Ivan, and his brothers Will and Jimmie, were the only boys still living at home. As a result, they had more work to do. They tended the animals and helped with the spring planting. In August, a fierce hailstorm dumped nearly five inches of rain on the county and ruined the crops at many farms. Luckily, the Hossack farm escaped without much damage and the family celebrated a good harvest in the fall. Thanksgiving of 1900 was a sharp contrast to the year before, with more than two dozen friends and family members, including the Truitts, the Henrys, the Kemps

Louie was by then eight months pregnant and Johnnie and his new girlfriend, crowding into the house for a feast. John Hossack was in an exceptionally good mood during what Ev Henry later called "a good old-fashioned Thanksgiving turkey dinner." Ivan and his siblings would tell the authorities that the two days between the holiday gathering and their father's attack passed completely free of conflict.

At the coal bank, Ivan and his father filled the wagon with fuel for the stoves and then headed toward the town of Medora. Hossack wanted to pick up mail and newspapers at the general store before going home.

At the farm, Will Hossack split logs for firewood after his father and Ivan left the house. Will was eighteen, muscular and broad-shouldered from farm work, and by December 1900, was the oldest boy still living at home. Will wanted to be sure the family had enough wood to make it through the weekend. The axe he was using was an old one, with a dent in the handle and a distinctive nick in the blade. He had used it just days before to kill the turkey for the holiday meal. As he was using it that morning, his sisters, Cassie and May, passed him on their way to the barn to milk the cows. His mother was churning butter in the kitchen.

Late in the afternoon, about the time that her husband was reaching the general store in Medora, Margaret Hossack walked across the road to the Nicholson farm, a half-mile away. Harvey Nicholson had died just ten days earlier, at the age of forty-five, after a long battle with typhoid fever. Mary Nicholson was now alone with three children and the burden of a farm to run.

Margaret had loaned Mary a wash boiler and she needed it back in time to do laundry early the next week. The two ladies chatted for a few minutes and then Mary remembered some sheets that she had borrowed from the Hossacks. They were clean, but she wanted to iron them first. Margaret cheerfully told her not to worry about the ironing, she would do it herself. She took the wash boiler and the sheets and headed home. When Mary later thought back to the visit, she recalled that Margaret seemed to be in a very good mood.

After stopping at the general store, John and Ivan drove the wagon along the dirt roads toward home. They arrived around 4:00 p.m. Both of them were hungry, having missed their midday meal, but they unloaded the wagon before going inside to eat. Margaret prepared supper for them, and they ate at the kitchen table as other family members came in and out of the house. Margaret and May went to the barn to do the evening milking just as dusk was falling. When he finished with his chores, Will came into the kitchen to wash up. When Ivan got up to leave the room, heading for the outhouse in the yard, Will remembered that he had left his coat outside. He asked Ivan to bring it inside for him.

John Hossack finished his supper but stayed at the table, reading the newspapers he had picked up in Medora. When he heard Will mention the woodpile, he asked whether the boys had put away the axe that afternoon when they finished chopping wood. He was concerned about the weather and didn't want the axe left out overnight. Will stepped out onto the porch and called to Ivan, "Pa thinks it will snow tonight. Get the axe at the woodpile and put it away."

When he was finished in the privy, Ivan trudged through the yard to the woodpile. He put the axe away and carried Will's coat with him into the house.

As darkness fell, Cassie and May helped their mother prepare supper for the rest of the family. The girls ate in the kitchen with their mother and the two older boys, while their father remained at the table with his newspapers. Hossack seemed to be in good humor. He talked to his family about stories that caught his interest in the papers while they ate, and then he played a game with Ivan, waving a whip back and forth on the floor as Ivan jumped over it. Hossack laughed and joked as he watched his son leaping and dodging. Will and Jimmie joined in the game and then the three boys moved to the sitting room, where the stove was warming the room, to toss a pillow back and forth. Their father followed them and picked up his newspapers again.

Cassie and May helped Margaret clean up and then the three of went to sit with the boys. The girls worked on sewing projects while Margaret mended clothes. Later, May recalled that the evening had been "harmonious," and that "father and mother were in unusual good spirits."

Will was the first to turn in for the night, climbing the stairs sometime between 7:00 and 8:00 p.m. to his room directly above the kitchen. Soon after, John Hossack declared that he was ready for bed. It was early for him, but he was tired from his long day. He undressed and lay down in bed in the downstairs room that he and Margaret shared, one of two that opened onto the sitting room.

Ivan and Jimmie continued playing, wrestling on the floor until their mother made them stop. They were making too much noise, she scolded, and their father was trying to sleep. The boys quieted down and soon climbed into the double bed they shared in their downstairs room. A few minutes later, Cassie went upstairs. May soon joined her, saying good night to her mother before climbing the stairs. Margaret was still sewing in her chair when May left.

The house grew silent and still, except for the ticking of the clock. It was 9:00 p.m.

According to testimony that she gave in the legal proceedings that followed, Margaret went into the pantry after the children went to bed and rolled some of the butter that she had churned that afternoon. When she returned to the sitting room, John was standing by the stove, pulling his pants on. He said that he was unable to sleep, so he sat in his chair, smoking his pipe and reading. They talked for a time about chores, the farm and plans to go to church the next morning.

Around 9:30, Margaret stated that she heard the dog barking and fussing outside, as he often did when the neighbors' livestock got loose or when someone approached the house that he didn't recognize. Margaret looked outside, but didn't see anything out of the ordinary.

At 10:00 p.m., she went to bed. Her husband came into the dark room a short time later and got into bed next to her. Nothing was said between them, but from the sound of his breathing, Margaret believed that John fell asleep before she did.

At various legal proceedings over the course of the next several months, the five Hossack children answered many questions about that Saturday night and the hours that immediately followed the attack on their father. Their recollections were consistent with one another's - and with their mother's - in every important respect.

According to their reports, it was shortly after midnight when Margaret Hossack called up the stairs to her three older children, asking them if they had heard a noise. Cassie replied that she had not and that her mother should go back to bed. But Margaret, standing in the kitchen at the foot of the stairs, called again: "I think somebody is in the house and something is the matter with Pa. Come down quick!"

This time, May, lying in bed next to Cassie, also heard her mother's plea. She had a strange sound in her voice, as if she was afraid. Both girls quickly got out of bed and rushed downstairs. Their brother, Willie, dressed in pants but barefoot, was just ahead of them. As they came down the dark staircase, Cassie heard the striking of a match and then another sound, a kind of groaning or choking sound, coming from somewhere downstairs.

Margaret was wearing only the chemise and drawers that she usually wore to bed and she was holding a small oil lamp that illuminated the kitchen. She was crying but she didn't speak as she led them to the bedroom door, where she handed Willie the lamp. In the dim light, the boy saw his father lying in bed, his head covered with blood and a gaping wound over his right ear. He turned to Cassie and told her to run to the Nicholson farm. Without a word, Cassie left the house and raced barefoot across the cold fields to the neighbor's house.

May woke up Jimmie and Ivan. They quickly dressed and followed her to where their father lay on his left side, facing the wall. His head looked disfigured, with his right eye bruised and swollen shut. The sheets soaked with blood. Ivan began to cry loudly.

John Hossack asked faintly, "Why is he crying?"

Willie choked out a response, "It's because you are hurt, Pa."

"No, I'm not hurt. I'm only sick."

"Who hurt you, Pa?" Willie asked.

"Nobody hurt me," his father replied.

Moments later, Cassie returned with their nineteen-year-old neighbor, John Nicholson. The young man came into the bedroom and took a long look at John Hossack. He asked Margaret where she found him. She didn't speak, but motioned toward her husband on the bed. Nicholson left without asking any more questions. He told the Hossacks that he was going to get a horse and ride to Liberty to take the news to the Henrys and Kemps.

After the young man left, Margaret dressed, putting on the blue dress that she had worn that day.

May and Jimmie left to seek help from Will and Rinda Haines, whose farm was located a half-mile to the north. The hurried along the dark road, worried that the intruder that their mother had heard in the house might be hiding somewhere, watching them. The climbed the Haines' front porch and knocked loudly on the door, calling out as they did so. In a moment, Haines, who was fully dressed, came to the door. Excitedly, May told him that her family needed help; her father had been attacked and was badly hurt. Haines looked toward the Hossack house, but after a moment's consideration, refused to come with them. He told them he'd heard a noise a short time earlier, about

11:00 p.m. He had lit a lamp and had seen a strange man standing on the porch just where they were now. It seemed that the man had gone away, but he couldn't be sure.

Unable to get Haines to come with them, May and Jimmie hurried back to the house where their father lay dying.

While his brother and sister were braving the cold night in search of help, Will stood watch over his father with his mother and Ivan. The blows to Hossack's head had left him paralyzed along the left side of his body, but he was able to move his right arm. He reached out weakly with it, saying that he was cold. Will realized that the fire in the sitting room had gone out. The temperature outside was well below freezing and the house had grown chilly. Will knew that he should go out and fetch a bucket of coal, but was fearful of going outside by himself. He decided to get the dog, Shep, to accompany him. He went out the south kitchen door, but didn't see Shep there, so he went around to the east porch, where he found him. When he called to him, Shep refused to move or pay any attention to him at all. It was very unlike the well-trained dog, so Will tried again, but to no avail. The dog simply didn't move at all. Confused and frightened, Will filled the bucket with coal and returned to the house.

Soon after May and Jimmie returned, neighbors began to gather at the Hossack house. Cassie went back across the fields and brought Mary Nicholson back with her, and at 2:00 a.m., Neil Morrison arrived. When Margaret told Morrison what had happened, he followed her to the bedroom to see the wounded man, now lying on his back in the middle of the bed, his face turned toward the ceiling. The terrible wound on the right side of his head could be clearly seen in the light of the oil lamp and he was still bleeding on the sheets. Hossack was breathing hard. Morrison thought he was unconscious, but then saw him slightly raise his right hand and move his fingers. Morrison watched as Margaret, silently weeping, wiped blood from her husband's face with a cloth. She gave him a small sip of water. When Morrison saw her open a bottle of camphor, a medicine used externally to ease pain, he stopped her, saying that he didn't think that John could stand having the stinging liquid applied to his open wounds.

Within an hour, Will Conrad, another neighbor, arrived. He stood with Morrison in the doorway and watched Margaret, who was sitting next to the bed. As Hossack moved slightly, he made a choking sound, as if he was having trouble breathing. In tears, Margaret looked at the two men and said, "Ain't this awful?"

Throughout the pre-dawn hours of Sunday, families in the vicinity were awakened and told that John Hossack had been attacked and was close to death. As the neighbors rose from their beds and dressed, they hitched their horses to their buggies and drove to the Hossack farm. A few of them came on foot, guided by moonlight or by the lanterns they carried.

About two hours after the attack, John Nicholson arrived at the Henry farm and told Annie and Ev that Annie's father was badly hurt and close to death. Annie and Ev woke and dressed their five young children and bundled them up in their buggy. They went to the Hossack farm as quickly as they could, and when they arrived, they found the house filled with light and crowded with people.

On their way inside, both of them noticed the family dog, lying quietly on the front porch. He acted strangely. Despite the many visitors and commotion, Shep was quiet and unlike his usual self.

May met Annie, Ev and their children at the kitchen door. She told them to be as quiet as they could.

"Is he killed?" asked Annie.

May replied, "No, he's not dead yet."

Dr. William Dean, a graduate of the medical school at Vanderbilt University, was thirty-nine years old in 1900 and had lived and practiced in New Virginia, Iowa, for six years. He had one of the few telephones in the area, but it didn't ring that morning. Instead, he was awakened in the early hours of December 2 by Charlie Nicholson, who had ridden seven miles on horseback to tell the doctor that John Hossack needed help. Dean had been the Hossacks' doctor for several years. He understood from Nicholson that the situation was urgent, but it took him some time to prepare to leave home and then an hour to travel by buggy to the Hossack farm. When he arrived at 4:30 a.m., Hossack had been lying wounded in his bed for more than four hours.

Dr. Dean arrived at the farm time at the same time as Lew Braucht, a local blacksmith. Braucht and Dean were met outside by Neil Morrison and Will Hossack. When asked what the trouble was, Morrison was quick to tell the doctor, "It's a bad case. A murder." He then led Dr. Dean inside and pointed to the bedroom door.

Dean went quickly to the wounded man, whose head was now covered with clothes and supported by several pillows. Margaret was at his bedside and the doctor later stated that he could tell she was very anxious. He carefully unwound the wrappings from Hossack's skull, and as he wiped away the blood, he could see a deep cut above the right ear and could tell that the skull had been smashed. It looked as though Hossack had been hit twice, first with a sharp blade and then with a blunt instrument, fracturing his skull. Brain matter had been leaking from the open wounds, making the right side of Hossack's head appear to be greatly enlarged. His right eye was swollen shut and the skin around it had a bluish tint. The pillows and sheets were soaked with blood. Dean noted that Hossack's wounds were still bleeding.

As a result of the brain injury, Hossack was totally paralyzed on the left side of his body and he appeared to be unconscious. His breathing was shallow and irregular and his pulse was weak. His entire body was covered in cold, clammy sweat. Aside from trying to keep him comfortable, there was nothing else that Dean could do for him.

As the doctor examined her husband, Margaret spoke, "Is there any hope for him?"

Dean shook his head. "No, there is no hope."

When he was later asked to testify about Margaret's reaction to the news, he said it was what one would expect from a grieving spouse. She wept, sobbing audibly, paced the room and then sat next to her husband, remaining at the bedside and holding his hand. At one point, Dean asked Margaret how Hossack's injuries had occurred. She said that she didn't know. She only knew that she had heard a sharp sound, like the striking of two boards together, then a sound like a door shutting and saw a passing light on the wall. She had called out to the children and told them that someone was in the house. When they came downstairs, they found Hossack lying in bed, terribly wounded.

George McIntosh, a twenty-five-year-old neighbor of the Hossacks who lived a half-mile to the east, rode on horseback to notify Johnnie about the attack on his father. The Truitt house, where Johnnie lived, was dark when McIntosh arrived and there was no response to his knock. He shouted several times and called out the young man's name before Johnnie came to the door. McIntosh quickly told him the news. Johnnie seemed shocked and surprised. He asked how his father had been attacked - what weapon had been used - but McIntosh told him that he didn't know anything more. Johnnie asked him to wait, saying he would ride back with him. He told McIntosh that he couldn't believe that such an awful thing had happened.

Like most of the neighbors, McIntosh knew that Johnnie frequently quarreled with his father and had moved off the family farm a year earlier. So, when the two men went to the barn to saddle a horse, McIntosh covertly checked to see that Johnnie's horse felt cool to the touch. It definitely had not been ridden in the past hour.

Alger Truitt had been awakened by his wife, Nancy, when she heard Johnnie talking to someone on the porch. He overheard the news that John Hossack had been attacked. Earlier that day, Johnnie had driven Truitt's wife and son, Harold, to Indianola, using his own horse and one of Truitt's grays as the team. Truitt knew that they'd stopped at the farm of Alonzo Odell and returned for supper around 6:00 p.m. Johnnie played cards in the sitting room for most of the evening and then, Truitt thought, he had gone to bed. Truitt was the last one to retire for the evening, going to his bedroom on the first floor just after 10:00 p.m. But he had a terrible feeling - what if Johnnie had crept out of the house later that night? He was also well aware of the animosity between Johnnie and his father.

After Johnnie and George left, Truitt went out to the barn. As McIntosh had done only a few minutes before, he checked all of the horses. None of them seemed as if they had been ridden during the night.

When Johnnie reached the Hossack farm, he went straight to his father's bedside. Dr. Dean watched the young man enter the room and stand for a moment, looking down at his dying father. Without saying a word, he turned and walked out of the room.

Will approached Johnnie and asked him if he had seen Shep on the porch. There seemed to be something wrong with him. Johnnie went to the porch and called the dog. Shep's eyes were open, but his body was limp. Johnnie reached down and took hold of him, pulled him to a standing position, and shaking him, talking to him as he did so. Shep limply fell back onto the porch. He seemed to be sick.

During the next few hours, others noted Shep's condition, and people began to talk about the possibility that the dog had been drugged by the same person who attacked John Hossack in his bed.

It would explain why the dog had not raised an alarm when the intruder entered and left the house. Shep was well-known for barking at strangers, but none of the children remembered hearing him bark before they were awakened by their mother.

While the sun was rising over the Hossack farm, more neighbors and family members were arriving. Will Haines walked down from his own house to join the other men outside. Soon, Louie, the fourth Hossack daughter, arrived with her husband, Joe Kemp. While Louie spoke with her sisters, Joe entered John's bedroom. Margaret once again began crying as she described seeing her husband in bed after the attack. Hossack, now with a bloody froth around his mouth, was obviously close to death. He was making choking noises, and Joe heard him ask Margaret for water. Joe took up his father-in-law's hand and grasped it in the traditional Masonic grip. He thought he felt the dying man respond to the handshake.

A few minutes later, Frank Keller, one of John's oldest friends and one of the county's original pioneers, arrived. He had been at the Hossack home just a few days before, on Thanksgiving afternoon, when he had stopped by to return a meat grinder that he had borrowed. Keller's wife was sick and he had spent the day at home, butchering. He was in dirty work clothes and hadn't planned to stay but Hossack, in a jovial mood, insisted that his old friend come into the house and join the party.

When Keller learned of the attack early on Sunday morning, his wife and daughter were badly frightened by the news and begged him not to leave them alone until the sun came up. Keller waited impatiently until dawn and then went straight to the Hossack farm. When he arrived, he went directly into the bedroom. Hossack's eyes were closed and he was almost motionless. The only sign of life was the slight rise and fall of his chest. Like Joe, Keller gripped his friend's hand in one of the secret Masonic handshakes and spoke softly to him. He asked if he could hear him and if John knew who he was. Keller thought he heard Hossack faintly say his name. Keller bent down, put his head close to John and whispered, "Put your trust in the Lord."

Hossack drifted in and out of consciousness for the next few hours. Neighbors and family members heard him speak several times, asking for a fire, his eyeglasses and water. He called repeatedly for Margaret, as well as for several of the children. Margaret stayed next to him through the night and into the morning. She held his hand, wiped his forehead and moistened his lips. To those who saw her, it seemed that she did everything possible to ease her husband's pain and to make him as comfortable as possible during his last hours of life.

But there was nothing she could do. At 9:45 on Sunday morning, December 2, 1900, John Hossack died.

Earlier that morning, Johnnie had searched for the murder weapon. Finding nothing around the house, he walked to the woodpile to look for the family axe. When he couldn't find it, he asked his brothers if they knew where it was. Ivan remembered that Will told him to put the axe away and told Johnnie to look inside the granary.

Lew Braucht accompanied Johnnie in the search. He was one of a number of people who were concerned that Johnnie might have had something to do with his father's attack. As they neared the granary, they saw a wooden handle protruding from the dirt under the shed. Yanking it out, Johnnie immediately recognized the nicked blade. Braucht thought he saw bloodstains on the handle and hairs stuck to the metal blade and was quick to conclude that they had found the murder weapon. Johnnie, though, was not so sure. The blood, he told Braucht, could be from the turkey that Will had slaughtered for Thanksgiving dinner just three days before. The axe might have been tossed in the dirt by one of his brothers, who often carelessly threw the axe under the granary instead of putting it inside. Johnnie put the axe back where they had found it and returned to the house with Braucht.

Ivan was in the yard and Johnnie told him that they had found the axe under the granary. But, Braucht later recollected, Ivan insisted that he had put the axe inside. The top section of the granary door had been open and Ivan said he had reached in and placed the axe next to a barrel. The implication was obvious: if Ivan put the axe inside the granary, then someone - possibly the murderer - had moved it during the night.

Braucht was convinced that the axe was an essential piece of evidence. He found Neil Morrison and asked him to come with him to the granary, where Braucht retrieved the axe and the two men examined it together. Then Morrison noticed Frank Keller walking away from the house and called him over. Keller looked the axe over and believed that he saw both blood and gray hairs on the handle and blade. He later stated, "Somebody says, well they had been killing turkeys with this axe. Well, says I, that is not turkey feathers..."

Keller cautiously touched the blood on the axe handle and it felt wet. A bit of it stuck to his finger. Just then Dr. Dean walked out of the house and Keller called to him, stating that they had found the murder weapon. Dean joined the growing group of men outside of the granary. Taking the axe in his hands, he, like the others, noticed the blood spots on the handle and several hairs on the blade. He also realized that the continued handling of the axe was compromising its value as evidence. He gave it back to Braucht and told him to return it to its original location and make sure no one else touched it. Braucht shoved the axe back under the granary.

Warren County Sheriff Lewis Hodson arrived at the farm around noon. He was accompanied by his deputy, Grant Kimer. The two lawmen saw the group of men gathered near the granary and walked toward them. Both of the men had been recently elected to their posts, and neither of them had ever investigated a murder. Lew Braucht stepped forward to explain that he was standing guard over the axe, which he and several other neighbors believed might be the murder weapon.

Sheriff Hodson pulled the axe out from under the small building and examined it closely. He noted the possible blood spots and three hairs on the blade. He removed the hairs and placed them in his pocketbook for safekeeping. He then wrapped the axe in newspaper and handed it to Deputy Kimer, instructing him to safeguard it. He told Kimer to go into the house and sit with the corpse in the bedroom.

Hodson spoke briefly to some of the neighbors, some of whom had been at the farm since the middle of the night. Frank Keller led the sheriff across the yard to the front porch, where he pointed out drops of blood that he had found on the steps. Then the two men went inside and proceeded to the bedroom where the murder had occurred. Hodson saw Hossack's body on the bed and looked over the ugly gash on the right side of the man's head.

Hodson turned away and went back outside. One of the neighbors approached the sheriff and suggested that perhaps bloodhounds should be put on the trail of the attacker, but Hodson was quick to dismiss the idea. "We don't want a pack of dogs yelping around the corpse," he said.

Shortly after Sheriff Hodson's inspection of the body and the bedroom, George Clammer, the county attorney, arrived. Clammer was the son of a Methodist minister, and unlike most of those gathered at the house, he was not a farmer. He had lived his entire adult life in Indianola, where he attended Simpson College and won acclaim as a scholar, orator and football player. After graduation, he pursued a career in law. Ambitious and self-confident, the handsome young man was twenty-seven years old and had recently been elected to his second term as county attorney. He listened as the sheriff told him what he knew so far and then allowed him to show him some things he had noticed on the porch. Hodson pointed out a half-dozen dark spots that looked like dried blood on the floor. A barrel of rainwater sat to one side of the porch and the door, leading into the kitchen, had a broken pane of glass.

The kitchen was fairly typical of those found in farmhouses of that era. It was simply furnished, with a clock on one wall, a table and chairs in the center and a cook stove against the west wall. The pantry was on the east side of the room; a second door on the south side led to the yard, and a staircase led to the upstairs bedrooms. Clammer examined the wooden floorboards, noting that they were clean and showed no evidence of blood.

He passed through the kitchen and entered the sitting room, where the few pieces of furniture had been pushed back to the walls. A coal stove stood in the center of the room and a small table and a chair were pulled up close to it. Two curtained windows were on the north wall. On the east wall was a portrait of John Hossack, a fair depiction of the farmer. On the west side of the sitting room were two bedroom doors. In one of them, Clammer saw a bed, a three-drawer chest wedged into one corner, and an oval mirror hanging above it. The bed was covered with a brightly colored patchwork quilt with a single word - IVAN - in neat stitches at the bottom.

Clammer then went to the doorway of the second room and looking into the bedchamber shared by the victim and his wife. The bed was against the walls in the southwest corner. The body lay in the middle of the mattress, surrounded by bloody sheets and blankets. The two pillows that supported the victim's head were also soaked with blood. Clammer saw a window at the foot of the bed, and noted that neither the sash nor the glass seemed disturbed. A sewing machine sat next to the dresser. A piece of carpet was on the floor next to the bed, marked with a small stain that looked like blood. A Winchester rifle leaned against the wall.

Sheriff Hodson told Clammer that Margaret had awakened - and before she knew her husband was hurt - she left the bedroom and went into the kitchen to call up the stairs to her children. Clammer was puzzled by this story. If the woman was startled awake and frightened in the night, wouldn't her first instinct be to awaken her husband, who was lying next to her?

Later in the afternoon, Dr. Harry Dale, the thirty-three-year-old county coroner, arrived at the scene. After discussing what they knew so far, Clammer and Dale decided to question Margaret Hossack together. They asked Dr. Dean, who had attended the victim in the hours leading up to his death, to be present. Perhaps attempting to make Margaret feel comfortable, they asked Sue Himstreet, a neighbor who'd arrived a few hours earlier, to be in the room during the questioning.

The group went upstairs to a bedroom where Margaret was waiting for them. Clammer noted that she was a large woman, about his own height, or perhaps an inch or two taller, and must have weighed at least one hundred and sixty pounds. She was in her late fifties, but years of farm life had made her raw-boned and tough.

When he asked her what had happened, Margaret told the same story that she had recounted several times before. According to Mrs. Himstreet, she answered Clammer's questions without complaint or hesitation and seemed "perfectly free" with her responses.

Did her husband have any enemies? No, Margaret didn't think so.

Did she know where the axe had been stored the night before? She responded that she had heard Will tell Ivan to put it in the granary on Saturday evening, but he was gone such a short time that she supposed he simply tossed it underneath, as the boys sometimes did, rather than taking the time to put it inside.

Did she know that the axe was found under the granary that morning? Did she know that the handle had blood spots on it, and was believed to be the murder weapon? No, Margaret answered calmly, she didn't know either of those things.

Did the family have troubles? Did she fight with her husband, or with the children? This brought the questioning to a difficult subject. Over the past decade, Margaret had told many of the neighbors that she was afraid of her husband and that he had frequently threatened her and the children. Undoubtedly she knew that word of these incidents had made their way to the authorities, but she refused to admit to any family problems to Clammer, just as she would not admit them to others who questioned her later. No, she replied, there were no problems.

Clammer asked if she had been hurt when he husband was attacked. Had the weapon struck her? No, she said, she had not been hit.

At the end of the interview, he asked about her clothes. What had she worn to bed that night? She replied that she had slept in a chemise and drawers, the same ones she was wearing now, under her dress.

Clammer made a bold request: could she remove her dress?

At this point, according to Sue Himstreet, Margaret hesitated for the first time. Clammer repeated that he wanted her to take her dress off so that the three men could examine the clothing underneath for blood spots. Finally, Margaret stated that she had no objection to removing her clothing, but that she hated to do it in the presence of the men because she hadn't changed her underclothes for a week and hated to have them see. But Clammer was not to be deterred. It was essential that the underclothes be inspected, but he agreed to leave the room and let the doctors conduct the examination.

Once Clammer was gone, Margaret stood and pulled her dress over her head as Drs. Dean and Dale watched. According to Mrs. Himstreet, she showed no hesitation or nervousness as she allowed them to look at the garments that she wore underneath. The two men scrutinized the clothing, and then left the room to report their findings to Clammer.

Once the women were left alone, Margaret, clad only in her underwear, asked Mrs. Himstreet to look at her clothing and see if she noticed any blood. Mrs. Himstreet studied the garments, noting a small amount of blood on the right shoulder of the chemise. She saw more spots on the back - at the bottom and at the center, near the top. She saw no blood on the front. When she told Margaret what she found, the other woman seemed surprised. She had never looked at her own clothing and had no idea that there was any blood on her at all.

The long and terrible day finally came to an end. Of the nine Hossack children, eight of them spent the night at the farm, including the three who lived nearby. Alex, the oldest son, was the only one not there. He had been notified of his father's death and would arrive the next day.

But the family was not alone. Neighbors continued to come and go, and most of the authorities in charge of the investigation remained throughout the night.

Clammer had asked his wife's cousin, E.A. Osborne, a druggist and amateur photographer, to come to the Hossack farm on Sunday to take pictures of the dead man. Osborne arrived after midnight with a friend, H.H. Hartman, a local attorney and fellow photography buff. They took four flashlight photographs of the body while Clammer and Dale watched. When they were finished, Deputy Kimer escorted them to their buggy and gave the axe, still wrapped in newspaper, to Hartman. He had been asked by Clammer to take possession of the axe and to send it to Dr. Eli Grimes in Des Moines.

Finally, around 4:00 a.m., the undertaker, George Moore, was permitted to perform his duties. He had been at the house since midafternoon and now entered the bedroom for the first time to carry out his work. He lifted the small piece of carpet on the floor and placed it under Hossack's head. He wiped the blood from the wounds, cleaned the body, and prepared it for the next day's official medical examination. Then he stuffed the carpet in a bucket of water, which also contained some bloody rags, opened the window at the foot of the bed, and placed the bucket on the ground outside. By the time Moore had completed his tasks, dawn was breaking on the horizon.

On the day after John Hossack's death, Coroner Harry Dale selected three men to serve as the inquest jury. T.W. Passwater was an Indianola resident with experience in law enforcement, once serving as deputy warden at the state penitentiary and as a deputy sheriff for the county. The other two men, C.D. Johnson and Fred Johnston, were farmers who knew the victim and lived near the Hossack farm.

Fred Johnston was an especially important choice. He was well-respected in the community and had been a close friend of the Hossack family for more than two decades. He and Hossack had served together as trustees for Warren County and as elders in their church - and Johnston knew about the domestic problems that had plagued the family for years. In fact, he had been one of the friends who had visited the family the previous year to urge them to reconcile and to keep their problems to themselves. As it turned out, he would be asked to describe that meeting under oath.

County Attorney Clammer and Dr. Dale joined the three members of the jury at the proceeding. W.A. Olive, a stenographer, had been hired to transcribe the questions and answers during the two days of the inquiry.

Robbery was not a suspected motive. The Hossacks had confirmed that nothing of value was missing from the house. Because of the history of domestic problems, family members were under suspicion and Dale made sure that none of them knew in advance the questions they would be asked, and that they were kept separated so that they could not discuss anything amongst themselves. The inquest began on Monday morning and during the proceedings, Margaret and the nine children were kept under guard in a single upstairs bedroom. They were not allowed to speak about the crime or the investigation. After testifying, they were sent to another room and kept away from those who had not yet testified. The only exceptions were made for Margaret's son-in-laws, Ev Henry and Joe Kemp, who were allowed to leave the house and return to their own farms for chores.

Dr. Dale brought the jurors into the downstairs bedroom, where the murder occurred. The corpse was still where the undertaker had left it, covered with a sheet and lying on a cooling board on the double bed. Dale pulled back the sheet and displayed the wounds and then pointed out the blood spots on the bedcovers and the walls, making note of the spatters in the southwest corner, a few feet from Hossack's head at the time of the attack. There was also blood almost nine feet away from the body on the east wall and on the door frame, the area behind where the assailant must have stood. The amount of blood on the walls, and the fact that it sprayed in four directions at once, indicated the force of the two blows.

The blood spatters suggested something else: that the killer, swinging an ax just a few feet from Hossack's head, must have been sprayed with blood, since the killer's body blocked the path of the spray to the east wall.

As the final piece of evidence, Dr. Dale held up the chemise that Margaret had been wearing on the night of the murder. He indicated the blood spots on the right sleeve and the back. Johnston and Passwater both recalled - and later testified - that there was no blood on the front of the chemise.

When Dale finished, he covered the body and led the men out of the bedroom, but Fred Johnston stayed behind. He held the chemise in his hands and saw that there was no blood on the front. To Johnston, almost all of the blood spots on the back looked as if they had been spattered against the cloth. Only one spot, a mark at the lower end of the right side, looked different to him, more like a smear, as if the cloth had rubbed against something. When Clammer called to him from the other room, Johnston dropped the chemise onto the sheet covering Hossack's body and left to join the other jurors.

None of the authorities remembering seeing the chemise again until it was found a few days later in the bottom of a bucket of bloody water, soaked and no longer viable as evidence.

The separate testimonies that are taken during any legal proceeding have to be put together as a sort of narrative for any defense attorney or prosecutor that is involved. Often the stories will have separate overlapping or contradictory tales that have to be woven together to create a single coherent chronology. From his investigation of the crime scene and his informal questioning of neighbors at the Hossack farm, Clammer had already formed his theory about the murder, and he strongly suspected that Margaret Hossack was guilty. Her story about sleeping through the attack didn't make sense to him, especially given the narrow width of the bed they shared. He believed that if she had been lying there, she would have been struck by the handle of the axe, or at least would have been awakened by the presence of the killer, who stood only inches away from her face.

To Clammer, Margaret had more than enough motive to want to kill her husband. She was reported to have said many times that she feared him and wished that he were dead. There was talk in the neighborhood that the couple had reconciled and had been living in peace for the last year, but this did not necessarily erase the decades of hostility that had gone before. Clammer did not believe that a one-year truce solved anything. If the neighbors were willing to testify about what Margaret had told them in the past, their statements could be persuasive to a jury.

The suspicion that Margaret had killed her husband was obvious during the inquest, starting with the questioning of Drs. L.H. Surber and Emmett Porterfield. Both were middle-aged physicians who practiced in Indianola, and they had performed the autopsy together. They were the first to testify.

According to both doctors, who testified separately, the first blow had resulted in a wound that was five inches long, striking the victim just above and in front of the right ear. The blow was powerful enough to drive the weapon, either a hatchet or an axe, about four and a half inches into Hossack's head. The second blow, about an inch below the first and resulting in a three-inch wound, was also delivered with great strength, causing pieces of the skull to be forced into the brain cavity. The doctors had examined the rest of the body and found no other unusual marks or signs of violence. They concluded that Hossack had been alive when he was struck, and although they could not pinpoint the time that elapsed between the two blows, they speculated that they had come close together.

The doctors were also asked for an opinion about whether the victim would have lost consciousness after the attack and if so, when he would have regained the ability to speak. The jury knew that Margaret claimed to have called the children only moments after being awakened by the assault on her husband, and that the children said that Hossack spoke to them shortly after they entered the bedroom. Would speech have been possible after such a violent attack? Neither doctor was able to offer a clear answer to the question.

Each was also asked if they thought the blows had been struck by a right-handed or a left-handed person. Both of them answered this question with assurance: given the position of the body in the bed and the nature of the blows, it appeared that the attacker was left-handed.

Margaret Hossack was right-handed. Perhaps Clammer had shared that information with jury members because they challenged the doctor's conclusions with a series of pointed questions, starting with asking if it was *possible* the killer had been right-handed. Dr. Surber replied that it did not seem possible. When it was Dr. Porterfield's turn in the witness chair, Passwater asked him to elaborate. Wouldn't his conclusion depend on the number of pillows supporting the head at the time the blows were struck and how close to the foot of the bed the attacker had stood? Porterfield resolutely refused to change his mind, responding, "My answer is that I thought they were left-handed blows."

It was a critical point. Still not satisfied, the jurors asked for a demonstration. Passwater lay down on the floor, acting the part of Hossack, and stuck two pillows under his head. He requested that the doctor stand next to him, showing how the blows might have been hit from that position. Playing the part of the attacker, Porterfield demonstrated how the ax was swung, in a left-handed fashion, to cause the wounds. The jurors kept pressing the point. Wasn't it conceivable, given the possible position of the assailant and the angle of Hossack's head at the moment he was struck, that the blows had been delivered with a right-handed stroke? Eventually, after having testified repeatedly that the murderer was surely left-handed, Porterfield conceded that yes - it was possible that the killer was right-handed.

It was later established that the only left-handed member of the household present on the night of the murder was Will Hossack.

Twelve neighbors were also called to testify at the inquest: eight men and four women. All of them had known John Hossack for many years, more than two decades in several cases. They knew him as a fellow farmer, community leader and friend. Yet almost all of them knew a different side of Hossack, one that had been revealed to them through conversations with his wife. Those conversations were of great interest to the jury members.

The neighbors were typically first asked about the night of the attack - when they had learned of the attack and what they saw and heard at the Hossack farm. Inevitably, though, the questions shifted to the Hossack family troubles. Many of them were reluctant to talk. Neil Morrison repeatedly said that he couldn't recall his conversations with Margaret Hossack. William Haines stated, "I never know anything more about anybody's business than I can help." Fred Johnston admitted that he knew about the turmoil, but it had been "hushed up" over the years. Ev Henry said that he had always understood that the family tried to keep their conflicts private. Clammer told them all that the time for secrecy was over. The inquest was serious business and now that a crime had been committed, the neighbors had a responsibility to tell the jury everything they knew.

It turned out that they knew a great deal. Neil Morrison confessed that he had heard from Margaret about the family's troubles for at least fifteen years. At first, he thought they were just problems between John and the children, but later he learned that the conflicts were also between husband and wife. Margaret told him that her life was a "misery" and that her husband "abused" her and she was "afraid for her life, afraid he would do something to her or the children." On one occasion, she stopped Morrison on the road and asked him to come to her house because John was "acting like a crazy man" and she feared for the safety of her family. Morrison tried to calm her, but she insisted. He put off the visit until the next day and by then, the trouble had passed.

Other neighbors agreed that they had also heard Margaret speak of her husband's frequent threats to her and the children, often made while holding a knife or a loaded gun. They told of her coming to their farms or running up to them on the road, crying and saying that he was "wild" and that she feared he would kill someone. Few of them knew of any specific acts of violence, although several heard reports that Hossack slapped and whipped his children, hit his wife with his fists and once, threw a heavy stove lid at her. All who testified said that the threat of violence from her husband had been a constant source of fear for Mrs. Hossack.

Frank Keller offered detailed testimony about having many discussions with Margaret about her husband's foul moods, violent temper and threats. She had talked to him many times and once - unlike the other neighbors, who saw the domestic violence as none of their concern - he went to the Hossack farm and tried to help. Margaret begged him not to say anything, though. She could not let her husband know that she had been talking about him. If he found out, he was apt to kill the entire family. Keller recalled her tears and her saying that there could not be any peace in the family as long as John Hossack lived. She wept and cried out, "Why is it that the Lord don't remove him out of the way?"

Will Conrad, another neighbor, testified that the conversations with Margaret had been "more frequent than we wanted them." On one occasion, one of the Hossack girls came to his farm to ask for help, saying that Hossack had ordered Johnnie to leave the place. Apparently, Hossack had tried to kick daughter Annie and Johnnie had intervened. Hossack threatened the boy with a hunting knife, stating that he would "cut your guts out." Conrad, like Keller, tried to intervene, but by the time he got to the farm, things had calmed down. He said that Hossack was distressed and seemed "very much broken down." It was the only time Conrad talked to Hossack about his family situation and Hossack told him that he felt they were all against him and that he was very "unfortunately situated." He was considering dividing his property and giving his wife and children a portion of their own, with the understanding that he would live separately from them. Conrad refused to offer his old friend any opinion about the matter.

Even after this, Margaret continued to talk to Conrad about her fears. She was afraid to go to sleep, she told him, and sometimes "there would be weeks at a time when she could not take her clothes off." She always seemed afraid that he would kill some of them, Conrad recalled. But like everyone else, Conrad told her not to worry. In other words, he didn't want to be bothered with their personal problems.

Privately, though, Conrad confessed that he feared someone would eventually get hurt. He said, "I rather expected that in some kind of a family row that someone would strike a harder blow than was intended."

Conrad wasn't alone in this fear. Others noted Hossack's unpredictable behavior and could tell by the wild look in his eyes when he was in a "spell." Fred Johnston said that Hossack could get "worked up over something so that he didn't seem to know what he was doing." Ev Henry had talked to Conrad about the possibility of having his father-in-law arrested so that he couldn't harm his family. Conrad agreed that "this might be the only way out of it." Fred Johnston had talked to others about the possibility of having Hossack committed to an insane asylum - but, of course, all of them were reluctant to intervene, and nothing was ever done about the situation.

Like other neighbors, Conrad had heard Margaret say that she wished her husband was dead, and both he and Keller said that she had even asked William Haines to kill him.

William and Rinda Haines were in their mid-thirties and lived just a half-mile from the Hossack farm. The couple was around the same age as the oldest Hossack children. On the night of the attack, Haines had told May and Jimmie that he'd seen a strange man on his porch, but he wasn't asked about that at the inquest. The questions posed to Will and his wife were mostly about their knowledge of the problems within the family. Both of them admitted that they had known John Hossack for many years and knew he had a "pretty high temper." Many times, when coming to visit the Hossacks, they could tell the family had been quarrelling. Mrs. Haines said, "Mr. Hossack would not talk, and you could see he was awful mad, and we just judged from his looks that they had been in trouble." She often heard Margaret say that it would be better for the family if her husband was dead and that "it would be God's blessing if he were taken."

But Haines denied that Margaret had asked him to kill her husband. On one occasion, he said, she had been "in a passion" and had told Haines that he and the other neighbors should come and "fix" her husband and "attend" to him. Haines never considered that she was talking about murder, only that her husband deserved a good beating for the way he treated his family - "one he would remember and make him afraid to do these things anymore." Haines told her that he would never do such a thing. He didn't want to "get into trouble by laying hands on my neighbors."

Rinda Haines had a theory about the source of the trouble between the Hossacks, based on a story that she had heard from John's mother. According to the older woman, her son had been in love with Margaret's sister, Jane, but "circumstances prevailed" on him to marry Margaret instead. The marriage had never been a happy one. Other neighbors speculated that Hossack was especially strict with his children, and that his rage was often triggered when his wife took their side against his. Some thought he was angry about the lack of discipline in the household.

Two of them suggested another motive: Margaret may have been jealous of her husband's relationship with another woman. It was suggested that this woman was Mary Nicholson, one of the only neighbors who claimed to know nothing of the Hossack family problems. John Hossack had visited her recently, she said, since he was helping her to collect insurance after her husband's death. She was grilled about these meetings. How many times had he come? When had he arrived? Who else was in the house when he visited? Mrs. Nicholson said that she had seen Hossack "about twice" since her husband had died, but six weeks later, during a grand jury hearing, her son, John, would learn that Hossack visited their house "nearly every day" after Harvey Nicholson had passed away. She later replied - to a number of vague questions - that she knew of no reason why Margaret Hossack would have been jealous in regards to anything to do with her relationship to Mr. Hossack.

The same questions were also put to the next witness, Mrs. George Grant, and she also denied knowledge of anything out of the ordinary. After that, the theory was dropped and the topic was not raised again except to ask Margaret if her husband had ever, to her knowledge, had any "affection" for another woman. She replied that she hadn't known of any feelings like that on his part.

Whatever the reason for the conflicts, many neighbors confirmed that Margaret often spoke of separating from her husband, claiming that she would have done so years before had it not been for the "disgrace" it would cause the family. John Hossack was a prosperous man, but not a generous one. All of the property the family owned was in his name. He had suggested dividing the farm and giving her and the children all of the land except for the west eighty acres, which he would keep for himself. Margaret was in favor of the split, but the necessary legal steps were never taken.

Talk of a separation had become serious about a year before Hossack's death, when a quarrel broke out between the couple on Thanksgiving Day. Hossack, angry with his daughters for making social plans without his knowledge, turned his rage on his wife when she took their side. When he went outside briefly, Mrs. Hossack left the house, and there was some suggestion that she escaped through an upstairs window. She fled to Will Conrad's house in the rain. She was terrified when she arrived and he took her to Ev Henry's house. The next morning, he gathered several men from surrounding farms, including Frank Keller and Fred Johnston. Together, they talked to Margaret and convinced her to return home accompanied by Ev and Annie Henry. After Hossack had angrily confronted Ev, insisting that the man leave his property, Keller and Johnston went to the farm to talk to the family and urge reconciliation. In their testimony, the two men admitted that their goal had been to convince the Hossacks not to divide their property and separate, and they believed they had been successful. Frank Keller naively told the coroner's jury: "My understanding is that we got the children to agree to try and behave themselves and Mrs. Hossack was to do the same and Mr. Hossack was to do the same and they could try to live peaceably together."

Fred Johnston concluded the discussion by exacting a promise from the Hossack family members. They were to "let the matter drop and never mention it among themselves, or to me or to Mr. Keller, and I told them I never wanted to hear anything more about it, and they were never to talk to outsiders." Keller also emphasized the importance of secrecy, saying "that from that time forth, they should tell no man or woman, not tell any person, about their troubles, were not to talk about it among themselves, were not to refer to it, and were, if possible, forget it." Both men testified that they believed that all of the conflict had been resolved by the time they had left the house.

But as they were leaving, Margaret begged Johnston not to go. She asked him if he would stay the night, just to be sure that tensions did not flare up again in the aftermath of the two men humiliating John Hossack by coming to the house and lecturing him about his duties as a husband and father. But Johnston refused. He simply wanted nothing more to do with the family's problems.

During the year between this intervention and Hossack's death, the neighbors who testified heard nothing more of the troubles in the family. When the Hossack children were questioned, they said that relations in the family actually had improved during those twelve months. As May said, "We have had some trouble since that, but nothing like we had been though."

Eight of the Hossack children, as well as two sons-in-law, were called as witnesses at the inquest. The five in the house on the night of the attack were asked to talk about events of that night and the preceding day. The questioners were most interested in their observations of their father's condition right after the attack, what he said and the appearance of the wounds. All of the children remembered that he spoke a few words, and Will observed that his father's eye was swollen and his head was covered with a blood clot "about the size of a tea cup." Cassie and May thought the clot was smaller, but they, too, had seen a lot of blood "piled" around the wounds, soaking into the bed sheets.

But more than anything the jury wanted to talk about the family's troubles in the years before the murder. For the most part, the children were reluctant to speak about that subject. The youngest boys said that they knew nothing of any troubles, while the others were only slightly more forthcoming. Will admitted that he remembered his father threatening Johnnie with a knife a few years earlier. May confirmed that relations between her parents were "quite bitter" at times and Annie acknowledged that her parents sometimes used "very cross words" with each other and that her father could be "quick tempered." But, she said, family members tried to refrain from discussing their difficulties with neighbors and tried to bear them alone. Annie and Ev Henry agreed. They both claimed that they tried to keep the conflicts between her parents away from the public.

Margaret was the last one to testify. The questions about the attack on her husband were very specific - how had she and her family spent the evening before? What had first alarmed her in the night? What had she done, seen and heard? Her answers were consistent with those of the children and with the version of events that she had already recounted several times before.

Eventually, the inquiries shifted. "Did you and Mr. Hossack ever have any trouble?"

She replied simply: "No sir, no more than we might sometimes get out of humor for a little bit, nothing much."

The questioner seemed surprised: "You never really had any trouble?"

She answered again, "No, sir." And then the lies really began.

During a long string of questions, Margaret claimed that she was never abused, that her husband had never struck her with his fists and that she had never told anyone that he did. He never abused the children, she claimed. He never had any problems with Johnnie or threatened him with a knife. He also never threatened any family members with a gun or threatened to kill any of them. And most of all, Margaret stated that she had never told any of the neighbors that she feared for her life. She never told anyone that she wished that her husband was dead. In fact, she said, the thought never even crossed her mind.

The worst thing that Margaret said about her husband was that "sometimes he was hard to get along with, but it would not take long to get over it." He could be a "hard man to care for when he was sick" and "when he got out of humor, he was a hard man to please." But he had been in better health over the last year and it had been a good time for all of them. The boys had done everything they could to please him and the family "never had a word of trouble." Margaret claimed that her husband had been devoted to her and their children - "there was not a man who thought more of his family than he did or would do more for them."

The jury was stunned by her replies and one of them even blurted out, "Why in the name of God don't you tell us everything you know about it?" Another of them sternly warned her, "The spirit of John Hossack now listens to every question asked you." They persisted with more questions about difficulties with her husband, but Margaret's replies stubbornly remained the same.

At the end of her testimony, she asked to speak: "Well, gentlemen, I hope you don't think I killed him. I wouldn't do such a thing. I loved him too much."

The witness testimony came to an end at 8:00 p.m. on Tuesday night. Clammer, who was not permitted to join in the deliberations, left the room so that the three jurors could discuss the case with Coroner Dale. If the inquest jury named a suspect in their verdict, Dale had the power to immediately order that person's arrest.

At 11:00 p.m., George Clammer was called into the sitting room to hear the verdict. It was a simple statement, signed by all three jurors: "We do find that said deceased came to his death by two blows one the head; one by a sharp instrument and one with a blunt instrument."

The jury had been unable to agree that Margaret Hossack should be named as a suspect. Passwater was in favor of identifying her as the person responsible for her husband's death, but neither Johnson nor Johnston would go along with it. The decision was unwelcome news for the county attorney.

Dale and Clammer consulted privately and then jointly dismissed the jurors, thanking them for their service and telling them that their work was completed. Neither of the authorities, however, remembered to attend to one important matter: they did not take possession of the blood-stained chemise.

On Wednesday morning, December 5, the corpse of John Hossack was moved from the cooling board and placed in a pine coffin in the same bedroom where he had died on Sunday morning.

The Hossack family faced the grim task of planning the burial at the same time they had to face the people of the community. Many of the men who had come to the farm on Saturday night and Sunday morning - fellow farmers, Freemasons, church members, political and business associates - would attend the services and pay their final respects. There would also be the inevitable curiosity-seekers who, by word of mouth or from newspaper accounts, had found out about the strange and terrible tragedy on the Hossack farm.

At mid-morning, the coffin was carried from the house and placed in the back of a farm wagon. Margaret followed it outside, wearing a black dress and a hat with a black veil. She was suffering from a head cold and fatigue and her eyes were puffy and red. She sat in the front seat of the buggy, with one of her sons next to her taking the reins. Then they started off down the cold road toward New Virginia.

At about the same time, Sheriff Hodson was meeting with Justice H.L. Ross, a magistrate in Indianola. Despite the jury's refusal to name a suspect, Ross had been persuaded by George Clammer earlier that morning to issue an arrest warrant for Margaret Hossack accusing her of murder in the first degree.

Sheriff Hodson went home, hitched a team of horses to his buggy and headed toward New Virginia. Seated next to him was his deputy, Grant Kimer. Marcia Bell Hodson, the sheriff's wife, joined the two lawmen for the drive from Indianola to New Virginia.

By the time the sheriff arrived in town, the funeral service at the Methodist Church was underway. A large crowd had gathered in the street. Onlookers whispered to one another, nodding and pointing to the sheriff. Hodson's arrival mean that some legal action - probably an arrest - was about to happen. Even so, Hodson had parked his buggy down the street from the church, trying to be as inconspicuous as possible, while waiting for the service to conclude. As much as he could, the sheriff ignored the crowd.

An hour later, the church doors opened. The Hossack family emerged first and once again loaded the casket into the farm wagon. Mourners poured out of the church, mingling with the anticipatory crowd outside.

Sheriff Hodson watched the scene from his buggy, while Deputy Kimer climbed down and crossed the street. Standing a good half-foot taller than almost everyone around him, Kimer was easy to spot. He angled through the crowd, greeting people and shaking a few hands. The older Hossack boys eyed the deputy cautiously.

With the Hossack family leading the way, the mourners formed a long line of buggies and people on foot, slowly moving in the direction of the New Virginia cemetery, about six hundred yards from the church. Kimer returned to Hodson's buggy and they followed the procession. It was a short drive to the cemetery and the mourners halted their teams at the top of a rise and tied them to the hitching posts by the gate. Hodson remained at the bottom of the hill, keeping a conspicuous distance from the funeral attendees.

The pine box containing Hossack's mortal remains was pulled from the wagon. The Methodist pastor led the procession with his head bowed. Pallbearers followed the pastor, with Margaret Hossack walking directly behind them. She clung to the arm of her elderly brother, Donald Murchison, a former sheriff from Illinois. As the mourners filed through the gate, a few of them turned and curiously looked down the hill at the sheriff and his deputy.

In the northeast corner of the cemetery, the new grave had been dug, a mound of soil piled to one side. The pastor signaled for the coffin to be lowered and the crowd moved closer, pushing in behind the family members and crowding around the adjacent graves of Hossack's parents and an infant son.

As the mourners settled into place, Sheriff Hodson moved his buggy forward, driving slowly up the hill. He turned the horses at the gate and stopped in front of the wagon that had carried the casket. Leaving Mrs. Hodson at the buggy, Hodson and Kimer walked up the path toward the service, then separated. The sheriff moved to the left side of the crowd; the deputy stepped to the right.

After the pastor concluded his remarks and dropped a handful of clotted earth onto the wooden casket, people stepped away and started back up the gravel path. The Hossack children formed a protective half-circle around their mother and then, moving in a group, they slowly made their way toward the gate and the waiting carriages. Nervous friends and neighbors followed in silence.

As Margaret approached the gate, the sheriff put himself directly in her path. She paused in front of him, took two steps forward, and then stopped. Hodson advanced to meet her and spoke plainly and clearly, telling her that she was under arrest for the murder of her husband.

A murmur rippled through the gathered group of mourners. Donald Murchison leaned over and spoke softly to his sister, explaining that it was necessary for her to go with the sheriff. A few second passed and Margaret lifted her veil and started to speak. But her face twisted with emotion and as she began to weep, the black veil dropped back, covering her features. Hodson reached out and placed a gentle hand on the widow's arm. Almost apologetically, he said, "This is not a matter of my choosing."

Donald Murchison stepped forward and, with Hodson, supported his sister as they walked through the cemetery gate to the sheriff's waiting buggy. She climbed into the back seat, where Marcia Hodson was waiting. It was there that Margaret finally broke down. She put both hands to her face and began to sob, her body shaking convulsively as she wept.

The sheriff took her away, traveling back along the road to Indianola. Left behind, the confused funeral crowd lingered for a few minutes and then prepared to leave for home. Some of them likely felt relief that a suspect was arrested and justice was being served. Others believed that Margaret could not possibly be guilty and that another person, someone still at large, had to be responsible for the crime. For those who believed that she had killed her husband - those who had listened to her horror stories of domestic violence and understood her fears - the moment of her arrest must have given them a pang of shared guilt.

It was nearly 8:30 p.m. when Sheriff Hodson and his passengers finally arrived in downtown Indianola. Aware of the public speculation already spreading about the case, the sheriff was relieved that the streets were calm. The presence of an accused murderer in custody - a woman, no less - was unusual enough to attract a lot of attention.

The county jail, located one block south of the courthouse, was a small annex to the sheriff's private residence, where Hodson lived with his wife and their young son, Paul. The jail wasn't used very often. Occasionally, federal prisoners were housed there for safekeeping, but the average number of Warren County residents jailed in a year's time was less than a dozen and most of those were for minor crimes.

Margaret Hossack became one of them. Hodson escorted her to her cell and asked his wife to check and see if she needed anything. She didn't. Instead, she would try to sleep and likely worry about the dark days that she was soon to face.

On Thursday morning, December 6, five men - Alex and Johnnie, the two oldest Hossack sons; Margaret's two son-in-laws, Ev Henry and Joe Kemp, and her brother, Donald Murchison - arrived in Indianola to hire an attorney. After tying their team to a hitching post on the southwest corner of the town square, they went into the Worth Savings Bank Building and to the suite of the Henderson and Berry law offices.

Senator William H. Berry and his partner, Judge John H. Henderson, had been in business together at various times for nearly thirty years. They were a force to be reckoned with in the community and the surrounding region, as successful in local politics as they were in the courtroom. Berry had served two terms as a state senator and Henderson, the son of the county's legendary founding father, Paris P. Henderson, had spent ten years as a district and circuit court judge.

It was Senator Berry who greeted the men. A towering, handsome man, Berry thrived in the public spotlight and was a powerful figure in the state Republican party. He had vast experience in legal practice, although he had only been involved in one previous murder trial, when he was hired by the county attorney to assist in prosecuting a murder case more than two decades before. Berry spoke to the men for two hours and eventually agreed to take the case. He was paid a $500 retainer and the family agreed that he would receive a $1,500 cash bonus if he was successful in achieving an acquittal.

By the time that Berry agreed to take the case, the murder and the ensuing investigation had already aroused strong feelings among the public. The crime was brutal and seemed premeditated and had been committed against a man with no chance to defend himself, one who was well-known in the community. Berry knew that the public would expect a swift resolution and a severe punishment and that the jury members who would decide his client's fate would be men who identified with John Hossack. Ample evidence existed to show that the couple had quarreled in the past, and marital conflicts were usually seen as a strong motive for one spouse to kill the other. On the other hand, no woman had ever before been charged with murder in the history of Warren County. There were strong feelings in that era about how women - members of the so-called "gentler sex' -- were supposed to behave and, right or wrong, Berry knew this would work in his favor. Potential jurors, men with grown daughters and wives at home, might be reluctant to believe that a woman could act with such malice and violence toward a sleeping man.

On the prosecution side, Coroner Dale and County Attorney Clammer were both young men. Neither was experienced in homicide investigations and people in the community wondered whether they were up to the task of the case. Many remembered that, years before in 1877, a man named Rueben Proctor had been accused of murdering a young woman. The county prosecutors had moved too slowly in doing their jobs and vigilante justice prevailed. A lynch mob grabbed the man as the sheriff was taking him to the courthouse and he was hanged from the wooden beam of a livestock scale. Now, all these years later, the county's citizens watched Dale and Clammer investigate the murder of John Hossack and wondered whether the legal process could be trusted this time. Some whispered that vigilantes were again prepared to punish the guilty party if the authorities were once again too slow.

On Friday, December 7, Deputy Kimer was sent back to the Hossack farm to look for additional evidence. Several of the Hossack children recognized him and came out to meet him. Kimer explained why he had come and mentioned that he was looking for one thing in particular: the blood-stained chemise that their mother had been wearing on the night of the attack. Johnnie, Cassie and Will offered to help in the search, and were soon joined by the very pregnant Louie. Later that same evening, she would give birth to her first child in the downstairs bedroom where her father died. The baby was named John after his murdered grandfather.

Kimer discovered the bloody mattress and sheets tossed in a heap in the yard. He searched an upstairs closet for Margaret's clothing. Downstairs, he looked in the couple's bedroom, but to no avail. Then, after several fruitless hours, he discovered the chemise. It was submerged under a few rags in a bucket of bloody water, on the ground under the Hossacks' bedroom window. Johnnie used a stick to pull the saturated garment from the pail.

Given its condition, the chemise now had no evidentiary value. In addition, Kimer found no other physical evidence that tied Margaret to the crime. Even so, Clammer and Dale would remain steadfast in their belief that she had committed the murder. Her story just didn't make sense, they insisted, and they were sure she was lying about what had occurred on the night of her husband's violent death.

However, many people were not so sure. The evidence of lies and half-truths that was cited by Clammer and Dale, which came from the inquest, was not as conclusive as they made it appear in the newspaper accounts after Margaret's arrest. Margaret's story of sleeping through the attack was difficult to believe, but it didn't necessarily prove that she was guilty of murder. The inquest jury heard the same evidence as Clammer and Dale, but had not charged her with murder. In one newspaper story, Dale explained the jury's decision by pointing out that the two jurors who refused to name her lived in the vicinity of her sons-in-law. They wouldn't want to "become embroiled in difficulties" with their neighbors. However, Dale didn't mention in that same story that *he* was the one who chose the jurors, believing the three men could be objective.

One could almost understand why the people of the region were concerned about how the wheels of justice might turn in Warren County.

On Saturday morning, Margaret was allowed to visit with her sons, Alex and Johnnie, but only in the presence of Deputy Kimer. They discussed farm business, notably the appointment of Fred Johnston as the administrator of John Hossack's estate. According to Kimer, they never talked about the murder.

That same afternoon, Senator Berry visited with his client for the first time, talking privately with her for more than an hour. When Berry left the jail, he was immediately questioned by waiting reporters. Their greatest interest was in the preliminary hearing, scheduled for Tuesday, when a judge would listen to the evidence against Margaret and decide if the case should go forward. Berry refused to divulge anything he had discussed with his client and ignored the speculation that the hearing would be waived, sending the case directly to the grand jury.

On Tuesday, December 11, several hundred people gathered in the streets around the courthouse, hoping to catch a glimpse of Margaret on her way into court. A little before 10:00 a.m., Sheriff Hodson, trying to protect his prisoner from the crowd, escorted her from the jail to the courthouse by way of a back alley, slipping into the office of Justice of the Peace H.M. Ross before the spectators realized what had happened.

With her children at her side, Margaret stood before the magistrate and listened as her attorneys stated that she wished to waive the preliminary hearing. Her lawyers expected the case would be heard by the grand jury at its next session, scheduled for January 8, 1901. Justice Ross refused to grant bail, but agreed to take the matter under advisement, promising a decision within a few days. The proceedings were over in a matter of minutes and Hodson, unable to avoid the avid crowd of onlookers this time, returned Margaret to the county jail.

A few days after the hearing, Justice Ross decided that Margaret could be released on bail. Unfortunately, it was not until a few days before Christmas that the family was able to raise the money. Thankfully, though, she would be able to spend the holidays at home with the family.

Between January 9 and January 17, the Warren County grand jury met behind closed doors. Clammer solicited testimony from more than fifty witnesses, including the Hossack children. Margaret was not required to give testimony and her attorneys were not allowed in the grand jury sessions.

On January 17, the grand jury returned an indictment against Margaret Hossack, charging her with murder in the first degree. Sheriff Hodson once again arrested her and she was taken back to the county jail, where she would remain until her trial.

On Monday morning, April 1, 1901, four months to the day after John Hossack was murdered in his bed, Margaret's trial began in district court with Judge James Gamble assigned to the case.

The day was dark and dreary, with rain expected, but a large crowd still formed in the town square more than an hour before the courthouse doors were opened at 8:30 a.m. Indianola residents walked from their homes, while horses and buggies brought farmers and their families from throughout the surrounding area. Farm work had been delayed by frequent storms in March, when snow, sleet and rain made labor in the fields impossible. It looked as though the weather in early April would follow suit.

When the doors opened, the crowd excitedly pushed into the courthouse and climbed the stairs to the second floor courtroom, quickly filling the rows of seats, anxious to get a glimpse of Margaret Hossack. Many who did not know her were curious about the mysterious woman who had spent months in the local jail. Knowing that she had been mistreated by her husband, there was great sympathy for her in some corners. For others, though, she was a character out of a horror story like one that might have been penned by Edgar Allan Poe - a woman so unspeakably evil and calculating that she had killed her sleeping husband with an axe. Now, the curiosity-seekers wanted to get a look and see if they could discern something about her for themselves.

To their disappointment, the defendant was not present, but her family was grouped near the defense table - all nine of her children, plus two sons-in-law and a half-dozen grandchildren.

Judge Gamble was seated in a high-backed chair at the front of the courtroom. He was dressed in judicial robes and wore a vest and a bow-tie. Sixty-four years old and white-haired, with dark eyes and a thick mustache, Gamble was a veteran of the Civil War, a devoted Freemason and a respected jurist with a stern demeanor. Although he had only been on the bench for four years, he was well-versed in the law, having previously served as Madison County Attorney.

Newspaper illustration of Margaret Hossack during the trial

Jury selection took a day and a half. One by one, the prospective jurors - male property owners over the age of twenty-one who were not acquainted with the principals in the case and who did not hold firm opinions about the outcome - were called to the witness box and questioned by the lawyers. As many feared, scores of them admitted that they'd already decided that the defendant was guilty - or, in a few cases, innocent - and so were excused from service. By late morning on Tuesday, April 2, a jury was finally impaneled. All of them were relatively prosperous and educated. Most were farmers, although one was a teamster and another, a brick mason. The eventual foreman, J.P.

Anderson, was a well-respected local merchant. Ten of the jurors were forty-five or older. Eight had been married for at least twenty years, and five of them had seven or more children.

In short, the men who had been selected to decide the fate of Margaret Hossack truly were a jury of her murdered husband's peers.

Shortly before noon on Tuesday, Margaret, escorted by one of the bailiffs, entered through a side door of the courtroom. Dressed in a high-necked black dress and matching gloves, her gray hair was pulled back in a tight bun and covered with a black hat tied under her chin. She walked to the defense table and took her seat, close to her children.

Judge Gamble called the court to order and asked the defendant to rise. Margaret stood with her lawyers and faced the bench. Behind her the gallery stirred anxiously. A row of white-haired farmers, friends and contemporaries of John Hossack, sat in a line at the front of the courtroom, bent forward and attentive. Gamble had a stern look on his face as the clerk rose and read the indictment, charging that Margaret Hossack had killer her husband with two deadly blows, "Unlawfully, feloniously, willfully, deliberately, premeditatedly, and of her malice aforethought." The defendant, the jury was told, had pleaded innocent to all charges. As the accused woman listened, her eyes filled with tears and her body shook with emotion.

When the clerk was finished, the judge nodded to the two attorneys for the state, George Clammer and Harry McNeil, a prominent Indianola lawyer who had been hired to assist the prosecution. Clammer, meticulously dressed in a suit and tie, rose to give his opening statement. His goal was to offer the jury a simple, chronological narrative of the crime and a framework for the evidence to come. Hatred was central to his tale - the passionate hatred of a wife who had been abused for thirty years until her emotions finally overwhelmed her one night and drove her to the brutal act of which she was accused.

To craft his story, Clammer used the words and recollections of his witnesses. One of the key witnesses, however, was absent from the trial. This was William Haines, a neighbor who had allegedly "gone insane brooding over the tragedy" and had been committed to an asylum at Chariton, Iowa, just nine days before the trial. The mental breakdown had occurred just a few days after Senator Berry had visited Haines to question him about the case. When Berry left, Haines had become distraught, saddling his horse and riding wildly from farm to farm. It had taken several of his neighbors to subdue him so that he could be transported to the asylum.

Clammer began by establishing the scene of the crime. He produced a large diagram of the Hossack house, the first of many physical props he would use in the trial, and put it on an easel at the front of the courtroom. Immediately, Berry was on his feet, arguing that the drawing was not to scale, but the judge overruled the objection when Clammer assured him that a uniform scale had been used for the entire diagram.

Clammer seemed confident as he continued, noting the many witnesses that he would call to testify about Margaret stating that she wanted her husband dead. He said that he would prove that her animosity continued right up to the night of the murder. Clammer declared that the testimony of the defendant's son, Jimmie, would show, "after the family had retired, father and mother were quarreling for some time..." It was a dramatic assertion and a statement that had not been reported in the press. The newspapers had reported that all nine of the Hossack children supported their mother and denied the tales of family arguments. Now, Clammer claimed that one of them told a different story.

The county attorney continued with his account of what happened on the night of the murder, providing the jury with a vivid narrative that he hoped they would not be able to forget. According to his story, the defendant plotted the murder of her husband while lying in bed next to him after their final argument, and then she crept out and retrieved the family's axe from the granary. She struck the sleeping man twice, first with the blade and then the blunt side, "crushing the bones of his skull deep into his brain." Walking across the sitting room, she carried the bloody axe, "holding her hand, or perhaps a rag, beneath the axe so that drops of blood would not stain her rug." She rinsed the murder weapon and put it away, but threw it underneath the granary instead of placing it inside. She was dismayed to find that Hossack was not yet dead when she returned to the bedroom. When he began to groan aloud, she decided on the lies that she would tell her children and then summoned them to their father's bedside.

The evidence was circumstantial, Clammer admitted, but it would prove beyond a reasonable doubt that the defendant was guilty of murder. The jury would see physical evidence to incriminate her, including photographs of the victim's body; the bed where the attack occurred, still covered with the bloody pillow and other bedclothes; and hair and blood samples taken from the family axe. Expert testimony would show that the axe was the murder weapon, a fact that would discredit the defendant's story about an intruder. Wouldn't an intruder have brought his own weapon to commit the murder? Author's note: This bit of faulty reasoning would be proven very wrong in 1911 and 1912 when a string of axe murders occurred in the Midwest, carried out by a killer who used the family axe to slay entire families. The most famous of the murders occurred in Villisca, Iowa, less than one hundred miles away from the Hossack farm. And then there was Shep, the family dog, who was strangely quiet on the night Hossack was killed. Wouldn't Shep have barked and alerted the family to the presence of a stranger?

The jury would hear from other experts: scientists and doctors who would show that the defendant was lying about other critical elements of her story - specifically, that she had been in bed when her husband was attacked and that she had called her children immediately after the attack. Medical testimony and physical exhibits, as well as simple common sense, would show that her claim was impossible to believe. But most significant of all, neighbors and even members of the Hossack family would testify to an irrefutable aspect of the case: Margaret Hossack hated her husband and wanted him dead.

Court adjourned for thirty minutes before William Berry addressed the jury on behalf of his client. Over the past few months, Berry had come to understand Margaret. She had lived for thirty-two years with a husband who was harsh and abusive to his family, prone to irrational rages and was, very possibly, mentally ill. But Berry would not tell that story in court. Those details of her life might generate support in the minds of some, but they were the same ones that the prosecutor would use to prove that she had a motive for murder.

So, Berry took a different tack. He focused on Margaret's character, describing her as a hard-working wife and mother who was devoted to her husband and children. Berry knew many of the older farmers in the room by name; some of them had been friends of his own father. They were among the original settlers of Warren County and were men who had known John Hossack and had done business with him. Speaking in a strong, clear voice, Berry told a straightforward story about the Hossacks, one that would resonate with the jurors because it was a story that most of them could have told about their own lives.

Margaret Murchison had been born in Scotland and came to America with her parents when she was a toddler. On her father's farm in Illinois, she met John Hossack, a man who had come to this country from Canada with nothing but "his hands, his head and good health." The two married and moved to Warren County, where John purchased land and built a home. They had struggled together, Berry said, to make a life for themselves, with John laboring on the farm and Margaret taking care of the home and raising a family.

Berry conceded to the jury that the couple had argued. Many neighbors would testify about that. And it was also true, Berry said, that Margaret had left home on one occasion after a quarrel with her husband during the Thanksgiving holiday of 1899. She was upset and she'd gone to her daughter's house. But Clammer was wrong when he claimed the ill feelings between the couple continued. As the jury would hear, Margaret had returned home the next day. She wanted to remain with her husband and the two of them had reconciled, agreeing to live together in peace. The reconciliation had been a great success and they had lived without conflict for an entire year before John was killed. Just days before the murder, the Hossack family had come together with friends and neighbors for Thanksgiving, with John and Margaret celebrating the restored condition of their marriage and their love for each other and their children.

By the middle of the afternoon, the sky outside the courtroom windows had darkened to a dull gray and a hard rain began to fall against the glass. The steady tapping of the rain provided a background for Berry's speech. When he came to the night of the murder, he offered the jury an alternative to the story that Clammer had told, raising his voice so that he could be heard over the storm.

Berry spoke: "You will hear from the defendant that she was awakened by a noise shortly after midnight on the night of the attack, and then, her children at her side, discovered her husband, wounded in bed. Throughout the long hours of the night, she stayed next to her husband and nursed him until he died the next morning."

Berry stood motionless before the jury box as he continued. The killing of John Hossack was an awful act, he said, and it was also a mysterious one. In order to convict the defendant of murder, the prosecution had to prove her guilt beyond a reasonable doubt, and that would not be possible.

The defense, he promised, would show that Margaret Hossack was an innocent woman.

Clammer called his first witness - Will Hossack. The large and awkward young man was not used to speaking in public and he stumbled his way through an hour of testimony. He said that he's used the axe on the day before Thanksgiving to kill the turkey for the holiday dinner, and on the night of the murder, he had told his brother Ivan to put the axe in the granary. He described being called by his mother in the middle of the night and seeing his wounded father after the attack, with a blood clot on the right side of his head that was "nearly as big as a tea cup." The area around his father's eye was blue and the eye itself was swollen shut.

Clammer then questioned Will about the history of the family's domestic troubles, but he was reluctant to answer. He said that he didn't recall much trouble in the past year. Clammer pressed him, asking how far back he remembered trouble in the family. At that point, Berry interrupted and objected to Clammer's questions. The troubles were too far in the past, he argued, and therefore irrelevant to the crime as charged. Given the ample evidence that the couple had reconciled after Thanksgiving 1899, the court should not allow the jury to hear testimony related to previous arguments. However, as he would throughout the trial, Judge Gamble overruled Berry's objection, allowing the jury to hear about past conflicts in the Hossack household. Whether they were relevant to the murder was a question the jury had to decide.

In spite of the judge's instructions to answer the questions, Will still shrugged off the seriousness of the arguments between his parents. The conflicts, he said, rose up occasionally and were over quickly. His parents would argue about something around the house or the farm, but, "then very soon it would be over as if nothing had ever happened. You would not know or notice that there had been any disagreement between them." A year earlier, according to Will, his parents had reconciled. The family had "agreed to let bygones be bygones and pay no attention to what had gone before."

Rinda Haines was the next witness to take the stand. Small and nervous, she was under great pressure from the prosecution. Her husband, William, had previously been identified as the "star" witness for the state, but now he was locked up in an asylum and she was expected to testify in his place. As Rinda Haines saw it - and as she told others - her husband's involvement in the case was against his will, and his inability to testify was the fault of the defense lawyer who had visited him, badgering him and triggering his breakdown. Although she was interrupted several times on the witness stand by Berry, who claimed that her stories were too old and not connected to the crime in question, Rinda answered Clammer's questions at length.

During her testimony, she spoke of being on very friendly terms with the Hossacks, visiting frequently with them. Two or three years before, Margaret had come to visit Rinda and William visibly upset and complaining that John had been causing trouble. Allegedly, Margaret suggested that William, along with a few other men, should come and straighten him out. The Haineses went to the Hossack house that night but nothing was said about the situation. John Hossack didn't talk to them at all, until they got ready to leave. Mrs. Haines added, "She once told me about them quarreling, and he hit her and she stepped out of the glass door, and she pulled the door to and broke the glass out. She told that he throwed stove lids and hit her on the foot and knocked her toenail off."

The next witness was Dr. Dean, the physician who had attended to Hossack in the last hours of his life. After Dean was seated in the witness box, Clammer approached him and handed him a model of a human skull. The doctor used the skull to point out the location of Hossack's wounds. He explained that he had found the victim unconscious when he arrived at the house, with a thready pulse, shallow and irregular breathing, and covered with cold, clammy sweat. He noted, "He was not conscious any of the time after I got there. He articulated a few words, but he held no conversation."

Clammer asked for a medical opinion about whether or not it was possible that Hossack could have spoken at any time after the attack? Dean couldn't tell him that, claiming there was no "hard and fast rule." There was also no way, he said in reply to another question, that he could know how much time elapsed between the attack and his examination.

When it was Berry's turn to question the physician, he asked Dean about the appearance of Hossack's wounds. Will thought he had seen a large blood clot on his father's head. Had Dean seen such a clot? No, Dean responded, he was quite sure that no solid clots had formed by the time he examined Hossack at 4:30 a.m., and certainly not a clot the size of a teacup. He had seen an enlarged place on the victim's head, just as Will had, but it had been a tangle of brain matter that was oozing out of the wound, mixed with blood and hair.

Berry asked about Hossack's brain injuries. Wasn't it possible that the wounded man could speak soon after the injury? Dean agreed it was possible that Hossack spoke after the attack, although that ability would have declined over time due to bleeding and pressure on the brain. In other words, it was likely that Hossack could have spoken soon after the injury.

During a break in the testimony, Berry spoke to reporters, saying that he regarded the testimony of Dr. Dean - a prosecution witness - to be of enormous value for the defense.

On Wednesday morning, Clammer called thirteen-year-old Ivan Hossack to the stand to tell his story about putting the axe away in the granary on Saturday night. He confirmed that he had done so. Under Berry's cross-examination, Ivan remembered that the evening before the murder had been a peaceful one. He talked about the laughter in the house and the games that he'd played with his father and brother. He stated, "I saw no indication of any disturbance or quarrelling between father and mother that evening. He and ma were playing with the children. I heard no trouble after I went to bed."

Regardless of this testimony, Clammer continued to pound away at the theme of family troubles, calling a procession of Hossacks to the stand, Cassie, May, Annie and Annie's husband, Ev, were forced into the witness stand and answered questions about the history of the battles between their parents. Like Will, they acknowledged there had been conflicts in earlier years, but they claimed that the arguments had ceased after Thanksgiving 1899. With the involvement of his friends and neighbors, they claimed, John Hossack was apparently embarrassed into keeping his temper under control and the bickering came to an end.

Each time that he cross-examined one of the Hossacks, Berry stressed the contrast between the two Thanksgivings - in 1899 and 1900 - and how much better the most recent one had been. At times, when addressing the Hossack children, Berry grew expansive in his questions, often mixing anecdotal details into his inquiries, then requesting the witness to simply affirm that his descriptions of the John and Margaret's reconciliation and the subsequent harmonious holiday dinner were accurate. Clammer objected strenuously to Berry's methods, claiming that the defense attorney was acting as a witness. His objections had little effect on how Berry conducted himself. As one newspaper articles stated, "This did not embarrass the big senator, however, and he proceeded to regale the judge and jury with Thanksgiving dinner stories until all that has ever been said on Thanksgiving dinners had been exhausted."

The next witness, Coroner Harry Dale, had publicly declared that he believed that Margaret Hossack was guilty of murdering her husband. When he was called to the stand as the final witness on Wednesday afternoon, he seemed eager to support the prosecution's case. He responded to all of Clammer's questions with assurance and great conviction.

After initial questions about Hossack's wounds, Clammer asked Dale for a medical opinion regarding Will's claim that his father's eye was swollen and bluish in color. How much time, in Dale's opinion, would have elapsed before this condition would occur?

Dr. Dale replied with certainty, "At least a quarter of an hour."

Clammer knew how the coroner would respond to the next question. The county attorney's voice was excited when he asked it: "Where a man is found suffering from two such wounds as you describe; where there is a clot of blood as large as a teacup and as thick as your hand; where the blood has ceased flowing; where the eye is discolored and swollen, and where the man when found asks and answers questions, what would you estimate as the length of time that had elapsed since the blow was struck?"

The courtroom was silent and still as Dale responded to the question in a theatrical manner. He paused, seeming to ponder the response that he and the prosecutor had already agreed upon. Then he turned and looked directly at Margaret Hossack as he spoke: "I should think that as least half an hour must have elapsed."

A smile of satisfaction creased Clammer's face as he sat down at the prosecution table. The implication of Dale's opinion - that the defendant was lying in her claim that she called to her children immediately - caused a stir in the courtroom. Reporters frantically scribbled in their notebooks and spectators excitedly whispered to one another.

At the defense table, Senator Berry leaned over to his co-counsel. The two men put their heads together and conferred quickly and quietly. A few moments later, John Henderson rose to conduct Dale's cross-examination. The tall, thin attorney with his long, waxed mustache that fashionably turned up on each end, walked up to the witness stand. He stood there for a moment in front of Dale, his hands in his pockets, staring almost defiantly at the coroner.

Henderson's plan was to show that Dale's conclusion, particularly about the length of time after the attack before the victim could have spoken, was nothing more than an educated guess. Had Dale ever treated a patient who had the same head injuries as John Hossack? No, Dale admitted, he had not treated anyone with those wounds. Then Dale's knowledge of the shock suffered by Hossack must be based on his reading, Henderson surmised, more than from his experience? Yes, Dale admitted that this was the case. But could he then tell the jury anything that was conclusive? No, Dale was again forced to admit, only a physician who was there with the patient could say with certainty when he returned to consciousness. Wasn't it true, then, that Dale was only guessing when he answered the hypothetical question that the prosecutor had put to him? Dale was unable to deny that this was the case.

Henderson then brought up another case, in which a man had suffered a perforation of the brain, when his head was pierced completely through by a large, thirteen-pound iron bar. The man, Phineas P. Gage, was a railroad construction foreman who, in 1848, had been working on the construction of the Rutland & Burlington Railroad, outside Cavendish, Vermont. An explosion sent the bar through his head. Unbelievably, the victim never lost consciousness. Although his personality changed temporarily, he soon recovered from the accident and lived for another twelve years without losing his mental capacities.

Henderson asked the doctor how Gage's case could be explained. Dale stated that it was an exceptional case, as were others where victims suffered severe injuries to the brain without the loss of their senses. Henderson asked, wasn't it possible that the same could be true of John Hossack - that his could be another exceptional case, in which the victim remained conscious after experiencing a severe brain injury? It was possible, Dale grudgingly conceded.

Henderson ended his cross-examination of the doctor with two last questions.

He asked, "Isn't it a fact that as a result of all this you are compelled to say to this jury that you don't know anything about when he could have recovered consciousness, whether he ever did, how long it would be, or anything about it, as a fact?"

"I would not make any definite statement as to the fact," Dale replied.

"It might have been early or late, or between times, or any other, isn't that true?"

"Yes," Dale said quietly, humiliated by the clever attorney.

It was another good day for the defense team in the Indianola courtroom. Predictions about the outcome of the case swung back and forth, and the relevance of key testimony was debated all over the area. Front-page newspaper stories were printed daily and thousands of readers in the region around Des Moines, who could not attend the trial in person, were kept updated on every change in fortunes for the prosecution and the defense. By midweek, the trial could realistically be compared to the ebb and flow of a boxing match.

On Thursday morning, Clammer turned to a subject that had generated intense speculation in the community since the murder: the blood and hair that had been found on the axe.

The public knew that the reports from the men who'd found the possible murder weapon differed. Had both the blade and the handle been covered with fresh blood and hair, or were there only a few spots of old blood on the handle and a few hairs stuck to the blade? Of course, most knew that the presence of blood and hairs didn't necessarily establish the axe as the murder weapon, especially given Will's testimony that he used it to kill a turkey only a couple of days before. But experts had analyzed the blood and hairs to determine if they were human or animal and those conclusions were eagerly anticipated.

Dr. John L. Tilton of Simpson College took the stand to reveal what he had discovered. In reply to Clammer's questions, Tilton gave a long and tedious account, detailing the difficulties of his analysis. It came down to the fact that he found no satisfactory evidence of human blood. Some of the blood had come from a fowl; Tilton was certain about that. The conclusion was, of course, consistent with Will's testimony about killing a turkey for Thanksgiving dinner, but it established nothing at all about the use of the axe for any other purpose.

Tilton had also studied the hairs from the axe. In great detail, he described his analysis. The first two had characteristics common to dog hair and human hair, while the third was "unlike that of any dog whose hair I have been able to examine," justifying his conclusion that "that hair was probably from a human being." Given that all three hairs were said to come from one source, Tilton said, it's likely that all three were from the same source.

Clammer asked him if the hairs that had been taken from John Hossack's head matched the hairs on the axe? Tilton conceded that they could have come from the same head.

One day in mid-December, Sheriff Hodson and George Moore, the undertaker, had dug up Hossack's coffin in the New Virginia Cemetery. Moore had used scissors to snip off a few strands of the dead man's hair. The hairs were, as Hodson later testified, as "near to the area of the wound" on the right side of Hossack's head as they could get. The evidence was placed in a small vial, and less than a week later, Hodson and Clammer had taken the sample to Professor Tilton for examination.

In Senator Berry's mind, the hairs on the axe were an important issue. He knew that Clammer would rely heavily on them to establish that the Hossacks' axe was the murder weapon, especially given the lack of definitive evidence regarding the blood on the axe. It was important for the defense to challenge Tilton's "conclusions" on several grounds, which Berry began to do with his cross-examination. He focused on the certainty of the professor's opinions. Under Berry's questioning, Tilton admitted that his conclusion that the human hair came from the same individual was little more than a guess. It was practically impossible, he said, for a scientist Tilton was a geologist, by the way, whose specialty was rocks and minerals to take a few hairs of unknown origin, compare them with hairs from a particular man and then to conclude without a doubt that the hairs were from the same individual. The most that the scientist could say was that they resembled one another. He thought the hairs in this case did, although hairs from two different individuals could also bear a resemblance.

Tilton's lack of certainty was a gift for the defense, but Berry had another, more important goal in mind: he wanted a ruling that the testimony about the hairs should be entirely disregarded by the jury. The challenge was a procedural one, based on the requirement that physical evidence could be admitted in a trial only after its chain of custody had been established. In this situation, the prosecution had to prove that the hairs introduced in the courtroom were the identical ones that the sheriff had removed from the axe, and Berry did not believe the state could do that. Berry also knew that Clammer would be especially sensitive to this challenge, since it directly implicated the conduct of the county attorney during the murder investigation.

When he began his cross-examination of the next witness - Sheriff Hodson - Berry raised the issue. With Hodson on the stand, Clammer took him through his story of obtaining and transferring the evidence. On the morning after the murder, he said, he'd taken the three hairs from the axe and placed them in his pocketbook. Some days later, he went to Clammer's office and the hairs were put in a vial. After that, he had helped with the exhumation of Hossack's body, placed hairs collected from the dead man in another vial and eventually, delivered both vials to Professor Tilton for analysis.

When it was his turn with the witness, Berry wanted to know more of the details. Exactly how long had the hairs from the axe been in the sheriff's pocketbook? Hodson thought it was a week or ten days, but he couldn't be certain. Who had placed the hairs in the first vial? Hodson didn't know, but thought it might have been Clammer or Dr. Dale. Clammer had kept the first vial in his possession until five or six days later. After that, Hodson and Clammer had gone to Tilton's office. Hodson have given him the vial of hairs from the body and Clammer had given him the other vial. But did Hodson know for sure that the hairs in the vial that Clammer gave to Tilton were the same ones he had taken off the axe? No, Hodson said, that would be impossible for him to say. He knew nothing for sure about what had happened to the hairs after they had been removed from his pocketbook and given to Clammer.

Berry latched onto Hodson's response. Immediately after Margaret had been arrested, the county attorney had publicly gone on record as saying he was convinced of her guilt - at the very time that he had in his private possession the hairs from Hodson's pocketbook. Unless Clammer was willing to testify under oath, which Berry knew was extremely unlikely, how could the jury be sure that the hairs examined by Professor Tilton were, in fact, the ones Hodson had taken from the axe? Establishing a chain of custody was an essential precondition of introducing any physical object into evidence. If the hairs were then inadmissible, it seemed obvious that Tilton's testimony, based on those hairs, should be disregarded as well. Without the hair, the only thing to tie the axe to the murder was the blood, and that had been inconclusive too. In Berry's mind, he had scored an important victory for the defense. He made a motion to withdraw the hairs from the jury's consideration. Judge Gamble agreed and sustained the motion. The hairs from the axe could not be shown to the jury.

Berry then made a second motion: If the hairs themselves were not proper evidence, he argued, then the expert analysis of them must also be inadmissible. But Judge Gamble ruled against him and allowed Tilton's testimony, which had occurred before Berry challenged the admissibility of the hairs, could stand. The jury would be allowed to consider his conclusions, such as they were. Berry silently noted that if the jury convicted his client, Gamble's ruling would definitely be grounds for an appeal.

Jimmie Hossack was called to the stand later that day. He took his seat on the witness stand, but before Clammer started his questioning, the young man looked directly at his mother. She sat quietly in front of him, her eyes fastened on her son. Jimmie put his hands on the armrests of his chair, as though bracing himself for what was to come.

Clammer started the questioning by asking Jimmie about the night of the murder, specifically where he slept and when he went to sleep. Jimmie said that he knew his parents were still in the sitting room when he went to bed between 7:00 and 8:00 p.m. Clammer paused then, before asking the significant question: "Did you hear them quarrelling for about an hour after you had gone to bed?"

Jimmie stared hard at the county attorney. In a firm voice, he replied, "No."

Clammer seemed jolted by Jimmie's answer. He turned quickly to the prosecution table and snatched up a small stack of papers. He shook them in the boy's direction. "Didn't you swear before the grand jury that you had heard them quarrelling before they went to bed?" he sputtered.

Jimmie looked at his mother and then down at the floor. "Yes."

Clammer flipped through the papers and thrust one at Jimmie. "For the purposes of refreshing your memory, I will ask you to read these lines from your testimony before the grand jury." Jimmie's hands were visibly shaking as he took the paper and looked down at it. He handed it back to Clammer.

The county attorney read the paper aloud: "'I heard Ma and Pa quarrelling after I had gone to bed. I did not hear what they said. He was blaming her for something. On Thursday evening, they had also been quarrelling for about an hour.'" Clammer paused and then turned to Jimmie again. He asked him, "Did you not also testify that he was blaming her for something and that she said he was almost driving her crazy?"

"Yes, I did," Jimmie replied in a low voice.

Clammer's face was stern as he looked at the boy. "And you said, too, before the grand jury, did you not, that you did not pay much attention to them, as it was a common thing for them to have quarrels?"

"Yes, I said that then. You got me to say it." Jimmie was now choking back sobs and by this time, one of the reporters in the courtroom wrote that his face had a look of agony on it, "like that of a hunted animal."

"Do you not so testify now?" Clammer demanded.

"No, I do not!"

Berry stood and objected to Clammer's examination of Jimmie. The prosecutor was cross-examining his own witness, he said, asking leading questions that should not be allowed. And Clammer should not be allowed to read testimony from the grand jury hearing once Jimmy denied it was the truth. Judge Gamble overruled the objections, stating that Clammer could continue.

But Clammer was unable to sway Jimmie from his current testimony. Several more times, he read aloud from Jimmie's prior statements and each time, Jimmie claimed they were false. Clammer had scared him, he said, and made him say things that weren't right. He hadn't heard his parents arguing. In fact, he hadn't heard anything from them after he went to bed. Yes, he said over and over, he had testified differently before, but he would not say those things now. By the time that Clammer finally sat down, Jimmie was crying openly.

Berry rose for his cross-examination. His large frame hid Jimmie from the rest of the courtroom, but it was obvious that the young man was still crying, gulping for breath and trying to calm down. When Berry spoke, his voice was kind and gentle. "Do you remember how many times they called you in and out of the jury room"?

"No sir," Jimmie answered, "but it was a great many. They would send me out and then after a while send for me again."

"Now, while you were being examined at one of those times before the grand jury, Jimmie, Mr. Clammer told you, did he not, that if you didn't change your testimony and testify differently from what you did before the coroner's jury, and tell all you knew about this, you would be prosecuted?"

"Yes, sir."

"And that you would be put under arrest?"

"Yes, sir."

"Now, Jimmie, I will ask you if you were alarmed and scared by this statement of the County Attorney?"

"Yes, sir."

The courtroom was silent as Jimmie was excused and went back to his set. The damage from his recantation had been done. When court reconvened a few minutes later, Judge Gamble ordered that all of the testimony that Jimmie had given in regards to his grand jury testimony was to be stricken from the record. He had recanted those statements and they could not be used in the trial. Reporters on hand in the courtroom that day were skeptical about the idea that Jimmie was now telling the truth. Most of them saw it as a ruse to cover for his mother, but was it? The fact was, none of the other children in the house that night, including Ivan, who was sleeping next to Jimmie, claimed to hear John and Margaret Hossack arguing. Perhaps, if Jimmie had told the truth to the grand jury, the voices of his parents had not been loud, or the discussion had been short and ended amicably before the couple went to bed. Or, perhaps Jimmie was telling the truth. Perhaps Clammer, the ambitious county attorney who had believed in Margaret's guilt from the start, really had bullied the boy into giving false statements.

Jimmie's actions in court were another blow to the prosecution, but this did not stop Clammer from continuing to hammer away at the stories of the Hossack family troubles. On Thursday afternoon, he brought more neighbors to the stand, including Neil Morrison, Will Conrad, Nora Cart and Eleanor Keller. All of them told the jury about their conversations with Margaret Hossack over the years, during which she alleged abuses by her husband. Berry jumped to his feet many times, objecting to the line of inquiry. The information that Clammer was seeking, Berry argued, was immaterial, unconnected to the offense charged, and too old to be relevant. Judge Gamble overruled his objections every time.

Eleanor Keller told the same stories that the others did: that Margaret said her husband was "very dangerous to my family" and "kind of crazy." She had "no peace and... wished he was dead." But Keller's testimony was especially significant because she had also talked to Margaret in January 1900, after the reconciliation was arranged at the prior Thanksgiving. She was still telling tales of woe, even after the troubles had supposedly come to an end, Mrs. Keller claimed. She even quoted Margaret as saying, "it ain't any better than it always was." She added that Margaret said that she still wished that her husband was dead.

On cross-examination, Berry asked whether Mrs. Keller thought the woman was having a "pretty bad time."

Mrs. Keller responded, "Yes, I did. I used to feel it when first she told me more than afterwards... I don't know what came over me. I didn't somehow ---"

We'll never know what Eleanor Keller was going to say next. Was she about to mention her sense of guilt about not helping Margaret, a woman whom she knew to be in a dangerous and unstable situation? Before she could finish her sentence, Clammer was on his feet, objecting. The witness was unresponsive. She wasn't answering the question she had been asked.

Judge Gamble agreed with Clammer and addressed the witness directly, telling her that she could only testify about the conversation between herself and Margaret Hossack, not what she thought. Mrs. Keller's testimony came to an end, leaving her thoughts unspoken.

On Friday, Good Friday before the Easter holiday, Margaret sat impassively at the defense table with her granddaughter, Ethel May Henry, cuddled in her arms. The toddler was three years old, a quiet little girl with curly hair and large, innocent eyes. To some in the courtroom, one of the many points of Berry's argument seemed obvious: that this kindly grandmother, showing so much affection to the child on her lap and with her loving and supportive children around her, could not have possibly committed the terrible murder of which she was accused.

Unfortunately, many people still didn't see it that way. Despite the setbacks suffered by the prosecution when it came to Dr. Tilton's evidence and Jimmie's recantation, the newspapers believed that Clammer was slowly drawing a noose of circumstantial evidence around Margaret's neck. Even those reporters who were sympathetic to her plight felt the case was going badly for her.

That afternoon, the county attorney called Frank Keller, neighbor and longtime friend of the Hossacks, to the stand. He was the final witness for the prosecution. After shifting around in his seat until his was comfortable, the tall, lanky man began a rambling account of his arrival at the Hossack house on Sunday morning, just before John died. As he spoke, he turned toward the jury, gesturing with his hands for added emphasis. Keller repeated the story that Margaret had told him about what had happened and it was consistent with the others. But Keller had new information to reveal: that after the murder, Margaret knew where the axe could be found. He'd asked her where it was and she'd answered, without hesitating, that it was under the granary. And she was right, of course. Keller and some other men found it exactly where she said it would be.

When Clammer encouraged Keller to tell what he knew about the family's domestic problems, he gave the court a lengthy account. Senator Berry, as usual, objected to the line of questioning but Judge Gamble again allowed the witness to testify about the conversations that he had with Margaret about her husband. On many occasions, Keller said, she had talked to him about her husband's erratic behavior, and she'd told him that John had threatened to kill the family. Another time, Keller had offered to accompany Margaret home and have a talk with John, but she'd refused. She was afraid of what John might do if he knew she was talking about family matters with the neighbors. Instead, she suggested that Keller and several friends should come one night and beat him near to death for abusing his family. When Keller refused, Margaret seemed to know that would be his reply. She couldn't live with him, she sighed, and wished to God he was dead. As she turned to go home, she cried out, "Oh, why is it that the good Lord won't remove him out of our way?"

Keller's story was eerily similar to the one told by Rinda Haines on the first day of the trial. Was his memory clear on this point? Or was he mixing up past conversations with testimony he knew Mrs. Haines had already given? At the coroner's inquest, Keller had never said anything about being asked to beat up his friend and neighbor.

It was hard for Keller to answer Clammer's questions without digressing, adding his own opinions and theories about the case. Keller's garrulous responses provided entertainment for the spectators but frustrated the judge. After one lengthy diatribe, the judge quickly silenced him and admonished him to respond only to specific questions.

Eventually, Clammer was able to steer Keller towards Thanksgiving Day 1899. Keller's memory was consistent with the story of Fred Johnston, who had testified earlier, except for one thing: Keller remembered that Hossack had referred to a secret between himself and his wife. As Keller recalled, Hossack said, "I want you to understand that there is a hidden secret in this family that nobody by me and Maggie and God knows anything about. When I die, I will die with this secret in my breast." Keller went on to say that he never learned what this tantalizing secret was. It was something, he believed, known only to the murdered man and his wife.

With her grandchild cradled in her arms, Margaret Hossack became visibly unnerved by Keller's words.

Henderson conducted the cross-examination for the defense. Keller's willingness to talk was evidence and Henderson soon had him discussing his relationship with the dead man: how they met, how they became friends, their participation in various social and political activities and so on. During his testimony, Keller admitted that John Hossack was sometimes emotionally and mentally unstable and "subject to tantrums and spells." Mrs. Hossack frequently asked him and other friends to come to the house "for the purpose of cheering him up." On only one occasion, Keller admitted, had Margaret suggested to him that the neighbors should consider beating John Hossack so that he would "quit abusing his family."

Just before he ended the cross-examination, Henderson asked Keller what he and Johnston had told the Hossack family at the time of the reconciliation. Keller replied, "We suggested that from that time forth, they should tell no man or woman, nor tell any person, about their troubles, were not to talk about it among themselves, were not to refer to it, if possible, to forget it. He and they all agreed to it."

It was a plan, which pretty much everyone could agree, had ended in disaster.

Keller left the stand, and at the end of that Friday afternoon, the prosecution rested its case.

On Saturday morning, Senator Berry walked to the courthouse with serious issues on his mind. For the defense to succeed, he had to convince the jury that it was at least possible that an intruder had committed the murder. But if a stranger had entered the house and killed John Hossack, why hadn't Shep barked and alerted the family? Berry planned to argue that the dog had been drugged, and he planned to call witnesses to support this idea.

But there were several other obstacles standing in the way of an acquittal. Clammer's version of events was winning over the jury because no other suspects had been named and no motive was suggested except for a wife's hatred over the abuses that she had suffered. The defense wasn't obligated to prove that another person was guilty, but it would certainly help the case if the jury could at least imagine an alternative to the prosecution's story. William Haines was an obvious choice. The man was certainly crazy and he wasn't there to defend himself. Berry planned to bring his name to the jury's attention in his closing argument.

The prosecutor's arguments were also effective because they appealed to common sense. How could the defendant have been in bed when the blows were struck and not woke up? How could she have not been hit by the axe? These aspects of her story were hard to believe and the defense would have to depend heavily on Margaret's performance on the witness stand. She had to persuade the jury that she was telling the truth.

The prosecutor's evidence of motive was the most damaging to Margaret. The jurors were not apt to forget the testimony that Margaret had said on frequent occasions that she feared her husband and wished that he was dead. The defense could only argue that her feelings had changed since she had said those things, stressing the reconciliation and relying on the testimony of the children. Their honesty, though, was in question, since they were obviously trying to save their mother's life. But, now that Jimmie had changed his story, they were at least all telling the same story. Perhaps the strong show of emotional support by all her children would have some effect in swaying the jurors in Mrs. Hossack's favor.

Berry was still trying to formulate his plan when he arrived at the courthouse. A crowd of spectators were waiting outside, hoping to find a seat in the gallery once the doors were opened for the day's proceedings. A few well-wishers and colleagues greeted Berry as the crowd parted to let him into the building. He nodded curtly, his face tight, and he made his way inside. It was time for him to go to work.

Berry opened the defense by calling an expert witness to the stand named Dr. T.S. Parr, a physician who had been practicing in Indianola for thirty-two years. Dr. Parr gave his opinion in great technical detail, but his conclusion was relatively simple: If Hossack had spoken at all, it was likely that he had done so very soon after his injury. It was basically what Berry had gotten the prosecution's experts to concede to already.

Next, Berry turned to evidence about Shep, presenting witnesses who described the dog's behavior on Sunday morning, claiming that he was not acting like his usual self. William Anderson, a schoolteacher who had boarded with the Hossacks for a time and had taken Shep hunting, noticed that the dog was behaving strangely, as did Will and Johnnie Hossack and Margaret's brother, Donald Murchison. All of them remembered that the dog was acting stiff and unnatural and was certainly not his normal self.

Berry did not expect Murchison to be his strongest witness about the dog. He merely used him because of his law enforcement background. Murchison had not visited the Hossacks in more than twenty years and had never seen Shep before. He only knew that he behaved as if he were drugged. Murchison was on the stand to speak about the early married life of John and Margaret Hossack. He bolstered the story that Berry told in his opening statement, about the young man working on the Murchison family farm, marrying his employer's daughter, and moving with her to newly purchased land in Iowa.

In was in this context that Berry asked a simple question, one to which he thought he knew the response: "When was the defendant, Margaret Hossack, married?"

Murchison hesitated before he answered. "I am not quite positive; I think it was in the fall of 1868."

Berry didn't acknowledge anything odd about Murchison's response, although he knew the Hossacks claimed that they were married in the fall of 1867. Murchison added that the couple had moved to Iowa in the spring of 1868, after they were married. Berry either didn't notice the inconsistency, or didn't think it was worth pointing out. In any case, the sword statement by the defendant's brother - that the Hossacks were married in the fall of 1868 - went uncorrected and became a part of the official transcript.

Clammer, however, noted the marriage date stated by the defendant's brother. Only moments later, when Alex Hossack was on the stand, Clammer asked his birthdate and Alex responded that he had turned thirty-two in August 1900. Clammer did the math. This meant the oldest Hossack child had been born in August 1868. Clammer believed that the secret shared by John and Margaret Hossack had just been revealed: their first child had been born out of wedlock. It was something that the prosecution could use to its advantage.

Although unaware of Clammer's thinking, Berry addressed the issue of the alleged secret between the Hossacks on Saturday morning with his final three witnesses. According to Frank Keller, Hossack had told him that he and his wife had a secret, and, as Keller repeated Hossack's comment, it seemed there was something more between the couple than just domestic quarrels, something bigger and perhaps stranger - perhaps a secret that warranted murder. But Berry hoped to dismiss that idea and replace it with another, impressing on the jury that Hossack only meant that his troubles were a private matter and that he didn't want others to know about the problems with his wife and family. Berry had witnesses who would testify to that effect.

Berry produced three witnesses in quick succession who said that they had overheard the conversation between Keller and Hossack, although they had not heard it as Keller remembered it. Louie Kemp had heard her father say that his troubles were a secret he would carry with him to the grave, but nothing about a secret known only to himself and his wife. Cassie Hossack confirmed her sister's recollection, and so did Fred Johnston, who had also been present. He added, "There was nothing said by Mr. Hossack about there being any secret known between him and Maggie and their God and that it would die with him. No mention of Maggie in connection with any particular secret at all."

At noon that day, Judge Gamble adjourned the trial for the remainder of the holiday weekend, reminding everyone that court would be back in session on Monday morning.

Margaret Hossack spent a lonely Easter Sunday in her cell at the county jail, although her day was brightened by visits from her children and grandchildren and by a bundle of lilies that May brought to add some cheer to her grim surroundings.

Throughout the months leading up to the trial, Berry had refused to say whether or not the defendant would take the stand, but, of course, rumors swirled about the possibility. Even so, it was a dramatic moment on Monday morning when Berry called Margaret Hossack as the final witness for the defense. In the crowded courtroom, spectators whispered to one another and craned their necks to get a glimpse of her as she made her way to the witness stand.

It seemed as though Margaret had aged several years over the course of the trial. The weathered features of her face sagged and her steel gray hair seemed to have whitened. For exactly one week now, she had sat erect and composed at the defense table, her hands usually clenched in her lap. On most days, she had a shawl draped over her shoulders and sometimes clutched a black handkerchief. Her sharp, blue eyes stared straight ahead and she never acknowledged the crowd behind in the spectator's gallery. When her name was called, she walked deliberately to the witness stand.

The defense attorneys knew that Margaret's appearance on the witness stand would be memorable for the jurors. They had seen her sitting in the courtroom, and they had watched her crying as her children testified, but they had not heard her speak. They still needed to be convinced that she was the woman that the defense claimed she was: a hard-working farmwife and mother, committed to her husband and children and incapable of committing the violent act of which she was accused.

Berry wanted the jury to relive the night of the murder from Margaret's point of view. He wanted her to present it in a simple, chronological narrative. He would not ask her about her relationship with her husband, either about their conflicts over the years or about their reconciliation. At the inquest, she had denied that she and her husband had any serious problems, and now, in the face of sworn statements to the contrary from so many neighbors, such testimony could only damage her credibility.

Speaking in a low, firm voice, Margaret answered questions without faltering or contradicting herself. Several times during her two hours on the stand, she began crying and had to stop speaking until she could regain her composure.

When asked about the night of the murder, she described preparing supper for her husband and Ivan when they returned from the coal bank, milking the cows with May, patching and darning while her husband played with the boys and then read the newspapers. Later, she rolled butter in the pantry. Several times she heard the dog barking outside, as if something disturbed him. At one point, she went out on the porch to see what was going on and didn't notice anything strange.

She'd talked with her husband that night, she said, about the work to be done on the farm. He wanted to butcher one of the hogs and build a new platform on the wells, and they'd discussed the boys going back to school. As she remembered their last conversation, her voice became shaky and tears filled her eyes. He'd told her, she said, that he felt better that night than he had in the morning and he was looking forward to going to church the next day.

Berry waited several minutes for Margaret to pull herself together. Once she did, she recounted what had happened after she went to sleep, telling the same story that she had told several times before. She had been awakened by a noise and got out of bed. Outside the bedroom door, she heard sounds from her husband and she thought that he had also been disturbed by the noise. But then she saw a light and heard the door to the outside shut. She ran to the door and found that it was not fully shut. It was then that she called her children, saying that she thought there had been someone in the house. She also called to her husband several times, but he didn't answer, and, hearing that he was breathing hard and choking, realized that he might be hurt. When he children came downstairs, she lit a lamp and followed Will into the bedroom, where they found John Hossack mortally wounded.

Margaret said that her husband first asked why Ivan was crying and then claimed that he was not hurt, only sick. He called for her and later, for Will and Johnnie. As she recalled her husband speaking the names of their sons, she began to cry again. She paused with her head bowed, sobbing and gasping to try and catch her breath. The courtroom was very still as people listened to the sound of her weeping and waited for her to regain her composure once more.

Finally, Berry asked her a series of pointed questions. Margaret never hesitated before answering each of them. He walked her through a series of denials. She did not strike her husband, she did not know who did, she knew nothing more than the sounds that awakened her, she didn't see anyone in the house that night except for her husband and children and she did not handle the axe or any other sharp or blunt instrument. When he was finished, Berry concluded his examination and stated that he had no more questions for her.

Harry McNeill rose from the prosecution table to conduct the cross-examination. For more than an hour, he took Margaret through her story again and again. He asked her to repeat much of what she's said in response to Berry's questions, challenging her memory several times and requesting more details. Margaret responded calmly, speaking in a low tone and without appeared to be upset or confused. She only contradicted herself one time, but it was on a point that seemed insignificant: at what time she had gone into the pantry to prepare the butter?

On a more critical issue, McNeill asked several questions about her testimony that she had heard the dog barking. Did she really hear him barking for an hour and a half? She told him that yes, this was her recollection.

Just as during the direct examination, the questions were limited to the hours surrounding the attack. The prosecutors hoped to challenge her story, but they weren't relying on her testimony to supply them with a motive. The neighbors had already given them everything they needed to do that.

Around noon, Margaret was finally allowed to step down from the witness stand. She nearly stumbled from exhaustion as she walked back to her chair. By all accounts, her appearance had been a success. Newspaper reporters agreed that, "there seemed to be the impression on the audience that she had told the truth."

Finally, on April 8, after all of the principals had made their appearances, the lawyers finally had the courtroom stage to themselves. That afternoon, a crowd formed on the courthouse lawn during the lunch recess. However, less than half of those waiting were admitted for the afternoon session. The seats were simply filled too quickly to let everyone inside. People stood three and four deep, pressing together to fill up all of the standing room. The dry facts had been presented and the testimony of the investigators, neighbors and family members had been heard. Now, the drama would truly begin.

Clammer was the first to address the jury. He spoke for four hours that afternoon, arguing the case with passionate conviction. He returned to the theme of hatred - an emotion that he stressed had been in the defendant's heart for years - and the images that he painted about what happened on the night of Hossack's murder were vivid and terrible.

He reminded the jury first about the proof of motive - that over a period of years, neighbors heard the defendant say that she feared her husband. She complained about him and sought to humiliate him with her stories. According to Clammer, she brooded for years about the idea that she would be better off without him and tried to get her neighbors to assault him. When this was refused, she decided to take care of him herself.

In dramatic fashion, Clammer recreated the events of the night of the attack, when the defendant changed from a typical farmwife into a wicked, evil killer. As he talked, he reminded the jurors of various pieces of evidence that were consistent with his version of the story.

The newspapers were happy to publish Clammer's script:

That night after they had gone to bed, she lay thinking it all over; how it would never be any better; how for years she had hated John Hossack. The man she despised was lying beside her in a deep sleep, she could hear his breathing; she wanted to stop it; she wished she could kill him. She thought herself into a passionate fire that night on December 1, when she said she was nervous and could not sleep and in a fit of desperation she got up. She walked about the sitting room; everybody else in the house was asleep. She lighted the lamp and by that time there was a demon in possession of her soul. With livid face she stood in the door of the sitting room and looked at John Hossack - how she hated him.

She had never been a loving wife, she had never been a woman of strong affections, and that night murder crept into her strange soul. She did the deed as a woman in such a moment of desperation and barbaric determination might be expected to do, crazily, clumsily with the family axe. She knew where the axe was, she had heard Ivan say in the evening that he was going to put it in the granary. She opened the door and walked out into the night. The good old family dog rose to greet her and she gave him a vicious cuff. She walked down to the granary with her heart full of hate. She did not stop to let herself think; she had but one purpose, for everyone was asleep and no one would ever know who struck him.

Clammer continued his rather breathless and melodramatic story, reveling in the details of what Margaret was thinking about and how she was feeling on that night. For good measure, he threw in the remark about how she was in such a bad mood that she hit the faithful family dog. Of course, there was no evidence of any of it, but there didn't have to be. Attorneys are allowed wide latitude in their closing arguments and Clammer was throwing in everything that he could think of, describing Margaret as being "crazed with her evil purpose" and plotting exactly how "she would kill him with one well-directed blow." Of course, since the killer struck Hossack twice, unable to kill him with just one blow, Clammer asked the men of the jury, "who but a woman would have done that?"

He went on to describe how Margaret had then cleaned off the ax and returned it to the granary. But, implying that she was an empty-headed female, she could not remember whether she got the axe from the granary or from under it. She then hurried back to the house, cleaned up the evidence of blood that had been left behind even though there was no evidence of anything being cleaned and when she heard her husband groaning, she gave the alarm, realizing he wasn't dead.

Clammer continued his story:

No human eye witnessed the killing of John Hossack. No man saw the light which flooded the sitting room and the bedroom where he lay. No man saw the stealthy figure creep to the side of the bed, no one saw the axe raised. No one saw the edge cleave his skull. No one saw the defendant step back a moment and set that axe upon a piece of carpet. No one saw that second blow, which crushed the head of John Hossack; no one saw the murderess walk stealthily from that house through the bedroom door across the sitting room door out across that porch; none saw the direction taken by the murderer.

And yet how are they going to explain it away? He was killed, and by what argument can you say he was killed in any other way? Will you kindly tell me how a stranger would know where to find the family axe? Would he use an axe at all; would he not bring his own instrument? The blood spots show that was axe was carried to the granary after the deed was done. The granary is one hundred and twenty feet from the house. A murderer slipping away in the dead of night would have never gone there. He would have taken the shortest road to get away.

The accuracy of the blows shows that they were never struck in the dark. I will merely leave it to your common sense. Would any man take a light into that house and raise and axe to strike John Hossack when he had to raise it over his wife's sleeping body and with her face toward him? We know he would not, and we know if he had, Margaret Hossack would have been awakened.

At one point in his closing, Clammer returned to Shep, offering the jury an absurd explanation for his unusual behavior. He had not been drugged, Clammer claimed, but was so ashamed by the fact that Margaret killed her husband that he "had a heaviness of the heart because his master had been killed." According to Clammer, Shep was the only witness to the crime, but because he was unable to tell what he'd seen, he was only able to appear lifeless and morose to those who were at the house following the murder.

In addition to this "astounding" revelation, Clammer also announced that he knew the reason why Margaret and John Hossack disliked each other so much. It was a revelation that would have been shocking to conservative rural people at the dawn of the twentieth century. Margaret had forced John to marry her because she was pregnant out of wedlock with their oldest child, Alex! Clammer called the jury's attention to the date of his birth and Donald Murchison's testimony that the Hossacks had been married either around the same time, or just after, Alex had been born. Margaret had forced John to marry her, they never got along.

While Clammer was speaking, the courtroom was very quiet and Margaret sat still, watching him as he spoke to the jury. After Clammer made his claims about the reason for the Hossacks' hatred for one another, a wild expression passed over her face, but then she collected herself and her features regained their rigid look. At the same time, Berry was bounding out of his chair with an objection. There was no evidence to say it had been a forced marriage and the county attorney was asserting this without any support. Of course, he had done that with several things in his closing statement - not the least of which were interpreting the thoughts of Shep - but this had put Berry on his feet.

Clammer was ready with a response. He was making a simple point, based on sworn testimony from witnesses at the trial. Margaret Hossack had her first child in August 1868 and, according to the statement of her own brother, that was before she and John Hossack were married. The conclusion was obvious and based on these facts, was irrefutable. The defendant had given birth to her first child out of wedlock.

As it turned out, Clammer was right - at least about the marriage date. The Hossacks had lied about the date of their marriage and Alex *had* been conceived prior to the wedding. But Clammer had stumbled on this by accident. Only two people in the Indianola courtroom actually knew when the Hossacks had been married - Margaret and her brother, whose misstatement under oath offered Clammer the opportunity to make this claim. Although the legal record of the date of the Hossacks' marriage was located less than two hundred miles away, in the Stark County courthouse in Toulon, Illinois, George Clammer never produced the marriage certificate as evidence. But whether this proved that John and Margaret hated one another is open to debate.

Clammer continued to hammer his points to the jury until late afternoon, when he suddenly stopped and rested his hand on the table next to him. He spoke to the jury, "Gentlemen, after all is there need that I should say more? Would it not be useless after all to stand here and talk to you of something so plain that it needs no more talking about? And yet there may be one man among you who says he is not quite sure. There may be one who wants more evidence. He shall have it. And when I have shown you this I have shown you what weeks of eloquence cannot argue from the minds of honest men."

Clammer turned and asked that the bed in the far corner of the room be moved over in front of the jury. The spectators rustled in their seats, craning for a better look, as the bed, covered in bloody sheets, was carried into position. After it had been placed directly in front of the jury box, the county attorney spoke in a quiet tone, "You see this bed. It is small. The furniture men call it a three-quarter bed. The evidence has shown you that John Hossack did not move after he was struck. We can see from the blood in what part of the bed he was lying."

With a dramatic gesture, he threw back the covers. On the bottom sheet, almost in the center of the bed but inclining slightly to one side, was a mass of blood where John Hossack's body had lain. Clammer stressed the fact that Margaret was a large woman and that in order for the killer to have struck her husband, the assassin would have been forced to lean over her body to deliver the deadly blows. Without blatantly saying it, he made it clear that he thought Margaret's story was a lie. He told the jury, "There is not a shadow of a doubt in this case. It is all wiped away; every bit of investigation points in the same direction. Not one syllable is introduced by the defendant to show that anyone else might have committed this crime. All points the same way. Not any doubt at all, gentlemen. Don't you worry about reasonable doubt. The Court will tell you what it means. It means a reasonable, not a foolish fallacy, not mercy or pity on this defendant. Pity her as she pitied John Hossack. Pity her as she pitied him when creeping into that room. Pity her as she pitied him when she raised that axe and twice brought it down on his head. What pity does she deserve at the hands of this jury?"

Clammer stepped back from the jury box and uttered his final words with certainty. "She did it, gentlemen, and I ask you to return it to her in kind, that having considered all this case as honest, honorable men, knowing as you do your enormous responsibility that you will return to her a debt at the hands of the law. She has forfeited her right to live; she should be where John Hossack lies, rotting beneath the ground."

As Margaret listened to the closing sentences of Clammer's argument, her face was twisted with emotion. One of the reporters present wrote that the words, vivid and terrible, seemed nearly beyond her endurance.

But the day was not yet over. Late that afternoon, Judge Gamble allowed the defense to make a brief statement. Henderson rose from his seat and faced the jury. In angry words, he denounced the county attorney for his charge against the character of Margaret Hossack. The claim that she had borne a child out of wedlock was not supported by the facts, but rested solely on a misstatement by Donald Murchison as to the marriage date. It was a contemptible accusation, intended only to inflame and prejudice the members of the jury against the defendant, making her appear to be a woman of loose morals. Interestingly, it seemed to bother the defense counsel more than the accusation that she had committed murder.

At 10:00 a.m. the next morning, Senator Berry began the defense's appeal to the jury. He spoke until noon, when the proceedings stopped for lunch. Many of the reporters who were present that day stated that it was "the master effort of his life." There were a number of times when the jury members were moved to tears by his speech, which expanded on the theory that William Haines, now confined in an asylum, may have been the one who committed the murder.

While Berry spoke, the jury couldn't help but notice that Margaret was surrounded by her children and grandchildren, all of whom finally seemed to appreciate the terrible position in which she was now in. Time after time, a tear-stained face would be raised and would gaze anxiously at the jury. Johnnie sat with his head bowed, as his large frame shook with emotion. At times when Berry paused in his closing, Johnnie's sobbing was audible throughout the courtroom. As one reporter noted, "its effect on the spectators can only be described by the word terrific." Even the prosecutors turned their heads away from the anguish of the family, fearful that it would "unman them" and give an impression to the jury that they could not remove.

When the court adjourned at noon for lunch, the *Des Moines Daily News* wrote, "fully two thousand people went out in the sunshine, their faces stained by the tears which had coursed down their cheeks during the period when Senator Berry closed his most pathetic appeal."

At 1:00 p.m., the court reconvened and Berry continued his closing arguments. He was attempting to counter the powerful images that Clammer had presented about the night of the murder. Berry's usual voice was loud and resonant, but now he spoke in low and somber tones about the closeness of the family and especially about the peaceful Thanksgiving holiday that they had shared. He then began to speak about Margaret and her commitment to her life and family. Berry told the jury, "All her life she has been a good mother. She has raised nine children and has helped her husband build up a home, with no criminal record behind her, with no criminal tendencies ever displayed. I want to ask you whether you would be justified in thinking that, with her husband sleeping by her side and her children asleep in the rooms above, with no provocation at all in the world, she lay there and deliberately planned a brutal murder. It was a crime that few men could have done. Jesse James might have done it, but from what you know of her, do you think it was within the power of Margaret Hossack?"

As Berry spoke, he turned to the defendant. She was seated at the defense table with her arms around the three-year-old grandchild who was sleeping on her lap. Tears fell from her eyes as she listened to her attorney. He had now raised his voice slightly, close to admonishing the jury:

If in the heat of sudden passion, she had committed this hideous crime, she would now be a broken woman. After she had taken that axe and thrown it under the granary she would never have returned to the house, to the husband she had murdered, and aroused her children to come and see her work. After she did it she would have been crazed. She would have wandered off into the night, anywhere, anywhere to get away. She could not have been guilty of that crime and contained herself all these months in the county jail, as she has done. In my heart of hearts I say I believe she is innocent of this crime and it is only the consciousness of that innocence which has no nobly sustained her.

Then Berry challenged the circumstantial evidence presented by the prosecution. The experts, he reminded the jury, were not conclusive on any of the important points. They could not say the blood or the hairs on the axe were human and, without that evidence, there was nothing to prove that the family's axe was the murder weapon. In fact, Berry argued, the evidence seemed to point against it. The family axe had a nick on the blade, and the wounds displayed no mark. As for the scientific evidence that challenged the defendant's credibility - John Hossack's ability to speak and the appearance of the wounds - the experts were also not in agreement. Some of the medical evidence presented by the prosecution actually supported her story and none of it conclusively proved that she was lying.

Berry stressed the testimony about the chemise that Margaret wore on the night of the murder. The garment had been soaked in a pail of water, compromising its value as evidence. The state was to blame for the fact that it had not been preserved in its original condition, but witnesses who had seen it while Mrs. Hossack was wearing it recalled only seeing blood spots on the back - the front was clean. How could that he possible if she had struck her husband with the axe? Would not the front of the chemise be covered in blood if she committed the murder? Berry asserted that this fact alone should provide the reasonable doubt about the prosecutor's story.

Berry spoke for the rest of the afternoon. He removed his coat, loosened his tie and rolled his rumpled shirtsleeves up past his elbows. His waved his hands about in the air. As he paced back and forth in front of the jury box, his boots thumped loudly on the wooden floor. He constantly wiped at his red and sweaty face with a handkerchief.

During Berry's emotional closing argument, his co-counsel, John Henderson, felt the strain of the proceedings to such a point that he was unable to stay seated at the defense table. He paced rapidly in the hallway outside of the courtroom, deep in thought, his hands clasped tightly on his head and Berry's words echoing from the room beyond the wooden doors.

Finally, at 5:30 p.m., as the sun was starting to dip below the horizon, Berry approached the jury box and made one last plea for understanding and mercy for this client:

I have talked to you longer than I intended. Maybe I have wearied you, maybe in my zeal I have said too much. I know that may be true, and yet, though night has now fallen and though the day for all of us has been one hard to endure, it seems that even now I cannot be content to say the final word. I have in my heart that fear that somewhere, sometime, in the course of these four months I have left undone something that night have aided the cause of Margaret Hossack. As I stand here now, with my work completed, I am oppressed with a terrible feeling that too late there will come to me something I might have done.

But I have done all I could. The time has now come for me to stop. And in your hands I leave the results of my work, to you I must consign the fate of this defendant.

Gentlemen, if any one of you is the only one on this jury who entertains a reasonable doubt of the guilt of Margaret Hossack, I ask that you obey the law and refuse to vote for her conviction. I was surprised at the zeal with which the county attorney demanded not only the conviction but the life of this defendant. He went far beyond what the testimony warranted. After four months of association with Mrs. Hossack and her family, I can stand before this journey and before my God and say that I believe her to be absolutely innocent of this crime. You are asked to hang her - oh, those bitter, those terrible words that were spoken in this courtroom.

In conclusion, I only say to you this - when your verdict is found let it be such as that you standing beside her on her gallows will have your conscience approve your decision when the rope is cut and she falls to the ground. Let your verdict be one that if you shall consign her to the felon cell for life you can say when the door has shut her out from the world forever, I have done right. Let it be one that whatever punishment you shall fix, when in the years that are to come you meet these daughters, these sons and these grandchildren and you can say, I convicted your mother, but I did what I thought was right. And if your verdict cannot be such a verdict, follow the law as it will be given to you by this court. Do not condemn this woman unless you can stand in the presence of these generations yet unborn without one qualm of conscience.

When you reach your jury room, consider the life of Margaret Hossack, its trials and burdens and those difficulties of wifehood and motherhood. Consider the tempests of unfortunate disagreements in the light of the reconciliation that followed. Find such a verdict as that when you meet her, as you someday will, in the presence of the judge who can judge, with all impartiality, you will have no regret for what you have done here. If you cannot say you are convinced beyond a reasonable doubt, remember that as ye would have others do unto you, do ye also unto them. If there is a doubt, put yourself in her place and remember the rule that should govern us all. Mercy, mercy... Justice we cannot always do, we can but do the best we can. As you know that someday you will answer for what you have done, but sure that you do not commit to the hangman or to the cell an innocent woman. It is better even that the guilty should sometimes escape than that the innocent be punished.

Never in all my life have I felt the responsibility as I have in this case. I have never dreaded a responsibility as I have this, and I pray no such responsibility shall ever be case upon me again. I am now leaving with you the fate of a woman who before high heaven I believe to be innocent.

Finally, Berry's voice trailed off and he stopped speaking. He stood before the jury for a few moments, silent, with his head bowed. Then he raised his head, as if he intended to continue speaking, but he stopped himself. He gazed directly at the twelve men in the jury box before he turned around and walked slowly to the defense table, where he sat down next to his client.

It was a great piece of courtroom theater and an effective one. The silence in the room lasted for more than a minute before Judge Gamble declared that the court was adjourned for the day. The crowd filed from the courtroom, talking quietly as they filed out. Some of them gathered on the lawn in the growing dusk to talk, while others started for home in silence.

The defendant, escorted by Deputy Kimer, followed the spectators out of the courthouse. Looking tired, strained and much older than when the trial had started, Margaret walked in silence. The dispersing crowd moved aside to let her pass, watching as she made her way back to the county jail.

The prosecution was allowed a rebuttal statement and it was made by Harry McNeil on Wednesday morning. It stretched into the late afternoon as he carefully went over the state's evidence once again, focusing first on the defendant's motive and then her lack of credibility. Standing next to the bed in which John Hossack died, he demonstrated to the jury how, if Margaret had been lying next to her husband, she would have been struck by the weapon. He spoke of the axe and reiterated how she knew where it could be found.

During most of his argument, McNeil was detached and quietly thoughtful, with an air of impartiality rather than the malice expressed by Clammer. Sometimes, though, when repeating arguments made by the defense, his tone became sarcastic and cynical. He laughed bitterly when he repeated the family's story that Shep had been drugged, despite the fact that it was less ridiculous than the prosecution's claim that the dog acted strangely because he was depressed over the murder. At other times, he spoke in a loud and angry voice. He also blamed Berry for driving William Haines into the insane asylum. Shouldn't the defense bear responsibility for his absence? Certainly, if the defense was going to finger Haines for the crime, it was convenient that Haines was not in the courtroom. Perhaps, McNeil suggested, the defense had arranged for that to happen.

Finally, McNeil brought his argument to a close. He stood directly in front of the jury box and lowered his voice almost to a whisper. His words could only be heard by the jurors, those at the defense and prosecution tables and a handful of spectators who were close to the front. He said to them:

The eloquent attorney for the defense stands before you and asks for mercy. I sat that in the light of all this evidence you no right to return a verdict for acquittal. They talk to you of generations yet unborn and of how you will feel when you meet the defendant in the world that is to come. I say to you that there is a duty you owe the people of Warren County...

I have no more sympathy for this defendant because she is a woman than I would have for a man who murdered his wife. And you have no right to acquit her because she is a woman or even because she is an old woman. Never since the crucifixion of Christ has there been a crime of a more hideous nature than this. If there are tears to shed, prepare to shed them for John Hossack. I have known John Hossack all my life. I can say of him as was said of Abraham Lincoln, 'God Almighty might have made a better man, but God Almighty never did.' Who in this country knows of any wrong John Hossack ever did? I have shed tears for him myself because there has been none shed for him by his family. They have cried little because they were afraid their mother was going to be hung, but they have not cried for their murdered father. If John Hossack's spirit is here today what must it think of this scene? What must it think of the hard, dogged face of the defendant? Gentlemen, Senator Berry has asked that you show mercy. I demand that you give justice.

If you, gentlemen of the jury, as I believe you do, believe this woman guilty, let no technical error bias your judgment, and let no sympathy for an unborn generation, as appealed to you by Mr. Berry, lead you to the wrong verdict in this case, because the good citizens of Warren County demand of you and they expect from your hand... that you will render that verdict which justice demands, and that verdict will be guilty with the punishment of death - death."

When McNeil finished, Judge Gamble read the instructions to the jury. There were thirty-one different instructions and the reading took slightly more than an hour. The jury was reminded that the defendant had been charged with first-degree murder and that she had pleaded not guilty. She was presumed to be innocent and the prosecution had to be prove guilt beyond a reasonable doubt. The jury was to judge the credibility of all of the witnesses for itself. Point by point, the judge explained the applicable criminal law for the jury, describing the weight to be given to different types of evidence. The jury could consider the testimony given by experts, although it should be cautious, the judge warned, in considering conclusions that were based on theories or upon less than personal observation.

The jury had several choices. If unable to conclude that the defendant had killed her husband, then she must be acquitted. If she had done the deed, then the verdict would depend upon a determination as to the defendant's state of mind at the time of the killing. If she had acted out of sudden passion, without a deliberate intent to kill, she was guilty of manslaughter. If she had not intended to kill, but to cause great bodily harm, then she was guilty of murder in the second-degree. She could be convicted of first-degree murder only if the jury found, beyond a reasonable doubt, that she had acted with premeditation, requiring a deliberate intent to kill with malice aforethought, meaning that she had acted with a "wicked and depraved heart." If she was guilty of first-degree murder, then the jury was asked to recommend the appropriate sentenced: imprisonment for life at the state penitentiary or death.

The jury listened to Judge Gamble with rapt attention. Directly in front of them was the bed in which Hossack had been murdered. The axe, which the state claimed had been the murder weapon, was resting against the bed. Other pieces of evidence, including several articles of clothing and a bloody square of carpet, were also nearby. Prosecution and defense lawyers, exhausted after the long days of the trial, sat at their tables in the middle of the courtroom. Margaret and her family, none of them crying now, were seated just behind the defense attorneys, clearly visible to the jurors.

At 5:30 p.m., the judge finally finished his task. The jury, he announced, would be taken to dinner and then would begin its deliberations. The twelve men in the jury box, their faces grim and serious, rose to their feet and, in single file, followed the bailiff out of the courtroom.

Margaret Hossack's fate was now in their hands.

No matter how you looked at it - even barring prosecution claims of depressed dogs and its bizarre comparison of an bad-tempered farmer to the Great Emancipator, Abraham Lincoln - the Hossack trial was a strange one. The jury had listened to five days of testimony and two days of arguments. The prosecution called forty witnesses to the stand; the defense called thirteen. Three people - Will and Cassie Hossack and Fred Johnston - testified for both the prosecution and the defense.

There were ten women called to the witness stand: five members of the Hossack family the defendant and all four of her daughters and five neighbors. The Hossack daughters were mainly asked about the night of the murder, were questioned briefly about the relationship between their parents and all reported that the family had lived peacefully for the year after the reconciliation. Four of the neighbor women who testified - Mrs. George Grant, Nora Cart, Sue Himstreet and Eleanor Keller - were on the stand for only a short time and were only asked a few questions about specific incidents. Only Rinda Haines, whose husband was unable to appear, was extensively grilled by the attorneys.

Mary Nicholson, who was questioned closely at the coroner's inquest, did not testify. Nor did the wife of Will Conrad, who reported Margaret Hossack's presence in their home at Thanksgiving 1899. Nancy Truitt, who knew the family well and attended the Thanksgiving party just days before the murder, was never called to the stand.

The narrative of the Hossacks' relationship and marriage was mostly told by the men who knew John Hossack, farmers whom Margaret had turned to for help - and who had ignored her pleas that they do something to make him stop mistreating her and the children. These witnesses offered the most detailed impressions of the defendant, recounting her complaints about her husband's behavior and in effect, blaming her for the problems in the family.

Throughout the trial, there were many women in attendance. One of the most noticeable was Marcia Hodson, the wife of the sheriff, who had apparently formed a close bond with the older woman while she was housed in the jail. During the trial, Marcia sat next to her at the defense table. To many of the men in the courtroom, John Hossack's abusive behavior toward his family was less damning than his wife's conversations with the neighbors, which, in their view, brought shame to the otherwise respected farmer. But among the woman who silently watched the proceedings, there was a subtle, but perceptible support for the accused. However, the stories of these women - neighbors who knew Margaret Hossack, as well as spectators who came to know her history at the trial - went largely untold in the courtroom.

While the jury was starting their deliberations, the Hossack clan was gathering at the county jail. Margaret was refusing to eat and wouldn't talk to anyone but her family and Marcia Hodson. The sheriff told reporters that she was more distressed and broken down than at any other time during the trial. Several of her sons visited that evening and afterwards, they paced up and down the street outside of the jail. Cassie remained with her mother throughout the long night.

Two blocks away at the courthouse, small groups of men gathered on the lawn. It was a mild spring evening with balmy temperatures and a sky full of bright stars. The men in the square stared up at the lighted windows on the third floor of the courthouse, behind which the jury deliberated. The farmers wanted the trial to be over. The fields were drying out and it was time to get back to work.

In the jury room, the first vote was taken and seven men voted for conviction; five for acquittal. Debate continued all night until all twelve jurors agreed on a verdict.

At 10:00 a.m., the jury sent a message to the judge that they had reached a verdict. The news spread quickly, and within ten minutes, a large crowd was rushing through the doors of the courthouse. The seats rapidly filled. A buzz was in the air. It was almost over, everyone knew. A rustle went through the crowd as the defendant was brought in. Her family took their seats in the row behind her and Judge Gamble resumed his place on the bench.

After the crowd settled into their seats, Judge Gamble gestured to Deputy Kimer, who stepped to the rear of the room and opened the door. Slowly and silently, the jurors filed in, many of them with their heads bowed and their eyes cast down. They all looked pale and exhausted. The judge soberly asked them if they had agreed upon a verdict.

The foreman, J.P. Anderson, got to his feet and responded, "We have."

Anderson handed over the verdict form, which had been signed by all twelve jurors, and the bailiff carried it to Judge Gamble. All eyes were on the judge as he unfolded the paper and, after silently reading the words written there, raised one hand to his forehead. He handed the verdict back to the clerk, who read it aloud: "We, the jury, find Margaret Hossack guilty of murder in the first degree and recommend that she be sentenced for life to hard labor in the state penitentiary."

As the words left the clerk's mouth, Margaret remained paralyzed at the defense table. It was not until the jury filed out that and the time had come for her and her family to leave the courtroom that they seemed to recover from the blow and allow grief to overtake them. As newspaper reporters later wrote, "The scene was terrible. Mrs. Hossack gave way to feeling with utter abandonment. Her daughters clung to her hysterically and her oldest son leaning his head against the window sobbed as only a strong man can sob. Finally the woman found guilty of the murder of her husband was led back to the county jail and for hours she cried with a violence that brought at length relief in utter hysterical exhaustion."

Senator Berry announced that he would move for a new trial.

Five days passed. Margaret Hossack next appeared in court on Tuesday, April 16 for formal sentencing by the judge. Once again, she was surrounded by her family.

First, Judge Gamble addressed a motion that had been made by Berry and Henderson, asking for a new trial. Stating that the defendant had been well-represented by her attorneys and given a fair trial, he denied the motion. Then the judge turned in the direction of the Hossack family. He said to them, "The jury has returned a verdict of guilty as charged in the indictment and now it becomes my painful duty to pronounce sentence as provided by law." Then, speaking directly to Margaret, he asked, "Have you any reasons to offer why the sentence as fixed by the jury should not be pronounced?"

Margaret slowly rose in her chair and attempted to speak, but she was so overcome by emotion that she slumped back into her chair without uttering any sound but a choked sob. While Judge Gamble waited, Berry leaned down and spoke quietly to her. Again she stood, this time leaning on Berry's arm for support. She raised her right hand, as if once again taking the oath to tell the truth, and spoke very softly. She said, "Before my God, I am not guilty."

A moment passed as Judge Gamble gathered his thoughts. When he finally spoke, the grizzled war veteran's voice cracked with emotion, "Sometime and somewhere in the providence of God, it will be revealed whether or not you have spoken truly."

Margaret's sentence was pronounced and the broken woman was ushered from the courtroom. According to the *Des Moines Daily Capital*, "The people from the vicinity of the Hossack home who were so constantly in attendance at the trial were present when the sentenced was delivered this morning and they gathered around her in large numbers this afternoon, attempting to offer some words of consolation."

On April 18, 1901, Sheriff Hodson, accompanied by his wife, arrived at the Anamosa State Penitentiary and turned over custody of Margaret Hossack to William Hunter, the warden. The Hodsons were assured by the warden that Margaret would be given a separate cell and the best medical attention and care. Before the couple left, Margaret once again pleaded her innocence. The *Daily News* reported that she said, "Sheriff Hodson, tell my children not to weep for me. I am innocent of the horrible murder of my husband. Someday people will know that I am not guilty of that terrible crime."

She was taken into custody by Warden Hunter, a Civil War veteran who had been the administrator of the prison for three years in 1901. He had very few female prisoners and none of them caused trouble. He knew that his newest ward was a convicted murderer, but he expected no threat from her. In fact, a few months after her arrival, Hunter would become convinced of her innocence.

Margaret was taken to the receiving room, where she was examined and questioned. She was given prisoner number 4654. She was expected to be incarcerated for the remainder of her natural life. Like all new prisoners, she was next escorted to the bathhouse, where she was washed and disinfected, and then taken to her cell in the female department.

The female department of the penitentiary, an imposing stone structure located in downtown Anamosa, was a community of mostly young women. Only one was older than fifty-seven-year-old

Margaret Hossack. This was a physician, seventy years old, who was serving a five-year sentence for performing an abortion. They were incarcerated for a variety of crimes, the most common offenses being larceny, prostitution and adultery. Margaret was not the only convicted murderer. Sarah Kuhn, a woman convicted of poisoning her husband, was also serving a life sentence at Anamosa.

Angie Waterman was in charge of the female department, having been hired as a matron by Warden Hunter in 1898. Described as a "Christian lady" who took "great interest in the unfortunates in her department," Mrs. Waterman was an attractive young woman with previous experience as a nurse. Prior to coming to the penitentiary, she had been employed at the Hospital for the Insane in Clarinda. She was, at heart, an optimist and a reformer who saw it as her duty to provide the women with practical and moral guidance. She evaluated the woman based on their behavior and divided them into classes based on that. The more privileged inmates, including Margaret, wore plain gray clothing. The second-class prisoners wore plaid and the third-class women wore stripes. The first-class inmates were given better clothing and food than the lower classes. The differentiation of the prisoners was said to encourage self-improvement and obedience.

The cells for the women were located in what had once been the insane ward. The cells, each occupied by one inmate, were small - approximately four and a half feet wide, eight feet long, and seven and a half feet high. Each cell was wired for electricity, with a single bare bulb hanging overhead. The building was kept warm in the winter with steam heat and indoor plumbing provided hot and cold water in the bathrooms. Inmates were allowed one hot shower per week in a communal bathhouse.

During that spring and summer, Margaret adjusted to the prison routine. After fifty years of grueling work as the daughter and wife of hardworking farmers, and as a mother to nine children, she now settled into a community of women with only simple domestic chores. The women, who never saw or interacted with the male prisoners, maintained their living quarters and followed a daily regimen of light work. They washed, they laundered, sewed clothes and cleaned the cellblock. They didn't cook for themselves. Hot meals were served to them three times each day. The women were forbidden to talk during meals, but the food was good and well-balanced. When they weren't working, the women remained in their cells, often reading books borrowed from the prison library. They were allowed to mail one letter per week. On Sundays, they were taken to the chapel for church services and the chaplain regularly visited the women in their cells for spiritual guidance.

For Margaret Hossack, it's not unthinkable to consider the idea that prison might have come as a relief when compared to the hard life she had lived for the past few decades.

The guilty verdict did not bring an end to the story of Margaret Hossack. As it turned out, the trial was merely one chapter in a story that continued to evolve.

Certainly, the verdict came as no surprise to Margaret's neighbors. From the beginning, many of them predicted it to reporters and to one another, and many served as witnesses against her at the trial. Yet, almost immediately, those some people - some of whom offered Margaret words of consolation after the trial - began to regret how things had turned out. They came to acknowledge their own role in what had happened. They had ignored Margaret's requests for help, or had failed to act in regard to the dangerous situation that they knew had existed in the Hossack household.

The family's emotional reaction at the time of the verdict contributed to the concern about whether Margaret had been fairly judged. As one newspaper reported, "The children seen genuinely to believe in the innocence of their mother, and this, while without much value as legal evidence, sways the private judgment." There was some speculation that perhaps Margaret was protecting the real killer, an idea that framed her in a more sympathetic light. Was she lying out of a mother's natural impulse to protect one of her children? Given the early reports that the Hossack sons had quarreled with their father, the thought was a logical one, although investigators never looked at any of the children as suspects. Maybe, too, Margaret's unwavering contention that she was innocent caused her neighbors to wonder if justice had been done.

Several days after the trial ended, an editorial in the *Des Moines Daily Leader* criticized the verdict, highlighting Senator Berry's rebuke of the county attorney for telling the jury that its duty was to find and punish the guilty party rather to focus on the reasonable doubt that existed as to the guilt of the defendant. The editor opined, "Perhaps the jurors unconsciously determined that, as a crime had been committed, it was their duty to fasten the commission of the same upon someone, and selected the only person it seemed possible to suspect." As the editorial noted, the evidence that pointed to Margaret as the murderer was only circumstantial, leaving substantial room for doubt that the jury ignored.

In June 1901, just a little over two months after her sentencing, the public feeling had shifted to such an extent that people in New Virginia and Warren County began lobbying for a pardon for Margaret Hossack. Many prominent residents of the region pledged to sign a petition that would be taken to the governor.

Life was moving on while Margaret was in prison. William Haines was released from the insane asylum and returned to his farm near the Hossack place. Margaret's attorneys, Berry and Henderson, had dissolved their law firm. Henderson was establishing a new one with his son, Frank, and Berry was practicing alone, but they were working together on an appeal for Margaret to the Iowa Supreme Court. The Hossack farm, where Johnnie and Will had been living and trying to maintain it, was ordered sold by the district court to settle John Hossack's estate. It was auctioned off in September 1901 and purchased by C.C. Taggart, a landowner who lived near Medora. Since John had died without a will, the proceeds of the sale were divided along his family. Despite her conviction for his murder, Margaret was legally entitled to one-third of the total amount.

In October 1901, Berry and Henderson filed their appeal with the Iowa Supreme Court, arguing that Margaret's conviction should be set aside and a new trial granted. In a lengthy brief, they claimed that various procedural errors had been made by Judge Gamble, mistakes in admitting evidence and giving instructions to the jury. According to Berry and Henderson, the expert testimony about the hairs - the most important evidence connecting the axe to the murders - should have been inadmissible. They also raised a number of other points where they claimed certain legal points were not correctly explained to the jury.

Almost one-third of the brief, however, was devoted to the broader claim that the evidence, viewed in its entirety, did not support the guilty verdict. The attorneys asked the court to carefully consider a number of specific points, including the unusual behavior of the dog, testimony from doctors that supported the defendant's story, evidence of the couple's reconciliation, and the lack of significant bloodstains on the defendant's chemise. All of this, they claimed, proved her innocence.

They also asked the court to take into account Clammer's final presentation to the jury, which was, they claimed, unfairly prejudicial and injurious to the defendant. The county attorney had been overzealous and his story, filled with vivid and horrific details, was not based on fact but on his "fertile imagination" as he sought to "secure a verdict at all hazard." Many of his statements, including the unsupported charge of illicit relations between John and Margaret Hossack before their marriage, were intended to "arouse the passions of the jury members" instead of appealing to reason. Clammer was guilty of misconduct, Berry and Henderson claimed, for the way that he had argued the case in the courtroom.

The lawyers cited earlier cases, in which the Supreme Court had recognized an obligation to reverse a jury verdict that was based on popular opinion and local prejudice and that resulted from "the heat and excitement of the trial." Berry and Henderson believed that this trial warranted that same judicial action. The conviction should be reversed and a new trial ordered.

Needless to say, the attorney general for the state of Iowa did not agree and filed a response, citing precedent to support Judge Gamble's rulings and instructions and defending the jury's verdict. The attorney general's brief echoed points made in Clammer's final argument and stated that it was not only evidence that supported the defendant's guilt, but also her less-than-satisfactory traits as a woman. She was not dainty and timid, as women rightfully should be. She was large, broad-shouldered and "masculine in appearance" and was an "inhuman wife and mother," since she had responded to the noise in the night by leaving her bedroom rather than by following the "natural impulse of a woman," which would have been to seek the protection of her husband. She was the mother of many children and yet she claimed not to have awakened immediately when the alleged intruder entered her house. The implication was clear - either she was lying or she did not properly care for her husband. Either way, the guilty verdict was well justified.

Oral arguments took place in front of the Iowa Supreme Court later that same month. After that, the nine justices would make the next decision that would decide Margaret Hossack's fate.

Six month later, on April 9, 1902, the Court rendered its decision, having voted unanimously to reverse the conviction and grant Margaret a new trial. Without addressing the charge of prosecutorial misconduct, the court based its decision on two rulings by Judge Gamble. These were allowing the jury to consider Professor Tilton's opinion on the hairs, which made it appear that the axe was the murder weapon even though no one knew for sure, and the judge's instructions about the reconciliation between the Hossacks.

Margaret was released from the Anamosa State Penitentiary on April 18, 1902, exactly one year after her arrival. One newspaper reported that she "expressed the belief that a new trial would clear her." She was transferred back to the Warren County Jail to await trial.

By then, Margaret was almost sixty years old and her health had declined during the year she was in prison. After being examined by a doctor, who stated that her confinement was worsening her condition of "nervous prostration and disease of the spine," a judge ruled that she could be released on bail if a bond for $15,000 was posted to guarantee her appearance at trial. Several of her former neighbors came forward to sign as guarantors of the bond. A few days later, Margaret was released from custody by Sheriff Hodson, and she went to live with Ev and Annie in the aptly named Liberty, Iowa.

In the late fall of 1902, at the urging of the family, Berry and Henderson petitioned the court for a change of venue for Margaret's second trial. Citing John Hossack's favorable reputation in the community, the circumstances of his death and the publicity surrounding the earlier trial, they claimed that it was impossible for the defendant to receive a fair trial in Warren County. The court agreed and ruled that the second trail would be held in Winterset, in Madison County, about twenty miles west of Indianola. The trial was scheduled for February 1903.

When his second term as county attorney having expired in the fall of 1901, George Clammer did not run for reelection. He went into private practice and served on a local school board. But when it was clear that Margaret Hossack would be tried again, he was asked to join the prosecution team for the new trial, with the hope that he could repeat his success and convince another jury that she had killed her husband.

The trial began on Thursday, February 12, 1903 at the Madison County Courthouse, a handsome stone building with a large second-floor courtroom that resembled a theater. Observers filled the seats in the balcony, which extended above the back half of the room, and spectators downstairs crowded into rows behind the wooden railing that separated the audience from the defense and prosecution tables. The jury had been selected the day before and were seated in the jury box. They were younger than the jurors of the first trial, although they had similar backgrounds. Eleven of the men were farmers and one was a harness maker.

The circumstances of the second trial were much different than the first. Two years had passed since the murder and the change of venue had a great impact. John Hossack was largely unknown to the people of Madison County and few, if any, of the jurors or spectators were personally acquainted with him. Their only knowledge of the family's domestic troubles came from the newspapers.

The sentiment toward Margaret Hossack was also different. The mistrust and suspicions that had colored the newspaper portrayals of her two years earlier had been replaced with compassionate stories of an elderly and even pitiable woman. The damning evidence that had been used by the prosecution to prove motive in the first trial - the many stories from neighbors about Hossack's cruel treatment of his family - now aroused sympathy for his wife and children. Reports that preceded the second trial focused on the defense more than the prosecution and Margaret's lawyers were frequently quoted as being optimistic about an acquittal. Some residents of Madison County - especially the women - openly declared their hope that Mrs. Hossack would not be found guilty a second time.

Clammer was joined at the prosecution table by Harry McNeil, his colleague from the first trial, and W.S. Cooper, the attorney for Madison County. Judge Edmond Nichols presided and once the court was convened, he invited Clammer to give his opening statement to the jury. Clammer spoke for nearly two hours. Well aware that many in the audience favored the defendant, he made a point of reminding the jurors of their duty under the law: to be objective and neutral in evaluating the facts of the case against the defendant.

As in the first trial, Clammer put up a large diagram of the Hossack farm and a layout of the interior of the house. He noted the history of the marriage, mentioning the couple's frequent quarrels over the years as evidence of the defendant's hatred of her husband, and repeated his version of what he believed happened on the night of the murder. When he reached the point when the victim's children first saw their wounded father in his bed, Margaret Hossack burst into tears. Clammer paused for several minutes, allowing her to regain her composure before he finished his account.

The prosecutor acknowledged that the evidence was circumstantial, but he was sure that the jury could see that it all pointed at the defendant as the murderer. They would see that the physical evidence incriminated her since the bed, the bedclothes and the axe had all been preserved from the first trial. They would hear witnesses testify about her motive for the murder. Throughout it all, the jury members must remember, he stressed once again, that they were obligated to put aside their sympathies and consider only the evidence and testimony presented to them.

After lunch recess, Senator Berry began his opening statement. Madison County was part of the state senatorial district that he had represented during his four years in the state legislature, so Berry was well-known, at least by name and reputation, to most of the people in the courtroom. He used this to his advantage, easily captivating the audience with his confidence and ease in the courtroom. At the first trial, he had started out with an appeal to the sympathies of the jury, relating the story of the difficulties of the defendant's hard life, but this time, he tried a different tack. He began by focusing on what he would continue to drive home during his questioning of the witnesses and in his closing arguments as being the real key to the case: that the evidence presented by the prosecution was simply insufficient to support a conviction. There was no witness to the murder. There was only circumstantial evidence against his client, and much of it, especially testimony from neighbors that suggested motive, was irrelevant and should not be considered by the jury. And Berry once again stressed the 1899 reconciliation between the Hossacks. If he could convince the jury that the husband and wife had put aside their differences and were living amicably together, then the jurors would be bound to ignore all evidence of domestic quarrels in the years before.

During the time that Margaret had been in prison, the family farm had been sold and the children had moved away. Johnnie had moved to Des Moines and had taken a job with the gas company. May had gotten married and now lived with her husband, Ira Coulter, near New Virginia. Will lived and worked at the Truitt farm, as Johnnie had once done, and Ivan, still in his early teens, had been sent to live with the family of George and Anna Van Patten on a nearby farm.

For the two weeks of the trial, the Hossack family was reunited in Winterset. They rented rooms at a private home only a few blocks away from the courthouse and just as they had done during the first trial, the family - sons and daughters, in-laws and grandchildren - surrounded Margaret with their physical presence. They walked into the courthouse together each morning and left together at the end of the day. In the evenings, they dined together at the boarding house before going to bed.

In the courtroom, the family watched as Clammer presented the case, listening to the same witnesses they had heard in the first trial. For the most part, there were few surprises or even changes in the testimony of the neighbors, family members or expert witnesses.

Margaret remained stoic and quiet throughout the proceedings. She stayed with her family, walking back and forth to the courthouse with them and sitting with them in the courtroom - an old woman surrounded by her children and grandchildren. She listened to the testimony but seldom turned to look at the audience behind her. She kept her eyes cast downward, or looked in the direction of the witness stand. She suffered from a bad cold during most of the trial, coughing frequently and holding a handkerchief to her mouth. She kept a shawl draped over her shoulders to ward off the winter chill.

Different than before, though, were the women and young girls who approached the defense table during the breaks in the proceedings. They came forward to speak to Margaret, offering comforting hands and words of sympathy to her. Their kindness did not go unappreciated.

On Tuesday, February 17, Clammer called Ivan Hossack to the witness stand. He was now fifteen years old and the separation from his family had been bitter and sad. He had resisted moving to the Van Patten farm, but his brothers and sisters told him that there was nowhere else for him to go. None of the brothers except Alex had homes of their own and Alex and his married sisters had no room for him. So Ivan had no choice but to accept the offer from the Van Pattens. At least their farm was not far from where he grew up.

The Van Patten farm turned out to be a good place for Ivan. They had a large home on many acres of land and accepted the boy as part of the family. He was treated very well, helped with the chores and attended school with the Van Patten children, Loyd and Nina. Ivan and Loyd became close friends.

On the day Clammer called him to testify, Ivan took the oath and swore to tell the truth. He took his set in the witness box and Clammer began asking questions, taking him through the events of the evening of the murder. Yes, Ivan remembered Will asking him to retrieve his coat from the woodpile on that Saturday evening around dusk. And yes, he remembered that Will called for him to put the axe away, and that he then met his mother coming from the barn and told her he was going to the granary with the axe. Did he remember putting the axe inside the granary?

Ivan said that he wasn't sure.

Clammer asked him to refresh his memory by looking at the transcript of his testimony from the first trial. At the inquest, Clammer reminded Ivan, he had been positive that he had put the axe inside of the granary and later, at the trial, he was fairly certain of the same thing. Ivan acknowledged that he remembered testifying at both proceedings, but now, he said, he couldn't be certain. He knew that sometimes he put the axe in the granary and other times, he simply tossed it underneath.

He didn't remember where he had left it on the evening of December 1, 1900.

During the second trial, women made up more than half of the courtroom audience. Many of them attended each day of the trial, returning to the same spots they had occupied the day before, as if the places had been reserved for them. The newspapers poked fun at this phenomenon, albeit in a good-natured way, suggesting that the women were neglecting their household duties to attend the trial, forcing their men "to go with a cold dinner or late supper or go to the hotel or lunch counter."

The women listened attentively to the opening arguments and the testimony that followed as each of the prosecution witnesses came to the stand. Paying the same careful attention to detail that he had in the previous trial, Clammer elicited testimony about the Hossack marriage and its long history of turmoil and violence. The witness accounts of the defendant's fears for the safety of her family were again presented as the strongest evidence that she had committed murder.

On February 18, William Haines took the stand. Newspapers reported that Haines had been "violently insane," and had spent a long stint in the state mental asylum. Although he had been unable to testify in the first trial, he was now ready to talk. Under questioning from Clammer, he told his story, stating that Margaret Hossack had approached him several times with reports about her husband mistreating the family. Haines recalled that she once asked him to come to her house and "settle her husband," and once he claimed that she said that she wished he would "finish" him. Haines swore, as he had at the inquest, that he had always refused her requests. Like the other neighbors, he didn't want to get involved in the family's squabbles.

However, Haines' testimony raised questions about his truthfulness. On the witness stand, he admitted that he had lied to May and Jimmie when they came to his door on the night of the murder and asked for help. Haines said under oath that his wife didn't want him to go out that night, so he had invented a story about seeing a stranger on his porch, making him afraid to leave the house.

Then, under vigorous cross-examination by Senator Berry, Haines confessed that he and John Hossack had a long history of disagreements. In fact, he admitted that they had quarreled in public about politics just a few weeks before the murder. This admission contradicted the testimony that Haines had given a few days after the murder, when he stated under oath at the inquest that they had not argued in nearly ten years. In truth, their most recent quarrel had occurred on Election Day in early November 1900, just weeks before Hossack was slain.

The inconsistencies in Haines' statement cast doubt on his credibility, and Berry suggested that perhaps his long history of mental instability had caused him to imagine, or at least misunderstand, his reported conversations with Margaret about her husband. Haines left the witness stand in confusion and it became clear to everyone that he was certainly not the star witness that Clammer had hoped he would be.

That afternoon, Clammer announced that the prosecution had no more witnesses to call and Margaret uttered an audible sigh of relief. The trial was not yet over, but many in the audience had already made up their minds. As court adjourned for the day, women from the galleries gathered and advanced to the front of the courtroom. They formed a line and walked forward, one woman at a time, to greet Mrs. Hossack at the defense table, taking her hand in theirs to offer her their unwavering support.

Margaret's second trial lasted four more days. The weather turned clear and mild, perhaps as a promise of an early spring, which would have been welcome news to the farmers in the jury. Things were also looking good for the defense attorneys. The prosecution had concluded its case, leaving the public unconvinced that their client would be convicted a second time.

In order to refute the claims made by the prosecution and raise doubts about the state's case, Berry began his defense by calling many of the same witnesses that he had questioned in the first trial, including the doctors, neighbors and the Hossack children. Berry also began offered the jury alternative suspects. Haines was one of them. His own testimony about his strange behavior on the night of the murder made him appear suspicious. Berry also had a tantalizing fact that had not been brought out at the first trial, which suggested that Haines might be involved. On the morning after the murder, Johnnie Hossack and Lewis Braucht had spotted footprints in the Hossack orchard. They led away from the house, heading north - directly toward Haines' house.

Berry also introduced an important new witness, a farmer named G.K. Burson, who lived three miles east of the Hossack farm. Burson told the jury that he had seen a mysterious rider on the night of the murder. The gallery paid close attention to Burson while he was on the stand, many of them leaning forward in their seats to take in every word. According to his story, the man had been on horseback, riding away from the Hossack farm, just minutes after Margaret claimed that her husband had been attacked. Burson said that he was startled by a noise, which sounds like the "rapid clatter of a horse's hoofs" approaching from the west. Burson rushed out of his house and watched as the horseman crossed a forty-foot wooden bridge and headed up the hill. In the moonlight, he got a good look at the horse and rider as they raced past. The rider was a man, short and heavyset, wearing a dirty, white hat that was pulled down over his eyes and a light-colored coat.

The prosecution subjected Burson to a brutal cross-examination, trying hard to show inconsistencies in his statements, while also attempting to suggest that it was a common thing for local boys to run horses down his road while returning from town late at night. Burson never buckled under Clammer's questions. In the end, the rider that Burson had seen so soon after the Hossack murder was never identified and the jury was left to wonder if the horseman, whoever he may have been, was involved in the murder or not.

On Friday afternoon, the defense called Margaret Hossack to the stand. The courtroom fell silent as she rose from the defense table and walked slowly to the witness stand. After being sworn in, she sat down and faced the audience.

Perhaps believing that a local lawyer would be more persuasive to the jury, Berry chose John Guiher, the former Madison County attorney who was assisting the defense, to question Margaret. The strategy of the questioning was clearly different than with the first trial, where Margaret had been asked nothing about her relationship with her husband. She had not talked about the difficulties of her marriage, or about the reconciliation. Thanks to the decision from the Supreme Court, the existence of the reconciliation was critical to the case. If the jury was persuaded that the couple had reconciled, then prior conflicts could not be considered as evidence of the defendant's motive. It was now important to the defense that Margaret testify that animosity between her and her husband had ceased in November 1899.

Guiher asked whether she remembered when Fred Johnston and Frank Keller came to her home on the evening after Thanksgiving 1899. She said that she did.

Guiher directed her, "State whether or not at that time it was agreed between you that you would let bygones be bygones; that you would forget the past, and all try to live without trouble in the future."

"Yes, sir," she responded.

Answering mostly in single syllables and in a voice so low that both the court reporter and Judge Nichols frequently had to ask her to repeat herself, Margaret stated that there had been no trouble between herself and her husband after Thanksgiving 1899. Her husband, she said, had been a good provider for the family and had treated their children kindly. The family had lived in peace for the twelve months prior to his death.

Guiher asked her about the night that her husband was killed and Margaret answered the questions the same as she had before, at the coroner's inquest just days after the murder and at the trial the following April. Her story had never changed and it was supported by the testimony of her children. Eventually, the attorney came to his last four questions - each of which Margaret answered clearly and calmly:

"Tell the jury, whether on the night of December 1, 1900, you struck John Hossack with an axe."
"I did not."
"Tell the jury with you struck him with anything else."
"I did not."
"Tell that jury whether or not you know who struck him."
"I do not."
"Tell the jury whether or not you saw any person strike him."
"I did not."

That evening, the *Daily News* proclaimed that an acquittal for Margaret seemed likely. Noting that the defendant's testimony was "convincing," the article concluded: "It is the general opinion here that the state has not produced sufficient evidence for conviction. Public sentiment is strong for the defendant and if she is convicted the community will be disappointed."

On Monday afternoon, the lawyers began their final arguments. Each of the six participating attorneys spoke, with the prosecution and defense taking turns. The final speeches were reserved for the lead attorneys, and it was late on Wednesday morning when Senator Berry faced the jury to begin what would be a five-hour argument for acquittal. As before, he stripped off his coat, loosened his tie and rolled up his sleeves. Sweat rolled down his face as he paced from one side of the courtroom to the other. Refuting the evidence and the conclusions of the prosecutors, he argued passionately for Margaret's acquittal. He had no doubts, he said. He believed in his heart and would say before God, that Margaret Hossack was not guilty of the terrible crime that she had been charged with. The jurors watched and listened intently. Many of the women in the crowd wept as they listened to Berry plead for the defendant.

George Clammer's turn came the following day. He was thorough in his presentation, proceedings logically from point to point and propping up his argument with references to the testimony. There was no other reasonable explanation, he argued, than the obvious one: that Margaret Hossack, after hating her husband for years, had killed him in his sleep. As at the first trial, the former county attorney relied heavily on his props - the bed and the axe with the bumped handle and the chipped blade. Once again, Clammer painstakingly went through the evidence, including the history of the troubled relations between husband and wife, Margaret's pleas for help to neighbors over the years, the family axe as the murder weapon, the narrowness of the bed, and the defendant's incredible claim that she slept through the attack.

When he reached the end of his argument, Clammer acted out the murder, placing himself in the role of the attacker. According to the newspaper reports of the trial, the spectators were as "still as death" as they watched his dramatic performance. Moving to the side of the bed, Clammer seized the axe. He raised it over his shoulder and brought the shaft down forcefully against the mattress and frame. The bed shuddered and the sound of the axe handle striking wood echoed off the walls of the room. Then he stepped back and waited, as if deep in thought. Then, suddenly, he sprang forward again, swinging the axe high over his head and bringing it down with a heavy crash against the bed frame.

He turned on his heel and faced the jury. He tersely concluded the stunt with only one line: "The defendant asks you to believe that she was not awakened by the sound of these blows."

When Clammer was finished, Judge Nichols read his instructions to the jury. They were almost identical to the ones provided by Judge Gamble at the end of the first trial, but with one significant difference: Nichols told the jurors that they must decide whether they believed that a successful reconciliation between the Hossacks had occurred. If they believed it, then they could not consider the earlier quarrels between the defendant and her husband as a motive for committing the crime.

With that point made clear, the jurors were turned over to the bailiff, who led them to a separate room in the courthouse to begin their deliberations.

Margaret and her children left the courthouse and returned to their rooming house. There, it was said, the beleaguered woman finally broke down, shedding the tears that she had been holding back almost from the very start of her ordeal.

A crowd gathered on the courthouse lawn, waiting for a sign that the jury had reached its verdict. In the courthouse, lights burned through the night. The twelve jurors took their first vote. Initially, nine of them were in favor of conviction, three for acquittal. The majority argued the case for the prosecution, trying to sway the three hold-outs to their side. The debate, reports later stated, was "long and heated." After thirty hours of deliberation, the three jurors refused to convict Margaret Hossack of murder. They never spoke publicly about their reasons, but they stood in unwavering opposition against the majority.

On Friday evening, they returned to the courtroom and the foreman informed the judge that it was impossible for them to reach a verdict. They agreed only on one thing: that further discussion would not result in a decision. Judge Nichols questioned the jury himself until he was certain that no consensus was possible. After that, he resignedly thanked them for their time and discharged them, announcing to the assembled crowd that court was adjourned.

Hours later, Judge Nichols predicted that the case would not be retried, and he was right. After two weeks, the Board of Supervisors of Madison County passed a resolution that it would not further aid in the prosecution of Margaret Hossack, stating its desire that the case be dismissed. W.S. Cooper, the county attorney, wrote to the board that he believed Mrs. Hossack was guilty of the crime, but he knew of no person and no additional evidence that could be produced against her, so that the "result of another trial is very doubtful." A year later, Cooper amended his statement, strongly requesting that the case be dismissed, citing lack of new evidence, the difficulty and cost of getting witnesses to testify yet another time, the publicity surrounding the two earlier trials and the "advanced years and enfeebled condition and appearance" of Mrs. Hossack. He did stress, however, that the case should be dismissed "not because of the innocence of the defendant, but because it will be impossible to secure her conviction."

Margaret Hossack never went back to court. Her legal troubles were over. No one else was ever arrested or publicly named as a suspect in the murder of her husband.

The question of her guilt lingered in the community. Most people who believed she was innocent also believed that she knew who had murdered her husband. The most prevalent theory was that she was covering up for one of her sons, who had attacked his father out of anger, or more likely, to protect his mother. That possibility was never explored by the investigators, who never wavered in their belief that Margaret was the killer. Over time, people came to realize that neither she nor other members of the family would ever discuss the case again. Even those who believed she was guilty, or that she knew more than she would admit, did not view her with animosity. She was not a threat to the community and she was seen as a woman who suffered greatly in her marriage - and one who may, or may not have, finally taken her revenge.

Time and history have laid waste to the aftermath of the Hossack story, leaving behind tragedy, pain, suffering, and even a lingering haunting.

George Clammer never gave up his belief that Margaret Hossack killed her husband. His failure to secure a conviction in the second trial haunted him for the rest of his life. To this day, John Hossack's murder remains unsolved.

Clammer gave up his political aspirations and his criminal law practice. Although he had lived in Iowa his entire life, he moved his family to Fort Collins, Colorado, in 1904 and was admitted to the Colorado bar two months later. But even so far away, Clammer could not forget the Hossack case. He remembered the violence of the crime, the cruel damage rendered by the two blows to Hossack's head and all of the grisly evidence that he was forced to look at for so many months. The memories, his wife confided to others, continued to upset him years after the case was abandoned.

Clammer built a successful civil law practice in Fort Collins, but after ten years, he moved his family again, this time to Manhattan, Kansas. He began practicing law with a local firm, earned respect as a civic leader, served as president of the Rotary Club and Chamber of Commerce and on the boards of several local businesses. He devoted his private time to his church, to writing, to music and to reading Shakespeare.

He died in 1938 at the age of sixty-four. In his obituary, he was praised as "a truly superior lawyer and a man of unimpeachable character." There was no mention of his early legal experience as a county prosecutor.

William Berry failed to prove Margaret Hossack's innocence, but his defense and eloquent arguments eventually won her freedom. Berry never had another case that attracted such widespread publicity, but he did stay in the public spotlight for the next two decades. In 1907, the governor named Berry to the newly formed Board of Parole, where he served as chairman for eight years. After the death of Justice Charles Bishop on the Iowa Supreme Court, Berry was considered the frontrunner to fill the seat. Both the Warren and Madison County bar associations supported Berry's candidacy, but the seat was eventually offered to someone else. In 1912, he was prominently mentioned as a potential candidate for statewide office but despite initial interest in him as a candidate, widespread support failed to materialize, and Berry withdrew from the race. He never again ran for public office, but he did serve as a trustee for Simpson College until 1917.

He continued to put tremendous energy into his legal practice and it thrived. He lived long enough to witness a landmark change in Warren County when, in September 1921, Jennie Smith and Una Overton became the first women in the county's history to serve on a jury. They were seated as jurors in a civil case in the same courtroom where Margaret Hassock had been tried two decades earlier.

Berry remained active until the end of his life, maintaining a full schedule of legal and political commitments. He went to work on this last day of life, March 25, 1923, and suffered a major heart attack just as he arrived at his office on the second floor of the Worth Savings Building.

The story of the Hossack murder remained a tale that was told long after Margaret Hossack's final trial, eventually turning into local legend.

A few people whispered that the Hossack family had found a way to bribe the three hold-out jurors in Winterset. Most people assumed that the family members knew more about the murder than they had admitted in court. A rumor started that May's husband, Ira Coulter, might have been the one who attacked John Hossack. William Haines, whose wife later sued him for divorce charging him with cruelty, remained a suspect for many people. No solid evidence ever emerged to support any of these theories, though, but the stories were passed down from generation to generation.

More than thirty years after the crime, a new allegation arose. In 1935, Ray Dickinson, a rural mail carrier, ran an advertisement on the front page of the *New Virginian*, a weekly newspaper distributed in New Virginia and the surrounding area. Upset about a foreclosure hearing the previous year, Dickinson claimed that one of his neighbors, John J. McCuddin, had committed perjury during the proceedings. In addition, Dickinson alluded to the strange death of a man named Ed Knotts. Several years before the Hossack murder, McCuddin and his brother, Charles, had twice been tried for killing Knotts, with the second trial ending with an acquittal. The case was never solved.

Dickinson's charges enraged McCuddin. A little over a year after the advertisement appeared, McCuddin allegedly threatened Dickinson with a snow shovel in an alley behind the New Virginia post office. On December 24, 1936, Dickinson published a second advertisement. It was directly addressed to McCuddin and warned him that the "other ghost that had its head chopped open may wake up and talk to you if you keep on the way that you have been. I want to let you know that I mean business and I don't mean maybe." It was a puzzling but seemingly pointed reference to the murder of John Hossack.

McCuddin had enough. He filed suit against Dickinson, charging him with libel and demanding damages. In a written interrogatory before trial, Dickinson was asked, "What did you mean by the statement in reference to a ghost that had its head chopped open?"

Dickinson replied: "By this statement is meant that the plaintiff J.J. McCuddin has knowledge of another homicide."

The case dragged on for several years. Eventually, McCuddin was awarded damages of $100, although the decision was later overturned by the Iowa Supreme Court. The authorities did nothing to re-open the Hossack case and Dickinson was never formally questioned about what he might know about the Hossack murder. Many people in the community dismissed the charges as part of a longstanding feud, but there were a few who wondered if there might be some truth to Dickinson's allegations.

At the time of the crime, the McCuddins lived just a few miles west of the Hossack farm, and both J.J. McCuddin and his father signed as sureties on a bail bond so that Margaret Hossack could be released from prison in December 1900. The families knew each other and the McCuddin brothers were about the same age as the older Hossack boys. None of the McCuddins were ever called as witnesses in the legal proceedings related to Hossack's murder.

During Margaret Hossack's murder trial, Don Berry, the son of defense attorney William Berry, was a young student at Simpson College. He earned great respect for his coverage of the case for the *Des Moines Register*. After graduation, he was hired by the paper, but only stayed for one year, leaving to take up farming. His father had helped him to acquire land and he farmed for nearly fifteen years. He married Bertha Sloan, a Simpson classmate, and started a family - but he never lost his love for reporting. By 1919, he was back in the newspaper business again. For the next forty years, he was the editor of the *Indianola Record-Herald*. When his mother, Alice Berry, died in 1928, he and Bertha moved their family into the Berry residence on Ashland Avenue and lived there until 1966.

As time passed, Don often heard stories about the Hossack murder. Fact and rumor were liberally mixed as the community continued to debate the guilt of Margaret Hossack and speculate about the involvement of others in the crime. Based on what he saw and heard during the trial in 1901, Berry developed a theory of his own. Near the end of his newspaper career, his interest in the county's history led him into a project with Gerald Schulz, the chairman of the sociology department at Simpson College. Together, they wrote a history of Warren County in 1953. In a chapter called "Crime and Other Social Problems," Schulz recounted the story of the Hossack murder case, including Margaret's dramatic arrest at the cemetery and the results of the two trials. Don Berry added a footnote to the story:

As a young reporter I covered the first trial of Margaret Hossack for the Des Moines Register. *While the testimony did not prove her "not guilty," to my mind it fell short of proving her guilty. In the years that passed since the trial, evidence has come to me still further casting doubt on her guilt; but I cannot repeat it here without casting a shadow on another party, now dead and against whom the evidence is not conclusive. However, I cannot allow this permanent record to go to press without saying more in defense of the name of Margaret Hossack than simply that the second jury disagreed. I do not believe she was guilty of the murder of her husband. D.L.B.*

Interested readers knew that by the time Berry wrote the note, most of the witnesses in the case, including William Haines, and all of the Hossack children, except for May Coulter, had died. Berry never publicly disclosed the evidence that he had received, nor did he indicate the name of the person he believed to be guilty of the murder, but near the end of his life, he discussed the case.

In order to give a recounting of the significant events of his life and the history of the Berry family, Don agreed to a series of recorded interviews with his son, Thomas. The stories were recorded on reel-to-reel tapes over several sessions. The last recording was made in 1970, when Berry was almost ninety years old. Near the end of the last tape, Thomas asked his father if he had any other stories to relate. Don replied:

John Hossack and his wife and children lived about a mile north of the road running from Medora to New Virginia. And John Hossack was murdered one night. His wife woke up in the night and found he had been hit in the head with an ax... and killed right there in the bed beside her. The axe was found the next morning under the corncrib and still had some blood on it. The grand jury indicted her for murder. My father was the attorney for the defense, defended her.

John Hossack was a good, I guess, straight old chap but he was pretty strict with his children and pretty crotchety... I think she could have cleared herself but I think it would have involved testifying against her own son, and what would any mother do if she told what she knew and her son would hang by the neck until dead. She'd keep still. And Mrs. Hossack kept still. And the general feeling was she either did it or knew who did it. I don't think there were any questions about it. And father tried that case and I covered it... That was the first big case I'd covered.

She was convicted and sent to the penitentiary. One night I was coming down on the train from Des Moines to Indianola, and the conductor came to me and said there's a lady back there who would like to talk to you. She's a sister-in-law of the warden up at Anamosa.

I went back to talk to her and she says, "I'd like to talk to your father but I can't stop." She was going south on the Q after she got to Indianola. She says, "The warden wants that woman out. He doesn't think she is guilty. He's never had another such case in his life and he thinks she's absolutely innocent. And he wants your father to get her out of there..."

I don't remember just what the grounds of the appeal was. Something in the summation of evidence. Then it came back and the prosecution asked for a change of venue and the case was taken to Winterset, tried over there, and it resulted in a hung jury. Now that was in 1903 because I remember that after the mail had come in we got a telephone call from Winterset there at the Register *that said the jury had hung. And I wrote the story...*

The Board of Supervisors decided she'd taken a good deal of punishment and they hadn't proved her guilty, and the county spent all the money it was going to spend prosecuting her. I don't think the old lady was guilty. I think one of the sons did it.

And that night shortly after the murder - do you remember when you go down to Medora and turn east on the pavement you cross a little hollow there in a little ways? Well, that hollow had a long wooden bridge over it and somebody heard a horse go across that bridge in about three jumps and that boy was apparently back at the farm where he worked and I've heard the report - I don't know this for sure - that the man found his horse sweaty the next morning. So I think the boy killed him because he was a crusty old chap and wouldn't do what his children wanted and she kept still rather than send him to the gallows. Any woman, any mother, would have done the same thing.

Margaret Hossack's brother, Donald Murchison, died in Elmira, Illinois in 1910. His obituary vaguely mentioned a surviving sister who lived in Iowa, but in subsequent years, the Murchison family attempted to expunge the name of Margaret Hossack from its history.

In 1938, a booklet that was published to celebrate the centennial of the founding of Elmira was printed with Margaret's name removed from the list of Alexander Murchison's children. It was taken out by Frances Murchison, the daughter of Margaret's brother, Alex, Jr. She considered herself the keeper of the family's history and took great pride in relating anecdotes about her ancestors for her nieces and nephews. But she told them nothing about her Aunt Margaret, nothing about her aunt's marriage, and nothing about the sensational murder trial at which her uncle Donald had testified.

Soon after the second murder trial concluded, the strong bond holding together the nine Hossack children seemed to suddenly snap, freeing them to move on with their own lives. None of them left a record of their thoughts about the murder for future generations.

Two of the daughters, Cassie and Louie, left Iowa altogether. Cassie married Will Skelly and they moved to Utah. Louis and her husband, Joe Kemp, also moved west, settling in Colorado. A few years later, 1909, Louie died of complications during the birth of her fourth child. Joe had her body returned to Indianola for burial and he arranged for the baby, named Margaret Lucretia after her mother and grandmother, to be cared for by Cassie in Utah. Cassie raised her and she spent the rest of her life out West, far away from her siblings.

Later on, Joe wrote an autobiography that was privately distributed to a few family members, but he had little to say about the murder of his father-in-law, noting only that a few days after Thanksgiving 1900, his wife's father was "called to his home on high which was a severe and sudden shock to all of us." To anyone reading it who knew nothing of the murder, it sounded like Hossack could have died from a heart attack, or as the result of some kind of accident. For Kemp, who had been instrumental in arguing for a change of venue in the second trial, he wanted nothing written about the event. When his oldest son, John Alger Kemp, who was born in the Hossack farmhouse six days after his grandfather's murder, moved to California as a young man, Joe told him that he should never tell anyone that his grandmother had been charged with murder. Still, the story was passed down through the family, and one of Kemp's granddaughters later referred to the murder as a "family secret" and admitted that she was "haunted by the thought of her tainted blood."

Annie Henry and May Coulter stayed in Iowa, close to where they had been born, and both raised large families: seven children for Annie and six for May. Annie, who died in 1923, was plagued by depression for many years. She always insisted that her mother was falsely accused of murdering her father.

Like her mother, May suffered through an unhappy marriage. Ira Coulter was a bitter man, much like John Hossack. He was impatient, strict and had a sharp temper. Eventually, May suffered a nervous breakdown and she left him. She lived the rest of her life in Indianola, lonely and unhappy. She was the last of the Hossack children to die, succumbing to heart disease in 1956 at the age of seventy-six.

Will and Johnnie Hossack, the two boys most often rumored to have been involved in the murder of their father, moved away from Iowa. Both suffered from mental illness before their deaths.

After the second trial, Will roomed and worked at the Truitt farm, as Johnnie had done before him. He shared a room with Harold Tritt, Ivan's friend. In an unpublished journal, Truitt, now grown to adulthood, wrote about Will:

Will Hossack worked for us for two years after the murder, and I believe he was a nervous man after that for a long time. I had to sleep with him when he was with us, and I learned soon after his arrival to arouse him before I got into bed with him, because I almost caught his fist in the middle of my face. I surely hated to sleep with him, but I was afraid to tell folks, so I lived with my cowardliness in silence.

Truitt later came to believe that Will was involved in the murder. He wrote, "Although I don't know about either Will or Mrs. Hossack's abilities to kill someone, I will say I am pretty sure Mrs. Hossack swung the axe and Will held the lamp for her to swing it by."

By the time that Truitt came to believe this, Will had moved to Colorado, where he found work in the mines and lost touch with his family. In his early thirties, Will was hospitalized in an insane asylum, as his brother Johnnie would be. In November 1918, unmarried and only thirty-six years old, Will died. On the death certificate, a physician noted that the cause of death was the "general paralysis of the insane." In other words, the young man died as a result of the third and final stage of syphilis. He was buried in a pauper's grave near Pueblo, Colorado.

Johnnie also left Iowa and broke off contact with his family. He left his job at the gas company in Des Moines and moved to the West Coast. He married a woman named Jessie and fathered two sons, eventually settling with his family in Rialto, California, where he found work in the oil fields. Johnnie died at Patton State Hospital in San Bernardino in 1936. His death certificate states that his cause of death was cerebral arteriosclerosis, accompanied by psychosis. He was fifty-eight years old.

After the second trial, Alex Hossack returned to Palo Alto County. His wife died several years later, leaving him with four young children. He lived an itinerant life, traveling alone across Iowa and to other parts of the Midwest, looking for odd jobs and never staying in one place for long. Unable to raise his children on his own, he left them in the care of his late wife's sister. His wandering sometimes took him to Mitchell, South Dakota, where his brother, Ivan, had settled. On occasion, Alex walked past his brother's house and talked to Ivan's young daughter when she played in the yard. He visited Ivan at his barbershop downtown and Ivan sometimes gave him money. Eventually, Alex returned to Iowa, spending the final years of his life in Dubuque, where he died in poverty in 1939.

Jimmie, who had shared a room with Ivan in the old Hossack house, lived in Indianola for most of his life and worked for the railroad. For a while he lived with his mother in a boarding house. He never married or had children, and he had a tendency to be disagreeable and mean-spirited, just like his father. His nieces and nephews disliked and were afraid of him. Jimmie, like Alex, stayed in touch with Ivan, who he occasionally wrote to, sending him the occasional postcard or photograph.

Plagued by drinking problems throughout his adult life, Jimmie died in 1945 and was buried next to his sister, Louie, in the Indianola Cemetery.

It turned out to be Ivan, the youngest of the Hossack children, who was most successful in creating a stable and happy life. A couple of years after the second murder trial, Ivan left the Van Pattens and joined up with the Ringling Brothers Circus, where he learned to be a barber. He later moved to Colorado and briefly lived near his brother, Will. After serving in the Army during World War I, Ivan settled in Mitchell, South Dakota, where he opened a barber shop and got married. He and his wife, Myrtle, lived modestly and occasionally returned to Indianola and visited the Van Pattens, Annie, May and Jimmie. Ivan never had much of anything to say about the past, preferring not to talk about his painful memories or his abandonment by his family. He held on to a few keepsakes, including the quilt that his mother had made with his name stitched at the bottom, but he rarely talked about his youth.

In 1922, Ivan's only child was born, a daughter named Maxine. He proved to be a devoted and fiercely protective father. One day, when the little girl was eight or nine years old, Ivan returned from the barbershop to see her talking to a strange man outside their house. The man turned and Ivan recognized him as his brother, Alex, who for some reason had not identified himself to Maxine as her uncle. Ivan spoke angrily to him, telling him not to come to the house. It was all right for Alex to visit him at the barbershop, he said, but he didn't want him stopping by his home or talking to his daughter. Maxine never recalled ever seeing her uncle again.

Ivan lived a contented life, taking care of his family, running his business, and managing the upkeep of his well-appointed home. He loved to hunt for pheasants, either alone, or with friends, in the fields outside of town. In his barbershop, he got to know the local farmers and merchants and was well-liked by all who knew him.

In the late 1930s, Ivan took Myrtle and Maxine with him to Iowa and they visited the home of May and Ira Coulter. It was the first time that Maxine, now a teenager, had met her cousins. Away from the adults, they sat outside and talked. Maxine was told a surprising story about her father's parents: that his father had been killed, hit in the head with an axe in the middle of the night! Maxine's father and four of her aunts and uncles had been living in the house at the time. A few days later, her grandmother had been arrested and charged with his murder. She was later sent to prison, but after another trial, she was set free when the jury could not decide on a verdict.

When Maxine asked her mother about the story, Myrtle reluctantly confirmed that it was true, but said that Ivan had never told her any of the details. He hadn't wanted his adored daughter to find out about that part of his life and it would be best if Maxine never let him know what she'd heard. Maxine never raised the subject with her mother again, nor did she tell her friends, but she wished she knew more. She finally understood, though, why her father had gone to live with the Van Pattens as a boy.

On only one occasion did Maxine ask her father anything about the murder. She phrased her question carefully so as to not reveal her knowledge, asking, "What did my grandfather die of?"

For Ivan, who had dealt with his family's past by staying silent for many years, he likely thought back to the events that surrounded his father's death - the brutality, violence, the cold winter day's trip to the coal bank, the late supper, the newspaper, the games in the kitchen, his trip to retrieve Will's coat and to put away the axe. He must have realized, all those years later, that his testimony in the second trial had helped save his mother from prison. He pondered his reply for a moment before he finally answered his daughter's question. "He died of meanness," he said.

After the jury in the second murder trial failed to convict Margaret Hossack, she returned to Warren County and lived there for the last thirteen years of her life. She and her bachelor son, Jimmie, resided in a boarding house on Boston Street in Indianola. Alger and Nancy Truitt, the Hossacks' neighbors, also relocated to Indianola and lived just a few blocks away. They were representative of a national trend of migration from farms to towns in the early 1900s. The Truitts had taken in three of the Kemp children after Louie's untimely death and Margaret sometimes visited her grandchildren there. She was a quiet, older woman, neither cheerful or outgoing, and even to her grandchildren, she seemed cold and withdrawn. It was almost as if life had beaten the happiness out of her.

There is no evidence that Margaret, at any time after the second trial, ever spoke of her husband's murder. No journals, letters or diaries have even been found in which she recorded her feelings about the trials of her knowledge of the crime.

Margaret died of natural causes on August 25, 1916, at the age of seventy-two. Dr. Surber, a witness at the inquest and for the prosecution at the first murder trial, attended her after her release from prison. He signed her death certificate, recording the cause of death as "acute dilation of the heart."

Survived by eight of her children and nearly twenty grandchildren, Margaret outlived her parents, her in-laws, her siblings, two of her children and, of course, her husband. Astonishingly, the obituary that appeared in the local newspaper a week after her death did not mention the central fact about her life: that she had been accused and once convicted of her husband's brutal murder. It focused instead on her qualities as a mother and her devotion to her church.

In late August 1916, Margaret Hossack was laid to rest in the northeast corner of the New Virginia Cemetery, a short distance from the spot where Sheriff Hodson had arrested her fifteen years earlier. On a small hill, John and Margaret Hossack, husband and wife for thirty-two years, are buried side by side. A simple stone, engraved with their names, is the only designation of the site. Whatever secrets they had, they took them to the grave.

And yet the story of the Hossack murder was not yet over.

The Hossack farm, purchased at auction by C.C. Taggart in September 1901, remained in the Taggart family for more than fifty years. Then, in 1953, in an odd twist of circumstance, ownership of the land, and the house in which John Hossack was murdered, passed to a relation by marriage of the Hossacks.

It was in 1953 that LaVere Burchett took possession of the farm. LaVere, a former marine who'd just returned from service in the Korea, was newly married to Marge Morris, whose uncle, Loyd Van Patten, was married to Ethel Henry, a granddaughter of John and Margaret Hossack.

The Burchetts moved into the old, drafty farmhouse, a place that had changed very little since the Hossacks first moved in, more than seventy years before. It still lacked modern conveniences - no electricity, no insulation, no running water and no indoor plumbing. In the winter, the only heat was provided by an old coal stove. There was a lot of work to do to make the house more modern and the Burchetts began making improvements, which continued over the next fifteen years. The first renovation was to tear down the partition separating the two small bedrooms on the first floor and combine the space into one large area. They tore down and replaced some of the older outbuildings, the barn and the chicken house, and in 1967, tore down the original Hossack farmhouse. The carpenters who dismantled the old house claimed that they saw places where John Hossack's blood had stained the bedroom walls and floor. On the site of the original house, the Burchetts built a modern one-story home of brick and clapboard.

LaVere Burchett knew the stories about the Hossack murder, as did everyone who had grown up in the area. He knew that Hossack had been slain in the middle of the night and while his wife had been arrested and tried for the crime, it had never been officially solved. After the Burchetts had lived in the new house for several years, LaVere awoke one night to find the grayish figure of a man standing at the foot of his bed. The figure seemed human-shaped and although it stood there silently, LaVere didn't get the sense that it was threatening in any way. In spite of that feeling, the apparition startled him. After a few moments, it vanished.

Over the years, Burchett encountered the form more than a dozen times - and it wasn't always standing at the end of his bed in the darkness. He saw the ghost, which he came to believe was that of John Hossack, in other parts of the house, including the hallway and the kitchen. Once, he saw him in broad daylight, sitting on the edge of his bed.

Rather than be unnerved by the dead man's presence, LaVere chose to think of him as a protective spirit, watching over the household where he had built a life and then met an untimely end. Perhaps because of the suddenness of his death - and the fact that his murder was never solved - John Hossack was never able to shake himself loose from the land that he loved with a passion that he was never able to extend to his wife and children.

1908: "COME PREPARED TO STAY FOREVER"

In old Indiana, not far from LaPorte,
There once lived a woman, a home lovin' sort.
Belle wanted a husband, she wanted one bad,
She placed in the papers a lonely hearts ad.
Men came to Belle Gunness to share food and bed,

Not knowing that soon they'd be knocked in the head.
But while they were sleeping, she'd lift the door latch.
She'd kill them and plant them in her tater patch.

From a 1938 folk song about the Indiana murderess

The hands on his pocket watch read just after 4:00 a.m. when Joe Maxson was roused from his sleep on the morning of April 28. The hired hand, who slept on the second floor of the farmhouse, had no idea what had awakened him at first. And then he smelled smoke. He rubbed his eyes and ran a hand down his face, smoothing the drooping brown mustache over his lip. Why would Belle be cooking breakfast so early? And if she was, had the stove caught on fire? He wearily swung his legs out of bed and reached for his pants, which were hanging on the post at the end of the bed. As he did so, he saw tendrils of smoke sifting up between the floorboards from the kitchen below. More smoke was drifting under the bedroom door. Maxson was now fully awake. This was not something burning on the stove - the entire house was on fire!

The farmhand stumbled blindly to the door and threw it open. Smoke filled the hallway and the ominous flicker of flames could be seen farther down the hall. He called out as loudly as he could for Belle and the children, but there was no answer. Belle's room was just steps away. The room was always kept locked and while he had been forbidden to enter, Maxson kicked at the door with all of his strength. It shuddered on its frame, but it refused to open.

Choking on the smoke, Maxson raced down the stairs, clutching his valise and a pair of overalls. These he left in a carriage shed about fifty feet from the property after he escaped the burning house. He tossed his belongings aside and ran back to the house. He called loudly for Belle and the children, shouting their names and pounding on windows. There was still no response from inside. In the thick smoke, and from what he could see through the windows, the house was dark and its occupants were unmoving. It was soon engulfed in flames and the fire spread wildly.

Maxson continued to run around the house, calling for help. He explained later, "I was yelling to attract the attention of Mrs. Gunness and the children, but I did not hear any sound except the roaring of the fire. I picked up bricks and threw them in the windows but no one showed up."

The nearest neighbor, William Clifford, lived about one-eighth of a mile from the Gunness farm. He was the first to arrive on the scene. Together with Joe Maxson, they smashed windows but dared not enter the burning house. Soon, others began to arrive, drawn by the light of the flames as they danced up into the sky. William Humphrey, who lived on the Russell farm to the north, placed a ladder underneath an upstairs window on the west side of the house. He climbed up and peered inside. He later said the bed in one of the rooms looked as though someone was sleeping in it. Maxson said that this was the room where Belle usually slept.

Other families from neighboring farms - the Nicholsons, the Laphams, and the Hutsons - arrived to offer what help they could. They tried in vain to wake the occupants of the burning house - if they were still alive. Maxson wasn't sure, but he thought it was shortly before 5:00 a.m. when he hitched a horse to a buggy and drove to the LaPorte, Indiana, jail to notify Sheriff Smutzer, his deputies LeRoy Marr and William E. Antiss, and the volunteer fire brigade. It was later reported that Maxson said that he was convinced that one of Belle's enemies had set fire to the house.

In less than one hour, the Gunness farmhouse and outbuildings were reduced to blackened rubble and heaps of scorched debris. The floors had collapsed and only uneven sections of the brick outer walls remained standing. The house had been utterly destroyed. By daylight, teams of men led by Sheriff Smutzer sifted through the smoldering ruins, searching for the bodies of Belle Gunness and her children.

Over the course of the next day, volunteers removed debris that had fallen down into the basement of the house. The work was nearly completed when searchers came upon the headless remains of an adult woman in the northeast corner of the cellar. The body of Belle's son, Phillip, was lying across the headless woman's body. His small form was wrapped in a blanket. The bodies of her two girls were resting on either side of the body. How had the bodies ended up so perfectly arranged after the chaos of the fire? This was just one of the mysteries revealed by the blaze.

Investigators thought that the positioning of the bodies suggested that they had been deliberately arranged that way before the house caught fire. The *LaPorte Argus-Bulletin* newspaper didn't think it was out of the ordinary, though. One of the reporters wrote, "It looked as though the mother in a desperate effort to save her children gathered them by her side with the youngest clasped in her arms and met death bravely."

But the image of the tragic death of a devoted mother was soon to change. In a matter of days, Belle Gunness would be branded a murderer. Who was responsible for the fire? And was the woman found in the ruins really Belle Gunness? Worst of all - just what had Belle been up to at her LaPorte County farm?

Those questions - and many more - would make newspaper headlines across the Midwest in the days and weeks that followed the fire. Many of them would never be answered. In a few short years, Belle Gunness would become a terrifying legend and over time, that legend has grown. She is considered today to be one of America's most prolific female serial killers, possibly doing away with two husbands, a number of suitors and boyfriends and even her children. She is believed to have killed as many as 20 people - some put the number at more than 100 --- and it's very possible that she escaped without a trace after that April 1908 fire and was never punished for her crimes.

Rudyard Kipling once wrote that the female of the species is much deadlier than the male. When it came to Belle Gunness, this observation certainly turned out to be true.

Belle Gunness was no stranger to mystery or to controversy. Her origins, like most of her life story, are shrouded in legend and deliberate inventions. Most of the accounts of her life state that she was born as Brynchild Poulsdatter Størset on November 11, 1859 in Selbu, Sør-Trøndelag County in northern Norway. Her father, Paul Pederson Størsetgjerde was a poverty-stricken peasant who maintained a farm in Selbu.

The farm belonged to distant relatives and Paul leased the land to grow barley, oats, and potatoes and raise a few sheep. During the winter months, he supplemented the family's meager income by working as a stonemason. Hunger and poverty loomed huge in Belle's early life and she was sent to work as a dairy maid and cattle girl, hired to shepherd the livestock to the mountain pastures for fresh grazing. Any money that she earned was turned over to her father to help with the family expenses.

Little is known about the day-to-day life of the struggling family, or what changed Belle into the woman she became. Brynchild's circumstances and her years in Norway were unknown until her crimes in America became a national story in 1908. Before that time, most people in the United States had never heard of Selbu or its remote corner of Norway. But the connections of the small community to the infamous Belle Gunness led to recollections that were picked up by the press of the day. According to one story, Belle was remembered by many, and most of what they had to say about her wasn't good. "She was a bad human being," the local newspaper *Selbyggen* wrote, "capricious and extremely malicious. She had un-pretty habits, always in the mood for dirty tricks, talked little and was a liar already as a child. People mocked her and called her '*Snurkvistpåla* ffiwhich meant spruce twigs and Paul's daughter - the girl collected kindling from the spruce trees for the family fireffl." The demeaning task and the cruel nickname subjected the young girl to mockery and ridicule from children and adults in the community. There was no question that Brynchild and her family occupied the lowest rung of the local social ladder. The resentments that she undoubtedly felt toward the more fortunate in the village built up in the young woman until a defining tragedy in her early life created a powerful anger that would return over and over again as a violent retribution towards men.

In 1877, when Belle was 17, a traumatic and life-changing event occurred that forever altered her feelings toward men and the raising of children. Brynchild, who had been raised in the Lutheran Church, discovered that she was pregnant, scandalizing her family and bringing even more shame upon herself. She was already an outsider in the community, and this gave the gossips something else to whisper about. After this scandalous news spread through the community, Brynchild attended a dance one evening and was physically accosted by the son of a wealthy local family - a man far above her own station in life.

But Brynchild was a sturdy young woman and she fought back against the man's sexual advances. Rebuffed by a woman he felt should have welcomed his attentions, the now-angry young man kicked her viciously in the abdomen. Brynchild miscarried, but officials in Selbu did nothing to prosecute her attacker. Strangely, though, the young man died a short time later, allegedly from stomach cancer. In light of her later crimes, there has been speculation that Belle poisoned her attacker and thus claimed her first victim.

Her part in his death will always remain a mystery, but what is known is that Belle was never the same after her miscarriage. Her personality was markedly changed. She became increasingly morose and resentful and all of the dreams that she once had of settling down with a loving husband in a happy marriage disappeared. As her sister Nellie later said, "Money was her god." She became intent on escaping the rural provinces of Norway for the America, where popular myth said that even a person of the most humble origins could make their fortune. Beaten down and angered by the poor conditions and the cruel people of her hometown, Belle convinced herself that America was her best chance at achieving a comfortable life.

A young Brynchild Størset, who later became Belle Sorensen Gunness

Over the next three years, she saved her money and worked hard to make her dream come true. She labored in pigpens, milked cows and tended horses until her older sister whose name, oddly, was also Brynchild, but changed to Nellie in the New World agreed to help her pay for passage to New York. Nellie had left for America in 1874 and married a Chicago man named John Larsen. By the time Belle arrived, the Larsens were well-established on Chicago's Northwest Side.

Identifying herself as Brynchild Petersen to immigration authorities, she boarded the steamship *Tasso* and made the Atlantic crossing on September 8, 1881. She made her way to Chicago and moved in with her sister and her husband for a short time. Life with the Larsens offered security but proved to be an uncomfortable arrangement. John Larsen did not like Belle as she called herself , which made her relations with her sister severely strained. Belle initially went to work as a servant but she was ambitious and longed for the finer things in life. She began searching for a husband and three years later, she found one.

In 1884, Belle married Mads Albert Sorensen. Much of what is known about her days in Chicago came from Anton O. Olsen, a close friend of her husband. Olsen was an engineer at the Munger Laundry Company in Chicago and a man with a curious connection to the Sorensen family. Around the time when Belle and Mads were married, Olsen lost his wife to typhoid fever, leaving him to care for their eight-month-old infant girl, Jennie Eugenia. Unable to care for an infant in diapers without a woman in the house to help him, he had given the girl up for adoption to Belle and Mads Sorensen. Mads was his good friend, and a night watchman for the Mandel Brothers Department Store. The couple had agreed to care for the child and provide for her as a foster daughter. He knew Mads to be a good and decent man, an immigrant who had come to America from his birthplace near Oslo in Norway. Olsen had become friends with Sorensen through the Wicker Park Chapter No. 121 of the Independent Order of Mutual Aid, a fraternal lodge associated with the trade union he belonged to that sold life insurance policies to its members. Mads assured Olsen that his wife, Belle, was the "right kind of mother" to raise Jennie in their loving home.

Olsen didn't know Belle very well at the time of the adoption, other than that Mads had married her in Chicago in 1884. The couple began their married life in Austin, then a quiet town west of Chicago, bordering the village of Oak Park.

In addition to the money that Mads brought home, Belle helped out by working in a butcher shop for a time. A physically strong and imposing woman, she was no stranger to hard work from having worked on farms in Norway. The skill in cutting up animal carcasses that she developed at the butcher's shop would later become useful in Indiana when she wielded her hatchet on the remains of a dozen murdered suitors.

Family members would have rather odd memories of Belle. She was prone to fits of violent rage, followed by an eerily quiet calm, seeming to be able to suddenly snap back into control. Her nephew, John Larsen, remembered that she had a "weakness for adopting children." He went on to say that Belle was "a queer woman and there was estrangement in the family with her for fifteen years. When first she met people she was cordial. Later she would appear indifferent to them." Nellie Larsen, John's mother and Belle's sister, was a quiet, reserved woman with soft features and a round face. She remembered that, even as a little girl, Belle caused problems in their family. When she first came to America, everyone noticed that there was something strange about her. Nellie said, "She was wild and flighty in her speech. Often she would mutter to herself and when we asked her what she said, she only laughed. My husband disliked her from the start and that also did much to keep us apart."

About three weeks before Jennie Olsen's mother died, a Lutheran minister drew up the adoption papers on December 10, 1890, outlining the agreement between the Sorensens and the Olsens. Anton Olsen, filled with guilt over the situation, wanted it understood that Jennie would legally remain his daughter and that she would eventually come back to live with him when he remarried.

Around the time of the adoption, Mads purchased a small confectionary store at 318 Grand Avenue, near Elizabeth Street, in Chicago's Austin neighborhood. The store had previously been owned by a man named Charles Christiansen. Mads took over running the business while Belle looked after children that other people did not want, or could not care for. In addition to Jennie Olsen, Belle would eventually have three children with her in Indiana - likely all adopted - Myrtle, Lucy and Phillip.

Strangely, Belle seemed to have a desperate need to take in boys and girls that no one seemed to want or those whose parents could not afford to clothe and feed them. Thanks to Belle's attack and subsequent miscarriage as a young woman in Norway, she was apparently unable to have children of her own. This seems to have fed her desire to adopt children off the streets, including Jennie Larsen, whose father had given her up because he could not care for an infant. Taking in unwanted children seems like a kind-hearted thing to do, but among Austin residents, rumors stated that the confectionary was a front for the real business that was being run out of that location. The real business, they claimed, was a "baby farm" - the buying and selling of infants.

Nellie Larsen was aware of Belle's fixation with children after Nellie's daughter, Olga, went to stay with her aunt for six weeks. When it came time for Olga to go back home to her parents, Belle offered to adopt the girl. Nellie refused and angry words were exchanged. The argument led to a serious falling out, and the two sisters did not speak for years.

A portrait photographer named R.C. Ganiere had a shop at 299 Grand Avenue. He later told the *Chicago Journal that* Belle Sorensen had been one of his best customers. He noted that she seemed obsessed with children. Belle made frequent visits to his studio to be photographed with children dressed in their Sunday best. He told the newspaper, "Although neighbors regarded Mrs. Gunness in the nature of a hermit, she appeared jovial whenever she came to my place. She dressed stylishly and was rather handsome. What troubles existed between herself and her husband I did not know, but there was much ill feeling, and the man, a midget in comparison with his wife, seemed to fear her."

Living in a small apartment above the confectionary shop, the Sorensens had a rather drab existence. Their life revolved around the shop, Norwegian fraternal societies, the Lutheran Church and their daily routines. It was punctuated by angry quarrels over money issues. Belle was unhappy with the store's income and warned Mads that they would have to give up the business if things didn't improve. Then she suggested to him that he might want to increase his life insurance coverage, just in case anything ever happened to him. She was sure that he would not want his family to starve in the event of some calamity.

Belle's complaints to Mads about the shop failing to prosper could be largely traced to problems that she created. She was sullen and rude to the customers, saying little and making as few acquaintances as possible. A number of local people noticed that Mads would almost cower when she approached him. He appeared to be deathly afraid of her. The two daughters that she had at the time were always dressed in the finest clothes, making people wonder where the owners of a small shop came up with the money to dress their girls in such style.

The confectionary was heavily insured - as was Mads --- and relations between Belle and her husband became increasingly strained. Mads' easy-going nature was constantly tested by the strange and often violent moods of his wife. In 1897, after nearly 13 years of marriage, Sorensen considered leaving his troubled wife for a life of adventure in Alaska as an employee of the Yukon Mining and Trust Company. Gold had been discovered in the Klondike River in 1896, starting a rush to the region by prospectors and adventurers from all over. However, Mads decided that is was best not to leave Chicago. His wife refused to allow him to go. Once again, the compliant man was beaten down by his wife's stronger will. This time, though, his decision to give Belle her way cost him his life.

*Belle Gunness's most famous family photo.
Belle with Phillip on lap , Myrtle and Lucy*

About a year after Mads had asked his wife about going to Alaska, the confectionary shop burned during a mysterious fire. Belle was alone with her children in the store at the time. She hurried them to safety in front of the building, where she began screaming at the top of her lungs. Belle claimed that a kerosene lamp had exploded and started the fire. No lamp was ever found in the ruins, but the insurance money was paid. The interior of the store was completely burned out, and the neighbors gossiped that Belle had been responsible. After the Sorensens received the insurance money, the charred building was sold back to Charles Christiansen.

The tidy sum paid for the store allowed Belle and Mads to move their family into large home at 620 Alma Street, between Chicago Avenue and Ohio Street, an area usually reserved for the well-to-do. They settled into the three-story, wood-frame home with the large back yard and began bringing in extra income by renting office space on the upper floor of the house to a physician. The house was only a few years old, but many regarded it as a creepy place - but perhaps only after the horrors of the farm in LaPorte County were revealed. In a May 1908 story in the *Chicago Tribune*, a young neighbor girl, who sometimes came to the house to play with Jennie, recalled that she was frightened by the "strange actions" of Mrs. Sorensen. The girl remembered, "It was a cold and dreary place. It made me shiver to go into it. I always was afraid. It seemed so mysterious. Now I feel like something terrible happened there."

The house at 620 Alma Street now Latrobe in Chicago's Austin neighborhood

Mystery followed the family to Alma Street. The origin of the Sorensen children continued to raise questions. Belle took great delight in parading her daughters about in the finest clothes they could afford. Many people knew that Jennie Olsen came to live with the family after her mother had died, but where had the other children come from? The sudden appearance of a baby boy named Axel in the Sorensen home raised a number of eyebrows. Belle passed off the infant as her own, but Dr. J.B. Miller, the North Avenue physician who rented space in the upper floor of the Alma Street home, later told a curious tale to the *Chicago Daily News*. "A few days before the appearance of little Axel I was asked by Mrs. Sorensen to hold myself in readiness to attend her for a confinement case ffia term of the time period for childbirth and the recovery period afterwardsffl. To me as a physician this announcement came as a surprise. When Mrs. Sorensen came to me with this statement I concealed my surprise and of course replied I would be ready to take the case."

A few days later, someone put a note under Miller's door advising the doctor that he was "wanted" immediately and to come at once to Belle's bedroom. Dr. Miller recalled, "This looked peculiar to me as I had passed the evening in my office and had slept in the adjoining room but had heard no one. I hurried right over to Mrs. Sorensen's room and there found her in bed with an infant. 'Why doctor,' she exclaimed: 'Where in the world were you? I aroused the whole town trying to find you and had to get somebody else.' There was nothing I could do but say I had been at home. I never learned with any degree of satisfaction what doctor attended the woman."

Belle claimed that she had given birth to four children, but it struck the neighbors as very peculiar that a woman who had failed to give birth in the first 11 years of her marriage had allegedly delivered four children within the span of the next three years. One neighbor, Mrs. William Diesling, stated that she had gone to the Sorensen house one day and had found an infant crying on the couch. She asked Belle why she didn't feed it and Belle replied that she didn't have time to take care of it. Mrs. Diesling asked who the baby belonged to and Belle said that a relative had sent it to her to look after. The next day, the baby was gone. Belle claimed the relative had returned for it.

But was this really the case? Did the baby meet with a more tragic end? According to burial records, it was discovered that Caroline Sorensen, a three-month-old girl, died on August 24, 1896, and an infant boy named Axel passed away in April 1898. Both children exhibited symptoms of acute colitis - inflammation of the large intestine - and both were buried in Forest Home Cemetery. It's very possible that the "colitis" could have been caused by the ingestion of poison. However, that's just a supposition. What is known for sure is that Belle collected significant insurance claims on the lives of both of the children.

Trouble followed the family to Alma Street. A second fire of mysterious origin broke out in 1898, causing flames to spread to the adjoining homes. Belle blamed the fire on a careless neighbor and denied that she had anything to do with the property damage. Another insurance check was collected and cashed and by this time, Mads' days were numbered.

By 1900, his health had badly declined. His doctor believed that it was a heart ailment, but Belle's sister Nellie later voiced her own suspicions in an interview with the *Chicago Tribune*. She recalled, "I do remember that the children were sitting on the porch and that Sorensen had been complaining of an illness. Then she Belle went into the house to prepare supper and later called her husband. She said he refused to eat and went upstairs to lie down on the bed. After a while my sister went upstairs to see how he was and then she told me she found him dying. Some of the neighbors had said Mrs. Sorensen had given her husband poison and murdered him. And I heard there was talk of exhuming the body, but my husband and I never mixed in the affair and I know little about it." But Nellie did add one ominous note to her statement: "It seemed she would do anything for money. I never saw such a money-mad person in my life."

Sorensen died on July 30, 1900, the day before his $2,000 life insurance policy with the Independent Order of Mutual Aid was scheduled to lapse. A few days earlier, he had notified the lodge that he planned to let his old policy lapse and would cease to make payments. The first physician to examine Sorensen, Dr. Charles E. Jones, thought that he had died from prussic acid poisoning. He noted the body had a strange appearance, almost as if Sorensen was not dead. His cheeks were pink and he looked so life-like that it almost appeared that he was in a trance. However, since Sorensen's own doctor had been treating him for an enlarged heart, the cause of death was listed as heart failure. Belle immediately began making attempts to collect on the life insurance policy.

Belle's actions fueled the suspicions of Sorensen's relatives and a court order for an autopsy was secured on August 30. The body was exhumed, but the intestines were never checked for traces of poison. No one, especially the dead man's widow, wanted to pay the cost of a thorough medical inquiry that could shed light on the mysterious death, and so the original cause of death was sustained. The insurance company awarded the widow $8,000, which was a huge sum in those days. Belle kept up appearances in the Austin neighborhood for another year, much to the chagrin of her neighbors.

Most of the local people were both frightened and intrigued by Belle, who many believed to be both an arsonist and a poisoner. The neighborhood children listened to the gossip that passed between their parents and took the whispers with them to the schoolyard, where they taunted the children whose "mama had killed their daddy." The children were tormented mercilessly and Belle was shunned by almost everyone in the community.

One woman, though, felt differently about Belle. In 1908, Mrs. Josephine Burkland told the *Chicago Tribune* that she had been close friends with Belle. She stated that years before, when Jennie had been burned in the fire at the Grand Avenue building, Belle had nursed her night and day. "She displayed the same affectionate interest in her daughter Myrtle when the child was ill," Mrs. Burkland said. "She always had a pleasant smile for everybody." She remembered a large reception that Belle held for the teachers and principal of the nearby Julia Ward Howe School at Laurel Avenue and West Superior Street. She received her guests with a pleasant smile and a warm handshake. The guests admired the lavish preparations that she had made and the teachers agreed that she was a devoted parent.

But how well did they know her? A number of people interviewed said they had noticed a change in her attitude, especially toward Jennie. After Mads had died, Belle was the head of the household and she became increasingly cold and aloof to the young girl. She was very demanding and critical, and became very impatient with everything that Jennie did.

Meanwhile, Anton Olsen had remarried. He made it known that he intended to take Jennie to his home on the South Side and make her the center of his new family. He was in for a surprise. In an interview with the *Chicago Tribune*, he said, "I asked Mrs. Sorensen, as she then had children of her own, to give Jennie up to me. She said that she would but did not like to do it quite then. A second time, when I asked her to give Jennie up to me, she said she would not. I told her I still had something to say about Jennie but she said she had me beat on that. Another time I spoke with her about the matter and her answer was that if I would I could go into court with it. She was then living in Austin. Soon after I went out to Austin again to see her, but she had left. I did not know where she had gone. I did not locate her again for about two years."

Around this time, Belle made a property swap with Arthur F. Williams, president of the Trade Circular Advertising Company, at 125 Clark Street on Chicago's Near North Side. In exchange for the house in Austin, Belle acquired the deed to a 60-acre farm that Williams owned outside of LaPorte, Indiana, on McClung Road. The deal was arranged through a real estate agent named M.E. Cole. He and Williams met with Belle on many occasions. Williams said later, "I remember her quite well. She appeared to be sharp and well-versed in business methods."

But Belle did not immediately move to Indiana. She was searching for a new husband, a man to work her new farm. With her children in tow, she set off for Janesville, Wisconsin, to look for wedded bliss. Her intended target was a man named Peter Frederickson. She hoped to convince him to sell his home, increase his life insurance not a good sign and move with her to LaPorte. She had placed a matrimonial advertisement in the local newspaper and, at first, Frederickson responded enthusiastically.

Belle had discovered that his home was completely paid off and worth at least $1,500. "You must come with me to Indiana where it is much nicer and there is so much to do," she urged him, but Frederickson stalled. A wedding supper was planned, but no one on his side of the family agreed to attend. Frederickson's relatives told him that he should reconsider the idea of marrying Belle Sorensen. He took their advice and called off the wedding.

Belle left Janesville disappointed, but refused to give up on her plan of snagging a new husband. She traveled to west-central Minnesota for an extended visit with a cousin who owned a dairy farm near Fergus Falls. In this heavily Norwegian, German and Lutheran region, Belle renewed a friendship with a widower named Peter S. Gunness, who had once lived in her house in Chicago, renting a room there while Mads Sorensen was still alive.

Gunness had immigrated to America in 1885 from Kongsberg, Sandsvaer, which was in in southern Norway, between Oslo and Bergen. After living for a short time in Chicago, he settled in Janesville with his two uncles before continuing north to Minneapolis, an area thick with Norwegian and Swedish immigrants. After settling down, he married Sophia Murch and they had a daughter together, whom they named Swanhilda. Gunness went to work for a grocer and they lived happily for a time. When Sophia died, though, Gunness found himself in the same situation as Anton Olsen - trying to take care of a little girl with no mother.

As Belle and Peter grew closer, objections were raised by Gunness's relatives about the planned wedding. His brother, Carl, later told the *Chicago American*, "We were all opposed to his second marriage. We knew he was afraid of the woman and we thought her influence over him was too great for us to prevail."

Planning to marry in LaPorte, the two departed for Indiana. Peter Gunness had no idea that he was on his way to his doom.

The town of LaPorte was founded in 1833, and its first permanent residents were Aaron Stanton and Adam Polke. Lured by cheap government land, others soon followed. The "original" old settlers included men like Walter Wilson, Hiram Todd, John Walker, James Andrew and Abram P. Andrew, Jr. They purchased 400 acres of land at the Michigan Road land sale in Logansport and LaPorte was officially incorporated a year later. The new town, despite its sparse population, became the county seat and the government offices became the largest source of local employment. The arrival of the Michigan Southern and Indianapolis, Peru & Chicago Railroads brought farmers, carpenters, mechanics and businessmen into the growing community. The greatest year in the town's development was 1852, when the Michigan Southern & Northern Indiana Railroad linked LaPorte to Chicago.

New settlers who built their homes on the south and west ends of town found large areas of fertile prairie lands that were dotted with outcroppings of beautiful oak groves. The north part of the township was heavily timbered. Within the woodlands and prairies were a number of sparkling lakes, one of the finest of which lay close to the location of Belle Gunness's new home. Commerce, industry, and the abundant farmland helped the town to grow after the Civil War, although it was eclipsed by Michigan City, its larger neighbor to the north. In spite of this, local publications called LaPorte "unquestionably the handsomest city in Northern Indiana, if not the state."

The news about Belle Gunness that broke in the spring of 1908 shattered the optimistic notion that this tranquil farm community was somehow removed from the clamor, noise and urban horrors of Chicago, and was somehow immune to the evils that lurked in the big city. But even before that, locals believed there was something strange about the farm that Belle purchased out on McClung Road. It was a place where even multiple murders might be considered commonplace.

Even today, a dispute lingers among the townspeople about the real history of Brookside Farm, the property that Belle Gunness purchased near Fish Trap Lake. There is even an argument about who actually built the place. The one thing that they can agree on, though, is that the land was soured even before Belle arrived and carried out her reign of terror.

The history of the property appears to go back to 1831, when it was purchased by Adam Polke, one of the first white men in the region. He bought the land from the government in November of that year, selling his interests to S. Treat, a cattle buyer, in 1842. Treat then transferred ownership of the land to his brother, George, who then sold it to Dr. B.R. Car, a homeopathic physician, who constructed a log house on the property in 1857. He lived at the site and conducted his medical practice there, setting aside a portion of the property for a private cemetery that became filled with unmarked graves. Frontier medicine was primitive in those days, and many patients didn't survive.

Dr. Car likely would have lived out his days in peace, caring for the sick and injured, if not for the actions of his son, G. Hile Car, the leader of a gang of Midwestern holdup men and outlaws. They began using the property on the shores of sparkling Fish Trap Lake as a rendezvous point. Based on the stories, the peaceful farm turned into the "terror spot" of Northwest Indiana. Illegal gambling, liquor distilling, horse racing and general lawlessness were everyday occurrences along McClung Road during this time. Eventually, the younger Car moved west to Denver, where he was killed in a shootout. Dr. Car, after attempting to make a living in the coal and lumber business, moved away from LaPorte in disgrace in 1875, leaving behind a stack of unpaid bills.

In 1877, the August Drebing family replaced the log cabin with a sturdy brick home, although some versions of local history have it that John Walker, one of the original settlers of the area, actually built the brick home for his daughter, Harriet Holcomb, and her husband John. Whoever built the house, it was obvious that they intended to make it the finest residence in the region, but they managed to fail miserably. The *Chicago American* interviewed a long-time resident of LaPorte, who stated that the house on McClung Road was always sinister in its appearance. He told a newspaper reporter, "When it was finished, it was an unpleasant looking building in spite of all the money and skill that had been lavished upon it. It was heavy and gloomy and forbidding with glowering windows and shutters that were always closed, and odd overhanging gables. It was depressing merely to put one's feet in the door. It seemed that nothing could brighten it up, not even the laughter of children. Even the sunlight seemed to lose its brilliancy when it streamed through those narrow, forbidding windows."

According to local legend, the Holcombs had been Confederate sympathizers during the Civil War, which put them at odds with the Northwest Indiana locals. They abandoned the tainted property and moved to King's County, New York, and in 1888, ownership passed to a farmer with the wonderful name of Grovsvenor Goss, who transferred it to his wife, Sarah. In 1890, a Chicago streetcar conductor turned land speculator named C.M. Eddy went to LaPorte and bought the entire lot from Mrs. Goss. She was eager to get rid of the cursed place after her son committed suicide by hanging earlier that same year. Eddy's hope for a quiet life in the country was crushed after his wife died in the house. In 1892, he sold the house to Mattie Altic, a brothel-keeper from Chicago, who decided to move her sporting house from the Custom House Place vice district in the city to LaPorte. Not surprisingly, her presence in the community became a terrible scandal.

Mattie, tall and striking in appearance, was unconcerned about gossiping old ladies, offended ministers and the opinions of the wives of her best clients. She spruced up the place and renovated it into a first-class resort. Most of her regular clients from Chicago visited the La Porte mansion and a dock, boathouse and large carriage house were added to make the place even more appealing. She installed new furniture, marble trim, a dance floor and spacious bedchambers to accommodate her patrons when the evening's revelry came to an end. Each night, the sound of dance music and the merry laughter of the patrons and prostitutes echoed into the quiet woods and across the nearby lake. This was no mere brothel; it was "Chicago Southeast," as Mattie proudly put it. LaPorte, a quiet, religious town, was horrified by the woman's brazen behavior.

But Mattie Altic would not be around to offend the town for long. She suffered a heart attack in the doorway of her house after a night of drinking and dancing. The official coroner's verdict blamed her sudden demise on heart disease. However, it was widely known that Mattie had been jilted by a suitor and there were whispers that she had committed suicide. Old friends came down from Chicago to pay their last respects. Her funeral in Michigan City was a lavish affair and a long procession accompanied the hearse to Pine Lake Cemetery for her burial.

Needless to say, Mattie's questionable life and tragic death in the house added to the unnatural pall that seemed to hang over the place. No one stepped forward to purchase it. In fact, its next owner ended up with it after foreclosure proceedings in 1894. Thomas Doyle never lived there and sold it to Arthur Williams in 1898. Williams moved his father-in-law, M.D. Train, into the house while he ran his business back in Chicago. Belle Sorensen finalized the property swap with Williams and his wife on November 1, 1901. Five months later, on April 1, Belle and Peter Gunness were married in LaPorte. They settled into the former bordello at Brookside Farm with plans to start their married life.

It was a marriage that would not last for long.

Meanwhile, poor Anton Olsen came into the picture again. After hearing of Belle's marriage to Peter Gunness from a neighbor in Chicago, Olsen contacted Belle again and once more demanded that Jennie be allowed to return home. By now, Olsen was remarried and was ready to resume his parental duties. According to an interview that he gave to the *Chicago American* in 1908, Belle allowed Jennie to come and live with him for about one month, with the understanding that Jennie could choose to live where she wanted. He enrolled his daughter at the Cornell School at 75th Street and Drexel Boulevard on the South Side. The girl seemed to be adapting to her new life - and then Belle came to Chicago to visit.

She went directly to Jennie's school, took the girl out of class, and sent Olsen a message that amounted to the fact that since Jennie didn't have any food or clothes at Olsen's house neither of which was true , she was taking her home with her to Indiana. Olsen said, "I persuaded her to let Jennie stay so I could talk to her. From that time on, she was unwilling to remain at my house because there were no fruit trees growing or places to play." Olsen reluctantly went along with his daughter's wishes and took her to the train station. Jennie had made it clear that she wanted to leave the city and return to Belle's care in Indiana. Whether she threatened the young girl - or merely persuaded her that life would be better in LaPorte - Belle had managed to turn Jennie against her father.

As the train pulled out of the station, Anton Olsen sadly watched it go. Belle had been very kind to him before she left Chicago, trying to ease his sorrow about the loss of his daughter, but that moment on the station platform, as the train pulled out of sight, was the last time that Olsen saw Jennie alive.

Later, after shovels wielded by grim-faced men began cutting through the mud and muck of the hog pens and back yard of the Gunness farm in LaPorte searching for human remains, Olsen vividly recalled the last words that Belle spoke to him before she took his daughter away. "I am a Christian woman," she said, "with a passion for God."

A picture postcard of the Gunness farm

In the spring of 1903, another child arrived at the farm on McClung Road. The little boy's name was Phillip, and he was alleged to be the son of Peter Gunness, Belle's husband. Unfortunately, his father - if he was his father, which is unlikely - didn't live long enough to see the baby born. On December 16, 1902, Peter met with a "tragic accident." According to Belle's account, Gunness was working in a shed when a part of a sausage-grinding machine fell from a high shelf, split open his skull, and killed him instantly.

But even with her husband gone, people in the community never wondered how Belle might get along working the farm by herself. She was not well-liked in LaPorte. In fact, "strong and self-determined" was likely the kindest thing that they had to say about her. Deliverymen, farmers, store owners and neighbors all told stories about her amazing physical strength. Some even speculated that she wasn't a woman at all, but a man in women's clothing.

In the *New York Daily Tribune*, the coroner of LaPorte County, Dr. Harry H. Long, admitted that, "Mrs. Gunness was a woman of unusual appearance. She was large, bony, powerful looking, with square jaws and black eyes. She was a woman who would attract attention anywhere from her lack of womanly characteristics. Her long strides, together with her remarkable countenance and her generally vicious appearance gave her an aspect that was almost terrifying." Neighbors would recall her "large, grotesque" hands, which were ideally suited to cutting up pig carcasses into bacon, ham and pork shoulders. The skills she learned at the butcher's shop in Chicago served her well. On butchering days, the men from the adjoining farms would gather together to shoot the animals, bleed them and gut them, and then the women would take care of the rest. Belle, however, performed all of this bloody work herself. Mrs. Frances Lapham, a LaPorte neighbor for almost nine years, later spoke of a wide leather belt that Belle wore around her waist. It contained pouches and various sizes of sheaths for the knives that she used to cut up the farm animals - and likely a number of human beings.

People may have whispered about Belle being a man, but there is no question that she was a woman. In fact, she knew how to use and manipulate her gender to suit her purposes and to achieve her aims. She may not have been attractive to most men, but some found her appealing. She was mannish and coarse to many but others, like Chicago photographer R.C. Ganiere, noted her stylish appearance and commented favorably about her maternal skills. Belle Gunness was simply a physically strong, criminal sociopath and a clever manipulator who used her womanhood to her advantage when she wanted to.

The questions about Belle's sexual identity began to be raised in LaPorte in the spring of 1903, when baby Phillip Gunness was born. A neighbor, Mrs. William Nicholson, came over to help Belle to deliver the baby, but she found the front door locked. She would not let anyone into the house to witness the birth. Another neighbor noted how odd it was that Belle was out in the yard chasing pigs and washing baby blankets in the cistern just two days after Phillip was born.

If Belle actually gave birth to Phillip, she would have been forty-four years old at the time. It was not a physical impossibility, but it was still unlikely. Midwife Mary Swenson told investigators that she remembered being called to the Gunness farm, but arrived too late to deliver the baby. When she saw the infant for the first time, she was amazed to find the child washed, clothed and appearing too old to be a newborn.

Women in rural LaPorte had the same suspicions that Belle's neighbors in Austin had that Belle Gunness was faking pregnancies and claiming other people's children as her own. No birth certificate for Phillip was ever found and many surmised that the boy had been "dropped off" at the Gunness farm in the middle of the night. Frances Lapham, the neighbor who talked about Belle's knife belt, boldly stated that she believed Belle had murdered a woman and took the victim's baby.

It's unlikely that we'll never know if that supposition is true, but what we do know is that Belle smashed the skull of her second husband, Peter Gunness in December 1902 - just nine months after their wedding. Peter's untimely death generated another $3,500 in insurance money for Belle, although most local people found it hard to believe that Gunness could have been so clumsy. Belle stated that the death of her beloved husband had been a terrible accident. On the night of December 16, he was sitting next to the kitchen stove and, while reaching for his shoe, he jarred a shelf above him, dislodging a meat grinder. It crashed down on his skull, causing a deep cut. Belle attended to his injury and applied Vaseline to ease the pain. Peter, who didn't lose consciousness after the blow, laid down on the couch to rest. He fell asleep and at about 3:00 a.m., Belle was roused from sleep by her husband's groans. She called for a doctor, but Peter died before he arrived.

Dr. B.O. Bowell, who worked as a physician for Coroner Long, determined that Peter's death was caused by a skull fracture. He measured the distance of the fall and weighed the machine, and while he could not explain why Peter was not knocked unconscious when he received his fatal wound, he concluded that there was no foul play involved. With no evidence to the contrary, the matter was dropped and Belle collected another hefty insurance check.

Gust Gunness, the dead man's brother who had argued with Peter about marrying Belle in the first place, traveled from Minneapolis to LaPorte. He later told the *Chicago Journal*, "I stayed there several days. Mrs. Gunness begged me continuously to stay with her and manage the farm. 'We can get along nicely together,' she said, 'and we will make good money here for I know you are a good farmer.' I didn't like her eyes and I didn't like the place so I refused. I didn't think we could get along. I had no money to speak of. I tell you - I'm glad I didn't take up that offer."

The following spring, Gust returned to LaPorte to retrieve his niece, Peter's daughter Swanhilda, from Belle's care. The girl was lonely and desperately wanted to go home to Minnesota, where the rest of her family lived. But Belle refused to let her go, assuring Gust that she would be well cared for at the farm. Failing in his attempt to hire a local attorney to sue Belle for a division of his brother's insurance policy intended to benefit the girl, Gust and his brother Carl decided to secretly remove the girl, right from under Belle's nose. In the middle of the night, they sneaked onto the property, packed up Swanhilda and spirited her away to Edgerton, Minnesota. Later, Swanhilda told the *Chicago Tribune*, "When my papa married that woman, he took us down there to live with her on a farm. She treated me all right when papa was around but all of us were afraid of her, even Myrtle and Lucy and Jennie Olsen was too. After papa died, she treated us worse than ever. Pretty soon after papa died that woman began having me to see her. I stayed there almost a year when Uncle Gust came and got me and I came away to where my grandma lived." The uncles were eventually convinced that taking the girl away saved her life - and they were undoubtedly right.

The surviving children - Jennie, Myrtle and Lucy - were afraid of Belle and knew better than to defy her authority. They were all considered to be sweet and well-behaved children. Each week, they attended Sunday school at the Methodist Church in a cart drawn by a little pony. Belle was often heard telling them, "Mother loves you more than all of the world and will make you rich women someday." Instead of embracing her with affection, though, the girls would often recoil and cast wary glances in her direction while they played.

Following the death of Peter Gunness, a succession of male visitors began arriving at the farm. Most of them were unattached men of Nordic descent who hailed from small towns across the Upper Midwest and Great Plains. They came in response to Belle's "lonely hearts" advertisements in the matrimonial notices of the *Skandinaven*, the largest circulating Norwegian-Swedish-Danish newspaper in the United States. Believe it or not, the newspaper had a tremendous circulation.

Arrivals from Nordic countries were a huge part of the immigration wave of the late 1800s and early 1900s. Tight-knit Nordic farming communities were scattered across the plains of Minnesota, northern Wisconsin and the Dakotas, while immigrants who did not make a living from farms tended to make their way to the big cities. Chicago was a hub of Scandinavian immigration and most of the men were engaged in the building trades. Large Norwegian and Swedish neighborhoods formed west and north of the central business districts. The Swedes moved up Clark Street and west of the Chicago lakefront. The Norwegians settled farther west in Wicker Park, Logan Square and the Austin neighborhood. To the rural Scandinavians, Chicago was seen as a frightening, crime-ridden hellhole that wore down its people in the factories, machine shops and slaughterhouses. They lived in highly segregated neighborhoods where their familiar languages were largely the only ones they heard spoken.

In these communities, whether they were in the city or on the plains, the foreign language press thrived. The weekly *Chicago Scandia* and the *Scandinaven* connected rural and urban immigrants who were separated not only from home, but from each other, across great distances. These widely circulated newspapers made it possible for men and women to socially interact with one another and even broker marriages through the placement of personal notices. The newspapers became an opportunity for Belle Gunness to look for potential husbands - and for victims.

Belle inserted her first advertisement in the matrimonial columns of both Scandinavian newspapers in the Midwest. One advertisement, which ran in Chicago, read:

Personal - comely widow who owns a large farm in one of the finest districts in La Porte County, Indiana, desires to make the acquaintance of a gentleman equally well provided, with view of joining fortunes. No replies by letter considered unless sender is willing to follow answer with personal visit. Triflers need not apply.

Several middle-aged men with large bank accounts responded to Belle's advertisements. They traveled to her farm, intent on proving that they were men of substance who were worth of the interest of a comely widow. They brought with them plenty of cash and deeds to their homes and farms.

Emil Greening, a seventeen-year-old carpenter who worked with his brother, Fred, doing handyman work at the Gunness farm, was infatuated with pretty, blond-haired, blue-eyed Jennie Olsen. Thanks to his crush, he was often at the farm to witness some of the strange comings and goings that occurred. He later told the *New York Daily Tribune*, "Mrs. Gunness received men visitors all the time. A different man came nearly every week to stay at the house. She introduced them as 'cousins' from Kansas, South Dakota, Wisconsin and from Chicago. Most of the men that came brought trunks with them but they rarely took trunks away. Mrs. Gunness kept the 'cousins' with her all the time in the parlors and her bedroom. She was always careful to make the children stay away from her 'cousins' who rarely tried to show them any affection. I believe that many murders were done right under my nose."

A view from the south side of the Gunness farm

Greening may have been lucky to escape with his own life for day laborers that were hired by Belle for seasonal work seemed to disappear just as quickly as her visiting "cousins." Olaf Lindboe was a thirty-five-year-old Wisconsin man who moved from a dairy farm in Rockefeller, Illinois, to accept Belle's offer of employment. He worked at the Gunness farm from March to May 1905 and then disappeared. A local man, Chris Christofferson, had befriended Lindboe and was puzzled by how one day at the height of plowing season - when Lindboe was most needed - he was suddenly gone. When he asked Belle about him, he was told that Lindboe had received a letter from a land grant that offered him a free trip to St. Louis where he could buy property. Christofferson thought it was strange that his friend had not told him goodbye, but Belle said he was in a hurry to leave. Later, Belle changed her story and told inquisitive neighbors that Lindboe had "gone back to Norway."

Henry Gurholt, another worker from Wisconsin, came to the farm after Lindboe. Like his predecessor, he lasted only a few months. Christofferson also made his acquaintance and happened to be at the farm on the day that Gurholt arrived. In August 1905, Belle had Gurholt cut some oats for her and then she asked Christofferson to stack them. She said that Gurholt had, after doing the initial work, gotten sick and had left the farm. Gurholt was never seen again, but he did have family who inquired after him. He had kept in close touch with them by mail as he traveled. Immediately after his disappearance, they demanded to know what had become of him. Belle pled ignorance. All she knew was that Gurholt had left her in August in order to go to Chicago and work as a horse trader in the Union Stockyards. He had abandoned his trunk and his fur overcoat and Belle claimed both of them. She was seen wearing the coat all over town during the following winter.

Lindboe had a reddish mustache and Gurholt had a thick, black one - descriptions that matched two corpses later unearthed at the Gunness farm.

George Berry, who came from Tuscola, Illinois, traveled to LaPorte in January 1906 with plans of working on the farm and eventually marrying Mrs. Gunness. He had $1,500 with him when he left home but both he and his money disappeared. An unidentified man in his fifties disappeared from the farm at oat-cutting time. He left behind a horse and buggy that Belle put to good use.

In 1907, Belle hired Ray Lamphere, a curly-haired, thirty-seven-year-old from Indiana, to do carpentry work and assorted odd jobs on the farm. Lamphere was a sort of jack-of-all-trades, a drifter who was talented with a hammer and saw but was mostly lazy, aimless and dull-witted. He claimed that he had worked as a builder for 20 years and carried a membership card with the Carpenter's Union in Chicago Heights. He heard about the work that needed to be done at the Gunness farm from a fellow carpenter and met up with Belle for an interview in LaPorte. She hired him on the spot.

Ray Lamphere

As their relationship unfolded, it seemed that there was nothing Lamphere wouldn't do to please Belle. By his own admission, the two became sexually involved, despite their twelve-year age difference. He said that as the relationship evolved, Belle proposed marriage to him on several occasions and encouraged him to take out a life insurance policy on himself with her as the benefactor. She offered to pay the premiums for him as long as he agreed to marry her. His refusal to agree to her terms   Lamphere was apparently not as dim-witted as he appeared to be   led to a bitter falling out between them, but during the time that he was still in her good graces, Lamphere kept her secrets and did whatever was required of him - up to the point of aiding and abetting murder. As a hired hand, Lamphere knew better than to try and break into Belle's "secret room" in the cellar of the farmhouse. Belle always kept possession of the only key to the basement. He may have shared her bed on occasion, but he certainly didn't share every aspect of her life.

Over time, Lamphere became very unhappy about his lot in life, even though it was the course that he had chosen. He was the ne'er-do-well son of William Lamphere, an elderly produce farmer who had once been the local justice of the peace and one of LaPorte's most respected politicians until hard times reduced his circumstances. William always said that his son was "a good boy" and the only thing wrong with him was his love for drink. And it's true - he had a deep and abiding passion for liquor. Almost every night, he could be found drinking alone or with one of his cronies in the saloons of LaPorte. When he was drunk - which, according to locals, was most of the time - he was gloomy and bitter as he contemplated his predicament as the keeper of Belle's secrets. He wavered back and forth between loving and fearing the woman, concerned that one day he might pay dearly for his role in her crimes - with punishment carried out by either Belle, or by the law. He would never tell what he knew about her because she would kill him or he would go to jail. Besides, Belle was one of few people who knew his secret that he was a bigamist with several wives scattered around the country.

The relationship between Belle and Lamphere was a strange one, but it was clearly one of evil codependency. The more that Lamphere knew of Belle's secrets, the more damage that he could do. Belle obsessed over what he might say if the mood struck him. These circumstances made her watch him even more closely, turning Lamphere into a nervous wreck. It likely made him shudder with fear as he worked on the farm and walked past the graveyard that had sprung up behind the house.

He knew that if he wasn't careful, he was liable to end up in the same patch of ground as his predecessors.

Over the years, there have been questions as to what accomplices that Belle may have had in addition to Ray Lamphere. Some believed that she was in fact operating a "clearinghouse" of murder in which wealthy men were being waylaid and killed in Chicago, packed into their steamer trunks and then shipped to LaPorte for burial. After an exhaustive search, though, no evidence of these trunks was ever found.

However, suspicions pointing to an agent in the Chicago matrimonial bureau acting on Belle's behalf seemed to be the only logical explanation for the disappearance and presumed murder of

Herman Konitzer, the wealthy son of a German family. The forty-eight-year-old man disappeared from a boarding house at 701 N. Halsted Street in Chicago in October 1905. Konitzer was a recent immigrant to the United States. He had been educated at a Berlin University and had managed the estate of a countess before coming to America with a sizable fortune. He had rented rooms at the Bismarck Hotel and was looking for extended lodging when he saw an advertisement for accommodations in a boarding house that belonged to Olive Johnston in a German-language newspaper. He transferred his belongings to the Halsted Street address and was accompanied there by a traveling companion, a Catholic priest.

Several weeks later, Konitzer left Chicago, bound for LaPorte, taking only a small suitcase with him. He told his landlady that he would return soon to retrieve his wardrobe, which was valued at several hundred dollars, but she never heard from him again. Mrs. Johnston believed that Konitzer was carrying between $5,000 and $10,000 in cash with him at the time of his disappearance. He had sold all of his possessions in Germany to fund his new life in America. The landlady was also positive that the female letter writer from Indiana who sent a note to Konitzer at the Halsted Street boarding house had been Belle Gunness. Konitzer had previously told Mrs. Johnston that he hoped to someday marry and settle down on a farm.

If the letter was indeed sent by Belle, how did she manage to make contact with a German immigrant, when all of her previous matrimonial notices had been placed in Scandinavian newspapers? The letter was supposedly written by Belle in German, which leads many to believe that she was operating through a confederate in Chicago who made it his or her business to inquire about the wealth, status and history of unmarried and unattached men of means.

Men with a trusting nature answered Belle's calls for companionship as they appeared in the lonely hearts ads of the ethnic language newspapers. One such man was John O. Moe, of Elbow Lake, a small farm town in West-Central Minnesota. He was a subscriber to the *Skandinaven*. After an exchange of letters that convinced him to travel to Indiana, where he expected to sample Belle's wonderful cooking, share her bed and run her thriving farm, Moe was last seen in Elbow Lake on December 20, 1906. He said that he was going east to Chicago, but offered no other details. Two days later, Moe showed up at the First National Bank in LaPorte with two drafts for $1,100 drawn on the National Park Bank of New York. According to Alfred Pegelow, the assistant cashier, Moe wanted to use the money in LaPorte to pay off a mortgage, but because he knew no one in town who could vouch for his identity, he was hoping that the bank could help him. Pegelow recalled, "He seemed very anxious to have the cash and we finally took the drafts for collection, sending them to our New York correspondent and asking them to wire us when the drafts were paid."

Emil Greening, who did handyman work on the Gunness farm, told the *New York Daily Tribune*, "Moe was with Mrs. Gunness almost constantly. When he left, his trunk stayed behind and no one saw him go. It was several days before Mrs. Gunness announced that he was gone. Moe's trunk was in the Gunness house on July 11, 1906 when I left the place. His was not the only one. There were about fifteen other trunks, and one room was packed full of all kinds of men's clothing which Mrs. Gunness said her 'cousins' had left and she was not certain if they would be back for them."

Other men followed, including Ole Budsberg, a widower from Iola, Wisconsin, who lived on a farm with his three grown sons, Mat, Oscar and Lewis. He left home on April 5, 1907 to "run the farm" for Belle Gunness. Budsberg was barely conversant in English. He received his news from the *Skandinaven* and it was from this paper that he made his first contact with Belle. She encouraged him to travel to LaPorte and he did so - with $800 in his valise and a draft for $1,000 in exchange for a promise of marriage. On April 6, he appeared at the LaPorte Savings Bank accompanied by Belle. He asked assistant cashier James Cartwright Buck to send a $1,000 mortgage note to the Farmer's State Bank in Iola, Wisconsin, for collection. The cash was counted out and this was the last time that Mr. Buck thought about the matter until October, when the bank in Iola sent a letter of inquiry concerning the whereabouts of Ole Budsberg. Apparently, his sons had not heard from him in months. Shortly after the letter arrived, Buck went to the Gunness farm and inquired about Mr. Budsberg. Belle said that he wasn't there. When asked when she had seen him last, she replied that she didn't know - she never kept track of dates - but the last she saw of him, he was on his way to catch a train to Oregon, where he planned to buy land.

To allay the suspicions of Budsberg's sons, Belle wrote a letter to Mat Budsberg, contriving a story to put him at ease and keep suspicion from being pointed in her direction. In it, she said that she had some letters and papers that had come for his father after he had left her farm. She wanted to know if Ole had returned to Iola so that she could send them to him there. Mat Budsberg later testified: "She said too, she hoped he was not offended by her not marrying him. She said she hoped if he was going out West, he would find some land as a homestead, but if she were in his place, she would go to the old country and visit."

Ole Budsberg had neither gone out West nor returned to his homeland. His remains were unearthed in the Gunness yard in May 1908. There was enough left of his face for Oscar and Mat to positively identify him.

Several other men visited the Gunness farm throughout 1907. All of them stayed for a short time, then allegedly left and were never seen again. Belle's favorite method of dispatching her victims was poison. She was an expert at poisoning, adding strychnine to the food that she served her victims, all of them single men who were probably delighted by the prospect of a lovingly prepared, home-cooked meal at her kitchen table. Strychnine, an alkaloid extract obtained from the dried ripe seeds of a small tree in the East Indies, has a dire effect on its victims within 20 minutes of ingestion. Strychnine is a common component of industrial rat poison and it causes a particularly horrifying death. The victim experiences muscle spasms that escalate into painful convulsions. These convulsions lead to the production of too much acid in the body, an abnormally high body temperature and the rapid breakdown of skeletal muscle. Death results from asphyxiation caused by the paralysis of the nerves that control breathing.

Once her victims were dead, Belle disposed of them in the same businesslike way that an ordinary person would attend to a bag of garbage. This was not only murder for profit, but murder for revenge - acts of pure hatred that went back years to the memory of the brutal assault that she had endured in Norway. It was that bitter childhood, and the attempted sexual assault, that drove Belle to dominate and then murder the men that came into her life. Her sister stated that Belle was always driven by money, but this was only part of the reason that she killed. She also did it because she could. For years, she got away with it.

After her victims were dead, Belle dragged them from the kitchen down into the cellar for butchering. In that cold, brick-lined room, she dismembered the bodies by the light of a single lantern. Inside this grim chamber, Belle installed a wooden table next to a vat filled with chloride of lime solution. Using the knives that she carried in her worn leather belt - the same knives that she used to cut up hogs - she severed the limbs of the men she had lured to their deaths. The blood-spattered basement room was kept off-limits to Ray Lamphere, any workmen who came to the farm and especially to the children.

Miss Jennie Garwood, a teacher at the Quaker School that the Gunness children attended, told the *Chicago Daily Journal* that she noted with alarm one morning that the girls were upset and had been crying. Miss Garwood asked Myrtle what was wrong and the girl said that their mother had beaten and whipped them. When the teacher demanded to know why this had happened, Myrtle tearfully replied, "Mama told us to keep out of the basement but while we were playing, we went downstairs. She caught us and before we got to the bottom of the steps she brought us back. She always kept the cellar door locked and got awful mad when anybody started near it. She told us that she would punish us worse if we ever tried to go downstairs again. Then she whipped us." Miss Garwood said that it was the first time that she had ever heard of the children misbehaving and she was very surprised.

Myrtle had also confided a deadly secret to one of her playmates shortly after Peter Gunness had been killed in the freak "meat grinder accident," a story that was later disclosed to LaPorte Police Chief Clinton Cochrane. The little girl had whispered to her friend, "If you never tell anyone, I will tell you something... My mama killed my papa. She hit him on the head with a meat cleaver, but don't you tell." Hearing of this later, LaPorte's mayor, Lemuel Darrow, was convinced that Belle had a corpse stashed away in the basement and had feared that the girls would discover it. Darrow had been suspicious of Belle for years. At the time of Peter Gunness' death, he insisted that the circumstances were questionable, but a serious investigation was never launched.

Once Belle dismembered her victims, she wrapped the pieces in gunnysacks and buried them in holes in her private graveyard. This was a piece of land that measured about seventy-five by one hundred and twenty-five feet and was circled by a double wire fence that stood eight feet high. To the south, the ground sloped downward into a marsh that had once been part of Clear Lake. Belle poured quicklime on the bodies to speed up their decomposition. Then, for good measure, she piled bricks on top of them to accelerate the action of the lime. Emil Greening remembered that during his time working at the farm, Belle had asked him and several other men to dig up tree stumps on the property and fill the holes in with soft dirt. Human body parts that were not buried in the graveyard - or fed to the hogs - were dropped into the shallow pits created by the removal of the tree stumps.

A nearby pond was another likely location for the disposal of human remains that were impossible to identify once they were discovered. John Zach, a house-mover employed by Belle on occasion, told the *Chicago Journal* that she hired him three times to move the hog pen to different locations on the property. He related, "I wondered why she was so particular but it never entered my head that bodies might be buried in the place where she wished it. Now I am convinced something was wrong."

Belle claimed numerous victims over a relatively short period of time, but only one of her invited guests is known to have escaped with his life. George Anderson, a thirty-nine-year-old Swede from Tarkio, Missouri, was told that he needed to come up with more money than he brought with him in order to pay off Belle's mortgage and marry her. Anderson owned a 32-acre farm back in Missouri and did not bring all of his money with him. He was a wealthy farmer and he longed for a wife. He was persuaded to make the trip to La Porte because Belle's eloquent letters intrigued him. Once there, he realized that she was not the beauty that he expected. In addition to her coarse features and sturdy form, she had a severe manner that, at first, did not appeal to him. Belle did make him feel at home, however, providing hearty meals and a comfortable guest bed in her home.

One night at dinner, Belle raised the issue of her mortgage and Anderson agreed to pay it off if she married him. Her obvious joy at this news led to him wire his bank in Tarkio and ask for the necessary funds to be transferred. But on this third night in the Gunness home, he had a change of heart.

He awoke that night from a restless sleep and looked up to see Belle standing next to his bed, looking down at him. She held a candle in her hands and the expression on her face was so sinister that he let out a loud yell. Belle ran from the room without making a sound. Frightened for his safety, he remained awake the rest of the night and at dawn, hurriedly dressed and fled from the farm. He didn't stop running until he reached LaPorte. Anderson went straight to the station and waited for the first train that would take him back to Missouri.

Indiana historians and those in LaPorte who have studied the case of Belle Gunness for years believe that Belle was responsible for up to forty-two murders during the eight years that she lived at Brookside Farm. It is impossible to know for certain if this number is correct. There were fourteen bodies that were eventually unearthed from the makeshift Gunness graveyard, including the mostly intact corpse of a man named Andrew Helgelein, who had been buried with obvious haste.

The story of the gruesome events that transpired on the farm on McClung Road, and the discovery of the graveyard, culminated with the unraveling of Helgelein's murder and the persistent efforts of his brother, Asle, to learn his fate. He refused to accept the lies and distortions told by Belle after his brother disappeared. Ironically, Belle and her rejected suitor, Ray Lamphere, were exposed from beyond the grave by Andrew Helgelein, a man so hesitant to commit to visiting the farm that Belle pursued him for months before he finally came to LaPorte.

Helgelein, a bachelor farmer from Aberdeen, South Dakota, came to town to win Belle's heart and "pay off the mortgage" on January 2, 1908. His arrival sparked a fit of irrational jealousy in

Ray Lamphere, who became convinced that Belle and Helgelein were plotting to kill him. He was so sure of this that he drilled a hole in the floor of the sitting room so that he could eavesdrop on their conversations from the cellar. In the depths of his paranoia, he suspected that Belle either planned to poison him or would attempt to commit him to an insane asylum because what he knew about her would send her to the gallows.

Andrew Helgelein, Belle Gunness's final victim

Once "dear Andrew" arrived at the farm, Belle kicked Lamphere out of her bed, fired him outright and then attempted to secure a peace bond restraining order against him. She claimed she feared that the angry ex-farmhand might attempt to kill her. Her real, even greater, fear was that he could expose her crimes. If she could convince the authorities that he was dangerous, any claims that he made against her would look like the lies of a disgruntled ex-employee.

Oblivious to all of this drama going around him, Andrew Helgelein walked into Belle's trap. He was to become the last of her prospective husbands and Belle's final victim. However, he seemed to come with great reluctance. It took months for Belle to nag, cajole and convince him to travel to LaPorte. She sent him more than a dozen personal letters that were filled with tender homilies, words of encouragement, loving affection, and sugary sweet entreaties.

Helgelein answered one of Belle's matrimonial ads in 1906. She became writing him back in August of that year, and her return letters were so warm and welcoming that a number of additional letters were exchanged. Almost immediately, she began asking him to come to LaPorte and visit the farm - and, of course, bring money. As Belle wrote, "You will have a much better chance to make use of your capital here, and you can be sure that nothing will happen to them, but will probably make you independent for the rest of your life."

When Andrew failed to come in September, the tone of Belle's letters became more urgent. She implored him to come to Indiana before the harsh winter weather arrived. She also addressed his concerns about his money. She wrote, "You talk of leaving some of your money up there. This I would not do if I were you, especially when you are going so far away, rather, sell your things. If you read only just a little every day, you find the newspapers are full of bank robberies and bank failures; it is either one or the other. I am sure you will find just as good a place for them here, as you will find up there." In hindsight, it's ironic that Belle was warning Helgelein about "robbers" that would take his money.

But Helgelein still hesitated. He did not make it down for the Thanksgiving dinner that Belle invited him to and soon her correspondence reflected a growing impatience. She sent him pressed roses and wrote longingly of a Norwegian Christmas. She drew pen and ink portraits of herself and Helgelein snuggling on the couch in front of her blazing fire, warm and snug as snow gently fell outside. The letters ran the gamut of emotions and began to show Belle's desperation.

Nearly 11 months more passed before Andrew could put his affairs in order and make up his mind to join Belle on her farm. In September 1907, she expressed her delight that Helgelein "gave them ffihis family in friends in South Dakota who objected to him leavingffl the slip" and was on his way to Indiana. In a letter that was sent in late 1907, Belle wrote:

To my very best Friend in the Whole Wide World:
No woman in the world is happier than I am. I know that you are now to come to me and be my own. I can tell from your letters that you are the man I want. It does not take one long to tell when to like a person, and you I like better than anyone in the world, I know. Think how we will enjoy each other's company. You, the sweetest man in the whole world. We will be all alone with each other. Can you conceive of anything nicer? I think of you constantly. When I hear your name mentioned, and this is when one of the dear children speaks of you, or I hear myself humming it with the words of an old love song, it is beautiful music to my ears. My heart beats in wild rapture for you, My Andrew, I love you. Come prepared to stay forever.

Helgelein might not have planned it that way, but he indeed came to stay on the farm forever.

Belle had finally broken down his resistance. Andrew agreed to come for a visit to see his potential home and then decide for himself if he wanted to move to Indiana. He caught a train to Minneapolis and connected to another that took him to Chicago. Before he left on his trip, he told his brother that he would be back in about a week; however, nine days passed and Asle heard nothing from him. Worried, he contacted Minnie Cone, a mutual friend of the brothers who lived in Minneapolis. Minnie repeated what Andrew had told her when he stopped to see her: that he was going to look over the Gunness farm with the possibility of settling there permanently. Andrew also told Minnie that he would be gone for only seven days. Disturbed, Asle then wrote to the postmaster of LaPorte and inquired about a local farm woman named Gunness, but there was no response. Growing more concerned, he contacted the bank where Andrew had deposited his savings in January. In a letter dated April 10, 1908, Frank J. Pitner, the cashier at the First National Bank, replied to say that he had conferred with Mrs. Gunness, who had told him that she would divulge all the information she had concerning Andrew.

Terrified and in a near-panic, Belle wrote several unconvincing stories in a feeble attempt to allay suspicion and explain away Andrew's disappearance to his brother. On March 27, 1908, she informed Asle that, "He wanted to take a trip to see if he could find your brother who had a gambling house in Aberdeen. He left Aberdeen the same day and he didn't find him in Minneapolis and he was going to make a thorough search for him in Chicago and New York. He always thought that he, the brother, went to Norway and he would go after him. I have waited every day to hear something of him."

By then, Belle had hired Joe Maxson to take over managing the farm, doing chores and feeding the animals, finally replacing Ray Lamphere, whom she had fired on February 8. Undeterred by threats of arrest and unwilling to leave Belle alone, Lamphere hung around the farm and was often seen following Belle when she was in town. Alcohol and jealousy turned out to be a bad mix for the squirrely little man. Acting on Belle's complaint that Lamphere had repeatedly trespassed on her property and had cut down a wire fence, the police arrested him on March 12 for committing an act of harassment. He was fined $1, a paltry sum that was allegedly given to him by Elizabeth Smith, a black woman that some of the people in LaPorte accused of practicing voodoo and the black arts. She would become an important part of the events that followed.

Belle filed a second complaint against Lamphere on March 28, and this time he was fined $19.10. Lamphere brought a lawyer, Wirt Worden, along to the hearing and he asked Belle a series of pointed questions about her first two husbands, all of which were objected to by Belle's attorney. None of the questions were ever answered. The *Chicago Daily News* later asked the judge in the case, Robert C. Kinkaid, about Belle's demeanor during her testimony. He said, "The woman, when the first questions were asked of her, was composed. Then she trembled and was agitated as the questions became more numerous. The questions were leading and not relevant and at the time seemed somewhat insulting to the woman by intimating that she killed two husbands for the insurance. She protested against the cross-examination and left the stand agitated, which might of course be true of any decent woman resenting insinuation."

Lamphere's fine was paid by John Wheatbrook, who owned a farm in Springville, six miles north of LaPorte. He put the shiftless drunk to work on his own farm to keep him away from Belle and out of trouble.

But having Lamphere out of town was not enough to satisfy Belle. With tears in her eyes, she begged the court to issue a peace bond against him, claiming that he followed her around town and showed up at the farm, both day and night, threatening her life. She claimed that Lamphere was not in his right mind and was a menace to the public. She asked the authorities to hold a sanity hearing, but her request was turned down. Belle complained to the sheriff that her former employee was a threat to her family, telling him that, "I'm afraid that he'll set fire to the place."

In desperation, Belle sought out her lawyer, Melvin E. Leliter, to have her will drawn up in the event that this "madman" actually succeeded in doing her harm. She was hysterical with worry and was sure, she told him, that Lamphere would murder her some night in her bed. Her lawyer advised her that her best course of action might be to "get a gun and shoot him" the next time he showed up, but Belle staunchly said that she "would rather die than do that."

During his time at the farm, Joe Maxson noted nothing unusual, He didn't believe that Belle was as worried about Ray Lamphere as she claimed to be to the police and her attorney. He told the *Chicago Tribune*, "I never saw Lamphere here except once and that was in the evening when he came out on the lawn but didn't go to the house. I saw him standing near the house when I came up from the barn that night and several other times. At these times, all Mrs. Gunness said was, 'There's Lamphere again,' or something like that and didn't get excited although she always locked the doors carefully."

At the same time that Belle had her hands full with Lamphere, she was also trying to fend off the prying inquiries from Asle Helgelein. The walls that she had built around her murderous operation were starting to crumble. Asle was unconvinced that his brother had ever left LaPorte, and he demanded more information from Belle, who fired back a lengthy reply to him on April 24. This letter was her final written correspondence. In it, she accused Ray Lamphere of stealing letters that Andrew had written to his brother before they could be mailed to South Dakota. She suggested that Andrew, in the "missing" letters, had invited Asle to come down to the farm so that he could see for himself what a paradise Indiana was. Belle was sure that this letter would silence her troublesome adversary.

Belle wrote that Andrew's whereabouts were as great of a mystery to her as they were to Asle. "It is very strange that the man should go away with all his belongings," she stated. She denied that Andrew was still in LaPorte and boldly told him that if he wanted to come and look for his brother, she would help conduct a search. However, she cautioned him that hunting for a missing person was often an expensive proposition. If she was to be involved in such an endeavor, Asle would have to pay her for her efforts. Eventually, Asle Hegelian did come to La Porte but not until May, when Belle's secrets were finally exposed.

Despite her daring words to Asle Helgelein, Belle was worried. Lamphere still represented a danger to her and Asle was making inquiries that could potentially send her to the gallows. She decided to make another attempt to silence Lamphere. Belle went to see her attorney and told him that she wanted to file her will very soon. She feared for her life and the lives of her children because Ray Lamphere had threatened to kill her and burn her house down. The will needed to be in place in case Lamphere carried through with his threats.

On April 27, Belle filed her last will and testament with George Link, the clerk of the circuit court. She appointed Wesley Fogle, a local farm implement dealer from whom she had purchased tools and equipment the previous year, to serve as the executor of her estate. Belle bequeathed her entire estate, valued at $13,000, to the children - Phillip, Lucy and Myrtle - but left nothing to Jennie Olsen. According to Belle's feeble explanation to Emil Greening, the girl had been sent to California in 1906 to continue her education.

Greening later told the *New York Daily Tribune*, "I wrote to her but I gave the two letters to Mrs. Gunness and I never received an answer." Lamphere's attorney, Wirt Worden, never believed that Jennie left LaPorte at all. He told a grim story. "Before she was supposed to be sent to school, Mrs. Gunness went to Chicago. She bought the girl an entire new outfit. After she had the clothes she took particular pains to show them to the neighbors. Then a short time after that Jennie disappeared."

John Widener, another would-be sweetheart of Jennie's, was given two addresses in Los Angeles to try and contact the girl, but the letters came back as undeliverable. He was interviewed by the *Chicago Journal* and said, "In October 1907, I met Mrs. Gunness again and she told me that she had just sent Jennie $100. I told her that I had written several letters and had received no reply. She laughed and said, 'That's alright. I wrote and told Jennie that you were married.' I told her that I had not been married and that it was my brother and asked her to write and tell Jennie I was still single. She said she would. Jennie never wrote to me."

Jennie's half-sister, Minnie Olander, was given an entirely different explanation of Jennie's whereabouts by Joe Maxson, who said that he believed the girl had gone off to Fergus Falls and was attending a Lutheran school there.

But Jennie Olsen was already dead - murdered by Belle because she had learned her secrets. Fearing that she would go to the authorities, Belle killed her. This was the reason she never bothered to add Jennie's name to the will. It was a sloppy mistake to make by someone who had been getting away with murder for years.

Only one person seemed to know Jennie's true fate before Belle's dark secrets were finally uncovered in early May 1908. This was poor Anton Olsen, Jennie's long-suffering father. According to his own account, he was awakened from a disturbing dream in the early hours of a morning sometime in late April. Olsen, a man not given to superstition, was so shaken by the dream that it gave him a terrible feeling of dread. He did not put stock in ghosts, séances and portents of evil, but in his dream he had witnessed a horrifying vision of Jennie lying in a shallow, unmarked grave. Rain was falling and the wet landscape around the grave appeared to be a farm. Terrified, he feared that the farm might be the place in Indiana where his daughter had been living with her foster mother for years.

Olsen had not seen Jennie in nearly five years, when she had gone off to live with Belle. But now he was looking forward to a reunion with his daughter on her 18th birthday, which was fast approaching on May 5. Perhaps his anticipation about this event had caused his unsettling dream. She was nearly a grown woman and he could not imagine what she looked like now. He admitted that he was nervous about seeing her again and perhaps this had been the source of the dream.

Anton Olsen turned over and eventually went back to sleep, dismissing the nightmare. He wouldn't think of it again until he got the gruesome word from Indiana about Belle Gunness' farm of horror. When he heard the news, he knew that he would never see his daughter again.

After the reports of Lamphere's threats were given to her attorney, Belle stopped talking about them. She never went to the police to report further threats, but she knew that word would spread, especially since she made sure to tell a few people that her will had been drawn up because she was afraid that her former hired hand would kill her family and burn down her house. Good gossip was impossible to pass up in LaPorte, and she knew that the stories would spread.

Belle was carefully setting the stage for the final act to follow.

On the night of April 27, 1908, the Gunness family was in a festive mood. There was nothing about that evening that would suggest that Belle had filed her will earlier that day, or that it was about to become a self-fulfilling prophecy with the terrible events that followed. The house was brightly lit that evening, and hired hand Joe Maxson, who slept on the second floor, later recalled "a happy family gathering." The children laughed and played games with Belle in the parlor. It was Belle's last chance to reprise her role as the caring and devoted mother. She sat on the floor and laughed and sang along with the children. Maxson went to bed shortly before 8:30 p.m. but he couldn't remember what time Belle put the children down for the night. Eventually, after everyone had gone to sleep, the house grew quiet.

During the early hours of the next morning, Maxson awoke to the smell of smoke. When he ran out of his room to see what was happening, he was confronted by a wall of flames. He screamed for Belle and called to the children, but there was no response. Even after he made it safely out of the house, he continued to call out and beat on the windows, trying to rouse the sleeping family. Neighbors who were alerted by his cries and the light of the flames joined Maxson as he tried to get Belle and the family out of the house. The fire burned quickly and no one was saved. Eventually, Maxson raced to town to get help, but by the time the fire department arrived, the old brick farmhouse was a pile of smoldering ruins.

As it happened, Ray Lamphere was also awake at the same time Joe Maxson was trying to escape from the burning house. He had spent the previous afternoon in LaPorte and bedded down for the night at the shack that belonged to "Nigger Liz," the alleged "voodoo woman" and one of the strangest characters in town. She lived in a ramshackle cabin on the south shore of Clear Lake. Lamphere left her place just after 4:00 a.m. and headed for the Wheatbrook farm, six miles away, where he was now employed. He just happened to be passing the Gunness farm and noticed fire and smoke billowing from the roof. Lamphere did not stop to help, nor did he notify any neighbors, but kept walking because, as he told the *Chicago Tribune*, "I was afraid I might be suspected of having set it on fire."

It only took a few minutes for the Gunness house to be reduced to burning ruins. The farmhouse and outbuildings were gone and most of the brick walls of the house had collapsed. As the fireman began poking through the debris, they found the four burned bodies in the cellar. Some suggested that as the upper floors had collapsed, the corpses had been dumped into the lowest level of the house. The bodies of Belle's children were easily identified but the other corpse, assumed to be Belle, was not so easy to recognize. In addition to being badly burned, the head had been severed from the body. Had Belle been murdered before the fire was set? Or did perhaps a falling beam somehow manage to cleave her head from her body after it had toppled into the cellar?

Ruins of the Gunness house after the fire

County Sheriff Al Smutzer, who had rushed to the scene with the fire department, examined the body for himself. He knew about Ray Lamphere's threats against Belle and her children and after taking one look at the wreckage and the mangled bodies, he sought out the former farm hand. Attorney M.E. Lehter also came forward and told the sheriff about Belle's will and how she feared that Lamphere would kill her family and burn down her house.

The first order of business, though, was trying to unravel the mystery in the cellar. Within a matter of hours, as soon as the ruins of the house had cooled down, scores of investigators, sheriff's deputies, coroner's men and volunteers began searching through the debris. The body of the headless woman became the most controversial piece of evidence. Sheriff Smutzer initially believed it was Belle's and he surmised that the ferocity of the fire had burned off her skull. However, this opinion was easily dismissed because Belle was known to have a gold bridge with false, porcelain teeth in it - teeth that were nearly impossible to destroy in a house fire. No teeth or gold bridge were found in the first search of the basement. Apparently, her head had been placed somewhere else. Belle's dentist, Dr. Ira P. Norton, said that he believed that if the dental work from the headless corpse could be located, he could determine whether or not it belonged to Belle. She wore a porcelain bridge, which Norton had made, and this might answer the question of whether or not she died in the fire.

Workers and law enforcement officers searching the ruins of the house for clues

A group of men dug deeper into the rubble but failed to find the skull. Frustrated, Smutzer called in Louis "Klondike" Schultz, a local man who had worked in the Alaskan gold fields as a prospector and miner. Schultz set up sluicing equipment and began using water to sift through the ashes and rubble in search of Belle's teeth. On May 19, to the complete satisfaction of Sheriff Smutzer, Schultz declared that the he had found the teeth and Belle's gold bridgework. Dr. Norton identified this as work that he had completed for Belle. But there were a number of people who were perceptive enough to ask a simple question: if Belle was callous enough to kill her children and set her house on fire, why wouldn't she simply leave her false teeth behind to make it look like she died also?

Sluicing for clues, bones and Belle's teeth and gold bridge in the ruins of the house.

Smutzer thought the fire was started by someone who had gone out the front door. Joe Maxson pointed out that an oil can that usually stood in the outside hallway in that part of the house was missing. The crime was deliberate. There were four bodies found, and the remains were taken to the morgue, where Coroner Charles Mack directed the postmortem. The four-man coroner's jury issued their findings based on the discovery of Belle's false teeth and bridge. They said they were confident in the belief that the headless body was that of Belle Gunness and the other remains were her children. Death, they ruled, was caused by suffocation, followed by burning. There was no evidence of any other wounds. The removal of the woman's head was due to the fire.

But Dr. Harry Long, who assisted at the postmortem, disagreed. And he was not alone in his opinion. Many of the neighbors who were present when the headless body was pulled out of the basement stated that it was not the body of Belle Gunness. Dr. Long measured the remains, and making allowances for the missing head, stated that the dead woman had been about five feet, three inches tall and had weighed no more than one hundred and fifty pounds. This was five inches and at least seventy-five pounds lighter than Belle! Neighbors went on record as saying that the body found in the basement was nowhere close to Belle's statuesque form. Detailed measurements of the body were compared with those on file with several LaPorte stores, who had made dresses for Belle. Dr. Long became convinced that the body was not Belle Gunness.

As the physicians argued over their findings, Sheriff Smutzer, who seemed sure the body belonged to Belle, focused his attentions on Ray Lamphere. He was aware of the bad blood between Belle and her former employee. Their strained relationship had already been confirmed by Belle's attorney, as well as by others who heard the gossip around town. When lawmen went to question Lamphere on April 29, he immediately raised the suspicions of deputies Antiss and Marr. Before they could ask him anything, Lamphere blurted out, "Did Widow Gunness and the children get out all right?" When asked if he meant from the fire at the edge of town, he replied yes. He was immediately arrested and taken back to town, but he denied having anything to do with it, swearing that he was nowhere near the farm when the blaze occurred. However, a young man named John Solyem stated that he had seen Lamphere running down the road from the Gunness house, just before the house caught on fire.

Belle's former lover and hired hand was arraigned on charges of arson and murder. With no attorney to represent him, he was bound over to the LaPorte County circuit grand jury. There was no doubt that Lamphere was the obvious suspect. He had argued with Belle, allegedly threatened her, and had been jealous over her relationship with Andrew Helgelein. At the time of his arrest, he was wearing an overcoat that had been the property of the missing John O. Moe and carrying a watch that had belonged to another prospective suitor of Belle's. From his cell, Lamphere bitterly told the *Chicago Tribune*, "She gave me these things. That woman - I knew she was bad. I always suspected that she killed Helgelein, but now I'm sure of it. Once she wanted me to buy Rough on Rats ffia poison for rodentsffl for her, and another time she wanted chloroform. I would not get them for her."

While all of this was taking place, Asle Helgelein arrived in La Porte. His first stop was the sheriff's office, where he explained that he believed his brother had met with foul play at the hands of Belle Gunness. Sheriff Smutzer seemed uninterested in searching through the ruins of the Gunness house again, but Helgelein insisted. It was not until Smutzer questioned Joe Maxson, Belle's hired hand, that he realized that something had been missed during the initial search of the property. Maxson told the sheriff that Belle had ordered him to bring loads of dirt by wheelbarrow to a large area near the hog pens. Maxson said that there were a number of deep depressions in the ground that had been covered by dirt. Belle had told Maxson that she buried her garbage there, and that she wanted him to make the ground level by filling in the depressions with fresh dirt.

Unfortunately, Smutzer had little incentive to open up the case again. He, along with State's Attorney Ralph Smith, just wanted to pin down the case, convict Lamphere and let the matter be forgotten about. Smith, a Republican, was facing a tough reelection campaign. The last thing that he wanted on his record was political embarrassment brought on by an outsider like Helgelein who was asking questions and making dangerous accusations. At this point, Belle Gunness was an merely an unlikable woman who had been murdered by her hired hand. What Helgelein was suggesting could turn the case into a nightmare. Sheriff Smutzer was in the same boat. He was retiring after four years in office and his deputy, William Antiss, wanted his job. A case like this would help him make a name for himself. Smutzer, another Republican in a heavily Democratic district, just wanted it over with. He grudgingly traveled to Chicago to confer with detectives from the Pinkerton Agency and solicited help from the Chicago Police, who sent detective C.J. Smith to aid in the investigation.

The local Democrats, eager to thwart and discredit the Republicans, saw the Gunness case as the means to salt away the next countywide election for their state's attorney candidate by pushing the theory that Belle had murdered her children, burned the house down, and then escaped the fire. Lamphere, they were convinced, was simply a patsy, cleverly set up by Belle to take the fall. Mayor Lemuel Darrow and his police chief, Clinton Cochrane, were in agreement on this point. Darrow, an important Democrat and wealthy landowner, was a distant relative of Chicago's Clarence Darrow, the famous defense attorney. Darrow's law partner, Wirt Worden, again agreed to be Lamphere's lawyer, likely as a favor to the defendant's father, the long-serving justice of the peace.

Darrow was in the middle of his five-term run as mayor. The Democrats had controlled the political landscape for two decades but were feeling vulnerable. The *Argus-Bulletin* was their local mouthpiece and the newspaper called for a broader investigation of the Gunness case as a means of building party credibility. It was at odds with the town's Republican newspaper, the *Daily Herald*, whose editors pounded away at Ray Lamphere.

But the one thing that neither side saw coming was that the Belle Gunness case was about to get worse - much, much worse.

Asle Helgelein -- who was little more than an annoyance to the authorities at this point, and at worst a crackpot - was not concerned about the politics of LaPorte. He was determined to find out what happened to his brother. This single-minded determination turned out to be the linchpin that revealed the horrors buried under the earth of the Gunness farm.

Working next to neighbors who lived along McClung Road, Helgelein led the men as they began to dig. At first, the usual scattered debris consisting of cans, bottles, broken glass was unearthed. Then a piece of gunnysack was found buried four feet below the earth. Sheriff Smutzer was called over as hundreds of curiosity-seekers watched with morbid fascination from behind the woven wire fenced that circled the yard. Within minutes came a grisly find: the mostly intact body of Andrew Helgelein. As the burlap was unwrapped from around him, Asle made a positive identification. Before sundown, the putrefied remains of four more victims were found. The crowd watched as workers unwrapped individual body parts, deteriorated by quicklime, from gunnysack cloth. They turned up eight men's watches, assorted bones and human teeth.

The skeletal remains of the missing Jennie Olsen were unearthed and the mystery of her disappearance was solved. Anton Olsen and the dead girl's sisters were immediately notified and summoned to LaPorte.

The town was shocked, and more volunteers came out to the farm to join in the search. On the following day, three more bodies were discovered. In all, fourteen of Belle's victims were pieced together, with a quantity of teeth, bones and personal items left over. The gruesome finds made headlines in newspapers throughout the Midwest and relatives of the victims began to appear from all over the region to claim bodies. All of them told of lonesome brothers, uncles and cousins who answered Belle's matrimonial ads and traveled hopefully to LaPorte with their life savings stuffed in their pockets. As relatives arrived, Deputy Antiss accompanied them all to the temporary morgue - a carriage shed on the Gunness property - to make positive identifications.

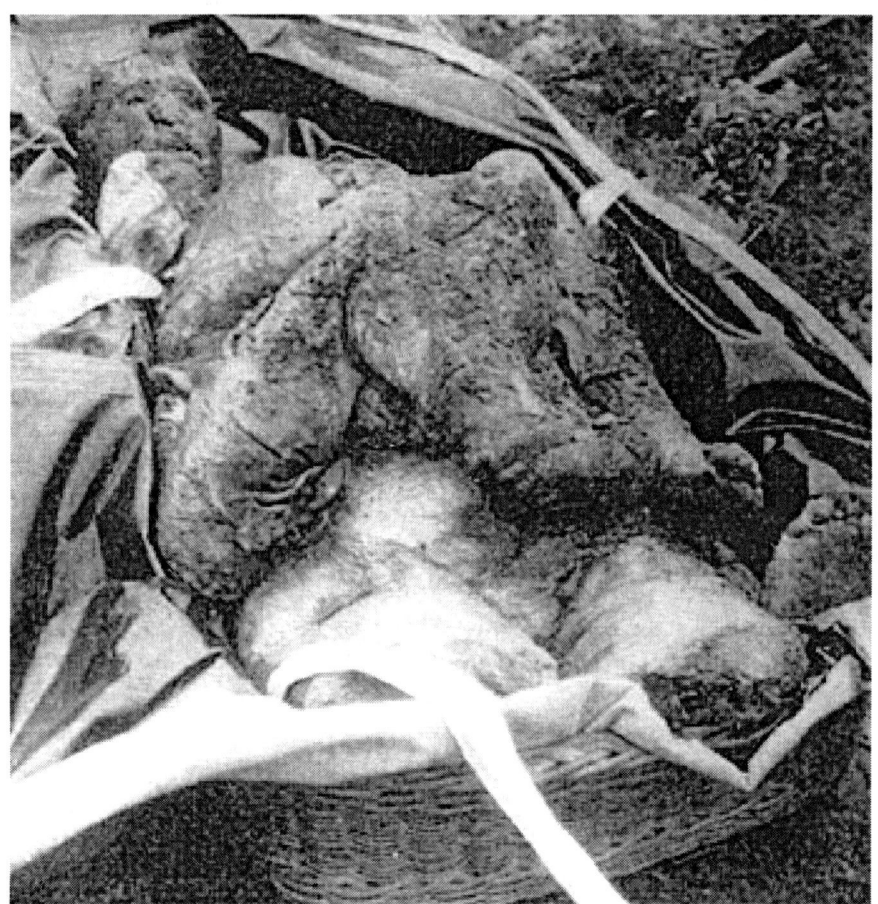

The mostly intact body of Andrew Helgelein was discovered buried in Belle's yard. This was the first evidence of the numerous murders that had occurred on the property.

Dr. J.H. William Meyer, who had formerly been attached to the Cook County Hospital in Chicago, took charge of the postmortem examinations. He told the *Chicago Tribune*, "It is horrible. I am at a loss to express an opinion on the whole case. I believe that nothing like it was ever encountered before. No jury of the foremost physicians of the country could say how long ago and just how these different people were killed."

Volunteers working at the farm to try and discover the bodies that had been buried all over the property. No one was prepared for the horror they would find.

As one day led into the next, and more victims were unearthed at the farm, the murders became national news. Reporters from every large paper in the United States descended on the small town of LaPorte, overwhelming not only the residents but the officials in charge of the case. The rush of visitors was so great that liverymen established a regular bus line from downtown LaPorte to the Gunness farm. The road was clogged with buggies, automobiles and pedestrians coming from every direction.

As estimated fifteen thousand people from all over Northwest Indiana, Chicago, Indianapolis and small town Illinois pressed onto the grounds. The mood was weirdly festive as the crowd was serviced by vendors selling sandwiches and drinks from roadside stands. Picture postcards of the studio portrait of Belle and her children were produced by a local printing house and sold for ten cents. Gruesome images of the recovered remains of Andrew Helgelein were also made into postcards and these sold even faster than the family portrait. Picnickers packed lunches and spread out blankets in the grass. Baseball games were played within a few hundred feet of the crime scene and pickpockets conducted a brisk trade by roaming through the crowds at the farm and on the train platform as visitors made their way home. Sheriff Smutzer sighed and offered a sad comment on the happenings: "Awful, isn't it? There does not seem to be any horror in these people. I never saw folks having a better time."

Sheriff Smutzer never backed down from his contention that Belle Gunness died in the fire. In fact, he blamed the idea that she escaped on a Hearst reporter named Arthur James Pegler, father of syndicated newspaper columnist Westbrook Pegler, despite the strong evidence that existed to say that Belle Gunness fled from LaPorte. According to Smutzer in a 1934 interview, it was Art Pegler who planted the notion in the public's mind that Belle plotted the crime, substituted a "body double" and vanished into the night. He said that Pegler, who worked for the *Chicago American*, came to him one evening and told him that he was going to send in a story that said Belle didn't die in the fire, just to give the case a new angle. The next day, the story was splashed over the entire front page of the paper and this started talk that Belle had escaped. "It had its origins in the mind of one newspaperman," Smutzer grumbled.

On May 6, 1908, the first newspaper story appeared to announce what many in LaPorte already believed: that Belle Gunness was alive. The headline read, "Woman Bluebeard Alive Says Coroner." According to Coroner Mack, "That woman is *not* dead." Nevertheless, he had escorted the caskets of the "supposed" Belle and her children to Forest Home Cemetery in Forest Park, west of Chicago, for internment. He added that he believed that Belle was not the body found in the burned house. The real Belle Gunness had fled. "She used another body for a ruse after she murdered her own children and set fire to the house," he claimed.

There were many who believed that Coroner Mack was right. Criminal forensics, even as primitive as they were in 1908, tended to disprove the contentions of the sheriff and the state's attorney who believed that Belle was dead. But was the story merely cooked up by Art Pegler? Amid the political controversies and the excesses of the yellow journalism of the day, there seemed to be only one truth that could be counted on in the investigation: that Belle Gunness, the seemingly loving mother who chloroformed her children and then burned them to death, was a predator unlike any previously seen in American history.

On May 10, the *Chicago Sunday Record-Herald* heartily agreed, "It is safe to say that in light of the disclosures of the past few days, Mrs. Belle Gunness, the LaPorte widow, has eclipsed the record of the prairie vixen of Kansas Kate Bender and that she undoubtedly holds the palm as the most extensive slayer, man or woman, of the age."

Steady rains during the early weeks of May temporarily put a halt to the excavations on the Gunness farm. But that made little difference to the reporters and curiosity-seekers; they had moved on to another attraction - the search for Belle Gunness. Despite fervent insistence from the Republican officials in LaPorte, few wanted to believe that the case was closed and Belle was dead.

Within a few days of the fire, there were reported sightings of Belle in Chicago and across the country. In Syracuse, New York, Cora Belle Herron, the widow of a chemical salesman from Chicago, was on her way from Franklin, Pennsylvania, to New York City, where she planned to visit her sister. Her journey was rudely interrupted when she was removed from a Pullman sleeping car, and dragged off to jail on suspicion of being Belle Gunness. The matter was straightened out, but the angry woman later filed a lawsuit against the police.

Andre W. Thompson of Paulina Street in Chicago furnished the police with a photograph of Belle and swore that she was hiding in plain sight in his neighborhood. It was hard to dismiss Thompson's claims as he had been a boyhood friend of the late Mads Sorensen and had been best man at Mads and Belle's wedding. Thousands of copies of the Gunness photo were made and sent to police agencies in the United States and Europe, but a search of Thompson's neighborhood failed to produce Belle.

From across the country, heart-breaking reports filled the newspapers. Friends, wives and relatives of missing persons held out faint hope that the Gunness farm might offer clues to a score of unsolved disappearances of loved ones. With each body that turned up, a forlorn hope filled the hearts of many, but for most, their loved ones remained missing.

The horrifying stories of the carnage discovered on the farm caused at least one person to become unhinged. On May 10, in Warsaw, Indiana, a seventy-year-old man named Jacob Pouch committed suicide while "temporarily deranged" after reading newspaper accounts of the Gunness crimes.

In Chicago, U.S. Attorney Edwin W. Sims ordered the arrest of every shady keeper of matrimonial agencies - the notorious "match-makers" who led young girls into brothels; middle-aged widows and spinsters into the arms of bigamists and con men; and lonely bachelors into death traps like the Gunness farm. The fallout from the Belle Gunness case sparked a wave of political action and a long-overdue crackdown against these shady storefront operators.

The murders encouraged tipsters to alert the police to old rumors about the house where Belle lived on Alma Street and the candy store that she had once operated. Lieutenant Matthew Zimmerman of the Austin district led a fruitless search for a druggist who allegedly sold poisons to Belle, while a post office inspector conducted a search for matrimonial bureaus that Belle might have used to find her victims. Sadly, he probably needed to look no further than the personals section of the Scandinavian newspapers of the day.

Chicago Coroner Peter Hoffman called for an excavation of the former candy store address at 313 Grand Avenue to see if Belle had buried a little girl named Lucy there. She was believed to have adopted the girl in 1894. No such excavation was ever conducted and no digging was done in the backyard of the Alma Street house either. The owner of the house at the time, David Nellis, was not anxious to see his yard torn up and worried about possible damage to the foundation of his home. He had used his life savings to purchase the house and the police, thinking practically, sympathized and called off the dig unless something more tangible than neighborhood gossip turned up.

Meanwhile, back in LaPorte, there was complete chaos. Digging continued at the Gunness farm as known victims those identified by family members were carried into the carriage shed, removed from the burlap wrapping and stacked like human cordwood. The stark horror of the scene inside the shed and the solemn faces of the volunteers who continued to excavate the grounds were in stark contrast to the laughter, baseball games, pony rides, picnics and souvenir sales that were going on just a short distance away.

Inside the fenced-in area of the farm, Sheriff Smutzer was encouraged by the discovery of three engraved gold rings in the sluice boxes of "Klondike" Schultz. The inscriptions on two of them read: "PG to JS Aug-23, 94" and "PS to JS, 5-3-96." Smutzer and Ralph Smith, the local prosecutor, believed that the rings belonged to Belle. They were found near where the corpse of the adult female was found after the fire. This "stunning new evidence" closed the case to the satisfaction of Ralph Smith.

But the initials were certainly not Belle's, even if the "S" stood for "Sorensen." No one could figure out the identity of the people who might have matched the inscriptions inside the rings. Were they left behind by Belle in her hasty escape? Or did they belong to the mysterious woman that Ray Lamphere claimed had been lured to the farm from Chicago and then murdered? Many believed that it was this woman's body - not Belle's - that was found in the burned-out cellar.

As the summer turned into fall, Ray Lamphere waited in jail for his trial. At some point, Lamphere made a partial confession to Reverend E.A. Schell, but on the advice of his attorney, he retracted it and said nothing further in the weeks following the fire as he waited in the recently opened LaPorte County Jail. He was said to be in a state of near nervous collapse as he waited for his murder and arson trial to begin.

It finally started on the afternoon of November 9, 1908. In the oak-paneled courtroom of Judge John Carl Richter, jury selection began. The actual trial started four days later - on Friday the 13th, which was also Ray Lamphere's birthday.

The trial itself was a contentious one and a bitter test of wills between political rivals, each determined to destroy the reputation and standing of the others. The Republicans had prevailed in the 1908 fall election. William Antiss had replaced his former boss, Albert Smutzer, as sheriff. Charles Mack was defeated for re-nomination as coroner in the LaPorte County Democratic Convention because he believed that the body of the woman in the cellar was Belle Gunness, which ran counter to the case that Mayor Darrow and Wirt Worden were building for Ray Lamphere's defense. Mack was unceremoniously dumped by the Democrats for going against the interests of the party. Prosecutor Ralph Smith defeated his challenger, Philo Q. Doran, following a blistering campaign in which the handling of the Gunness case was called to account by the Democrats and defenders of Ray Lamphere.

Wirt Worden continued to push the theory that most people had come to accept as the truth: that Belle had escaped from the fire. His arguments were backed up by some pretty convincing facts. Ralph Smith was equally confident in his strategy of pinning the murders of Belle and her children on Lamphere after he scrapped his original plan of trying the accused man for the murder of Andrew Helgelein. He gave an irritated interview to the *Chicago American* just before the trial. He said, "I am tired of this silly rot that she is alive! I am going to put a stop to all this talk about her being seen in forty different places in the country by every Tom, Dick and Harry who thinks he is a detective!" When it came to Lamphere's trial, he was confident about the outcome. "There is no possibility in my mind that the verdict will be anything other than guilty. I anticipate a good deal of trouble securing a jury owning to the wide publicity that has been given the case but a special venire of seventy-five men have been drawn. That the dead woman found in the house was Mrs. Gunness we have conclusive proof. I have the evidence to hang the man in my office! The effort to make political capital of the case failed."

Smith would first have to overcome the compelling findings of Dr. Walter Haines, an eminent Chicago toxicologist. Haines was called to LaPorte to conduct an analysis of the three bodies of the children dug out of the basement. He identified sufficient quantities of arsenic and strychnine in the stomachs of the victims to cause death. Based on what Haines told the court, it would be very difficult for the state to establish that Lamphere first poisoned the victims and then set fire to the house, especially with Joe Maxson on the premises.

The strong feelings about the case in the community, as well as the widespread publicity surrounding it across the region, caused an estimated five hundred people to jam into the courthouse, hoping to gain admission to a room that only seated 300. Numbered tickets were given out to spectators on a first-come-first-served basis in an effort to try and prevent overcrowding. It was noted that women far outnumbered men among the courtroom spectators.

It was evident from the moment that the judge's gavel banged to signal the opening of the trial that extraordinary measures had been taken to ensure an acquittal for Ray Lamphere. The drunken, ne'er-do-well had not a dollar to his name and yet his legal team consisted of Wirt Worden, Mayor Darrow and Darrow's co-counsel, Ellsworth E. Weir, one of the most distinguished lawyers in the state. Asked later where he was going to get the money to pay his legal fees, Lamphere shrugged his shoulders and said that he didn't know. The scruffy Lamphere had been cleaned and scrubbed for his courtroom appearance. He was washed, shaved and dressed in a suit, looking more like a respectable bank clerk than a lowly farm hand with a bad reputation. His elderly mother - estranged from his father for years - made a tearful plea on her son's behalf. She evoked sympathy from nearly everyone in the room when she told of her son's early circumstances and the terrible poverty they had endured.

The daily courtroom proceedings were unpredictable and lively, especially when the flamboyant Ellsworth Weir asked the circuit clerk to issue a summons for Belle Gunness to appear on November 14, an action that provoked anger from the prosecution and laughter from the audience. But Weir was serious. In the *LaPorte Daily Herald*, he was quoted as saying, "In my opinion the woman is not so far away that she could not answer the subpoena and her coming into court or otherwise will depend largely on the advice of her counsel. It might not be so easy of a matter to convict Mrs. Gunness of a crime as many people seem to suppose."

As the trial continued, eyewitnesses recounted startling stories of the strange events that went on at the Gunness farm. On the fifth day of testimony, jurors were told about a late-night visit to the farm house by Addie Landis, a young woman who was to meet with Belle about a possible job. A buggy driver, Leo Wade, said that he had driven Miss Landis to the house and watched as she left the carriage, went to the back door and looked into the window. Suddenly, the girl let out a scream and ran back toward the buggy - falling down several times on the way. Obviously upset, she demanded that Wade take her to the home of Pearl Corey, another prospective employer. Weeping, she cried out, "I've seen the most awful thing I ever expect to see!" According to the testimony of the hack driver, Corey refused to let Miss Landis into her home and so he let her off downtown. He found out the next day that she had taken the train to Valparaiso, Indiana. Within a week, Addie went mad and had to be institutionalized at the Logansport Hospital for the Insane. Pearl Corey verified the driver's story and said that Addie was supposed to come to her house that evening about a job. She would have let her in, she said, but she was raving like a maniac about what she had seen at the Gunness house. She told the court, "I could not make much sense out of what she said except that it was about cutting up a body and I believed the girl was a lunatic. In light of other developments, I am inclined to think that what she saw that night drove her crazy."

Joe Maxson took the witness stand and offered testimony about events at the Gunness house on the night of the fire. He claimed to have spotted Lamphere lurking in the trees near the house and then running across a nearby field. He recalled Belle's apparent nervousness that night and said he believed that she had injected dope into an orange that she gave him in order to put him to sleep. A strange feeling of drowsiness came over him soon after eating the fruit, he said. After going to bed, he never heard any sounds downstairs and he was lucky to have awakened when he did. Maxson wholeheartedly believed that Belle had intended for him to die during the fire.

A grocer's clerk named George Wrase recalled selling Belle some supplies in town on the day before the fire. Her purchases included two gallons of kerosene in a five-gallon oil can. As she was paying for the items, Ray Lamphere came into the store to purchase a five-cent plug of chewing tobacco, and for a long moment, the two of them stared at one another. Wrase thought that they looked at one another with hatred, but could some other kind of silent communication have passed between them? It was very disturbing, the grocer's clerk recalled. The oil can was later found in the ruins of the cellar, under a pile of bricks, a few yards away from the four bodies.

Peter Colson, who had worked on the farm for two years, told of Lamphere's obsession with Belle - and his fear of her. Colson admitted to sleeping with his employer. "She made such love to me!" he rapturously exclaimed, as loud murmurs from the largely female audience in the courtroom interrupted the proceedings. Colson said that he was both attracted and repelled to Belle. Eventually, he left the farm and said that he spent the next six months sleeping in a haymow on a farm a half-mile away."

The prosecutor was encouraged for a moment by Judge Richter's ruling to admit Coroner Mack's verdict that Belle had perished in the fire, but Richter reconsidered the matter and then reversed his ruling. It was a setback for the state, but the jury and the audience still had the vivid and gruesome reminder of the horror in a grisly display of jars that were sitting directly in front of the downcast Lamphere. The jars contained human bones, fragments of flesh, bits of cloth and other evidence that had been pulled out of the burned farmhouse and from the tainted grounds.

There were forty prosecution witnesses called to the courthouse, but only one - Louis "Klondike" Schultz, who was in Arkansas - failed to show. Former Sheriff Smutzer, the most important part of the prosecution's case, identified the three rings that were found in the ruins of the house as those that he had seen Belle wearing when she came to his office shortly before the fire to complain about Ray Lamphere. Smutzer hotly denied an allegation suggested by Wirt Worden that he had any "special interest" in the case, other than a duty to the community. He denied that his testimony had anything to do with politics.

LaPorte dentist Dr. Ira P. Norton testified that the teeth found in the burned house were, without a doubt, those of Belle Gunness. He had attended to her dental needs and knew the woman well. The teeth seemed to provide the physical evidence needed to convict Lamphere. The hired hand's jealousy, Belle's broken promise to share Helgelein's money with him, and this thirst for revenge provided ample motive, or so it seemed. According to the prosecution, Lamphere not only set fire to the house but had also witnessed the murder of Andrew Helgelein.

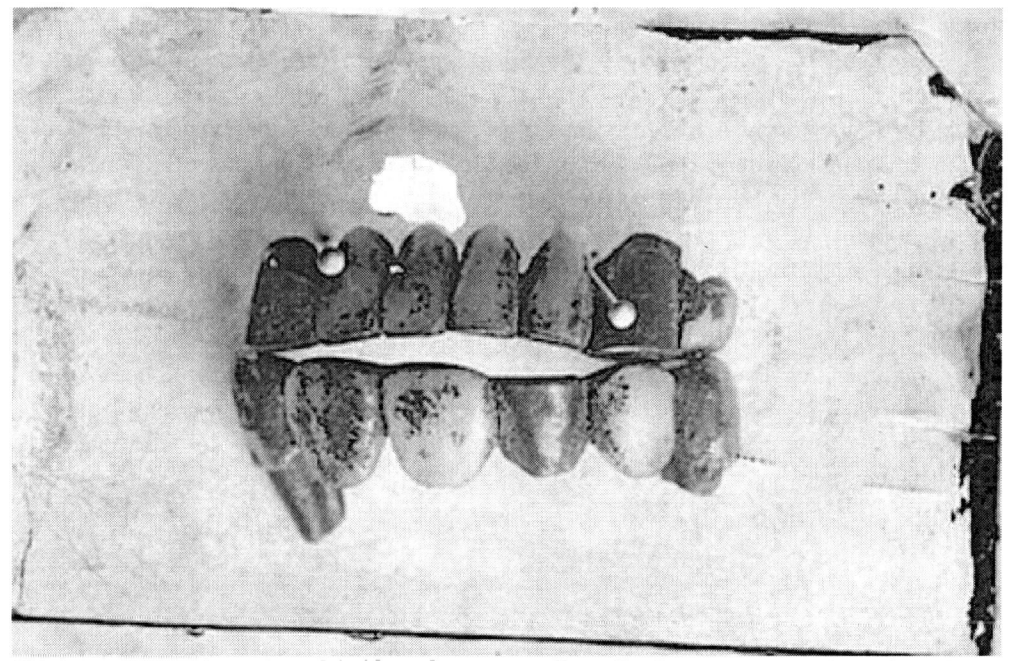

The controversial teeth and bridge that were allegedly found in the ruins of the house.

But the defense had another theory about the mysterious teeth and bridgework. Wirt Worden developed evidence that contradicted Dr. Norton's identification. A local jeweler testified that the gold in the bridgework had emerged from the fire almost unscathed, even though the heat from the blaze had damaged several watches and other pieces of jewelry that were recovered from the ruins of the house. Doctors replicated the conditions of the fire by attaching a similar piece of bridgework to a human jawbone and placing it into a blacksmith's forge. The real teeth crumbled and fell apart; the porcelain teeth came out pitted and marked; and the gold parts melted out of shape. Both of the artificial elements were damaged to a greater degree than those in the bridgework that had confirmed Belle's identification. Joe Maxson and another man claimed that they had seen "Klondike" Schultz take the bridgework out of his pocket and plant it just before it was "discovered." As mentioned, Schultz was conveniently out of town when Lamphere's trial began.

After Worden wrapped up the defense's opening address to the jury, the *Argus-Bulletin* reported that "several of the jurymen edged to the front of their seats as if drawn toward the speaker like a needle attracted by a magnet. When he had finished, there was a profound silence. The spectators realized that Worden had made assertions and made them in such a masterly manner that if he proved able to back them up by the testimony of witnesses, Ray Lamphere's neck would be saved from the noose that William Antiss, Sheriff-Elect of LaPorte County, placed around it yesterday afternoon.

All of the circumstantial information tended to prove that Belle had faked her own death and substituted someone else's body in the place of her own. Worde's next words must have electrified the jury. He told them, "We will prove by testimony that on the afternoon of April 27, Mrs. Gunness had a conversation in front of the First National Bank building with a certain man in which she said, 'It must be done tonight and you must do it!' Something *was* done that night. A torch was applied to the Gunness house and the bodies of the three Gunness children were found in the ruins. We will produce a witness who saw Mrs. Gunness drive out to her house on the Saturday preceding the fire in the company of a woman who has never been seen since unless it was her body that was found in the ruins of the fire."

In his closing remarks, prosecutor Smith warned the jury not to be sidetracked by the crimes of Belle Gunness as they deliberated over whether or not Ray Lamphere was guilty of the crimes for which he was charged. The *Chicago Tribune* quoted his words to the jury: "The badness of Mrs. Gunness is no defense for Lamphere. She was as bad as hell. Lamphere was associated with her. Lamphere was going to marry her. It was Lamphere who came upon her the night she was killing Helgelein and helped her dispose of the body." As Smith finished his remarks, his face was red and he was shaking in fist in anger. He concluded, "The defense wants to know where the miner Schultz who found the teeth is. I ask: Where is 'Nigger Liz'? Why don't the defense bring her here and prove their alibi by her?"

As a matter of fact, Elizabeth Smith had a lot to tell the court, but she was never called to testify. The intolerant racial attitudes of the day, and her reputation as an addled eccentric, simply didn't allow the defense to bring her to the stand. Without Smith to account for his presence at her shack that night, the case for Lamphere's acquittal was on shaky ground, but there was little his lawyers could do that hadn't been done already.

The jury retired to consider its verdict on November 25. Each side was confident that the outcome of the case would be in their favor - but what happened was unforeseen and did not end up in a clear victory for either the Republican or the Democratic faction of the politically charged trial. On Thanksgiving evening, after 19 ballots and 22 hours of deliberation, the jury compromised and decided that Lamphere was guilty of arson, but they cleared him of the murder charges. Judge

Richter read the sentence and pronounced an indeterminate sentence of two to 21 years in the penitentiary.

The prosecution appeared to be satisfied by the outcome of the case but Worden, Darrow and Weir seemed to take the verdict harder than Ray Lamphere did. Lamphere seemed strangely unconcerned. After the trial ended, he told the *LaPorte Daily Herald*, "I have no particular complaint to make. The evidence was pretty strong against me and I am willing to take my medicine by my own conscience is clear and that helps some." That night, with the suspense finally over, Lamphere slept better than he had at any time in the previous five months. His mood was almost upbeat the next morning after a visit from his mother and two sisters inside of his cell at the county jail.

Later that week, he was escorted to the state penitentiary in Michigan City by Albert Smutzer. During the trip, Lamphere acted as though he was resigned to his fate. A reporter for the *LaPorte Argus-Bulletin* caught up with him before he was taken out of town and Lamphere told him, "I'm lucky to be here. Why? I might have been chopped up and put in a hole in old woman Gunness' chicken yard. I'm going to prison with a clear conscience. I didn't do any more than hundreds of others in my place would have done." Asked by the reporter if he ever planned to make a clean breast of things and reveal what he had witnessed on the night that he cut a hole in the floor of the parlor so that he could spy on Belle and Andrew Helgelein, Lamphere looked irritated. He replied, "No, I don't think I ever will."

Lamphere remained silent - or so the official words on the subject stated - all the way to the end of his life. He eventually died in prison from tuberculosis that he contracted while waiting in jail for his trial to start. Lamphere passed away on December 30, 1909, soon after attempts to get an eleventh-hour pardon from Indiana Governor Thomas R. Marshall failed.

Soon after Lamphere's death, a convict named Harry Myers came forward with stories that he claimed were told to him by Lamphere after he became convinced he would die from tuberculosis. To this day, no one knows if the stories were true. The warden of the penitentiary dismissed Myers as a crank, but many took the account seriously. Myers said that Lamphere described to him Belle's escape from LaPorte. Lamphere himself had driven her in a buggy to a point nine miles from town, where she met a man who was to take her to Chicago. According to Lamphere, she had carried two large valises with her and a small tin box containing stacks of one-hundred-dollar bills, expensive items of jewelry and other valuables with which she apparently intended to finance a new start in life.

Lamphere also claimed that the woman who had perished in the burning house was from Chicago. Belle had met her on State Street during one of her frequent shopping expeditions to the city. The unknown woman had been seated on the stairway of a building, looking downcast. Belle struck up a cheerful conversation with her, promising to give her a good-paying job as a housekeeper in Indiana. The woman happily agreed and traveled with Belle back to the farm.

In his account to Myers, Lamphere then allegedly stated that Belle had asked him to build a wooden box measuring two or three feet square, which would large enough to hold the severed head of the Chicago woman. After the woman was murdered, Belle brought him the head, wrapped in a rug, and placed it in the box. She nailed the lid shut and ordered Lamphere to bury the box in the orchard. Myers said that Lamphere could not remember the exact spot where he had buried it, which, of course, was seized by prison officials to raise doubt about the validity of the story.

Even though prison warden James Reid disavowed Myers's claim that he had learned this far-fetched story from Lamphere and expressed little confidence in the words of a convicted burglar and thief, Wirt Worden decided to look into it further. "I arranged for the parole of Harry Myers and employed some other men to dig in the orchard for the box," he said. "Although considerable time was spent on the farm in digging for it, the box was never located. It was a difficult task to begin with, and merely a matter of guess work."

On January 14, 1910, Reverend E.A. Schell came forward with a confession that he claimed that Lamphere had made to him before he succumbed to tuberculosis. In this confession, Lamphere spoke about Belle Gunness, whom he called a "human monster." Lamphere told Reverend Schell that he had not murdered anyone but that he had helped Belle bury many of her victims. When one of her "suitors" arrived, Belle charmed him with intimate carriage rides, a warm bed and good meals. After she had his money, Belle would drug the man's coffee and then split his head open with a meat cleaver. Other times, she simply waited for him to go to bed and then would chloroform her sleeping victim. Belle then carried the body to the basement, placed it on a table and butchered it the way that she would the carcass of a hog. The bodies were usually buried near the hog pen, but sometimes Belle varied her methods of disposal. Sometimes she dumped the corpse into the hog-scalding vat and covered the remains with quicklime. Other times, when she was feeling tired, she merely chopped up the bodies and, in the middle of the night, fed the remains to her hogs.

According to Schell's account, Belle really was dead. It had been her body in the fire. A liquored-up Lamphere and his companion, "Nigger Liz," had entered the Gunness house one night with plans for stealing Belle's money. Together, they chloroformed Belle and the three children, but Lamphere denied starting the fire. He had no idea how it could have started, unless he or Smith had accidentally knocked over the candle that they had carried into the house to light their way.

Was this story true? Many doubted it. Lamphere had a penchant for lying and Wirt Worden and the physicians that Worden consulted wondered how it was possible that a woman of Belle's size and strength could be so easily subdued by Lamphere and Smith. She would have certainly awakened during their attempt to chloroform her, and shouted to the children and Joe Maxson while fiercely resisting. The story was simply not plausible and Elizabeth Smith emphatically denied it when she was taken into custody for questioning and then released.

The version of events that has been accepted as the truth by most people in the years that followed the Lamphere trial is one that tends to conform to the testimony of Daniel Hutson, a Gunness neighbor who had briefly worked for Belle before buying his own farm on adjacent property. During the early evening hours of July 9, 1908 - two months and 11 days after Belle was supposedly consumed in the flames of her burning farmhouse - Hutson was making his way home in his wagon when he saw a man and a woman walking on a hill. The couple was in plain sight near the ruins of the Gunness house and Hutson was no more than 50 feet away from them. He told his story to the *Chicago American* in November 1908. It is reprinted here:

As soon as the woman saw me she said something to the man and they both got into the buggy. It was a side-bar buggy and the horse the woman was driving was a dapple gray weighing, I should say, 1,250 pounds. They seemed in a hurry to get away and were whipping the horse. As they passed out of the gate they were very close to me and I saw at once that the woman was Mrs. Gunness. I tried to shout to her but I was so taken aback by the sight of her that I was unable so say a word. They drove on down the road to Michigan City as hard as they could drive and I made all haste I could after them but was driving a hayrack and it was difficult to keep up. I noticed that the man sitting with Mrs. Gunness in the rig had streaks of gray hair under his hat on the sides. Mrs. Gunness was dressed in black and had two veils, both of black net. The one veil was rolled up so the other did not conceal her features. I should have known the woman anywhere because of her off physical characteristics. She is as broad as a man and has an odd way of turning her head. It is a furtive way, as if she had to fear something from behind. They kept whipping that horse until there were a good distance ahead of me and had passed the gate entering my farm. I knew it was no good to pursue in the dark so I turned into my farm and for fear of frightening my wife, said nothing. Later the child of one of my neighbors, Martha Scheffer, came over and without knowing I had seen the Gunness woman, told of meeting her driving along the road with a man and described the same horse and buggy.

Hutson said that his daughters, Eldora and Evaline, also saw Gunness, Many years later, as elderly women, they stuck to their story. A farm hand named Frederick Lambright also backed Hutson's story. He claimed that he had spotted Belle on the night in question and provided additional details. Lambright said that the woman and the man with her had parked their buggy near the southeast corner of the ruined house. The man stood next to the buggy and held the hitch in his hand as he talked to the woman that Lambright believed was Belle Gunness. Lambright told the *Chicago American*, "I distinctly heard her say 'That money ain't there.' I saw Mrs. Gunness as she bent over feeling for something on the ground. I told of my experience a few nights later to William Humphrey."

When Hutson told his story to the police, Sheriff Smutzer refused to take his statement. The farmer told the newspaper that he wondered why the police were being so close-minded about the matter. He began to suspect that the whole thing was a cover-up or worse, that some of the local officials had been in league with Belle Gunness. Of course, the farmer knew nothing of the political controversies that were mixed up in the case. Even so, he was angered when Sheriff Smutzer laughed at him and said, "Belle Gunness is dead and she ain't coming back. You sure you didn't see a ghost?"

Time passed. Stories changed as witnesses died or were forgotten.

Elizabeth "Nigger Liz" Smith, the daughter of Virginia slaves, Ray Lamphere's lover and the reputed worker of voodoo who fooled the people of LaPorte into thinking that she was some sort of witch, died on March 17, 1916. After her death, it was discovered that her old shack out on Railroad Street was filled with junk, including 980 pounds of old carpet. No one knew how old she was when she died. As workers began to tear down and haul away the pieces of the eyesore in which she had been living for decades, they found torn and dirty letters from men with whom she had corresponded through matrimonial agencies, a book about hypnotism and recipes for spells and incantations. They were also shocked to find life insurance policies, a bank account with a sizable amount of cash in it and the deeds to six properties in LaPorte. She had lived like a hermit, shunned by the locals, but it turned out that she was worth a small fortune. It was said, however, that her accumulation of wealth had come to her after the fire at the Belle Gunness house.

They were also shocked to find a skull that had been stashed under her bed. Of course, rumors immediately started that it was the head of the woman found in the Gunness basement after the fire, but it turned out to be much older than that. A few locals claimed that Liz had used the skull to work her magic, and that she had purchased the thing long before Belle came to LaPorte. It turned out that Liz had bought it from a traveling conjurer, who claimed that he had retrieved it from the battlefield after the massacre at Little Big Horn. He said it was the skull of an Indiana Indian chief. There was no way to know if this was just some colorful tall tale or not, but it had nothing to do with Belle Gunness - although it did keep the story alive.

What did Liz know about the Gunness case? We'll never know, for she took her secrets to the grave with her. This was despite the fact that she had promised Wirt Worden that she would someday tell him all that she knew - but only when she was near death. Unfortunately, Worden was in Louisiana at the time of Smith's death. He rushed back home as quickly as he could but by the time he arrived in town, Liz was already dead. She had stubbornly refused, even on her deathbed, to tell her secrets to anyone but Worden.

Wirt Worden left criminal defense behind after the Lamphere trial and became a LaPorte County prosecutor. He was elected as a judge of the circuit court in 1934 and served on the bench until his death from a heart attack at age 68 in 1943.

Albert Smutzer left law enforcement behind after his term in office ended. He left LaPorte to work in the building trade in Chicago. He later returned to LaPorte to live out the rest of his days with his daughter in 1933. Four years before his return to Indiana, his deputy and successor, William Antiss, died at the age of 60. Smutzer died in October 1940, never able to escape the notoriety that he received from the Gunness case.

Belle's sprawling home on Alma Street now Latrobe Avenue in Chicago's Austin neighborhood was torn down years ago and for a long time, it remained an empty lot. Like many other locations that have been connected to crimes or notorious people, the land was considered to be cursed for years. Eventually, though, the empty lot on North Latrobe Avenue was redeveloped and a new home was built on the site in 2003.

The fire debris was eventually cleared away from the farm on McClung Road, leaving only the brick cellar of Belle's house behind. The land became overgrown and neglected and prospective buyers steered clear of the property after they learned the history behind it. Then, just about everyone in LaPorte was startled when John Nepsha built a new home atop the old foundation in 1923. Bad luck followed. Nepsha's wife later divorced him, stating that she couldn't live there, and in 1936 a surveyor dropped dead in the yard as he was measuring the private cemetery on the property. Visitors came from all over the country to see the place where the infamous murders occurred, showing up at all hours of the day and night, and asking to take home souvenirs.

Other owners have come and gone over the years. In 2006, an interview with the owners at the time revealed that their son "saw dead people" on the property. It was a revelation that shouldn't come as a surprise, based on the number of people who died on the land and the number of unmarked burial sites that are likely still waiting to be found.

The LaPorte County Historical Society Museum features a disturbing Belle Gunness exhibit in the lower level of the building. A life-size figure of Belle is posed next to a side panel from one of the woodsheds that had been located on her property. There is a large collection of photographs and artifacts, including a skull that is purported to belong to one of her many victims. The skull is not on public display, and it is unlikely that it will ever be interred because records that identify the location of the potter's field where Belle's unknown victims were buried was never recorded. What happened to them - and just who those men were - will always remain a mystery.

But, of course, the greatest mystery of all is, if Belle Gunness did not die in the fire, what happened to her?

For decades, she was spotted in cities and towns across the country. Friends, amateur detectives and those with wild imaginations caught sight of the murderess or someone they thought looked like her on the streets of Chicago, New York, San Francisco, Denver, and beyond. For more than 20 years, the LaPorte Police Department received an average of two "Belle sightings" a month. She had taken her place in the ranks of the most infamous killers in American history.

In April 1914, Sheriff Antiss traveled to New York City to see a local woman that the police were holding because they believed her to be Belle. There turned out to be nothing to it. Other officers followed what seemed to be promising leads for many years, but each sighting turned out to be bad information, rumors, outright lies and cases of mistaken identity. After scores of baseless sightings and reports, Antiss and his successors in office simply abandoned the hunt and allowed the story to settle into the realm of legend and folklore, a tale of horror about how Belle was still out there somewhere, looking for her next victim.

Law enforcement officers in LaPorte gave up on the story after chasing one bad Belle Gunness lead after another, but as the years passed, new information emerged to suggest that maybe the stories of Belle's survival had been right all along.

In the spring of 1931, Deputy District Attorney George Stahlman of Los Angeles contacted LaPorte County Sheriff Tom McDonald to tell him about the arrest of two elderly women. These ladies - Esther Carlson and Anna Erickson -- had been nicknamed the "Arsenic and Old Lace Killers." They had recently been picked up for the poisoning murder of Carl Arthur Lindstrom, a wealthy 81-year-old man. It was all too familiar to those with knowledge of the Gunness case because everyone involved was Scandinavian.

Mrs. Carlson if that was her name worked as a housekeeper for the old man. Anna Erickson was a close friend of Carlson's. The first person to become suspicious about the seemingly harmless pair had been the victim's son, Peter Lindstrom, who reported the disappearance of a $2,000 joint savings account that his father had opened with his housekeeper. Peter opened an investigation that led to a drug store in Long Beach, where it was found that Carlson had tried to purchase arsenic.

Arrested and indicted on a murder charge, Carlson said that she had lived in Hartford, Connecticut, from 1892 to 1909 and denied any connection to LaPorte, Indiana. She had several friends in Los Angeles who vouched for her. They said she was born Esther Johnson in Sweden, not Norway. Carlson became ill with tuberculosis during her time in jail, waiting for her trial to start. The doctors stated that her condition was terminal. She was hospitalized and fading fast when, at Wirt Worden's request, Los Angeles homicide investigators produced witnesses from LaPorte and Chicago to provide some possible identification. They located R.C. Ganiere, the former photographer who had taken photos of Belle and her children 33 years before, and was now in the grocery business in California. He was positive that the woman dying in the hospital bed was Belle Gunness.

This opinion was shared by two other men, who saw Esther Carlson after she died. These men were L.E. Silvery of Monterey, formerly of LaPorte, and John "Dennis" Daly, a 70-year-old retired boilermaker who appeared at the county morgue at the behest of Sheriff McDonald. Daly importantly claimed in the *Chicago Tribune* that he was "one of the few men alive" who had actually seen Belle flee the LaPorte crime scene in 1908. He said, "With me was a friend - neither of us knew the Gunness farmhouse had burned during the night - and we saw a heavily veiled woman in black hurrying across the tracks toward the railroad station. I said to my friend, 'there goes Belle Gunness.' I had an impulse at that time to stop her but I didn't. When we went into town a few hours later, we learned that the farmhouse had been burned and it was believed she burned with it."

Was the body in the L.A. morgue Belle Gunness, or was it Esther Carlson? Photographs that were published in 1931 in the *Chicago American* do bear a strong resemblance to Belle, although Carlson's face was thinner than Belle's, possibly due to the passage of time. Carlson and Gunness shared the same forehead crease. Their eyes were alike and both had long earlobes. If this really was Belle Gunness, then she had evaded death either in a house fire, in prison or at the end of a hangman's noose, and survived more than three decades before passing away quietly in a California hospital bed.

It became one of the greatest mysteries in the annals of American crime - and one that some remain determined to solve.

In November 2007, a team of forensic anthropologists and researchers led by LaPorte native Andrea Simmons, a historian and Indianapolis attorney, and Dr. Stephen Nawrocki, a board-certified forensic anthropologist and a professor from the University of Indianapolis, opened the grave of the woman who had been buried next to Mads Sorensen and Belle's children in Forest Home Cemetery. Their purpose was to conduct scientific testing on the skeletal remains and to hopefully solve the mystery that had been baffling LaPorte residents - and crime buffs the world over - for years. The fragile remains were removed and taken to the University of Indianapolis Archaeology and Forensics Laboratory, where DNA was extracted. Those samples, along with the original envelopes from Belle's letters to Andrew Helgelein, were sent to the State Police Forensics Laboratory in Indianapolis for analysis. Later, additional samples were sent for DNA testing to a university laboratory in Texas.

Results were hoped for by April 28, 2008, the 100th anniversary of the fire at the Gunness farm, but they were, unfortunately, inconclusive. Attempts are ongoing, though, and the team involved continues to wait patiently for fresh results. If it turns out that the body belongs to Belle and she really did die that night in the fire, it raises many questions about what happened on that April night in 1908. The tests will also reveal whether or not the children who died that night were actually Belle's offspring, or if they were adopted. If the charred bones don't belong to Belle, Simmons and her team hope to find the funding to exhume the remains of Esther Carlson in Los Angeles.

But, for now, the mystery of Belle Gunness remains unsolved.

1908: GHOSTS OF THE RAY COUNTY POOR FARM

Resting quietly on the edge of the small town of Richmond, Missouri, is the Ray County Museum. The massive red brick building has a long history in the area, dating back to 1908, when it opened as the Ray County Poor Farm. During that era, poor farms were county-operated residences where indigent, elderly and disabled people were supported at the county's expense. They were common in America, starting in the middle part of the nineteenth century and declining in use after the Social Security Act took effect in 1935. By 1950, they were forgotten relics of yesterday.

Most were working farms that grew some of the produce and grain and raised the livestock whose meat the inmates consumed. The residents were expected to provide labor to the extent that their health allowed, both in the fields and in providing housekeeping and care for the other inmates. Rules were strict and the accommodations were sparse. The poor farms were often a place of last resort for those who could no longer care for themselves, and the inmates were too poor, too sick or too old to make it on their own. The counties where they resided reluctantly took them in and offered just enough for them to survive - at least in most cases.

County poor farms were the last stop in a wretched life for many people. They died unknown or at least forgotten, and were buried in pauper's graves. Not surprisingly, many of the old farms have left ghosts and spirits lingering behind.

The Ray County Poor Farm was started in September 1908. The centerpiece of the farm was a menacing, fifty-four-room brick building that would provide housing for the inmates who were unlucky enough to end up at the farm. By May 1910, the farm had opened its doors to about fifty residents, all of whom had been moved there from an older and smaller establishment about eleven miles outside of town. At the time, the new structure, which offered both electricity and steam heat, was the most modern building in the county. Sadly, though, instead of being a haven of modest comfort, the farm was a place of despair, heartbreak and desperation, and one that few of the inmates ever left alive.

The old Ray County Poor Farm building

The farm was situated on twenty-three acres of land, and was large enough for growing a wide variety of garden crops. There was also room for cattle, hogs, horses and chickens, as well as a slaughterhouse, a smokehouse and a small pond in front for fishing and swimming. The farm was meant to be self-sufficient so that it would operate as cheaply as possible. The residents were expected to help with the day-to-day operations, with planting and growing the food, caring for the animals, milking the cows and gathering eggs each morning. Nearly every able-bodied inmate was given an assignment or was quickly taught a skill that would aid in the function of the farm. When necessary, the goods grown and raised on the farm were traded or sold in nearby towns so that items like salt, flour, beds, blankets and other basic needs could be purchased.

While life on the farm sounds like an idyllic experience, it was anything but that. The inmates were abandoned by their families, had lost their homes or simply could not care for themselves. They were totally dependent on the little comfort that was offered to them by strangers, and it was a sad and lonely existence. As the occupants died, they were buried in what grew into two cemeteries on the grounds. One of them contains a potter's field, filled with the unknown, indigent dead. Who these people may have been in life remains unknown.

The Ray County Poor Farm was normally filled to capacity with fifty residents. It continued operating until 1959. A year later, the building opened again, this time as the Elms Park Rest Home, which saw a drastic increase in the number of residents. Greedy owners packed as many people into the place as possible, squeezing four or five beds into rooms that had been built for two. It became impossible for people to walk through the rooms and pass between the beds. The overcrowding, which caused negligent care and squalid conditions, continued until the place was closed down in 1971.

Today, the old poor farm is home to the Ray County Museum, a historic site that offers a look at western Missouri's fascinating past. But the staff members do not work in this building alone. Over the last several years, stories have widely circulated of the ghosts that remain. It seems impossible that these spirits could be happy, since this was once a place of sadness and misery, but regardless of why they are here, they refuse to leave. Apparitions, voices and footsteps are often reported, but who are these spirits? Are they the nameless poor who were once housed on the farm, or have some of their identities been revealed?

One of the ghosts is believed to be that of Goldie Riser, who spent the majority of her life at the poor farm. She lived a heartbreaking existence, with her tale of sorrow beginning on October 16, 1896, when her mother, three-year-old sister and eighteen-month-old baby brother were brutally murdered. Goldie, by all accounts, had been deaf and mute her entire life and in those days, was unable to help the authorities with information about what she might have seen during the murders.

There is little known about Goldie before she came to the area with her mother, Eva, and her stepfather, Jessie. They had moved to Missouri from Hicksville, Ohio, but with no friends, relatives or business prospects in the area, it is unclear why they chose to move to their small, one-room cabin in 1892. Goldie's mother had left her first husband, Goldie's father, and had married Jessie Winner shortly before leaving Ohio. During their time in the small cabin outside of town, Eva had given birth to two more children, and it has been rumored that Eva was pregnant again at the time of her death, but no records exist to document the story.

It was an early Tuesday evening in October when a neighbor, M.D. Street, was walking down the road near the Winner cabin and saw six-year-old Goldie in the yard acting strangely. Street quickly noticed a group of hogs that were surrounding and feasting on something in the yard, just beyond the fence. He took a closer look and was startled to see that it was the body of Goldie's mother, still in her nightclothes. After driving the hogs away, Street alerted other neighbors. He led a small group of men into the cabin and made a gruesome discovery. Goldie's three-year-old sister was lying on the bed with her throat cut. On the floor were the remains of the little boy. His throat has also been cut in the same manner as his sister.

The police arrived and searched in vain for clues as to who had committed the murders and a motive as to why they might have been committed. Robbery was quickly ruled out. The cabin only contained a bed, a cook stove and a few chairs. There was nothing hidden away of any value. The killer, or killers, had left nothing behind. Goldie was taken into town in an attempt to learn if she had witnessed the murders or could identify the killers, but no one could get through to her. Uneducated and likely terrified, Goldie could only wave her hands about and make choking noises. In those days, in rural Missouri, there was no method of communication that the handicapped girl could use to communicate with the authorities.

Jessie Winner was a coal miner who often spent many days away from his family, working in nearby towns when mine work was available. He spent his off time at home, raising corn on his small farm. He had been away from the family for several days at the time of the murders, and was planning to return home soon to harvest his corn crop. Before he could return, he received the terrible news that his entire family, except for his step-daughter Goldie, had been violently murdered. Later that same day, Winner was placed into custody by the police. Investigators had no clues and they didn't want to take a chance of Winner getting away from him if it turned out that evidence turned against him.

Neighbors were questioned by the investigators. A Mrs. Hankins lived a half-mile from the Winner cabin, near the original county poor farm, where her husband was the superintendent. She stated that she heard three screams late in the night, but assumed that there was a ruckus at the poor farm and paid little attention to them. When pressed by the police, she admitted that the screams might have been those of Eva Winner. It sounded like her voice, she said. But other neighbors, who lived closer to the Winner cabin, said they didn't hear anything out of the ordinary that night.

Evidence gathered at the murder scene indicated that Eva had been involved in a long struggle with her attacker. Blood was spattered in several places on the floor and the fight looked as though it may have started near the stove. There were several broken pieces of a chair nearby. Outside, about eight feet from the cabin, and near the body of Eva, was a large piece of wood that was covered in blood and strands of hair. It looked as though she had been beaten with it, but it was not the murder weapon. She had been killed with an axe. After the other attempts to kill her had failed, the attacker delivered a strong blow to the top of her head with the axe and then left her lifeless body in the hog lot. The animals would have likely consumed her corpse if Mr. Street had not passed by the house that evening.

Within days, the police arrested Lon Lackey, a close friend of Jessie Winner. By this time, they were convinced that Jessie had murdered his own family, with help from his friend. A preliminary hearing was held for the two men on November 9, and they were both charged with the murders of the Winner family. Defense attorneys for both men asked that the matter go before a grand jury, and with both cases continued, they were returned to the local jail.

Large crowds had gathered outside in hopes of attending the trial and hearing the gory details of the murders. By early afternoon, it was clear to everyone that a trial would not take place that day. Thwarted, the crowd turned into an angry mob. Hoping to maintain the peace, Sheriff Holman deputized fifteen to twenty men to keep back the crowd. After threats were exchanged between the mob and the lawmen, the crowd slowly dispersed. Inside the jail, though, rumors spread that the mob would be back later that night, larger than before.

The rumors turned out to be true. Later that evening, about one hundred men gathered outside the jail with plans to lynch Jessie Winner and Lon Lackey. As the lynch mob milled around outside, demanding that the men be given up, Sheriff Holman went outside to try and calm things down. The mob demanded that he turn over the keys but the sheriff told them that he had sent the keys home with one of his deputies. This sent a large part of the crowd to the deputy's house but when they arrived, they were told that he had left town. Returning to the jail house, they made a few more demands and then, still being turned away by the sheriff, they gradually drifted away.

Knowing that the prisoner's lives were in jeopardy, the two men were secretly moved to the Lafayette County Jail, across the river in nearby Lexington. But it was not far enough. On the night of December 9, an angry crowd attacked the jail, broke open the cell door locks and removed the two inmates. The alleged murderers were taken back across the river in a rowboat and lynched. Their bodies were discovered the next morning, hanging side by side from a burr oak tree.

Jessie Winner's body was later buried in the graveyard at the former county poor farm. His remains were placed near the final resting place of his murdered wife and his two children.

There is little known about the next few years of Goldie's life. Local papers reported that during the hearings of Jessie Winner and Lon Lackey, her uncle arrived in town to speak with the child, but he did not take her away with him. Local residents stated that Goldie was temporarily taken in by a kind elderly couple, who sent her to the Fulton School for the Deaf for one year. It is not known why she only stayed at the school for one year, what happened to the couple, or how she ended up at the county poor farm. Most believe that one or both of the elderly people died, and Goldie was sent home when her tuition at the school could no longer be paid for. Her new residence, at the original poor farm, was only a half-mile from the cabin where her family had been killed.

Several postcards were mass-produced in the wake of the murders, as was the ghoulish custom in those days. One card was that of the small cabin where Goldie had lived with family - and which became the murder scene. Another clearly featured her murdered mother and siblings displayed on tables with onlookers staring at their stiffening bodies. Another grisly postcard shows Jessie Winner and Lon Lackey after they were lynched, still dangling from ropes. These shocking postcards were sold to the public, and the proceeds were given to the poor farm to offset the cost of Goldie's room and board.

Goldie was among the first occupants of the new poor farm in May 1910. According to the 1920 census, she was still a resident there and was unable to read or write. Her illiteracy was not that uncommon for the time and place, especially when her handicap was factored into the equation. She spent the rest of her life at the farm, working in the kitchen and on the grounds. She died on March 8, 1941 from pneumonia. She had been suffering from tuberculosis for five years prior to her death.

If there is any resident most likely to remain behind at this forlorn place, it is that of Goldie Riser - a sad, lost little girl whose only hope for a good life was taken away from her at a very young age.

Strange encounters continue to be reported at the former poor farm to this day. It is a place of tragedy and pain, where the spirits of the past cling tenaciously to the life that is carried into the building by the staff members, volunteers and visitors who walk through the doors of the imposing structure. They communicate in any way that they can, through bumps and thuds, knocking, footsteps, voices, whispers and on occasion, spectral manifestations that vanish almost as quickly as they appear.

1909: THE MURDERING PHYSICIAN

In nineteenth- and early-twentieth-century Michigan just like in the rest of the country arsenic was easily obtainable. It served as a rat poison and an insecticide. Even children's stuffed animals were dusted with it by the manufacturers to prevent infestation by pests. Arsenic was found in green lampshades, wallpaper, cosmetics and copper cookware. It was used to color candy and glaze fudge. Cheese makers sometimes tossed in a pinch or two into the cheese-making vats in hope of killing ptomaine.

Arsenic was even an ingredient in many patent medicines of the era. As late as 1921, the American Medical Association was still finding arsenic in patent medicines with innocuous names like Blue Bell Kidney Tablets, Botanic Blood Balm, Wildroot Dandruff Remedy, Dr. Miles' Restorative Nervine, La Franco Vitalizer No. 200 and many others. Arsenic was also used in mainstream medicine as a treatment for syphilis.

Seemingly omnipresent, arsenic was used to dye stockings, underwear, curtains, decorations, artificial flowers and cloth linings for baby bassinettes and cribs. Green flannel boot linings impregnated with arsenic allegedly killed several California gravel miners in 1875.

In the farms and orchards of Michigan during this era, arsenic was extensively used as an insecticide called "Paris Green." It was dusted on tomatoes, potato plants, cabbage, cucumbers, grapes, melons and sprayed on fruit trees.

There were a number of symptoms to show that someone was suffering from arsenic poisoning, from skin ulcerations to headaches, abdominal pain, diarrhea, discolored patches of skin, hair loss, coughing, convulsions, and paralysis in the hands and feet. The problem was, in those days, the same symptoms pertained to a range of diseases. Arsenic poisoning was often diagnosed as conditions that included "general debility," neuralgia, consumption tuberculosis, cholera, rheumatism, gastritis, dysentery, or paralysis - all of which commonly appear as causes of death on old Michigan death certificates.

Of course, sometimes the lethal symptoms were not caused by long-term exposure, but by sudden conditions that were deliberately and maliciously created.

In the summer of 1846, the *Oakland Gazette* reported that suspicion surrounded the death of a woman named Harriet Russell. Her remains were disinterred and her stomach and intestines sent to the University of Michigan in Ann Arbor for testing. Silas Douglas of the chemistry department tested the samples and found arsenic. Russell's husband was taken into custody.

In the summer of 1861, the *Grand Traverse Herald* reported another suspicious death. The university analyzed the stomach contents of Nicholas Frankinburger of Traverse City, once again finding a large quantity of arsenic. The chemistry lab was contacted again in 1865 for the Haviland murder case in Battle Creek, in which Sarah Haviland was accused of poisoning three children. The lab's findings led to her conviction.

Toxicologists and pathologists from the university went on to serve as expert witnesses in many arsenic poisoning cases. In the middle and late nineteenth century, axe murders were so prevalent because the deadly weapons were common tools that could be found close at hand in most households. Arsenic was also readily available, and so for many rural killers, it became a weapon of choice in getting rid of troublesome family members.

Another use for arsenic in those days was as an ingredient in embalming fluid. This was a lucky break for poisoners, because post-mortem embalming could hide ante-mortem poisoning attempts. In the spring of 1892 the wife of Matthew Millard, a leading businessman of Ionia County, took ill and died. Her husband, a one-time undertaker, embalmed her with injections of arsenic in her mouth and rectum before having her buried. Due to suspicions of poisoning, Mrs. Millard was exhumed about three months later, and several tissue samples were analyzed. Mrs. Millard was re-buried, then re-exhumed again so that more samples could be taken. This time, arsenic was found in her internal organs.

The case went to court. The leading toxicological textbook of the day taught that arsenic could not spread to internal organs after death; therefore, said the prosecution, Mrs. Millard's husband must have poisoned her. Robert Kedzie and University of Michigan toxicologist Victor Vaughn testified for the defense, saying that arsenic could indeed spread throughout the body after death. They maintained that the presence of the poison in the internal organs did not necessarily indicate ante-mortem poisoning. To prove it, Vaughn duplicated the arsenic injection procedure on a corpse and buried it. When exhumed, it was found that the arsenic had spread to the internal organs. Millard was ultimately acquitted.

In 1895, a New York woman named Mary Alice Fleming was charged with murdering her mother with poisoned clam chowder. Vaughn testified for the defense. The June 11, 1896 edition of the *New York Times* wrote, "Dr. Vaughn is the discoverer of tyrotoxicon, the ptomaine poison found in stale milk, and enjoys a world-wide celebrity for original research in toxicology and physiological chemistry." The story went on to say that Vaughn testified about the types and classifications of poisons, and described in detail the symptoms of arsenic poisoning. He agreed that it appeared that Mary Alice's mother had apparently died of arsenic poisoning. Though the prosecution's case was strong, popular sentiment of the time ran against the death penalty for women, and Mary Alice was acquitted.

Victor Vaughn, along with pathologist Alfred Warthin, also provided analyses in what would become one of the most infamous series of murders in Michigan's so-called "thumb" on the east side of the state. The Sparling family poisonings in Ubly, near Bad Axe, involved a father, John Sparking, and three of his four sons, Peter, Albert, and Scyrel. The four of them died from arsenic and strychnine poisoning in a case that was mired in infidelity, insurance fraud and tragedy. The alleged perpetrator was a trusted family physician that Vaughn and Warthin believed was a killer.

Was he? We may never know, since he was later suspiciously pardoned by the governor.

The rustic little village of Ubly is located in the wilds of Michigan's rugged thumb. Just south of Bad Axe, it was first known as Sidon, being north of Tyre as the city in the bible. Later it was called Pagett's Corners after Alfred Pagett, who started a general store on the west side of the settlement in April 1870. In 1880, a number of men met to talk over applying for a post office. They wanted to call it Pagettville, but Mr. Pagett modestly declined. He suggested instead that the town be named Ubley, after a little town that he was fond of in England. When the application came back, though, whoever had filled out the form in Washington had spelled it Ubly. The name stuck.

One of the most respected community members of Ubly was a man named John Wesley Sparling. The hard-working, god-fearing farmer was forty-seven years old and was in the best of health. The rest of his family could say the same about themselves. The family included his wife, Carrie, four sons and one daughter. Sparling was a regarded as a kindly, traditional man and he kept his farm neat and up-to-date. His broad, level acres were plowed and harvested with the best modern machinery. His barn was clean and well-stocked. He paid all his bills on the day they were due and he always had money in the bank. The merchants of Ubly and Bad Axe were always glad to see Sparling or any of his family come into their place of business.

Sparling's family was as well-regarded as he was. His daughter, May, was a lovely girl and had married and moved away from home. The four boys, Peter, Albert, Scyrel apparently a fancy spelling for "Cyril" and Ray, were strapping young men who spent their days swinging scythes, splitting wood and heaving bales of hay into the upper loft of the barn. So great was their energy that often at night, the Sparling sons retreated to the barn, where they had built a makeshift gymnasium. Lifting weights, doing chin-ups and working on the exercise rings burned up some of their considerable energy. When John wasn't around, some said the boys enjoyed taking a few swigs of drugstore tonics, which contained a high percentage of alcohol. The daily work of the farm kept the boys lean and trim, and they caught the eyes of all of the young women in the community.

But work on the farm was not all there was to the lives of the Sparlings. They were sent to school in Ubly and then to Bad Axe for high school. Every Sunday found the family at the Ubly church.

Some still wonder if the scandal that soon reached the townsfolk would have come to light had Carrie Sparling not developed an eye affliction in January of 1909. Traveling by horse and carriage, Mrs. Sparling went into Ubly to seek the help of Dr. Robert MacGregor. The doctor was an energetic and popular figure who had come to town in 1905 to take over the practice of an elderly doctor who was retiring. MacGregor came from London, Ontario, and soon earned the trust of the small community. Handsome and trim, he was an athlete as well as a physician, and often played baseball on the Bad Axe town team.

When Carrie arrived at the doctor's office, he ordered a complete physical exam, even though only her eyes were ailing her. Afterward, the handsome MacGregor proclaimed Mrs. Sparling's trouble was not serious. He administered eye drops, and before she left for home, he promised to call on her at the farm in a week or so to see how she was getting along.

True to his word, barely a week had passed when Dr. MacGregor hitched his horse and headed southward over the Huron County line en route to the Sparling family dairy farm. John Sparling greeted him upon his arrival, and the doctor indicating he had come to look after Mrs. Sparling's eyes. After a thorough examination behind a closed bedroom door, Dr. MacGregor administered more eye drops and bid Mrs. Sparling a good day. As he climbed in his buggy, John Sparling caught up with him, inquiring after his wife's illness. MacGregor said he was perplexed. He wasn't quite sure of the cause of Carrie's eye infection, and would need to keep an eye on it, as it were. He told the farmer that he would gladly stop by the farm to check on her whenever he happened to be in the neighborhood.

As it turned out, the doctor just happened to be near the Sparling farm many times over the next several months, or so the neighbors said.

As spring gave way to the warmer days of June, John worked hard making hay. Strong as an ox and healthy as his sons, John at first tried to ignore his rebellious stomach. He had never before quit work mid-day, but that's exactly what John Wesley did this day, clutching his aching stomach as he made his way to the house. He would just lie down for a few minutes, he told himself. He was convinced he would feel better after some rest. He crawled into bed - and never got out of it again.

The following morning, Peter rode to Ubly to fetch Dr. MacGregor. Morning and night, the doctor stayed nearby, trying to ease the patient's suffering. John vomited for a week, unable to keep any food in his stomach. The doctor diagnosed him with Bright's disease, a fatal kidney ailment. John Wesley needed more care than the family doctor could provide, so Dr. MacGregor made arrangements for John Wesley to seek treatment in an Ontario hospital. He never improved and on July 8, 1909, John Sparling died.

The people of Ubly and Bad Axe crowded into the small church in town to hear the minister pay tribute to Sparling. The whole community gathered in the Tyre Cemetery, where John Wesley was laid to rest next to an infant son who had died in January of 1894. John had seemed to be in the prime of his life, but tragedies often happened. Or that was what most people believed. There was only one person who questioned Sparling's sudden death, and that was his uncle, who was also named John. The uncle was a veterinarian and auctioneer and had once served as a state senator. His nephew had been a strong and active man, and his strange death just didn't make sense. No one paid much attention to his comments - at least, not yet.

As tragic as John Sparling's death was, at least it didn't leave the family in bad straits. Peter Sparling, who was twenty-five, stepped into his father's shoes and took charge of all of the farm work. When it came to the finances, however, Peter was advised by his mother; and she, in turn, it soon became evident, was advised by the family physician. No one considered this to be odd at the time. Asking for and accepting the advice of the family doctor in matters other than health was not uncommon then, especially in rural communities, where the local doctor was considered one of the wisest men in town. In addition to advising Carrie in financial decisions, he also made numerous trips to the Sparling farm to examine her eyes. As far as the neighbors could see, her affliction never improved, but it never got worse, either. Soon, it became apparent that Dr. MacGregor was spending more time at the farm than an eye affliction and financial advice seemed to warrant - and tongues in Ubly began to wag.

One of the pieces of advice that MacGregor gave to the new widow was to consider buying life insurance policies for each of her sons. Carrie agreed, for she had some to depend on the doctor for his assistance. The boys, though, didn't think that insurance was necessary. They were all fit and in the prime of life, but so was their father, the doctor reminded them. They reluctantly agreed. As it happened, the doctor's father, who lived in Canada, sold insurance policies through the Sun Life Association, and he was more than happy to accommodate the Sparling sons. Dr. MacGregor examined each of the boys and gave them a clean bill of health. He explained that each of the boys needed to appoint a beneficiary for their insurance policies and since each was a bachelor, he suggested they name their mother. When the paperwork was completed, Carrie Sparling was the sole beneficiary on all four polices.

When Dr. MacGregor wasn't caring for his patients - or spending time at the Sparling farm - he and his wife, Ida, enjoying visiting and playing cards with their good friends, Xenophon Boomhower and his wife. Boomhower was a promising young prosecutor working in Bad Axe, and the two couples spent many hours together. After dinner, the men often retired to the sitting room to discuss their work.

One night, Boomhower asked after the Sparling family and the doctor confided his concerns about Peter Sparling. As the attorney was aware, Peter was a thriving young man. He worked hard and had great drive, but had slowed down as of late. He was easily tired and no longer exercised with his brothers in the barn at night. MacGregor feared that Peter had acute pancreatitis.

Within two months, almost as the doctor predicted, Peter's condition worsened. Like his father, Peter had never quit working in the fields at mid-day, but he became so sick that he stumbled into the house, clutching his stomach. One of his brothers rode off to fetch the doctor, but it was too late. In a few short days, Peter was buried next to his father in the Tyre Cemetery.

Folks in the neighborhood - especially Uncle John Sparling - speculated about how the father and son, both hard-working and clean-living men, could have died within such a short span of time. No one dared to believe the obvious. Such a suggestion was unthinkable - or was it? For Uncle John, something was seriously wrong on the farm, and he vowed to get to the bottom of it.

For Carrie Sparling, losing her husband and her eldest son so quickly was unimaginable. Everywhere she looked in the family farmhouse, she could still see John and Peter. Dr. MacGregor, always the helpful friend, suggested to Carrie that perhaps the remaining Sparlings should move to a new farm. The physician continued to guide her in business matters and found the perfect farm for her in Huron County. It was on a portion of land owned by Robert and May Hurford, Carrie's daughter and son-in-law. Since this farm was located closer to Ulby - and closer to his office - he would be nearby if she needed him, especially for the persistent eye irritation, which was still troubling her.

Carrie purchased the forty-acre farm in March 1910 and soon moved herself and her three remaining sons to the property. To aid her in keeping the house, Mrs. Sparling hired a young girl who lived in the neighborhood named Annie Pieruski. She soon became largely responsible for all of the housework, laundry, cooking and baking for the family.

Things were quiet for a while. The Sparlings got used to the new farm and Albert took over as head of the family. The boys worked hard and they provided an ample living. Ray and Scyrel did their fair share and life at the new farm entered a comfortable routine - at least for the next year or so.

During this time, Dr. MacGregor remained a close friend to Carrie, continuing to help her in many financial matters, including assisting her to follow through in another suggestion about life insurance. With Peter passing away at such a young age, he advised her to insure her three surviving sons for an additional $1,000. One never knew when tragedy might strike. Carrie purchased three more policies, this time with the Gleaners Life Insurance Society.

Around this same time, Dr. MacGregor confided in his faithful attorney friend, Xenophon Boomhower, that Albert Sparling had not been feeling well as of late. The doctor was concerned that if anything happened to Albert, suspicions of foul play might be placed on Mrs. Sparling. He was greatly concerned about this because Mrs. Sparling was a close friend and an admirable woman. He couldn't bear to see her good name slandered.

By April 1911, local farmers were anxious to get into their fields. It had been a wet spring so far, though, and most had to content themselves to working in the barn and anxiously watching the overcast skies for sunshine to break through the clouds. The farmers were not the only ones eager for spring - so was Dr. MacGregor. He decided to go to Bad Axe and purchase a new automobile. His "horseless carriage" would be one of the first in the area, and would allow him to make his house calls in style. It should be noted that many folks around the area wondered how the country doctor, who earned a good portion of his pay in bartered eggs, jams and produce, could afford an automobile. When he did receive cash, the typical house call in the country earned him about $2. However, when he bought the automobile, he didn't bat an eye at the price of more than $600, informing the salesman that he'd pay for it in cash within a month's time.

On the Sparling farm, the three sons were getting ready for another year of planting. But in the middle part of May, Albert began complaining of stomach pains. He took to his bed and was soon vomiting and unable to keep food down - much the same as Peter had done just two years prior. Diagnosed with acute pancreatitis, Dr. MacGregor surmised that he had injured this organ when he had fallen from the apple tree. Others speculated young Albert perhaps suffered internal injuries after he strained himself lifting a heavy piece of farm machinery. Regardless of what happened, Albert died in June and was buried next to John and Peter in the Sparling family plot.

Uncle John also ranted about this suspicious death, and while many dismissed his claims, others were starting to listen.

After Albert's death, Dr. MacGregor decided to take his wife on vacation to Ontario. While they were gone, Carrie Sparling purchased a house in Ubly for $5,000, placing a down payment of $1,000, proceeds from one of the insurance policies, to close on the investment. Some thought it was good that Mrs. Sparling was moving off the farm after facing so much misfortune. Others, perhaps influenced by the questions being asked by John Sparling's uncle, began to wonder what had really happened on the two family farms. Their tongues wagged a bit more when Dr. MacGregor and his wife returned from their trip and moved into Carrie's recently purchased house, using a portion of the space to set up his office.

Carrie apparently had no intention of living in the house at all. She remained on the farm with Ray and Scyrel but often went into town to check on her new real estate investment. The folks who kept track of her comings and goings guessed that her eye ailment must have been causing her a good deal of grief.

Meanwhile, Dr. MacGregor made good on his debt to the automobile dealer in Bad Axe. Gossip at the bank followed shortly after, for Mrs. Carrie Sparling had endorsed her check from the insurance company's proceeds - the Sun Life policy from Albert's death -- over to the good doctor. He, in turn, signed off and walked away with $1,000 in cash - a large portion of which he dropped off at the auto garage.

Tragedy continued to follow the Sparling family. On August 4, not long after the boys had harvested the oat crop, Scyrel, the youngest of the sons, went to his bed complaining of severe cramps and nausea. The day before, he had helped a neighbor with his harvest, and the night before, on August 3, Scyrel and his friend, Lem Douglas, along with their girlfriends, spent the evening in Bad Axe, where they frequented the town's ice cream parlor. There seemed to be no reason for his illness, and yet he was paralyzed by pain.

With his father's and his brother's deaths in mind, some folks though that Carrie should get someone other than Dr. MacGregor to care for her son. At best, his treatments were faulty and at worst, well - something strange seemed to be going on in Ubly.

But Carrie, like so many times before, sent for her friend, Dr. MacGregor. He came at once and after consulting his medical books, diagnosed Scyrel with liver cancer. To be sure, the following day he called in Dr. Willett J. Herrington, requesting a second opinion. Unbeknownst to Dr. Herrington, Dr. MacGregor also contacted Dr. Daniel Conboy for his opinion, who, in turn, didn't know Dr. Herrington had just been consulted as well. Dr. Conboy had extensive training in toxicology. While he had been consulted in Albert's death and had previously agreed to the diagnosis of acute pancreatitis for Albert, something hadn't seemed quite right. After Albert's death, he continued to research the young man's symptoms. He soon found that they indicated something else entirely: arsenic poisoning.

After a joint exam of Scyrel, Dr. MacGregor, perhaps anticipating the thoughts of Dr. Conboy, surprisingly asked Conboy if he suspected arsenic might be the cause of the patient's aching stomach, itchy extremities and the irritation in his nose, mouth and throat. Dr. Conboy agreed and made it clear that he also suspected that the same thing might have killed Albert Sparling.

Concerned about Scyrel's situation, Dr. Conboy paid a visit to Xenophon Boomhower in Bad Axe, giving him an update on the boy's condition. He had serious worries, he told him. He believed that Carrie Sparling had poisoned Scyrel - and perhaps even her husband and other sons - for the insurance money.

After Conboy and Boomhower conferred, the pair then traveled together to Ubly to see Dr. MacGregor, where they learned from the physician that Scyrel's condition had grown worse. There was no question that the young man was near death. Boomhower told MacGregor to notify him immediately if Scyrel died. He wanted to order an autopsy, and Drs. Conboy and Herrington would assist. MacGregor agreed, but then added a hasty dismissal of any postmortem. He wouldn't be surprised, he said, if any autopsy showed signs of arsenic. He knew that the Sparling boys consumed patent tonics, which all contained arsenic. It was a common ingredient for just about every medicine at the time.

But Dr. Conboy was now swayed by this. If the boy had been poisoned, the arsenic levels in his system would be much higher than any patent medicine could produce. Dr. MacGregor then suggested they hire a nurse from the Port Huron Agency to keep an eye on Scyrel. Dr. MacGregor wasted no time and hired Marguerite Gibbs the following day. She was his personal choice and soon the attractive young woman began tending to Scyrel, administering his medicines, monitoring all of his food and drink and, in her spare time, searching the Sparling home for poison. Two days later, the nurse discretely showed Dr. MacGregor a cardboard box in the Sparling kitchen that was filled with arsenic. Dr. MacGregor dutifully delivered the box to Boomhower. Of course, the implications were clear: Carrie Sparling had poisoned her husband and three of her sons.

After MacGregor left, Boomhower contacted the local sheriff, Donald McAuley, and asked him to look into the case. Sheriff McAuley began talking to people, and learning all he could about the Sparlings. He soon learned a great deal more than he had expected. Neighbors told of an alleged affair between Dr. MacGregor and Carrie Spalding and asked a lot of questions about several mysterious deaths over such a short period of time. The sheriff also got more than he bargained from Uncle John Sparling, the seventy-year-old former senator who insisted on his suspicions being taken seriously. McAuley had no choice but to dig deeper into the situation - and look harder at Mrs. Sparling and Dr. MacGregor, a man once seen as above reproach.

Sheriff McAuley had no experience with murder cases, but he was a good investigator. He soon learned from the bank that each time Mrs. Sparling had profited from an insurance check, Dr. MacGregor's accounts showed that he profited as well. It didn't take a big-city detective to see that something was wrong. Had MacGregor purposely thrown suspicion on Carrie Sparling in order to divert the investigation away from himself?

On August 10, Dr. Conboy, at the request of prosecutor Boomhower, paid a surprise visit to the Sparling home. When he arrived, he found Mrs. MacGregor assisting the nurse in bathing Scyrel, who drifted in and out of consciousness. Dr. MacGregor was comforting Carrie. It was painfully obvious to everyone that Scyrel wouldn't last much longer.

On August 14, Dr. MacGregor called Drs. Conboy and Herrington back to the Sparling home. They brought with them Dr. Eugene Holdship. Only Dr. Conboy knew the complexity of the case, for he had been familiarizing himself with the side effects of poison late into the night for the past ten days. After examining Scyrel, all agreed that he could not live much longer. The doctors departed, except for McGregor and Holdship. Before leaving, Conboy reminded MacGregor to summon him if things took a turn for the worse. He and Herrington had been tasked with performing a postmortem by the prosecutor.

A few hours later, Scyrel died.

Almost immediately, Dr. MacGregor suggested to Dr. Holdship that they should go ahead and perform an autopsy. Holdship was unaware of the orders that had been given by the prosecutor about the examination and went outside to fetch Ulby's undertaker, Hector McKay. He had been summoned to the house hours before and had been sleeping in a hammock in the Sparlings' backyard. When McKay came into the house, Dr. MacGregor asked him for his knife and he then handed the blade to Holdship, informing him that he should make the cuts.

In the dark of night, Carrie Sparling held the lantern with as steady a hand as she could manage while Dr. Holdship sliced into the body of her son, following the direction of Dr. MacGregor. Dr. Holdship removed the liver, spleen, pancreas and part of the upper intestine, noting that the liver appeared swollen and ruptured. Dr. MacGregor diagnosed the cause of death as cancer of the liver, promptly asking Dr. Holdship if the organ appeared diseased. Dr. Holdship nodded his agreement. When Dr. Holdship inquired as to whether he should dissect the stomach, Dr. MacGregor indicated that Scyrel's stomach looked fine; there would be no need to disturb it.

At first light. Dr. MacGregor drove to Bad Axe, carrying with him home canning jars that contained Scyrel's organs. Boomhower, who had been preparing to leave for the Sparling home so that he could be present at the autopsy, was surprised when MacGregor arrived at the courthouse. Boomhower was there with Sheriff McAuley, Dr. Charles B. Morden, the Huron County coroner, and Drs. Conboy and Herrington. The men were stunned when MacGregor handed over the jars of organs to Boomhower, who had previously stated that the contents would be sent to the University of Michigan for analysis. Boomhower demanded to know why MacGregor had performed the autopsy. The doctor was quick to explain that it had been no trouble at all; he was happy to help.

The coroner inspected the jars, questioning the absence of the stomach, for pathologists at the university would require it for their analysis. If arsenic had been present, the mucous membrane would show signs of irritation and inflammation - a fact that Dr. MacGregor was well aware of. But MacGregor assured the coroner that there was no need for concern. He said he had opened up the stomach himself, and the organ showed no indication of arsenic.

But Boomhower, friendly with MacGregor or not, was not satisfied. He immediately had Scyrel's organs sent to the University of Michigan, where they were examined by Victor Vaughn and pathologist Alfred Warthin. Both men agreed that traces of arsenical poison were present.

Furthermore, their conclusions as to the symptoms of the poison upon a dying person stated with almost certainty that Scyrel had been poisoned.

This still posed a question, though. Was the arsenic present through Scyrel drinking patent medicine, as Dr. MacGregor had suggested, or was it the result of a criminal act by a party or parties unknown? MacGregor reiterated the fact, in light of the university's findings, that he had collected a large number of patent medicine bottles in the house and had thrown them out. The whole family was addicted to such medicines, against his advice, and many of the so-called cures contained arsenic.

And there the case rested for a time. Dr. MacGregor continued his practice in Ubley, although it may have fallen off a bit. Some of his patients would have been put off by the four deaths in one family under his care.

Ray Sparling now worked the farm alone. Without his brothers, though, his heart was no longer in it. Mrs. Sparling decided to leave this farm, and they put the place up for sale. James R. Turnball auctioneered the sale and nearly everything they owned was disposed of, including livestock, wagons, sleighs, work tools, egg incubators, an almost-new Empire cream separator and all of the latest mechanical farm devices that John Sparling had once been so pleased to own. Inside the house, Mrs. Sparling sold off three heating stoves, four bedsteads, three kitchen tables, six chairs, a rocking chair, one dish cupboard and even the organ. Carrie Sparling seemed a broken woman.

Meanwhile, Xenophon Boomhower prosecuted a number of cases, but he never got the Spalding mystery out of his mind. Nor did Sheriff McAuley. The two men often talked about the strange deaths and little by little, they compiled enough evidence to turn the case over to a grand jury. Among other things, they had the body of Albert Sparling exhumed and had a postmortem performed by Drs. Vaughn and Warthin at the University of Michigan. They also found arsenic in Albert's remains, just as they had in Scyrel's. Their report clearly stated, "He came to his death in substantially the same manner as Scyrel."

On January 12, 1912, County Attorney Boomhower filed murder charges against Dr. Robert A. MacGregor. At the same time, he charged Carrie Sparling and nurse Marguerite Gibbs with being accomplices. While they were being arrested, Boomhower secured all of the papers and books in Dr. MacGregor's safe and took them to his office for study.

The trial turned out to be the greatest sensation in Bad Axe history, before or since. On April 12, 1912, the small town was flooded with local residents, visitors from out of town, and reporters. Fearing that the town's dilapidated courthouse, one wall of which was already partially caved in, might collapse, Judge Watson Beach announced that the trial would be held on the second floor of the *Huron County Tribune* building, which may have been the reason that the newspaper's account of the trial was so complete.

Dr. MacGregor and the two women pleaded not guilty, and the doctor's trial began first. Judge Beach's expectation for the large crowds turned out to be justified. The hall was filled to capacity.

FEBRUARY 1, 1912.

POISON MYSTERY DEEPENS

WIFE, DOCTOR, NURSE HELD

Four men of Sparling family believed to have been poisoned and the doctor and two women who are in custody on charges of murder.

CYRIL SPARLING

PETER SPARLING

ALBERT SPARLING

J. W. SPARLING

MRS. J. W. SPARLING (STANDING) MAY SPARLING SITTING

DR. ROBERT A. McGREGOR

Four Deaths Are Found to Have Resulted From Use of Arsenic.

TEE, Mich., Jan. 31.—A coroner's jury today conducting inquests to determine the cause of death of John Wesley Sparling, Sr., and his son, Peter Sparling, decided that both men came to their death from poisoning. Dean Vaughn of the University of Michigan reported he found traces of arsenic in both stomachs.

Some time ago University of Michigan chemists, who examined the viscera of Cyril and Albert Sparling, the other two sons, reported they found arsenic.

MORE INDICTMENTS TO BE HANDED DOWN

Alleged Bribery of Jurors in Los Angeles Promises to Develop Into Big Scandal.

By International News Service.
LOS ANGELES, Jan. 31.—The admission by Assistant District Attorney W.

Attorneys Joseph Walsh and George M. Clark acted for the defense and Prosecutor Boomhower was assisted by E.A. Snow as special counsel.

Jury selection in the case turned out to be a cumbersome process. Everyone in the county, it seemed, had heard of the Sparling deaths, and either adamantly defended the reputation of Dr. MacGregor or were ready to see him hanged. It took two full weeks to find twelve men who had not already formed an opinion to serve as jurors.

Judge Watson Beach presided. He informed the court that Dr. MacGregor was being tried solely for the death of Scyrel Sparling, though circumstantial evidence regarding Albert Sparling could be taken into consideration. Testimony regarding the deaths of John and Peter Sparling would not be admitted at this point. The jurymen would be stay at the Steadman Hotel during the course of the trial.

Boomhower had carefully prepared his case, although all of the evidence was circumstantial. There were no eyewitnesses who could attest to seeing the doctor poison any of the Sparlings. Step by step, though, the prosecutor, by the introduction of many witnesses, built up a continuous line of thought with the jury. It would show that shortly after the death of John Sparling, insurance had been taken out on the lives of his four sons, and that the policies had been written by the doctor's father. Dr. MacGregor himself had examined the boys twice and had found them fit both times.

Peter Sparling had died. Albert Sparling had died. Mrs. Sparling bought a house in Ubley and never lived in it - but the doctor did. Boomhower made the most of this situation, ridiculing his old friend. "And I have never been able to find record where Dr. MacGregor paid Mrs. Sparling a penny of rent," he told the jury.

Boomhower also took up the matter of the doctor's new automobile. He made a point of the date when MacGregor first talked of buying the car and of MacGregor's remark that he would pay for it "in about three weeks." The prosecutor stated that he timed it well since "Albert Sparling died twenty-two days after that remark was made."

The prosecution went deeply into the doctor's financial records. The daybooks and other papers were produced to show that amounts of cash paid, or given, to MacGregor by Mrs. Sparling could not "by the greatest feat of the imagination be attributed to professional services," as claimed by the defense. Boomhower estimated aloud for the benefit of the jury that if all of the money had been for services, then the doctor must have made at least four calls daily on the woman for over a period of four years - including Sundays and holidays. Even then, the prosecutor said, the rate per call would be much higher than what was customarily charged by other doctors in the region.

Link by link, the prosecuting team continued building their case against the defense. Dr. Conboy testified that Dr. MacGregor had placed the blame for Scyrel's poisoning squarely on Mrs. Sparling. Dr. Holdship testified he, in fact, did perform Scyrel's autopsy, but it had been under the guiding hand of Dr. MacGregor. Furthermore, Dr. Holdship testified that Dr. MacGregor had specifically told him not to cut open Scyrel's stomach during the post-mortem, while Dr. MacGregor not twenty-hour hours later had told the prosecutor that he himself had slit open the stomach.

Annie Pieruski, the young woman who had been hired to help Carrie with the housework, testified to the many visits by Dr. MacGregor. It wasn't uncommon for Dr. MacGregor and Mrs. Sparling to go behind a locked bedroom door to conduct their thirty-minute business. Oddly enough, on the rare occasions when Mrs. MacGregor accompanied her husband to the Sparling farm, the doctor had no need to go into the bedroom with Mrs. Sparling.

A farm hand named Henry Bacon who had worked for John Sparling took the stand. Bacon claimed that he had seen Dr. MacGregor and Mrs. Sparling go into the bedroom together a week before John Sparling died. Dr. MacGregor locked the door behind him and the pair remained in the bedroom for a period of at least twenty minutes.

The combined testimony of Pieruski and Bacon, no doubt, caused tongues to wag in town, but Dr. MacGregor emphatically denied any undue intimacy between himself and Mrs. Sparling. There were few who believed his denials, however.

The most compelling testimony in the circumstantial chain of evidence came from Drs. Vaughn and Warthin from the University of Michigan, the pathologists who analyzed Scyrel's organs. The level of arsenic found could not be explained away by the consumption of patent tonics. In their combined expert opinion, Scyrel Sparling had been poisoned.

Another sensation occurred when Sheriff McAuley testified that Dr. MacGregor told him that Mrs. Sparling and all of her sons were "suffering from some unfortunate disease." This suggested, as the prosecutor stressed to the jury, that Mrs. Sparling might have been the next to come down with an "incurable condition."

A good number of people came in support of Dr. MacGregor. His father attended court each day it was in session. Carrie Sparling, too, who had also been charged in the conspiracy, still believed in the goodness of her family doctor. Carrie stated that she sprayed plants with arsenic, explaining the box of poison found in her house. She insisted the doctor was not responsible for her loved ones' deaths.

Ray Sparling, Carrie's last surviving son, also defended the doctor, stating that the brothers naming Carrie as the representative on each of their life insurance policies had been their own idea. They wanted to ensure that their mother would be properly cared for in the event that they passed away before she did. When Prosecutor Boomhower asked the surly young man how many times Dr. MacGregor frequented the Sparling farm, he snapped, "more than a half-dozen and less than three thousand."

Scyrel's nurse, Marguerite Gibbs, was called to the stand by the defense and told of finding poison in the Sparling cupboard when she was at the house caring for the dying young man. In rebuttal, the prosecution maintained that the poison had been planted there to divert suspicion away from the doctor.

The doctor's wife, Ida MacGregor, took the stand on behalf of her husband and proved to be a valuable witness, testifying with righteous honesty. Though she couldn't change the facts, Ida MacGregor did testify to the relationship in question between the Sparlings and the MacGregors. The families exchanged Christmas gifts and took turns entertaining in each other's homes. The

Sparling boys made themselves at home when visiting the MacGregors, and Ida helped Carrie in any way she could during the Sparlings' harvest season. If anything improper had been going on between Dr. MacGregor and Mrs. Sparling, it became evident to the jury that Ida MacGregor had been completely unaware of it.

When Dr. MacGregor took the stand, he faced a grueling five days of questioning. He had an answer for everything, though his statements directly contradicted the testimony of Drs. Conboy, Herrington and Holdship, as well as the county coroner and the sheriff. He was tripped up again and again in his attempts to account for the various sums of cash he had received from Mrs. Sparling. He couldn't explain why he was living in her Ubley house rent-free. But he did explain that Mrs. Sparling's eye ailments required multiple visits to the farm. The endorsement by Mrs. Sparling on Albert's insurance proceeds merely paid off debt that the family owed to the doctor. He was unable to explain why he was unable to alleviate Carrie's eye ailment.

But Boomhower believed that he had the answer. The jury sat with rapt attention when the prosecutor called Nick Prezinski to the stand. Prezinski, a neighbor, testified that the bottle that Dr. MacGregor drew drops from to administer to Carrie Sparling's eyes contained atropine. The drug dilated the pupils and could cause temporary blindness. Had Dr. MacGregor purposely been impairing Mrs. Sparling's vision so that he would have an excuse to come to the farm?

Dr. MacGregor and his counsel did all that they could to blame the death of Scyrel Sparling as well as the other Sparling men on the family's "constant taking of patent medicines." This caused the poison to build up in their bodies, they claimed, and eventually caused their deaths.

But, by the time the defense closed their case, the jury had heard all they needed to hear.

In all, over one hundred witnesses had testified in the case, and on June 6, 1912, the opposing attorneys completed their final arguments and the case was turned over to the jury. The trial had started with jury selection on April 2 and by the time it ended, the Sparling murder trial had been the longest criminal case in the state of Michigan.

At fifteen minutes after midnight, on June 7, the jury sent word to the judge. They had reached a unanimous decision.

In spite of the hour, Bad Axe came alive as reporters and locals, who hadn't dared return home for fearing missing the verdict, hurried back into the makeshift courtroom on the newspaper's second floor. Anticipation of the verdict silenced the large room.

Robert Bowman, foreman of the jury, rose to give Judge Watson Beach their verdict: "We find Dr. Robert A. MacGregor guilty as charged of murder in the first degree; of murdering Scyrel Sparling by arsenical poisoning."

While the courtroom erupted in loud exclamations, MacGregor sat expressionless and strangely quiet.

Judge Beach sentenced MacGregor to life imprisonment; he would serve his time at Michigan's state prison in Jackson.

In December of 1912, Dr. MacGregor's attorney requested a new trial. New evidence supposedly came to light in the form of a written statement by a Mr. J.W. Douglas of Bingham. In the statement, Douglas alleged Scyrel had consumed dangerous amounts of patent tonics. Douglas saw a bottle fall from Scyrel's coat pocket - the bottle was allegedly filled with an arsenic concoction. In addition, the defense claimed the jurors had not been sufficiently sequestered at the Steadman Hotel. It was alleged that letters were handed to them on the street. Further, the defense claimed jurors had been seen talking to various persons on the street numerous times. Judge Beach considered the information presented before him but denied Dr. MacGregor a new trial.

MacGregor was not yet willing to give up. His attorney pressed the matter, and took an appeal to the Supreme Court in Michigan. The court upheld the lower court's conviction and this seemed to settle the question of guilt, at least officially, for a time.

And then the real mystery of the case began.

Dr. MacGregor had gone to prison in June 1912, but in November 1916, Michigan Governor Woodbridge N. Ferris granted him a full and unconditional pardon on the grounds of complete innocence. Not only that, but the governor took the very unusual and extraordinary course of having the prisoner brought to Lansing by the prison warden and granting MacGregor's pardon in person.

When he made a statement to the press, Governor Ferris made an even greater mystery out of the deaths of the Sparlings. The governor told reporters, "For more than two years I have been investigating his case. I have had the assistance of some of the best authorities in Michigan, and I am firmly convinced that Dr. MacGregor is absolutely innocent of the crime for which he was convicted. I am satisfied that in sending him to prison, the state of Michigan has made a terrible mistake."

Why had Governor Ferris ignored the verdict of a jury? Why, too, had the governor ignored the opinion of Michigan's highest court? When pressed as to the reason why, Governor Ferris refused to reveal the evidence on which the pardon was granted. But the statement said that the murderer of the Sparlings was still at large - or that the father and three sons had committed suicide.

After the pardon, Dr. MacGregor was a free man. Traveling to Ontario with his wife, he thought he'd pick up his life and start anew in Canada, but it didn't work out that way. Locals knew of his past and wanted nothing to do with him. Unable to get work, he turned to Governor Ferris, who appointed him as the official physician for the state penitentiary in Jackson - ironically the same place where he had served four years as an inmate. He held that post until his death in 1928.

No one was ever punished for the deaths of the Sparlings. Prosecutor Boomhower had dropped the charges against Carrie Sparling and Marguerite Gibbs in 1912, due to insufficient evidence. Mrs. Sparling and her surviving son, Ray, moved to Port Huron to escape the never-ending speculation of her involvement in the deaths of her husband and three sons. Carrie Sparling died in 1933.

Officially, the Sparling murders remain unsolved. The question remains of what exactly happened to the Sparlings, and who really was responsible for their deaths? Why did the governor grant a full pardon without offering evidence of his decision? If Dr. MacGregor was indeed innocent, and his only crime was falling in love with Carrie Sparling, who then, had poisoned the Sparling men? Had the sheriff, the townspeople and the prosecutor been so busy investigating Dr. MacGregor and Mrs. Sparling that they failed to look to see if anyone else had something to gain?

It's at this point that some historians speculate about Ray Sparling. The first death in the family had been John Sparling. Peter, the next oldest male then died, followed by Albert, who fell in line by age behind Peter. If the killer had been following a pattern by murdering the oldest male Sparling down to the youngest, Ray should have been next. Yet, he wasn't. Scyrel became the next to die.

There is little information that can be found about Ray Sparling. Little is written about him in the accounts of the murders and the trials, and no allegations were ever made against him, although perhaps they should have been. Who knows?

It is interesting to note that on November 10, 1911, after Carrie Sparling held the auction to sell off her home and farm implements, she didn't sell her property. Instead, she deeded it to Ray. Six years later, in March 1917, Ray sold the farm to William Elliott for $4,000. He became the only person other than Carrie - aside from the gifts given to Dr. MacGregor - to ever profit from the deaths of John Sparling and his sons. Was it a motive for murder?

We'll probably never know.

1928-1934: THE PENNSYLVANIA "HEX" MURDERS

A pair of rural murders that came to be known as the "Hex Murders" - and the subsequent hex scare that followed - marked a substantial turning point in Pennsylvania history, especially in the way that the public perceived the practice of "powwowing" and folk magic in the region.

In the early twentieth century, before the two famous murders in York and Schuylkill counties, the belief in and practice of folk magic was seen by the press and intellectuals as a quaint holdover from less sophisticated times. It was not until the murders occurred that it began to be seen as a threat. Practitioners were no longer seen as backward or ignorant; now they were dangerous. Medical professionals sought to educate the people of rural areas and eradicate the old ways. The false treatments were keeping the sick from getting the real medical care that they needed, it was believed. There was little room for superstition, hex doctors and "quacks" in the modern world.

The danger of "superstitious" beliefs had become readily apparent after blood was spilled. Folk healers began to be regarded as witches and "a threat to the social order." They were chastised for their unscientific methods and paraded before the general public in the newspapers as lunatics. It seemed impossible to believe in the civilized world of the 1920s and 1930s that anyone still believed in magic.

But among the back roads and farmlands of Pennsylvania, magic was alive and well.

Pennsylvania hex magic dated back to the earliest days of the colony, linked largely to the Pennsylvania German or Dutch, as they are often called immigrants and their descendants. Scores of German-speaking immigrants flocked to the Pennsylvania colony to take advantage of the economic opportunities and religious freedoms that they could not find in Europe. They soon spread throughout the state, seeking fertile farmland and natural resources. The German settlement was especially dense in the southeastern corner of the state, not far from Philadelphia. This eventually became known as Pennsylvania Dutch Country to legions of tourists who still flock there today. The Germans held strongly to elements of their culture, and blended customs of the Old and the New World to form a distinct identity. Even their language became a unique dialect.

Though there were a great many different religious denominations among the German settlers, there was a common tradition of folk magic that was practiced by all, with the exception of the "Plain Dutch," such as the Amish, who rejected the practice. For large numbers of these Germans, the belief in folk magic was entwined with their Christian beliefs. Occult practices had always been more accepted in Germany than in England. At one end of the magical spectrum was the practice of *brauche* or *braucherei*, more commonly known as powwowing not to be confused with the Native American ceremonial practice of the same name . Powwowers performed magical-religious folk healing and drew their healing power from God. At the other end of the scale was *hexerei* or witchcraft. Practitioners of black magic drew their power from the Devil or other ungodly sources. Powwowers and hex doctors often worked against one another, with the common person caught in the middle. It was in this setting that folk magic flourished for more than two centuries.

Powwowers played an important role in Pennsylvania in days gone by. Before the arrival of modern medicine, they offered relief from ailments and, perhaps more importantly, a degree of hope. The use of folk magic provided a sense of control in a world that was often beyond control. Generally, Powwowers provided cures and relief from illnesses, protection from evil and the removal of hexes and curses. They also located lost objects, animals and people, foretold the future, and provided good luck charms. To carry out their practices, they used charms, amulets, incantations, prayers and rituals. It was generally believed that anyone could powwow, but members of certain families were especially adept at it. These families passed the traditions down from generation to generation.

The opposite of the powwower was the witch, who used dark magic that was beyond the normal use of the folk healer. The witch harassed neighbors and committed criminal acts with supernatural powers that did not come from God. Sometimes witches were called hex doctors. The term "hex doctor" can be confusing because it can imply many things. At times, the term was applied to powwowers who were also knowledgeable in the ways of *hexerei* and were skilled at battling witches and removing curses. These hex doctors fell into a sort of gray area between a witch and a powwower. Sometimes they cast hexes for a price or out of revenge. It was not uncommon for someone to seek out one hex doctor to remove the curse of another. For many Pennsylvania Dutch, and certainly for outsiders, powwowers and witches could not easily be placed into categories. There were many who labeled the use of any folk magic as witchcraft that was strictly forbidden by their religious beliefs.

Since no one ever went around readily identifying themselves as a witch, it is not always clear how one learned the art of *hexerei*. It was generally assumed that the witch made a pact with the Devil, from whence the witch's power allegedly came. There was also a book of spells and incantations that was usually associated with *hexerei* called *The Sixth & Seventh Book of Moses*. The book had a sinister reputation, which will be discussed shortly, and was rumored to be in the library of every witch and powerful hex doctor.

Witches targeted their victims in many ways. Since *hexerei* was based around a farming society, many of the witch's attacks were directed at animals and crops. They were often blamed when cows did not produce milk, when seemingly healthy animals mysteriously died, or when crops failed. It a large hairball was found in the stomach of a dead animal, it was referred to as a "witch ball," and it might be attributed to the work of a local witch. When witches went after humans, they used a variety of torments. They were commonly suspected of causing illnesses, especially conditions that lingered and caused a person to waste away over time. A witch could also use spells to launch invisible attacks, causing seizures or fits, the sensation of being pricked or stabbed, or the feeling of being choked or strangled. Witches could also cause a run of bad luck for any individual that they attacked. The witch could even appear in the form of an animal, like a black cat, so that they could move about undetected and harass their victims. Needless to say, just about any type of misfortune could be blamed on a witch.

But how was the good and bad magic actually practiced? Powwowers, hex doctors and witches all used similar techniques, whether healing, hexing or conjuring. There were many prayers, incantations and spoken charms. Powwowers frequently invoked God, Jesus and the Holy Ghost, along with other religious figures. They generally believed that all of their abilities were a gift from God. Witches, of course, did not call on God, but they usually did not invoke the Devil either. The words, whether spoken loudly or softly, were often accompanied by hand gestures or the laying on of hands on the body.

In addition to spoken words, the written word was also used for magic. Written amulets and charms were common, and many Pennsylvania Germans carried them on their person. Amulets usually included a written version of a protective charm and perhaps verses from the Bible. The paper they were written on was usually folded into triangles. If not carried personally, such amulets might be hung in a house or barn.

Ritualized objects were also used. These objects were actually mundane items, but they often acquired a special purpose. Sometimes the objects would be used as a surrogate for the afflicted or for the disease itself. Much of German folk magic depends on the principles of contagion and transference. Basically, the idea is that the evil or the disease is contagious, and can be transferred away from the afflicted person and into an object. The object could then be disposed of in a prescribed manner to keep the contagion from spreading. Traditionally, this kind of magic is known as sympathetic magic - and it often worked, as long as the person afflicted truly believed that it would.

As mentioned earlier, many powwowers and hex doctors depended on charms, recipes and incantations that were passed down through their families. These "recipe" books contained the collective knowledge of a family line of powwowers. By the middle 1800s, these homemade volumes were joined by published volumes that came into common usage. Folk healers had always invoked and used the Bible in their magic, but they increasingly supplemented their knowledge with sources published by other powwowers.

The most famous and widely read of these books was compiled by a powwower named John George Hohman in 1819. Hohman was a German immigrant who settled on a farm in Berks County, Pennsylvania. As a side business, he published broadsides and books about the occult and medicine aimed at the local German population. In time, he published the most widely read grimoire book of magic in America. The compilation of spells, charms, prayers, remedies and folk medicine was called *Der lang verborgene Freund,* or *The Long Lost Friend*. It was the first book of powwow magic to achieve wide circulation. It has been in print in either German or English continuously since 1820.

Aside from being a collection of charms and recipes, the book itself became a talisman. In what was an example of a resoundingly successful early marketing ploy, buyers of the book were told they would be protected from harm merely by carrying it. In the front of each edition was an inscription that read, "Whoever carries this book with him, is safe from all enemies, visible and invisible; and whoever has this book with him cannot die without the holy corpse of Jesus Christ, nor drown in any water, nor burn up in any fire, not can any unjust sentence be passed upon him. So help me. "

The bulk of the book consisted of remedies and charms to cure common illnesses, fevers, burns, toothaches and other ailments. It also contained recipes for beer and molasses and even had a charm for catching fish. Many of the charms in the book were meant to provide protection from physical harm from weapons, fire, witches and thieves. It also provided instructions on how to keep animals in a certain location, heal livestock and cattle and even cure rabid animals. *The Long Lost Friend* soon became the primary reference for anyone attempting to understand the practice of powwow, and it gained a place of honor on almost every powwower's and hex doctor's shelf.

As an opposite number to the helpful charms of *The Long Lost Friend* was the far more dangerous book of witchcraft, *The Sixth & Seventh Book of Moses*. Drawn from the tradition of European grimoires and ceremonial magic, *The Sixth & Seventh Book of Moses* were purported to have been written by Moses himself, and allegedly contain secret knowledge that could not be included in the Bible. Described as two separate books, they are almost always published together in one volume, first appearing in Pennsylvania in 1849. The book soon gained an evil reputation among the German population and those who were familiar with its lore. It was associated with hexing because the text provided instructions on how to conjure and control spirits and demons. It also contained spells and incantations that were beneficial to the user, as well as spells that would duplicate some of the biblical plagues of Egypt, turn a staff into a serpent and other miraculous happenings. Much of the volume is made up of reproduced symbols that were allegedly copied from old woodcuts. Some copies were printed, at least partially, with red ink. A few hand-copied editions were alleged to exist that had been written in blood.

Though hex doctors frequently acquired the book to enhance their reputations, merely owning the volume was believed to be dangerous, and if a hex doctor actually read it - that could be fatal.

Reading the book was believed to attract the attention of the Devil or at the very least, cause the reader to become so obsessed with the book that they could do nothing but read it. The only way to break the obsession - should such a thing occur - was to read the entire book in reverse, starting at the end and working back to the beginning.

To modern readers, all of the stories and claims of spells, hexes, magic books and incantations may sound rather silly, but rest assured, they were all common traditions of the Pennsylvania Dutch Country of the late nineteenth and early twentieth centuries. It might sound hard for us to believe today, but people at that time and place readily accepted such ideas. And that turned out to be the most crucial point of the murders that followed: those involved truly believed in the magic that was said to exist. They believed that it worked and could ruin their lives.

And they would do anything to try and stop that from happening.

The Rehmeyer Hex Murder

The first and most famous Hex Murder, the strange killing of Nelson Rehmeyer, captivated the people of the region and sold newspapers across the country. The story began with a young powwower named John Blymire, who was born in 1895 and learned the art of German folk magic at a young age. His family had been powwowers for at least three generations and probably longer. Although he did poorly in school, Blymire established a good reputation as a healer in York County. Starting at the age of seven, he began providing healing remedies and cures. Despite his early success, though, he began to believe that there was a shadow hanging over him.

One day, as he was leaving the cigar factory where he worked, an apparently rabid dog began running toward some of his fellow workers. Blymire approached the dog and spoke some words of a spell. The dog's mouth allegedly stopped foaming and the animal became subdued. Blymire patted its head and the animal followed him excitedly for several blocks. The other workers were amazed at the dog's apparent cure. But soon after, Blymire's luck began to turn bad. He soon became ill and he started to believe that another practitioner of folk magic had placed a hex on him, possibly out of jealousy. He soon found himself unable to eat, sleep, or work his powwow magic. Blymire used several of his own magical charms to try and remove the hex, but he was unsuccessful. It was difficult to remove a hex if one did not know the identity of the witch who placed it.

Then one night, as he lay in his bed trying to sleep, the answer came to him. Just as the clock struck midnight, an owl outside hooted seven times. It was then that the idea came to Blymire that he had been hexed by the spirit of his great-grandfather Jacob, who had been a powwower and the seventh son of a seventh son. Since he could not fight back against a spirit, he decided that he would move away from his ancestral home and the cemetery where his great-grandfather was buried, hopefully breaking the spell. It seemed to work, and soon Blymire's luck began to improve - at least for a time.

In addition to his work as a folk healer, Blymire performed a variety of odd jobs. He soon met a young woman named Lily and they married. The couple had two children, but both died in infancy. The youngest only lived for three days. These tragic occurrences led Blymire to once again believe that he had been hexed. Unable to determine the source of the new hex, he turned to other powwowers for help. One of them was a man named Andrew Lenhart, who convinced him that the source of the hex was someone that he knew well.

John Blymire

This claim caused Blymire to become suspicious of everyone around him, even his wife. Lily had reason to fear for her safety because, in 1922, one of Lenhart's other clients murdered her husband after receiving similar information. The client, Sallie Jane Heagy, shot her husband, Irving, in bed after Lenhart was hired to "drive the witches" from her home. Sallie did not believe the treatment worked and was in terrible physical pain. She finally snapped one day, killed her husband, and later committed suicide in jail.

After consulting lawyers, Lily was able to obtain a judge's order to have Blymire committed to an insane asylum. The doctors determined that he was obsessed with hexes and magic and needed to go to the asylum for treatment. Soon after, Lily filed for divorce and it was granted. Blymire didn't remain locked up for long. Forty-eight days after he was committed, he simply walked out the door one day and vanished. No one even bothered to look for him.

Blymire went back to work at the cigar factory in 1928. While he was there, he met two other people who also believed that they were suffering because of someone who had hexed them. One of them, fourteen-year-old John Curry, was trapped in an abusive household and felt that a malevolent force was causing the trouble at home. Another man who believed he had been hexed was a farmer named Milton Hess. Hess and his wife, Alice, had been successful and prosperous until 1926, when a series of unfortunate events began at their farm. Crops failed, cows stopped producing milk and they lost a large amount of money. The entire family believed that they had been hexed by someone, but they didn't know who it could be. The talk of hexes reinforced Blymire's own belief in spells and he became terrified by the idea that someone was out to get him. He began to consult other powwowers again, attempting to track down the source of the lingering hex.

Blymire turned to a well-known powwower in the region named Nellie Noll, the so-called "River Witch of Marietta." The elderly woman identified the source of Blymire's hex as a member of the Rehmeyer family. When Blymire asked which of them had cursed him, she told him to hold out his hand. She placed a dollar bill on his palm and then removed it. When Blymire looked at his hand, an image appeared. It was the face of Nelson Rehmeyer, an old powwower whom Noll referred to as the "Witch of Rehmeyer's Hollow." Blymire had known Rehmeyer, a distant relative, since he was a small child. When Blymire had been five years old, he became seriously ill. His father and grandfather, unable to cure him, took the child to Rehmeyer, who healed him.

Unable to understand why Rehmeyer wished him harm, Blymire went to see Noll again. She confirmed that it was Rehmeyer who had hexed him, and added that he was also responsible for the curses on John Curry and Milton and Alice Hess. Blymire told the other two men what he had learned, and also revealed a solution for ending all of the hexes. Noll had stated that the men needed to take Rehmeyer's copy of *The Long Lost Friend* and a lock of his hair and bury them six feet underground.

Blymire and Curry decided to go together to Rehmeyer's Hollow and obtain the needed items. On November 26, they were driven by Hess' oldest son, Clayton, to the Hollow. They stopped at the home of Rehmeyer's former wife, Alice, who said that Nelson could be found at his own home, which was about a mile down the road. The men went to Rehmeyer's door, and Blymire asked to speak with him for a few minutes. He later said that the older man was much larger and "meaner-looking" than Blymire remembered. They went into the parlor, and Blymire asked him questions about *The Long Lost Friend* and other elements of powwowing - never mentioning, of course, the true reason why he and Curry had come. After talking for a while, the men realized that it was late, and Rehmeyer offered to let them sleep downstairs. They agreed and while Rehmeyer slept, they looked for his copy of the spell book, but were unable to find it. They debated on whether or not to try and obtain a lock of his hair, but finally decided that Rehmeyer was too big for them to hold down while they cut his hair. The pair left in the morning after agreeing that they needed more help.

Nelson Rehmeyer, the man that Blymire believed had "hexed" him.
The Rehmeyer house in 1928.

Blymire told Milton Hess that he needed a member of his family to help them subdue Rehmeyer. Hess and his wife offered their eighteen-year-old son, Wilbert, as an assistant. The next evening, November 27, the three of them arrived at Rehmeyer's house. He let them in and they went into the front room. Rehmeyer never got the chance to wonder why they had come back for another visit. When his back was turned, the men tackled him to the floor and attempted to tie his legs with a rope they had brought with them. The exact details of what happened next varied slightly depending on which man told the story, but during the struggle, Rehmeyer was beaten and strangled to death. It's possible that Blymire intended to kill Rehmeyer once he reached the house that evening, but if he did, he did not reveal his plans to the other two men.

When they realized that Rehmeyer was dead, they took all of the money in the house, hoping to make it look like a robbery. They left behind the book and the lock of the old man's hair. He was dead - the hex had been lifted. But if that was true, Blymire's luck certainly didn't improve. The three men doused the body with kerosene and lit it on fire, hoping the flames would spread throughout the house and burn it down. When they left, Rehmeyer's body was engulfed in flames, but somehow, the fire mysteriously went out. Some believe that perhaps the hex doctor was not yet dead when he was set on fire and that he might have moved enough to extinguish the flames, but had been burned too badly to survive. Regardless of what happen, evidence of the crime was left behind.

Two days later, a neighbor discovered Rehmeyer's body. The shocking crime stunned the community, but the terror and excitement that followed was nothing compared to the story that soon emerged. Alice Rehmeyer informed the police of Blymire and Curry's visit, and they were soon picked up as suspects. As details of the events emerged, newspapers across the country covered the story of the "York Witchcraft Murder" with great interest. Every bizarre detail of Blymire's hex-obsessed life was described for the public. When the men went to trial, there were daily reports of the proceedings. Hess received ten years, but Blymire and Curry ended up receiving life sentences for the murder. Both were eventually paroled and lived uneventful lives. Curry, the youngest, served in the military during World War II and became a talented artist.

The "Hex Murder" in York County received wide coverage, and while the local authorities did not launch any official assault on folk magic in the area, the press and authorities in other parts of the state eventually would. The sensationalistic newspaper coverage of the case brought intense scrutiny to folk practices, and they were labeled a form of witchcraft. The press maligned all practitioners of powwowing, even if they only practiced the most benign healing services. Lurid descriptions of magic and strange beliefs filled the newspapers and shocked Americans who were unaware that such things were still taking place in the twentieth century.

Law enforcement officials, doctors and educators began working together to put an end to what they considered superstitious and dangerous practices. Many of them began attributing supernatural motivations to any strange new cases that they encountered. During the Rehmeyer murder trial, York County Coroner L.V. Zach claimed that the deaths of five children in the previous two years had been caused by powwowers. He said that the children's parents took them to folk healers when they were sick, instead of real doctors and, as a result, they died. He did admit there had been no formal investigations of these cases, but that they were a matter of common knowledge. The *New York Times* featured the coroner's questionable claims in an article under a dramatic headline that read, "Death of 5 Babies Laid to Witch Cult." The newspaper quoted unnamed officials of the York County Medical Society, who said that the coroner's count of deaths attributed to witchcraft was much too low.

Soon, any death that was even vaguely connected to a powwower - or rumored to have a connection - was labeled a "hex murder." In March 1929, the body of Verna Delp, 21, was discovered in the woods at Catasuqua, near Allentown. On her body were three pieces of paper with magical charms written on them, supposedly to protect from murder and theft. A coroner's report identified three poisons in her body, and it appeared that she had taken them voluntarily. The young woman's adoptive father, August Derhammer, revealed to the police that he had recently learned that Verna was taking treatments from a powwower and that she had been planning to visit him on the day that she died. The powwower was identified as a man named Charles T. Belles, and he was arrested thanks to the fact that the police were sure they had another hex murder on their hands. At first, Belles denied treating Verna, but later admitted that he was treating her for eczema. He claimed to only be a faith healer, not a hex doctor. The authorities didn't believe him, and even though they could find no evidence to link him to the crime, continued to hold him in jail. As the investigation continued, it was discovered that Verna was pregnant and she had not seen her boyfriend, a truck driver named Masters, for several months. She had not yet told her family of the situation and was possibly looking for a way to end the pregnancy. Even after this new information came to light, the police still believed that Belles was partially responsible for her death. The obsession with hexes and powwow distracted the police from other possibilities in the case, including a botched abortion attempt, suicide or murder by someone other than Belles. By April, they still had no evidence that Belles was involved with the murder, but he was charged anyway. He finally received a hearing in mid-April after lawyers filed a writ of habeas corpus. He was released on $10,000 bail, and charges were eventually dropped. The murder of Verna Delp was never solved.

The press jumped on another case of "murder by powwow" in January 1930. Mrs. Harry McDonald, 34, a housewife from Reading, died after receiving severe burns in her home. She had apparently been given some sort of ointment from a hex doctor with instructions to rub it on her skin. At some point in the night, her body went up in flames when she got too close to her stove. She was seriously injured, and when he husband, who worked the night shift, found her in the morning, she was on the verge of death and could not be saved. The woman's brother told reporters that he believed the lotion she was using was flammable and caught fire, killing his sister. He had no evidence of this, but the press latched onto this theory and kept the story alive with "occult" connections for weeks.

Another "hex panic" murder occurred on January 20, 1932, when the body of a Philadelphia man named Norman Bechtel, 31, was discovered in Germantown under a tree on a temporarily vacant estate. The accountant and Mennonite Church worker had nine stab wounds in and around his heart. Some of the wounds appeared to form the shape of a circle, and were delivered with such force that they not only penetrated his suit and overcoat, but his eyeglass case in his pocket, as well. A crescent-shaped cut was made on each side of his forehead and a vertical slash ran from his hairline to his nose. Two additional cuts ran off the vertical slash in the direction of the crescent cuts. All of Bechtel's valuables had been taken and his car was later discovered six miles away. From the bloodstains in the automobile, it was clear that Bechtel had known his attacker well enough to let him or her into his car. The case gave all the appearances of a robbery gone bad - but then there were those pesky facial cuts, which detectives surmised might have special occult significance. When it was learned that Bechtel had grown up on a farm near Boyertown, where powwow was common, the police immediately started searching for evidence of another hex murder. Captain Harry Heanly, the chief investigator, had the victim's apartment searched for any possible connection with folk magic, but all they found were Mennonite books and pamphlets. After following a few more leads, the police still had no answers, so the press began calling the "mystery" a "hex murder."

Then in April 1937, William Jordan, 36, confessed that he and four others had killed Bechtel, who they had been attempting to blackmail. Most of the details of Jordan's confession were not publicly released, as Bechtel had been involved in "several love affairs" and had a large life insurance policy. Needless to say, the case had nothing to do with magic.

If these cases had been the only ones tied to powwow, it's likely that the hex scare would have died out sooner and the public would have lost interest. That was not mean to be, though, for another actual hex murder occurred in 1934, which sealed the fate of folk magic in the state for decades to come.

The Shinsky Hex Murder

The last true hex murder in Pennsylvania occurred in Pottsville, in Schuylkill County, on Saturday, March 17, 1934. A shotgun blast ended the life of Mrs. Susan Mummey, 63, as it tore through her living room window while she was standing next to her adopted daughter. Mummey was attending to the injured foot of her boarder, Jacob Rice, who was seated in front of her. The oil lamp that her daughter was holding shattered as the shot tore through the window. Mummey was killed and the other two took cover, not knowing if more shots would follow. They waited all night in fear, thinking that an assassin was lurking outside. Finally, as morning approached, Rice decided to make the two-and-a-half-mile trip to Ringtown to report the crime.

Initially, the police thought the murder was the result of some backwoods feud that turned violent. But soon the case took a bizarre turn when Albert Shinsky, 24, confessed to the killing. He claimed that the killing had been self-defense, and that Mummey had placed a hex on him seven years earlier when he was working in a field across from the Mummey farm. There had been a dispute about the property lines and one day, Mrs. Mummey came over the fence and stared at him for a long time, he said. He claimed that he then felt cold perspiration come over him and his arms went limp. From that point on, he was unable to work - but that was just the beginning of the torture.

Shinsky claimed that whenever he saw a sharp object, it would change into the shape of a black cat with flaming eyes from which he could not look away. The cat also appeared to him sometimes when he was in bed at night. It would creep slowly across the room and jump onto the bed. The appearance of the cat made him so cold, he claimed, that he had to get up and run around the room in order to get warm again. He sought help from several powwowers, but nothing worked. His family thought that he was lying and was just too lazy to work, but Shinsky seemed to genuinely believe that he was hexed. Eventually, when he could take no more of the supernatural harassment, he killed Mummey. He told the police that the minute she died, he felt the curse lift from his shoulders.

Prosecutors wanted to give Shinsky the death penalty for the murder, and the press once again emphasized the danger of the strange beliefs and practice of folk magic. Over objections from the police and the prosecutor's office, a commission of doctors ruled that Shinsky was insane, and he was sent to Fairview State Hospital. He remained in mental institutions for most of the rest of his life.

The case seemed to confirm in the public eye that the belief in witchcraft was some sort of threat to society. Practitioners of powwow still had a few defenders, though, and they retained plenty of clients, but the tide of public opinion had turned against them.

Thanks to the two high-profile murder cases - and the many suspected cases that were inflated by the newspapers - Pennsylvania's school system declared war on the belief in hexes, especially in the rural areas where it seemed most prevalent. It was hoped that within several years, a new focus of modern medicine and science could erase the superstitions that seemed to plague the countryside. State authorities also launched a campaign against powwowers and hex doctors directly, arresting and prosecuting them for practicing medicine without a license. Combined with the sensational stories in the media, and the assault on folk magic in general, many of the remaining powwowers went underground. Except for the few who retained public storefronts, most of those who continued to practice avoided the public spotlight and downplayed their work to non-believers. They continued to provide services, however, to those who sought them out. As time went on, fewer members of the younger generations showed interest in learning about the old ways of healing and hexes, but the practice refused to die out completely. Many modern healers still exist today, and while they may not be linked to any kind of witchcraft, German folk magic remains alive and well - although believers in the craft today seem far less likely to be driven to murder.

1928: A DREAM OF MURDER

Mabel Schneider sat on the edge of the sofa, looking anxiously out the front window of her home near Mount Morris, Michigan. She could see the winding Dixie Highway, glistening with hard-packed snow. It was 11:20 a.m., time for her five-year-old daughter, Dorothy, to come home for lunch.

There was no reason for Mrs. Schneider to feel tense and nervous, and yet she did. Her heart was pounding as she watched an old-model Dodge slow down just over the edge of the hill. The driver of the robin's egg blue car seemed to be having difficulty picking up speed on the slick, snow-covered road. Then the automobile turned slowly onto Stanley Road, gaining momentum. In seconds, it was out of sight.

When Dorothy was still not home from kindergarten after 11:30, Mrs. Schneider started walking towards the school. She paused for a moment at a filling station and asked Mrs. Sid Hodges, the wife of the owner, if she had seen the little girl on the road. Mrs. Hodges said she had seen the child pass by the gas station on her way home, just a short time before. If she had passed by the station, then her mother should have seen her along her route.

Now starting to panic, Mabel used the gas station's telephone to call Dorothy's teacher and then B.B. Fox, the superintendent of schools. Fox immediately contacted Deputy Sheriff Harry Gleason who, along with Thomas McCarthy, started a search. Both men were close friends with the Schneider family and knew little Dorothy well. Leslie Schneider, the child's father, was called home from his factory job, and he also joined in the search.

It was a terrible time for a young girl to go missing in America. It was January 12, 1928 - less than three weeks since a little girl named Marion Parker had disappeared in California. Marion had been kidnapped and held for ransom, but tragically, her dismembered body was found a short time after she had vanished. Newspaper headlines across the country screamed the gruesome details of the little girl's kidnapping and murder - and now Dorothy Schneider was nowhere to be found.

Deputy Gleason and the others immediately went to work, tracing Dorothy's footsteps from school, past the filling station and on towards home. Somewhere along the way, she had disappeared and the only clue connected to her vanishing was the blue automobile that had been seen by Mrs. Schneider through her front window. The driver might have seen the girl, and if she had been taken, they might have seen something. Or, worse, the driver of the car might have been involved in her disappearance.

The searchers took up the trail, examining ever dirt side road for telltale tire marks. Three miles west of Mount Morris, about one-half mile north of Stanley Road, and on the outskirts of Flint, they came upon a spot where a car had been mired in the mud. Archie Bacon, who owned a farm near the spot, confirmed the fact that a light blue car and been stuck there. In fact, he had helped the driver to get the automobile out of the mud and back onto the road again.

The officers and volunteers spread out over the scene and discovered a man's footprint embedded deep in the mud. He had left a trail behind. They followed the tracks to a fence on the opposite side of the road, where they found small imprints of a child's overshoes. After circling the twenty-acre field on the other side of the fence, the searchers resumed the trail, where the man's footprints led toward a small wooded area which ran along Benson Creek. Along the trail, more heartbreaking clues began to appear: a child's cap, a coat and a sweater. Leslie Schneider tearfully identified them as belonging to his daughter.

By now, Deputy Gleason had sent word to the station that more officers were needed. A large group of them, led by Sheriff Frank A. Green and joined by volunteers and friends of the Schneiders, quickly arrived on the scene and started searching along Benson Creek. Sweeping out in a long line, the men walked through the wooded area, pushing aside brush, lifting tree branches and beating the bushes for clues. They repeatedly called Dorothy's name, hoping that perhaps she was just lost in the woods.

But deep down, they feared the worst. And those fears quickly came true.

Next to an elm tree that hung out over the cold waters of the creek, they found a severed section of Dorothy's body. Another severed piece had been hurled across the creek and was discovered in the snow. A third section was found on the riverbank. The child had been literally torn apart.

One of the officers discovered a wrapper from a package of chewing gum, leading the sheriff to believe that she might have been lured away by her killer with the promise of candy. They also found a cork, about the size that would fit a two-ounce bottle, lying next to a crumpled handkerchief. Sheriff Green theorized that an anesthetic - possibly chloroform - had been used to render Dorothy unconscious. The men thoroughly searched the area but were unsuccessful in finding the murder weapon. They assumed that it had been thrown into the creek, which was now swollen by the thaw of the recent heavy snowfall.

It was nearly dark when Sheriff Green and his men came upon the last section of the naked, dismembered body of Dorothy Schneider. It had been thrown into the river and was washed downstream, but happened to catch on a log.

After night fell, Green returned to the nearby farm and question Archie Bacon, who was eager to try and help any way that he could. The farmer gave the sheriff a complete account of what he had seen that day. Around noon, Bacon explained, he had seen the light blue car as it turned north on Stanley Road near his house. He saw the driver get out of the car and walk towards the fence. It looked as though he was carrying some kind of bundle in his arms. Three hours later, he saw the same man trying to get his car unstuck from the frozen mud at the side of the road. A short time later, he walked up to Bacon's house to ask for help.

Bacon told the sheriff, "The man had little to say. He spoke about the weather. His car had become mired because he tried to turn up a side road where a man lived that he wanted to see, he told me. I asked him where he lived and he said near Saginaw. When I asked whether he lived near the Cornell farm, he replied that he did not live 'too far from there.'"

Bacon added that the man seemed nervous, and that he had given him a dollar for his trouble. He said that William Lawrence, a neighbor, also had helped the stranger move his car back to the road and together, they had watched it disappear at a point where the Stanley and Clio Roads intersect, about one mile east of the Bacon farm.

Archie Bacon described the automobile as an old model, four-door Dodge sedan, robin's egg blue in color. It was so spattered with mud from being stuck that he had been unable to make out the license plate number. The man himself, he told the officers, was stoop-shouldered and wore a gray overcoat with a grease stain on it, and a gray fur cap. He was about fifty years old, five feet, eight or nine inches tall.

As word spread about the murder, public anger grew to a frenzy. People began taking it upon themselves to join in the investigation, eager to do whatever they could to help. Because of the wanted man's nondescript appearance, suspect after suspect was picked up, only to be released. For the next four days, Archie Bacon's powers of observation were tested to their limits. The case had, in fact, altogether too many clues. So many men fitted Bacon's general description and there turned out to be far too many dilapidated four-door Dodge sedans painted robin's egg blue on the road.

One of the first suspects arrested drove a blood-stained Dodge sedan, but the bloodstains were soon explained by the man's wife, who told the authorities that she had just transported a freshly slain pig from the market. More suspects were picked up. Many of them were suspicious characters with known criminal records. Some of them had records for sex offenses against children. They were, in other words, the rural Michigan version of the "usual suspects." But every one of these men turned out to have no connection to the kidnapping and murder of Dorothy Schneider.

Dr. Donald R. Brasie, the Genesee County Coroner, headed the medical team that performed the autopsy on Dorothy's horribly mutilated body. Dr. Brasie stated grimly that the crime was "the most fiendish in local history." He added that the dissection indicated that the killer had considerable knowledge of anatomy and was clearly, a "pervert of the most depraved type." After stabbing the little girl in both sides of the abdomen, causing her death, he had cut the body into pieces for seemingly no purpose other than his own gruesome pleasure.

Meanwhile, the clues continued to pile up. Ray Boston, a truck driver from Battle Creek, reported an altercation with a driver of a car similar to the one described by Archie Bacon. Boston had been on his way to Flint when he saw an old blue Dodge stuck in a ditch four miles west of Williamston. Boston stopped his truck and got out to help, but the driver of the car pulled out a revolver and threatened him with it. "Move on, that's the only way you can help me," the driver reportedly snarled. By the time that the state troopers that Boston had contacted arrived, the car had vanished. All of the roads leading out of Flint were heavily patrolled, but this clue, like all of the others, came to nothing.

It was suggested that only an escaped mental patient could have carried out such a horrible murder, so the state asylum in Pontiac was investigated in a search for the killer's identity. But no patients had escaped in the last several weeks and none of those missing from before that time even remotely matched the description of the man they were searching for.

Michigan Governor Fred Green added to the growing reward fund with $1,000 from his own pocket. He stated publicly, "This crime is so atrocious, so terrible, that for its perpetrator to remain at large would not only be a stain on the name of law enforcement and decency in the state, but it would represent a menace to every citizen, father, mother and child." He also stated that the manhunt for the killer would be further intensified, and volunteered to remain overnight in Flint and personally supervise the investigation of a "new order of things." Green expressed his opinion that a definite leadership, correlating the efforts of all law enforcement officers engaged in the search would lend impetus to the hunt.

One suspect who was picked up matched the wanted man's description, even to the grease stain on his gray overcoat, and his car was an old Dodge with a blue finish. Fortunately, Archie Bacon was adamant about his repeated insistence that "there is something about his face that I can't describe. I will know him the instant I see him, and there will be no mistake." Thanks to the farmer's clear memory of the man and his sense of responsibility in helping any way that he could with the case, no innocent man was ever held for long, regardless of the circumstantial evidence against him.

With assistance from Roy O. Perry, the deputy secretary of state, Michigan newspapermen compiled a list of all Genesee County cars that matched the description of the Dodge that Mrs. Schneider and Archie Bacon had seen. Three airplanes were loaned to the police from the Selfridge Field Air National Guard base and were flown over the countryside, looking for any automobiles that might have been abandoned.

In just four days, between fifty and sixty suspects were brought in for questioning and then released. Suspicious characters that showed up at the funeral home for Dorothy's burial services were also apprehended. One of the men was a curiosity-seeker who was posing as a physician, asking to see the body. He was arrested on those charges, but was cleared of her murder.

But then a strange event took place that would change the course of the investigation and would eventually lead to the arrest of the killer.

Early on the morning of January 16, Harold Lotridge woke up to the sound of a jangling alarm clock in his home in Owosso, some thirty miles from Flint. As he blinked himself awake, he found himself troubled by a dream that he vividly recalled. In his dream, the name Adolph Hotelling was sharply imprinted in his mind. He had no idea why this would be. He knew Hotelling fairly well because he was a fellow deacon at the Owosso Church of Christ, but Harold was very concerned about why he would be dreaming about him. The previous night, Hotelling had presided over a communion service at church, but this was not why the man was stuck in his head.

Harold woke up with the knowledge - not knowing where it had come from - that Adolph Hotelling was the murderer of Dorothy Schneider, the little girl whose death had lately filled the newspapers!

Harold was no psychic. The level-headed young man was in his middle twenties with a wife, Lillian, and three young children. He worked as a carpenter and had no interest in anything out of the ordinary. The newspaper stories about the little girl's murder had only caught his interest because he had children of his own. Harold was a member of the church choir, as well as a deacon, which is how he knew Hotelling. The older man was a strict, very devout man who was, on occasion, hard to get along with. But for some reason, Harold could not get the idea that Hotelling was the killer out of his mind.

He was still troubled by the dream when he went to work that morning. Both Harold and his father, John, were working on a new school project in Flushing, about nine miles west of Flint. Harold told his father about the eerie dream, and explained that he felt sure that Hotelling had killed the little girl. Strangely, the description of the man - right down to his blue Dodge - fit Hotelling almost perfectly. Had Harold subconsciously made the connection, perhaps after reading a newspaper story before bed, or had he actually received some sort of psychic vision.

Harold and John didn't know what to think. The whole thing seemed unbelievable. Hotelling was a respected and upstanding family man, with children of his own, and was considered a pillar of the church. One of his sons was a well-known Boy Scout leader in the community, two of his daughters were happily married, and he also had a young daughter who was around Dorothy Schneider's age. Surely this couldn't be the depraved killer who had torn apart that poor little girl, they thought.

While they worked, the Lotridges discussed the dream from every angle. Harold fought against attaching any important to a mere dream, but he couldn't shake the feeling that something was seriously wrong with Adolph Hotelling. However, going to the police did not seem feasible. The public had become increasingly disturbed by the case and by the lack of progress by the police. The authorities were finding it more difficult each day to deal with the seething emotion in the community. In Mount Morris, a local resident was badly beaten because he made a remark that the murderer probably had his own reasons for committing the fiendish crime. Governor Green was still publicly admonishing the lack of progress by investigators and people were becoming upset. The Lotridges feared that if Harold went public with his concerns about Hotelling, it might get an innocent man into trouble.

Little did they know that their conversation was overheard by a fellow construction worker named Sheldon Robinson, who just happened to be a neighbor of the Schneider family. He lost no time in going to the Flint police with his "tip." The reward fund had grown to $8,000, which was a lot of money in 1928. He knew that Harold's information had come from a dream, but the authorities were following up every clue.

Later that same day, Genesee County Sheriff's Deputies Mark Tailthorpe, Henry Munger and Thomas Kelly arrived at the modest Hotelling home in Owosso. Mrs. Hotelling was doing laundry and her husband, dressed in overalls, was attending to odd jobs around the house. When he was questioned by the deputies, Hotelling vehemently denied any connection with the crime. His wife insisted hysterically that her husband "never did a thing like that. If he had, I would be willing to help kill him myself."

The officers went out to inspect Hotelling's car, an old model Dodge that had a shiny new black finish. When a signet ring worn by one of the deputies "accidentally" scratched the paint, he could clearly see robin's egg blue under the black paint. This changed everything, and within minutes, the officers found the clothes that had been described by Bacon and Lawrence. In one of the pockets, they found a blood-stained clasp knife and a handkerchief that was similar to the one found at the crime scene. They also found a list of women's names from the region. Among them was Mabel Schneider.

Hotelling, a carpenter and building contractor, admitted that he had been in Flint on the day of the crime, but that was all. He had nothing to do with the murder, he claimed. But his denials soon became irrelevant. Placed under arrest, he was placed in the back seat of a squad car so that he could be transported from Owosso to Flint. While en route, Hotelling tried to slash his own throat with a rusty nail that he had managed to get into the car. He was only able to inflict a slight wound.

Word quickly spread of the arrest and a crowd began to gather around the jail in Flint. About one hundred National Guardsmen were ordered out with fixed bayonets and tear gas on hand. They cordoned off the jail to keep the frenzied crowd in check.

Once at the jail, Hotelling quickly confessed. He insisted that the Marion Parker case in California had gotten into his head and that "something must have snapped." He told the police, "I don't know what came over me. I was driving along and saw a pretty little girl. I got her in the car, thinking I would drive her home. She cried. I drove to Snyder Road which was muddy and my car became mired. I carried her part way across the field. She still cried and wanted to go home."

He placated her with a stick of chewing gum. When they reached Benson Creek, with Dorothy walking, she continued to cry and said that she would tell her father what he was doing. Hotelling chloroformed her and stabbed her twice. Once dead, he raped her corpse and then cut her body apart. His knowledge of anatomy came from a brother-in-law who was a veterinarian. During his confession, Hotelling also admitted to two unsolved sex crimes against two small Owosso girls. He had used chloroform to render one of them unconscious.

After spending the night in jail, Hotelling retracted his confession. But it was too late. Governor Green stated publicly, "He has made a confession. He is guilty without question whatsoever."

The authorities knew they finally had their man. And so did the public. The mob outside the jail had grown, and officials knew that their suspect had to be taken elsewhere. He was spirited out of Flint and taken to Lansing, but word of his presence spread, and as crowds once again began to form, he was taken away again. Hotelling was being held at the reformatory in Ionia as another infuriated mob tried to lynch him. The National Guard had to be called out again to disperse the mob.

When Harold Lotridge heard that Hotelling had been arrested and that he had confessed to the horrible crime, he reported to the county jail in Flint to claim the reward. To his surprise, the prosecuting attorney ordered him to be locked up. He was detained overnight, accused of "withholding information." Lotridge told authorities that Sheldon Robinson had suggested that they split the reward between them, but Lotridge refused to do so. He later told about the elements of his dream to the *Owosso Argus Press*.

> *I was awakened Monday morning by the alarm clock, with Hotelling's name on my mind. I couldn't forget him and it made me nervous. In my dream I didn't see Hotelling commit the crime, but I couldn't get it out of my mind that he was the slayer. On the way to Flushing where my father John Lotridge and I have been working on a school house, I confided in him. Hotelling seemed to fit the description so well and my father knew that he had the old blue car, that when we got to Flushing we called Floyd Fortman, the foreman, to one side and told him the story. He advised us to go to Flint and tell the officers.*
>
> *Sheldon Robinson, one of the workmen who lives next door to the Schneider family, and who is now claiming the reward, overheard the conversation and asked who it was we suspected. When we refused to tell him, he left, saying that he was going to Flint. When he returned, he had the state trooper with him and he questioned me, and I told him all I knew. However, he asked me what kind of wheels the Dodge sedan owned by Hotelling had, and I told him wooden wheels. He said that the slayer's sedan had disc wheels and I concluded that my tip was wrong."*

But Harold wasn't wrong. His dream had been accurate, as police investigators and attorneys found out. The Genesee County Circuit judge ruled out a change of venue for Hotelling's preliminary hearing. It turned out to be his only court appearance. At the Ionia reformatory, Sheriff Green and his deputies loaded Hotelling into a car and brought him to Flint. He wore the same clothes that he was wearing when he was arrested. Accompanied by his attorney, W.A. Seegmiller, Hotelling faced the court to plead guilty and have his sentenced pronounced. Mrs. Hotelling was absent. She had suffered a nervous breakdown.

Leslie Schneider was in the courtroom that day, and he waited quietly for the proceedings to start. When the handcuffed prisoner passed him, he dealt a smashing blow to the man's face - something he had wanted to do since the day his little girl vanished.

Adolph Hotelling was sentenced to life in prison, without parole. It was the severest penalty possible under Michigan law at the time. Immediately after the hearing, he was taken away to the Marquette prison, where he would spend the remainder of his life. He died in 1955. His surviving family members changed their names, hoping to avoid the bloody stain left behind by their husband and father.

The end to most intensive manhunt in Michigan history up to that time brought nothing but grief to Harold Lotridge. Sheldon Robinson claimed that Harold told him that the young man told him that he was going to "turn in the murderer when the reward got big enough." This was strongly denied by Lotridge, who retained an attorney to bolster his claim to at least a portion of the reward. The other contenders to the money were Robinson and farmer Archie Bacon. As far as is known,

Harold never collected his share of the money. Even if he had, he would not have had long to spend it. Harold Lotridge died just four years later, in 1932.

What happened to Harold that would have caused his unusual dream? He was a normal young man. He had never suffered from any seizures or "spells." The vision that came to him that night was just like any ordinary dream. In the end, the reward is of little importance to the story. What matters is that Harold's dream was real, and it was eventually taken seriously by the authorities. In less than one day after Harold Lotridge woke up with the name Adolph Hotelling in his mind, the murderer was behind bars. Hotelling might well have committed the perfect crime - remember, this was not his first assault - or it could have taken months, or even years, to identify the nondescript man had it not been for a dream voice that spoke to Harold Lotridge in the night.

1929: A DEADLY FAMILY CHRISTMAS
The Lawson Family Murders

Charlie Lawson was a simple man with simple aspirations. He was a husband, a father and a North Carolina tobacco farmer. He had worked hard and now owned most of his land free and clear. He had followed the path set forth by his parents, just as his brothers had. Charlie wasn't wealthy by any means, but his debts were low and he food on the table and a roof over his family's heads. Seven of his eight children were growing up straight and strong. There had been only one real sorrow, when William, his third child, had died from pneumonia. It seemed that all was right with the Lawson world, but as we all know, appearances can be deceiving.

They certainly were in Charlie's case.

Charles Davis Lawson was born on May 10, 1886 in Stokes County, North Carolina. His father was a tobacco farmer, and Charlie, like his younger brothers, worked his father's tobacco fields. In 1911, Charlie married Fannie Manring and they started having children. First to arrive was Marie in 1912. She was quickly followed by James Arthur in 1913, and by William in 1914. After a brief respite for Fannie, Carrie arrived in 1917.

Charlie's younger brothers, Marion and Elijah, decided to set out on their own, but they didn't go too far. They moved their families to an area closer to Germanton but still in Stokes County. In 1918, Charlie decided to follow their lead, so he loaded up Fannie and their four children and moved near Germanton to be closer to his brothers. Charlie found work as a sharecropper, but his dream was to own his own tobacco farm. Sadly, he and Fanny lost their son William to sickness in 1920, but continued adding to their family. Daughter Maybell was born in 1922, followed by James William in 1925 and Raymond in 1927.

1927 was a banner year for the Lawson family. Not only was their son Raymond born strong and healthy, but after scrimping and saving every penny, they had put together enough money to buy their own farm with a house and a barn. Their new farm was located on Brook Cove Road, just outside of Germanton. With their farm in Stokes County, they were close to many Lawson and

Manring families. It was important to them to always be near family, and their children could grow up with a multitude of cousins. However, they weren't finished yet, as in 1929, their baby daughter Mary Lou arrived.

The Lawson home, taken some time after the murders.
The barn can be seen behind and to the left of the house.

The house wasn't much to look at, but it was of sturdy log construction. The family didn't need much, and it a step up from their sharecropper's shack. There was room for the entire family, and it was warm and dry. Fanny worked hard to make the house a home for her husband and seven children.

Charlie was a hard-working man and a good provider. He had a good reputation among his neighbors. Most people thought he was a nice man and that he treated his family well. He met the two main standards of the day for any man to be considered a 'good man' in that he was honest and he paid his debts. But Charlie had another, darker side. It was a side that was largely kept from the public eye. Charlie had a bad temper. When he was angry, he could "fly off the handle and get really carried away." One neighbor explained that when one of Charlie's children got a whippin', they REALLY got a whippin'. And this applied to his wife Fannie, as well. Though they tried to keep this ugly trait a secret from their friends and family, it was impossible to hide it from everyone all of the time. But in the 1920s, people had a tendency to turn a blind eye to "that sort of thing." People generally believed that it was none of their business what a man did in his own home. And so, Charlie continued his iron-fisted rule over his family unhindered.

1929 – A Year in Hell

Fannie Lawson had joined a new church in Germanton, and she took the children with her when she attended services, except for Arthur known as "Buck" to friends and family , who stayed with his father. Charlie wasn't happy about this change in his family life. He was a devout member of the Primitive Baptist Church, and couldn't understand why his wife and children felt the need to change, but he allowed them to continue. For Charlie, his strict religion meant stability in his life, and he found within it justifications for everything he said and did. Primitive Baptists believed in predetermination, which is the belief that God has predetermined everything that is going to be said and done in every person's life before they are born. Conveniently, that made everything Charlie did and said to his family, or anyone else for that matter, preordained and therefore approved of by God. He was also taught, through the Primitive Baptist faith, that as a husband and father, he was the head of his household. Furthermore, his wife and children were his personal property to do with as he pleased. These strict beliefs were great if you happened to be a man who demanded unquestioning obedience, but they didn't always make for a happy family life. Charlie's beliefs may have partially influenced his actions on the terrible Christmas Day that was to come.

During the summer of 1929, two events occurred that changed the order and flow of life in the Lawson family. Early in the summer, Charlie and Buck were breaking up 'new land' soil that had never been cleared or cultivated before . Charlie was breaking up clods of dirt with a mattock when it became entangled in some wire. When it sprang free, the mattock swung up and hit him in the head an occurrence that a cynic would say was surely predetermined by God. He didn't seem severely injured at the time, but several weeks later, he started seeing the local doctor for what he described as blinding headaches and trouble sleeping. Some people in the community believed that he was never the same after the accident.

Later in the summer, when Charlie and his older sons were working in the field, he became enraged with his son, Buck, and attacked him. Buck, now a strong and wiry 16-year-old, defended himself until Charlie was forced to back down. Buck made sure his father knew that he would never let him beat him or the rest of the family again. Charlie was, of course, outraged, but had little choice other than to accept it as his son was bigger and stronger. After that, Buck took to sleeping in his clothes, in case he would need to jump from his bed at a moment's notice if Charlie lost his temper with anyone. Buck had taken on a very heavy load: that of his family's protector.

This did not mean that there were no happy times in the Lawson household. Other than Charlie's occasional outbursts, they went on with their lives in much the same manner as every other farm family they knew.

The fall of 1929 came and went with relative calm. Buck was watchful and Charlie held his temper. As December arrived and the days grew colder, farm chores changed and the children spent more time indoors. Mary Lou was growing quickly and was starting to smile as she approached her fourth month. A little less than two weeks before Christmas, Charlie announced that he had a big surprise for his family. They were all to get bundled up in warm outerwear, as they were headed to town. Any town trip was exciting for farm children, but with the promise of a surprise, the little ones could hardly sit still. When they pulled into Germanton, the nearest town, they all piled out and Charlie sent them on a shopping trip. He told them that they should shop for new sets of dress clothes, and they should pick whatever they liked and not worry about the cost. Many of the children had never had new clothes before, so this was a very special treat. When everyone had selected and donned their new outfits, Charlie revealed a second surprise. He led his family to the studio of town photographer, where they posed for their first-ever family portrait. After they had been photographed in their new clothes, they changed back into their farm clothes and left for home.

You'd think alarm bells would be ringing at his point in the mind of the ever-vigilant Buck, as his father was acting very unlike his usual self. Whether or not they young man was worried by his father's sudden generosity is unknown, but he should have been.

As Christmas approached, the Lawson children grew more and more excited. The family wouldn't have much by way of presents, especially since they had already received new clothes, but Christmas Day was always very special. First, there would be food. Lots and lots of really good food. Traditionally, Christmas Day was a day where they could eat to their heart's content and enjoy special foods that they only had once a year. Family and friends would spend the day visiting back and forth. For the Lawson family, an extra-special Christmas supper was planned because they would be sharing it with the Manrings: Fannie's parents and family.

As often happens in much of the country, but not usually in North Carolina, it snowed on Christmas Eve. By Christmas morning, there was a six-inch blanket of snow outside. It was certainly a beautiful Christmas gift, but it made travel very difficult in the typically snowless countryside. Christmas Day started with a hearty breakfast, shared with Charlie's nephew, Sanders, who had stayed the night. At the same time, a few miles across the county, another Lawson family was having breakfast; one they would never forget. John, Charlie's brother, had a premonition that something horrible was hovering over the family. His feeling was so strong that he started to cry and had to leave the table. It would not be long before his premonition had been correct.

After breakfast, Charlie, Buck and Sanders joined a group of men from the area in their yard for a friendly shooting competition. Meanwhile, inside the house, Fannie and Marie were busy preparing Christmas supper. As a special treat, Marie baked a raisin cake with plenty of raisins inside and on the frosting. She was looking forward to pleasing her Manring grandparents. Unable to make it through the snow, Fannie's family would not be there for supper. The Lawson children would never know about that disappointment, but it had been a very happy day so far.

Outside, the shooting competition continued until the men started running low on ammunition. Most of the men headed for home at that point, and only Charlie, Buck, Sanders and a neighbor remained. Charlie said that he had plans to go rabbit hunting later in the afternoon. As their neighbor headed home, Charlie sent Buck and Sanders into town to buy more ammunition. It was Christmas Day and none of the stores would be open, but it would not be too difficult to get a shopkeeper to open up long enough to make their purchase. Buck and Sanders headed off without a worry in the world. By the time they came back, their lives would never be the same.

The Lawson family portrait, taken in December, 1929, shortly before the massacre. Back Row: Arthur Buck , 16; Marie, 17; Charlie, 43; Fannie, 37; Mary Lou, 4 months. Front Row: James, 4; Maybell, 7; Raymond, 2; and Carrie, 12.

Charlie had been planning something big, and with all the men gone, it was time to put his plan into action. Inside, the dishes were done and the house was in order. Carrie and Maybell had asked to walk to their uncle's house to visit with their cousins, so Fannie bundled them up and sent them on their way.

Charlie hid just inside the barn door as he waited for his daughters to walk by. In his hand, he held a loaded shotgun. As the girls walked pass the barn, he raised the gun, aimed, and fired twice in rapid succession. The two girls dropped to the ground, sending a fine spray of blood all around them in the snow. When Charlie walked out to see to his girls, they were still moving. Both had survived the shotgun blast -- Carrie's to the head and Maybell's to the upper back and head. He used the butt of the shotgun as a bludgeon, striking their heads again and aging in until all movement stopped. He dragged his dead daughters, one at a time, into the barn. After laying them side by side on the floor, he found two large, flat rocks and placed them like pillows under their heads. After crossing their arms neatly over their chests, he walked out into the daylight and closed the door.

Fannie had walked out into the yard to gather firewood for the stove. As she walked back toward the house with a small load of wood in her arms, Charlie raised the shotgun and fired again. Fannie dropped like a stone, dead before she hit the ground. Charlie dragged Fannie to the house and laid her on the front porch floor.

Marie had been inside helping her mother with the cooking when she heard a shotgun blast very near the house. She looked into the yard, saw her father dragging her blood-covered mother toward the house, and began to scream. When Charlie walked into the house, Marie was able to hold him off for a while but he broke free, shoved her toward the fireplace and fired his shotgun once more. He shot Marie dead with a point-blank blast to her chest. The pellets had pierced her heart, and the mantle clock behind her. Both stopped instantly.

The two little boys, four-year-old James and two-year-old Raymond, had been playing quietly in the house. They heard the shots, and saw their sister first fight back and then fall. Terrified, they both ran and hid, but not before their father saw them. He went for James first. The little boy ran to his bed and crawled underneath, and wiggled as close to the wall as he could get. Sadly, it wasn't far enough. Charlie reached under the bed, pulled James out, and slammed the butt of the shotgun into his head until his skull was nearly crushed. Raymond had run in the opposite direction and crawled behind the stove, wedging himself into the corner. Charlie first tried to pry him out with the shotgun and then was somehow able to coax the child from the safety of his corner. Raymond's short life ended with the butt of Charlie's shotgun, just as his brother's had, leaving his skull fractured in several places.

Only one child remained alive in the house -- the baby. Little four-month-old Mary Lou, was lying in her crib. Her only saving grace was that she was too young to understand what was about to happen. Her father raised his shotgun above her and slammed the blood soaked bludgeon down on her head, over and over again, until she joined her brothers, sisters, and mother in death.

With no time to spare, Charlie went quickly to work, preparing the bodies to be found. Family members might start arriving at any minute for a Christmas visit. He brought Fanny into the house from the porch, laid her out straight on the floor, and placed the baby in her arms. He laid Marie, James and Raymond alongside their mother. The last thing he did was to take pillows from the beds and place them under their heads, crossing their arms over their chests, just as he had done with his daughters in the barn.

Charlie had annihilated his entire family, with the exception of his oldest son, whom he had sent away. It had taken but a few minutes to snuff out the lives of the seven people he should have loved the most. His work done, he left the house, stumbled past the barn and into a grove of trees, still carrying the shotgun.

Elijah Lawson, one of Charlie's younger brothers who lived in the area, was out hunting rabbits with two of his young sons that Christmas afternoon. They had plans to meet up with Charlie and Buck to continue the hunt with them. As they approached the house, Elijah's son Claude stopped and carefully leaned his gun against a nail in the rear outside wall of the house before entering. He knew to never bring a loaded rifle into a house. As he entered from the back door, he was stunned into motionless silence. What lay before him on the floor was more than his young mind could process. Hearing a noise across the room, he saw his father opening the front door. He had seen the pool of blood and drag marks on the front porch. Something was terribly wrong at Charlie's house. Elijah on one side of the room, and Claude on the other, stood for several moments, taking in the scene. It was obvious that everyone was dead, and had not been dead for long. Blood pools on the floor were still moist and slowly dripping down through the cracks between the floorboards. They had arrived just minutes after Charlie had killed his last victim and left the cabin.

Charlie Lawson murdered four of his children in this room: Marie, James, Raymond and Mary Lou. The clock seen on the mantle is the clock that was stopped when Marie was shot.

Their first thought was that an intruder had entered the cabin, and for some unknown reason, had killed the family. But where was Charlie? Realizing they'd walked into something horrible, they backed out of the cabin. Claude later told the sheriff, "Some was layin' in the house dead - blood runnin' every which way." His father said, "Man, we left a-runnin"

And run they did. They first ran to the top of the hill overlooking the Miller farm, the closest house to the Lawson farm. Elijah stood on the hill and yelled down to Mr. Miller, "Come here. Someone has killed Charlie Lawson's whole family!" The Millers telephoned the sheriff and the near neighbors. Within minutes, the Lawson house was converged upon by everyone within running distance. As the news spread across the county, more and more people arrived. The dead girls in the barn were discovered as people fanned out to look for Charlie. It didn't take long to figure out that there had been no intruder. Charlie had done all the killing that day. Sanders and Buck returned from town with the ammunition they were sent for. Elija broke the news to Buck and he collapsed in the front yard.

As hours passed with no sign of Charlie, worried men sent word to their homes, instructing their wives and children to prop chairs under the doorknobs, and to let no one inside until they returned home. Few people in the vicinity had locks on their doors . The word went out that "Charlie Lawson has killed his whole family and they can't find him!" No one knew if Charlie would stop with slaughtering his family, or if everyone was in danger.

Dr. C.J. Helsabeck was called to check the bodies, including the four children, whose births he had attended. The shock of the brutality with which Charlie had destroyed his family was almost more than the country doctor could handle. He, like anyone who entered the house, found himself in need of fresh air soon after entering. The initial reports were accurate. Everyone was dead and Charlie was nowhere to be found.

At some time after 10:00 p.m. on that terribly long Christmas Day, a shot rang out from the woods beyond the barn. All activity around the house suddenly stopped and everyone looked anxiously towards the woods, and then to the sheriff. Believing that Charlie had fired the shot, and fearing that anyone entering the woods would be risking his life, the sheriff didn't move. Eventually, one of the men ventured into the woods. Moments later, he called back that Charlie was dead.

The scene in the woods was a strange one. Charlie had evidently been there for hours, walking around and around a single tree. He had circled the tree so many times that the snow had melted, forming a sort of path. He had eventually sat on the ground at the base of the tree, leaned back, put the gun barrel in his mouth and pulled the trigger. Charlie Lawson had taken his eighth and final life.

With the murderer dead and no intruder to search for, the only thing left was to take care of the dead and try to figure out why it had happened in the first place. Charlie had left two notes behind on the ground near his body. They consisted of just sentence fragments, seemingly addressed to no one. One note read: "Blame nobody but." The other note was just as cryptic, reading: "Trouble will cause." There was nothing else. Some believed that Charlie had started to explain his actions that day, and then decided against it. Perhaps, in the end, he decided to leave everyone guessing. No one will ever know exactly what was on Charlie Lawson's mind as he hid in the barn, lying in wait for two of his daughters to walk past within close range of his shotgun.

But why did Charlie spare his eldest son by intentionally sending him away that afternoon? Did he have a special place in his heart for the boy? Did he love him above his wife and other children? Or did he want his son to suffer, as the only surviving member of his family? No one would know for certain, but the most likely answer is that once Charlie had made up his mind, he wouldn't allow anyone to stop him until he put his plan into action. Buck was the only one who had stood up to him. Buck would have fought to his own death to protect the rest of the family. Charlie probably considered Buck to be the only possible obstacle in his deadly plan. And so, he sent Buck off into town, never suspecting that the next time he would see his family, they would be lying in their coffins.

The annihilation of the Lawson family was big news, not just in Stokes County, but across the nation, and eventually across the Atlantic. People flooded into town from miles around, first to see the house and then to see the bodies. Cars were lined up for miles along Brook Cove Road. Large groups of people would stomp through the fields, trying to get close to the Larson house, some walking for miles through the snow. The crowds were beyond anyone's expectations, certainly beyond the poor farming community's ability to control.

The Lawsons were not wealthy. Trying to bury eight people at one time was well beyond their means. It was through the kindness and generosity of many friends and neighbors that the slaughtered family received a proper burial. The Browder family donated a large plot in their family cemetery. With so many people to bury, it was decided that each member would have individual coffins, with the exception of baby Mary Lou, who was buried in her mother's arms. Men from the community, young and old alike, gathered together to dig a trench long enough to hold eight coffins side by side. It took a trench over twenty feet long to hold the dead Lawsons. William, the child who had died nine years previously, was moved to be with his family. Charlie was buried at the head of the grave, alongside his wife and children. In accordance with strict Primitive Baptist rules, the family was buried in a section of the graveyard that had not been consecrated. No one having committed the terrible sin of suicide was allowed to be buried on hallowed ground. Since Charlie was buried with his family, they too were sequestered from that blessed soil.

On December 27, the day of the mass funeral, the ground still held a blanket of snow. Eight white coffins were propped up on sawhorses, the largest on the left, and growing smaller down the row. Buck was inconsolable and had to sit through the ritual. Relatives feared that he might try to join his family in death, so he had two men with him at all times. Friends and family were allowed closest to the gravesite, and strangers fanned out beyond. An estimated 5,000 people attended the Lawson funeral. Several people had arrived early and had climbed the trees surrounding the small family graveyard to get a good view. People stood in the snow for hours, waiting to join the procession filing past the coffins. It was over five hours before the coffins were finally lowered into the grave.

Left : The Lawson family funeral with eight white coffins lined up before the mass grave.
Right : The Lawson family gravestone.

The mystery of why Charlie had done it hung over the community like a dark, angry cloud. It was the topic of conversation at every meeting, at every table in the local diner, and at every dinner table. Everyone wanted to know; needed to know. As people talked and shared bits and pieces of the puzzle, different theories began to surface. Unfortunately, some of the pieces belonged to an entirely different puzzle.

Some people refused to believe that Charlie had killed anyone, yet alone himself. He was a good man, a hard worker, and he loved his family. They theorized that he may have witnessed some sort of organized crime activity, perhaps a mob murder. His family must have been killed in retaliation, and Charlie's suicide had been staged to throw suspicion off the bad guys. But since Stokes County in central North Carolina wasn't exactly a hotbed of activity for gangsters, this theory just didn't hold up.

Others were inclined to believe that Charlie's head injury was at the root of the cause. The injury must have been far worse than the doctor had thought, and Charlie had gone insane as result. Another idea linked to the head injury held that Charlie had become convinced that he was going to die and he wanted to take his family with him. He must have reasoned that they would be helpless without him and would suffer greatly. In this delusional state, he must have killed his family to spare them from pain and suffering resulting from his death.

Charlie was a devout Primitive Baptist and followed their teachings without question. Another thought was that he had become deeply angered when Buck had defended himself that summer. He could have felt that Buck had stripped his authority within his home by interfering when Charlie chose to punish his wife or children. He felt he had to regain control of his family and to do that, he must demonstrate that they belonged to him and he could do whatever he wished with or to them.

Or could it be that when Buck halted Charlie's escalating pattern of violence during that summer, his anger festered and built up until he finally blew up on that snowy Christmas Day? The events of the day, as they unfolded, indicated a well-thought-out premeditation, as he was able to get Buck away from the farm and therefore out of his way before setting his plan in motion.

As neighbors and relatives discussed these different possibilities, a much more sinister idea took form, but it did not take solid form until nearly sixty years later. The information was related by several Lawson and Manring relatives who were around the family before the murders and were still alive all those decades later to tell what they knew and what they believed. There had been talk between Fannie and her sisters after a family funeral, overheard by a few cousins. She was concerned about Charlie's behaviors toward Marie, her oldest daughter. She had been growing more anxious through the previous year. The consensus was that Charlie had developed an incestuous relationship with his daughter. Another woman, a former close friend of Marie, revealed that just a few weeks before that deadly Christmas, Marie had told her that she was pregnant. Charlie was the father and both her parents knew. Adding to that, when Hill Hampton, possibly Charlie's closest friend and neighbor, was interviewed for a book about the murders, "He said that he knew of serious problems going on within the family, and he knew the nature of the problem, but that it was personal, and he chose not to reveal what it was." If this could possibly be true, Charlie may have felt trapped by the reality of his incestuous actions. Maybe the only way out that he could see was to destroy all evidence and all witnesses. This might not have been a far reach in his case, as his Primitive Baptist belief was that everything he could possibly do was preordained, and that he really had no choice. God had intended for him to do this from before he was born.

The only thing that anyone involved would ever know for sure was that this was an unsolvable mystery.

The identity of the killer was known. The killer was dead. The family was buried. The small Germanton farm community was still reeling from the shock of the horrific events that had happened to some of their own. However, they were of strong, sturdy stock, and life had to go on. They determinedly set about getting back to their usual routines, but the public wouldn't let that happen. There was to be no peace in the tiny rural community for a very long time.

Marion Lawson, one of Charlie's younger brothers, made a decision. Just a few days after the murders, Marion, his sons, and other Lawson men arrived at the farm on Brook Cove Road and started planting posts in a circle around the house and barn. Then they strung chicken wire, two layers high, around the posts, effectively fencing in the site of the murders. Townspeople and neighbors thought that Marion was trying to keep curiosity-seekers away, but Marion had a vastly different idea. With all the interest in the killings, he decided that they would use that interest to make a profit. He proceeded to charge people to tour the house and surrounding property.

The following article appeared in the *Winston-Salem Journal* on January 30, 1930:

The home place of Charlie Lawson, Stokes county farmer, who slew his wife and six children and then killed himself on Christmas Day is being commercialized and members of the family have roped off the Lawson home, locked the doors and are charging an admittance fee of 25 cents. They are even advertising the "attraction" in the daily newspapers. The excuse for such conduct is given that the money is needed to help pay off the indebtedness on a tract of land that Lawson was owing for and that the money raised in this manner will be applied to the debt for the benefit of Arthur Lawson, 19-year-old-youth, the only surviving member of the ill-fated family.

The charge of 25 cents to enter in and look on the scene of the gruesome tragedy has not deterred the morbid and the curious and visitors are there daily. Sometimes as high as 100 people making the pilgrimage. On a recent Sunday, before the home was roped off and locked up, it is said that at least 500 people visited the scene of carnage.

No report has come from the Baltimore hospital regarding the examination of the brain of Lawson but it is expected most any day and is awaited with intense interest.

Aside from Arthur's Buck's age being incorrect he was 16 at the time, not 19 , the story was accurate. Fannie's family, the Manrings, were outraged. As a group, they met with Marion Lawson and begged him to stop the outrageous display and promotion of their daughter and grandchildren's' death scenes. Marion was unmoved, and the tours continued. He told them that people were going to come to see the site anyway, so someone should benefit. It is unknown how much of the money raised through the tours was given to Buck.

The general consensus of the residents of Germanton was that the tours were shameful, and Marion was embarrassing them all. A few even approached him, asking him to stop. They received the same answer as the Manring family had -- a firm and resolute NO.

Interest in the murders and the murder site fell off slightly after the first few months, but it held steady for a surprisingly long time. People living around Germanton felt that the interest stayed so high because the murder house had become legitimate attraction in the minds of those who flocked there, like an alligator farm, or an amusement park. People could pay their quarters, walk right in, and gape at the bloodstains on the floors and walls without having to sneak in at night. Because of all this, interest in the place stayed strong, long after it would have waned naturally. The Lawson Family Murder House remained an active tourist attraction for several years. The community grumbled for a while, but only until they began to see that all those visitors were stopping in town to buy gas, to buy food, to eat in the diners, and stay in the new hotel. With the money Germanton was taking in from tourists, the little town began to thrive during an era when most of America was suffering. As morbid as it may sound, local historians believe that Charlie Lawson saved Germanton from the great Depression.

Stella Lawson Bowls, Marion's daughter, was just fourteen when her uncle murdered her aunt and cousins. When her father opened the house for tours, he enlisted family members as tour guides and workers. In her elder years, Stella recalled working in the house, cleaning up at the end of tour days. Later, she graduated to giving tours, following a dramatic script depicting the details of each horrifying death. She remembered resenting having to give up her Saturdays to work while her girlfriends were enjoying themselves. But this was now the family business, and like it or not, she was expected to pitch in and do her part.

Marion insisted that visitors sign the register before entering the house. Whether this was to compare the number of signatures with the receipts for each day, or to maintain an historical record is unknown, but it does make for interesting reading. Many celebrities of the day walked through the door of the farmhouse to view the bloodstains and hear the lurid details of the murders. There were state and federal politicians, a couple of governors, actors and actresses, singers and possibly one outlaw. In 1933, the sheriff of Stokes County received a letter from John Dillinger, taunting him and telling him that he had visited his county. The register at the Lawson house did indeed carry the signature of a John Dillinger. Whether it was *the* John Dillinger or an impostor is unknown, but it certainly was an interesting historical reference. A review of the register also revealed a bit of irony in that many of the first paying visitors to walk through the house were the same neighbors who had initially complained.

When relatives and early visitors were asked what it was like working in the house or taking a tour, one story was repeated many times. On that fateful Christmas Day, Marie had made a raisin cake for dessert. After the bodies had been removed from the house, nearly everything was left just as it was. When the house was opened for tours just days after the murders, the cake was still sitting on the cupboard. As time passed, the cake became hard, but there it stayed. The family members working in the house began noticing that the raisins on the cake were disappearing, so they agreed to keep watch. What they saw amazed them. As visitors made their way through the house, occasionally one would reach out and pluck a raisin from the cake. People wanted to have a little piece of morbid history, whether to prove they had been there, or to take home and display as a gristly souvenir. The cake eventually crumbled into bits and was thrown away.

After interest finally started to fall off at the Lawson farm, parts of "the display" were packed up and taken on the road. A circus promoter had taken the tour toward the end of its popularity. He saw a future for the remaining artifacts so he offered to buy whatever they would sell. He was allowed to purchase some of the recognizable items. As for the rest, the items they would not sell, he found his own and passed them off as the originals. The Lawson family tragedy had been transformed from a small town attraction, to a circus side show. The man who bought the items from the Lawson house designed a side show tent and wrote an enticing patter to coax a dime or a quarter from the pockets of the curious public. He purchased a shotgun and displayed it as the actual murder weapon. And on a small table, he put a raisin cake. A whole new group of people were being exposed to the tragic story of how the Lawsons died. No doubt, this new story was as chock-full of well-placed embellishments as the cake was full of raisins.

After a few more years of the Lawson story being bandied about as entertainment, the public finally moved on to other things. No one knows what happened to the items sold from the Lawson home. They were probably junked long ago, or are sitting in some old attic with no indication as to their history.

The "attraction" may have been closed and the side show discarded, but it appeared that at least some of the deceased Lawsons were not able to rest. Perhaps it was the suddenness of their deaths. Perhaps it was sadness or anger that made them cling to their old home. Maybe Charlie was still looking for Buck, to finish what he started. Whatever the reason, rumors spread of strange goings-on in the Lawson farmhouse late at night, after the doors were locked and everyone had gone home. Articles began to appear in the local newspapers about the house being haunted. At night, people parked on the road, watching the house. They waited to see the mysterious lights dance from window to window, or to hear the moans and bangs heard by others.

In life, Charlie had been an active member of the local branch of the Junior Order of United American Mechanics, known simply as "The Juniors." Even in death, he remained an active member -- of sorts. The word "junior" in the name held no association with the age of the members, just as "mechanics" had no association with actual mechanics. In Germanton, this organization was simply a fraternal society and social club for men. After reports of the hauntings began circulating, The Juniors started including Charlie in their initiation ceremonies. There were two basic initiation challenges for new members, designed to test their courage and give older members some fun. The initiate would be asked to go the Browder Graveyard at midnight and take a pebble from the Lawson headstone. For the second challenge, the group would proceed to the old Lawson house. With all the fellows watching, the initiate would walk around the house in the dark -- at midnight, carrying nothing but a lantern. The lantern was not only to light his way, but to provide proof to the members watching from afar, that the initiate had actually carried out the challenge.

As the decades passed and the house fell into decay, children and adults alike might wander through the premises, looking for ghosts or just exploring. On many occasions, people left the house with a feeling of extreme sadness, even if they had been light-hearted going in. Spontaneous tears were a common occurrence. Most visitors did not stay inside long. Cameras would sometimes stop working inside but work just fine when taken outside again. Other times, cameras and flashlights stopped working altogether when batteries would suddenly go flat.

Buck Lawson, his family's sole survivor, eventually married and started a family of his own. Buck and his wife, Nina, had a son and three daughters, of which Buck was terribly proud. His son, Arthur, was his namesake, and two of his daughters were named for his dead sisters. Buck tried to live his life well, and he did have some happy times, but deep down he had been broken on Christmas Day in 1929. His friends said that he turned to alcohol for comfort and to try to forget the memories of his past. When things got really bad, Buck would get depressed and lock himself alone in a room, playing a particular record over and over. The record was definitely not one that would lift his spirits, but he played it anyway. In 1930, The Carolina Buddies, a well-known Bluegrass group, had recorded the song "The Lawson Family Murders." Years ago, it was common to sing ballads about murders and tragedies, and this was no exception. When he was suffering most severely, a bottle of booze and that song were his only companions.

Buck's life was spared in 1929 but he was not to grow old. On May 10, 1945, he and another man were driving in a work truck when it struck a deep groove that had been cut in the road for repairs. Witnesses believed that they had not seen the warning signs as they drove toward the excavated area. The other man in the truck was severely injured but survived. Buck was killed instantly.

Buck had worked hard to move past the tragedy that tormented him. He had built his own life and had his own family. But sadly, he had largely lost his identity when his father had murdered his mother and siblings. He was no longer Buck Lawson; he was Charlie Lawson's son. This was never demonstrated better than in Buck's obituary. The first three paragraphs were a recount of his father's actions in 1929. Buck's life and death were not mentioned until the fourth paragraph. Arthur "Buck" Lawson was laid to rest in the Browder Family Cemetery, alongside the family who had left him sixteen years before.

By 1980, the old Lawson house was no more. Some of the wood was salvaged for a small bridge a few miles away, but nothing was left of the Lawson farm. The present owners do not welcome trespassers on their land. The site where the old house and barn once stood is now under a cultivated field. There is nothing to see and nothing to explore.

But that doesn't mean that the hauntings have stopped entirely. The site of the Lawson's nearest neighbors, the Hill family, is now a lovely, resorted farmhouse. The current owners operate it as the Squires Inn Bed and Breakfast. Shortly after moving into the house, the owner looked up and noticed a little boy and girl peering back at her through the glass in the one of the doors. She rose to see them better, at which point they vanished into thin air. After seeing the pair several more times, she decided to do some investigating. After discussing her experiences with a local historian, she was shown the Lawson family portrait, taken shortly before they died. The woman immediately recognized her young visitors in the photograph. She had been visited by Maybell and James Lawson. The historian told her the Lawson children had frequently crossed the field to play with the Miller children. The woman still sees the children, and though saddened by their fate, she finds some peace in that they are together.

At least they still have each other.

1931: "THE BLUEBEARD OF QUIET DELL"

Harry Powers, as he became known, was in the words of Evan Allen Bartlett, his only real biographer, "the most fiendish human being of his day." Powers, said Bartlett, was the perpetrator of "one of most monstrous mass murders in world history, the most horrible tragedy in American annals." Melodramatic words, and yet, for the most part, aside from folks in some parts of West Virginia, most people have never heard of him. During the early years of the Great Depression, his crimes appalled and fascinated thousands of people, but he is barely remembered today - much like the methods that he used to find his victims.

In the days before online dating services, single men and women who were looking to meet prospective mates often availed themselves of the services of matrimonial bureaus. These were mail-order matchmaking agencies that provided subscribers with lists of potential partners. "Lonely hearts" columns appeared in newspapers, and there were classified ads in true-romance magazines. One such agency, the American Friendship Society of Detroit, used advertisements like this one:

LONELY HEARTS - Join the world's greatest social extension club, meet nice people who, like yourself, are lonely many wealthy . One may be your ideal. We have made thousands happy. Why not you?

Among the scores of desperate love seekers who replied to such ads was a fifty-year-old Danish-born widow from Oak Park, Illinois, named Asta Buick Eicher. She was the mother of three children: fourteen-year-old Greta, twelve-year-old Harry and nine-year-old Annabelle. Asta was a cultivated, artistically-inclined woman who had inherited a tidy sum from her late husband, a prosperous silversmith. She was lonely and hoped to find a man to fill the hole that had been left in her life by the death of her husband. She wrote a letter in response to an ad that she saw in one of her romance magazines, and in early 1931, she received a reply from a gentleman who identified himself as Cornelius O. Pierson of Clarksburg, West Virginia.

According to his letter, Pierson was a successful civil engineer with a net worth of $150,000 more than $2 million in today's money. He had a "beautiful, ten-room house, completely furnished." Because his hectic work schedule and his many responsibilities prevented him "from making many social contacts," he had turned to a match-making service to help him "make the acquaintance of the right type of woman." From the information listed about Mrs. Eicher, he felt that she might be a suitable partner for him. He wrote, "My wife would have her own car and plenty of spending money."

Over the next several weeks, the two embarked on a long-distance, mail-order courtship. As their hand-written romance heated up, Pierson plied the full-figured widow with his particular brand of sweet talk. In response to a photograph of herself that she had sent, he exclaimed over how "well-preserved" she was and assured her that he "preferred plump women." He also let her know that he understood the deepest needs of the opposite sex. He wrote, thrillingly, "The great trouble is that men are so ignorant that they do not know that women must be caressed."

At some point in the spring of 1931, at Mrs. Eicher's invitation, Pierson made the first of several trips to her home outside of Chicago. There is no record of how she reacted to her first look at her long-distance suitor. From his letters, she expected a tall, handsome, distinguished-looking man with dark, wavy hair and "clear blue eyes." What she saw was a bespectacled, beady-eyed, moon-faced fellow who stood barely five feet, seven inches tall and weighed nearly two hundred pounds. One contemporary described him as "squat, pig-eyed and paunchy." Nevertheless, she must have been won over by his personality because she invited him back for several more visits and proudly introduced him to her neighbors as a man of substance with investments in oil and gas wells, farm property and "stocks and bonds paying from six to forty percent dividends."

On June 23, Pierson returned to Oak Park. After staying for two days, he and Mrs. Eicher departed on a trip together, leaving the three children in the care of the family nanny, Elizabeth Abernathy. Five days later, Miss Abernathy received a letter from Mrs. Eicher telling her that Mr. Pierson would be coming soon to pick up the children.

He arrived on July 1 and spent the night at the Eicher home. The next day, he sent one of the children to the bank with a note and a check, which had been allegedly signed by Mrs. Eicher. The note instructed the bank clerk to fill the amount of the bank balance in on the check and give it to the child. However, the bank refused to do so because the signature on the check did not appear to be that of Asta Eicher. When the child returned without the money, Pierson quickly packed up the car, loaded the three children and drove off, refusing to explain anything to Miss Abernathy.

She didn't know it at the time, but none of the Eichers would ever be seen alive again.

Three weeks after leaving Illinois, Cornelius Pierson arrived at the home of Mr. and Mrs. Charles Flemming of Northboro, Massachusetts. He was there to meet the object of a long and passionate correspondence, Mrs. Flemming's sister, Dorothy Pressler Lemke. The next morning, Cornelius and Dorothy stopped by two banks, where she withdrew $4,000 before departing for Iowa, where they planned to be married. Along the way, they stopped at a railway station, where Pierson shipped Dorothy's trunks.

At the time, no one noticed that the trunks were not shipped to Iowa but instead were sent to Cornelius Pierson in Fairmont, West Virginia. A man named Harry Powers claimed the trunks several days later.

It was the nanny, Elizabeth Abernathy, who first alerted the police that something was wrong. Searching the home of Asta Eicher, they discovered twenty-seven letters that had been written to her by Cornelius Pierson. On August 26, 1931, Oak Ridge police officials contacted the Clarksburg, West Virginia, police chief, Clarence Duckworth, and requested that he take a local resident named Cornelius Pierson into custody for questioning about the disappearance of Mrs. Eicher and her three children. The only problem was that there was no one with that name who lived in Clarksburg. The police chief turned the man's name and description over to detective Carl Southern, and asked him to try and track the man down.

On a hunch, Southern went to the post office at the corner of Third and Pike Streets, and there he learned that a man named Cornelius Pierson had rented a post office box and had given his home address as 111 Quincy Street. It turned out that the man's name was not Pierson at all - it was Harry F. Powers. And far from being a wealthy bachelor with money coming in from oil wells, dairy farms and high-yield bonds, he was a married vacuum cleaner salesman whose wife, Leulla, supplemented their meager income by selling sundries from a little shop adjacent to their house.

At first, Powers denied that he knew Mrs. Eicher, but when confronted with the more than two dozen love letters that he had written to her, he admitted that they had corresponded, but nothing else. He insisted that he didn't know anything about her disappearance.

Powers was arrested on the Illinois warrant and taken into local custody. The arrest was reported in the *Clarksburg Telegram,* and was read with interest by a woman named Louis Watson. She telephoned Harrison County Sheriff Wilford B. Grimm, to tell him that Powers had a garage on property that adjoined land belonging to her mother at a place called Quiet Dell, a small village nestled in the hills just a few miles outside of Clarksburg.

Harry Powers - the "Bluebeard of Quiet Dell"

Sheriff Grimm obtained a search warrant for the property on August 28, and State Police Corporal Dorsey Bailey, Police Chief Duckworth and Detective Southern headed for the garage. At Quiet Dell, they were joined by John Bond, a former Elk District Constable. The officers quickly found Powers' rural property. A tumbledown wooden bungalow stood in the center of the site, and it had clearly been vacant for years. Directly across a narrow dirt road, though, stood a large, shed-like structure that appeared to be a newly built garage. The door was secured by a pair of heavy padlocks that were pried open by a crowbar supplied by John Bond. The interior was big enough to accommodate three automobiles, but there were no cars inside. In the middle of the dusty concrete floor was a pile of trunks and boxes that turned out to be packed with the personal belongings of Mrs. Eicher and her three children.

One of the officers noticed a trapdoor in the concrete floor. Swinging it open, he was slapped in the face by a heavy stench that came wafting up from below. Shining their flashlights down into the darkness, several officers cautiously descended the creaking wooden steps. As they looked around, it became painfully clear that the cellar had been used as a prison. The space was divided into four cramped cells, each of them fitted with a heavy wooden door. Small, iron-grated openings in the exterior walls allowed some weak rays of sunshine to penetrate the gloomy interior. Otherwise, there was no light and no ventilation. And there were no furnishings - just a bare, filthy mattress on the floor of each cell.

In one of the rooms, they found a bloody footprint and other signs of violence, including bloody clothing and strands of human hair. A partially burned bank book was retrieved from some ashes near the building, but there was no sign of any victims.

The hopes of the authorities for the Eicher family began to fade.

Sheriff Grimm put in a call to the Clarksburg Fire Department to assist in pumping out an old well that was located nearby. It was filled with rocks and water - but no bodies. Handcuffed and heavily guarded, Harry Powers was brought to the farm and shown the bloody footprint in the cellar. Although officials demanded that he reveal the location of the bodies, he maintained his silence.

The news spread rapidly across the area, and by late afternoon, more than three hundred people had gathered at the farm to watch what was taking place. Among these bystanders was a fifteen-year-old boy who told Sheriff Grimm that he had recently helped Powers dig a ditch from the garage to the creek. Officers from the sheriff's department and the state police grabbed shovels and went to work. As the excavation progressed, a road gang from the county jail was brought in to help. Soon, a terrible odor began to emanate from the trench.

Asta Eicher's body was discovered first. She had been strangled and wrapped in a burlap bag before being buried in the ditch. The bodies of the three children were found later in the afternoon. That same evening, the diggers came upon the remains of a fifth woman. She was later identified as Dorothy Lemke of Northboro, Massachusetts, who had disappeared the previous month when she withdrew more than $1,500 from her banks and went off with her "lonely hearts" fiancée, Cornelius Pierson.

Based on the autopsy results, authorities concluded that Mrs. Eicher had been starved and tortured before being murdered. Evidence in the "death dungeon" - as the newspaper started calling the cellar - suggested that Asta had been hanged from a ceiling beam, perhaps in full view of her children. When the boy, Harry, who had been bound with rope and gagged with "garbage waste," had tried to struggle free and save his mother, his skull had been beaten in with a hammer. He had been castrated before he was buried in the ditch. His sisters, like Dorothy Lemke, had been strangled.

When he was told of these grisly finds on his property, Powers continued to maintain his innocence, insisting that they must have been buried there by someone else. At that point - around

8:30 p.m. on Friday, August 28 - his interrogation took a turn for the worse. Officials from the Park Ridge Police Department, Harrison County Sheriff's deputies and Baltimore & Ohio railroad detectives took turns "questioning" Powers with their fists, boots, burning cigarettes, a rubber hose and even a ball-peen hammer. He was jabbed with needles, his left arm was broken and hot boiled eggs were pressed into his armpits. Finally, around 4:00 a.m. on Saturday morning, he broke. He sobbed to the detectives, "I did it. My God, I want some rest." Photographs taken of Powers over the next two days show his badly swollen face, black eyes, bruises, burns, puncture wounds and welts - all of which his captors insisted were obtained by "falling down the stairs" during questioning. In the jail's infirmary, he signed a confession to the murder of Mrs. Eicher and her children "by using a hammer and strangulation."

During the time when Powers was being interrogated, the body of Dorothy Lemke was also found in Quiet Dell. She had been strangled with the belt that was still twisted around the neck of her corpse. Authorities in Massachusetts contacted her family, and the Flemmings traveled to Clarksburg to identify the decomposed body.

While searching through Powers' home, they found hundreds of letters that "Cornelius Pierson" had received from lonely women and widows around the country. Each of them had poured their hearts out to him, and he had professed his own love in return. On the basis of the letters, the authorities contacted Mrs. Edith Simpson of Detroit, who expected Pierson to marry her in September. She had already purchased her wedding dress and was making arrangements to leave town with him. When shown a letter that Powers had written to Asta Eicher, Mrs. Simpson was amazed to see that it was an almost exact copy of one that he had sent to her. She refused to believe that "her Connie" had done anything wrong until they showed her photographs of the bodies of his victims. It's likely that Edith was to be the next victim on Powers' list.

While all of this was happening, news of the atrocities was spreading across the region. The people became fascinated with the "Bluebeard of Quiet Dell," as he was dubbed by the newspapers. Throughout the first night after Powers was taken into custody, hundreds of people streamed through the Romine Funeral Home in Clarksburg for a glimpse of the five victims, who had been laid out in open caskets. On Sunday, August 30, an estimated thirty thousand curiosity-seekers overran the "murder farm," turning the hot, end-of-the-summer afternoon into a "morbid holiday." A dozen county deputies were dispatched to the scene to direct traffic, but they were soon overwhelmed. A couple of enterprising local promoters attempted to erect a six-foot wooden fence around the property and charge admission to get inside. Outraged at having the site of a tragedy transformed into what one observer called a "mass murder amusement park," someone soaked the fence with gasoline during the night and set fire to it. A second fence was promptly torn down by a mob and from that point, "everyone was then free to visit the death spot without charge or restraint."

Over the following weeks, leading up to Powers' indictment for murder, investigators dug into the background of the "Bluebeard of Quiet Dell." It was soon learned that "Harry F. Powers" was merely another of the man's aliases - one of the many that he had employed over the years. His real name was Herman Drenth. He had been born in Holland in 1892, and had come to America in 1910. Over the next dozen years, he had roamed the country, spending time in Indiana, Ohio, Illinois, Virginia and Pennsylvania before ending up in West Virginia in 1926. During those footloose years, he had done two stints in jail: once in Iowa for burglary and the second in Indiana for defrauding a widow of $5,400.

In 1929, he had married the former Leulla Strother of Clarksburg. The forty-one year old divorcee had an unfortunate marital history in that she had been previously married to a local farmer named Ernest Knisely, who was arrested and tried for murder after fracturing the skull of a neighbor during a violent disagreement. It was not long after she and Powers were married that he dreamed up the "lonely hearts" scheme. He joined a number of matrimonial mail-order services and secured the names of several hundred potential victims. At the time of his arrest, he had five letters that were sealed, stamped and addressed to women in New York, Maryland, Michigan and North Carolina that were ready to be mailed.

As the investigation dragged on, rumors began to circulate that the angry citizens of Clarksburg planned to take matters into their own hands. The threat became real on the night of Saturday, September 19, when a lynch mob of more than four thousand men and woman surrounded the jail, crying out for Powers to be turned over to them. The Clarksburg Fire Department was called to the scene to try and help dispel the mob with water hoses. But the angry crowd tore lengths of hose from the trucks to keep them from operating, and several members of the mob tried unsuccessfully to upset one of the fire trucks. The crowd was then confronted by a contingent of heavily armed lawmen - the sheriff and his deputies, the entire city police force, and a detachment of state troopers - who warned them to stay back, or be shot. Ignoring the threat, the mob surged forward. After firing a few warning shots over their heads, the police let loose a barrage of tear gas. Despite the fact that the tear gas canisters were already unleashing smoke before they reached the crowd, members of the mob were not reluctant to pick up the canisters and hurl them back at the officers. Tear gas permeated the downtown district for hours, burning the eyes of bystanders more than a block away. In the confusion that followed, eight of the rioters were arrested, while the rest, "choking and crying from the fumes," fell back and eventually dispersed after it was learned that Powers was no longer in the jail.

During the confusion, Powers had been hustled out of a rear exit and into a waiting automobile. Escorted by two state police cars, he was driven to the state penitentiary at Moundsville, where he would remain in solitary confinement until his trial.

But he would not spend his time there completely alone. Anticipating an insanity plea by the defense, prosecutors called in a well-known forensic psychiatrist, Dr. Edwin H. Meyers, to examine Powers. After examining him in his cell for several hours, Meyers pronounced him legally sane. In other words, he was someone who knows right from wrong, but was clearly psychopathic. He was "possessed of an exaggerated lust to kill which dominates his entire personality." Although motivated partly by financial greed, Powers derived his greatest gratification from planning and carrying out his murders - "tormenting, torturing, and punishing his victims before strangling or beating them to death." He was driven, in short, "by the mere love of killing."

In 1931, Harrison County was without a courthouse. The old, red brick building had been torn down and a new courthouse was under construction. The temporary courthouse, which would later serve as the City Hall and police station, was not nearly large enough for the number of spectators that were sure to flock to Powers' trial, so county officials made arrangements to hold it in the largest venue available, which was Moore's Opera House. It had a seating capacity of five hundred, and every seat would be filled during the five days of the trial.

The trial began on December 7, 1931 with the principal performers - the judge, jury, witnesses, defendant and his lawyers and the prosecutors - all on the opera house's stage. During its five days, the audience watched in rapt attention while Powers, by contrast, seemed bored with the whole thing. Prosecutor Will E. Morris and his associate, William G. Stathers, were seeking the death penalty and were confident that they would get it. Even though the defendant had been indicted for five murders, the prosecutors had elected to try the case based solely on the Lemke murder because there was a more direct link to Powers.

They had a damning list of witnesses, including James E. Smith, a contractor who testified that he had constructed the garage at Quiet Dell for Powers. Detective Carl Southern testified that Dorothy Lemke's body had been found in the ditch near the garage. He also stated that he had seized letters addressed to Cornelius Pierson from the possession of Powers. City and county officers testified about bloodstains, clothing and trunks found at the scene. County Coroner Dr. Leroy C. Goff testified that Mrs. Lemke had been strangled with a leather belt. Mr. and Mrs. Charles Flemming identified Powers as the man who had left their home with Dorothy, while claiming to be Cornelius Pierson. Employees from the express company in nearby Fairmont testified that Powers was the man who had picked up trunks and other baggage sent to Fairmont on behalf of Mrs. Lemke. Three bank officials of the Second National Bank of Uniontown, Pennsylvania, identified Powers as the man who had cashed two checks totaling $4,287.21 drawn on the account of Mrs. Lemke. Three residents of Quiet Dell swore that they had seen Powers shoveling dirt into the ditch near the garage between July 30 and August 1.

Powers testified briefly on his own behalf, but he offered only a confusing mixture of denials and accusations about two men who allegedly carried out the murders. He claimed to only be an acquaintance of Dorothy Lemke, and to have cashed her checks for one of the "real" murderers. He seemed totally disinterested during his time on the witness stand.

His expression remained impassive even when the jury returned a guilty verdict on the afternoon of December 11, after less than two hours of deliberation. On December 12, the judge pronounced a sentence of death on the gallows. Powers accepted his sentence without any noticeable reaction.

On the day of his execution, Powers was nattily dressed in a black pinstripe suit, white shirt and a gaudy blue necktie. He calmly walked up the steps to the gallows without assistance and looked out dispassionately at the forty-two witnesses who had assembled to watch him die. Asked if he had any last words, he calmly replied, "No." A moment later, at precisely 9:00 a.m. on Friday, March 18, 1932, three attendants stationed by three buttons pushed them simultaneously, and Powers dropped to his doom. None of the three men would ever know which button actually sprang the trap. Neck broken, Powers dangled at the end of the rope for eleven minutes before the prison physician pronounced him dead.

Even though Harry Powers is largely forgotten today, he has managed to live on in infamy, at least in a fictional version. In 1953, his life and crimes inspired a best-selling book called *Night of the Hunter* by Davis Grubb, a West Virginia native who grew up near Powers' home in Clarksburg. He set the novel in Moundsville, where the "Bluebeard of Quiet Dell" was incarcerated in the state penitentiary. Set during the Depression, Grubb's novel tells the story of a psychopathic ex-con named Harry Powell, who passes himself off as an itinerant preacher. In his relentless hunt for $10,000 in stolen cash, he courts, marries and murders a widowed young mother, then pursues her orphaned children, who run off with the money.

Two years after Grubb's novel was published to great commercial success and critical acclaim, a dark movie version directed by renowned actor Charles Laughton and adapted by James Agee appeared in theaters. Robert Mitchum played the serial sex killer with the words "love" and "hate" tattooed on his knuckles. It turned out to be one of the best, and most sinister, roles in his career.

1932: SHE WALKS THESE HILLS
The Story of Mamie Thurman

Although more than seventy years have passed, the spirit of a woman named Mamie Thurman lives on in the mountains of West Virginia. The legends say that when the winds wail in the dark of night, Mamie's ghost walks the hills of Logan County. There are stories of an apparition that has been seen, while motorists claim to have picked up a young woman walking near Trace Mountain, only to find later that the seat beside them in the car is mysteriously empty.

But why does she still walk? Many say that her spirit cries out for justice, having died under circumstances that combined murder, mystery, a missing grave and sexual depravity. It is a story of dark hearts and minds, and one that touched the homes of the area's most prominent citizens in 1932. The legends say that Mamie's ghost still touches them, even now.

On June 22, 1932, the lifeless body of a pretty, dark-eyed brunette woman named Mamie Thurman was found dumped along a roadside near Trace Mountain — now referred to as 22 Mountain — in Logan County, West Virginia. The gruesome discovery was made by a deaf-mute man named Garland Davis, who stumbled over the body while picking blackberries. Mamie's murder made startling news in the region, galvanizing a community that had just begun to feel the pain of the

Great Depression. At a time when many families could barely afford to put food on their tables, the strange death of Mamie Thurman would provide a sad but well-needed distraction.

R. L. Harris, the undertaker at the Harris Funeral Home who also acted as coroner, arrived on the murder scene that afternoon. He later stated that Mamie's corpse was found facing downhill, and that she might have never been discovered if some bushes had not kept the body from sliding down the mountainside. She was found wearing a dark blue dress with white polka dots and one shoe. The other shoe was found lying near the body. Also nearby was her purse, which contained a pack of cigarettes and about $10. She wore a watch, a diamond ring and her white-gold wedding band, which seemed to rule out robbery as a motive for her death. Upon examination, Harris learned that her neck had been broken and that she had been shot twice in the left side of the head with a .38-caliber weapon. Both bullets had passed through her brain and had been fired at close range, leaving powder burns on her face. Her throat had also been cut from ear to ear. Harris commented that she had been dead for several hours when she was discovered, matching later investigation notes that reported her last being seen the previous night around 9:00 p.m.

Harris removed the body to the morgue on Main Street, where he embalmed it later that afternoon. He believed that Mamie had already been dead when her throat was cut, and that she had not been killed at the scene. Most likely, the killer did not expect the corpse to be found for some time, if ever. In such a rural area, where paved roads were virtually non-existent, it was more likely the killer thought animals would carry away the remains long before they would be discovered.

On the same day that Mamie's body was found, an arrest warrant was issued by Magistrate Elba Hatfield. That evening, a local man named Harry Robertson and his African-American handyman, Clarence Stephenson, were both arrested.

Robertson was a local politician and was well-known in the community. He worked at the National Bank of Logan and served as the treasurer for the local public library. He was also a prominent sportsman and was liked by nearly everyone who knew him. In addition, his wife was active in society circles, such as they were in Logan County. She was the treasurer of the local Women's Club, and with her husband, was active in church. Stephenson was a native of Chattanooga who had been in Logan County for the past nine years. He had worked in several mines before going to work for Robertson. Prior to his being arrested for Mamie's murder, he had never been in trouble with the law. He mainly worked around the Robertson house, acting as caretaker and doing odd jobs. His primary responsibilities were to feed and care for Robertson's hunting dogs.

What led the police to Robertson's door is unknown, but when questioned, he admitted to that he had been having an affair with Mamie Thurman. He explained that he had arranged to rendezvous with her with the help of his handyman, Stephenson. He would tell his wife that he was going hunting and then they would take his guns and drive off in Robertson's Ford. Stephenson would then drive Robertson to one of the places where he had arranged to meet Mamie.

News of the arrests quickly spread through Logan County. Rumors flew, and many formed their own theories about who killed Mamie. The stories varied as to what the dead woman had actually been like. Most considered Mamie to be an active church worker, a young woman of quiet demeanor who was "a very nice lady who minded her own business." Unfortunately, though, Mamie was said to have a darker side. It was one that was not so well known to her friends and neighbors, but apparently was closer to the truth. She was sometimes referred to as the "Vixen of Stratton Street" in the days following her death and tongues wagged about her encounters with married men, her sexual escapades and about the fact that she was a "temptress." More facts, equally as unseemly, would be revealed in the days to come.

Mamie Thurman had been born in Kentucky on September 12, 1900. Her husband, Jack, was also from Kentucky, and was sixteen years older than his wife. The Thurmans had lived in the town of Logan for eight years, and they rented a two-room garage apartment behind Harry Robertson's house on Stratton Street. Jack Thurman had a job as a city police officer, landing the position just fifteen months before his wife's murder. The job came about thanks to the efforts of Harry Robertson, who was the president of the city commission. This would not be the only item in the case to show that the families, friends and political positions of the town were hopelessly entangled. It would not be the only odd "coincidence" that still has local conspiracy buffs talking all these years later.

Mamie's funeral took place just two days later, on June 24. Without a doubt, it was probably one of the most bizarre services ever held in Logan County. Strangely, the cost of the funeral was more than $7,200, a staggering amount in 1932. The services were paid for in cash by her husband, who as mentioned, was employed as a city patrolman. At that time, he would not have that amount in a year.

The funeral was attended by five hundred and fifty women and about thirty men, and was conducted at the Nighbert Methodist Church, where Mamie was a member. The pastor of the church, Reverend B. C. Gamble, and Reverend Robert F. Caverlee of the First Baptist Church both officiated. Oddly, Gamble did not deliver a sermon. Instead, he read a scripture from the Book of John. The verses told of a woman that was brought before Jesus, having been caught in the act of adultery. It was the intention of her captors to stone her to death. Jesus replied that the one of them without sin should cast the first stone, and the abashed crowd left the woman alone. In the moments that followed, Jesus didn't condemn the woman for her actions, but simply told her to go and sin no more.

"This is the text," Reverend Gamble said. He paused for a few moments for the words to sink in before he added, "develop your own sermon on that basis." His words were met with stunned silence from the congregation. Only the sound of weeping could be heard. After that shocking moment, Mamie's obituary was read aloud and the service was concluded. What happened next remains a mystery to this day.

Mamie's death certificate filed at the courthouse stated that she was buried at Logan Memorial Park in McConnell. Strangely, since she had been shot twice in the head, it listed her cause of death as "unknown." According to records and a search of the cemetery, though, Mamie was never buried there. To make matters even more confusing, records at the Harris Funeral Home showed a charge of $35 for moving Mamie's body to Bradfordsville, Kentucky. However, the cemetery in Kentucky had no record of her being interred there. So, where is Mamie Thurman buried? No one knows, marking yet another unsolved mystery in this perplexing case.

On the day of the funeral, West Virginia State Troopers searched the home of Harry Robertson. They made a number of disconcerting discoveries. In the basement, they found several bloodstained rags and a number of places on the floor where it looked as though someone had attempted to clean something up. That "something" was believed to be blood, a belief that was later confirmed by a Charleston chemist named T. A. Borradaile. His tests showed the blood to be human; however, none of his tests were admitted as evidence by the court during the trial that followed. The troopers also found a razor hidden in the basement, and they discovered a hole in the wall that appeared to have been made by a bullet.

The investigators also found bloodstains on the window, fender and seat of Robertson's Ford sedan. The car was mostly used to transport hunting dogs when Robertson made the trip up to Trace Mountain, where he owned a hunting cabin. The back seat of the vehicle had been removed and a tarp had been placed over the back of the front seat and on the rear portion of the vehicle. This was supposed to protect the seats from the dogs when they were in the back, but investigators also believed the Ford made a perfect transport vehicle for Mamie's body. Her corpse had been found about one mile from Robertson's cabin.

On June 27, Harry Robertson was released from jail on $10,000 bail that was guaranteed by his defense attorney, C. C. Chambers, Bruce McDonald of the McDonald Land Company, T. G. Moore and C. L. Estep. He would be back in court on July 29 for the hearing into the case.

Somehow, during all of the investigations, Jack Thurman was never suspected in Mamie's death. In fact, the Logan Police Department had granted him a furlough after his wife's funeral. Before the hearing and trial, he traveled to Louisville, Kentucky, where he visited Mamie's two sisters at an orphanage. The children had been placed there after Mamie's father was killed in a gun battle with police in Ashland, Kentucky. It is assumed that he broke the news to them about Mamie's death and gave each of them $2, which would be worth about $34.50 in 2014.

On July 5, the *Logan Banner* announced that Judge James Damron of Huntington would aid the prosecution in the Thurman trial without pay. He was one of the state's most distinguished criminal lawyers and judges. In a letter to the county's prosecuting attorneys, L. P. Hager and Emmett F. Scaggs, he wrote, "Mamie Thurman's brutal murder was a drastic deed and the handiwork of a well-laid-out conspiracy." He also said that he believed the perpetrators of such a "foul and damnable murder" should be apprehended and brought to justice. The district attorneys readily agreed to his sentiments and gave him a seat at the prosecutor's table.

In the meantime, the investigation into the murder continued, and detectives were making some rather unsavory discoveries about some of the county's leading citizens. One allegation even stated that there was a "club" in Logan where men would meet with their girlfriends and carry on affairs in secret. Mamie was said to be a member of this "club," and had been involved with many of the area's politicians and businessmen. The case was getting heated, and pressure was being felt at the district attorney's office from all sides.

In a press statement on July 26, Assistant D.A. Emmett Scaggs announced that his office had no intention of dragging the names of anyone into the case merely for the purpose of satisfying the curiosity of prurient citizens. He knew that many people were more interested in a potential sex scandal than in finding out who killed Mamie Thurman, but his office was not. In addition, he assured the public that just because some "prominent people" might be involved, his office was moving forward on the case as quickly as possible. Scaggs added, "Murder carries an extreme penalty, while adultery is only a misdemeanor." They would, he promised, get to the bottom of the case.

Scaggs followed this with another startling announcement. Believing that many honest people in the county could shed some light on the case, but were afraid to get involved, he had asked the court to offer a $1,000 reward for new evidence that would lead to a conviction. Mamie's murder, Scaggs stated, was the "most brutish crime in Logan County history" and he was determined to see it solved.

Not surprisingly, a number of people came forward with information. One of them was Oscar Townsend, who rented a room from Harry Robertson and had worked with him at the bank. He said that there had been "ill feelings" between Mamie Thurman and Mrs. Robertson, and that the two ladies, who had formerly been friends, had not been "going around together" for some time. He also informed the police that he had traded a .38-caliber pistol to Harry Robertson in exchange for a smaller pistol some time back.

Shortly after receiving this information, another search was carried out at the Robertson home. Police found a .38-caliber pistol under Robertson's pillow. They also found a knife and a bloodstained piece of canvas that led them back to Robertson's car. Inside the vehicle, a more thorough search revealed a blood clot underneath a rubber floor mat. It appeared that an attempt had been made to wash out the car, but the blood clot was missed because it was attached to the underside of the mat.

Things looked bad for Harry Robertson but it was not because of information given to the police by Clarence Stephenson. Even though he had been named as a co-defendant in the case, and had the same attorney as Robertson, Stephenson was not released on bail prior to the hearing. However, he didn't seem to hold this against his employer. From his cell, he sent a letter to his sister, Josie Carpenter, who was a maid at the Pioneer Hotel. He wrote that he "would die before he would lie on" Robertson and his wife. He asked that Josie get a message to Mrs. Robertson, and tell her that he had been moved to the Williamson jail to keep anyone from seeing him. He also wanted her to know he "will not do anything to hurt Mr. Harry or her." He wanted Josie to tell Robertson's wife to stand up and help him and Mr. Harry. He knew that things would go hard for himself and his employer, but he said that the police didn't know anything to hurt them.

On July 29, huge crowds of people, many carrying chairs, began gathering in front of the Logan County courthouse. Some came as early as 6:00 a.m., hoping to gain admittance to the hearing. The hearing attracted more than one thousand people to the courthouse that morning.

Magistrate Elba Hatfield was in charge of the proceedings. He was already in place on the bench when Jack Thurman arrived, and when Harry Robertson and Clarence Stephenson were brought in under guard. Stephenson had his hands cuffed in front of him, but Robertson's hands were free. Both men sat calmly at the witness table. Stephenson stared straight ahead. Robertson constantly wet his lips and looked around the room.

A few minutes later, Mrs. Robertson was escorted into the grand jury room by Robertson's boarder and police witness, Oscar Townsend. She walked to her husband's side and kissed him lightly on the cheek. Then she sat down next to him, placing an arm around his shoulders. Huddled close, they proceeded to whisper back and forth to one another for about ten minutes. They were then joined by Judge Estep and C. C. Chambers, attorneys for Robertson and Stephenson. Prosecutors Hager and Scaggs sat down at the other end of the long table. The hearing was about to begin.

The grand jury was made up of many of the county's prominent citizens. Many of them were associated with Harry Robertson. Instructions were given to the jury, and it was again stated that the murder of Mamie Thurman was one of the most gruesome in the county's history. The grand jury was charged, "If there is enough evidence to indict the parties responsible, the court expects you to do so."

Testimony was then given concerning the discovery and autopsy of Mamie's body, and the collection of the physical evidence in Robertson's house and car. Later, Harry Robertson himself was called to the stand. His testimony was the most shocking of the day. On the stand, Robertson recalled an almost two-year affair between himself and Mamie Thurman. He testified that he and Mamie often met at the "Key Club," located in the heart of Logan. He explained that the club was frequented by a number of well-known and wealthy businessmen and their "lady friends." Both male and female members had pass-keys to the place where, in private rooms, they enjoyed parties, illicit affairs and drunken orgies. Robertson said that Mamie gave him a list of sixteen different men with whom she had engaged in sex. She had given it to him about a year before, when they had worked together at the Guyan Valley Bank. He noted, "One of the men is dead, all except three live in the city of Logan and all are married but one."

Robertson went on to say that he continued to see Mamie, even though she refused to stop sleeping with other men. He testified that Clarence Stephenson was often the "go-between" for his trysts with Mamie, and Stephenson later corroborated this. He admitted having had "improper relations" with Mamie on many occasions, and said he had last seen her at around 8:00 p.m. on the night she had been killed. He did not see her again after that, he said, and he had nothing to do with her murder. The jury seemed pleased with Robertson's testimony but apparently, Stephenson was not as convincing.

During his testimony, the handyman refuted the charges that he had been involved in Mamie Thurman's death. He corroborated his employer's testimony, and denied seeing Mamie on the day she was killed. He also told of being moved from the jail in Logan to Williamson. He was driven by state trooper along an isolated road over Trace Mountain. At a bend in the road, they came upon two cars that were parked off to the side and surrounded by several men. Shots were fired in their direction and one of the troopers told Stephenson that it was a mob, and asked if he was afraid. They urged him to tell all that he knew, or it was likely that he would be "taken off." Stephenson replied, "If I was making a dying statement it would be, I don't know any more than I've told."

One odd incident took place during Stephenson's testimony that has never been explained. At one point, he suddenly stopped talking and pointed out into the courtroom as though he were deathly afraid. However, he would not tell what he saw. The prosecutor asked, "What do you see – Mrs. Thurman?" But ghost or not, Stephenson refused to answer.

At the end of the session, Magistrate Hatfield told the grand jury that all the evidence was circumstantial, but claimed it was very damaging against both defendants. The jury ended a four-day inquiry on September 15. The next day, a newspaper headline screamed: "Harry Robertson Not Indicted!" Clarence Stephenson, it was decided by the jury, would stand trial alone for the murder of Mamie Thurman.

The community was stunned and angered. Although it's doubtful that any mob violence was actually planned during the incident with Stephenson and the state troopers, there was talk of vigilante action after the hearing. There were a number of Ku Klux Klan members in the community. Not only would they want revenge on the black handyman for his alleged killing of a white woman, but also because they believed that he was having sexual relations with her. This was contrary to Harry Robertson's statement, but rumors and whispers of violence continued to spread. Nothing ever came of them, however, and Stephenson remained safely locked away in jail.

Stephenson's trial began on Monday, September 10 at the Logan County courthouse. Hundreds of spectators packed into the building, the balcony, and the public gallery and lined the hallways. Many others waited outside, hoping to get a seat inside at some point during the proceedings. A man who left his seat in the gallery would find it immediately filled.

The first witnesses were R. L. Harris and a Dr. Rowan, who had examined Mamie's body. They described the location where the corpse was found and the condition of the body. They again pointed out that Mamie had been killed by two bullets to the head before her throat had been cut.

They were followed on the stand by Jack Thurman, the husband of the deceased, who stated that he had worked his regular shift from 6:00 p.m. until 6:00 a.m. on June 21. He said he had last seen his wife at 5:30 that evening. He testified, "I was working my beat with Hibbard Hatfield and I telephoned my wife shortly before one in the morning. When she didn't answer, I went home and found that her bed had not been slept in." Thurman would not see his wife again until the next day, when he identified her body at the Harris Funeral Home.

Throughout his testimony, Thurman had to constantly be told to speak up, as his voice rose and fell in volume. Even when he was cross-examined by the defense, who tried to portray his relationship with his wife as rocky, Thurman remained quiet. He stated that he and Mamie did not argue on the afternoon of her death, and that they were on good terms. He had also believed, prior to her death, that his wife had been faithful to him and had been at home while he was on duty. In fact, he praised her many times during the course of his testimony. He said, "Mamie was the perfect wife to me, and I cannot realize why she would do the things that she had been accused of." A newspaper writer described his comments as "pitiful."

The next witness was Fannette Jones, a black woman who lived on High Street. According to her testimony, Robertson and Mamie often met at her house for their rendezvous. Jones testified that Mamie had come to her house about 8:00 p.m. on the evening that she was killed. She had stayed for about ten minutes and then left.

Other witnesses included Mattie Bell, a black laundry woman who worked for Mrs. Robertson. There was also Nadine Mabney, a drugstore employee who sold Mamie a pack of cigarettes at about 8:30 p.m. on the night of her death; Jack White, a teenager who said that he saw Mamie shortly before dark, and Clyde White, who testified to seeing Mamie enter the house of Fannette Jones and stay there "several minutes." All of these witnesses were used to create the prosecution's timeline of events on the night of the murder, as was the testimony of W. L. Brand, who saw Mamie about 9:00 p.m. on the night of her death.

The next witnesses were much more damaging to Stephenson. The first was E. F. Murphy, a local businessman who lived close to the Robertsons. He testified that he saw Stephenson alone when he came home from work on the day Mamie was killed. He also stated that he saw Stephenson and Mamie together around 6:00 or 7:00 p.m. that evening. Another witness, Sherman Ferguson, also claimed to have seen Mamie with Stephenson that same night. He spotted the handyman driving a Ford sedan while he was downtown that evening.

The most stunning testimony of the entire trial was provided by Harry Robertson, Stephenson's employer and Mamie Thurman's admitted lover. The newspapers reported that Robertson's testimony "almost brought the crowded courtroom to its feet on several occasions when he revealed the sordid details of his relationship with Mamie Thurman."

Robertson slowly began to reveal the truth behind his "hunting expeditions" with Mamie Thurman, and the two-year deception that he and Mamie had perpetrated on his wife and Jack Thurman. He began by testifying that he had known the Thurmans for seven or eight years and that he and Mamie began their affair while working at the Guyan Valley Bank. His relationship with Stephenson had been as a friend and an employer. The defendant maintained an apartment in the attic of the Robertson home and they often went hunting together at the cabin on Trace Mountain. Stephenson usually accompanied him to the cabin, bringing along the dogs in the back of the sedan. Stephenson had always been welcome to use the automobile when it was not being taken to the cabin.

Robertson testified that the last time he saw Mamie around 8:00 p.m. on the day she was killed. He left his house shortly after that to take his children to a swimming pool in Stollings. That was the last time that he saw her, he said, but added that Stephenson was in the house at that time. After returning to town, he said that he dined at the Smokehouse Restaurant until 9:00 p.m. with his son, where they had listened to a prizefight on the radio. The Ford was gone when he returned home. His wife later confirmed his whereabouts on that evening.

Robertson explained that he and Mamie would often meet at the mountain cabin, and that sometimes she would take a taxi to meet him incidentally, all of the taxi bills were found to be charged to Jack Thurman . Mamie always returned home around 11:00 p.m. After leaving the cabin, Stephenson would meet her and take her back to Logan. He said that Mrs. Robertson didn't know about the routine but probably "suspicioned."

He also said that he went hunting at Crooked Creek the Saturday before the murder, and that Mamie was with him at the time. He said that he had no "engagement" with her at that time but later went to Fannette Jones' house and was with Mamie for about an hour. Stephenson then took her home. He testified that this was the last time that he had sex with her before her death. He and Mamie had planned to go on another "hunting trip" the following Tuesday, but he said he had called it off on the afternoon of her death.

On October 13, Louise Robertson took the stand. The newspaper reported that the crowd anxiously awaited her testimony and that "they strained to hear every word." She stated her name and address, and said that she had been married to Harry Robertson for eighteen years, and that they had a fourteen year-old daughter and an eight year-old son. She admitted that she knew Mamie Thurman, and had been friends with her, but the relationship had cooled off. She said, "I stopped going around with Mrs. Thurman last January... I had reasons to believe that she and my husband were intimate and I wouldn't be around with a woman that was intimate with my husband."

When questioned about where her husband was on the day Mamie was murdered, she explained that her husband had left for work that morning, returned home for lunch, and then came home in the evening at the usual time. She added that he took the children to the swimming pool in Stollings that evening. After their return, all of them had dinner together and then Robertson drove his second vehicle, a Packard, "around the block," because he had recently had some work done on it. After that, he and his son left to go listen to a prizefight, promising to be back around 9:00 p.m. She went on to say that her husband had uncharacteristically washed the dishes after dinner. This was a job that was usually done by Stephenson, but her husband told her that the handyman was ill. She also noted that she saw Stephenson in the dining room after her husband left, and that he "was in the kitchen a time or two." She said that she heard him leave the house later on and that he returned a little while after the family went to bed. She told the prosecutor: "I heard him come upstairs and close his door. I never heard Clarence anymore that night after 11 o'clock."

The defense, still trying to throw suspicion onto Robertson, questioned Louise about the guns that her husband kept in the house. She simply answered that she didn't know anything about guns, other than that they were kept put away and out of the reach of the children. She stated, "My husband had a gun but I don't know what kind, as I don't know anything about pistols."

Mrs. Robertson's response when questioned about her husband's alleged affairs with Mamie was described as "very unusual." She replied to the questioning, "I learned they were intimate with each other because I had cause to believe they were. A woman doesn't have to be told these things." She claimed that no one told her about the affair; it was her "woman's intuition" that caused her to become suspicious. She was then asked if she had ever spoken to Mamie about the affair. She replied,

"No, but I was talking to Mrs. Thurman once and she told me that someone had told her that she had better watch her husband. I told her that if her husband is ever untrue to you, you won't have to be told, you'll know it. I had an enmity toward Mrs. Thurman. Of course, I cared and was hurt... but what was the use to be mad about it?"

While there was nothing really very damaging in Mrs. Robertson's testimony for Clarence Stephenson, the same could not be said for the police officers that testified. Of course, it should be pointed out that these men were friends and co-workers of Jack Thurman and undoubtedly wanted to see the man they believed to be the killer properly punished. That's not to say that they lied about the investigation, but things certainly became heated during the examinations. One intense moment came when defense attorney Chambers began baiting Logan patrolman Bill Bruce about the bloody rags found in Harry Robertson's basement. He suggested that the police had planted them there and Bruce became angry. He shouted at Chambers, "If it wasn't for paying a fine, I'd slap your face!"

Chambers snapped back, "Oh, no . . . you wouldn't slap my face here or any other place!"

The judge banged his gavel and shouted down to them, "If you men don't hush, I'll have you both sent to jail!"

In addition to Bruce's testimony, Police Chief Smeltzer testified that he saw Stephenson cleaning out the inside of Robertson's Ford Sedan at about 8:00 a.m. on Wednesday, the day that Mamie's body was discovered. Patrolman Bruce was with him when they drove by the house.

After both the defense and the prosecution rested in the trial, the judge began his final instructions to the jury. It was then that a rather strange event occurred. Several women discovered two envelopes in the gallery that were addressed to one of the prosecutors, John Chafin. The notes were signed "A Voter" and "A Citizen." Each claimed that the writer had seen the murder of Mamie Thurman committed. They also went on to state that the writer believed the crime would be "white washed" and would go the way that other crimes had gone in Logan County. The notes added, "We believe there are people here who saw that woman get in the car and go to her death. We believe there are those who saw her get into the car and go up Trace Mountain." The prosecutors later announced that they didn't think there was anything to the letters.

Stephenson was allowed to make a statement to the court before the jury began its deliberations. He insisted, "I am not guilty. I have no knowledge of the crime that I am accused of. I tried to tell the truth.... I hope the law won't stop until they find the guilty parties."

The jury was only out for fifty minutes before returning with a "guilty" verdict against Clarence Stephenson. They did pass on a recommendation of mercy, however, charging against the death penalty and opting for life in prison instead. A life sentence was handed down on October 13, and Stephenson was given ninety days to appeal to the Supreme Court.

On November 15, pleas from the Logan County Branch of the National Association for the Advancement of Colored People NAACP went out across the county to raise the $600 needed for Stephenson's appeal. Many churches in Logan began accepting donations, and more than three thousand people attended a meeting in Stephenson's support. The money was raised, but despite all of the efforts on his behalf, the Supreme Court turned down his appeal in 1933.

Stephenson remained in the Logan County Jail for some time before being transferred to the West Virginia State Penitentiary at Moundsville. The state prison was a horrible place in those years, but Stephenson strangely never served "hard time." One Logan resident, Normal Sloan, who served time with Stephenson both in the Logan County jail and at Moundsville, said that Stephenson actually received catered meals while incarcerated in Logan County. Sloan said, "Everything was carried to him three times a day from the New Eagle Restaurant."

After being transferred to Moundsville, Stephenson served as Warden Oral Skeens' chauffeur. In this way, he was excused from the often-brutal conditions of the prison. According to Sloan, Stephenson continued to deny that he committed the murder, but he did admit that he played a hand in Mamie Thurman's demise. Sloan recalled many years later, "He told me he was hired to take the body to 22 Mountain, and that he didn't do anything to Mamie Thurman. He never did say who killed her, but he said that he didn't do it. Stephenson told me it was all politics."

On June 11, 1939, Stephenson was transferred out of Moundsville and was sent to the Huttonsville Prison Farm, where he died of stomach cancer on April 24, 1942. He never spoke to the authorities of the things that he knew about Mamie's death, choosing to carry the secrets of the crime to his grave. As time has passed, most have come to believe that Stephenson was little more than a scapegoat in the case, and that Mamie Thurman's real killer was never punished.

A number of strange events, mysteries and unanswered questions have followed Mamie to the grave. Investigations into her death have continued for years and still continue today. There are dozens of questions that still linger over what took place in 1932. Many of these questions will never be answered, thanks to the fact that many of the details were so conveniently erased from history shortly after the trial occurred. Even the courtroom transcripts and seventeen deposition copies have disappeared.

Many believe that Stephenson took the blame for events that were set into motion by prominent citizens of the area, who were working to cover up their own illicit activities. Who killed Mamie, and why so brutally? Was her death caused because of something she knew, or something she had done? Was her broken neck a key to her death? Was her slashed throat, so unnecessary after two bullets to the head, intended as a warning to others about talking too much? Why was the list naming sixteen men that Mamie had supposedly slept with suppressed at the trial? What was Harry Robertson's real role in her death? Why didn't Louise Robertson divorce her husband after learning of his affair with Mamie? Why wasn't Louise Robertson ever suspected for the murder of the woman who was sleeping with her husband? The list of questions goes on and on....

Later inquiries, while not answering any of these questions, have discovered a number of rather unusual things that took place after the trial of Clarence Stephenson. Regrettably, many of these strange facts have triggered even more unanswered questions.

After the trial was over, Prosecutor Chafin appeared before a board of city commissioners on behalf of Jack Thurman, who had been refused permission to return to work as a police officer. After a closed-door session, Thurman was returned to duty as a Logan patrolman. It was reported that he died a number of years later in an insane asylum in Louisville, Kentucky.

Although Mamie's funeral services were conducted at the Nighbert Memorial Church, and were described as "the most unusual ever in Logan County," a check of the records at the church showed no listing of Mamie Thurman ever having been a member. There was no record of her being baptized there or married there. Defense attorney C. C. Chambers had been placed in charge of these records. Shortly after the murder case, the Rev. Gamble of the Methodist Church left Logan and was not heard from again. R. F. Caverlee, pastor of the First Baptist Church, who also officiated at Mamie's funeral, transferred to a church in Fredericksburg, Virginia, soon after the trial.

On Friday, December 30, 1932, a road crew discovered several bloodstained garments and a long-bladed hunting knife near the spot where Mamie Thurman's body was found. The knife was covered with what was thought to be blood. Foreman Joe Buskirk said, "It is only a miracle that my men discovered the rags and knife." Whatever became of these items is unknown. Could they have cleared Clarence Stephenson? We will never know.

And things got even stranger in 1985. In that year, a man named George Morrison, who was a half-brother of Mamie's, came to Logan looking for his sister's grave. Morrison lived in New Mexico, and had only just learned about his half-sister and her violent death. He wanted to erect a proper headstone on her grave, and it was at this point that it was learned that her correct burial records were missing. Some said that she was buried in the Logan Memorial Park in McConnell while others claimed that she had been moved to Kentucky. No cemetery records existed to prove this, and no markers could be located to show where she had been interred.

Morrison placed a legal advertisement in the *Logan Banner*, searching for information. He received several calls resulting from the ad -- all of them distinctly strange. A caller who refused to identify himself claimed that he had been paid by a prominent doctor to exhume Mamie's body back in 1962. A woman called and said that she had once owned a cemetery map that marked the location of Mamie's grave. She no longer had it because someone had purchased it from her for $1,000. The man who bought it did not give his name. Another man wrote in reply to the advertisement and asked Morrison to phone his home. He gave his name simply as "George." Morrison said that the man sounded elderly, and he claimed to be a retired Logan businessman. He also claimed to know everyone involved in the original case, including Mamie, the Robertsons, Stephenson and others. "George" told Morrison that a woman had killed Mamie and that the deed had been covered up. Morrison was skeptical about all these odd calls, and began to realize that Mamie's death was a mystery that would probably never be solved.

What really happened to Mamie Thurman? How did she spend her last terrifying moments? We will never know for sure and perhaps for this reason, her ghost has long been reported to walk the hills around the town of Holden. Some believe that her ghostly appearances are caused because she cries out for justice, while others believe that she wants her final resting place to be found. Perhaps it is both. Regardless, her crying phantom has long been a part of local lore.

The ghostly tales began not long after the dark events of the murder trial started to fade from immediate memory. Hikers, motorists, and even Boy Scouts who had any reason to be near Trace Mountain began to tell of seeing a woman dressed in white wandering in the woods near where Mamie's body had been discovered. The reports claimed that she could be heard crying and that the smell of flowers always accompanied the sightings. The scent would even occur in the winter, when no flowers were in bloom.

A man who used to deliver supplies to a coal mine located near the murder site once had a rather startling experience in his truck. One night, as he was driving along the old road, he was suddenly overwhelmed by the smell of flowers, and an ice-cold chill swept through the cab of the truck. He had never heard the stories of Mamie Thurman's ghost but when he mentioned the incident to a friend, she quickly filled him in on the legend. He decided then and there that he would never travel that road again.

According to some, the old bridge near where Mamie was found is also haunted by her ghost. The road across the bridge leads back to some old coal mines, and a driver must travel down a steep incline before reaching the bridge. The stories say that if a car is parked on the bridge and shifted into neutral, the vehicle will roll backwards up the hill. No one has been able to explain why this occurs, but local lore has it that it is caused by the spirit of Mamie Thurman.

And these are not the only stories. Perhaps the most famous, and most commonly told, are the accounts of a spectral woman who has been picked up along the old mine road. She is described as wearing a white dress and having dark hair that falls just above her shoulders. The pale woman is often given a ride, back in the direction of Logan, but then she vanishes from the car long before it reaches its destination.

Could this phantom hitchhiker be Mamie Thurman? Many believe so, and a general belief in hauntings would suggest that it might possibly be. But then again, what about the tale of Mamie Thurman is truly as it seems? That is another question about this strange case that will probably never be answered.

1934: THE "AMERICAN TRAGEDY KILLER"

In the summer of 1906, a young woman named Grace Brown - twenty years old, single and several months pregnant - believed that she was traveling to the beautiful Adirondacks region of New York so that she could become a respectable married woman. She had spent the last several months at her parents' farm, writing desperate letters to her boyfriend, Chester Gillette, a co-worker at an upstate skirt factory. Convinced that her life would be ruined if her delicate condition became obvious, she begged him to marry her. In one letter, she wrote, "Oh Chester, please come and take me away. I am so frightened, dear."

Even though Chester claimed that he loved the pretty young woman, he seemed to be in no rush to settle down. He had attended Oberlin College and, although he came from the poor side of the family, his uncle owned the factory where he and Grace both worked. He considered himself to be several rungs higher on the social scale than Grace, whose parents owned a failing farm. Having seduced Grace, his thoughts turned toward forming an alliance with one of the daughters of the rich men in town. These men were friends with his uncle, and with luck, he could marry into a wealthy family and never have to work in the factory again.

With Grace away visiting her parents, he happily pursued other women, including a well-to-do beauty named Harriet Benedict. When Grace learned of his flirtations, she threatened to expose him publicly as a heartless seducer. If her life was ruined by a pregnancy, she wrote to him, she would make sure that his life was ruined too.

The warning seemed to have the desired effect. In early July, Chester invited her on a vacation to the Adirondacks. Grace, believing they were setting out on a sort of pre-wedding honeymoon, was ecstatic when Chester arrived at the hotel where they had agreed to meet. Soon they would be married, and raising a baby together. On July 6, the couple checked in at the Glenmore Inn, a picturesque hotel on the shore of shining Big Moose Lake in Herkimer County. After signing assumed names in the hotel register, Chester - carrying his suitcase and tennis racket - escorted Grace down to the water, where they rented a rowboat.

What happened during the next few hours will never be known. The pair was spotted on the lake several times that afternoon by other boaters. At one point, were seen picnicking on a beach. When they failed to return at sundown, Robert Morrison, the man who rented them the rowboat, was not especially alarmed. Tourists often didn't realize just how large the lake actually was. Finding themselves too far away to make it back before nightfall, they sometimes rowed to the closest shore and spent the night in one of the cabins that ringed the lakefront.

But when they were not back by late the next morning, Morrison became seriously concerned. A search party set out in a steamer, and scoured the water and shoreline. They eventually came upon the rowboat, floating upside down in the water. Looking down into the depths of the water, one of the searchers spotted an object caught in the weeds at the bottom. Using a long, spiked pole, they managed to haul up the drowned corpse of Grace Brown.

Three days passed before Chester Gillette, still using an alias, was arrested. At first, he claimed that Grace had drowned accidentally when the boat overturned. He later changed his story, claiming that she had deliberately thrown herself overboard. "She got up and jumped in the water - just jumped in," he said. The boat capsized and he nearly drowned trying to save her before managing to swim to shore. Neither explanation accounted for the terrible wounds on her head, which had been caused - according to the autopsy report - by some kind of bludgeoning implement, very possibly a tennis racket.

The question of what really happened to Grace remains in doubt, however, due to her body being embalmed before the autopsy was conducted. Isaac Coffin, the aptly named Herkimer County coroner, admitted on the witness stand that the damage to her head could just as easily have come when her body was recovered from the lake.

Chester's trial became a media sensation. District Attorney George Ward pulled out all the stops to secure a conviction. He read pleading letters from Grace that had been obtained from Chester's room without a search warrant. As a *coup de grâs,* he brought into the courtroom a glass jar containing the fetus that had been removed from Grace's body during the autopsy. Chester's lawyer objected to the fetus being displayed in court, as Chester had admitted he was the father, but the damage was done. Despite the uncertainty surrounding Grace's death, the jury only took six hours to find him guilty. Sentenced to the electric chair, Chester went to his death in March 1908, still claiming that he was innocent.

Even though it was notorious at the time, the sad tale of Grace Brown and Chester Gillette likely would have faded into obscurity had it not been for author Theodore Dreiser. For years, Dreiser had been poring over newspapers in search of a crime that embodied his own personal obsessions with sex and social ambition in America. In the person of Chester Gillette, he found the perfect material for a book. The result was his 1925 classic *An American Tragedy.* The book became an enormous bestseller and brought Dreiser great fame and fortune. In 1931, he achieved even greater fame when the book was turned into a Hollywood movie by the same name later remade as the Academy Award-winning *A Place in the Sun,* starring Elizabeth Taylor and Montgomery Clift. The story of a trusting young woman and her murderous, social-climbing beau became a part of American culture.

On the evening of July 30, 1934, Robert Allen Edwards - a clean-cut, church-going, twenty-one-year-old, with striking good looks that made him very popular with the opposite sex - took his girlfriend, a homely but outgoing twenty-seven-year-old named Freda McKechnie for a drive. The young couple stopped by to visit Freda's seven-year-old niece, and then they went on to Harveys Lake, a popular resort located about twelve miles west of Wilkes-Barre, Pennsylvania.

Freda and Bobby - as everyone called him - both came from respectable families. They Lived around the corner from one another in Edwardsville, Pennsylvania, and attended the same church. The young couple spent a great deal of time together -- much more time, in fact, than their parents suspected. Besides the usual small town activities like church socials, picnics and movie dates, they passed many hours in various secluded romance spots, including the town cemetery. Despite the difference in their ages and the glaring disparity in their physical attractiveness, everyone assumed the two sweethearts would eventually get married.

Bobby, though, had other ideas. Three years earlier, he had gone off to Mansfield State Teachers College now Mansfield University , where the popular, black-haired young man was elected president of the freshman class. While there, he met a talented singer and pianist, a senior named Margaret Crain. The bespectacled brunette came from a middle-class family from East Aurora, New York. Though Margaret was, by all accounts, even less attractive than Freda, Bobby was entranced with her. Margaret was flattered by his attention. No young men had been interested in her before, and she soon succumbed to her handsome lover's charms. Before long, they had started a passionate affair.

With American still in the grip of the Depression, Bobby was forced to drop out of college in his junior year. He moved back home to live with his parents, and took a job with the Kingston Coal Co., where his father and Freda's father both worked. By then, Margaret had graduated and was working as a high school music teacher in Endicott, New York. Although separated by more than two hundred miles, they kept up a steady correspondence, sending fervent, heartsick letters back and forth. In his letters, Robert called her "my dear wife" and made pledges of future matrimony.

Bobby Edwards and Freda McKechnie

Eventually, Margaret gave Robert one hundred dollars to make a down payment on a used 1931 Chevrolet, which they nicknamed "The Bum." The car would be jointly owned, and Bobby would use it to travel to see her. Sometimes, they would meet midway for trysts at the Plaza Hotel in Scranton. Over the next year, Robert made regular weekend trips to Margaret's family's home, where he impressed her parents as a fine young man who would be a worthwhile future son-in-law.

But what Margaret and her parents didn't know was that during his time back home in Edwardsville, Bobby was still sleeping with Freda McKechnie. This affair would likely have remained a secret if not for the fact that, on July 23, 1934, Freda had gone to a doctor and learned that she was four months pregnant. When she broke the news to Bobby the following day, he agreed to do the right thing and marry her. They would elope to West Virginia. The date was set for August 1, just a week away, after Bobby received his next paycheck. Thrilled, Freda began assembling a trousseau. Many would recall later that they had never seen her so happy.

On Monday night, July 30, after a dinner at the McKechnie home, Bobby and Freda went out for a drive. Even though the sun had set and a hard rain was falling, Freda - giggling with excitement over the upcoming wedding - proposed that they go for a swim at Harveys Lake, one of their favorite trysting spots. They arrived there shortly after 9:00 p.m. and parked at a spot called Sandy Beach. They changed into swimsuits and waded out into the water.

An hour later, Bobby left the beach alone.

Early the next morning, a fifteen-year-old girl named Irene Cohen was canoeing on the lake with her younger brother and one of her friends when she spotted a woman's body, wearing an orange bathing suit, floating face-down beneath the water. Terrified, she paddled over to Sandy Beach and got two lifeguards, who plunged into the water and pulled the lifeless body out onto the sand.

The police were summoned, along with a local physician, Dr. Harry Brown, who quickly determined that the woman had not drowned. She had died from a savage blow to the back of her head with a blunt instrument. When he removed her bathing cap, clotted blood came out, and he could see a laceration on the top of her head. The murder weapon was discovered a short time later when investigators, who scoured the beach, found a leather-covered blackjack in the sand. By then, the victim had been identified as Freda McKechnie, whose parents had spent a sleepless night wondering why their daughter had never returned home from her drive with Bobby Edwards.

Within hours, Edwards had been picked up by the police on suspicion of murder. At first, he denied that he and Freda had gone to the lake at all. He told the police that after driving around for a little while, he had dropped Freda off in town. Then had gone to meet some friends whose names he could not remember. When investigators revealed that the tire tracks found at the crime scene matched the tires on his car, he sheepishly admitted that he had been lying and offered to tell "what really happened."

He admitted that he and Freda had, in fact, driven out to Sandy Beach. Even though it was raining and there were flashes of lightning in the sky, they decided to go swimming. After changing into their bathing suits, they "went into the water and waded to the float." This was a wooden platform floating on top of metal barrels that offered swimmers a place to relax in the sun. Edwards went on, "I got a notion to dive. I dove. When I came back up, my hand struck her under the chin. She fell backward and hit her head against the float." Stunned but still conscious, she had swum out farther into the water. A moment later, according to his wildly implausible account, Edwards saw "her white bathing cap disappear. I went out for her but couldn't find her. I went back, got in my car and drove away."

On the morning after his arrest, police officers took him out to the crime scene to get his version of the events once more. He revised his story again. This time, Edwards admitted that he had hit Freda with the blackjack. But he insisted that she was already dead when he hit her.

In this version of events, he and Freda had taken a rowboat out to the float. After swimming for a little while, Freda complained of being cold. As she stepped back into the rowboat to return to shore, she suddenly collapsed. Edwards tried to revive her but was unable to find a heartbeat. Panicking, he swam back to shore and ran to his car. As he climbed in, he thought of the blackjack. It belonged to his father, and he had put it in his glove box -- for protection, he said. He told the investigators, "It occurred to me that if there was some mark on Freda's body, it might look like her death was an accident and I would be left out of it. I knew Freda was pregnant. I knew she was not allowed to swim. When I returned to the boat, she was in the same position. She had not revived. I could do nothing. I put her head on my left arm and struck her on the back of the head with the blackjack. I didn't even realize what I had done, and I carried the body out to the water up to my chest and let it drop."

By this time, the investigators knew that Edwards was in a relationship with another woman and had a compelling motive to do away with Freda, who was secretly pregnant with his child. When they confronted him with all of the circumstantial evidence against him, he finally broke down. This time, he revealed the truth of the murder. He choked, "Freda didn't faint. She didn't fall and hurt herself. I had been thinking of doing this since she told me she was to become a mother - because I wanted to marry Margaret Crain. We swam for a while. We talked about her having a baby. The water was a little over four feet deep, and when she ducked down once, she came back up with her back to me. I pulled out the blackjack quick and hit her on the back of the head. I hit her with the blackjack and then I left her in the water."

After tossing the murder weapon into the lake, Edwards got dressed and drove home. He even stopped along the way at an all-night drugstore to buy some chocolate bars for his mother. Before going to bed, he hung his swimsuit on the backyard clothesline to dry. He slept soundly that night and got up and went to work the next morning as if nothing had happened at all.

No one knows which reporter first dubbed the case the "American Tragedy Murder." Newspapermen from two Philadelphia papers, the *Record* and the *Bulletin*, both claimed to have dreamed it up, as did a writer for the United Press syndicate, and a reporter from the *New York Times*. It's not hard to imagine that all of them latched onto the idea independently, since the details of this latest tragedy were strikingly similar to the case that spawned Theodore Dreiser's bestselling book and the recent film. Within days of Edwards' arrest, newspapers all over the country were suggesting that the novel - or more likely the movie version of it - had provided the confessed killer with the blueprint for his crime.

As is the case with just about every work of literature or mass entertainment that has been blamed for inciting a murder, there turned out to be no truth to the accusation. By all accounts, Edwards had never read the book or seen the film. Still, the startling resemblance between the murder of Freda McKechnie and Dreiser's fictionalized version of the Chester Gillette-Grace Brown case turned the story into a national sensation.

Dreiser himself saw the Edwards case as "an exact duplicate of the story which I had written" and wondered whether "my book had produced the crime." When the *New York Post* offered to pay him to travel to Pennsylvania and cover the trial, he eagerly accepted. On the opening day of the trial, October 1, 1934, he was one of fifty reporters who jammed into the Luzerne County Courthouse in Wilkes-Barre. The scene, he wrote, was "quite a spectacle."

The hundreds of spectators who pushed and shoved their way into the courtroom, hoping for an exciting show, were not disappointed. The questionable high point came when the district attorney read a series of Bobby's steamy love letters to Freda McKechnie. The contents were allegedly so salacious that, according to one observer, they made John Cleland's pornographic classic *Fanny Hill: or the Memoirs of a Woman of Pleasure* "look like a toned-down version of *Little Women.*"

By then, Edwards - whom the papers were gleefully calling "the Playboy of the Anthracite Fields" - had recanted his confession and gone back to his claim that Freda had died accidentally. His testimony failed to persuade the jury, and they took only twelve hours to convict him and sentence him to death.

Theodore Dreiser was unhappy with the verdict. He believed that Edwards, like his predecessor Chester Gillette, was a victim of tremendous American social pressures. Dating back to his days as a newspaper reporter in Chicago, Dreiser had "observed a certain type of crime in the United States." It was one that "seemed to spring from the fact that almost every young person was possessed of an ingrowing ambition to be somebody financially and socially." This distinctly American brand of crime, according to Dreiser, involved "the young ambitious lover of some poorer girl who had been attractive enough to satisfy him until a more attractive girl with more money or position appeared and he quickly discovered that he could no longer care for his first love. What produced this particular type of crime was the fact that it was not always possible to drop this first girl. What usually stood in the way was pregnancy."

To support this claim, he pointed to a half-dozen such murders, including the Gillette-Brown case of 1906 that had served as the basis for *An American Tragedy*. It wasn't a perfect fit, as Margaret Crain's family was not rich; she was a high school music teacher and her brother was a Baptist minister, but still, the two cases had much in common. Dreiser blamed the crimes committed by these men on American society and its "craze for social and money success." He believed that Edwards was just another in a long line of such killers. Dreiser was one of hundreds of people who wrote to Governor George H. Earle in a futile attempt to win a pardon for the condemned young man.

Just after midnight on May 6, 1935, after spending hours reading his family Bible, Edwards walked calmly to the electric chair at Rockview Penitentiary in Bellefonte, Pennsylvania. According to one reporter, he was murmuring a prayer as the black hood was placed over his head.

1934: "BABES IN THE WOODS"

Kings Gap Estate was a lovely wooded property owned by steel magnate James McCormick Cameron of Harrisburg, Pennsylvania. Cameron had amassed over two thousand acres of land about 45 minutes south of Harrisburg, where he built a thirty-two room stone mansion in 1908 for use as a summer home for his extended family. The estate, located on a slope of South Mountain in the Blue Ridge mountain range, was donated to the state of Pennsylvania for the establishment of Kings Gap State Park in 1973.

But in 1934, the eyes of the nation were focused on Cameron's secluded summer hide-a-way. It wasn't Cameron, or any of his politically connected family, that caused all the fuss. It was because of three little girls, who would become forever known as the "Babes in the Woods."

It was November 24, 1934, two days after Thanksgiving, and the weather was steadily growing colder. John Clark, the caretaker of the Kings Gap Estate, and his friend Clark Jardine, were walking through the woods on the southeastern edge of the estate, gathering a load of firewood. As they neared the edge of the property, about fifty feet from Pennsylvania Route 233, Clark noticed a stained green blanket lying on the ground. It appeared to be covering something lumpy. Poaching was common in the area, so the men at first thought that someone had shot a deer and left the stripped carcass behind. But why would poachers bother to cover a deer carcass with a blanket? It just didn't make sense. The two men walked to the spot and pulled back the rain-soaked blanket. Though it took a moment for them to process what they saw, it would be indelibly etched in their memories for as long as they lived. Before them, on a second blanket that was folded underneath, lay three little girls.

Three little *dead* girls.

The men ran to the nearest phone and called the authorities. Their ghastly discovery set off a chain of events that became one of the most sensational criminal cases of the 1930s.

When Police Chief Harvey Kunhs from nearby Carlisle arrived, closely followed by county coroner Haegele, they were better able to assess the condition of the girls. The three seemed to be huddling together, lying side by side on a blanket. The youngest of the three seemed to be snuggled in the arms of the older girl. They appeared to be well-dressed, with shoes, socks and warm coats. Taking into account the girls' matching gray eyes, freckles and light brown hair, Chief Kunhs believed that they must be sisters.

News of the discovery rapidly spread across the countryside, and hundreds of people flocked to the scene; some with ghoulish curiosities and others hoping against hope that none of their own missing children were among the dead girls. Even more people traveled to Carlisle to inquire about the girls during the days that followed.

Unable to determine the cause of death at the site, the bodies were transported to Carlisle for autopsies. Dr. W. Baird Stuart conducted the postmortem examination. He estimated the ages of the girls to be between 7 and 16. Though police had speculated that the girls may have died of carbon monoxide poisoning, the doctor came to a different conclusion. All three girls had been "suffocated to death, either by strangulation or suffocated by external means." Two of the girls appeared otherwise unharmed, but the middle age girl had been attacked in some way, though no evidence of this was recorded in the formal report. They appeared emaciated, and Stuart determined that they probably had not eaten in the 18 hours prior to their deaths. He estimated that the girls had been murdered three days earlier, on November 21.

On Sunday, November 25, the day after the bodies of the three unknown girls were found, the Pennsylvania State Police called for volunteers. They wondered if the bodies of the parents might be found in the area. The state police planned and conducted a massive search covering the whole of South Mountain. No more bodies were found. The children had been murdered and their bodies abandoned without any sign of their parents. The position and condition of the bodies were troubling to the chief investigators. They had been killed; it could not have been an accident, but it seemed that whoever had done the terrible deed must have loved them. They were posed in a gentle manner, as if they were snuggled up together in sleep, and their bodies were covered from the elements. This did not jibe with the expectations of the police. Killers did not usually care for those whom they murdered. This case would prove to have many exceptions to the norm before the questions were answered.

Photograph of the three little girls as they were found in the woods on November 24, 1934. The photograph was published in newspapers across the country in an attempt to identify the girls.

Other than the name of the killer or killers, the most important issue for the authorities was to identify the girls. They felt strongly that they could not solve their murders if they didn't know who they were or where they came from. They published the photograph of their bodies as they were found in newspapers around the country. A farmer thought the girls might be his nieces, believed to be in the custody of his sister-in-law who was estranged from his brother. They turned out to be alive and well. A woman who operated an orphanage in Baltimore traveled to Carlisle to see if they were three of the five children who had gone missing. They were not. Another woman thought they might have been her sister's daughters, but they were found to be alive and well. The police became so desperate to identify the girls that they allowed the general public to view the remains at the funeral home. An estimated 10,000 people filed past the three coffins, but no one came forward to say they knew who they were.

Just a day after the girls were discovered, John Naugle was hiking near Pine Grove Furnace, about three miles from where the bodies were located. He came across a black Gladstone suitcase that appeared to have been tossed into the woods near the road. It contained fifteen girls' dresses of three different sizes, and a school book with the name "Norma" written in a child's hand. The suitcase also contained some adult women's and men's clothing, a washcloth and towels. This discovery led police to believe that the case had belonged to the girls, and possibly their parents. The clothes were put on display and photographed for the newspapers, in case someone might recognize them. This was another dead end but they felt strongly that the "Norma" from the school book now lay in a Carlisle funeral home.

The newspaper photo of some of the girls' clothing found in the suitcase.

After a week had passed with no clue as to the identities of the Babes in the Woods, as they were beginning to be called, they were buried, but they were certainly not cast aside or forgotten. The people of Carlisle had embraced the girls and taken them in as three of their own. The Carlisle American Legion Post 101 organized a funeral, largely paid for through donations from the citizens of Carlisle. Not knowing which religious denomination the girls had been raised to follow, several of the local clergy worked together to perform the burial rites. Thousands of people attended the funeral and burial in Westminster Cemetery. Boy and Girl Scouts from area troops served as pall bearers for the three small white coffins. The girls were buried side by side, as they had died. Later, after the girls had been identified, a bronze plaque was added to their tombstone with their names and ages. Their epitaph read:

Babes in the Woods
Sleep tender blossoms, folded so close
In slumber which broken shall be
By His gentle voice whispering low
"Little Children Come Unto Me"

Preparing for the funeral procession for the three unknown girls.

Before the girls were laid to rest, casts were taken of their faces to create death masks. Police thought that as the girls had not been recognized from the photograph of them, someone might eventually come along who could recognize them from their death masks. A photograph of these masks was published in national newspapers, again to no avail.

The murder of the three little girls was not the only strange murder case in Pennsylvania at that time. In fact, on the same day, and at about the same time as the girls' bodies were found, the bodies of two adults were found just 100 miles away.

The bodies of a man and a women were found at the deserted Spring Meadow flag station on the Holidaysburg branch of the Pennsylvania Railroad, just outside of Altoona. The woman had been shot in the chest and head. The man had a single gunshot to the head. A rusty .22-caliber rifle lay on the ground between them. It was evident that the man had first killed the woman, then killed himself. No identification was found on either body. However, the police had a few clues to work with. They had found an abandoned car near McVeytown, not far from Altoona. The serial numbers had been filed off, and all identification had been removed, but the license plates were still on it. The car was traced to a man named Elmo Noakes. A search of military records indicated that Noakes had served in the Marines, and the Navy had copies of his fingerprints. The body of the unknown man was positively identified as Noakes through his fingerprints.

The license plates on the car gave the police more helpful information. Noakes had registered the car just a few weeks earlier in Roseville, California. When the police in Roseville were contacted, they questioned his extended family and discovered that he had left town earlier in November, heading east. With him were his 18-year-old niece, Winifred Pearce, and his daughters, Norma, 12, Dewilla, 10, and Cordelia Noakes, 8. The "Babes in the Woods" had finally been identified.

Over time, the police were able to piece together some of what the family had been through and where they had been. When the identifications were made and photographs of Elmo Noakes and Winifred Pearce were published in newspapers, several people came forward with stories of their encounters with the family.

Elmo Noakes' story was not an uncommon one, but the choices he made certainly were. After serving honorably in the Marine Corps, Elmo had married Mary Isabella Hayford in 1923 in Salt Lake City, Utah. Mary had a daughter, Norma Sedgwick, from her first marriage, which had ended in divorce. Elmo and Mary had two more daughters: Dewilla, born in 1924, and Cordillia in 1926. They were apparently a happy family living a contented life until Mary died in 1932 from hemolytic septicemia blood poisoning, reportedly brought on by a self-induced abortion . When Norma's father learned that her mother had died, he petitioned for custody of his daughter, but Elmo packed up the three girls and moved to California before he could be served.

Elmo settled in Roseville to be near his family. He was raising his own two young daughters and a step-daughter alone and he needed help. His three sisters and a brother, Robert, all lived in Roseville. He hired his niece, Winifred Pearce, the daughter of his older sister, to be his housekeeper and babysit the girls while he worked at the Pacific Fruit Express company. Everything seemed to be going smoothly. Elmo worked hard and was doing well at his job. He was respected by his friends and co-workers. The home he provided for his children was comfortable, and there was always plenty of food on the table. When Winifred turned 18, she moved into the Noakes home to work for Elmo full-time. This was over the strong objections of her family, who were starting to grow distrustful of Elmo's relationship with his niece.

During the fall of 1934, two years after his wife's death, Elmo quietly made some changes. First, in September, he purchased life insurance policies on his children. He already had a life insurance policy on himself, but he changed the beneficiary to his sister, Winifred's mother. At the end of

October, he purchased a bright blue, 1928 Pontiac Essex for $46. Then on November 11, the 32-year-old Noakes packed up the three little girls, and Winifred. No one knew if Winifred went along simply to help take care of the girls, or if she had become Elmo's lover. Elmo left without collecting $50 owed to him for the previous two weeks' work from his job at the express company. It was unheard of for anyone to walk away from a nice home and a steady job, as well as two weeks' pay in the depths of the Great Depression.

Elmo Noakes and Winifred Pearce

There was some speculation as to why Elmo took his family away so hurriedly. His sisters bickered, argued and fought incessantly, to the point of police involvement, and they frequently tried to pull Elmo into their disputes. As a result, his brother Robert believed that he left to get away from his sisters. He explained that his sister and her husband, Winifred's parents, did not get along, and Elmo had given the girl a peaceful home. Other family members suspected that he left so that he and Winifred could be together, something they could not do openly in Roseville around so many members of their extended family. Another reason for his leaving so abruptly was proffered by a few of Elmo's friends. They believed that the only way that he would take off so suddenly, leaving everything behind, was because he was being chased by gangsters. Organized crime figured prominently in the newspaper headlines, radio dramas, and motion pictures of the day; perhaps that's where Elmo's friends got the idea that the mob was involved somehow. In any event, they knew of no reason why gangsters would be after Elmo, but they couldn't think why else he would pull up stakes so suddenly.

The route the little clan took as they headed east is unknown. None of them had any ties with anyone in Pennsylvania, but that's where they ended up. November 17 was the first time they were known to have been in Pennsylvania. They spent the night in a tourist home in Gettysburg, registering under false names, then left the following morning. Mrs. Anna Lafauvre told the police of her encounter with the family on Sunday, November 18. She and her son were eating in a restaurant in Philadelphia. Elmo, Winifred and the three girls came in and sat down at the table next to them. She overheard Elmo explain to the girls that they only had money for one meal, and the five of them would have to share it. Mrs. Lafauvre took pity on their dire circumstances. She invited Cordillia, the youngest of the children, to eat with her and her son. The adults happily accepted, and their one meal was shared by four rather than five. Cordillia told the woman: "Daddy is looking for work. I'm kind of tired and this food tasted awfully good." Lewis Ellis, the restaurant's owner, said that he also remembered the family coming into his place. Before they left, Elmo asked Ellis if he knew of any jobs that were available. He would do any kind of work. But there was nothing to be had, and so the family left. After spending the day looking for work in Philadelphia, the family stayed the following night in a camper park in Langhorne, a suburb of Philadelphia. The next two nights, November 19 and 20 were spent in another camper park just outside of Langhorne. Everywhere they went, they continued to register under false names. The owner said they all slept in their car as they had no camper.

There is no record of where they spent the next two nights, but they likely had little or nothing to eat. The police speculated that as Noakes had found no work, he had run out of money and was becoming desperate. His friends and neighbors in Roseville described him as a kind, loving father who cared deeply for his daughters. Police believed that Noakes' desperation turned to panic and depression. He must have decided that he could not watch his daughters starve to death. He would kill them quickly to save them a drawn-out and painful death. It is unknown whether he considered wiring back home to Roseville for money from his family or friends, or if he thought of placing the girls in an orphanage. There were plenty of children with one or both parents living who were sent to orphanages during those lean times, but in the end, Elmo did neither of those things. It is unknown whether Winifred Pearce was an active and willing accomplice, or if her part in the murders was a passive one. She had to have helped in some way, as Elmo couldn't have killed the girls without help of some sort, even if it was just keeping them distracted as he killed them, one at a time.

After the terrible chore was done and the dead children were deposited in the woods, covered with their only two blankets, Elmo and Winifred climbed back into the Pontiac and drove away. Were they already planning their own deaths? That was highly likely, as everything they did after abandoning the girls' bodies led them straight down that path.

They drove east from that lonely spot in the woods of Kings Gap. Seventy-five miles later, they ran out of gas near McVeytown and abandoned the car on the side of the road. Now their only option was to hitchhike. A truck driver picked them up and drove them another hour and a half to Altoona. Once there, the couple checked into a rooming house using false names for the last time. Without a cent left to their names, there was not much they could do, and they were weak from hunger. Elmo tried to sell his spectacles, but was not able to find a buyer. They walked to a secondhand store where Winifred was able to sell her coat for $2.85. Elmo used the money to buy a rusty .22-caliber rifle and a handful of ammunition. From there, they walked along the railroad tracks till they arrived at the abandoned flag stop. They entered the station and ended their own lives with an act of murder-suicide. They had lived just one day longer that the girls.

Elmo Noakes had served his country as a Marine. His Navy records had become known after he had been identified. Regardless of his actions, the members of the Carlisle American Legion decided to take care of their comrade in arms and the woman he carried with him into the next life. Elmo was buried with full military honors in the same cemetery as his daughters, though in a different section. Just as Winifred Pearce had lain next to him as they died, she would lay next to him for eternity. The entire family would stay in Pennsylvania.

During the ensuing months, further speculation brought forward additional possible explanations as to why this otherwise kind and respectable man would take the lives of three daughters, his niece and possible lover and himself. The strangest suggestion was that the girls were killed by members of a cult. A mark seen on Norma's forehead in the death photograph of the girls was thought, by some, as a "mystical mark," but was later determined to be an injury. Another suggestion was that Noakes had become mentally ill. Imagining something or someone evil was after him, he suddenly took his family and fled to Pennsylvania. He had killed his girls to protect them from the evil. Unfortunately for those of us needing clear explanations, many of the most perplexing questions will forever go unanswered.

For a long time, Norma, the oldest of the three girls, was believed to be Elmo's daughter and her name was recorded as either Norma Sedgwick Noakes or just Norma Noakes. She was, in fact, Elmo's step-daughter, and half-sister to Dewilla and Cordelia. It took decades, but in 2004, the family of Roland B. Sedgwick, Norma's biological father, succeeded in having Norma's last name officially change to Sedgwick on all official documents pertaining to her murder.

There are many reasons why a person's spirit might linger after death, feeling trapped and tied to this world. Elmo Noakes and Winifred Pearce would have certainly had reasons to be among those who never left this earth, including infanticide, suicide, desperation, depression and perhaps even incest. They had many reasons and many fears at the end of their lives. If you were to find yourself walking along an old railroad bed, one running out of Altoona, Pennsylvania, take care and keep a close watch. You may find that you have company that you didn't expect. A man and a woman may appear, seemingly out of nowhere, dressed in old-fashioned clothes. They may seem to not notice you, and they probably won't. They share with each other a sorrow that you will not want to share. They will stand still, facing each other, clasping each other's hands. Wait quietly, as it will not be long before they fade back into nothingness. Elmo and Winifred were seen where they died for many years, stretching into decades. It may be that they no longer return as often, or it may be that there is rarely anyone in that lonely spot to witness their appearance.

It is difficult to know just who it is that haunts the woods on the edge of the Kings Gap State Park, near where Route 233 passes by. If you happen to be watching in the right place, at the right time, you will hear the sound of quiet weeping. These are sobs that seem to come from everywhere. The air in this area is heavy and thick. At times, visitors may feel heavy in their chest, hard to breathe. The sadness permeates everything until the crying fades to stillness. This section of the woods has been called haunted for decades. Scout troops camping in the woods nearby have used this spot as a test of courage. Who can sit there, alone, in the dark? Even if they don't hear gentle sobs, the feeling of sadness can be overwhelming. Is it Elmo, crying over the deaths of his daughters by his own hand? Does Winifred have deep regrets over her part in taking three innocent young lives? Is it Norma, saddened by her inability to protect her little sisters? Or is it Dewilla or Cordelia, unable to face the loss of their lives and futures? Maybe they are missing their daddy? The misery of the place will leave visitors with a lasting sense of loss.

The spot is easy to find. In 1968, highway workers erected a large, blue and yellow memorial sign to mark the location. Lest someone forget...

Note from René: The phrase "Babes in the Woods" has been used for over a century in legends and in the media to refer to children who are murdered, lost, or abandoned in rural wooded areas. The name could be no more appropriate than in the murders of the three innocent little girls: Norma, Dewilla and Cordelia.

On a personal note: as a young child growing up in the Midwest, I often thought of children, taken into the woods and left behind. To this day, I still remember the words to the haunting song sung to me as I sat on the knee of my beloved grandmother. It was a song she knew from her own childhood. Her song was not about this particular case, but instead, it was a song for all the lost children, forever in the woods. When I close my eyes and picture my grandmother's soft, kind face, I can still hear her gentle voice...

My dear, do you know how a long time ago

Two poor little children whose names I don't know
Were stolen away, on a fine summer's day
And left in the woods, as I've heard people say

Poor babes in the woods, poor babes in the woods,
Oh don't you remember poor babes in the woods.

And when it was night, so sad was their plight
The sun, it went down and the moon gave no light
They sobbed and they sighed, and they bitterly cried
Those poor little babes, they laid down and died.

Poor babes in the woods, poor babes in the woods,
Oh don't you remember poor babes in the woods.

And when they were dead, the robins so red
Brought strawberry leaves and over them spread
And all the day long, they sang this sweet song
Poor babes in the woods, poor babes in the woods.
Oh don't you remember poor babes in the woods.

1957: DEPRAVITY IN THE HEARTLAND

Even today, nearly six decades after his crimes were unearthed, Edward Gein remains one of the most depraved killers in American history. Books and films like "Psycho," "Texas Chainsaw Massacre" and "The Silence of the Lambs" used his deviance as the means to terrify several generations of readers and movie-goers. In addition, Gein is the perfect example of the horror that can lurk in the American heartland. Among the quiet woods, acres of farmland and lonely houses at the end of long dirt roads, evil can -and does - sometimes hide.

Ed Gein and the Gein family farm house, located outside of Plainfield, Wisconsin

Edward Theodore Gein grew up on a farm a few miles outside of the small town of Plainfield, Wisconsin. His father, George, was a hard-luck farmer with little talent for working the soil and a taste for alcohol. He sometimes worked as a carpenter and tanner to supplement the family's income. He also had a tendency to be quick with his fists after he had been drinking. But as rough as he was, he was no match for his wife, Augusta.

Augusta had been raised in a fiercely religious home and with her, this sort of influence developed into a raving opposition to anything related to sex. All around her, she saw nothing but filth and depravity. How she managed to become pregnant with her two sons, Eddie and Henry, remains a mystery. Shortly after Ed's birth, she forced her husband to leave the "sinkhole of filth" she called LaCrosse, Wisconsin, and move the family to what she believed to be a more righteous location, Plainfield. However, this small, God-fearing town turned out to be no better, at least in Augusta's eyes. She considered the place to be a "hellhole" and kept her two sons on the farm and away from anything she considered to be a sinful influence, namely whorish women and the wickedness of carnal love.

In 1940, George Gein dropped dead from a heart attack. Most likely, he was not sorry to go. The years spent with Augusta had undoubtedly taken their toll on him. The two boys were left alone with their mother, and soon Ed was even deeper under her terrible spell. Henry attempted to break away and have a normal life, but his rebelliousness came with a price. In 1944, he was found dead on the Gein property. It was reported that he had suffered a heart attack while trying to put out a brush fire, although this did not explain the bruises that were discovered on the back of his head.

Ed finally had his mother all to himself. In 1945, Augusta had a stroke and was confined to her bed. Ed tended to her day and night, although even his constant attentions were found lacking. Augusta alternately screamed at him and cajoled him, calling him a "weakling and a failure." He would never be able to survive without her, she constantly railed at him. Her screams would echo through the farmhouse for hours. Then she would grow quiet and call Eddie lovingly to her side. She allowed him to crawl into bed next to her, and she would whisper and speak softly to him as he slept. Ed prayed that his mother wouldn't die and leave him to face the world alone.

The most terrible event that Gein could imagine occurred in December 1945. Augusta died after suffering another, more serious, stroke. Eddie, now thirty-nine, was left alone to fend for himself. It was at this point that he began his descent into dark and unfathomable madness.

For some time, no one seemed to notice. Even in a town as small as Plainfield, Ed Gein was a loner and rarely ventured off the farm. Hidden behind the ramshackle walls of the old farmhouse, he only appeared in town when he needed to run an errand, perform some handyman chores or stop in for an occasional beer at Mary Hogan's tavern. No one seemed to think that he was any stranger than before. He had always been an odd little man, in need of a bath, but he seemed no different than he had been before his mother's death.

It would be later - after the horrors of his farmhouse were revealed - that Gein's peculiarities seemed to stand out. Local folks would later recall his barroom discussions of articles that he had read in the pulp men's magazines. These were stories of Nazi atrocities, island headhunters and sex-change operations. His jokes seemed to be a little on the cruel side, as well. When Mary Hogan, the oversized tavern owner, suddenly disappeared, Ed began kidding that she was staying overnight at his house. Mary had vanished from the roadhouse, leaving nothing but a puddle of blood behind, and many thought Gein's jokes about the poor woman were tasteless, but nothing more. Even the stories about the strange things going on at Ed's house didn't faze anyone. Some local kids, peeking in Gein's windows, spread rumors that they had seen shrunken human heads in his living room. Ed laughed and explained that his cousin had served in the South Seas during World War II, and had sent the heads to Ed as souvenirs.

Eddie Gein would never hurt anybody, the townspeople thought. He was a strange little guy who disliked the sight of blood. He wouldn't even go deer hunting with the other fellows in town. That's what everyone in Plainfield said - until Bernice Worden disappeared.

She vanished on November 16, 1957. Late that afternoon, Frank Worden returned to town from an unsuccessful day of deer hunting and stopped by the hardware store that was owned and operated by his mother, Bernice, a fifty-eight-year-old widow. Strangely, his mother wasn't there. She had apparently just walked out, leaving the front door unlocked and the back door standing open. Frank then discovered something terrifying: a trail of blood leading from the storefront to the back door. A quick search revealed a receipt that had been left behind. The receipt was for a half-gallon of antifreeze. It had been made out to Ed Gein.

Frank notified the police, and officers went to Gein's farmhouse to question him about Mrs. Worden's whereabouts. Ed had not been expecting company, as was evidenced by what they found

Left One of the rooms that once belonged to Augusta Gein. Ed sealed it off from the squalor in the rest of the house. Right The horrific state of Gein's kitchen.

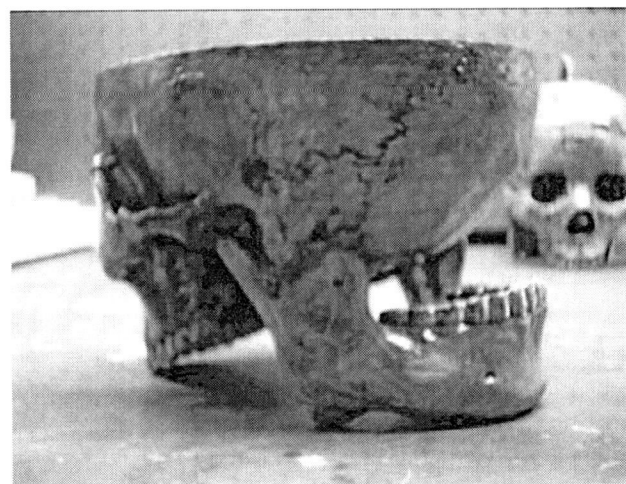

Left The naked body of Bernice Worden was found at Gein's home upside-down and dressed out like a deer carcass. Left One of the skulls, discovered by police, that Gein had shaped into a bowl.

in the summer kitchen behind the house. In the broken-down little building, they discovered the body of the missing Bernice Worden. She was naked and hanging by her heels from an overhead pulley. She had been beheaded and disemboweled, and was dressed out like a butchered deer.

The stunned and sickened officers immediately called for reinforcements. A short time later, more than a dozen lawmen were combing the farm and exploring the contents of what would become known as Ed Gein's "house of horrors." What they found that night was like nothing that had ever been recorded in the annals of American crime.

Soup bowls had been made from the sawed-off tops of human skulls. Chairs had been upholstered in human skin. Lamp shades had been fashioned from flesh, giving off an eerie and putrid glow. A box was discovered that contained nothing but human noses. A belt had been made from female nipples. A shade pull had been decorated with a pair of woman's lips. A shoe box found under a bed contained a collection of dried, female genitalia. The faces of nine women, carefully stuffed and mounted, were hanging on one wall, peering down at furniture that had been constructed out of human bones. On a table was a bracelet of skin, a drum made from a coffee can and human flesh, scattered pieces of human remains, and more. The refrigerator was stocked with what turned out to be frozen human organs, and a human heart was found in a pan on the stove.

Perhaps the most disturbing discovery was a shirt that had been sewn from a female human torso, complete with breasts. The skin had been taken from a middle-aged woman and tanned like deerskin. Gein would later confess that he often put the shirt on at night and pretended to be his mother.

The local sheriff estimated that the various body parts added up to fifteen women, maybe more. Around 4:30 a.m., after hours of sifting through the hideous and horrifying debris, the investigators discovered a bloody burlap sack. Inside it was a freshly severed head. Inserted into the ears were large nails connected with twine. The head belonged to Bernice Worden. Gein had planned to hang it on the wall as a decoration.

During the many hours of confession that followed, Gein admitted to the murders of two women: Bernice Worden and tavern owner Mary Hogan although his confession to the Hogan murder would not come until later . The rest of the gruesome remains in the house had been scavenged from the local cemetery. For the past twelve years, following the death of his mother, Gein had been slipping into the Plainfield cemetery at night and robbing graves. His macabre collection had been gathered from the bodies of the dead. In his quest, Gein had enlisted the aid of a dim-witted farmer named Gus, who had helped him dig up the bodies. Once back at the house, though, the work had all been Ed's. When Gus had been committed to an old-age home, Gein became desperate for fresh trophies. At this point, he was driven to murder.

For months after Ed was taken away, neighbor boys threw rocks at his abandoned farm house. To many, the place was seen as a symbol of evil and perversity. It was avoided at all costs. Eventually, notice was posted that the contents of the house and the farm itself would be auctioned off. The townspeople were in an uproar, but little could be done about it, or so it seemed at first. On the night of March 20, 1958, Gein's home mysteriously caught fire and burned to the ground. Arson was suspected, but no matter how it had burned, the people of Plainfield were delighted to see it gone. There were many in town who believed that perhaps even greater horrors may have been hidden away somewhere in the building.

The destruction of the home assured Plainfield residents that their town would not become a showplace for the madness of Ed Gein. However, it did not stop the procession of cars that drove slowly past the place, or the curiosity-seekers who came to witness the auction of the remaining property. Much of the rusting machinery was purchased by scrap dealers. The land was sold to a Sun Prairie real estate developer named Emden Schey. Within months, Schey would raze the charred remains of the farmhouse and re-forest the property with more than sixty thousand trees - erasing all traces of the "murder farm."

The only oddity from the sale came with the auction of Ed Gein's car, which he had been driving on the day of Bernice Worden's murder. This item started a bidding war with fourteen different people competing. In the end, the eight-year-old Ford sedan sold for $760, about $7,545 in 2014 dollars, or about twice what it cost when it was new, based on the price of the average new car in 1949. The buyer was a mysterious bidder identified variously as "Koch Brothers," "Cook Brothers" and even "Kook Brothers" from Rothschild, Wisconsin. The buyer later turned out to be an enterprising carnival sideshow operator named Boniface "Bunny" Geibbens from Depere, Wisconsin. The "Ed Gein Ghoul Car" made its first appearance in July 1958 at the Outagamie County Fair in Seymour. It was displayed in a canvas tent with huge sign on it, proclaiming, "See the car that hauled the dead from their graves! Ed Gein's crime car! $1,000 reward if it's not true!"

That first weekend, more than two thousand people paid the twenty-five cent admission to see the dilapidated automobile.

Word spread of the macabre attraction and controversy erupted. Plainfield residents, along with officials for the Wisconsin Association for Mental Health, were outraged. Geibbens, however, was thrilled with the free publicity and was unfazed by the uproar. Soon, though, his display began to run into trouble. At the Washington County Fair in Slinger, Wisconsin, the death car had been part of the sideshow for only a few hours before the sheriff arrived and closed the show down. Soon, county fairs all across the state banned the attraction and Geibbens headed south to Illinois, where he hoped to find more open-minded and perhaps more ghoulish crowds.

Eventually, interest died out and according to Bunny Geibbens' grandson, the "Death Car" is in storage on the old family farm near Pulaski, Wisconsin. It's officially retired from the sideshow circuit.

By the time Ed Gein died of lung cancer on July 26, 1984, he had become a legend, even though he spent the rest of his days locked in a mental institution. His body was taken to Plainfield and buried in the local cemetery, where, true to form, souvenir-seekers chipped away pieces of his gravestone. What was left of the stone was stolen in 2000, and recovered in 2001 near Seattle.

But Ed Gein's story didn't end in the cemetery where, years before, he had made his nocturnal grave-robbing excursions. His legend lives on. Even during his lifetime, Gein had become a creature of nightmarish myth, thanks to local legends and his Central Wisconsin reputation as the "Mad Butcher of Plainfield." This dark creature of children's imaginations was immortalized in 1960 by director Alfred Hitchcock in his film, "Psycho." The film had been inspired by a book of the same name by Wisconsin author Robert Bloch, who had fashioned the "bare bones" of the story of Norman Bates from the Ed Gein case.

Since that time, the Ed Gein story has inspired other movies, including *Ed Gein: The Musical,* books, songs among them Slayer's "Dead Skin Mask," and Mudvayne's "Nothing to Gein", documentary films, plays and even a comic book. The case was unlike anything ever experienced before in the history of America, and some would say that it began a new era, creating a thirst for death, depravity and a voyeuristic fascination with serial killers. Who can say? Regardless, the "strange little man" who lived on a lonely Wisconsin farm has never been forgotten, and his presence will doubtless continue to be felt for many years to come.

1959: A NIGHTMARE IN KANSAS
The Slaughter of the Clutter Family

The village of Holcomb sands on the high wheat plains of western Kansas, a lonesome area that other Kansans call 'out there.' Some seventy miles east of the Colorado border, the countryside, with its hard blue skies and desert-clean air, has an atmosphere that is more Far West than Middle West. The local accent is barbed with a prairie twang...and the views are awesomely extensive with grain elevators rising as gracefully as Greek temples.
Truman Capote, In Cold Blood

It was to the tiny Kansas village of just 270 people that Richard 'Dick' Hickock and Perry Smith drove on November 14, 1959. They left Olathe, Kansas just after noon and had driven the four hundred or so miles to Holcomb in an almost straight run, stopping only for gas, food and a few supplies. Supplies they would need for the evening's planned activity. They purchased rubber gloves and one hundred feet of cord in Emporia, and in Great Bend, they stopped for duct tape. The other supplies they would need, a .12 gauge shotgun and a large hunting knife they had brought with them and stowed in the trunk of the old black '49 Chevrolet that Dick had tuned up just for the trip. What lay ahead of these two men was a confluence of people and events that would shock a nation, horrify a state, terrify a prairie town, and fascinate a diminutive novelist from New York and his childhood friend, Nell. The events of that terrible night, as they unfolded, and those of the weeks and years that followed, would be forever remembered in Holcomb, and neighboring Garden City. They would have undoubtedly been remembered for decades by many people in Kansas. But because of novelist, Truman Capote, and his award winning 'non-fiction novel' which he titled *In Cold Blood,* the events would be forever immortalized in print.

Hickock and Smith were, thus far in their short lives, career criminals. Between the two, they had committed numerous robberies, frauds, and Hickock's specialty, paper hanging. Both men were well practiced at writing bad checks, but Dick had turned the practice into an art form. Though these two men committed their most horrific crimes together, and died together, they had started their lives out very differently.

Richard Eugene Hickock was born into a farm family in Olathe, Kansas on June 6, 1931. Mr. Hickock was a hardworking farmer, but with only forty acres, he was just able to support his family, and not much else. But the family, Walter, Eunice and sons Walter, Jr. and Richard, had been a loving family with a solid home. Hickock had been a popular young man during his school age years. Athletics were his forte and in high school, he had lettered in several sports. He was a good looking boy and was a favorite of the local girls. When he graduated from high school, he would have liked to go to college, but there was not enough money for that, so he got a job and went to work. He began courting Carol Bryan, a young girl still in high school, marrying her when she was just sixteen. The young couple rented a large house and had three sons in rapid succession. He held a variety of normal jobs, working as a mechanic, ambulance driver, and car painter. Then, it 1950, Hickock was in a car accident in which he received a severe head injury. He was in a coma for a short time and his face was left slightly disfigured, after which he suffered from frequent migraine headache. After growing up handsome, his facial deformity seemed to sap his confidence, leaving himself conscious and he over-compensated by behaving irrationally and getting into trouble. Constantly overspending, he and his young wife were soon in heavy debt. Hickock became restless and found another lover. When his mistress, Margaret Edna, became pregnant, he left Carol and moved in with Margaret. Carol divorced him and he married Margaret, all before he was twenty-five years old. Unable to keep up his payments and support his sons, Hickock began to indulge in criminal behavior on a regular basis, until was finally caught, charged and sent to prison.

Born in Elko County, Nevada on October 27, 1928, Perry Edward Smith was the son of rodeo performers, traveling from rodeo to rodeo as stunt riders known 'Tex and Flo'. John 'Tex' Smith was a red-headed Irishman and Julia 'Flo' Buckskin was full blooded Cherokee, a bazaar mix. Perry definitely took after his mother in appearance with straight black hair and dark eyes. The Smith's had four children, two boys and two girls. Their home life was horrific at best. Tex was an alcoholic, abusive husband and father. Flo, also an alcoholic, philandering wife and only a marginal mother. Their oldest daughter, affectionately known to her siblings as 'Bobo' did the lion's share of parenting, while their parents were either stumbling drunk or absent. On more than one occasion, Tex found Flo with another man and nearly beat her to death. When Perry was six, Flo packed the children into a car, and left for San Francisco.

Perry did not fare any better in his new home than he did in his old one. He soon began getting into trouble and was first caught stealing at age eight. His mother placed him in a Catholic orphanage where he was abused by the nuns who were supposed to care for him. They were frequently enraged by his chronic bed wetting, which plagued him for the rest of his life. Back and forth between his mother and father, he spent more time inside institutions than out of them. He joined the merchant marines at sixteen, then the army at eighteen. After serving in Japan and Korea, he was honorably discharged after which he set out to find his father. But before they could meet up, Perry was in a motorcycle accident which left him with two badly broken legs and a broken hip. After several months in the hospital, Perry was able to leave, but he would need crutches for many more months. He would walk again, but his legs were mangled and twisted and he suffered chronic pain for the rest of his life. He had no organized schooling past the third grade, but as an adult, he worked hard to self-educate himself, reading English books to improve his grammar, dictionaries to expand his vocabulary and penmanship books to learn to write with a beautiful hand.

After Perry's legs were nearly healed, he was finally able to join his father. Tex owned some property in Alaska and the two of them built a rustic hunting lodge, equipped to house and feed up to twenty guests at a time. With all their money spent on construction, they opened the lodge and waited for the money to come rolling in, but nobody came. On occasion someone would drive up to the lodge, but only for a photo, then leave. The two men, father and son, found themselves flat broke and with no foreseeable way out. With no money coming in, the two nearly starved to death. Tex blamed Perry for all of his problems and threw him out. Wandering around the country, broke and having difficulty getting by on odd jobs, he returned to his old criminal ways. He made his way to the small town of Phillipsburg, Kansas, where he and another man were caught after robbing a livestock sale barn. Following a brief stint of freedom after breaking out of the Phillipsburg county jail, Smith was recaptured by the FBI, charged, and sent to the Kansas State Prison in Lansing.

Dick Hickock was sentenced to 2-5 years for fraud and robbery. Perry Smith was already serving 5-10 for grand larceny, burglary and jailbreak, stemming from crimes he had committed in Phillipsburg, Kansas. The two men found themselves sharing a cell in Lansing. At first, Hickock didn't think much of his squat, limping, greasy-haired cell mate, but Smith admired Hickock. He saw him as masculine and seemingly full of confidence. In order to impress Hickock, Smith made up a story about killing a black man, just for the fun of it. This story worked as Hickock viewed Smith in a new light and the men became close until Smith was paroled on June 6, 1959 and told never to set foot in Kansas again.

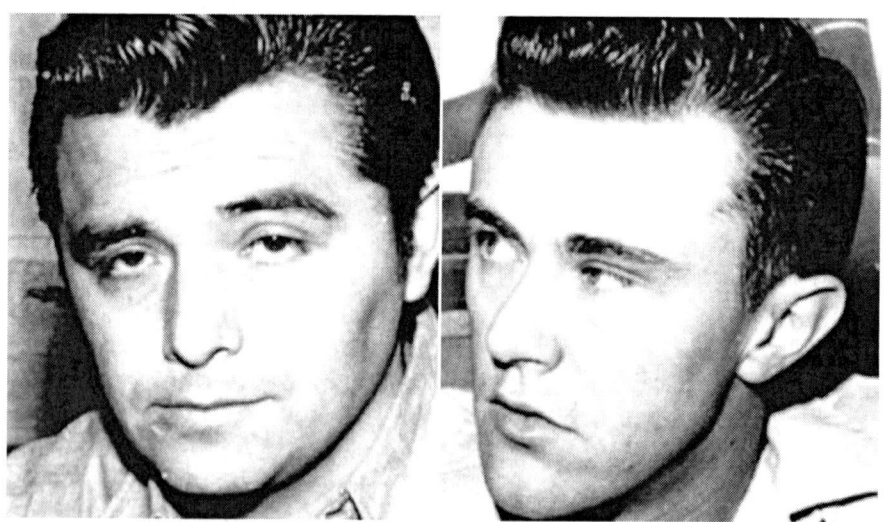

Richard 'Dick' Hickock and Perry Smith in 1959

But the fickle hand of fate was not yet finished. There was one more player to bring into the mix in the person of Floyd Wells. Wells was just another young man, who had left an unhappy home at an early age, to find his way in the world alone. Hitching rides and hopping box cars, he had made his way to Kansas. Hearing of a rich farmer needing more farm hands, he found his way onto the River Valley Farm, owned and operated by Herb Clutter. Wells worked for a full season for Clutter as a picker. He had been treated well by the Clutter family and had received a $50 bonus and a new wallet for Christmas. He was appreciative of how he had been treated, but moved on shortly after. Wells should have stayed with the Clutters, as his life afterword was nothing to be proud of. He got married, divorced and served a stint in the army, after which, he took up a life of crime, until he too got caught. In June of 1959, he was sentenced to 3-5 years for breaking and entering, and was sent to the Kansas State Prison in Lansing.

Perry Smith was paroled from Lansing and the vacancy he left behind in the cell he had shared with Dick Hickock was soon filled with the arrival of Floyd Wells. Hickock was due to be paroled in August, but that still gave the men time to strike up a friendship, where they regaled each other with colorful accounts of their exploits, both criminal and sexual. As their talks moved from bragging to historical, Wells told Hickock about a time, ten years earlier, where he had worked for a wealthy farmer in western Kansas. Clutter was his name and he had a handsome family and home. The farm was prosperous and he held as many as eighteen hired hands at a time. He would have had to keep thousands of dollars on hand just to keep the operation flowing smoothly. Hickock was intrigued, asking dozens of questions about the farmer, his family and his house. He wanted to know every detail Wells could remember. He had Wells draw out a diagram of the house and the farmyard, every barn and silo. Most importantly, he had Wells mark the spot where farmer Clutter kept his safe.

Hickock was an idea man; a schemer. As he listened to Wells, a plan was forming in his head. One that would get him out of the hole he had dug for himself. A plan that would take him from poverty and the nickel-and-dime crimes he was used to. While he had shared a cell with Smith, the two had talked of going to Mexico, buying a finishing boat and taking rich American fishermen onto the ocean to fish. They could finally have the wealth they had long deserved. With the story of the Wells' rich farmer ringing in his ears, Hickock smiled in his bunk. He knew what he was going to do. He just needed a partner. He needed Perry Smith.

On August 13, 1959, Dick Hickock was paroled from Lansing, on the condition that he live with his parents, hold a steady job, and not associate with any other Lansing convicts. All of these he swore to, as he plotted to break his word in every instance. Soon after arriving home, he went to work as a mechanic and was doing well. His parents welcomed him with loving arms and tried to keep him on the right path. But he had already written to Perry Smith in Idaho. In this letter, he told Smith about a 'cinch job' he had lined up where they were going to score a take of at least ten grand.

With some misgivings, Smith boarded a Greyhound bus in early November and headed back to Kansas, the state he had sworn never to return to. Dick picked him up at the bus station and took him home to meet his parents. He asked if Smith could stay with them till he could 'get settled' but Mrs. Hickock saw Smith for what he was, one of her son's prison buddies and she would not allow it. Smith also made her uneasy. There was just something about that man that she didn't trust. Hickock took Smith into Olathe where he took a room in the Hotel Olathe. Hickock, using his parents' name as collateral, purchased a new .12 gauge shotgun, model 300, and told his family he wanted to hunt rabbits. Their plan was not only taking shape, but was now set in motion.

Herbert William Clutter was a true self-made man. Herb started his life as the son of a humble Kansas farmer. He had worked hard and attended Kansas State College, majoring in agriculture. He returned to western Kansas, his head filled with new-fangled ideas for farming and ranching, but no money or land to use them on. He took a job as an advisor in the local agricultural service, and was able to rent some farm land. Herb was a very hard worker and was dedicated to the land. After a few short years, he was able to buy land of his own near the tiny hamlet of Holcomb.

Holcomb had suffered greatly during the depression, as most of the country had, but it was struggling to come back to life. Folks in Holcomb had a school, a Post Office of sorts, a cafe to keep local gossip alive and a gas station. The Santa Fe Railroad had tracks that ran past the edge of town carrying passengers and cargo, but it rarely stopped in Holcomb. They were a tight knit community who watched out for each other. Trust ran so deep that it was a rare occurrence for anyone to lock their doors, even at night. The nearest 'city', ten miles distant, was Garden City, the Finney County seat. Eleven thousand residents called Garden City home. Herb was a frequent visitor but he was a staunch community supporter and did as much of his business as possible in Holcomb.

In a little over two decades, Herb had amassed several hundred acres, and his farmyard held huge barns for livestock and silos to hold his grain. He was so successful, that he was hand-picked to serve as an advisor on President Eisenhower's Agricultural Board. He was known to be a fair man and was highly respected in his community and around the state. He was devoutly Christian, did not drink coffee or alcohol, and was never seen out late at night. Herb's idea of spending time with the gals and the fellas, was to attend the 4H meetings that he usually led.

At any given time, Herb had a dozen or more employees, but only two whom he and his family completely trusted. Mrs. Helm, their long time housekeeper, kept a watch over the family, Monday through Friday. Keeping an eye on the farmyard was Alfred Stoecklein. Alfred was the only employee who lived on the farm. He, his wife and their three young children lived in a tiny house just one hundred yards from the main house, just the other side of the largest out building.

As a young man, Herb had married Bonnie Fox, the sister of a schoolmate and the love of his life. Together, they had four children, three girls and the last, a boy. In 1948, he designed and built a beautiful brick ranch house on their River Valley Farm, so named for the Arkansas River that ran along their property. The house was spacious, over 4,000 square feet, and contained five bedrooms and two bathrooms, quite an indulgence in 1940s Kansas. The children were happy and much loved.

They were a relatively wealthy family, but the children were not spoiled. They each had their daily chores, and when there was extra work to be done they all pitched in. Herb and his children thrived.

The Clutter home on their River Valley Farm

But Bonnie was not as hale as Herb and lost much of her vitality, almost from the beginning of their life together. Following the birth of their first daughter, Bonnie fell into a severe bout of postpartum depression, taking years to recover. As each successive child was born, her depression worsened until, after the birth of her son, she moved from their master bedroom into one of the small, vacant bedrooms upstairs. Bonnie would never again return to the strong vital woman Herb had married. On occasion, she would leave the family, for short stays in a psychiatric hospitals, or to visit clinics for various treatments, but nothing seemed to help. Days would go by without the children even seeing Bonnie. Though she stayed in her room for long periods of time, her family would hear her sobs through the door. They did what they could, caring for her in every way they knew, and Herb did his best to be mother and father to his children.

By the Fall of 1959, the two oldest Clutter daughters were grown and had moved on to their own lives. First born Eveanna was married and living in Mount Carroll, Illinois. Ten months earlier, she and her husband had presented Herb and Bonnie with their first grandchild; a son named Tracy. Their next eldest daughter, Beverly, was busy attending nursing school in Kansas City, Kansas. She was engaged to a young biology student who was very much in favor by her parents. They were planning a large family wedding in Holcomb during the week of Christmas.

Sixteen-year-old Nancy was the starlet of Holcomb High School. She seemed to be able to complete any task asked of her and excelled in everything she tried. A prize winning baker at the Kansas State Fair, she also played in the school band and loved to make her own clothes. In academics, she was the favorite of all her teachers and a permanent fixture on the Honor Roll. Whoever said: "If you want to get something done right, ask a busy person" must have had Nancy Clutter in mind. She had been going steady with the same boy, Bobby Rupp, since she was thirteen, and seemed to be devoted to him. Unfortunately for them both, Herb had been pressuring her to break it off with Bobby, or at least to slow things down considerably. He sincerely liked the boy but he was a Catholic. Herb had raised his family to be devout Methodists, and as Nancy knew, she would never be allowed to marry a Catholic. Herb felt that the sooner they faced up to that fact, the better off they would be in the long run. But Nancy's heart belonged to Bobby Rupp, and his belonged to her. Time would tell if they would find a way to stay together. Nancy, and her best friend Susan, were looking forward to attending the Kansas State University in Manhattan together. Many a solid relationship has fallen apart when college gets in the way.

Kenyon, the lone boy in the family, was much like his mother, tender hearted and sensitive. He was tall and thin, but very strong. He had grown up working on a farm, and at fifteen-years-old, he had the physique to prove it. But he was a sensitive young man. Everyone liked Kenyon, but he had only one really good friend, and they had done almost everything together; hunting, camping along the river, and riding horses. The year before, Herb had allowed him to buy an old truck with a Model T engine to fix up. That truck was among his most prized possessions. Whenever anyone saw a cloud of dust rising off a country road, accompanied by loud hoots and yelps, they knew that Kenyon and his buddy Bob Jones were out and about.

As 1959 was moving through November, the Clutter clan was preparing for a massive Thanksgiving celebration with fifty or more relatives due to arrive, but on November 13th, Thanksgiving was still a week and a half away. Preparations for the festivities were already underway, but there was still much to do in their everyday life. On this night, the Holcomb Hight School auditorium was set for their performance of "*Tom Sawyer*", starring none other than the lovely Nancy Clutter. It was an extra special night for Nancy as her mother, Bonnie, had found the strength to leave the house and witness her daughter's performance. In Nancy's heart, she knew that she was playing to just one person in the audience, her mother. After a long line of congratulations and expressions of awe at the youngsters' portrayal of the kids from Hannibal, Nancy asked her father for permission to attend a late movie with Bobby and other friends in Garden City. Herb, typically insistent upon a 10:00 pm weeknight curfew, agreed and Nancy was off for a night of teenage fun. The rest of the family returned to River Valley Farm, Herb to his office, Kenyon to his room to read, and Bonnie to her bed.

The family was up early on the morning of the 14th. It was a Saturday so there was no school, but this was a farm family. They were used to rising early. The only one who was allowed a sleep in was Nancy, so recently the star of the school play. But by 9:00 am, she was up and busy as usual. She had quite a day scheduled for herself and she worried that she would not get everything done.

First, Mrs. Katz, who lived in Holcomb, had called Nancy, asking her to teach her young daughter Jolene how to make a fruit pie. This she happily did, then left to give another young girl a flute lesson, followed by errands for her mother. As her afternoon wound down, she found herself helping Kenyon clean up the small garden under their mother's window. Bonnie loved her little garden, but she so rarely had the energy to work in it. Knowing this, her children worked to keep it nice for her, something bright to look upon in her time of sorrow. But in mid-November, the plants were dried and brown, and needed pulling.

Herb, Bonnie, Kenyon and Nancy Clutter

Kenyon finished his chores in the morning and had spent his afternoon finishing a hope chest he was making as a wedding present for his sister Beverly. He had just put the final coat of varnish on the finely sanded mahogany. Kenyon was a skilled craftsman and he was proud of the work he had done on the chest. Waiting for the final coat to dry, he had met up with Nancy in the garden. They discussed the upcoming family gathering at Thanksgiving and their sister Beverly's wedding. They days had grown short and the temperature was getting chilly. They teenagers went inside to prepare dinner for the family.

Herb had been occupied all that afternoon with a gentleman visitor and had not left his office for nearly three hours. Although he had just had an insurance physical the week before, reassuring him that he was in outstanding health for a man of 48, he had recently become concerned about his family should something happen to him. His last two children still at home were nearly ready for lives of their own, but they would need him for a few year yet. And they there was his dear sweet Bonnie. She could not possibly make it on her own, and would never be able to handle managing the affairs of the farm. He had decided that it was time to invest in a life insurance policy. He had spent that very afternoon with his insurance agent and he had written a check for a $40,000 policy with double indemnity. Should his death be from anything other than natural causes, the policy would pay out double. The agent slipped the check into his jacket pocket, shook Herb's hand and drove away.

After the meal was finished and the dishes were washed, Bobby Rupp called to invite Nancy to a movie, but Herb said no. They had gone out the night before and that was enough for one week. Bobby was welcome to visit, but Nancy was to stay home. Bobby accepted the invitation and drove the three miles to the Clutter home. He had always been proud that his girlfriend lived in such a nice home and came from a good and proper family, but he worried about the problems their different religions were sure to cause. But that was an issue he would worry about later. For tonight he would just enjoy spending time with his girl. They watched three or four television programs in the family living room. Herb, mostly just interested in his newspaper, only perked up for two telephone calls and when the weather came on. After the news was over, Bobby rose to leave. Nancy walked him to his car, and giving him a quick kiss on the cheek, she ran back into her house. Teddy, the Clutter's collie, gave a soft woof in Bobby's direction, then walked off around the corner of the house. Bobby touched his cheek where Nancy had kissed it, climbed into his car, and headed for home. That would be the last time he would see Nancy alive.

Inside, the Clutter house was settling in for the night. Bonnie had been closed up in her room since early afternoon, but would not come out again this late. Kenyon went to his room, planning to read himself to sleep. Herb retired to the main floor master bedroom. Nancy went upstairs to her room to start her Saturday night beauty routine. She washed her hair and put lotion on her face and legs. Just before crawling into bed, she made her final entry in the diary she had been keeping for the past three years, never missing a day.

As Nancy prepared for bed, a black '49 Chevrolet was slowly rolling down the tree lined drive toward the Clutter house, headlights doused. Inside were two men; men who had driven a very long way to visit this house. They parked in the dark shadows of the trees and waited. A light was on in the hired man's house. It went out, then came back on again, then a short time later, it went out again and the little house stayed dark. The Stoeckleins had been nursing a sick child for the past two nights. The two men in the car, Dick Hickock and Perry Smith, put on the rubber gloves. They slowly opened their car doors, got out and quietly pushed them closed again. Hickock carried the knife and Smith carried the shotgun. They carefully walked to the house, keeping close to the shadows. It was 12:30 a.m. on November 15, 1959 when the men entered through the unlocked door to Herb Clutter's office.

As quietly as they could, they began their search for the safe that Floyd Wells had described to Hickock only a few months before. They had found the office, just where Wells had said it would be, but there was no safe. Search as they might, they just couldn't find it. They decided to rouse Mr. Clutter and have him show them where the safe was and force him to open it. Walking through the main floor of the house to the master bedroom, the heavy boots the men wore made a thumping sound on the hard wood floors, no matter how stealthy the men tried to be, but the household remained asleep. Hickock opened the door to the bedroom and shined the flashlight into his sleeping face. He woke with a start, and coming from a deep sleep, he must have thought that Bonnie was looking for him. His first words were "Is that you, Honey?" It wasn't Bonnie.

The men forced Herb from his bed and dragged him to his office. He was wearing stripped pajamas, but remained barefoot. They had not given him time to put on his slippers. Once in the office, he repeatedly denied owning a safe. He had never owned a safe. They were welcome to any money that might be in the house, but it would be very little. With such a large operation, he did nearly all of his business by check. He tried to explain to them that he had no need for a safe. Smith was beginning to believe the man, but Hickock became irate, punching and slapping him repeatedly. He called Herb every foul name he could think of, using his favorite; 'lying son-of-a-bitch' most often, but to no avail. He still insisted there was no safe. While Hickock continued trying to get Herb to give up the information he wanted, Smith pulled the telephone wires from the wall, and stepping closer to the door into the main part of the house, he heard floorboards creaking overhead. He stepped into the hall and looked up the stairs, where he saw a figure standing at the top, outlined by moonlight streaming through a window behind. The figure moved from his view. Smith found another telephone in the kitchen and cut the wires. While there, he noticed another purse and riffled through it, looking for money. He found a silver dollar, but it fell to the floor and rolled under the table. He got down on his aching knees and crawled under the table to retrieve the one dollar coin. As he did so, it struck him that they had driven four hundred miles for a big score, and here he was, crawling on the floor for a buck. Standing up, he headed back towards the office but found that Hickock had pulled Herb by the collar, back into his bedroom. Grabbing Herb's wallet, Hickock pulled out $40, stuffed the bills into his pants pockets and tossed threw the wallet aside.

Hickock was growing angrier by the minute. They had entered the house to find a safe stuffed with cash, then found there wasn't any cash. There wasn't even a safe! He asked Herb if his wife might have any money. Hearing the mention of his wife nearly sent him into a panic. He begged the men not to disturb her, explaining that she had been very sick for a long time and he feared a shock like this might send her over the edge. With a total lack of sympathy for his wife, Herb was forced to lead them to her bedroom. When the three men entered the upstairs hallway, it was empty and all of the doors were closed. Walking to the last door, Herb entered. Lighting the lamp on the night stand, he woke Bonnie with a voice and words as calming as he could muster. "Don't worry Honey, these men just want to know if we have any spare money. I told them they're welcome to anything we have in the house. They won't hurt us." Terrified, Bonnie began to sob into her husband's chest. Hickock opened her purse and riffled through it. Finding only a few dollars, and shoved them into his pocket and tossed the purse onto the floor.

They needed to check the other rooms on the second floor, presumably more bedrooms. But first, they had to find a way to confine Herb and Bonnie. They decided to lock them in the bathroom. Smith realized that Bonnie really was quite ill, so he took a chair from the hallway and put it in the bathroom so that she might sit while she waited.

In next room, they found Kenyon fast asleep. They woke him up. He seemed to be frozen with fear, so Hickock had to pull him from his bed and onto his feet. Wearing only a T-shirt, Smith grabbed a pair of jeans and tossed them to the boy, telling him to put them on, and fast. They searched Kenyon's room but didn't find a cent. Looking around, Smith spotted a small gray Zenith transistor radio. He liked it, so he took it. Finding nothing else of value, the men shoved the frightened boy toward the bathroom, so he could join his parents while they moved on to the next room. But before they had a chance to open the final door, a young woman stepped into the hallway. She looked at the men, and said: "Good grief, is this some kind of joke?" Nancy quickly realized it wasn't a joke when Smith shoved the barrel of the shotgun in her face and ordered her into the bathroom, along with Kenyon.

The fear that must have gone through the Clutter's minds must have been terrific, as they waited, crammed into the family bathroom while two strangers roamed around their house. Outside the bathroom, Hickock and Smith were confused as well, not sure what they should do next, when they struck upon a plan. They would tie up each of their captives and take them to different rooms in the house. They would move from person to person, waving the knife and gun in their faces, trying to scare them even more. Then, they would threaten to kill them all unless Herb would tell them where he had all the money hidden. Smith had become convinced that there was no safe and there was no stash of cash, but the situation was escalating, becoming more violent. He just wanted to get out of there, but things had gone too far to simply walk away.

The men returned to the bathroom, and pulled the Clutters out, one at a time. Hickock covered them with the shotgun as Smith bound their wrists so they couldn't fight back as they moved them around. Smith pointed the knife at Herb's throat and took him to the basement and into the furnace room. Unwilling to have the gentle man lying on the cold, dirty concrete floor, he kicked over a mattress box and told Herb to lay down on his stomach. Smith had always been good with ropes and knots. He trussed him up with the rope tied around his neck at one end, and the other around his ankles in such a way that if Herb struggled or worked to get untied, the rope around his neck would grow tighter and he would slowly begin to strangle.

Next, Smith brought Kenyon into the basement. At first, he had him in the furnace room with his father, tying his hands to a pipe overhead. After thinking better of his plan, he cut the boy down and moved him into the adjacent playroom. There was an old sofa along one wall and Smith had him lay down there. He tied the boy's hands and feet to the arms of the sofa. But as he was leaving the room, Kenyon started coughing and gagging, obviously having a hard time catching his breath. He returned to the boy and placed a pillow under his head, allowing him to breathe easier.

Next, it was Bonnie Clutter's turn. Smith took her into her own bedroom and had her lay down, where he tied her hands and feet to the bed. She continued to sob, never believing they would come to no harm. She didn't seem concerned for herself however, her tears and her pleas were for her daughter. She was convinced that the other man meant to hurt her sweet girl. Smith promised her that he would not let Hickock touch Nancy, then put duct tape over her mouth. He told Bonnie to go to sleep, and when she woke up, they would be gone and someone would come and untie her.

When Smith returned to bind Nancy, he found that Hickock had already taken her into her bedroom and had forced her onto the bed. He was sitting on the edge, stroking her and seeming to try to calm her with a soft, cajoling voice. When Smith came into the room, he stopped. Working together, they tied Nancy's feet and hands to the bed and told her to lie still as they went into the hall to talk. Once in the hallway, Hickock told Smith: "I'm gonna bust that little girl, and when I'm done, you can bust her too." Smith hated that kind of behavior and the two men began to scuffle, right there in the hallway. Smith told him that there was no way he was going to let him touch that girl. He was angry that he had to do all the work, climbing up and down those stairs on his aching legs, and all Hickock wanted to do was rape a teenager.

In the end, the two men left Nancy alone and went to the basement where the men were being held. Having grown tired of the search and the events of the night, they decided to leave with what they had. They hoped to get as great a head start as they could before the law got after them, so they wanted to make sure the men were still securely tied. Herb appeared to be quite a strong man and Hickock was worried that he might work his way free and call the police "before they had a chance to clear the county." He started to wrap Herb's entire head in duct tape, around and around, leaving only a space for his nose. The idea was that if he did get loose, he would need to pull the tape from his head and face first and it would hurt like hell. At the very least, it would slow him down. As he wrapped the tape, Hickock continued to swear and call him names, telling the man that he was damn lucky to be alive, and that if it were up to him, he would wipe out his whole family.

Smith had grown weary of Hickock's big talk and his temper began to flare. He grabbed the knife and thrust it at Hickock, telling him: "You're so damned hard, you kill him!" Hickock stopped talking and looked sheepishly at Smith, refusing to take the knife. Smith later recounted how he reacted: "I guess my mind snapped. I didn't realize what I'd done till I done it. Shoved it in an sliced Clutter's throat - God the sound, like somebody screaming under water! At this point, Dick panicked and wanted to run, but I knew I couldn't leave Clutter like that; I hadda put him outta his misery. I aimed the gun and shot - hell, he would've died anyway. Everything kinda exploded after that." Much later, Smith told KBI agent Alvin Dewey: "I didn't want to harm the man, I thought he was a very nice gentleman. Soft spoken. I thought so right up to the moment I cut his throat."

That first shot set off a chain reaction of violence. Smith charged into the playroom, place the barrel of the gun against Kenyon's cheek and pulled the trigger. Then the two men raced up the two flights of steps to the bedrooms. "I made Hickock do the shooting on Nancy and her mother; I told him I'd had enough."

After collecting the spent shells, the two men left the house through the same door in which they had entered it. With them, they took the remaining rope and duct tape, their knife and shotgun, Kenyon's little transistor radio, Herb's binoculars, and just under $50 in cash. They had averaged about $12 per life that night. Hickock turned the car around and they headed back the way they had come, fleeing in the night, away from the blood bath they had left on the Kansas prairie.

They had driven several miles down the highway, when Hickock pulled the car over near a barren wheat field. Using the knife, he dug a hole and buried the shells, rope and duct tape. With that they were on their way home, laughing and making jokes. They arrived in Olathe just before noon. They had made an 800 mile round trip, robbed a farm house and killed four innocent people in a bit less than twenty-four hours. Hickock dropped Smith at his room at the Hotel Olathe, then drove himself home. He walked into his home, propped the gun against a corner of his bedroom, put the knife on his bureau, and hugged his mother. Before he left the previous day, he had told his parents that he was driving Smith to see his sister in Fort Scott. She was holding a lot of money for him. His share of the profits when his father had sold their property in Alaska. Suspecting nothing out of the ordinary, his parents welcomed him home and they all sat down to Sunday dinner. After they had eaten, the men moved into the living room to watch a basketball game on the television. Within a few minutes, Dick was fast asleep. A wonder, his father thought. He would never have believed that Dick could sleep through a basketball game.

On November 20, five days after the murders, Hickock and Smith moved through Kansas City, visiting clothing stores, appliance stores and pawn shops. Hickock wrote bad checks in as many as twenty stores that day, as Smith acted the straight man. After they had pawned what they had bought, they had amassed nearly fifteen hundred dollars. They had their stake, and they jumped into Hickock's car and headed for Mexico where they would lie in the sun, get drunk and sleep with as many Senoritas as they could buy. They were happy men, without a care in the world.

Holcomb, November 15, 1959

Clarence Ewalt was not a religious man, but his daughter Nancy enjoyed going to church. She was best friends with Nancy Clutter and Herb was kind enough to take his daughter to church with his family, saving him a round trip drive to Garden City and back on Sundays. As they drove through Holcomb, Herb and the kids would pick up Susan Kidwell, Nancy's other best friend, then continue on to the Methodist church in Garden City. And so, just as he did every Sunday morning, Clarence drove up the quarter mile long driveway to the Clutter house at 9:00 a.m. sharp to drop his daughter off. He had a habit of waiting till Nancy was inside the house before leaving for home. His daughter ran to the kitchen door and rang the bell. The Clutters kitchen door was always open to any neighbor, but she hesitated as she didn't feel comfortable just walking in. Looking back toward her father's car, he motioned for her to try another door. Nancy moved to Mr. Clutter's office door and she knocked. The door, which had been standing slightly ajar, swung inward. Nancy looked into the quiet office and backed away. Her father was becoming as concerned as she was. It was not like the Clutters to sleep in, especially on a Sunday! He decided to drive to the Kidwell apartment to call the Clutters from their phone.

Susan Kidwell was standing at the window, watching for the Clutter's car when Clarence and Nancy Ewalt pulled up to the Kidwell's apartment building. Susan quickly called the Clutter's number but the telephone on the other end just rang and rang. Susan had no idea that the Clutter's phones lines had been cut. It was decided that Ewalt would drive both girls back to the Clutter home, as they would feel more comfortable going inside together to awaken the sleeping family. Again, he waited in his car as he watched his Nancy and Susan open the kitchen door and walk into the house. Susan recalled: "We saw right away that the Clutters hadn't eaten breakfast; there were no dishes, nothing on the stove. Then I noticed something funny: Nancy's purse. It was lying on the floor, sort of open. We passed on through the dining room, then started up the stairs. The sound of our footsteps frightened me more than anything, they were so loud and everything else was so silent. Nancy's door was open. The curtains hadn't been drawn, and the room was full of sunlight. I don't remember screaming. Nancy Ewalt says I did - screamed and screamed. I only remember Nancy's teddy bear staring at me. And Nancy. And running..."

Seeing the girls run from the house, screaming that their friend was dead, Mr. Ewalt went into the kitchen to call the police, but when he picked up the receiver, he saw that the line had been cut. He backed out of the kitchen, loaded up the girls, and returned to Kidwell home to call for help. Larry Hendricks, an English teacher at the Holcomb High School, lived with his family in the apartment directly above the Kidwell's. His wife had been out doing laundry when she rushed in, telling him that there was something terribly wrong at the Kidwell's. The girls told him what they had seen at the Clutter house. Mr. Ewalt wanted to stay at the Kidwell home with his daughter, Susan Kidwell and her mother. Mr. Hendricks felt that someone should wait at the Clutter house for the police to arrive, so he went.

Shortly before ten in the morning, Sheriff Robinson and Undersheriff Meier arrived from Garden City. Hendricks relayed the vague description given him of what the two girls and seen in Nancy Clutter's bedroom. He explained that he knew the Clutters, and was one of Nancy and Kenyon's teachers. Believing that he could be of some help, he asked if he could accompany the officers into the house. Together, the three men went into the house through the kitchen. Sheriff Robinson and Hendricks went up the stairs to the bedrooms, and Undersheriff Meier went on to search the main floor and the basement.

The first room they came upon was Nancy's. She was laying on her bed, facing the wall. The back of her head had been blown away and blood splattered the walls and furniture. There was what appeared to be cord, or thin rope, binding her hands behind her back and ankles to the bed frame. She had apparently not gone to bed yet when she was killed. She was wearing a robe over her pajamas. It did not appear to the men that she had been sexually molested.

Visibly shaken, the men backed out of Nancy's room and looked into Kenyon's room, expecting to find him in the same condition as his sister. His room was empty and seemed to be undisturbed.

At the end of the hall was the last bedroom. This room's door was the only one that had been closed. In this room, they found Bonnie Clutter lying on her back, dead; her white night gown stained a deep red. Hendricks described what they saw: "She'd been tied too. But differently - with her hands in front of her, so that she looked like she was praying...The cord around her wrists ran down to her ankles, which were bound together, then ran on down to the bottom of the bed, where it was tied to the footboard - a very complicated, artful piece of work...She'd been shot point-blank in the side of the head. Her eyes were open, wide open, as if she was still looking at the killer. Because she must have had to watch him do it - aim the gun."

In the basement, the undersheriff had discovered the bodies of Kenyon and Herb Clutter. Kenyon, still tied to the sofa, no longer had a face. It had been completely obliterated by a single shotgun blast. He had been tied in the same fashion Nancy, with his hands and tied to the ends of the sofa.

Herb, they found in the furnace room, lying face down on the floor. Hendricks again described the scene: "I took one look at Mr. Clutter and it was hard to look again. I knew plain shooting couldn't account for that much blood...He'd been shot all right, the same as Kenyon - with the gun held right in front of his face, but his throat had been cut, too. His mouth was taped; the tape was wound plumb around his head...He was sprawled in front of the furnace. On a big cardboard box that looked like it had been laid there specifically...A thing I can't get out of my head."

He wasted no time in getting the investigation started by questioning Mr. Stoecklein, the only employee allowed to live on the farm. He said that he and his wife had heard nothing that night, explaining that they had gotten little sleep for the past two nights. They had been up and down all night with a sick, crying child. He wasn't surprised that they had heard nothing. It had been a cold night so the doors and windows were shut tight in both houses, and the out buildings between the two houses would have likely absorbed or deflected some of the sounds coming from inside the big house. The man was beside himself with fear and grief.

The county sheriff quickly realized that a crime of this magnitude was well beyond his experience or his means. In very short order, he requested that the Kansas Bureau of Investigation KBI take over the case. As a result, Alvin Dewey 47 was assigned to head up the investigation. Dewey was familiar with the area and he had been friends with Herb Clutter. His experience far exceeded that of anyone else in the area. He had served several terms as Finney County Sheriff before moving on to the FBI. After a variety of posts around the country, he transferred from the FBI to the KBI and moved back home to Garden City. Even with all that Dewey had experienced and seen in his career, he was quoted as saying: "I've seen some bad things, I sure as hell have. But nothing so vicious as this." Later, speaking directly to the press, he said: "Even if I hadn't known the family, I wouldn't feel any different about this crime. However long it takes, it may be the rest of my life, I'm going to know what happened in that house; the why and the who."

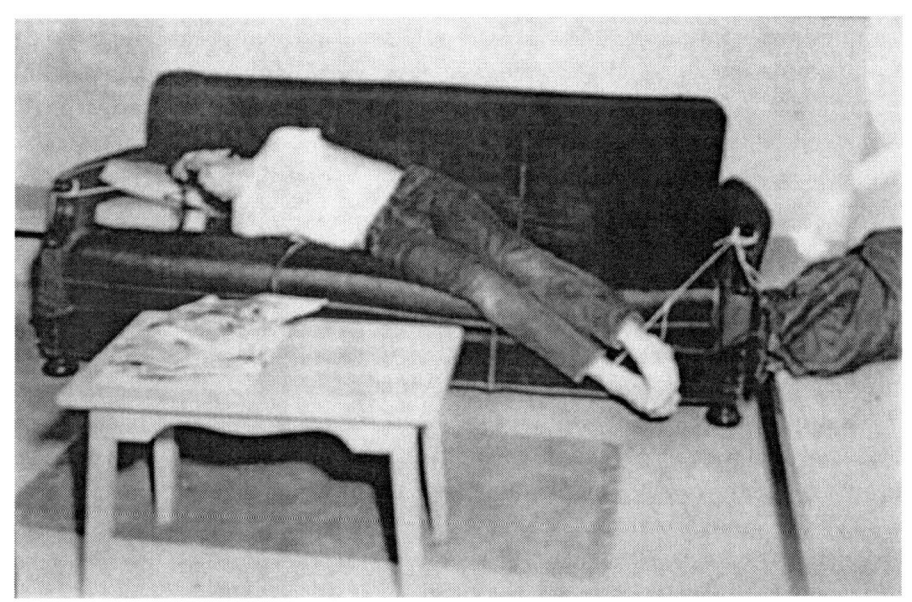

Kenyon Clutter, as he was found on the sofa in the basement.

Herb Clutter, lying on a cardboard box; his throat cut and shot in the head.

Sheriff Robinson radioed in to his office, and before long, the area around the house was filled with "more police, ambulances, doctors, the local minister, newspaper reporters and photographers."

Working from his office on the second floor of the county court house, Dewey put together a team of eighteen of the best men he knew, including Harold Nye, Roy Church and Clarence Duntz. They would work night and day, and seven days a week when necessary. A few of the men would not see their families for days at a time. They began questioning people within a few hours of the discovery of the bodies. There wasn't a minute to spare. They believed from the onset that there must have been at least two killers but they kept this belief from the press. But this theory left one overriding question in Dewey's mind: "How could two individuals reach the same amount of rage at the same time, the kind of psychopathic rage it took to commit such a crime." They also proceeded from the theory that the murders had been committed by someone local; someone who knew the surrounding landscape and were familiar with the layout of the Clutter home. That the killings were most probably done in a fit of revenge, and that Herb had likely been the target. It had appeared that Herb had been tortured before he was killed.

The KBI team questioned hundreds of people in their search for the killers. They talked to Nancy and Kenyon's teachers, classmates, friends, and anyone who worked for the school. They contacted anyone who knew or had given Bonnie any sort of medical attention or treatment. Herb's business associates, 4H associates and every member of their church were questioned. The KBI accumulated a list of everyone who had ever worked for the Clutters; farm workers, pickers, landscapers, carpenters, plumbers, electricians, mechanics...In short, anyone who had ever had any contact with any of the Clutters went on the list to be questioned. The list was long, but the men were determined to speak with everyone.

Even as the KBI was launching the largest manhunt in the history of the state, Holcomb, and the surrounding community began to grieve the loss of some of their own. The elder Clutter daughters were the first to be notified. Eveanna left her home in Mount Carroll, Illinois and headed for Holcomb. Beverly had been visiting her fiancé in Winfield, KS when she got the call. She, and dozens of relatives from Bonnie side as well as Herb's, flocked to Holcomb and Garden City when they got the terrible news of their great loss.

The funeral was held five days after the murders. The KBI men assigned to the case only took time off to attend the funeral services. The Phillips' Funeral Home in Garden City was overwhelmed with the crowds. The Holcomb High School had suspended classes for the day so that Nancy and Kenyon's friends and fellow students could attend their funeral. All told, over six hundred mourners walked past the four matching coffins on the day of the funeral. Only close family and very close friends were allowed to view the bodies before the funeral service. They were horrified at what they saw. Because of the extreme damage done to their faces, each of the Clutter's heads had been "encased in a cocoon-like cotton wrapping shading the physical appearance of each face." The cotton had been sprayed with some sort of fixative that had a type of shine to it, so the cotton sparkled like snow. Susan Kidwell was stricken when she saw her dear friend lying in her casket wearing her new red dress, the one Nancy had made for herself just weeks before her murder. Susan had helped her pick out the fabric.

The murdered Clutters, lying side by side in identical caskets.
It was, by necessity, a closed casket funeral.

With the family reverently returned to the earth, the KBI agents were back at it full time. The crime scene had been a large one, covering nearly every room in the house. And with four victims and all that blood, there were remarkably few pieces of evidence left behind. There was no way of knowing who had been the target, if anyone had been. No way to tell in what order they were killed. No fingerprints. No shell casings. No bloody palm prints. Just one bloody boot print. When the crime scene photos were developed, Dewey noticed a second boot print, creating an impression in the cardboard under Herb's body, invisible to the naked eye. One boot sole bore a diamond-shaped pattern, and the other, a distinctive cat's paw symbol. These would not help identify the killers while they remained unknown, but once they were found, these prints just might help put a noose around their necks.

The investigation was entering its second week and there were still no real leads. The KBI agents had questioned hundreds of people but no one had the slightest idea who the killers might be. Holcomb was the last place on earth that anyone would expect a crime like this to happen, and the Clutters were the last people anyone would expect to be murdered. Agent Dewey was still working from the theory that the murders had been committed by someone local, someone with an axe to grind. But as the days passed his pool of possible suspects got dramatically shallower.

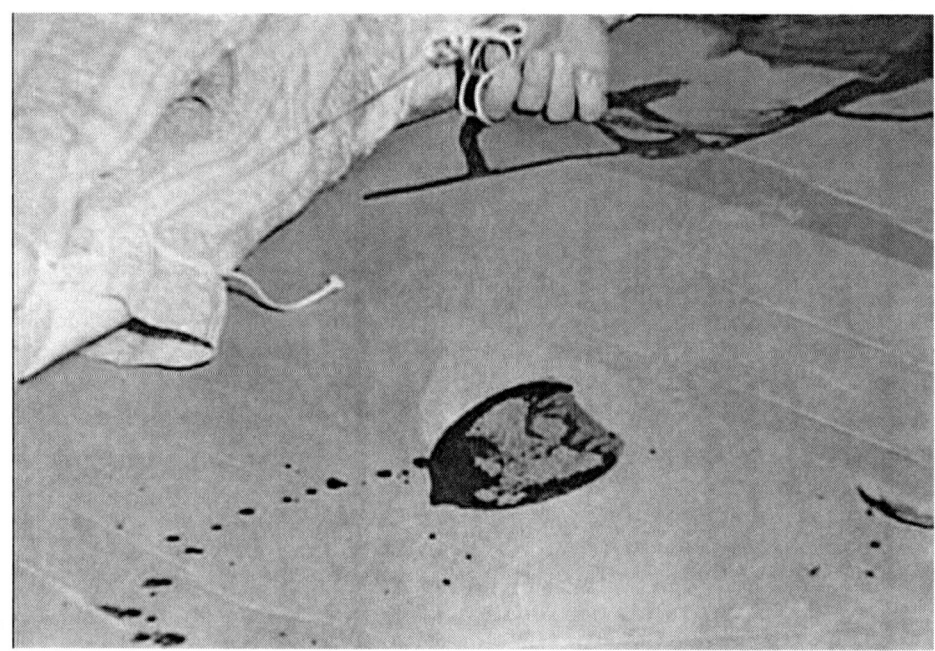

The bloody boot print found on the cardboard next to Herb Clutter's body.
The print was from Perry Smith's motorcycle boot.

While the KBI agents fanned out across the region, Hickock and Smith were traveling across Mexico at a frenetic pace. They spent time in Mexico City, then on to Acapulco, and back to Mexico City. They had burned through their money much faster than expected. Booze and women, women and booze. Hickock went as far as to try to get a job at a mechanic's shop, but was disillusioned with the offered fifty cents an hour he was offered. "How's a man supposed to eat on that!" It was time to go home, back to the good 'ole USA. The problem was that they had sold their car, and pawned almost everything they could just to pay for the dump they had been living in. The boys would be riding their thumbs home.

Everywhere he went, Smith had lugged along his old Gibson guitar and two heavy boxes of books, magazines, maps and odd treasures he had collected over the years. If he and Hickock were going to hitchhike back to the States, he would not be able to keep the boxes with him. He would not part with his guitar but Smith agreed to ship what they could not carry. The two men packed up a large cardboard box of their belongings and Smith mailed it to Las Vegas, In Care of General

Delivery. That was the one place where he knew they would eventually return. With their 'affairs' settled in Mexico, they set out for California.

Hickock and Smith traveled a strange route once they returned to the US. It seemed as if they didn't really care where they were going or where they would end up. They simply went where ever their ride would take them. If they were ever picked up by a solo person in a decent car, they had planned to attack, rob and kill the unfortunate driver, then steal the car. They never had a chance to put their plan into action though. Something always seemed to happen that prevented them from carrying it out.

Hitching one ride after another, the two men landed themselves walking along a lonely country road in rural Iowa when it started to rain. The men were soaked through and freezing cold when they saw a barn on the other side of a field. The barn was the only shelter around, so they made their way across that muddy field and forced their way inside. The barn was no warmer than the outside air, but at least they were out of the rain. Hickock rambled around the barn, looking for some random piece of dry clothing. He turned a corner to check out a horse stall and nearly walked right into the front grill of a black and white 1956 Chevy. They couldn't believe their luck when they looked inside and found the keys were in the ignition. The boys had found their next ride. As they stood there, shivering inside their wet clothes, they decided that they were going to spend Christmas on some sunny beach in Miami, Florida. But first, Hickock wanted to return to Kansas, to see his mother and father one last time.

Floyd Wells was sitting on his bunk in the Kansas State Prison. He was bored. He leaned across the narrow cell and switched on the small radio sitting on the shelf. When the radio came on, the announcer was in the midst of a big news story. Wells suddenly sat up straight, his eyes wide. The story was about a Kansas farm family who had been slaughtered in their home in the middle of the night the previous week…The Clutter family. The announcer said the police still had no leads. Wells' body suddenly slumped, his head hung low. Other than the killers themselves, he was probably the only person on earth who knew who they were. He had liked the Clutter family very much and wanted to see the killers brought to justice. However, Wells as in a precarious position. As an inmate, he did not want to be labeled a 'snitch'. It was often a death sentence to be labeled a snitch. Wells stayed remained silent. The following day however, he learned that a $1,000 reward had been offered for information leading to the capture and conviction of the Clutter family killers. This created the impetus he needed to break his silence and speak to the authorities. He discussed his dilemma with a trusted fellow inmate who was able to get a message to the warden that Wells had information about the murders.

Alvin Dewey was home getting ready for dinner when the phone rang. He closed his eyes and waited for his wife to call him. Their phone had been ringing almost incessantly since the murders. People called him at any time, night or day, to explain their theories about the murder or to share what would most likely prove to be a false lead. His men called with results of interviews or new thoughts of their own. And several times a day, someone from the media called hoping for an update. Dewey was dog tired. He had not slept for more than a few hours a night, puffed through three packs of Lucky Strikes a day, and had lost nearly twenty pounds since the that terrible Sunday morning. He was beginning to dread the sound of his ringing phone, but he still found himself racing for the receiver. It seemed as though there was never good news, but this time was different. When Dewey took the receiver, the voice on the other end said: "This might be nothing, but the time being, write these names down: Richard Hickock and Perry Smith."

The next day, Dewey drove to Lansing to interview a prisoner. He met with Floyd Wells in the Warden's office. He was about to hear a story that would break the case wide open. " I don't exactly recall how Mr. Clutter first got mentioned. It must've been when we were discussing jobs. Anyway, I told him how I worked at a considerable wheat spread in Western Kansas. Dick wanted to know if Mr. Clutter was a wealthy man. Yes, I said he was. From that point on, Dick never stopped asking me about the family. How many was they? What ages would the kids be now? Exactly how do you get to the house? How was it laid out? Did Mr. Clutter keep a safe? I won't deny it, I told him he did…right behind the desk in the room that he used as an office. Next thing I knew Dick was talking about killing Mr. Clutter."

Wells paused, suddenly seemingly unsure of himself; not sure what to say next. With the warden's urging, He continued with his story. "Well…he said he and his friend Perry was gonna go out there and rob the place and was gonna kill all witnesses and anybody else that happened to be around. He described to me a dozen times how he was gonna do it, how him and Perry was gonna tie them people up and gun them down. I never believed for a minute he meant to carry it out. I thought it was just talk, like you hear plenty of here in Lansing. Nobody takes it serious. That's why when I heard the broadcast on the radio in my cell - you know, how those Clutters were butchered - well, I didn't hardly believe it. Still and all, it happened. Just like Dick said it would. Just like Dick said it would."

When Wells stopped talking, the room fell dead silent. Dewey looked at the warden, stunned. He couldn't believe what he had just heard, but it had to be true. Now, the pieces were starting to fall into place. Turning to Wells, he quietly asked: "What made you tell us all this, Floyd?"

Wells responded immediately: "It kinda tortured me, 'spector. It's more than the reward you're offering. Nothing's worth taking the chance that others inside will know I tattled - convicts don't talk about each other, it's kinda a code – and, well…if somebody finds out, then my life won't be worth a dead coyote, will it? But a friend o' mine, he's a Catholic, kinda religious-like, when I told him about what I knew, he convinced me to speak out to somebody. I was scared, still am, but I remember Mr. Clutter and that little wallet with $50 inside. That meant a lot to me."

Dewey raced back to Garden City with the story and the names. He put his men to work, ferreting out any information they could on Smith and Hickock. That, combined with the copies of their prison records he carried back from Lansing, led him to a pretty fair biographical sketch of the two men. Dewey had learned long ago that studying a man's history can sometimes help him figure out that man's next move, or where he will end up.

KBI Agent Harold Nye was dispatched to Olathe, Kansas to talk to Dick Hickock's parents. Agent Roy Church was tasked with locating and interviewing Perry Smith's only surviving sibling;

a sister named Barbara, Bobo for short. Smith's only brother had shot himself in the head just hours after his wife had done the same. His sister Fern had died after she jumped, or fell, from a hotel balcony in a drunken stupor.

Harold Nye had discovered that Hickock had written bad checks all over Kansas City five days after the murders. He visited every store where Hickock had 'hung paper' and showed the clerks photographs of Hickock and Smith. They were both identified in every instance. Nye learned that Hickock had done all the talking and writing while Smith remained mute. Next, he visited Hickock's parents' home in Olathe, just a thirty minute drive from Kansas City. On the pretext of looking for their son for a parole violation, Nye questioned Mr. and Mrs. Hickock about his movements since he had been paroled. They were plain, caring people and they talked openly with Nye. They described how Dick had changed after his head injury, and what a good son he had been before. Mrs. Hickock spoke of her distrust of his friend from prison, Perry Smith, and how she blamed him for all the trouble he son had gotten into since Smith had arrived.

Nye listened politely as he carefully directed their conversation toward their son's activities on the weekend of November 15. They recited the tale Dick had spun; of driving Smith to Fort Scott to collect the money his sister was holding for him. They told Nye that their son had left on that Saturday at noontime, and that he had returned the next day at about the same time. Nye quickly calculated the time it would have taken the men to make the 800-mile round trip between Olathe and Holcomb. He figured they could complete the trip, with a few hours to spare. Time enough to kill the Clutters. Nye asked to see Dick's bedroom, if they didn't mind. When Mrs. Hickock opened her son's door, Nye nearly caught his breath. Propped up in the corner, was a .12 gauge shotgun, and on the dresser lay a large hunting knife. Quickly regaining his composure, Nye asked if the gun belonged to Mr. Hickock. "No, that's Dick's gun. He likes to hunt rabbits." Nye backed out of the room and closed the door, leaving the gun and knife where he had seen them. He would not risk getting probable evidence tossed out of court because of an overanxious and illegal search and seizure.

Agent Nye drove to the KBI office in Kansas City and called his boss, Alvin Dewey. He had news...Big news! First, Hickock and Smith were on a road trip the night of the murders, and the time line fit the murders. Second, Nye had actually seen a .12 gauge shotgun and hunting knife in Hickock's bedroom. Third, Hickock and Smith were back in town. They had returned and Hickock was up to his old tricks, writing bad checks. They had enough to bring the men in for fraud, at the very least. But their excitement was to be short lived. By the time the KBI had discovered that Hickock and Smith had been back in Kansas City, they were already on their way to Florida. The investigators never had a chance. The search would continue.

Dewey knew that just because they didn't have their suspects locked up, it didn't mean that they couldn't gather the evidence they would need to convict them when they finally had them in handcuffs. Perry Smith's sister, Barbara, was found and interviewed. She was entirely cooperative and answered everything she could, which wasn't much. She had not seen or heard from her brother in over four years. As far as she knew, he didn't know where she lived and she wanted to keep it that way. She told the investigator that she was frightened of her brother and had been for a very long time. He promised to keep her whereabouts a secret from Smith.

Knowing human nature as he did, Dewey believed that like bad pennies, Hickock and Smith would show up again, returning to places they knew; places where they were comfortable and in their element. Through a series of discoveries, uncovered by relentless police work, Dewey and his men learned that the men had stolen a car in Iowa, driven it to Kansas City and had replaced the Iowa license plates with stolen Kansas plates. And the prize...They had a full description of the car and the Kansas plate numbers. With this information, Dewey put out an 'all-points bulletin' on the car in every city men were known to have spent any time. They had also obtained a warrant to seize the shotgun and knife from the Hickock home. Christmas was fast approaching and everyone involved with the case hoped for their own Christmas miracle...Smith and Hickock behind bars.

Smith and Hickock were indeed behind bars; the kind of bars that served alcohol. They had finally made it to Florida and checked into a hotel in Miami Beach. Hickock, always thinking himself the ladies' man, enjoyed spending time on the beach, hustling women, young and old. Smith on the other hand, was not a fan of the beach. He was embarrassed about his twisted and scarred legs, he would not go without full length pants in public. He wouldn't even take off his boots and socks. Feeling conspicuous in the sand, he preferred to stay around the hotel. It didn't take long for the men to run out of money again. Broke and bored, they checked out of their hotel on December 19 and drove north. This is significant because on that very same date, a young farmer, his wife and two small children were shot to death on their farm near Sarasota, Florida. Smith and Hickock's close proximity to these murders, the date of the murders, and a similarity in victims would later cause Florida police to wonder if they had bloodied their hands again as they passed through their state. But that is a story for another time...

The vagabonds had been able to keep hold of the car they had stolen, but they were having trouble keeping gas in the tank. After leaving Florida, they crisscrossed their way through adjoining states as they generally headed west, picking up hitchhikers who were willing to pay for enough gas to get them where they were going. At one point, while driving through Texas, they discovered that there was money to be had by picking up discarded pop bottles, lying on the side of the road just waiting to be picked up. After a long afternoon and night of ditch picking, they had collected over 400 bottles, getting them enough money to carry them all the way to Las Vegas. Hickock knew of a cabin style motel where they could hold up for a while. They had been driving for five days straight.

On December 31, a black and white 1956 Chevy Bel Air with Kansas license plates pulled into a parking space in front of the Las Vegas Post Office. A short, dark haired man walked out of the Post Office carrying a large box that the post master had been holding in the General Delivery storage room. The man loaded the box into the back seat and climbed into the front passenger seat. Before the driver had time to start the car, both men felt the cold steel of a revolver pressing against their cheeks. Un-noticed by either of the men, a police car had pulled in just a few spaces from where their Chevy was parked. Officers Ocie Pigford and Francis Macauley of the Las Vegas Police

Department had spotted the car they had been watching for all week and the license plate matched the numbers on the "hot sheet." Pigford and Macauley were about to make the arrests of their lives. Without firing a shot, they had Perry Smith and Dick Hickock in handcuffs. Inside the box that Smith had carried out of the Post Office, the officers found, among other things, two pairs of boots. One with a diamond pattern on the soles and on the other pair, cat paws. If the officers had arrested the men just a few minutes earlier, they would have missed two vital pieces of evidence. Hickock and Smith had been back in town for less than an hour.

News of the arrests traveled through Kansas with lightning speed. Barely taking the time to pack a suitcase, Dewey, Nye, Church and Duntz were in a car speeding toward Las Vegas. Dewey had called ahead, requesting that Hickock and Smith be kept apart and he wanted them to worry. He didn't want them working out a story, but most importantly, he didn't want them to know the true nature of Dewey's suspicions. For now, all they were to know was that they were to be interrogated for fraud and parole violations.

Agents Nye and Church questioned Hickock in one interrogation room while Agents Dewey and Duntz questioned Smith in another. They started questioning the men at two in the afternoon and continued well into the night. At first, both men were cool and relaxed, answering every questions, almost proud. At a predetermined time, the agents in both rooms sprang the question: "What do you know about the Clutter murders?" and watched for their reactions. The truth was written all over Smith and Hickock's faces. They had their men; the search was over. The next morning, the grilling continued on what would have been Nancy Clutter's seventeenth birthday. The irony was not lost on the agents.

Hickock was the first to break. He confessed to everything they had done; before, during and after the murders. He described to the agents the roll he had played in the crimes, but insisted that Smith had done all the killing. When Smith was told that Hickock had confessed, he hung his head in disgust, but refused to confess himself. Both men waived extradition to Kansas so the transfer between states would happen quickly. The KBI agents kept the men separated by driving them back to Garden City in separate cars, each riding with the men who had originally questioned them. On the long drive back, Smith finally opened up and delivered his own confession to Dewey and Duntz. His account matched Hickock's in nearly way, except for the actual killing. Smith admitted to killing the father and the son, but said that Hickock had killed the two women.

The men were still kept away from each other, even in the Garden City jail. In order to do so, Hickock was held in one of the cells for men, and Smith was held in the one cell they had for women. The wheels of justice turned very quickly in the 1960s. Hickock and Smith were to be tried together for the same crimes. Jury selection was held on March 22, 1960 and the trial started the next day. Another irony of timing was hard to miss. The Clutter's farm machinery and livestock was auctioned off on March 21, the day before the jury was selected for the men who had killed the Clutters. Both men entered the same plea; not guilty by reason of temporary insanity. The two surviving members of the Clutter family, daughters Eveanna and Beverly were not present for any of the court proceedings. The family was represented by only one person, Arthur Clutter, Herb's brother. Arthur told anyone who would listen that he wanted to watch as those two boys were hanged.

Perry Smith is escorted into the Finney County Courthouse by two KBI agents.

After a string of witnesses, including Floyd Wells, the county coroner, FBI agents and KBI agents, ballistics experts, evidence experts, and a series of doctors who proclaimed both men sane, the prosecution rested its case on Friday afternoon. It had taken three days. At ten o'clock on Monday morning, the defense presented their case. By noon, the court had adjourned and the jury was charged. They deliberated for forty minutes and returned a verdict of guilty on all counts. Judge Tate looked straight at the two men standing before him and sentenced them to be hung by the neck until dead.

The next day, Hickock and Smith were transferred to their new homes on death row in the Kansas State Prison. They were back in Lansing. Their stay was to be brief, with their execution date set for May 13, 1960. But May 13 came and went and they were still on death row. Through a series of appeals, three more execution dates passed, October 25, 1962; August 8, 1963; and February 18, 1965, and the men still lived. Then, their last chance at life was denied when the Kansas Supreme Court ordered that Richard Hickock and Perry Smith were to be executed between midnight and 2:00 a.m. on April 14, 1965. There would be no more stays.

April 14 was cold and rainy. The Kansas State Prison's execution chamber was not much more than large warehouse-like structure on the far side of the prisoners' baseball field. In the far corner of the warehouse was a tall, stout wooden structure that served as the prison gallows. Present for the execution, in addition to the warden and the executioner, was a member of the press, the prison doctor, the prison chaplain and the four KBI agents who had been the most responsible for the capture and conviction of two murderers. Alvin Dewey, Harold Nye, Clarence Duntz and Roy Church had all requested to be present for the executions. No relatives of the murdered Clutters were present to witness the hangings. Arthur Clutter had chosen to stay home.

Richard 'Dick' Hickock was the first to be led into the warehouse, with his hands shackled to a thick leather belt strapped around his waist. Seeing the four agents, he went to each and shook their hands, then mounted the stairs of the gallows. When asked for any last words, Hickock looked out across the small cluster of witnesses and said: "I just want to say that I hold no hard feelings. You people are sending me to a much better place than this has been." The executioner quickly fitted a light black hood over Hickock's head, tightened the noose around his neck, and sprung the trap door, just as the chaplain called out: "May God have mercy on your soul." Dick Hickock dropped straight down, his descent stopped with an audible 'crack' as his neck snapped. It was twenty minutes before the doctor declared him dead at 12:41 a.m. Ten minutes later, Hickock's corpse was loaded into a waiting hearse and driven away.

Minutes after the Hickock's body was removed from the warehouse, Perry Smith was led in, wearing the same belt and shackles. Just as he had done throughout his trial, Smith was chewing gum. He paused when he saw Dewey standing near the entrance. He winked at Dewey and walked on. At the top of the gallows platform, Smith stated to no one in particular: "It would be meaningless to apologize now, but I do apologize." Then he went on to explain that he didn't believe in capital punishment; that he might have been of some value... The executioner repeated his grim process in preparing the prisoner for execution; the fitting of the hood, the tightening of the noose, and the loud thud as the trap door dropped. Perry Smith was declared dead at 1:19 a.m. and his body was taken away in a second waiting hearse. The witnesses quietly filed out of the building and went home.

No one came forward to claim either Smith or Hickock's bodies. Perry Smith's remaining family wanted nothing to do with him while he was alive, and they certainly wanted nothing to do with him after he died. Hickock's father had died of cancer shortly after the trial. His mother had lost the farm, and was left destitute. She spent her remaining years, living with various relatives. His brother was still alive, but he had spent the years following the trial trying to distance himself from the stigma of being the brother of a mass murderer. Both men were buried by the state, although $250 was paid toward Smith burial by the military for his service in Asia. They were interred in the

Mount Muncie Cemetery in Lansing, Kansas. The same cemetery where all the bodies of all unclaimed inmates are buried. And there they rested, until they were both disinterred in 2012, just long enough for DNA samples to be extracted, then reburied.

Truman Capote had been writing the story of Herb, Bonnie, Nancy and Kenyon, Hickock and Smith for six long years, ever since a short, 300 word article about the murders was printed in the New York Times. Shortly after the story came to a dramatic conclusion with the execution of the killers, his literary work, *In Cold Blood* was published in 1966 to rave reviews and awards to follow. Capote had risen to the pinnacle of his profession, but he was a broken man. Many of his friends believed that he had never fully recovered from the experience.

The Clutter home had been an important part of this saga, and that role continues to this day. Shortly after the farm auction in March of 1960, Eveanna and Beverly sold the land and the house to Mr. Bob Byrd, a business man from the east. Byrd owned several large farms and spent very little time at River Valley Farm. Shortly after the publication of In Cold Blood, the story slated to be made into a movie starring Robert Blake and Scott Wilson. When approached by the producer and director for the movie, Byrd agreed to rent to the house for the location set for the family and murder scenes. Released in 1967, the movie had an added chill factor when the audience realized that they were watching the actors murder and be murdered in the same rooms where the actual murders had taken place. Even the photographs on the walls were of the real Clutter family.

Byrd owned the house for thirty years but spent very little time there. His son daughter-in-law live there for the last few years, until Byrd committed suicide, thankfully somewhere else. In 1990, the house, a detached garage and seven acres was purchased by Leonard and Donna Mader, a Holcomb couple. Both Leonard and Donna had clear memories of the Clutter murders, but they had spent time in the home, and appreciated its size and location. Looking past the house's morbid history, the couple moved in, believing that no one would remember that history. They were very wrong. They soon learned that people were still interested in the site of the murders made famous by Truman Capote. During any given week, between five and twenty five sight-seers will wander onto their property, usually snap a few photos, then leave. Occasionally though, the intruders will actually come up to the house and peer in the windows.

After living in the house for a short time, and experiencing the unwanted visitors, the Maders decided to embrace history in the interest in their home. They opened the house up for tours and charged $5 a head. This plan only lasted a few months as people in Holcomb, and relatives complained that the practice was disrespectful and downright ghoulish. After receiving numerous pieces of hate mail, and tiring of keeping the house neat and tidy every minute in case someone might want a tour, they stopped.

Donna has described the home as warm and welcoming. Her children and grandchildren have spent countless happy hours with their parents and grandparents. The basement playroom that was the domain of the Clutter children, continues as the playroom for her grandchildren, despite the fact that Kenyon Clutter was brutally shot there. She had denied for years that anything 'supernatural' ever happens in the house, but visitors tell a different story. Nancy Clutter has remained where she died. She has been seen and heard numerous time, roaming the upstairs rooms and hallway. Her presence is in no way menacing, merely sad. In her old bedroom, and the place of her death, things are found mysteriously moved from place to place an on occasion, a young woman's sigh is drawn softly through the air. The Maders have converted her bedroom into a computer room. Donna said: "We used to have a bed in there, but the kids won't sleep in there."

Kenyon seems to have remained as well, but in the basement. He too is tied to the place of his death. No one has ever admitted to seeing Kenyon down there, but he seems content to rattle around, banging and tapping. Perhaps he is working on another project for one of this sisters. It is heart breaking to think that the youngest of the victims are still unable to find peace.

More than fifty years after the night Dick Hickock and Perry Smith entered that darkened house, few of the people involved are still alive. The house made famous by Capote's book and two movies still draws the curious and the kooks, psychics, ghost hunters, kids on a dare and gangs. Will the passage of a few more decades allow people to see the house as just a house, or will it forever be the Clutter murder house? Only time will tell for those who remember, but hopefully, the passage of time will finally see Nancy and Kenyon at peace.

1959: "YOU CAN T GO IN THERE --THEY RE ALL DEAD!"
The Walker Family Murders

Don McLeod was devastated, exhausted...and worried. He knew that the glaring eye of suspicion was focused on him. As a rule, the first person to find a murder victim, or in his case, victims, is also the first to be suspected of the killings. Sitting in a car outside the home of his good friend Cliff Walker, he had been grilled by Florida State Attorney Mack Smiley for over an hour. McLeod repeated softly, "The itty bitty boy – he called me Uncle Don – was shot." He didn't know how fortunate he was that he had not seen little Debbie, just 23 months old, lying face-down in the bathtub.

Had it really been just that morning that he had walked into that horrific scene inside his friend's house? That he had found Cliff, his wife, Christine, nicknamed "Tilly," and their two children murdered? It still seemed like a nightmare to Don, one that he dearly wished he could wake from. When he was finally allowed to leave, he walked into his house, hung his head and said, "They're all dead." His wife thought he meant the hogs...

And so began the longest day that Don and the many men prowling around the Walkers' small wooden house and dooryard could remember. It was a clear but chilly Sunday morning. Christmas was just five days away. The year was 1959.

Cliff, 25, and Christine Walker, 24, had both grown up in Arcadia, Florida, and had met in DeSoto High School. Christine was a pretty girl with soft brown curls, whose ready smile showed off a gold-capped front tooth. Those who knew her in her teenage years remembered her as having been "very well built" and that she would have "given Marilyn Monroe a run for her money." She was an outgoing, flirty girl who had the pick of the boys who were vying for her attention.

Christine grew up poor. Her father had deserted the family and her mother took in other people's laundry. Christine and her younger sister, Novella, got jobs at a McCrory's five and dime store to help out, and to earn a little spending money. Other girls, those from middle-class families, might dream of going away to college, or getting a glamorous job as an airline stewardess and seeing the world, but Christine knew what her future held for her; it was the same as that of most of the other girls in her graduating class. She would marry right out of high school and start a family, spending the rest of her life caring for her husband, children and home. It would be nothing special. But she had been special in high school. She had been head drum majorette for the school marching band. This had been the highlight of her short life, and she clung to it dearly. Her majorette uniform was her most prized possession. When visitors came to her austere little house, she would often take it out from where she kept it carefully folded in her cedar chest and show it off, saying that she was saving it for when she would pass it on to her own daughter someday.

Christine in her drum majorette uniform

Cliff, a tall, lanky young man, was different from the other boys at school. He was quiet. He loved the outdoors and enjoyed working hard. He smoked but rarely drank, and when he did, it was always in moderation. He was not the type to get into trouble. Cliff was the serious sort that Christine knew would make an attentive and hard-working husband.

And so the young couple got married. Within two years, Cliff had a job working for the wealthy Palmer family. One of the perks of the job was a house where they could live rent-free. It wasn't anything fancy, but they didn't mind. Not many young couples barely out of high school had their own house. Soon after, little Jimmy was born. A year after that, Christine brought home the daughter she had dreamed of, a beautiful little blonde darling they named Debbie.

Other than sporadic visits from friends, and the occasional family cookouts, the Walkers' life was a quiet one. They lived at the dead end of two miles of dirt road, roughly a mile and a half northeast of Osprey, Florida. Cliff was a modern-day cowboy. He and his buddy Don McLeod both worked as cow hands on the 14,000-acre Potter Palmer Ranch, which took up most of southern Sarasota County. The Walkers lived on one end of the ranch and the McLeods lived on the other, in another of the small houses that came rent-free to ranch employees. The job didn't pay well -- only $55 per week for hard work from dawn to dusk -- but Cliff loved working outdoors, and he'd always dreamed of being a cowboy. By the end of 1959, he and Christine had been married five years. They had lived in the little house at the end of the road for more than three of those years. It was the only home their children had ever known.

Left Cliff and Christine Walker's wedding picture
Right Cliff, Jimmie, Christine and Debbie shortly before their deaths.

Cliff's salary left very little for extras. Their home was simple, having not much more than what it took to get by. The rooms were sparsely furnished, but the young family had what they needed. When they could save up a little extra spending money, they usually treated their children. They didn't have much to spend on "fun" for themselves, but they did pass many Saturdays at local rodeos, where Cliff competed in the calf-roping competitions. Cliff's only real vice was that he was a hard-core smoker. He had to have his Kools; he bought them by the carton.

With Cliff off working all day, Christine occasionally found herself lonely at the end of that long dirt road, their nearest neighbor a mile away. She had talked about this feeling of isolation with her mother, but said that she knew her husband and children were happy there. This didn't mean that Christine was a prisoner in her home, however. She and Cliff were still able to visit friends and family, and Sarasota was only a short drive away.

As 1959 was drawing to a close, and Christmas fast approaching, the young family was preparing for the holiday. They already had a Christmas tree set up on their enclosed porch. Although it was not yet decorated, Cliff and Christine had managed to put a few brightly wrapped gifts for the children under the tree. They were excited, planning a holiday trip to Arcadia to spend Christmas with their families. Christine had written her mother that they would arrive on Christmas Eve. She was excited to show off the new red dress she had bought for little Debbie. She missed her mother, sister and young half-brother and was looking forward to seeing them.

December 19th was a Saturday, and the Walker family had plans for a very full day. Cliff put on his best jeans and shirt, and his "going out" cowboy hat. Christine was wearing a pretty red and white dress with matching high heels. She liked to look good and was proud of her figure, still slim and shapely after two babies. In fact, some of the Walker relatives thought Christine enjoyed the admiring glances that she got from men a little too much. Debbie, just a month shy of her second birthday, looked sweet with her blond locks curled. Three-year old Jimmie got into the spirit of things by insisting he wear his green cowboy hat, just like his dad.

Christine had been upset with Cliff for the past few days. He had apparently gotten into a fairly serious brawl on Thursday, which was not like him. But in the end, she was determined that they would enjoy their day out. First, they drove into Sarasota to look at cars at Altman Chevrolet. Cliff was considering trading in their car for a newer one. After test driving a two-tone 1956 Chevy 210 sedan, he passed it up; he just wasn't happy with it. Next, they went to a nearby hardware store, where the children were treated to cookies, candy and drinks. At their next stop, Cliff and Christine purchased the groceries and supplies they would need for the coming week.

The last stop was a visit to the McLeod family. Christine enjoyed visiting with Lucy, Don's wife, and the children played well together. After a short while, the men left to check on some cattle in the Cow Pen Slough area of the ranch. Christine and Lucy spent the time chatting while keeping an eye on the children.

When the men returned, they stacked a load of cattle feed in the ranch's Jeep for Cliff to drive home. Christine said she wanted to get home to put the groceries away and get supper started. The kids loved riding in the Jeep, so they begged to stay and ride home with their dad. Christine said goodbye to the McLeods and left alone in the family car about 3:45 p.m., heading for home. Taking into account the twenty-minute drive between houses, Christine should have arrived home about 4:05

p.m. The McLeods invited Cliff to stay a while, but he'd had a long day and wanted to get home. He and the kids piled into the Jeep and left about fifteen minutes after Christine. But they didn't go straight home; instead Cliff drove to the nearest filling station and put air in the Jeep's tires. It was later estimated that he would have arrived home no later than 4:35 p.m.

Early the next day, Don McLeod hooked the horse trailer up to his old GMC pick-up, loaded up his horse, and headed out for Cliff and Christine's house. He arrived well before sunrise to collect Cliff because the two of them were going hunting. A few days earlier, they'd been digging a fire line on the ranch when they spotted some wild hogs rooting in some brush. They made plans to go out early Sunday morning to hunt them down. Wild hogs were dangerous and not the kind of animals you wanted roaming around. Don and Cliff agreed to leave before dawn, hoping to catch the hogs returning to wallow in the mud after a night of foraging.

When he arrived at the Walker house, Don was a little surprised that Cliff was not yet up and about, and that he smelled no coffee brewing. If Cliff said he would be ready, then he would be ready. He could be counted on like clockwork. However, on this crisp December morning, Don thought he had caught Cliff sleeping. He chuckled and planned to give him a good teasing about it.

But as he looked around the dooryard, he began to grow worried. It really wasn't like Cliff to not be ready when he said he would be. Something just didn't seem right. The cattle feed was still in the Jeep, the windows were down and Cliff's loaded rifle was still on the window rack. Don knew his friend would never leave those things out all night. Both doors to the little house were locked, and this too was strange. Don banged on the door to the enclosed porch but received no answer. He made a circuit of the windows, shouting and banging on them. Still no answer. The house was quiet and dark, and he could see no one moving inside. Now he was really worried and panic was setting in. Using his pocket knife, he slit the screen on the porch door and popped the lock. The inside door was unlocked. He went in and flipped the light switch.

The light bulb shone dimly into the adjoining room, and Don's worries were confirmed. The first thing he saw were Christine's bare feet. She was lying on her back in the doorway between the living room and dining room with her skirt pulled up around her waist. Don's first thought was that the pilot light had gone out on the old gas stove and they had all suffocated. Stepping farther into the room, he was hit with the realization of what had really happened. Cliff lay on the floor just inside the living room door, with little Jimmie lying next to his legs. Large pools of blood had formed around their heads. All three, Cliff, Christine and Jimmie, had been shot dead, and blood was soaking into the bare wooden floorboards.

McLeod backed quickly out of the house and ran for his truck. Realizing that the horse and trailer would slow him down, he jumped into the Jeep and headed into Osprey to call for help. He first went to the pay phone outside the IGA grocery store, but the store was closed and he had no money for the phone. He quickly drove to the local cafe, which was just opening up, and asked the cook if he could use the phone. He told him, "There's some people who have been hurt, and I want to call the law." Having no phone, the cook gave him a dime to make the call. Back at the pay phone outside the grocery store, Don was finally able to call the Sarasota police department. The dispatcher told him to call the sheriff's office instead. Panic-stricken and frustrated, McLeod yelled into the phone: "Don't you hang up on me because I don't have any more money. They're all dead!"

Had it not been for the horrors within the house, the scene outside might have looked slightly comical. It was by far the largest number of people ever assembled at the home of Cliff and Christine Walker. Sarasota County Sheriff Ross Boyer and many of his deputies were the first to arrive, at about dawn. They were soon followed by several police officers from DeSoto County, Lee County and the Florida Sheriff's Bureau. Soon after, fingerprint and ballistic experts arrived at the scene. Someone brought in bloodhounds to search the area around the house. What appeared from the outside to be chaos, turned out to be exactly that. Inside the Walker house, four people lay dead, all murdered.

With the rush to the crime scene, and the large number of people arriving within the first few hours, the blunders started immediately. The Sarasota County Sheriff's Office typically chased down drunk drivers and poachers. They didn't have much in the way of investigative training or equipment, including a functioning camera. Needing crime scene photographs to be taken as quickly as possible, Sheriff Boyer recruited the local newspaper photographer to take pictures in exchange for inside information. As a result, along with the many police, deputies, and crime scene experts, a newspaper reporter and his photographer were also wandering through the house and yard. Another problem was that with so many vehicles driving right up to the house after the initial call went out for help, any tire tracks or footprints that the killer or killers left were obliterated. There was little evidence collected from inside the house. Sadly, it will never be known how much other evidence may have been missed, compromised, filched or destroyed with so many people walking through the scene.

Christine had been beaten and raped on her son's small bed before she was killed. She had been shot twice in the head while still on the bed, but her body was found lying in the doorway between the living and dining rooms. Cliff was lying lifeless on the living room floor. He had been shot in the face, the bullet entering the corner of his right eye. He was found flat on his back as he had fallen, cowboy hat still on his head. The coroner believed he was dead before he hit the floor. Three-year-old Jimmie was lying near his father's legs, dead. He had been shot in the head three times. Amazingly, it appeared that he had not died instantly. Maybe the saddest of all was Debbie, who had not yet reached her second year. A pool of blood near Christine's body was later found to belong to the little girl. A trail of blood led detectives to the bathroom, where they found Debbie's body, floating face-down in the bathtub. She had been shot once in the head and then drowned. Even the most seasoned of the police officers at the scene were stunned by what they saw. Several officers had to leave the house until they could regain their composure. Many of them were seen with tears on their cheeks before the day was over.

The evidence inside the Walker home was sparse, but the devastation was tremendous. Detectives found one of Christine's high-heeled shoes, covered in blood, on the floor of the enclosed porch. The other shoe, also bloody, was in the living room. A brick that was used as a doorstop for the dining room door was also bloody, but there was no sign that it had been used as a weapon. An apparent bloody fingerprint was found on the bathtub faucet, and on little Jimmie's bed was a bloody pillow that was covered with a quilt, as if to hide the blood. One brown hair and one long blond hair were found in the living room. A tear strip from the cellophane wrapping on a cigarette pack was found on the living room floor. The strip was a different color than the ones on Cliff's packs of Kools. Other than these, the most significant piece of evidence that was discovered was a bloody footprint, identified as a cowboy boot print. Much was made of this print, trying to relate it to another family murder case. However, years later, it was discovered that a deputy had accidentally stepped in a pool of blood and left the print himself but had been too embarrassed to admit his mistake. Lastly, there were seven .22-caliber slugs left behind: one in the wall of Jimmie's bedroom wall, one in Christine, one in Cliff, three in Jimmie and one in little Debbie.

After every possible analysis of evidence that could be done was done, and after hundreds of interviews and over one hundred polygraph tests, the police were able to develop what they believed was a good theory as to what had happened inside the Walker house that afternoon of December 19, 1959.

Christine Walker had left the McLeod house before her husband and children, so she arrived home alone. According to several friends and family members, she had parked the family car in an unusual place, next to where she would normally have parked. The police believe that this is because someone was already there when she arrived at the house, and had parked in her usual spot. They further believe that the person must have been known to her, and she may have invited him inside without suspecting what was about to happen. There was evidence that once inside the house, she went about her normal routine. She took the time to hang up her purse in the kitchen, put the groceries away, and place the Christmas card they had gotten from Don and Lucy McLeod that afternoon on top of the refrigerator where it could be easily seen.

What happened next is unclear. Perhaps the visitor, finding Cliff wasn't home, decided it was a good time to make advances toward Christine. She apparently resisted, and the situation got ugly fast. Christine was punched in the face. She desperately fought back, using the only weapon at hand: her high heeled shoes. As the shoes were found in two different rooms and covered with blood, she may have been able to injure her attacker before being subdued. Ultimately, they ended up in Jimmie's room on his bed, where the attacker beat and raped her. He pointed the gun at her head and pulled the trigger. His first shot only grazed her, leaving a crease across her skull just above her hairline. Seeing that Christine was still alive, he pulled her into a sitting position, placed the muzzle of the gun pointing straight down at the top of her head, and fired again. Christine fell back onto the bed, dead. The attacker then pulled her off the bed and threw a quilt from the bed over the pillow, hiding the blood. He grabbed another quilt and wiped the blood from Christine's legs.

For some unknown reason, the killer began dragging Christine into the living room but stopped part way. It was at that point, police believe, that Cliff and the kids drove through the gate, possibly startling the attacker into dropping her where she was later found. Cliff may have been surprised when he saw another vehicle parked in front of the house because he got the kids out of the Jeep, but didn't unload the cattle feed in the back, as he normally would have. He must not have sensed trouble because he left his loaded rifle in the Jeep when he went into the house.

Cliff never had a chance. He probably never knew what happened. He was shot immediately as he walked through the living room doorway, falling dead, flat on his back. A single slug had entered his brain, just at the corner of his right eye. Now, only the children remained alive. Jimmie must have been next. Following the belief that the killer was no stranger to the Walker family, the children would have to die as well, fearing that they would be able to identify him. The killer placed the muzzle of his gun just inches from Jimmie's head and fired. Jimmie dropped to the floor but he wasn't dead. The blood around his body was smeared. It looked as if he had thrashed around and dragged himself a short distance to be near his father where, after two more shots to the head, he had curled up and died.

While Cliff and Jimmie were being murdered, Debbie must have crawled to her mother. The pool of her blood that was found there indicated that Debbie was near her mother when she, too, was shot in the head. Like her brother, she survived the first shot, but she was not shot a second time. It is unknown if the killer was out of ammunition or if the gun jammed, but Debbie came to a very different end than her parents and brother. Lying on the floor, bleeding, Debbie was carried into the bathroom. An old sock had been stuffed into the broken drain and the tub was filled with about four inches of water. She was placed face-down in the water and drowned. Police theorized the killer held her down till she stopped moving.

With the entire Walker family dead, the killer had time to do as he wished, but it took a while for the detectives to determine just what that was. What they did know was that he walked out of the house, taking his weapon and a few mementos with him, including a pocket knife belonging to Cliff and the children's wrapped Christmas presents. He locked the door behind him, and seemingly disappeared into thin air.

A few days after the murders, Christine's mother in Arcadia received two more blows. First, she received a letter from Christine, telling her when they would arrive on Christmas Eve and how much she missed her. As it happened, Christine, Cliff, Jimmie and Debbie were buried on Christmas Eve. If that wasn't bad enough, a few days after that, a truck pulled up outside her home and unloaded the few possessions belonging to Christine, including the cedar chest where she kept her prized majorette uniform. When the chest was opened it was empty. No one had seen the uniform. Other family members who were allowed to enter the Walker house noticed that the only thing that the young couple had hung on their walls - their framed marriage certificate - was missing.

A few months after the murders, three women found a pile of bloody clothes stashed in an old shed a few miles from the Walker house. Included were two shirts, a skirt, a blouse, a pair of pants and a man's handkerchief, all belonging to Cliff and Christine. Could the killer have taken these items with him to help clean off the blood from his clothing?

These three discoveries served to reinforce the police theory that the murders were committed by some local man, someone known to the Walkers. Could a stranger possibly have known of the special love Christine had for her majorette uniform? Why would a stranger take Cliff and Christine's marriage certificate? How could a stranger know about the shed where the bloody clothes were found? There were many questions, and almost no answers.

There were suspects, lots of them. Wives suspected husbands, cousins suspected cousins, neighbors suspected neighbors, brothers suspected brothers, and two daughters thought it might have been their father. Of this growing unease in their community, one person noted that they used to live in a place where people waved at each other when they passed in the street. But with the focus of the search being on a local person, the community turned against itself, and everyone viewed his neighbor with suspicion and distrust.

Don McLeod, by virtue of being the person who found the bodies, was placed at the top of the list of suspects. He was one of the first to take and pass a polygraph test. The list of suspects grew quickly, as detectives had time to interview more of the Walkers' friends and family members. At one time, there were nearly 200 names on that list, but eventually, that number dwindled down to the most likely.

There were several names that came up of men who were not terribly likely, but very interesting just the same.

Mike Cutter was on the list because he had a reputation of being peculiar. He also owned a .22-caliber firearm, and was said to have carried a photograph of Christine.

Clay Cross was suspected for a time because his ex-wife said that in the early 1950s, he had shot her with a .22 rifle. He had also been arrested for beating an ex-wife and a former mother-in-law with a crowbar. He was provided an alibi by his new girlfriend, who happened to be his dead brother's wife.

Butch Dennison was on the list because a woman told a deputy that Butch not only lived near the shed where the bloody clothes were found, but that he had threatened to kill the Walkers. She further explained that his father had concealed his guilt by burying his bloody cowboy boots. Both Butch and his father passed a polygraph test.

Delose Smith's ex-wife suggested that he was the murderer because he had once talked to Christine, and that he had tried to have sex with her teen-aged daughter. Though the accusations were flimsy, detectives tried to interview Smith but he refused to return from Tennessee, where he was then living.

Mosby Henry Fulton made the list because he had been arrested several times for rape and for fondling young girls. It was even suggested that he had raped a woman in front of her wheelchair bound husband. One has to wonder if this was true, why was he free to continue his raping and fondling?

Cliff's sister had married a man named Ozie Youmans. Ozie had, at one time, made sexual advances toward Christine. He had served two years in jail in the nineteen-thirties for assault and attempted rape. He also passed a polygraph and was cleared.

The strangest suspect may have been Stanley Mauck. Mauck worked for the electric company as a meter reader, and had visited the Walker home once a month to read their meter. In addition to knowing the Walkers, he was also mentally ill. He began seeing a psychiatrist because he was having trouble fighting off a nearly uncontrollable urge to kill his wife and children. Mauck had no problems or issues with the Walkers, but he came under suspicion because he also read the meter of a murdered man in Sarasota. In his case, coincidence caused fingers to be pointed at him, but no other link was ever found to tie him to either murder.

Of the more likely suspects, there were several names that stayed on the list the longest. Some have been cleared over the years, while others remain viable.

The man who seemed to be the best fit was Wilbur Tooker. At the time of the murders, he was 65 and retired from the railroad. He was a bitter man, much of his bitterness stemming from the fact that he got a $101 pension check each month, but had to pay his ex-wife $75 in alimony. He was the Walker's nearest neighbor, living one mile from their house. Early on, he had been a welcome guest in their home, but over time, he had worn out his welcome by making sexual advances toward Christine, even going as far as grabbing her and attempting to fondle and kiss her. After she told Cliff about the things he had done to her, Cliff became enraged and wanted to beat him up. But after cooling down, Cliff warned Tooker to stay away from their house "because he couldn't behave like a gentleman." Over a dozen of Christine's friends and family told the detectives of her fear of Tooker. The police learned that he had been out of town for part of the day, but he couldn't account for the time in which the murders had taken place. With all this, they still were not able to directly tie Tooker to the murders. He died in 1963 in the Veterans Memorial Hospital in Bradenton and was buried in Illinois.

Another of the chief suspects was Curtis McCall, only 21 at the time of the murder. His brother called the police, informing them that Christine and Curtis had dated in high school and that they were having an affair up to the time of her death. He was positive that his brother had killed the family. Curtis had a history of violent behavior and had owned a .22 rifle. Sheriff Boyer and a deputy went to Americus, Georgia, where he was living, to interview McCall. He denied dating Christine but did say he had seen her a few weeks before the murders. He said Cliff was with her at the time. He agreed to take a polygraph test and passed on everything but the question: "Have you withheld any information from the law enforcement officers about the Walker murders?" Today, McCall's whereabouts are unknown.

The third most likely suspect was Elbert Walker, Cliff's cousin. Elbert knew the family well as he and Cliff had been as close as brothers growing up. After Elbert had been discharged from the military earlier that year, he had lived with Cliff and Christine for over a month. He said they had gotten along very well during that time. He had been suggested to the police as the possible murderer by several members of his immediate and distant family. They recalled how he had acted strangely on the day the crime had been discovered. He was seen in Osprey acting peculiarly, looking as though he had had a rough night. He went so far as to ask a gas station attendant for directions to the Walker home, which was strange as he had been there several times for family cookouts and had even lived there for a time. Upon arriving at the Walkers' place, he raced to the door, trying to force his way in, but was stopped by deputies who told him, "You can't go in there...They're all dead." Elbert then retreated to Christine's car, leaned down across the hood and cried, with his head on his arms.

Elbert's family thought he was behaving very strangely at the funeral, wailing and sobbing uncontrollably. He fainted twice during the ceremony, the second time when he passed Christine's coffin. Many of those in attendance who knew Elbert believed he was faking his sorrow, and this made them suspect that he might have done the deed himself. They thought he might have become infatuated with Christine while living with her and Cliff, and had returned to act upon his feelings. They further theorized that she had rebuffed him, and he became enraged and killed them all. In 1962, the police brought Elbert Walker back from where he was working in Ridgely, Tennessee, to the Sarasota County Sheriff's office. They questioned him thoroughly before offering him a polygraph test -- which he passed. Despite the results of the polygraph, many members of the investigating team were not convinced of his innocence and Elbert remained a suspect.

The last suspects of note have become criminal celebrities of a sort. Perry Smith and Richard Dick Hickock, two transients who were paroled from the Lansing State Prison in Kansas, became suspects in the Walker murders after they were arrested in Las Vegas, Nevada, on December 31, 1959. They had been sought for the brutal murders of four members of the Clutter family in the early morning hours of November 15, 1959 - just thirty-five days before the Walker family murders -- outside of Holcomb, Kansas. Herb Clutter, a prosperous wheat farmer had had his throat cut and was then shot in the head with a shotgun blast. His wife, Bonnie Mae, daughter Nancy, and son Kenyon, all bound and gagged, were then killed with shotgun blasts to the head. The murders of the Clutter family during a home invasion were later made famous with the 1966 publication of Truman Capote's *In Cold Blood* and the subsequent movie of the same title. Smith and Hickock had become household names.

Within a day of their arrest, both Smith and Hickock confessed to the murders with one exception: Smith said that he and Dick had shared in shooting the Clutters, but Hickock blamed Smith for all of the murders. They were returned to Kansas where they were questioned in greater detail about the planning of the intended robbery, the actual murders, and where they had been over the past month and a half.

The pair were both forthcoming about their movements after the Clutter murders. They had traveled several thousand miles between the murders and their arrests, including a stop in Miami, Florida, after having stolen a car in Tallahassee. In fact, they checked out of a hotel in Miami Beach, just four hours south of Osprey, on the morning of December 19th, the very day of the Walker murders. The men said later that they had read about the Walker killings in the newspaper and had joked that some "lunatic" had probably read about the Clutter murders and decided to copy their actions.

There were certainly similarities between the Clutter and Walker murders, the most obvious being that in both cases, a farmer and his wife and their two children were killed while living on an isolated ranch. Authorities in both Kansas and Florida wondered if Smith and Hickock might have more than just the Clutters' blood on their hands. Alvin Dewey of the Kansas Bureau of Investigation KBI conferred with Sheriff Boyer in Sarasota. They decided that there were too many similarities between the two crimes to be mere coincidence. In both cases, everyone in the house had been killed. They had all been shot in the head the Clutters with a shotgun, the Walkers with a .22-caliber rifle or handgun . There had been a boot print left at both crime scenes, though it was later determined that the print left at the Walker scene was that of a deputy. Semen had been found on Christine Walker and Nancy Clutter, although Nancy had not been raped. Most importantly, Smith and Hickock could have been in the vicinity of Osprey on the day of the murders.

However, there were just as many inconsistencies. The Clutters had never met Smith or Hickock but evidence pointed to the Walkers being killed by someone known to them. Consideration for their comfort had been shown toward the Clutters, but not so with the Walkers. And perhaps most importantly, the Clutter murders were the result of a planned robbery of a wealthy farmer, taking only money or small items that could be easily pawned. In the case of the Walkers, they were quite poor and had very few possessions. No one could have mistaken them as people with anything of value to steal. The only things taken from the Walker home were Christine's majorette uniform, a framed marriage certificate neither of which has ever been recovered , a pocket knife, the children's wrapped Christmas presents, and a pile of random clothing that was likely used to mop blood from the killer's clothing.

The KBI provided Florida investigators with copies of Smith and Hickok's fingerprints. Both men, having immediately confessed to the Clutter murders, vehemently denied killing the Walkers. They further denied that they had ever been near or through Sarasota as they traveled north. Sheriff Boyer made the trip to Garden City, Kansas, where Smith and Hickock were being held pending trial. He personally questioned both men, though there is no official record of their meeting, and the KBI administered another polygraph test concerning the Walker murders. Both men passed, and their fingerprints did not match those found on the Walkers' bathtub faucet. Sheriff Boyer returned to Sarasota and told his men that he had sat across from the pair of killers face-to-face and felt satisfied that, "They didn't kill the Walkers."

Smith and Hickock were executed in 1965, but doubt whether they truly didn't murder the Walkers still lingered with some.

In 1960, Sheriff Boyer received what at first seemed to be a great windfall: a confession. Serial killer Emmett Monroe Spencer, dubbed the "Dream Slayer," confessed to the Walker murders from his death row cell in Florida State Prison in Raiford. He seemed to have inside, detailed knowledge of the killings, but after three years of careful investigations and hundreds of man-hours, Sheriff Boyer announced that he was discrediting Spencer's confession, calling him an "informed liar." It turned out that Spencer was in another state in December 1959, and that he had gleaned all of his information about the murders from newspaper articles and detective magazines.

Sheriff Boyer at first stated that he was sure that they would solve the Walker case quickly. Later, he stated that he hoped that the case would be solved by the time he retired. As he was retiring from office, he noted that his new wish was that the case would be solved within his lifetime. Sadly, this was not to be.

In 1987, Max Skeens, the Sarasota Sheriff's Office's polygraph expert, became concerned about the validity of the more than 200 polygraph tests that had been administered during the Walker murder investigation over the past 28 years. He explained that the polygraph machines of the era were essentially worthless. And if that wasn't bad enough, he said that the training in use of the machines was just this side of worthless. According to Skeens, the training consisted of a ten-minute lesson from the machine salesman. He considered all of the department's polygraph tests from the 1960s and even many from the 1970s to be of no value. This information prompted a new round of tests with all the remaining suspects that could be located, using the most up-to-date machines and highly trained technicians. Of the main suspects, Don McLeod and Elbert Walker both willingly accepted the invitation to be retested, and both men passed completely. Of the other two prime suspects, Wilbur Tooker was dead, and they could not locate the whereabouts of Curtis McCall.

The case was no closer to being solved than it had been before.

True Detective ran a detailed story about the Walker murders, including murder scene photographs.

The Walker case is the longest-standing cold case in Sarasota County, but it has not been forgotten. Over the first fifteen years, as many as nineteen officers or deputies worked full-time on the case. After that, the case was reviewed routinely, but no one worked it full-time. As the years continue to roll by, the Walkers have been resurrected by numerous newspaper articles, mostly on the anniversary of the murders. Occasionally, these articles bring in a tip or two, but thus far there is still no resolution.

Lt. Ron Allbritton, a detective in the Sarasota Police Department and a distant cousin to Cliff and Elbert Walker, became determined to get the case solved before he retired. He had grown up hearing about how his relatives had been brutally murdered. He had also heard the whispers that the family suspected another of their cousins, Elbert, as being the murderer. It was as if the case had haunted his family and the community for over forty years. In 2004, he took action that resulted in DNA extraction from semen evidence taken from Christine's clothing. The state agreed to test the evidence, but because it was a cold case, it took more than a year before they could test the material. In 2006, they were able to develop one complete DNA profile and one partial profile. The next step was to collect DNA samples from suspects to test against the profiles.

Following contact with the *Sarasota Herald-Tribune*, DNAPrint Genomics, a local lab, agreed to develop DNA profiles of any suspect samples that were submitted, free of charge. This dramatically sped up the process. The first two suspects profiled were Don McLeod and Elbert Walker, both still living and both still suffering after nearly fifty years of being under suspicion. Both men were cleared as a result. Elbert said that he had no idea that his own family had suspected him; he thought it had only been the police. He said that he forgive anyone who had suspected or accused him, then added "Thank God for DNA!" Twenty more samples have been tested with no matches found. The case remains unsolved.

Unsolved but not dropped. In 2012, Sarasota police detective Kim McGrath delivered a sealed document to the Kansas Bureau of Investigation, requesting that the skeletal remains of Perry Smith and Richard Hickock be disinterred so that DNA material, in the form of dried bone marrow, could be extracted. Her hope is that it would be possible to develop DNA profiles to compare with the DNA profile of the Walkers' murderer. She stated that she "felt it in her gut that these men were guilty." Smith and Hickock were buried in the Mount Muncie Cemetery, near the Lansing State Prison in Kansas. The bodies of all executed prisoners left unclaimed by their families were buried there . The KBI complied and the disinterment took place, away from TV and newspaper cameras. The material was extracted and the bodies were reburied the same day. After testing, it was publicly announced that a match could not be made because the extracted DNA material was too degraded to develop a full profile. Despite the inability to provide a match, both men could not be ruled in or ruled out...so the suspicions continue.

Little remains of any of the key locations associated with this horrific crime. The Palmer Ranch has been subdivided and sold off to developers. Don McLeod's former home site now sits under a McDonald's parking lot. As of 2006, the humble home of Cliff and Christine Walker and their two children had been for many, many years an unrecognizable pile of rubble. That was soon to change, as the land was slated for development. There would be nothing physical left to mark where the young family once lived and hoped and dreamed. There are few reminders left. A niece of Christine's still cares for her cedar chest, wishing that it still contained her aunt's prized majorette uniform, but that's about all there is.

The murder case has long grown cold, but it remains open. As generations of retiring detectives pass the seven binders of materials on to younger detectives, hoping that fresh eyes will find something they missed, the Walkers' memories are kept alive. An older detective once said that looking at the binders feels like Cliff and Christine are there in the room, pushing and prodding, hoping the case will someday be solved and they can then rest easy, with their babies at their sides.

1969: MURDER IN DREAMLAND

If you were going to write a script for a "B" horror movie, here are a few suggestions: First, the victims should be an attractive young couple, the girl still in her teens. In keeping with traditional camp-fire horror stories, have the couple parked on a desolate back road known for being a lovers' lane. They're snuggled up together, all cozy, when they are kidnapped by... well, let's see... how about a motorcycle gang! Make these guys really scary-looking, with cruel, hard faces and long, shaggy beards. The gang should have an intimidating-sounding name, like the "Pagans." Then, put the young couple through hours of terror in the back of a panel truck, as one of the Pagans drives the truck around a bunch of dark, creepy country roads. Throw in the gang rape of the girl while her boyfriend watches helplessly. The whole thing could end with the young couple's gruesome murder. Make the location for the murder scene an old abandoned amusement park. And to give it that retro feel, set the night of terror in 1969.

If you don't want the movie to end there, you could throw in a few courtroom scenes. Have the bikers turn on each other so that two of them get to walk free. Then, add a final scene, where one of the guys who got away with the crime becomes a well-to-do businessman who shoots and kills a teenage boy years later, and finally goes to jail.

Too much, right? A movie like that would never make it to the big screen, probably not even as a straight-to-video "B" movie. There's just way too much going on. Too many story angles. Crazy story lines and characters. No one would believe it because it could never happen.

But it did happen - every single part of it.

Dreamland Park was a small amusement park in a rural area in Berks County, north of Reading, Pennsylvania. It was an odd place to build an amusement park, out in the woods, in the middle of nowhere. There seems to be no clear record as to exactly when the park opened, but a good guess would be in the mid-1930s. To be sure, Dreamland was no Disneyland Disneyland had yet to exist, remember? but it was a nice little place, surrounded by a large stand of shade trees. There were only a few simple rides, including a carousel with its own building. There were concession booths for food and games of skill, a roller rink, and a midget racecar track. A popular spot in the evenings was a large theater, where local and touring bands would play on weekends. If all this excitement was just too much, visitors could relax in the charming picnic grove.

This was the official face of Dreamland Park, but it wasn't where the real money was made. The park's real business was an illegal gambling racket. Ralph Kreitz, Dreamland's owner, had buildings set up for the sole purpose of housing card games and gambling devices. The largest of these was the Dreamland Clubhouse. Years later, the clubhouse would shelter a group that was very different from Depression-era gamblers looking for to make a big score.

Eventually, Ralph's operation was busted up by the police. With the illegal gambling operation shut down and the gamblers gone elsewhere, he wasn't interested in keeping the park open. Dreamland Park closed in the 1950s. Eventually, the property changed hands. By the late 1960s, some of the park buildings were abandoned and had fallen into disrepair while others found new uses. The few houses and apartments were rented to couples and families. The old Dreamland Clubhouse became another kind of clubhouse, one that housed the newly formed area chapter of the Pagans Motorcycle Club. The Pagans were classified by the FBI as an "outlaw motorcycle gang." Founded less than a decade before, they were still building their reputation. As a result, they were frequently involved in violent conflict with the Hell's Angels, and other less well-known clubs. The Pagans did what any outlaw bikers worth their salt did by trying to instill fear in all who encountered them.

James Eways had lived a privileged life in Sinking Spring, just a ten-minute drive east of Reading. He came from a wealthy family, but his aspirations proved to be unsavory to his parents' tastes, although there was reason to believe that not all of his father's business associates were on the level. In 1969, Eways' father, Musa Eways, had owned the defunct Dreamland Park for a few years. He was either renting the old clubhouse to the Pagans, or simply allowing them to use the building as their chapter headquarters for free. James Eways spent quite a bit of time at the old park, and followed the gang's escapades with longing. As he entered his twenties, he became a wannabe Pagan, doing his best to be accepted into the fold. James was eventually delighted to be assigned the gang name A'rab. He was on his way to becoming a full member!

Already a full Pagan member, Leroy Stoltzfus had grown up under vastly different circumstances from Eways. Raised on a farm in Leola, Pennsylvania, his family were strict Mennonites, and his father was a bishop. There are many different Mennonite groups, each with its own bishop. As soon as Leroy was able, he left his distinctly unexciting life among the Plain People and enlisted in the Air Force. After being discharged from the service, he slowly migrated back to his home state, where he entered with gusto into a violent lifestyle. Between frequent brawls and general lawlessness, and his love for riding motorcycles, he soon fell in with the local chapter of the Pagans and given the nickname "Elroy." He was twenty-four years old in 1969 and fully involved in the gang life.

In early August of 1969, a group of Pagans from Florida drove north to attend a concert and arts festival that was to be held on a farm outside Woodstock, New York. On their way to Woodstock, they decided to stop and check out a new Pagans chapter in Pennsylvania. The chapter was headquartered in Dreamland Park, where some of the local Pagans also lived. They partied long and hard for a few days. On the evening of August 12, 1969, they decided that they were lacking something that would make their party complete. Some females would give the proceedings that certain extra-special something! But where to find them? Several of the men divided up, sending one group to the Kutztown Fair and the other toward Reading to find women to bring back to the party. Two of the locals; Eways, Stulzfus, and Robert "Juice" Martinolich, who was visiting from New York, piled into a panel truck belonging to the Florida Pagans, with Harlan "Wolfman" Bailey, one of the Florida Pagans.

Dreamland Park aerial view taken in the mid to late 1960s. The buildings were still largely intact.   Dark in the Park

Meanwhile, Glenn Eckert, 20, had been on a date that evening with his Marilyn Sheckler, 18. Marilyn was from a suburb of Pittsburgh, and he wanted to show her the lights of Reading. They drove to the top of a hill on Skyline Drive, overlooking the city, and parked. This location was not

391

just popular for the scenic view, it also happened to be a well-known lovers' lane. Feeling romantic, Glenn and Marilyn decided to make use of the quiet and seclusion of the country road. This decision would turn out to be the worst of their short lives.

Glenn Eckert and Marilyn Sheckler in 1969

The Dreamland Park entrance was on Pricetown Road. Just a few miles down Pricetown Road, driving south toward Reading, there was a fork in the road. The panel truck carrying the four stoned and drunken Pagans took the left fork onto Skyline Drive -- the same Skyline Drive that overlooked the lights of Reading.

Glenn and Marilyn were enjoying their romantic interlude when suddenly, the car doors burst open and three burly, smelly men forced their way inside. The headlights of a truck parked behind them came on, blinding the couple. One of the men stuck a gun in Glenn's face and told him to drive. The young couple's unexpected and certainly unwelcome company was "Juice" Martinolich, "Elroy" Stultzfus and "Wolfman" Bailey. "A'rab" Eways, behind the wheel of the panel truck, drove it in front of the car, and Glenn was ordered to follow the truck. Eways led them to Leesport, a small town on the Schuylkill River about five miles north of Reading. There they abandoned the car at the train station, and the bikers forced the couple into the panel truck.

The next few hours were pure hell for the terrified young couple, with the gang members driving the truck around the area's deserted dirt roads, so they could take turns raping Marilyn. After climbing into the back of the truck, they had forced the terrified young woman to take off her clothes. Holding a gun to Glenn's head, they forced him to watch as the four men gang-raped her over and over, stopping only to switch drivers.

After the four Pagans had their fill of Marilyn, they decided to return to the clubhouse in Dreamland, so the rest of their friends could have their turn with her. Marilyn and Glenn were taken to Dreamland Park, but they never made it as far as the clubhouse. Just outside the entrance to the park, the bikers stopped the truck, dragged their victims out, and walked them into the woods. The Pagans walked back out a short time later, without their captives. It would be over two months before Glenn and Marilyn would come out of those woods. They would be carried out in body bags.

The Pagans eventually made it back to the party, where they carried on with their friends, getting high, boozing and brawling. Martinolich was arrested in the park later in the day, on August 13, for a barroom stabbing the previous night. He was soon released, and he made his way back to the clubhouse, as if nothing had happened.

Glenn Eckert lived with his parents in Robesonia, just eleven miles from Reading. He and Marilyn had left for their date on the evening of the 12th, and had not returned that night. When they still had not returned by the next morning, their friends and family started getting seriously worried. Some of Glenn's friends speculated that he and Marilyn had taken off for Woodstock, but it wasn't like either of them to go away and not tell anyone. A search was mounted for the pair. A few people went so far as to go to Bethel, New York, the following weekend, to search the Woodstock festival for them. But the turnout had been overwhelming and with the massive confusion, it was an impossible task.

On August 19, six days after the couple was reported missing, the 1964 sedan that Glenn had borrowed while his car was in the shop was discovered in Leesport. Among the items in the car were two pairs of loafers - a man's and a woman's -- Eckert's t-shirt and prescription sunglasses, and a bag containing $489.23. The money was the Aug. 12 take from Boscov's East, a restaurant in the Boscov's Country Kitchen chain that was operated by Eckert's father, Charles. Glenn worked for his father, and part of his job was to pick up the day's receipts for deposit in the bank the next day. Marilyn had a summer job at Boscov's North as a cashier, and Glenn had come in at closing time to take her on a date.

Charles Eckert later said in a newspaper interview that his son was engaged to another girl, with the wedding set for Dec. 7. Marilyn was to start her freshman year soon at Mt. Union College in Alliance, Ohio. She had told her mother that she wanted to stay on at her summer job until school started because she'd "met a boy." Perhaps their summer romance, like lots of summer romances was fun, but nothing serious. Perhaps they planned to get on with their separate lives when summer ended; Marilyn going off to college and Glenn marrying his fiancée. Whatever their plans, they were about to be cruelly shattered.

There was no indication of where the young couple might have gone, or with whom. Marilyn's brother, Grant Sheckler, was the last known person to have seen them, beside their killers. Around 9 p.m., they stopped by his trailer in Linstead, where Marilyn was spending the summer. They chatted for a few minutes before driving off again. Grant said Marilyn introduced Glenn as her boss. She told him that they'd be out for "a little while."

A massive hunt started from where the car was found, and worked its way outward in all directions. Hundreds of local police, state police and volunteers spent countless hours searching. They found nothing.

In September, state police detectives had gained enough information to arrest two men in the couple's disappearance: Leroy Stoltzfus and Robert Martinolich. Around the same time, two other men were detained by the police: James Eways and Harlan Bailey. The four were held in custody for questioning and suspicions relating to the disappearance of Marilyn Sheckler and Glenn Eckert. At some point, James Eways was allowed to go home. Rumors spread quickly through the area that his wealthy father had a hand in getting him released.

The search for the missing couple continued with no clue as to their whereabouts. The men in custody weren't talking. Then an anonymous tip was turned in to the state police, telling them that the bodies of Glenn and Marilyn would be found in the woods surrounding Dreamland Park. The search was not going be easy, as the woods were thick and terribly overgrown, but now at least they had a place to search.

State police bring in mine detecting equipment to aid in the search for the missing couple.
Reading Eagle

State Trooper Robert Kaunert went out to the Dreamland woods to check out the tip. It was a crisp autumn day, and he was enjoying being outside in the fresh air. As his footsteps crunched through the brightly colored fallen leaves, he spotted something glinting in the sunlight, and the day suddenly became less enjoyable. It was a pair of men's eyeglasses. Underneath was a skull with two small holes in it. Glenn Eckert had worn eyeglasses. It looked like he was no longer missing. More troopers descended on the woods, and Eckert's body was found, just as the tipster had said it would be. He had been shot to death and hurriedly buried under branches and brush. He was wearing the button-down striped shirt and cutoff jeans that he had worn on the night of his disappearance. His 1966 class ring from Conrad Weiser High School lay near his left hand. It was October 23, 1969, two months and ten days after he had gone missing. The following day, buried under a pile of rocks taken from a nearby stone wall, the body of Marilyn Sheckler was found. She was still wearing the yellow mini-dress she had worn on her date with Glenn, only now it was in shreds. She had been savagely beaten with a large rock until her head was nearly crushed. Encased in body bags, Glenn and Marilyn finally left the woods.

The investigation into what was now known to be a double homicide kicked into high gear. Things were moving fast. Three of the suspects were already in custody, and James Eways was called back in for questioning the day Glenn Eckert's body was found. He made up a flimsy story, covering his actions on the night of their disappearance, and was again released. This time, Eways didn't hang around. He immediately left Pennsylvania. State police searched for him for two months but failed to find him. Finally, in December of 1969, Eways surrendered to the FBI in Houston, Texas. He was returned to Pennsylvania, where he was taken into custody.

With the four Pagans in jail for the kidnap and murder of Sheckler and Eckert, questioning intensified and became more specific. It didn't take long for two of the suspects to make a deal with the prosecutor's office. And they made a great deal. It can't really be called a plea bargain because in the end, the two men didn't end up bargaining away anything. James Eways and Harlan Bailey turned state's evidence, and would testify against Martinolich and Stultzfus.

With information gained from Eways and Bailey -- or a pack of lies, depending on who was telling the story -- Martinolich and Stultzfus were bound over for trial. Stoltzfus was indicted for the first-degree murder of Marilyn Sheckler and Martinolich was indicted for the first-degree murder of Glenn Eckert. Stoltzfus' lawyer requested the two defendants be tried separately, and the request was granted. Martinolich would be tried in June, followed by Stoltzfus in September of 1970. There was no direct evidence linking any of the men to the murders, so the prosecutor's case for both men rested almost entirely upon the testimony of Eways and Bailey.

By the time the first trial began, Eways and Bailey had been cleaned up. They came into the courtroom with their hair cut, beards shaved and wearing new clothes. Some spectators remarked that they now looked like college professors. The two testified during both trials that the four of them had abducted Marilyn Sheckler and Glenn Eckert together, gang-raped Marilyn as they drove around, then drove them back to Dreamland, where the rapes were to continue. But when they arrived, the entrance was blocked by two state police cars. The police were there to investigate a fight that had happened earlier in the day. With the entrance blocked and police swarming all over the park, there was no way for them to get the truck with their prisoners inside back into Dreamland and join the party in the clubhouse. Instead, they stopped the truck a short distance from the entrance. Stoltzfus, Bailey and Martinolich climbed out and, with their captives, they ran into the woods. Eways drove off with the truck, intending to hide it until the police left. With this testimony, he had conveniently separated himself from the murders, by testifying that the couple was alive when he left.

Left Robert Martinolich left and Leroy Stoltzfus right being taken to his arraignment. Right James Eways left and Harlan Bailey shortly after the bodies were discovered at Dreamland.

Bailey had a lot more to add. He explained that when he had entered the woods with the others, it was to hide from the police, not to kill anyone. After a time, it was decided that he would sneak out and try to find transportation for the little group, so they could get out of the area until things cooled down. He, like Eways, said Glenn and Marilyn were alive when he left them with Stoltzfus and Martinolich. He further testified that he had three separate conversations about that night with Stoltzfus while in jail awaiting trial. Bailey said he had asked him what had happened to the boy and girl. Stoltzfus allegedly replied: "Don't worry about it, we took care of them. Just forget you ever saw them." Bailey followed that testimony by recounting their second conversation, when Stoltzfus explained how he tried to choke Marilyn but that she just wouldn't die. He was forced to beat her in the head with a rock and that did the trick. During their final conversation, Bailey said he told him how they Stoltzfus and Martinolich had covered the girl's body with rocks from a stone fence.

Stoltzfus supposedly followed that by saying: "They might find the boy's grave, but they would not find the girl's grave."

Both men charged with murder pleaded not guilty. They insisted they really had not killed the couple. Stoltzfus took the stand to defend himself during his trial. He claimed that he had been walking in the woods on the night of the murder, hiding from the police because he feared arrest on an unrelated incident. He said that he unexpectedly came upon Bailey and Eways holding a young man and woman captive. He said that Eways had grabbed him and held a knife to his throat while Bailey struck the woman down and beat her in the head with a rock until she was dead.

Dr. George P. Desjardins testified that he had performed the autopsies on the young couple. He stated that Glenn Eckert had died of a gunshot wound. Of Marilyn, he said: "My opinion is that this young lady died as a result of a blow to the left side of the head, producing a depressed skull fracture." He further explained that her body had been in an advanced state of decomposition when it was found, and he was not able to examine her vital organs to gain any additional information. For this same reason, he was unable to verify or disprove Bailey's claim that she had first been strangled.

Robert Martinolich and Leroy Stultzfus were found guilty of first-degree murder. They were both sentenced to life in prison. They were transferred from the Berks County Jail to separate prisons to live out their days behind bars. As for James Eways and Harlan Bailey, they weren't even charged with a crime. They each testified under oath that they had taken part in the abduction of Glenn and Marilyn, and that they had each taken part in the gang rape of Marilyn, but that's where they stopped. They were adamant that they had not taken part in the murders. They had bargained away their murder charges by testifying against the other two Pagans. The prosecutor had initially charged them with kidnapping and rape, but later dropped those charges, claiming that there wasn't enough evidence to prosecute. Apparently, their testimony was enough to put two men away for life for murder, but not enough for them to be prosecuted for kidnapping and rape. Eways and Bailey walked out of the courthouse as free men. They could go anywhere they liked. Bailey returned to his home in Wilton Manors, Florida. Eways went home to his parents in Sinking Spring, just twenty minutes down the road.

Stultzfus and Martinolich did not accept responsibility and fade off into the correctional system, admitting they had done wrong and willing to accept their punishment. Instead, they steadfastly maintained their innocence. Both men appealed their sentence, claiming prosecutorial misconduct. They also claimed that they had been convicted of a crime they didn't commit. They claimed that none of the four Pagans had left Dreamland to look for women. Instead, the state police had burst into the area to investigate an incident that had happened earlier in the day; a fight in which a young man had been stabbed. Stultzfus, Eways, Martinolich and Bailey had all run into the woods to hide from the police. After a while, Eways and Bailey became impatient and left to find a vehicle they could all use to escape the area, or at least until things cooled down and the police left. Martinolich moved closer to the edge of the woods to keep eye on what the police were doing. Stultzfus stayed where he was to wait for Eways and Bailey to return with a vehicle.

After quite some time, possibly even a couple of hours, Eways and Bailey returned and met up with Stultzfus in the woods. But now, they had a terrified young man and woman in tow, being held at gunpoint. The captives looked as though they had both been roughed up, but the woman was in much worse shape and her dress in shreds. Eckert, by then, probably believed that they were about to be killed. He fought to grab the gun away from Eways. Bailey grabbed Eckert, struggling to regain control. The gun went off, killing Eckert. Stultzfus did not know if Eways had shot the young man intentionally or if it had been a horrible accident. Either way, the result was the same. Eckert lay dead on the ground before them and Marilyn Sheckler had witnessed the killing. Bailey grabbed her, threw her to the ground, and tried to strangle her. He grew upset and spit out, "she just won't die!" In a panic, he grabbed a large rock lying beside her and repeatedly smashed it into her head, crushing her skull. Stultzfus said that the two men then turned the gun on him. They didn't shoot him, but instead forced him to help bury the young couple under branches, brush and rocks. Stultzfus insisted that Martinolich was not there when the men had returned or when the killings had taken place. He had remained at the edge of the woods, watching the police. He had a particular interest in their activities, since he had been involved in the fight they were investigating.

Over the years, their version of that terrible night started to seem more and more plausible, causing many to wonder if the wrong two men had been convicted of the killings. Regardless of who said what, the case was essentially one of contradicting stories told by equally bad men. If the crime had happened today, there might have been a scientific solution to determine who the real killers were. However, in 1969, DNA analysis was decades away. The police were also hindered by the severely decomposed condition of Glenn and Marilyn's bodies, and that the crime scene was a wooded wilderness area that had been exposed to the elements for over two months. Evidence did not have a factor in determining guilt in this case. Guilt had likely been determined by who was quickest to make a deal with the prosecutor's office.

All appeals brought forth by Stoltzfus and Martinolich were summarily denied. At every parole hearing, freedom was denied to them. At some point, they both ended up in the State Correctional Institution SCI Laurel Highlands in Somerset, Pennsylvania. This particular prison houses about 1,000 inmates. It also provides special services for elderly prisoners and those with medical problems. The final appeal on behalf of Martinolich was made in 2004. Once again, he petitioned for a new trial, but the judge ruled that it was just too late. His rights to appeal for a new trial had expired in 1997. Martinolich also requested that he be released so he could have surgery on his back, claiming that he wasn't getting proper medical care at SCI-Laurel Highlands and that he would soon be paralyzed without the surgery. This too was denied, as prison officials declared that he was receiving proper care.

Robert Martinolich, inmate AM0803, remains in prison as he approaches his seventies. Currently, he is the longest continuously serving inmate in any Pennsylvania SCI, having entered the system in 1970. As of 2014, he was transferred, and is now serving out his days in SCI-Mahony in Frackville.

The citizens of Reading were not completely naive to the criminal ways of the world, but this case was still a startling wake-up call. It was several years before teenagers again started driving to the top of the hill on Skyline Drive to make out, but residents were not particularly worried about locking their doors at night. They perceived the actual crime as being far removed from their small city. Their main concerns were relative to their newfound fears that they were going to be invaded by violent biker gangs. They were now aware that their otherwise peaceful countryside was a haven for the Pagans. And who knew what type of criminal element the Pagans would draw into their quiet midst? But as time passed, the whole ordeal began to fade in their memories, kept alive only by occasional newspaper stories, reminding them of the crime on the anniversary, or if one of the convicted killers was in the news for an appeal or parole hearing.

Leroy Stoltzfus died on March 28, 2010. He was 61 years old. He had been very ill for several years prior to his death. He was still technically a prisoner of the state, but he had been admitted to a Johnstown hospital, where he quietly passed away. He had served forty years for the murders in Dreamland Park. He continued to proclaim his innocence right up to the point that he was unable to speak. He had told family and friends that he deserved to be in prison for some of the things he had done, but not for murder. When his family submitted Leroy's obituary to be printed in the *Reading Eagle*, the heading read: "Free at Last." Ronald Stoltzfus, Leroy's older brother said of him: "He's not in prison anymore for a murder he didn't commit. He didn't kill anyone." Both of his parents predeceased him, but while they were alive, they never stopped praying for his release and redemption. Leroy's funeral was held in the Millwood Mennonite Church and he was buried in the Millwood Cemetery. A large contingent of Pagans attended the funeral and provided his body a motorcycle escort to the cemetery.

After the trial, Harlan Bailey may have returned to Florida, never to be heard from again in Pennsylvania anyway. James Eways shrugged off his connection to the murders and the Pagan's Motorcycle Club and returned to his comfortable life with his wealthy family. He attended Lehigh University and graduated with a degree in engineering. In time, Eways worked his way up to being considered a prominent, if not respected, businessman in the Reading area. He eventually became the president of a Reading engineering consulting firm.

In the early 1990s, Eways moved into a house that had been converted from an old church. His new home in Wernersville was on a quiet, rural street. Quiet, except when area teenagers decided to visit the "man who got away with murder." People may have ignored his former association with the Pagans, and his connection to a huge murder case when it came to money and business, but that doesn't mean they didn't sit around the supper table, repeating dark tales of kidnapping, rape and murder. Eways' house became an attraction for rowdy teens and curiosity-seekers alike. Teenagers heard the stories and sometimes took it upon themselves to harass Eways for what he had done, and what they thought he had gotten away with.

In the early morning hours of June 15, 1995, five young men climbed into a car and headed for Eways' house. They drove up and down his street; honking, shouting obscenities and threats, and shining lights into his house. After several trips past his house, Eways came outside, holding onto his loaded .357 magnum handgun. In his rage, he pointed his gun at the car and fired twice. One shot went wild, but the other found a mark. The bullet entered the car through the passenger side window, where one of the teens was sitting. The young man was shot. Twenty hours after James Eways walked out his front door and fired his gun, Michael A. Abate III died of a gunshot wound to the head. He would have turned 18 the next day.

Eways first denied shooting the boy. He denied firing his gun at all. Eventually, he admitted to firing the gun but said he only wanted to scare the kids, and the gun went off by accident --twice. Eways was arrested and charged with first-degree murder, third-degree, voluntary manslaughter, involuntary manslaughter, aggravated assault, simple assault and recklessly endangering another person. It appeared that the prosecutor had no intention of allowing Eways to get away with this crime.

Left   Michael A. Abate III of Ephrata, PA, victim of James Eways   Reading Eagle
Right   James M. Eways, after his 1995 arraignment for the murder of Michael Abate.
John A. Secoges, Reading Eagle

Eways' lawyer requested a change in venue because of intense pre-trial publicity and his client's connection to the Dreamland murders. The request was granted, and in September of 1996, James M. Eways went on trial in Erie, Pennsylvania. After deliberating for seven hours, the Erie jury delivered their verdict on October 1st. They acquitted Eways of both murder charges, the voluntary manslaughter charge and all assault charges. But Eways would not walk away this time. He was found guilty of involuntary manslaughter and five counts of recklessly endangering another person. The judge sentenced him to serve two to five years in state prison, but allowed him to be released on $500,000 bond, pending the outcome of his appeals.

In September of 1998, his appeals exhausted, James Eways finally walked into prison. He served the full five years of his sentence, the maximum allowed for involuntary manslaughter. Released in 2003, with ten years of special probation, Eways returned home, to the same house where he fired that fatal shot into a teenager's head. Like the proverbial phoenix, he reassembled his professional life. As of 2008, he has worked as Senior Process Engineer at Dutchland, Inc.

Left   The inside of the carousel building circa 1992   Nancy DiSanta
Right   The inside of the carousel building circa 2004. The roof collapsed under a three-foot-deep snow load in 1996.   Dark in the Park

Dreamland Park is still privately owned property. A few families still rent the small homes that were built when the park was in operation, and the clubhouse remains intact. The remainder of the buildings are in decrepit conditions. Left to the elements, they have slowly crumbled into nearly unrecognizable piles of rubble and random walls.

Some of the trees have been cleared, and there are a few more houses along nearby roads. But the woods are still there, and they continue to hold their secrets. For years, people have been sneaking into those woods; some on a dare, some out of morbid curiosity. Still others come seeking spirits. In the very early hours of occasional summer mornings, a mist floats through the trees, a shapeless undulating mist, sometimes so thick that it blocks the light, then turns as transparent as fine gauze. The mist is cold, very cold. If someone happens to be in the woods at the right time and the right place to observe the mist, they will find that it is accompanied by an irrepressible feeling of overwhelming sorrow so deep that the witnesses may find their cheeks soaked by tears. Others wandering the woods in the night, or even sometimes during the daytime, talk of a strange feeling that overcomes them. The feeling is hard to describe, but it is distinctly uncomfortable. Creepy, eerie and sometimes even frightening are words most commonly used to explain how it feels. The feeling goes away as soon as they step out of the woods and onto the road. Are Marilyn Scheckler and Glenn Eckert still together, walking between the trees? Have they found peace together in such a lovely spot, or are they still bound by the terror of the night they died? Has Leroy Stoltzfus returned to the place where his life changed forever? Is he vengeful about a wrongful conviction, or repentant for a life he took so many years ago? Perhaps the truth will be known someday, but for now, the woods remain possessive of their dark secrets.

What is left of the old Dreamland Park is slowly disappearing, as nature takes the land back. The entrance to the former amusement park is marked with a "Dreamland Park Drive" sign, but it is not a welcome sign. Posted all around the entrance and along the edge of the woods are large "No Trespassing" signs. It is common knowledge that if strangers are seen roaming the property, the residents will call the police. So if anyone were to venture into Dreamland, be warned. If the police won't get you, someone else just might.

1981: WHEN MONSTERS CAME IN THE NIGHT
The Keddie Resort Murders

Deep in the foothills of northern California's Sierra Nevada mountain range, scenically situated along Spanish Creek in the Feather River Canyon, was a stunningly beautiful vacation spot. The Keddie Resort was established in 1910 in this lovely area of Plumas County. Access to the resort was made easy by its close proximity to a railway line that carried passengers between Salt Lake City and Oakland. It lies eighty-seven miles west of Reno, Nevada. The nearest town is Quincy, six miles distant. The resort was isolated, and its guests liked it that way. There were thirty-three cabins, most of sturdy log construction, and a small general store for the convenience of the guests. The rustic, two-story Keddie Lodge had rooms to rent, if a cabin wasn't your style, and had a restaurant that was considered to be one of the finest for miles around. People were said to have driven hundreds of miles to dine at the lodge, where elk and trout were the specialties of the house. Afterwards, they might spend the night in one of the well-appointed rooms upstairs, or in one of the rustic cabins. The tables were filled with happy diners year round, and most of the cabins and rooms remained occupied through the spring, summer and autumn months by fishermen, hikers and those who just wanted to relax and get away from it all.

The Keddie Resort prospered for many decades. But over time, the demand for the cabins began to decline, and they slowly fell into shabbiness. By the 1970s, longtime owner Gary Mollath was forced to offer the cabins to low-income families on an extended rental basis. The increasingly down-at-the-heels resort also became the temporary home for many students who were attending Feather River College in Quincy. Nearly all the families living there were permanent or semi-permanent residents, forming a community of sorts, and for several, their rent came out of monthly welfare checks. The only real remnants remaining of the old resort were the general store, the restaurant in the lodge and the bar on the lodge's lower level. The restaurant maintained a good reputation and continued to draw out-of-towners from many miles away. The bar however, catered largely to locals. Keddie was soon thought of as a tiny town, rather than a resort, set off on its own among the towering pines. There was only one road to enter or leave Keddie, but for at least four members of this small community, well...many believe they never left.

The Sharp family during happier times. Back: Johnny, Greg, Sue mother and Sheila. Front: Tina and Ricky

Glenna "Sue" Sharp had not had an easy go of it. She was married to a cruel man and their relationship was rocky at best. Soon after giving birth to their fifth child, her husband threw her and the children out of the house. Sue took the kids to her sister's home, where they stayed for over a year. Her husband asked her to come back to him, and wanting a home of their own for her children, she relented and went back. Apparently, their separation had not made his heart grow fonder, as the old saying goes, and Sue once again found herself and the children alone and on their own. Late one night, she loaded herself and all five kids onto a train and headed north, toward Quincy, to be near family.

And so, needing to make a change in her life and a home for her children, Sue found and rented one of the run-down cabins at the Keddie Resort. They moved into the yellow clapboard Cabin 28 in November of 1980. Their stay would be a short one.

Sue was only thirty-six, and was trying to do her best to raise her family on her meager welfare check. There wasn't much left after the rent was paid, but she was struggling to make it work. Living with her in the tiny cabin was her fifteen-year old son Johnny, fourteen-year-old daughter Sheila often called Sassy , twelve-year-old Tina, and young sons Ricky, ten, and Greg, five.

The house was a tight fit for six people. There was a living room, kitchen and two small bedrooms. To stretch the space, Sue created a makeshift bedroom in the basement. Johnny, being the oldest, claimed the basement room for himself. Sue, Sheila and Tina shared one of the main floor bedrooms while Ricky and Greg shared the other. It was crowded, but it was the best Sue could do at the time.

In early 1981, roughly sixty-six people called Keddie home. It was described as a fairly tight-knit community, where people watched out for other people's kids and almost no one locked their doors. There were rumors of drug activity in the area, but this was no more than one might find in any small, isolated low-income community. And most of those rumors were only about marijuana. It was nothing terribly concerning for the residents of Keddie.

When the Sharp family moved into Cabin 28, it took a while for them to be accepted into the community. Sue made friends with Marilyn Smartt, who lived across and down the road from her in Cabin 26. Marilyn's husband Martin Marty and her two sons from a previous marriage also lived in the cabin. Other than visiting with Marilyn, Sue didn't stray too far from her cabin, though later, some people reported that she might have been earning a little extra money on the side, either by dealing drugs or having sex with men who came and left Cabin 28 at all hours. But these rumors floated to the surface after... And sometimes the things one hears "after" are not necessarily gospel.

Cabin 28 from the front.

Cabin 28 from the rear right showing the basement where Johnny had his bedroom. The basement bedroom could only be reached from the outside entrance. The nearest cabin was just 15 feet away.

The children were a different story. They seemed to make friends easily, as children often do. Ricky and Greg had several friends at Keddie, and living in such an isolated community, they had the run of the place. They had grown especially close to Justin Eason, one of Marilyn Smartt's young sons by a former marriage. The three were often seen roaming amongst the tall pines, playing fort, cowboys and Indians, pirates or whatever they imagined for the day. As many youngsters do, they frequently slept over at each other's homes.

Sheila, the oldest of the girls, was lucky to make a close friend, Paula Seabolt, right next door. In fact, their two cabins were a mere fifteen feet apart. Zonita Seabolt, Paula's mother, was suspicious of Sue Sharp. A strict Mormon, Zonita disapproved of the way Sue was raising her children. She was aware that Sheila had given birth at just thirteen to a baby fathered by her fifteen-year-old boyfriend, Richard Meeks, who also lived at the rundown resort. The baby, a girl, was placed for adoption. Mrs. Seabolt thought Sue should have kept a better eye on Sheila. As a result, Paula was never allowed to sleep over at Sheila's house, but Sue's children were always welcomed at the Seabolt house. As a result, Sheila and Tina slept over at the Seabolts' nearly every Saturday night.

Tina was a sweet, somewhat shy child. She did have friends, but she was not as outgoing as her siblings and often preferred to stay close to Sheila when she could. At school, Tina was well below her grade level and could not keep up. She was soon placed in a special education class. Her teacher was able to give her more one-on-one attention and she began progressing, though, her teacher complained, Tina received no support at home. But at home and around Keddie, she was simply seen as a normal kid, one who was small for her age, but just one of the kids. After...it was learned that young Tina's life in Keddie was troubled, more troubled than any twelve-year-old's life should be.

Johnny tended to spend his spare time in Quincy, where the children of Keddie were bused to school. He had made a best friend in seventeen-year-old Dana Wingate. They were often seen hanging out together around Quincy, visiting friends, drinking soft drinks at one of the local gas stations, or hitchhiking back and forth between Quincy and Keddie. Johnny quickly became well-known in the school, and his shaggy blond hair and handsome face made him very popular with the girls. But their parents were not so quick to accept the young man into the fold. He was obviously poor, living, as he did, in Keddie, and his choice of Dana for a best friend didn't help matters. After...there would be gossip about the two young men and their rumored involvement with drugs.

Dana Wingate spent a good amount of time with the Sharp family. Dana had been a premature baby and suffered many physical difficulties as a result. He had many struggles growing up. He was a beautiful little boy, so beautiful that he was occasionally confused for a girl. His older sisters sometimes dressed him up in their clothes for fun. As Dana grew older, he began to withdraw from his family. His father worked long hours and was not often at home. Dana became "one of those boys" -- one of those boys who seemed always to be "up to no good." Eventually, he was moved into a group home for boys in Quincy that was run by a high school teacher named Dan Dorris and his wife, Pat. Dana seemed to be doing better. He got along well with the Dorrises and with other boys in the home, and he had found a good friend in the new kid in town, Johnny Sharp.

Saturday, April 11, 1981 started out as an average day for Keddie residents. Sue Sharp, in particular, and her five children were having their usual Saturday. Johnny had gone into Quincy to meet up with his friend Dana. Sheila had asked if Paula could sleep over at her house, but Mrs. Seabolt wouldn't allow it. Instead, Sheila would spend the night next door with Paula, as she did most Saturday nights. Usually, Tina stayed at the Seabolts with her, but on this night, Mrs. Seabolt decided that the older girls needed some time to themselves. Tina would sleep at home. The younger boys, Ricky and Greg were having their own sleepover in Cabin 28 with their friend, twelve-year-old Justin Eason from just down the road. Sue planned to stay

Dana Wingate

in and ride herd on the gang. Justin arrived with his PJs and pillow, and Sheila headed next door with her slippers and sleeping bag.

Johnny and Dana spent some of the afternoon at the group home where Dana lived then Dana asked if he could spend the night with Johnny in Keddie. The Dorrises gave permission, but on one condition -- Pat made the boys promise not to hitchhike to Keddie. It was promise they would break.

The boys next spent some time at the home of a girl from school, arriving about 6:30 p.m. They told her they were planning to hitchhike to Keddie later that evening. She asked them to stay over at her house, but Johnny said no; his mother would be expecting him, and so they left, completely sober. The strongest thing they had had to drink was a diet TAB. Close to 7:00 p.m., a friend saw both boys standing outside the Quincy Country Store. He gave Dana a ride on his motorcycle to the Exxon station, where he waited for Johnny to catch up. Around 7:50 p.m., another local man saw the boys, thumbs out, on the side of the road, just beyond the Exxon station. He was only familiar with Dana, but his description of the other boy matched Johnny Sharp. What they did for the next two hours is unknown, but a girl both boys knew from school saw them shortly after 10:00 p.m., hitchhiking along highway 70 toward Keddie. She pulled over and visited with them for a while then drove on, unable to drive them to Keddie because she didn't want to be late coming home with her parents' car. The boys walked on down the road as she drove off in the opposite direction. They were alone when they were last seen.

Sue made popcorn for the kids, and they watched the TV show "The Love Boat." Later, she got the three boys quieted down and put them to bed. Tina also had gone to bed. Sue finally had some time to herself when there was a knock on the door. It was her friend Marilyn, with her husband Marty and his friend, Bo. John Boubede, known as Bo, was a shady character who had been staying with the Smartts for nearly two weeks. He and Marty had met at the VA hospital in Reno, Nevada, where they were patients in the psychiatric ward. They stopped by to see if Sue wanted to go with them to the Back Door bar at the lodge for a drink. Sue declined. The bar wasn't really her scene, and besides, she despised Marty for his abusive treatment toward Marilyn, and Bo was just plain creepy. Her three visitors finally left, and Sue was alone again.

Sometime between 10:00 and 10:30 p.m., Johnny and Dana finally made it back to Keddie, and they walked into Cabin 28 for the last time.

Sunday morning, Sheila Sharp, her arms wrapped around her sleeping bag, made her way home from her friend's cabin next door. With her mind on nothing in particular, she opened the door to the darkened living room, where the curtains were still drawn. As she looked into the dimly lit room, she could just make out the shapes of three bodies on the floor. There was blood everywhere! She ran screaming from the cabin and returned to the Seabolts'. She breathlessly told them that there were dead people in her house. With their terrible injuries combined with the low light, she hadn't been able to recognize her own mother and older brother among the victims.

While Mrs. Seabolt called the sheriff, Sheila returned home, worried about her little brothers. She ran down the right side of the cabin until she reached the boys' bedroom window. After waking the young boys and telling them not to leave the bedroom, she and Mr. Seabolt lifted them out the window and led them next door. She didn't know if the killer might still be in the cabin and if the boys could be in danger. Barring that, Sheila didn't want them to see the horrific scene in the living room.

When the police arrived from Quincy, the true magnitude of the horror inside Cabin 28 was discovered. As they carefully entered the cramped living room, what lay before them stunned them into silence. Three lifeless bodies were sprawled across the bloody carpet. The victims had been bludgeoned and slashed so badly that they were nearly unrecognizable. Sue Sharp, her son Johnny and his friend Dana were dead.

Sheriff Doug Thomas was told that the three victims hadn't been the only people in the house that night. Three little boys had been in the side bedroom and were unharmed. They had slept through the carnage without waking. All accept Justin Eason. Sheriff Thomas found Justin and questioned him in a police car, though the boy was nearly hysterical. Justin tried repeatedly to tell him that Tina was gone, but the sheriff just would not hear him. After several minutes, Justin's mother stepped in and made the sheriff stop and listen. He finally got the message. Not only were there three dead people on the floor of the cabin, but a little girl was missing.

All three victims had been tortured extensively before they were killed; tortured in a manner that could have taken hours. Sue was found lying face-down, next to the sofa, naked below the waist. She had been covered with a yellow blanket taken from her bed. Her hands were tightly bound with adhesive tape and her ankles were tied with electrical cord. Her torso and head had been slashed and sliced repeatedly. An old blue bandana had been used as a gag and several of her teeth were broken. She had been stabbed deeply in the chest multiple times, but her most devastating injuries were inflicted with a claw hammer. The hammer had smashed through her skull again and again, until it barely resembled a human head.

Johnny's body, though fully clothed and left lying on the floor face-up, had been bound and assaulted in a manner almost identical to his mother, with the added insult of having his throat slit. Dana had been treated a bit differently before he was killed. A sofa cushion had been pulled to the floor and placed under his head. He had tape wrapped around one wrist and electrical wire tied to one ankle, but his hands and feet were not bound together. He had been beaten with a weapon other than the hammer and he had been manually strangled to death.

The room was in disarray, but it seemed that little else in the house was touched. The phone had been left off the hook, and a few of the smaller pieces of furniture had been toppled. Large pools of blood were congealing on the carpet and blood was splattered on every wall. The killers seemed to have gone into a frenzy, slashing and stabbing at the walls with knives and punching holes with the hammer. A steak knife belonging to the Sharps was found on the floor. The ferocity with which it had been driven into one of the victims had caused the blade to bend at a 25-degree angle. The bloody hammer and a large knife had been left behind.

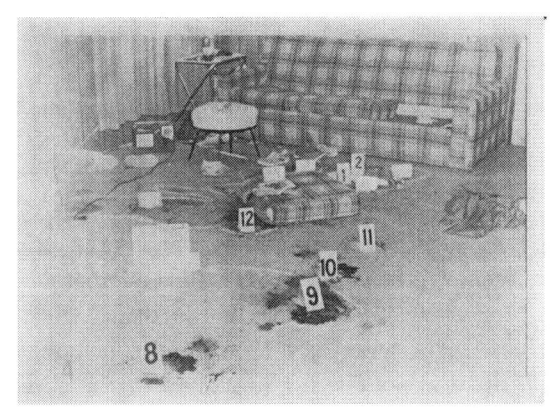

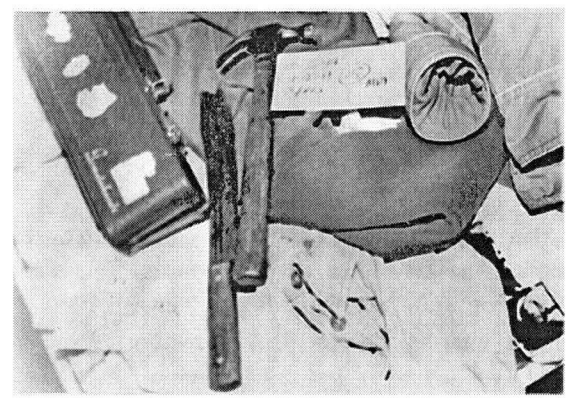

Left The scene of the crime - the living room of Cabin 28
Right The hammer and one of the knives used as murder weapons and left at the scene

The crime scene was utterly confusing, with no clear indication of who had been killed first, second or last. Sue had blood on the bottom of her feet, as if she stepped in a pool of blood before she was killed. The times of death were loosely determined to be between 10:00 p.m. and 2:30 a.m., offering the police little help. Cabin 28 was located in the center of a cluster of cabins, none of them very far away. Despite the proximity to dozens of sleeping residents, no one heard anything that caused them any alarm. One young woman thought she heard a slight scream sometime between 2:00 a.m. and 2:30 a.m., and as he walked home after closing, the bartender at the Back Door thought he heard a series of unidentifiable thumping sounds about that same time. No one else reported hearing anything at all.

There was one set of clues that at first looked promising. Justin Eason, one of the three boys who had been sleeping in a rear bedroom, may have actually been an eyewitness. He insisted he had seen nothing, but the bedroom door was found slightly ajar, with a blood smear on the door handle and a view of Sue's semi-naked body covered with a blanket. Justin was found with blood on the bottom of his feet, and blood on one hand. It was theorized that he had heard a commotion and had opened the door to see what was happening. At some point, he must have left the bedroom, walked into the living room, possibly covered Sue with the blanket, and then gone back to bed. If he had awakened before the killer or killers left, he may have seen them. But Justin had nothing to tell the police, insisting that he had slept through the night until Sheila had appeared at the window the next morning. He was either too frightened to talk, or the emotional trauma of the night of horrors had left him with no memory of the events.

Sheriff Thomas was desperate. He called in a professional hypnotist to question Justin. While under hypnosis, the boy told of seeing two men in the living room who were striking something on the floor. He was able to give the police a rough description of the men, enough for a sketch artist to provide drawings. Justin's statements have become problematic over the years, as he has changed his story many times.

A search was launched for little Tina. The only evidence left behind was a small amount of blood in her bed; not nearly enough to indicate that she had been killed in the cabin. Tracking dogs were brought in but they found no scent of her to follow. It seemed that all traces of Tina Sharp ended at the front door. The search for Tina turned nationwide as fliers were distributed to police departments around the country. With the exception of a few unsubstantiated sightings, Tina was simply gone.

If the residents of Keddie were asked to describe the place they lived in, they would have talked about the peaceful environment among breath-taking scenery, the care they felt for one another or the feeling of safety they all felt. This may have been true for some of them, but in reality, Keddie held its own dark secrets. At the time of the murders, there were any number of questionable characters living or visiting in Keddie or in the immediate area. The list is truly disturbing. The Sharp family thought they were moving into a little patch of paradise, but the reality was that they were surrounded by convicted child molesters, professional criminals, corrupt businessmen and transient thieves. The resort's owner had even been linked to a murder, though he was never arrested, and the resort's caretaker, Sue Sharp's next-door neighbor James Seabolt, was described by some of the residents as a habitual "peeping tom." Tina wasn't even safe at school, as one of her teachers was later found to be a pedophile and is now a registered sex offender.

With all the strangeness going on beneath its smiling exterior, Keddie had much in common with the fictional town of *Twin Peaks* in the 1990-91 television series of the same name.

As unbelievable as it may seem, there was even a serial killer in the area at the time of the murders. Robert Silveria, Jr., known as "The Boxcar Killer," is currently serving two life sentences without parole in Oregon. He was also convicted of murders in three other states and is suspected of murders in several others. He has been directly linked to at least fourteen murders and confessed to twenty-eight. He spent over fifteen years riding the rails, killing other transients along the way. Silveria was briefly employed by Plumas County and later in the Quincy lumber mill. He was undoubtedly in Keddie several times. Years later, Silveria was believed to have killed a man in a hobo camp just around the bend in the railroad tracks from Keddie. He confessed to the murders in Cabin 28, but his confession was quickly disproven. Food for thought, though: his methods of murder were stabbing or bludgeoning.

Two suspects, at least with nearly everyone but the police, surfaced the day the bodies were recovered. Martin "Marty" Smartt was married to Sue's friend Marilyn and was Justin's stepfather, the same Justin who was the only possible eyewitness to the murders and had been left unharmed as he slept next to Greg and Ricky Sharp. Marty's presumed cohort was his houseguest, "Bo" Boubede.

Both men were called in for an interview almost immediately and were briefly questioned. Tapes still exist of both interviews, and they are almost comical in their ineptness. Both men answered questions with several lies and contradicted themselves. At one point, when questioned about the fact that his stepson Justin was sleeping in the Cabin 28 during the murders, and that he might have witnessed something, Smartt actually states: "He is quiet enough to where he could have noticed something without me detecting him." Whether this was a slip, indicating that Smartt himself had been in the cabin committing the murders, or if he merely misspoke, is unknown. The detective failed to question him further on the point. Later in the interview, as the detective is describing the murders, Smartt volunteered the following: "Ah, I don't know. I'd like to see the hammer; I've been in Sue's house. The only hammer I ever knew that came out of there was a wooden-handled one. Ah, my hammer is missing." Again, the detective failed to follow up on this strange statement. Smartt also stated that he thought the whole thing was "overkill." He continued by describing how he would have committed the murders. He explained that he would have killed them all quickly and gotten out as fast as he could, instead of staying around to torture them.

Boubede's interview was nearly as strange. Although the murders had been committed just yards from where he had been staying, and Cabin 28 had been surrounded by dozens of officers and official vehicles, he told the detective that he had no idea where the murder cabin was located. He told them that he had never met Sue Sharp and had never been to her cabin, when he had been there just the night before on the way to the bar. He further told police that he had been living with the Smartts for well over a month, instead of the twelve days that he had actually lived with them.

Note: If the police would have taken the time to investigate Boubede more deeply than a cursory interview, they would have found he had a very interesting history. He had mob connections with close ties to a known mob enforcer. With his uncle and his sister, who acted as a getaway driver, he had been a violent bank robber. If that weren't enough, he was a scam artist, a car thief, and was one of Chicago's "Candy Bandits," involved in robbing the homes of wealthy women. When Boubede was questioned, he lied and claimed he was a former cop. He was also in possession of a false ID.

Both men were released. Boubede left Keddie that same day, never to return. Shortly after the murders, Marty was arrested for being involved in a knife fight. When he was released from jail, he was told to get out of town. Marilyn Smartt never saw her husband again. The morning the murders were discovered, she moved in with a Keddie neighbor, Wade Meeks. Wade was considerably younger than she was, and was the brother of Richard Meeks, the father of Sheila Sharp's baby. Marilyn consistently said that she believed that Marty and Bo had committed the murders. These two degenerates weren't the only suspects, but in retrospect, they were certainly the most likely. Years later there would be even more reason to believe in their guilt.

Theories about the crime began to emerge, along with rumors and public speculation. It was believed that the murders had been committed in one of three ways.

Theory One: The killer or killers were already in the cabin when Johnny and Dana entered. Sue may have already been killed or was being attacked. She was the only victim who was gagged, so the boys may have had no clue as to what was going on inside the cabin when they walked in. Johnny and Dana would have rushed in to save Sue and were attacked and subdued. Or, they may have come in and were surprised by the intruders, attacked and subdued. Once they were bound, the killers could take the time to torture and kill the three victims.

Theory Two: The killer or killers picked up Johnny and Dana as they hitchhiked to Keddie, and drove them home. Then, they were either invited in or coerced the boys into taking them inside, where Sue was probably up waiting for their return. The three were attacked, subdued, tortured and killed.

Theory Three: The killer or killers were invited inside, either by the boys or by Sue. Something happened to enrage the visitors and they attacked. The rage continued through the torture and eventual murders.

The only constant with all three theories is what happened to Tina, but certainly not why it happened. They believed that Tina was awakened by the commotion in the living room, came out to see what was happening, and was kidnapped to eliminate her as a witness. No one could explain why she was taken and not killed like the others.

It was also supposed that as Dana was treated differently than the others, having a cushion placed under his head, he had been viewed by the killers as an unexpected and innocent person in the house. He had been beaten as the other two had, but it appeared that he had suffered less actual torture with the knife and in the end, he was strangled.

The motive for the murders was equally confusing. As with many violent crimes, tongues wagged after the fact. Various members of the Keddie community, as well as people living in Quincy, were busy trying to figure out the motive. Some thought that Sue was the target because she was believed to be dealing drugs out of Cabin 28. Was it a drug deal gone wrong? Some people speculated that Sue was the target because of the rumors that she had been prostituting herself to help support her family. Had a "customer" gotten angry and the boys walked in on a rage murder? Still others believed that John and Dana were involved in drugs, and this was the result of one of their drug deals gone wrong, or possibly the boys had ripped someone off and this was revenge. Regardless of the supposed target, every possible scenario and motive held that Tina was an unexpected witness who had to be silenced; but still no one could think of a reason for her being taken from her home.

At least some of the motive theories were quickly put to rest. Following the autopsies, the coroner announced that no drugs were found in any of the bodies. Neither could the police find any evidence of prostitution on Sue's part, and no evidence that there had been any drugs in the house.

The living room of Cabin 28 was a disaster. There was blood everywhere; blood pools, blood spatter and blood smears on the carpet, furniture, curtains and walls. There was blood cast-off on the walls and ceiling, and knife slashes and hammer holes in the walls. It was as if brutally killing the victims wasn't enough to satisfy the killers, and they had tried to kill the house as well. Were the authorities seeing rage, frenzy or a bizarre sort of fun? They just didn't know. The living room was disassembled and taken to the sheriff's office. The walls were pulled from their studs, the carpet was rolled up, parts of the ceiling were pulled down and even some of the floor boards were removed; all hauled away for further study. The house was sealed and left to sit empty, at least for a while.

The search for the killers and the search for Tina continued. Some former Keddie residents, including Marilyn Smartt, recall that during a search, Tina's bloody jacket was found under the crawlspace of the Smartt cabin. Another recollection was that an old shed, used by many Keddie children as a club house, was found mysteriously scrubbed clean and missing several floor boards, leaving many to believe that Tina had been held, and likely killed, in the shed. Although several people remember these discoveries, there is no official record of such, and the sheriff at the time of the murders said he didn't remember anything like that happening. However, these records may have been among those destroyed by a leaky roof in the sheriff's office.

As the investigation continued, an interesting police report came to light. Tina had been repeatedly sexually molested by a "dirty man" in the resort. In filing the report, Tina was assisted by an unnamed advocate. She described the molestation in fairly good detail, despite being young and developmentally delayed. At the time, it appeared that she had not been raped, however, the man's assaultive behavior was escalating, and it looked like it would be just a matter of time. No name was noted in the report, suggesting that either Tina didn't know the name of her molester or she was too frightened to say. After the murders and Tina's disappearance, there were suspicions that Tina may have been pregnant, or had been given a sexually transmitted disease.

Suddenly, there was an entirely new theory as to the motive for the murders.

Theory Four: Tina may have been the intended target from the start. Possibly, Sue was expected to be there, but the boys were a surprise. The reason Tina had to be taken from the house was to hide the proof of her molestation. However, this new theory left no explanation for the torture of Sue, Johnny and Dana.

Three years after the murders, almost to the day, Tina was found. A couple of bottle hunters were searching through an old trash dump near a secluded area on the Feather River known as Feather Falls, fifty miles from Keddie. One of the men saw a human skull that looked as if it had been placed atop a rubbish heap. The skull, that of a child, had been picked clean by animals and bleached white by the sun.

Feather Falls was in Butte County, where a young boy had disappeared. Officials at first believed the skull belonged to him. Instead, the skull was identified as being Tina Sharp's. A local anthropologist suggested that the area where the skull was found should be carefully searched, as animals would have scattered her bones. After a thorough search, all that was found were a couple of teeth. All of Tina Sharp that was recovered was a skull, jawbone and teeth. No other remains were ever found. It was impossible to determine if her head had been severed and her body disposed of elsewhere, or if she had been left at the dump and animals had carried off the rest of her remains. If Tina had been the target of the attack at the cabin, the killer or killers would need to ensure that her body wasn't found for a very long time. But this didn't explain why her head was left in a different dump site, unless it was intended to slow identification, should her body be found too soon.

The cause of death was impossible to determine, but the anthropologist proffered the belief that Tina had not been held captive for any length of time, but had instead been killed soon after her abduction.

Sue, Johnny and Dana had been buried in the Quincy Cemetery. Now Tina joined them, but no one believed that they were at rest while their murderers were walking free. It didn't take long for many people to come to believe that at least some members of this sad quartet had never really left Cabin 28.

Weeks passed. Months passed. And still there was no resolution to the mystery. No arrests. No convictions. Life went on for the residents of Keddie and Quincy, but life there would never be the same.

Cabin 28 was spruced up. The boards that covered the windows were removed. Drywall was installed on the living room walls and ceiling. The floorboards were replaced, and new carpet went down. A cursory cleaning took place in the rest of the house, and a "For Rent" sign went up in the front yard. Surprisingly, the sign did not remain for long. Within two years, the first of a steady succession of families moved into the "murder house," as it was called. Many stayed for an extended period of time, and one family lived there for nearly three years before moving to a larger cabin. Sheila Sharp visited Keddie in 1986 and was surprised to see that a family was living in her old house. She said that she was grateful that it had become more than just a murder scene.

The Seabolts continued to live next door for well over a decade after the tragedy in 1981. But this does not mean that Keddie continued as a thriving little community. A pall had been cast over Keddie. The restaurant saw fewer and fewer customers, until it finally closed, along with the general store. The bar struggled on for a few more years before it too closed.

In 1981, all thirty-three cabins making up the Keddie Resort were inhabited, but over time, the cabins began to empty, one by one. Several families and a few intrepid college students kept the place alive, but only just. In the early 1990s, the water supply was found to be contaminated and more cabins were left empty. Plumas County inspected the property between 1993 and 1994, and many of the cabins were condemned and boarded up, including Cabin 28, which had been empty for the last few years. There is no record of when the last occupants moved out, but the cabin was inhabited at least through 1989.

As the years passed into decades, Keddie continued to deteriorate, though it was never completely abandoned. There has been no time since the resort opened in 1910 that someone hasn't lived there. At times, the population has dipped dramatically, but there has always been someone left to claim Keddie as home. There have been reports of owner Gary Mollath getting inspired and getting to work fixing the place up. He tried to sell the property in 1994, but couldn't find a buyer. He eventually fixed up a few of the decaying cabins and continues to rent them. Rumors of new owners surfaced in the early 2000s, with a promise of a refurbished Keddie, but that has yet to come to pass.

After Cabin 28 was condemned in 1994, the only visitors were people with a morbid curiosity to see the Keddie murder house. At night, the property was prowled by ghost hunters.

Cabin 28: Boarded, condemned and abandoned.

Was Cabin 28 haunted by the spirits of Sue, Johnny, Dana and possibly Tina? Many believed that it was. Most of the people who called the cabin home through the decade following the murders said they loved living there; that it was a nice little cabin and the surroundings were beautiful. In spite of these seemingly happy memories, there were reports of strange goings-on both inside and out. Kids didn't come into the yard to trick-or-treat on Halloween and neighbors hesitated when invited in for a visit. At least one former occupant reported there was a heavy, foreboding feeling around the living room closet, and the basement was said to be downright creepy. A man who had lived in the basement for a time with his new wife, while her parents lived on the main floor, said he was never so happy as when he finally got out of that house. He had no specific complaint it was a basement after all , but he was never comfortable inside the house, especially in the basement.

Children living in the cabin seem to have been affected the most. More than one child described seeing something white and fluffy floating through the living room. A former resident described how her children slept in the back bedroom, the same room in which Ricky, Greg and Justin were sleeping on the night of the murders. Her children began having night terrors and would wake up screaming. Her oldest child would occasionally wake up terrified, telling her there was a "man with a green face" looking at him through the bedroom window, even though that particular window was at least eight feet off the ground.

When the cabin was empty, passers-by would cross the road to avoid it. Strange noises were said to emanate from inside. For years, Keddie residents and visitors alike reported hearing moans and bangs floating out from between the boards over the windows. The cabin became a hot spot for ghost hunters and daring teenagers full of liquid courage. Occasionally, the boards were ripped from the door and curious people would spend the night inside, waiting for a ghost to appear. Late one night in 1991, three teenagers were seen running from the cabin, screaming as they raced to their car. They jumped in, and sped off. No one ever learned who they were or what they experienced while sitting there in the dark.

Cabin 28 was reduced to rubble in 2004

The caretaker did his best to keep the curiosity seekers, ghost hunters and psychics away, but to no avail. Tired of the negative attention toward the deteriorating structure, and fearing a lawsuit should someone get hurt while traipsing around in the dark, the owner had Cabin 28 demolished in 2004. He promised a memorial garden would be planted in its place, but the site remains empty. Some people were outraged when the cabin was pulled down. They pointed to the fact that the murder case remains open, and there might still be evidence inside. But this was a pretty feeble argument, considering the passage of twenty-three years, and all the families who had lived there since the murders. Others objected to the loss of a reputedly haunted house. It was even suggested that the cabin should have been turned into a kind of tourist attraction to help revive the area and bring money into the community, much as the previously mentioned Lawson murder house did in North Carolina during the Great Depression. The advertisements could have invited the daring to "Spend the night in a haunted house! Spend the night in the Keddie Murder House...if you dare!"

Cabin 28, along with the cabins on either side, has been gone for a decade, but people still cross the street to avoid walking too near. Children don't play in the grassy area where the cabin once stood, but strangers still occasionally visit at night, with their cameras, digital recorders and tri-field meters, hoping to catch a glimpse of one of the Sharps, or hear Dana's voice, calling out for justice.

Many people felt that a crime of that extreme nature was beyond the capability of the local police force to solve, and that Sheriff Thomas had waited too long to call in outside help. Sadly, when the outside help did arrive, they seemed to be nearly as inept as the local police. Dozens of people were interviewed and houses were searched, but to no avail. Transcripts and recordings of interviews were confusing, and strong leads were left unexplored. Over the years, evidence was lost or destroyed when a leak in the roof of the Plumas County Sheriff's Office went undetected. It was almost as if this terrible crime was never supposed to be solved. No one has ever been arrested for the Keddie murders. As we pass the three-decade mark, the possibility looms large that we many never know exactly who did it, or maybe even more importantly, why.

After the murders, the remaining Sharp children, Sheila, Greg and Ricky, were homeless. Their father, James Sharp, had come to Sue and Johnny's funeral, but insisted that he could not care for his surviving children, so they were left behind. They were taken in by Sue's sister, Jackie Holbert. She tried hard to care for them, but with six children of her own, she was not able to keep them. They were eventually put into the foster care system and spread across the Pacific Northwest.

When Sheila visited in 1986, she also paid her respects at the Quincy Cemetery. Her mother, brother and sister had been buried side by side, but she was dismayed to see that although Sue and Johnny had simple headstones, Tina's grave was marked only with a small tin plate, pushed into the ground. In 2002, Sheila arranged for a stone to be placed for Tina, and a memorial service was held at the cemetery for family and friends. She returned again to Keddie several years later with psychic Donna Raymond. The cabin was gone by then, but they stopped at the site where her former home once stood. Donna told Sheila that her mother was there with them and she had a message for Sheila. Sue wanted her daughter to know that she loved her very much but she wanted her to leave and never visit the site, or Keddie, again.

Normally, news of the torture and brutal murders of three people and the kidnapping of a young girl would typically have made headlines across the country. In this case, news of the tragedy barely made it across California. The tragic event in Keddie was overshadowed by other news. President Reagan was returning to the White House after recovering from being shot during an assignation attempt by John Hinckley. In the South, a succession of young African American boys were found naked and murdered in a series of killings that became known as the Atlanta Child Murders. In

Canada, the newspapers carried stories of poisoned infants in the Toronto Sick Children's Hospital. For the first two decades following the Keddie murders, they seemed to be one of California's best-kept secrets, and there was very little pressure to solve the crime.

In 2004, Josh Hancock and Amanda Glover released the first part of a two-part grassroots documentary titled "Cabin 28: The Keddie Murders." The intent of the documentary was to garner attention to the murders in order to hopefully solve the mystery. One revelation that came out of the documentary was a purported confession. A former therapist at the Reno VA Hospital who had worked with Vietnam veterans suffering with what we now know as Post Traumatic Stress Disorder came forth with a strange story. The therapist said he was treating Marty Smartt, who suffered with rage issues he believed stemmed from his years of service in the military. During their sessions, Marty told the therapist that he had killed Sue and Tina. He said that he was angry with Sue for trying to convince his wife to leave him. He became enraged and struck out at her. Tina walked in at that point, and he had to kill her to keep her quiet. He didn't elaborate on why he took Tina with him when he left the cabin. Marty's buddy Bo had allegedly gone along with him that night, and he left it for the therapist to assume that Bo had killed Johnny and Dana. The therapist further explained that he had discussed the confession with the police, but never heard back from them. Records indicated that this man had indeed contacted the police through a friend in 1981, but when the time came, he denied that Smartt had confessed to him.

Then in 2008, a major motion picture called *The Strangers* was released, and national attention was finally shining on this unsolved murder case. All this turned out to be both a positive and a negative thing. Trailers for *The Strangers* included that tempting phrase: "Based on a true story," and the Keddie murders were indicated as one of the "true stories." The reality is that the phrase should have read: "Very, very, very, very loosely based on a true story." But suddenly everyone wanted to know more about the Keddie murders. Unfortunately, many people decided that the whole thing was fantasy; no one was killed and it was just hype, a gimmick perfected by the producers of an earlier movie, "*The Blair Witch Project.*"

But Sue, Johnny and Tina Sharp, and their friend Dana Wingate were real people. They did live in Cabin 28 in the Keddie Resort. They were tortured, butchered, bludgeoned and murdered on April 11, 1981.

SIDE NOTE: Anyone looking for justice for the murder victims and their families will be disappointed. Martin Smartt, who left the area immediately after the murders, ended up remarried and living in Oregon. He died in 2000. Not as much is known about what happened to "Bo" Boubede, Smartt's likely partner in crime. At one time, he was living in Holiday, Florida, but he, too, is believed to have died.

Bibliography:

Alt, Betty & Sandra Wells - *Wicked Women*; 2000
Avery, Ron - *City of Brotherly Mayhem*; 2003
Bartlett, Evan Allen - *Love Murders of Harry F. Powers*; 1931
Bass, Arnold - *Up Close and Personal: A History of LaPorte County*; 2006
Baughmann, John - *More Strange & Amazing Tales of Raystown County*; 2003
Baumann, Edward & John O'Brien - *Hell's Belle;* 1987
Bryan, Patricia & Thomas Wolf - *Midnight Assassin*; 2005
Burt, Olive Woolley - *American Murder Ballads*; 1958
Capote, Truman -- *In Cold Blood*; 1965
Churchill, Allen - *Pictorial History of American Crime*; 1964
Cipriani, Frank - *Madame Bluebeard! The Crimes of Belle Gunness of Indiana's Murder Farm;* 1936
Coffeen, Robert F. - *The Gunness Murder Mystery*   LaPorte County Public Library Collection
Davis, F. Keith - *The Secret Life & Brutal Death of Mamie Thurman*; 2001
De la Garza, Phyllis - *Death for Dinner*; 2008
Dennett, Andrea Stulman - *Weird & Wonderful;* 1997
Dorwart, Doris M. and Snyder, Robert. - *The Dreamland Park Murders*; 2005
Hardy, Allison - *Kate Bender, the Kansas Murderess*; 1944
Hill, A. F. -- *The White Rocks: A tragedy of the Mountains*; 1865
Holbrook, Stewart H. - *Murder Out Yonder;* 1941
James, Ellen - *The Meeks Murders; Chariton Collector,* Spring 1982
James, John Towner - *The Benders in Kansas*; 1913
Jones, Bruce J. and Smith, Trudy J. -- *White Christmas - Bloody Christmas*; 1990
Keglovits, Sally, McCrary, Gregg and Ramsland, Katherine -- *Solvability and Risk Factors: A Cold Case Investigation. The Forensic Examiner.* Summer, 2013.
Kilgallen, Dorothy - "Sex and the All-American Boy" *True Crime;* 2008
Knudsen, Milli S. - *Hard Times in Concord, New Hampshire*
Kulczyk, David. -- *Death in California*; 2009
Langlois, Janet L. - *Belle Gunness: The Lady Bluebeard*; 1985
LaPorte County, Indiana Historical Society - *The Gunness Story*
Lewis, Arthur - *Hex*; 1969
Lindberg, Richard - *Heartland Serial Killers;* 2011
Marimen, Mark - *Haunted Indiana;* 1999
------------------ James Willis & Troy Taylor - *Weird Indiana;* 2008
McCormick, David - *The Bloody Benders' Grim Harvest*; Wild West; 2012

McQueen, Keven - *The Axman Came from Hell*, 2011
Mrs. Gunness Mystery: A Thrilling Tale of Love, Duplicity & Crime, 1908
Mysterious Murder of Pearl Bryan, or: The Headless Horror, 1897
Nash, Jay Robert - *Bloodletters & Bad Men*, 1995
------------------- - *Look for the Woman*, 1981
------------------- - *Murder, America*, 1980
Official Detective Stories, Inc.   December 1, 1934
Pistorius, Micki - *Fatal Females: Women who Kill*, 2004
Reiter, Joan Swallow - *The Old West: The Women*, 1978
Roth, Randolph - *American Homicide*, 2009
Rule, Leslie -- *When the Ghost Screams: True Stories of Victims Who Haunt*, 2006
Shepherd, Sylvia Elizabeth - *The Mistress of Murder Hill*, 2001
Smith, Trudy J. -- *The Meaning of Our Tears: The Lawson Family Murders of Christmas Day 1929*, 2006
Stanley, Neville - *The Dream that Named a Murderer*, *Fate*, March 1964
Taylor, Troy - *Dead Men Do Tell Tales*, 2008
Vronsky, Peter - *Female Serial Killers*, 2007
West Virginia Gazette - *Bluebeard of Quiet Dell*, 2009
White, Thomas - *Witches of Pennsylvania*, 2013
Wood, Fern Morrow - *The Benders: Keepers of the Devil's Inn*, 1992

Personal Interviews & Correspondence

DOCUMENTARIES
The Keddie Murders Part I and Part II
A Christmas Family Tragedy: The Charlie Lawson Family Murders

NEWSPAPERS
Allentown Morning Call
Altoona Herald
Altoona Mirror
Carlisle Sentinel
Chicago American
Chicago Daily News
Chicago Evening Post
Chicago Examiner
Chicago Journal
Chicago Record
Chicago Tribune

Columbia-Wrightsville Merchandiser
Decatur Daily Herald
Detroit Free Press
Detroit News
East York Community Courier
Fayette Tribune-Review
Fayetteville Observer
Feather River Bulletin
Gettysburg Times
Grand Rapids Press
Harrisburg Patriot-News
Hays Daily News
Huron County Tribune   Michigan
Johnstown Tribune-Democrat
LaPorte Argus-Bulletin
LaPorte Daily Herald
Lehigh Valley Newspaper
New York Daily Tribune
New York Times
Philadelphia Daily News
Philadelphia Inquirer
Plumas News
Reading Eagle
Reno Evening Gazette
Roseville Press Tribune
Sacramento Bee
San Francisco Daily Journal
San Francisco Examiner
Sarasota Herald-Tribune
Sarasota News
Tampa Bay Times
The Stokes News
Uniontown Herald-Standard
Wichita Eagle
York Daily Record
York Dispatch

WEBSITES

http: www.www3.familyoldphotos.com
www.abcnews.go.com
http: www.accomacinn.com restaurant our-history
https: archive.org
http: www.atlasobscura.com
http: www.ccpa.net
http: www.cor.state.pa.us
http: www.crimearchives.net
www.crimelibrary.com
http: www.crimemagazine.com cold-case-keddie-murders
http: www.culinnovation.net
http: en.cyclopaedia.net wiki Walker-family-murders
http: www.dcnr.state.pa.us
http: www.democraticunderground.com
www.dnalabsinternational.com
http: www.darkinthepark.com Dreamland dreamland.htm
http: en.potiori.com Charlie Lawson.html
www.forensicdnaethics.org
http: www.gcpolice.org History Clutter Pictures for Clutters.htm
http: www.hauntedcolorado.net In Cold Blood House.html
http: hauntedstories.net ghost-stories north-carolina lawson-family-murders
http: hauntsandhistory.blogspot.com 2008 03 johnny-coyle-and-accomac-inn.html
www.heraldextra.com
http: bycolakegal.tripod.com photos.html
www.huffingtonpost.com
http: imgarcade.com 1 the-keddie-murders-crime-scene-photos
http: incoldblog.wordpress.com
http: keddie28.com news.html
http: krazykillers.wordpress.com
http: lancasteronline.com
www.laurajames.com
http: www.linkedin.com
http: members4.boardhost.com
http: www.mudcat.org
www.murderpedia.org
http: www.murderbygaslight.com
www.mysuncoast.com

http://www.pajack.com
http://www.rarenewspapers.com
http://roadsidewonders.net
http://www.robinsonlibrary.com
http://www.sarasotasheriff.org
www.sfgate.com
https://sites.google.com/site/hauntsandhistory/pennsylvaniadutchhaunts&history
http://www.statementanalysis.com/cabin-28-murders/Smartt
http://www.stateparks.com/michaux.html
https://suite.io/kenneth-dillinger/3c3j26n
http://www.thedailybeast.com
http://travelersjournal.com
www.treasurenet.com
http://www.treasurequestxlt.com
http://www.yearsoftears.org

SPECIAL THANKS TO

Jill Hand - Editor
April Slaughter - Cover Design, plus Continued Advice & Patience
Troy & Rene will just thank each other, so let's get that over with.

Family:
Rachael Horath   who put in extra hours on this one
Elyse & Thomas Reihner
Bethany & Jim McKenzie
Haven & Helayna Taylor
Janet Jordan   who freaked out everyone in Moweaqua asking about the Portwood murders
Orrin Taylor

Friends & Assorted Characters:
John Winterbauer
Melissa Telesha
Katherine Ramsland
Ginger Collins Justus
Hannah Grey
Lisa Taylor Horton   & Lux

ABOUT THE AUTHORS

TROY TAYLOR
Troy Taylor is an occultist, crime buff, supernatural historian and the author of more than 100 books on ghosts, hauntings, history, crime and the unexplained in America. He is also the founder of the American Hauntings Tour company. When not traveling to the far-flung reaches of the country in search of the unusual, Troy resides part-time in Decatur, Illinois.

RENE KRUSE
Rene' Kruse has lived in small towns in the Midwest and Texas but has lived in southwestern Pennsylvania for the past 20 years. She holds a PhD from Texas A&M and teaches Applied Engineering and Technology at California University of Pennsylvania.
Rene' has been fascinated in ghosts and all things haunted for as long as she can remember and has been actively investigating haunted sites for over 30 years.

Troy And Rene' have co-authored two other books on history and hauntings:
AND HELL FOLLOWED WITH IT and **A PALE HORSE WAS DEATH**
Two titles about American disasters and the hauntings that followed in their wakes

See their other titles at: **www.whitechapelpress.com**

CPSIA information can be obtained
at www.ICGtesting.com
Printed in the USA
FSOW02n1804060416
18862FS